CW01664997

The Fold of the Land

The Fold of the Land

New Zealand's National Parks from the Air

Lloyd Homer and Les Molloy

Somewhere in a blanketfold of the land
Lies the golden strand

Allen & Unwin

Department of Scientific and Industrial Research
New Zealand Geological Survey
New Zealand Soil Bureau
Department of Conservation

Published by Allen & Unwin New Zealand Limited
(60 Cambridge Terrace, Wellington, New Zealand)
and the Department of Scientific and Industrial Research
(Private Bag, Wellington, New Zealand).

Allen & Unwin Australia Pty Ltd,
NCR House, 8 Napier Street, North Sydney, NSW 2060, Australia.

Unwin Hyman Limited,
15–17 Broadwick Street, London WIV 1FP, England

Allen & Unwin Inc.,
8 Winchester Place, Winchester, Mass. 01890, USA

© Crown Copyright (New Zealand) 1988

This book is copyright under the Berne Convention.
No reproduction without permission. All rights reserved.
Inquiries should be made to Allen & Unwin New Zealand Limited.

ISBN 086861 491 2

Title page quotation: from 'Arawata Bill' by Denis Glover,
reprinted by kind permission of the Estate of Denis Glover and
Ray Richards Literary Agency.
Front cover photograph: Rock avalanche, Arthur's Pass National Park
Back cover photograph: Beehive Island, Maritime Parks of the North
Photographic prints: DAC Productions Limited
Maps: Department of Survey and Land Information Map Licence 1988/9.
© Crown Copyright Reserved
Typeset by NZ Soil Bureau (Department of Scientific and Industrial Research)
and the Government Printer, Wellington
Printed by Mandarin Offset, Hong Kong

CONTENTS

PREFACE AND ACKNOWLEDGEMENTS

'Fold of the Land' is an exciting initiative for the Department of Scientific and Industrial Research (DSIR). It sets out to convey the fascination that earth scientists have for the New Zealand landscape, not in the complex language of scientific journals but through large format colour aerial photographs and a less technical text.

In 1984 DSIR were approached for scientific contributions to mark the centennial of New Zealand's national park system, to be celebrated from July 1987 to June 1988. One of the projects suggested by DSIR was a book of Lloyd Homer's aerial photographs of the parks. As a member of the Commission organising the centennial year I was asked to follow this up. Lloyd was not only a personal friend of long standing but a photographer with high professional standards, tireless energy and an outstanding collection of oblique aerial photographs of the New Zealand landscape. Such a book seemed the ideal opportunity for DSIR to produce a high quality publication on a neglected dimension of the parks, a book with the right balance of aesthetic impact and scientific information.

The idea would not have progressed any further without the support of three colleagues: the Director of the NZ Geological Survey, Dr Ian Speden, who generously gave his support and guidance to the project from the very start; my former Director (of the NZ Soil Bureau), Dr Mike Leamy, who also encouraged me to write the text of the book and oversee its scientific content; and the former Chief Director of the resources divisions of DSIR, Dr Hamish Thompson, who successfully promoted this ambitious and rather different project through the head office of DSIR.

Throughout 1985 and 1986, Lloyd and I navigated our way from North Cape to Puysegur Point, filling the gaps in the essential photographic portfolio of landforms. The rigours of many days of fixed wing flight, often above 3000 m altitude with the door off and the mid-winter air temperature well below zero, were adventures we were privileged to share with many pilots whose skills were essential to this enterprise. For both of us it was a nostalgic odyssey, to float far above the peaks and valleys that we had explored in our youth. The excitement returned but it was different, the satisfaction of recognition and understanding that comes with middle age tempering the wonder and anticipation that we once felt as novice explorers. We identified strongly with Arawata Bill's lifelong quest. The golden stand still lies somewhere in the blanketfold of this precious protected land, for others to re-discover and interpret in their own way just as we have done.

As a soil organic chemist I felt inadequate to handle the detail of what was essentially a geological challenge. I am grateful, therefore, to the following colleagues (most of them from NZ Geological Survey) who so generously commented on my interpretations of the landforms:
Graham Bishop (Fiordland, Mt Aspiring and Mt Cook); Michael Johnston (Nelson Lakes, Abel Tasman and Marlborough Sounds); Simon Nathan (Westland, Paparoa); Murray Cave (Arthur's Pass); Vince Neall (Egmont); Malcolm Laird (Paparoa); Bruce Houghton (Tongariro); Phil Moore (Urewera); Hugh Wilde (Whanganui); Bruce Hayward (Maritime Parks of the Far North).

The high photographic standards were complemented by the cartographic efforts of the team who produced the set of innovative maps which express the vegetation in the colour tones of the photographs. We are especially grateful to Terry Connor, draughting manager of the central office of the Department of Conservation, who so readily appreciated the artistic goals of the book. He cheerfully worked to severe deadlines to produce these maps, with the assistance of Chris Edkins, Leigh Moore and Phil Dickson. In addition, the Department of Survey and Land Information were very helpful in providing base information, technical advice and photo laboratory assistance.

The manuscript was typed by Shelley Witters of the Department of Conservation and Tessa Roach of NZ Soil Bureau. Dr Rod Furkert of NZ Soil Bureau organised the production of type, and the whole publication was guided by Bridget Williams of Allen and Unwin, and designed by Lindsay Missen. Once again, I have benefited from their professionalism and understanding of what we were trying to say in word and picture.

Aerial photography is not without its dangers and stresses no matter how often the safety margins are checked. My acceptance of a senior position in the Department of Conservation early in 1987 added to the pressure on my family, because I was trying to cope with the demands of a new department while still finding time to make the creative input to the book. I am sincerely grateful to my wife Sonia, and to my DOC colleagues, Ken Piddington, Alan Edmonds, Chris Collins and Wren Green, and my own staff, for their support during a very difficult year while this book was completed. I believe the result bears out their trust in both of us.

Les Molloy

For me this book is the culmination of a 20-year apprenticeship in aerial photography for geological research. Yet photographing our extraordinarily diverse landscape has always been more than just a job for me and I needed to share my awe and satisfaction with a broader readership who love the New Zealand land. Until Les joined me and made it happen it always seemed an alluring but very distant goal.

So many people helped me in this long journey:
Firstly, my wife Sheryl and children Clayton and Kirsten carried the inevitable domestic disruption – years of interrupted meals to watch weather forecasts, late night phone calls to pilots, the worry over safety margins, and the frustration of so many postponements.
My colleagues from the Survey – especially Wendy St George, Diana Russell and Peter Wood and so many others – accompanied me on flights over two decades, sharing the fun and the frustrations.
The final group that I owe a big debt to are the pilots. In particular, the Marlborough Aero Club (especially Warren Hamilton and Gerard Healy with whom I shared nearly 10 years of flying) and, in recent years, the Nelson Aero Club (especially Stuart Holland).

Although two thirds of the photographs in the book were taken on flights with Les during 1985/86, the foundation of the project had been laid down years earlier through the support of all these friends and colleagues. The book is dedicated to all of you.

Lloyd Homer

INTRODUCTION

New Zealand's twelve national parks and three maritime parks make up an impressive 9% of the land area of the country. They are held in high regard internationally and, since 1987, three of them (Fiordland, Westland and Mt Cook National Parks) have been considered important enough to warrant World Heritage site status. On the 23 September 1987 New Zealand celebrated the centennial of the gifting of its first national park, Tongariro, to the people by the paramount chief of the Ngati Tuwharetoa, Te Heuheu Tukino. Since 1887, eleven more national parks and three maritime parks have been 'preserved in perpetuity .... in their natural state .... for their intrinsic worth and for the benefit, use and enjoyment of the public' (National Parks and Reserves Act 1980).

Each park has its own landscape character, its landforms reflecting the geological history of the area, the prevailing rock types, and the climatic environment. There are 'hard rock' parks; Fiordland with its fiords and superb U-shaped valleys, and Abel Tasman with its granite coastal headlands. Whanganui, by way of contrast, consists of an intricate network of drainage channels eroding soft 'papa', or mudstone. Glacial landforms predominate in most of the South Island parks ranged along the Southern Alps. Each alpine park has its hallmark; the hanging valleys and intermontane riverflats in the schist rocks of Mt Aspiring; the glaciers, piedmont moraines and lakes of Mt Cook and Westland; and the screes and fans of the typical 'greywacke parks' – Arthur's Pass and Nelson Lakes. Volcanoes are a distinctive feature of several of the North Island parks – Tongariro, Egmont and many separate islands or cones in Hauraki Gulf and Bay of Islands maritime parks. Paparoa and the tableland of Abel Tasman are different again – karst landscapes with extensive networks of underground caves still partly unexplored. In addition to these differences in rock types, there is the dynamic influence of crustal movement along the boundary between the Pacific and Indian-Australian Plates affecting virtually all the parks and generating new landforms through the powerful forces of mountain uplift, earthquakes, volcanism, or the tilting of whole blocks into the sea (such as the Marlborough Sounds).

The following fourteen chapters are a journey through the landforms of these parks, beginning in the deep south with the stupendous scale of Fiordland and finishing with the island jewels strung around the coastline of the far north. We cannot yet claim that the parks are scientifically representative of the landform diversity of New Zealand, for they are heavily biased towards mountainous landscapes and lack important features such as the block mountains of Central Otago, the glacial lakes of Canterbury and Otago, geothermal areas, lowland plains and our most accessible coastlines. Nevertheless, they do contain some of the best examples of our natural heritage and their landforms are as much a cause for celebration in this centennial year as their vegetation and wildlife.

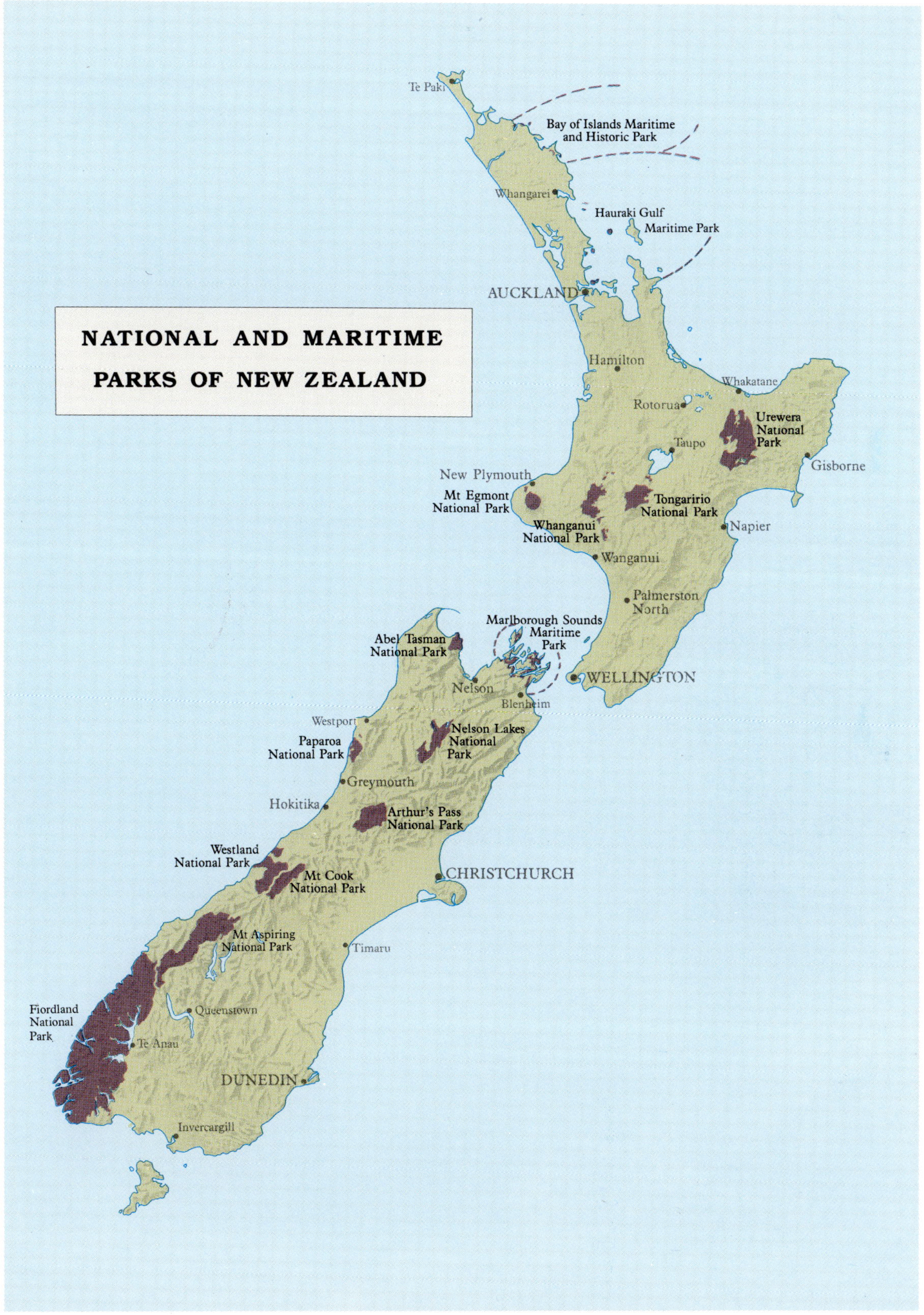

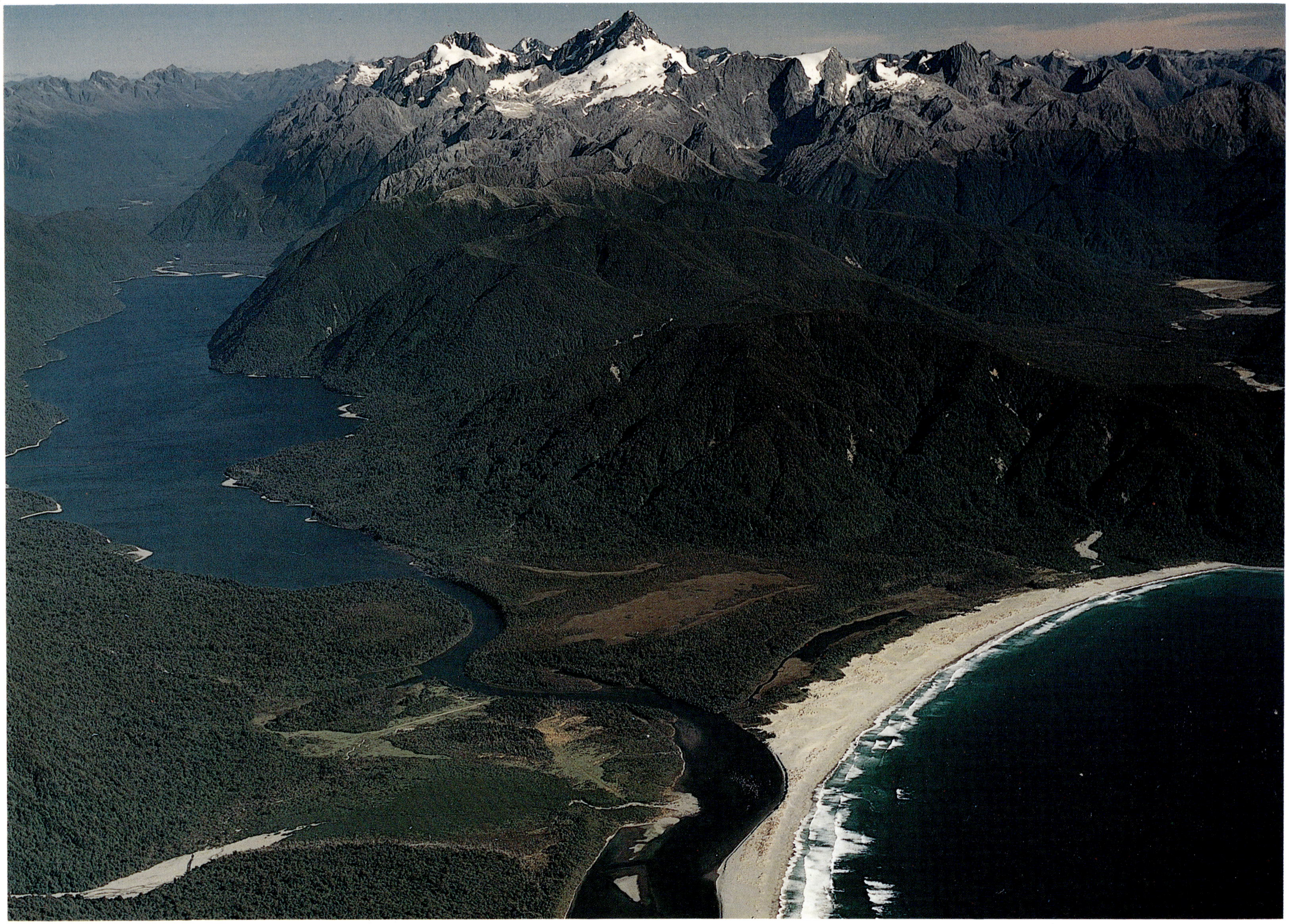

1

FIORDLAND NATIONAL PARK

Fiordland National Park is New Zealand's great wilderness park. Its area of over 1.2 million hectares is nearly 5 percent of New Zealand. Most visitors can only probe the northernmost corner of the park, yet that road journey to Milford Sound and back is an exhilarating experience. Regardless of the weather, the scenery along the Milford Road is of such a scale and grandeur that it has been world famous for more than a century. The view from the road is impressive, but it is limited by sheer rock walls at every turn; from the air the full extent of the park's thousands of peaks, lakes, rivers, waterfalls and fiords is simply mind-boggling. Unesco has recognised Fiordland's international importance by adding the park to its list of World Heritage Areas.

Three environmental factors have combined to produce Fiordland's distinctive landscape: its rocks, their rate of uplift, and the climate. Fiordland is New Zealand's largest area of hard, crystalline, plutonic igneous and metamorphic rocks. These hard rocks crystallised deep in the earth and they have been lifted to the surface because they lie close to the plate boundary along the Alpine Fault. As they were uplifted, the covering of younger, softer, rocks was eroded away. Fiordland sits astride two degrees of latitude in the higher 'roaring forties', causing the moisture-laden westerly winds (that prevail at these latitudes almost the whole year round) to release annual rainfalls sometimes as high as ten metres at sea level in Milford Sound. During the Ice Ages this precipitation fell as snow and built up into enormous glaciers which carved glacial landforms – now largely preserved in the hard rocks which have resisted erosion over the 10 000 years since the end of the last glaciation.

1 At the northern tip of Fiordland National Park, the lower Hollyford River flows behind a prominent sandspit to enter the sea at the northern end of Martins Bay. Between the beach and Lake McKerrow, the McKenzie Lagoon and pakihis occupy the hollows between the now forest-covered older sand dunes parallel to the beach. The Hollyford valley beyond the lake marks the transition from the schists, sandstones, argillites and volcanic rocks of the Humboldt and Ailsa Ranges (left, distance; see Fig. 17, Mt Aspiring) in Mt Aspiring National Park, to the hard granite, diorite, and gabbro rocks of the Darran Range (centre right), the imposing mountain range encircling Milford Sound. The prominent peak (centre) directly south of the bay is Mt Tutoko, the highest (2746 m) peak in the park. The flats of the Kaipo River (Fig. 3) can be seen centre right; one source of this river rises in an impressive cirque, the prominent 'Kaipo Wall' just to the right of Mt Tutoko.

THE WESTERN FIORDS

The western coastline of Fiordland is deeply indented with fiords which mark the troughs of former glaciers filled by the sea as it flooded back when the glaciers melted. Lake McKerrow is the northernmost fiord, its former open outlet now almost closed by the sand bar of Martins Bay. For the next 230 km, the coastline stretching to the south-west is breached by fifteen fiords, some of the largest ones, like Doubtful, Breaksea and Long Sounds, extending up to 35 km into the heart of Fiordland's mountain chain. Most of this mountain chain consists of gneiss, a hard, coarse-grained metamorphic rock. The peaks show a remarkable accordance in height as they gently slope down from 1700–1900 m in the north around Milford Sound to 1200–1400 m in the Cameron Mountains to the east of Preservation Inlet.

Unlike the parks underlain by schist and greywacke rocks further north along the Southern Alps, there is no pronounced 'grain' controlling the direction of the ridges in Fiordland; the maze of 'U'-shaped valleys running in all directions reflects the lack of regular orientation of the zones of weakness in the gneiss. Everywhere the valley walls are steep with little evidence of talus slopes. The challenge for any explorer is often to scale the sheer valley walls, whereupon travel on the open tops is often relatively easy.

The walls of the fiords have a superficial look of stability because forest is able to cling to the shallow soils (often only 25–30 cm of litter and peat over weakly-weathered rock) on these 55–60° slopes. But subtle differences in forest composition and colour indicate the paths of previous debris avalanches of water-saturated vegetation and soil. Some of these avalanche paths drop over 1000 m to the valley floor or fiord; they heal relatively quickly because of the mild, very wet climate.

DARRAN MOUNTAINS AND EASTERN LAKES

The Alpine Fault cuts across Lake McKerrow at the northern tip of the park and its trace can be clearly followed out to sea at the mouth of Milford Sound. On the southern side of the fault a block of plutonic igneous rock (diorite and gabbro) has been pushed up as a spectacular wall of mountains; these are the Darran and Wick Mountains which surround the Milford Road, between the Hollyford valley, Milford Sound and Lake Te Anau. Here occur the greatest concentration of present-day glaciers in the park, and the tourist features of Homer Tunnel, Milford Track, Sutherland Falls, Mt Tutoko and the Cleddau Chasm. The cirque glaciers on the upper south-eastern slopes are now mere remnants of the great glaciers, like the Hollyford which once curved around the southern end of the Darran Mountains to flow another 50 km north to Martins Bay (and probably even Big Bay). So large was this glacier that it overtopped the Main Divide at Key Summit and two lobes flowed to the south – one to Lake Wakatipu via the Greenstone valley and the other to Lake Te Anau via the Eglinton valley.

The large lakes of Te Anau and Manapouri occupy the down-faulted eastern margin of the park, where Ice Age glaciers excavated troughs so deep that the bottoms of both lakes are hundreds of metres below sea level. Beyond the park boundary, the eastern shores of both lakes consist of glacial outwash and moraine surfaces. The head of Lake Te Anau and the Earl Mountains provide an interesting contrast with the rest of the park. In this locality large tilted blocks of Tertiary sediments have survived, forming massifs with long smooth dip slopes and escarpments.

MARINE BENCHES OF THE SOUTH

In the remote south-western corner of Fiordland, from Dusky Sound to Sand Hill Point at the western end of Te Waewae Bay, the mountains slope down to a 10–15 km wide old marine platform. The underlying granite and Tertiary sandstone is generally mantled with well-rounded gravels and cut into flights of up to eleven uplifted marine benches, each marking a former shoreline. The oldest benches can now be recognised at altitudes of up to 1000 m above the present sea level, and the present wide wave-cut platform east of Puysegur Point is a contrast with the coastlines to the north where the fiord walls plunge straight into the sea. These densely-forested uplifted marine terraces (including those of the Waitutu locality on the park boundary around the outwash surfaces of the glaciers that produced Lakes Hakapoua, Poteriteri and Hauroko) are unique within New Zealand and internationally recognised.

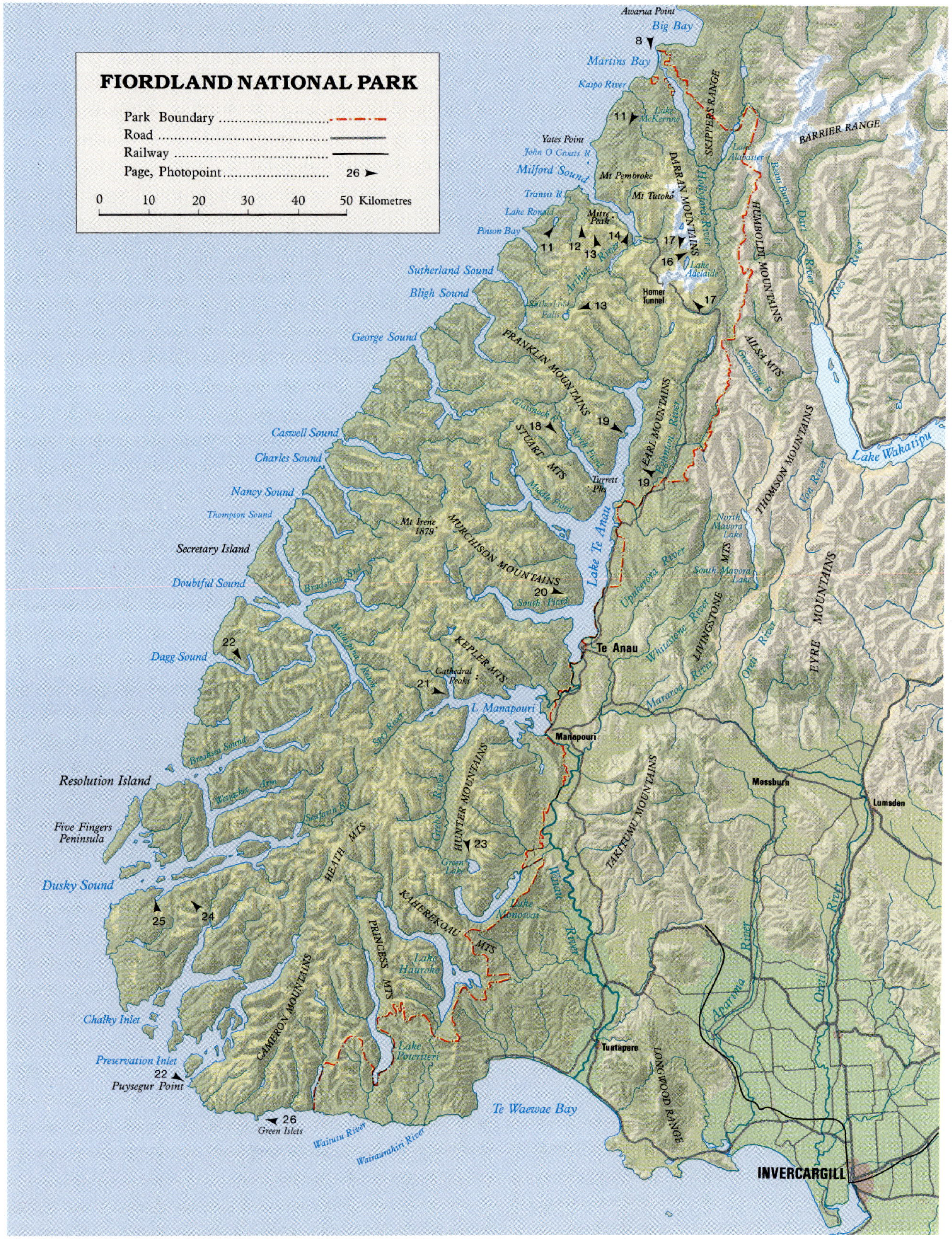

2 Lake Ronald nestles in a thin belt of ultramafic rock on the south-western side of the Transit valley (centre) and the entrance to Milford Sound (middle distance).

The ultramafic rock is only lightly vegetated with 'serpentine scrub', similar to that in the Red Hills area west of Mt Aspiring National Park (see Fig. 8, Mt Aspiring); an outcrop of this ultramafic rock at Anita Bay at the entrance to Milford Sound was the source of the Fiordland greenstone, a translucent bowenite known to the Maori as 'takiwai'.

3 The Alpine Fault can be traced out to sea in this view south-west across the Kaipo Slip and the lower part of the John O'Groats valley towards the entrance to Milford Sound. The slip occurs in rocks crushed and shattered by movements along the fault.

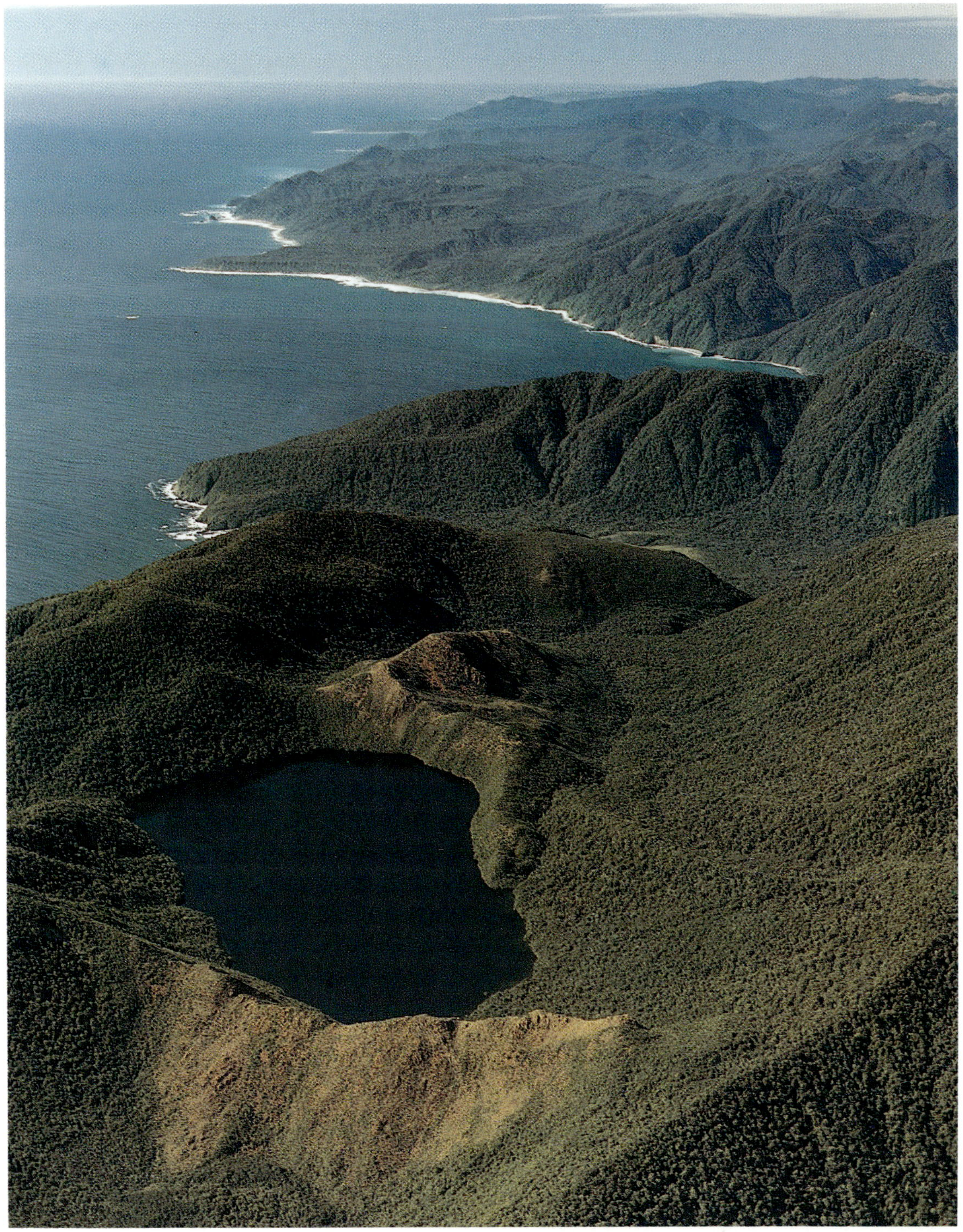

2

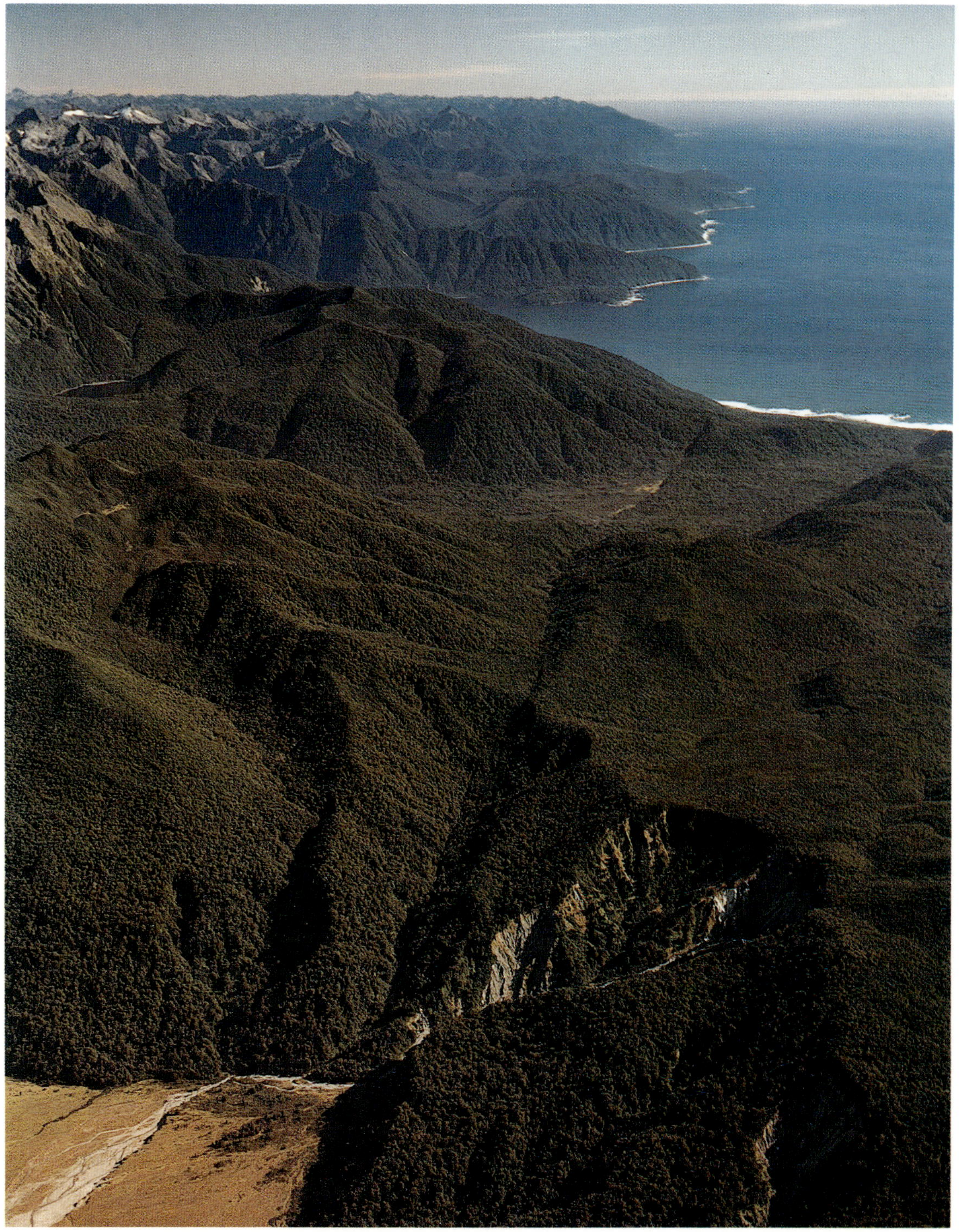

3

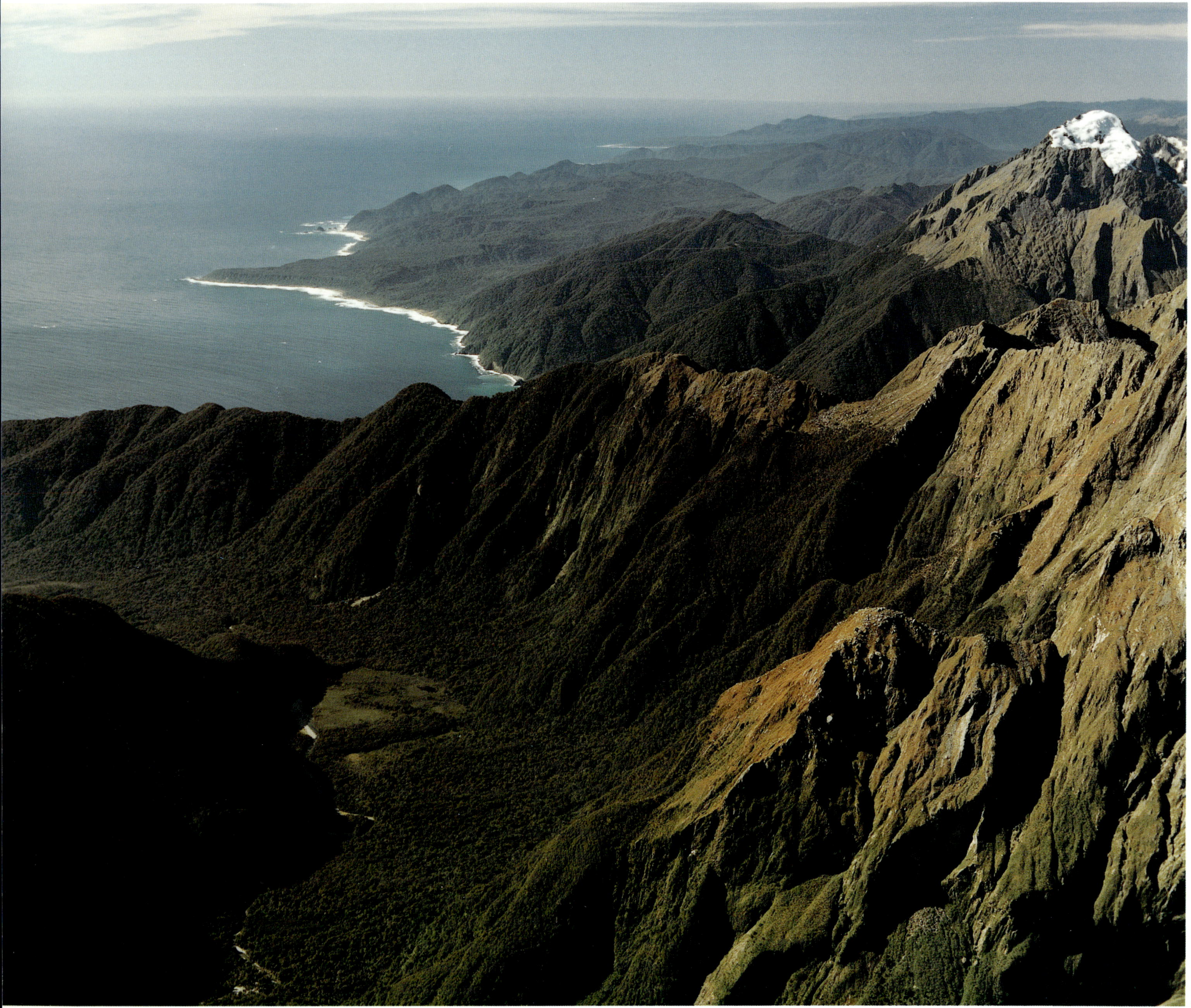

4

4 The steep rock walls of the mountains around Milford Sound rear up above the intensely folded and sheared rocks around the Alpine Fault to the west. The Transit River flows through the glaciated U-shaped valley in the foreground; the glacier-capped peak in the top right is Mt Pembroke (2000 m) on the far side of Milford Sound. Further north, the gently-sloping marine benches and glacial outwash surfaces between the Kaipo valley and the coast near Yates Point can be seen beyond the entrance to Milford Sound (see Fig. 2).

5 The Llawrenny Peaks (1932 m) are on the southern side of the entrance to Milford Sound, with Yates Point, on the northern side, visible in the distance. These ice-festooned peaks are only 5 km from the open sea, so rapidly does the land rise from the coast. The cirque basin on the shady south-easterly slope in the foreground has been plucked out by ice which previously flowed down from the peak. With glacial retreat, the basin is now partly filled with melt water. The crevassed ice in the basin has been augmented by spring avalanches of ice and snow from the slopes above. Eventually, climatic warming will ensure that this icy basin will become an ice-free lake, like the thousands of others at lower altitudes throughout the park.

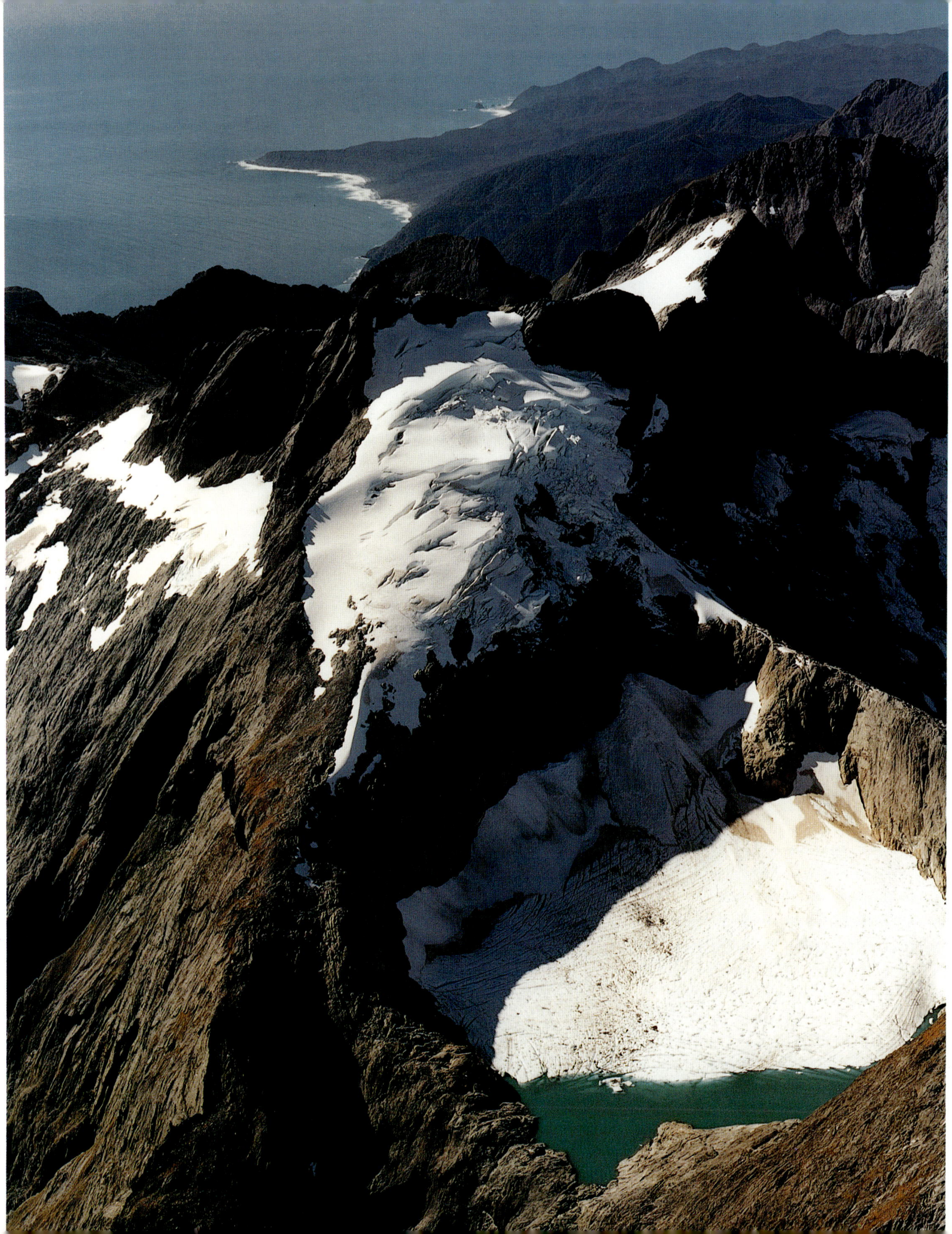
5

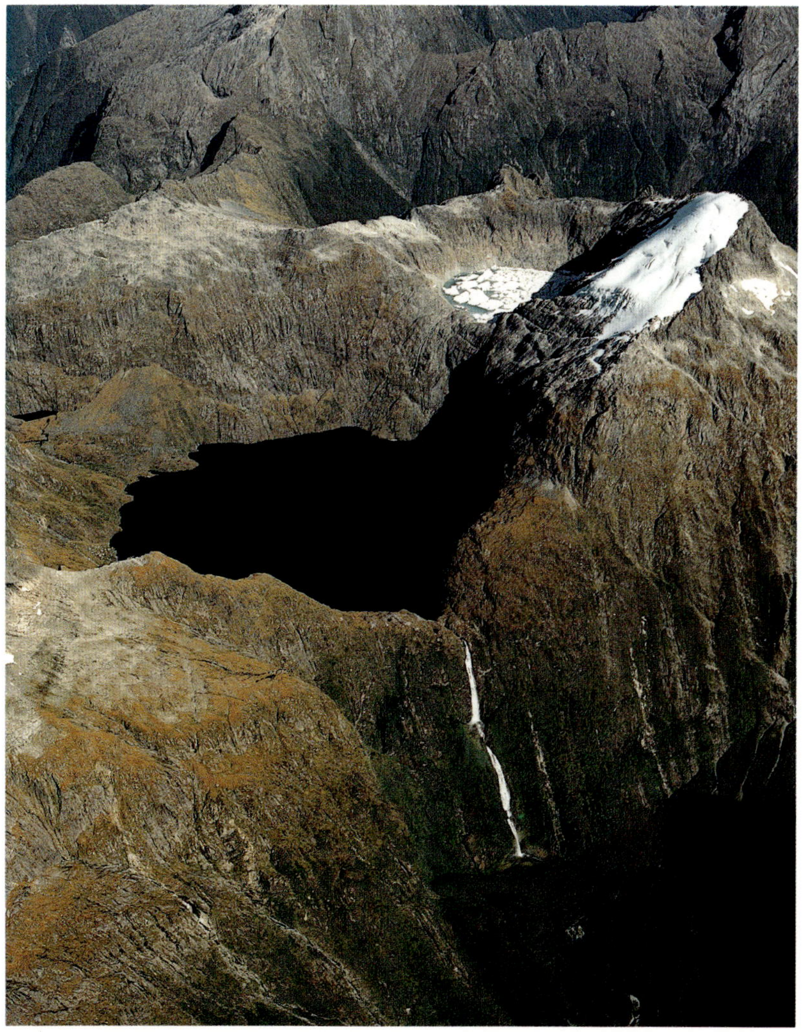
6

6 The Sutherland Falls, which plunge nearly 600 m in three leaps down the southern wall of Staircase Creek, are the highest waterfall in the park and an international tourist attraction.

Their immediate source is a moderately large cirque lake, Lake Quill, but their ultimate source is another cirque lake 350 m higher. This spectacular iceberg-filled lake lies in a cirque at the foot of the glacier-covered south-east slopes of a 1900 m unnamed peak. Note the similarity of the upper cirque lake to that under the Llawrenny Peaks (adjacent photograph).

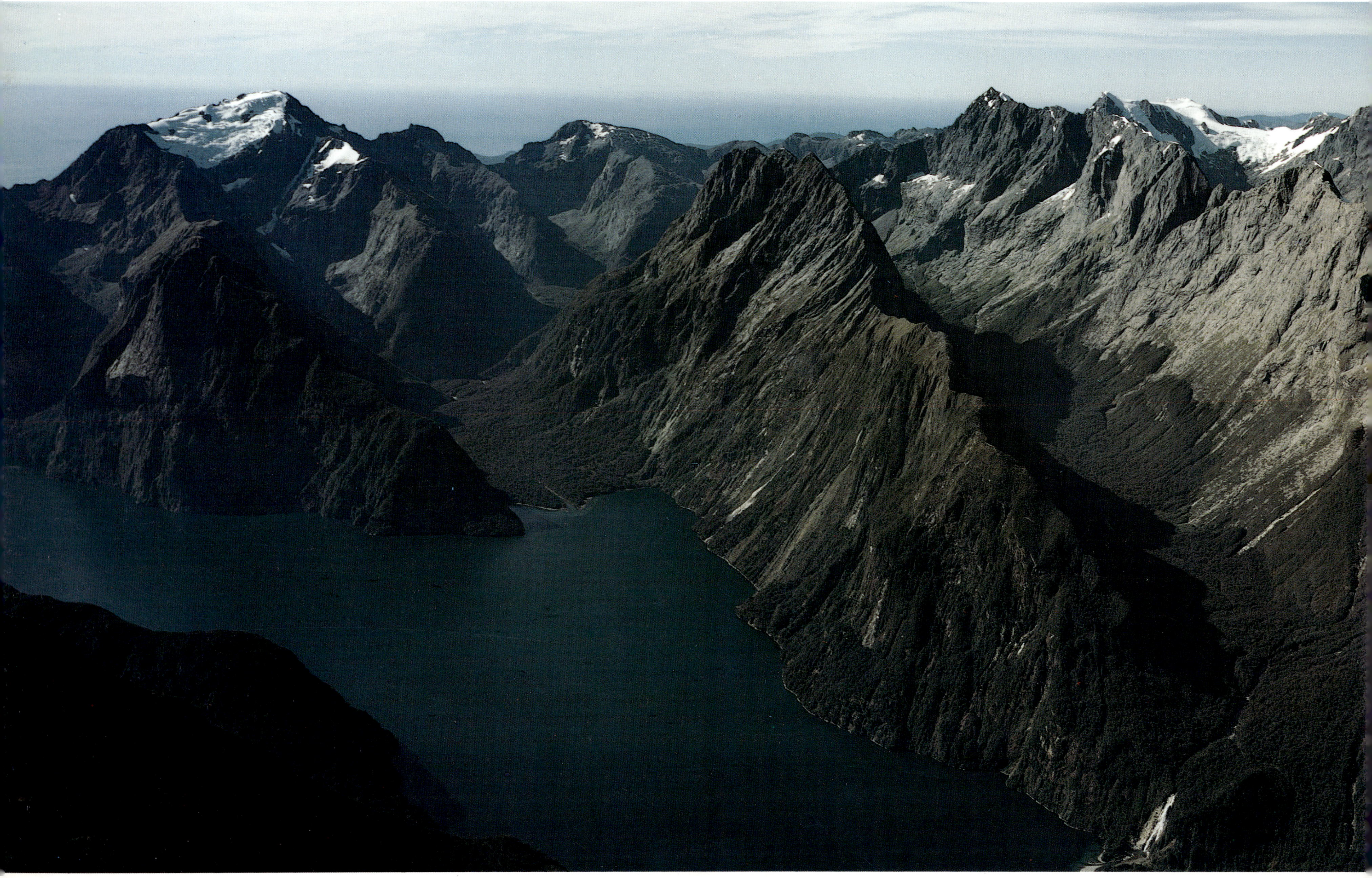

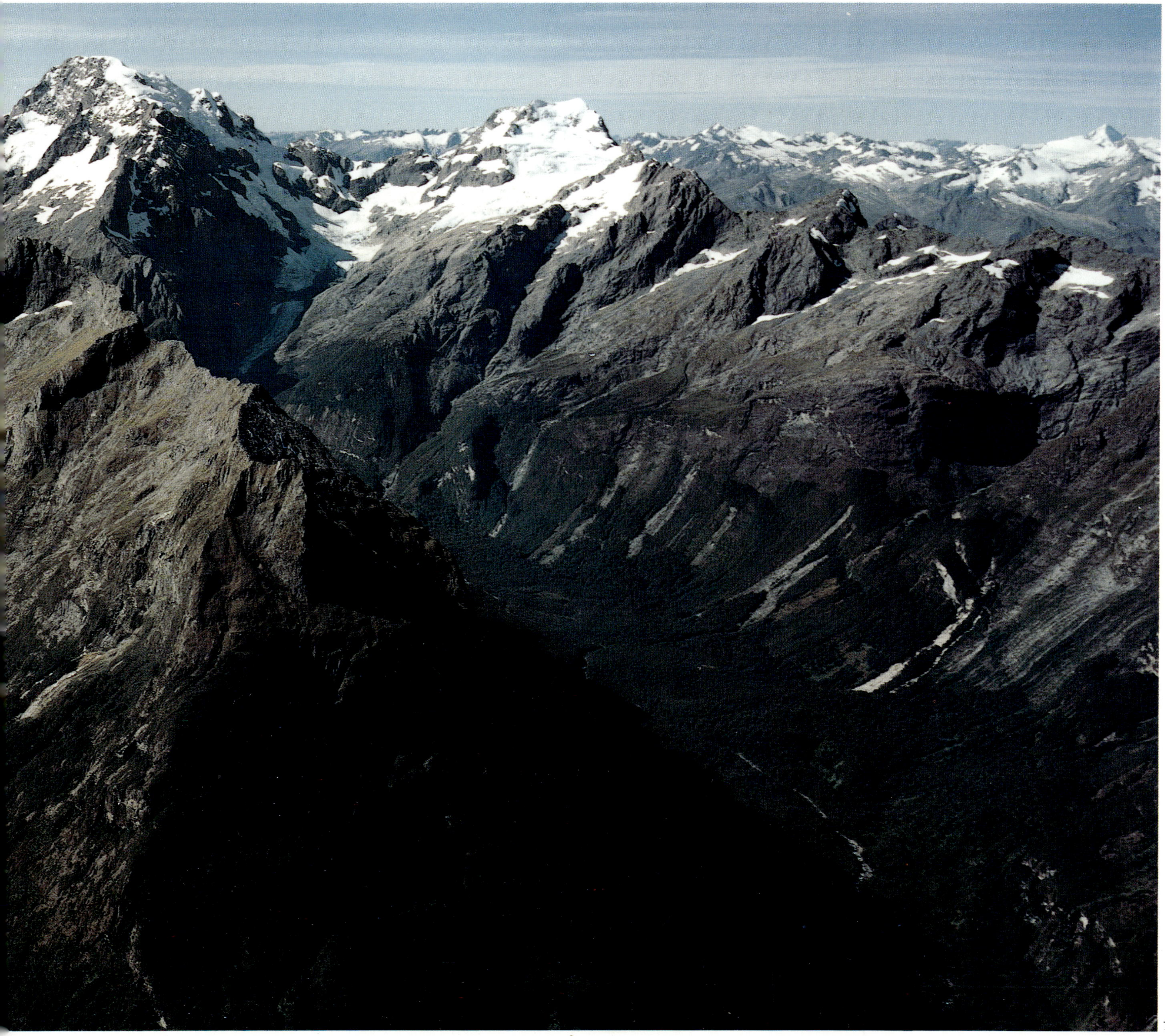

7

7 Milford Sound, and its tributary U-shaped valleys of the Harrison (left), Bowen (centre) and Tutoko (right), is an eloquent memorial to the great glaciers that carved this, the most breathtaking of Fiordland's fiords. The former Harrison and Bowen Glaciers, in particular, have honed the intervening rock ridge down to a razor-backed spine; this ridge plunges down to Bowen Falls which have built up a small rock fan (centre, foreground). Note the scars from avalanches and landslides on the slopes, some of them extending 1000 m from bushline to sea level. Rainfall here can reach 10 000 mm per annum, and occasionally the whole saturated mantle of forest, soil and rock fragments slides off the bedrock under its own weight.

In this view to the north-west, three glacier-bearing peaks tower above the canyons: Pembroke (left), Tutoko (centre right), and Madeline (right). Route-finding up the debris-strewn, densely-forested valleys and precipitous rock walls presents a considerable recreational challenge to anyone with intentions of climbing these peaks.

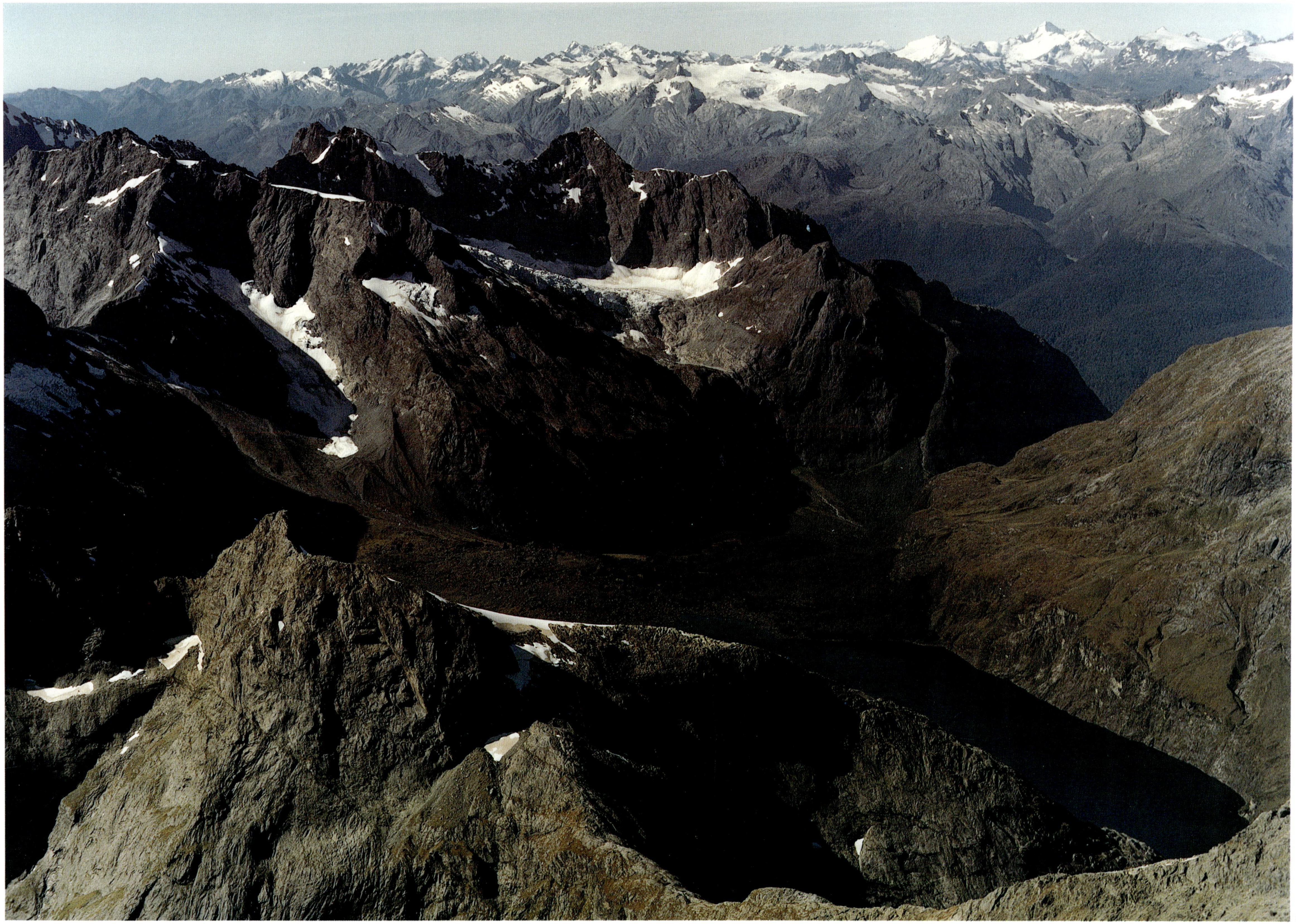

8 Lake Adelaide in the head of Moraine Creek is the largest of the cirque lakes in the gabbro rocks of the Darran Mountains on the northern boundary of Fiordland National Park. The hanging valley of Moraine Creek drains to the Hollyford River (centre, right), but the lake, which is impounded behind a dam of moraine and rockfall debris, only has an underground outlet. Note the difference between the ruggedness of the hard crystalline rocks of Fiordland and the smoother shapes of the softer rocks of Mt Aspiring National Park along the skyline on the far side of the Hollyford valley.

9 View, looking north-west, into the cirques at the head of the Hollyford valley at the southern end of the Darran Mountains. The Milford road can be seen until the point below Mt Talbot where it turns west into a cirque and enters the Homer Tunnel. The four prominent peaks on the skyline are (from left to right): Mts Pembroke, Grave, Tutoko and Madeline.

There is little regular orientation to the jointing in these hard, coarsely crystalline rocks, so there is no 'grain' to the maze of zig-zagging ridges that the glaciers have carved. Note the preponderance of glaciers on the near slopes of the peaks and the modest fringe of talus slopes at the foot of sheer walls (contrast the preponderance of talus slopes in the greywacke mountains of Mt Cook, Arthur's Pass, and Nelson Lakes National Parks).

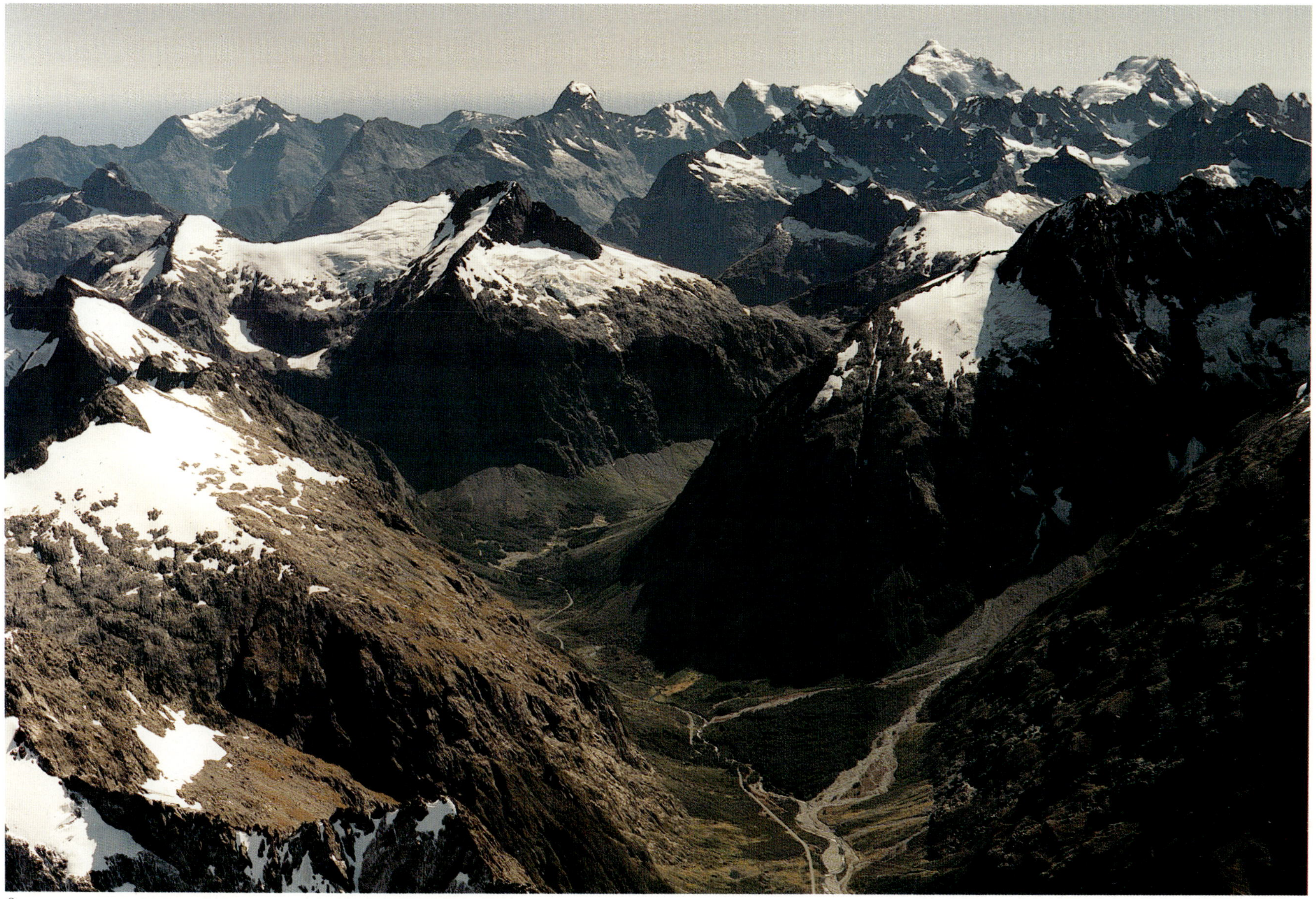

9

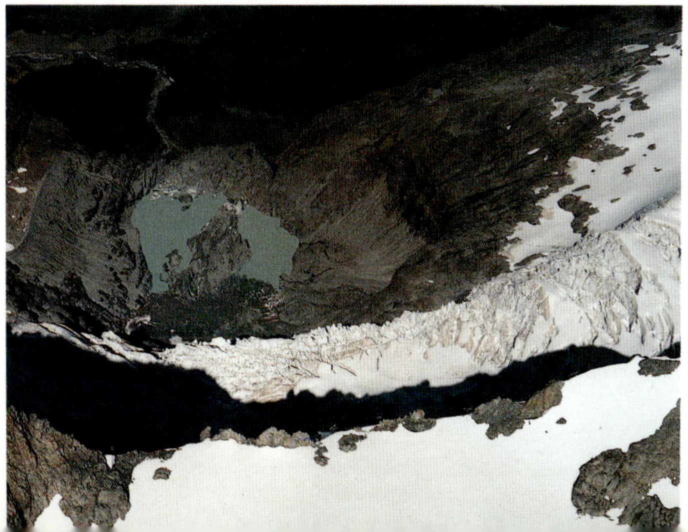

10

10 The retreat of a shrinking cirque glacier is well illustrated in this vertical view of the Korako Glacier (Fig. 8, opposite). The icefall now terminates in a dirty grey, moraine-filled lakelet in the bottom of the amphitheatre. The small smooth ridge of lateral moraine on the left of the lakelet marks the level of the glacial ice prior to the onset of the last major stage of glacial retreat.

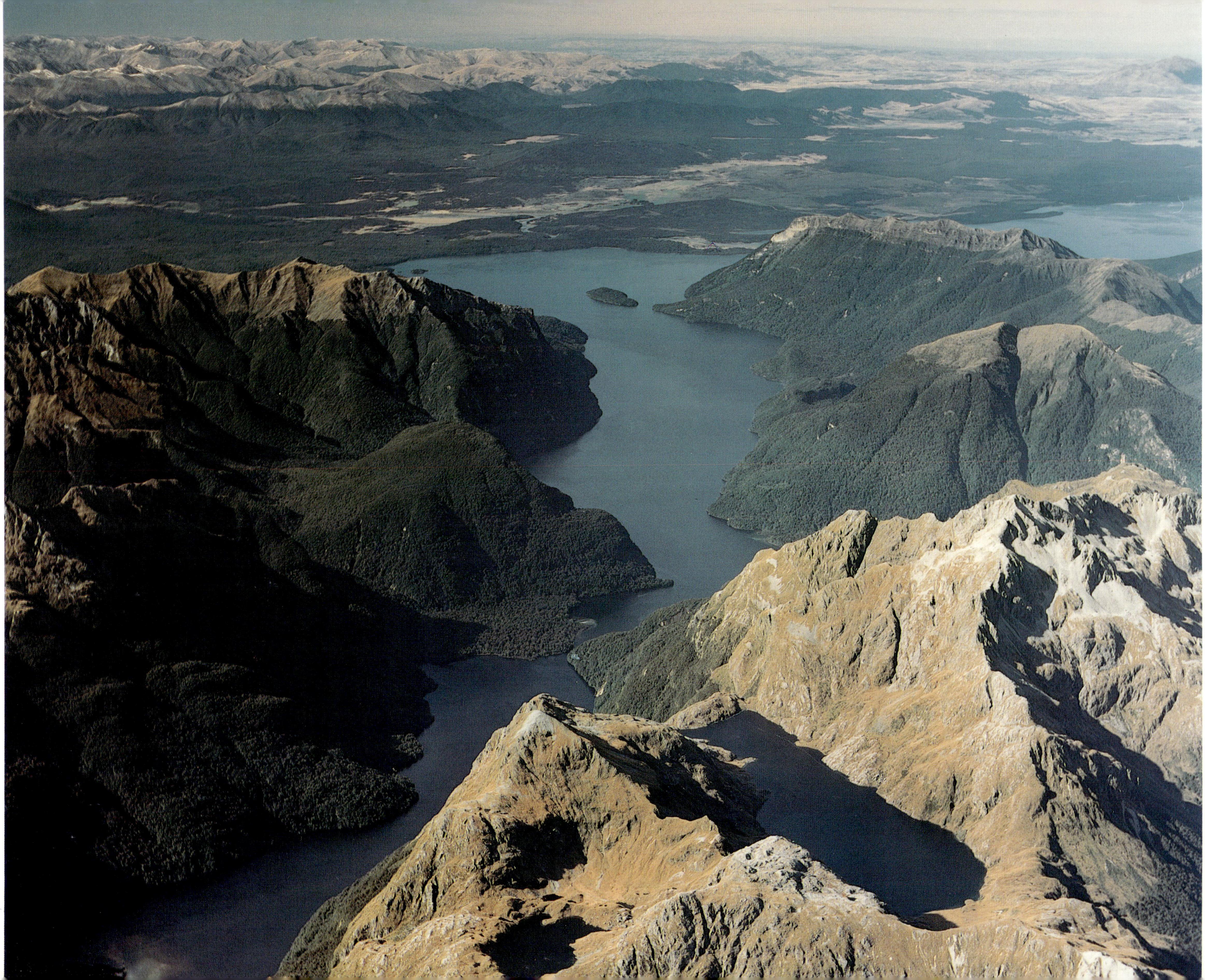

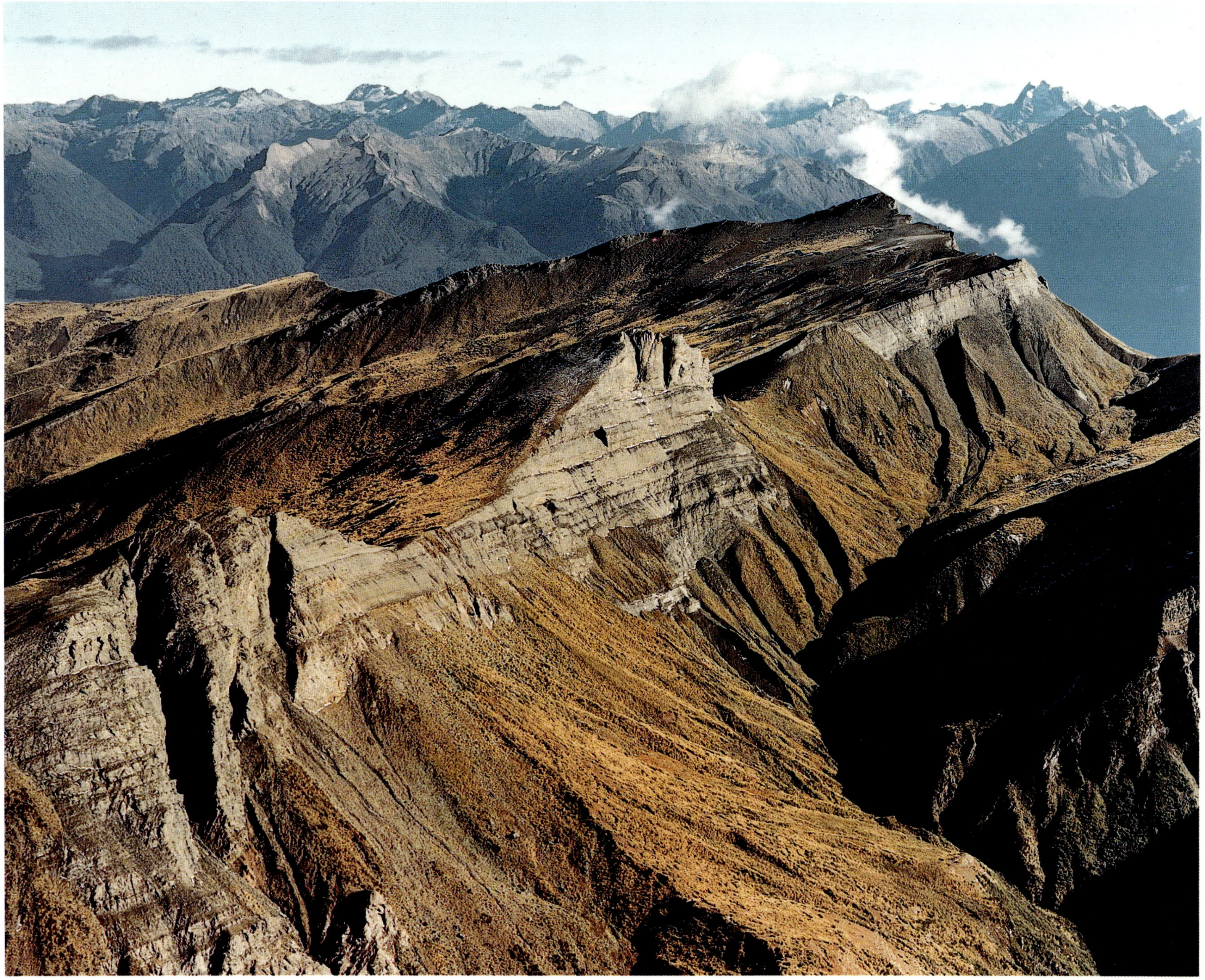

12

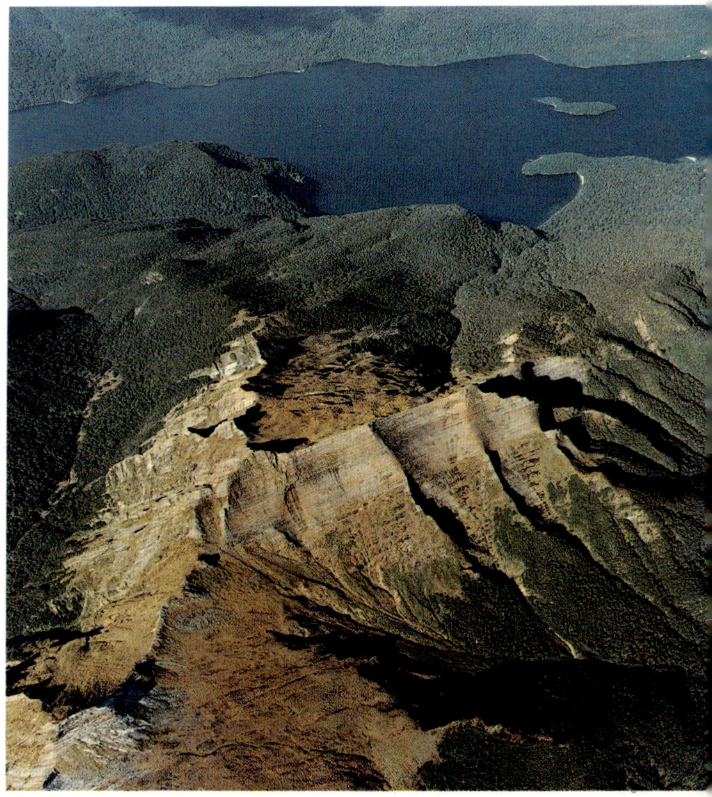

13

13 At the eastern end of the Franklin Mountains, a Tertiary sandstone formation similar to that at Annick Peak (see opposite) forms a spectacular escarpment above the valley slopes of the Billy Burn. Note the hummocky outcrops in the notch of the 'V' above Safe Cove of Lake Te Anau.

11 The view south-eastwards down the North Fiord of Lake Te Anau illustrates the sharp break in topography between the mountains of the park and the down-folded Te Anau basin. Lake Roxburgh (foreground) lies in an ice-cut cirque on the northern side of Mt McDougall (2036 m), above the Narrows. The Eglinton River enters the lake on the opposite side of Lake Te Anau, and the Livingstone Mountains are ranged along the skyline. The lowlands beyond the lake – the Te Anau Downs – are mantled with glacial deposits.

12 The Annick Peak scarp, at the southern end of the Earl Mountains, is one of the most spectacular landforms in the Tertiary sandstones and conglomerates that ring the northern end of Lake Te Anau. In this view looking north-west, the sandstone strata can be seen dipping gently to the south-west. Compare these dip slopes and escarpments in Tertiary rocks with the upright peaks (like Castle Mt, 2131 m, on the right skyline) and U-shaped valleys in the hard basement rocks to the west.

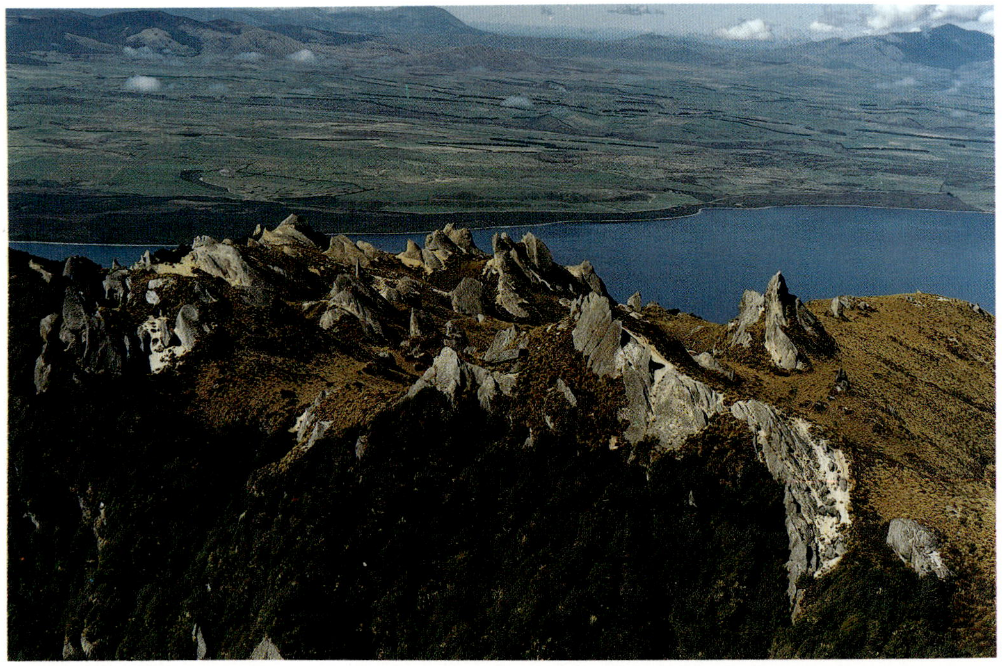

14

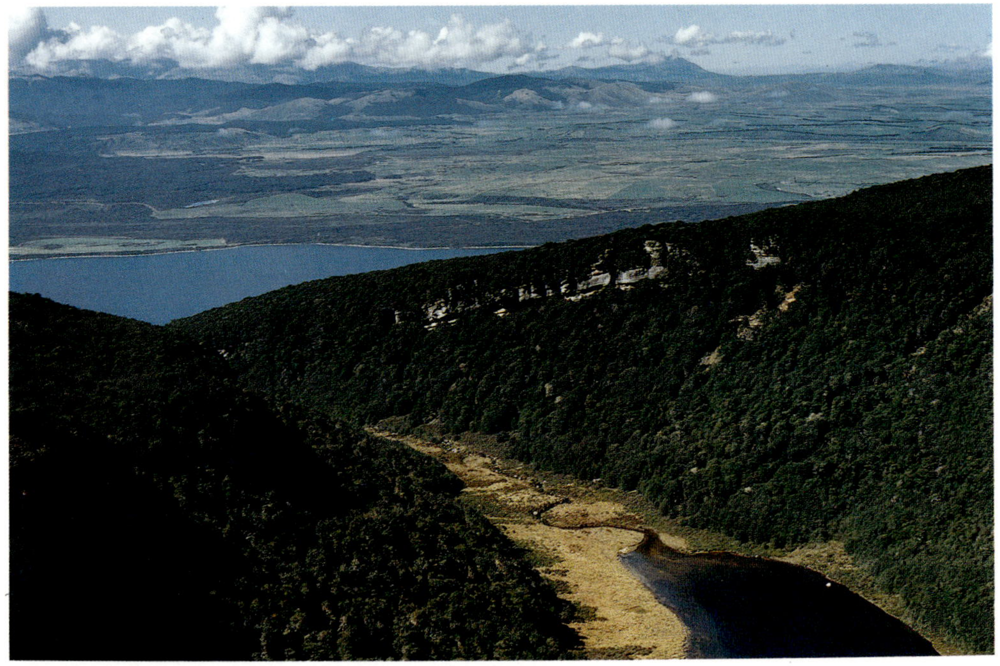

15

14 Spectacular tors occur on the ridge between the Point Burn, Murchison Mountains, and the South Fiord of Lake Te Anau. They have formed in granitic rocks of the Fiordland 'basement'; the limestone seen in the photo of Takahe valley has been eroded off the granite.

The farmland around the Upukerora River on the eastern side of the lake (distance) is covered with a thick layer of moraine and outwash gravel.

15 The Tunnel Burn drains Lake Orbell in the Takahe valley in the western Murchison Mountains. The rare rail, the takahe, was rediscovered here in 1948. At this point the granite rocks are capped by a sheet of much younger limestone (of Oligocene age). The limestone cliffs on both sides of the valley indicate the extent to which the Tunnel Burn has eroded down through the limestone sheet. This drainage system is linked to the Te Ana-au glowworm caves 650 m below on the shores of Lake Te Anau.

16 Island-studded Lake Manapouri (top, right) occupies a large glacial trough between the Kepler and Hunter Mountains, and extends out into the down-warped Waiau basin between Fiordland and the old volcanic rocks of the Takitimu Mountains (right, distance). This view, looking south-east across Norwest Lake, shows the typical rugged mountainous landforms which have developed on the rocks of southern Fiordland. The head of North Arm can be seen centre right, and the Cathedral Peaks are the prominent ridge cutting across the middle distance. Note the forested, ice-mammillated slopes beyond the North Arm and the ice-smoothed surfaces of the islands in Lake Manapouri.

The surface of Lake Manapouri is only 175 m above sea level but it is the deepest known lake in New Zealand, extending 270 m below sea level.

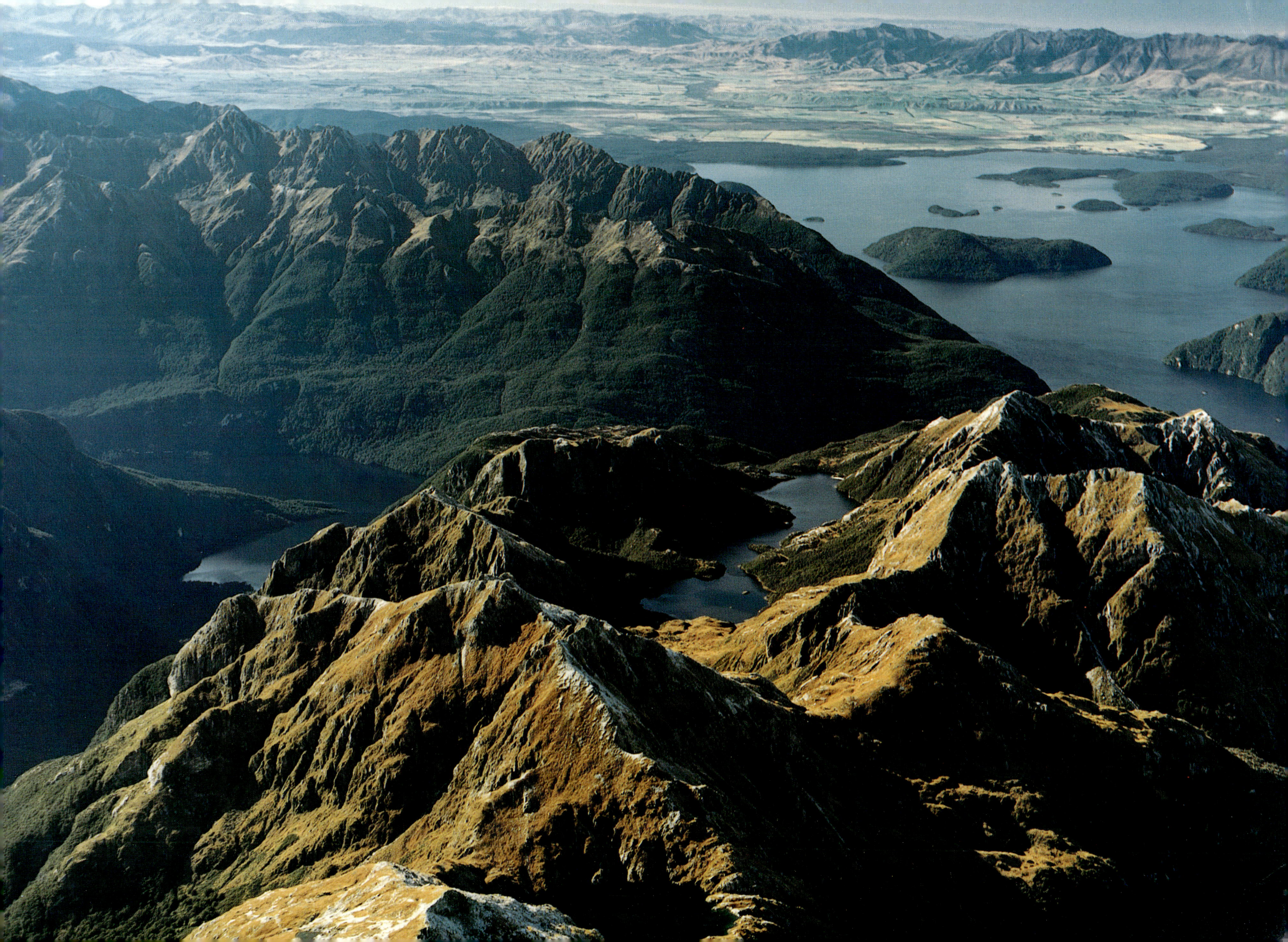

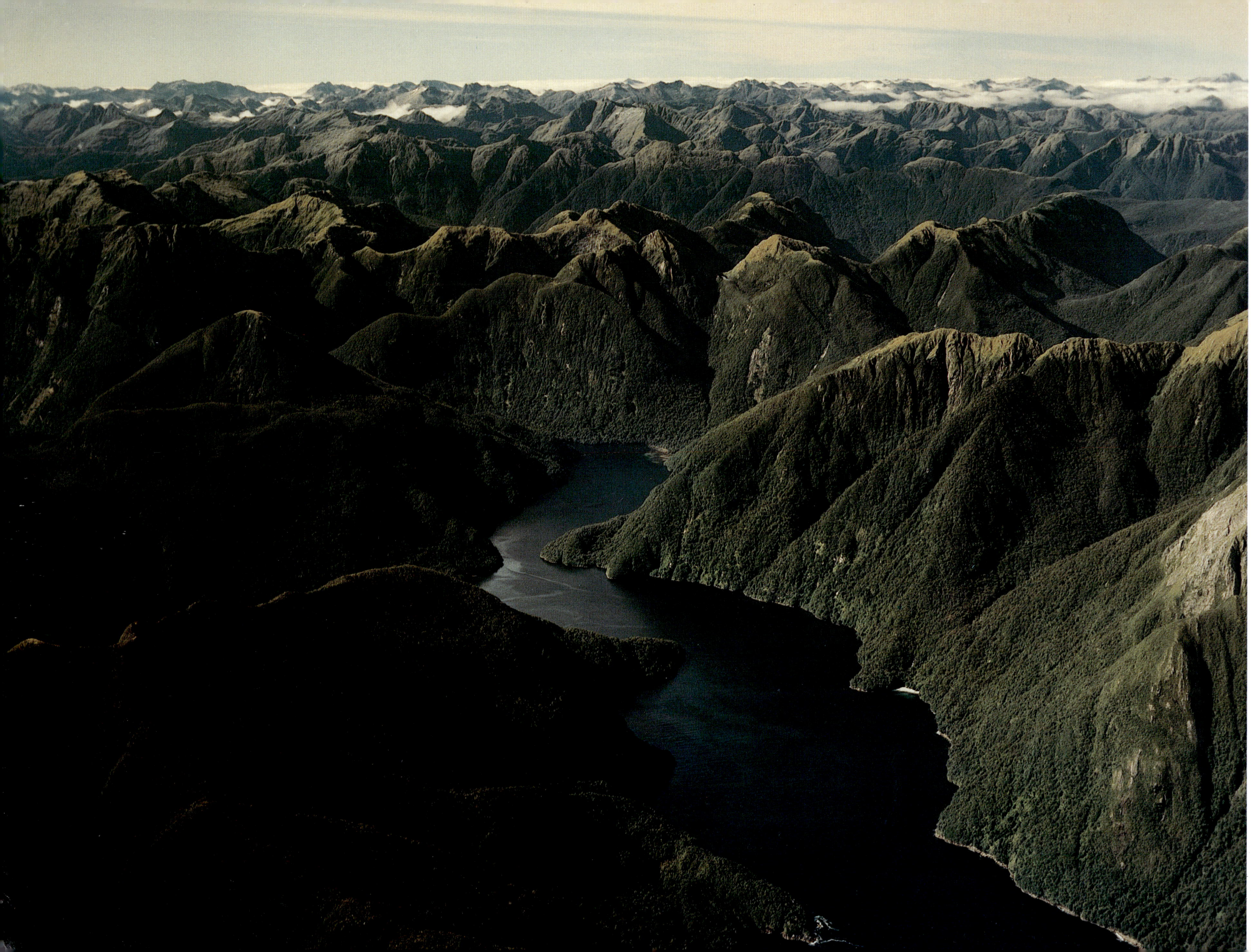

17 The peaks around the head of Dagg Sound rise only about 1100–1200 m above sea level yet the precipitous walls of the fiord make them look higher. This landscape is typical of the great western fiords – Doubtful, Breaksea and Dusky Sounds – carved in hard igneous and metamorphic rocks. This view to the south-east shows the bewildering maze of mountain ridges (all of a similar height) between the Tasman Sea and Lake Manapouri (under the cloud in the centre distance). The fiords penetrate so far into this mountainous hinterland that arms of both Doubtful and Breaksea Sounds extend back behind the first line of ridges at the apparent head of the sound.

18 Green Lake (larger) and Island Lake (smaller) nestle in a hummocky landscape resulting from an enormous ancient landslide; this large basin is 600 m above Lake Monowai which can be seen beyond the prominent notch in the encircling ridges. To the east-south-east in the distance lie the lower Waiau valley, the southern spurs of the Takitimu Mountains and the plains of Southland.

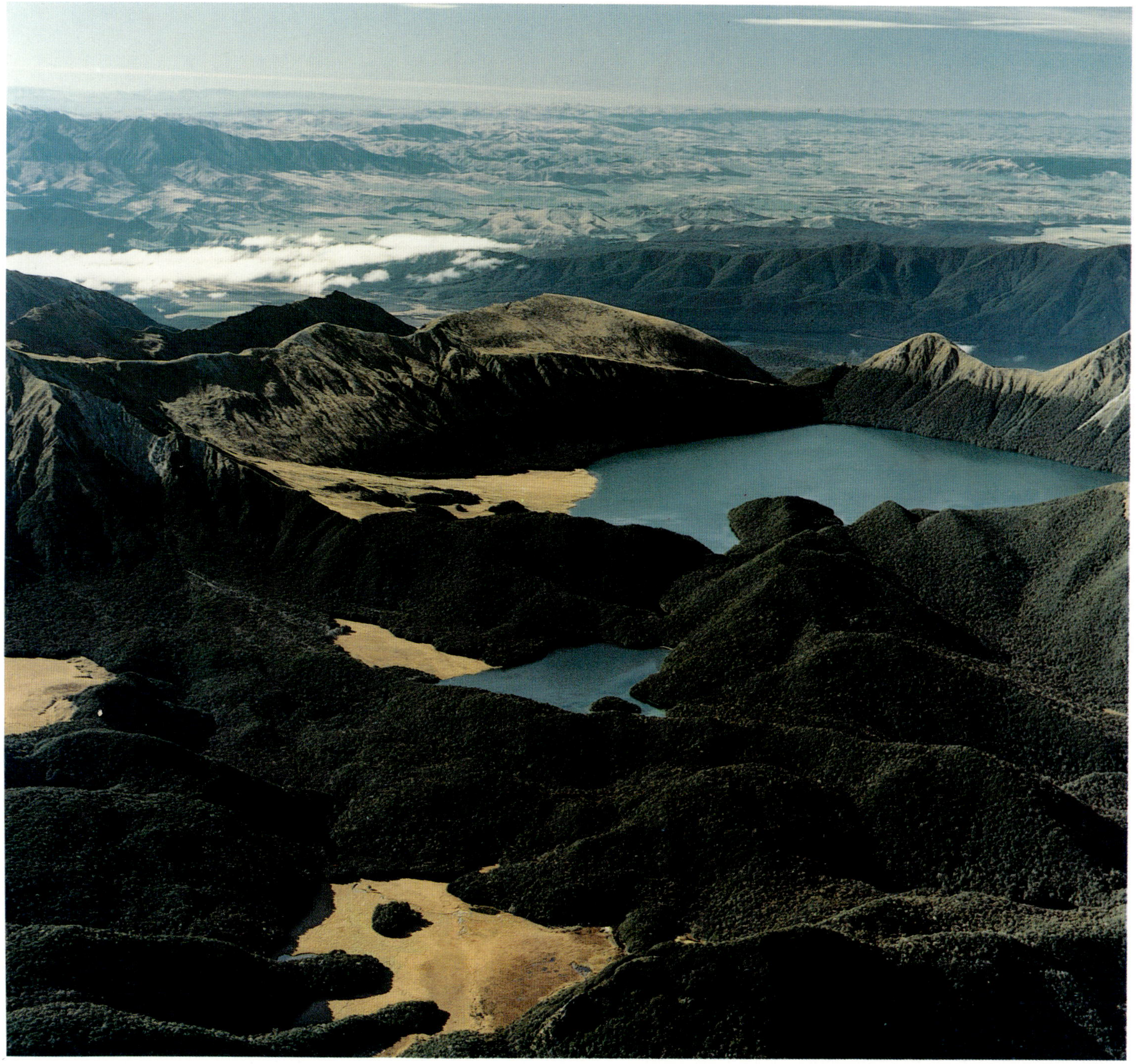

18

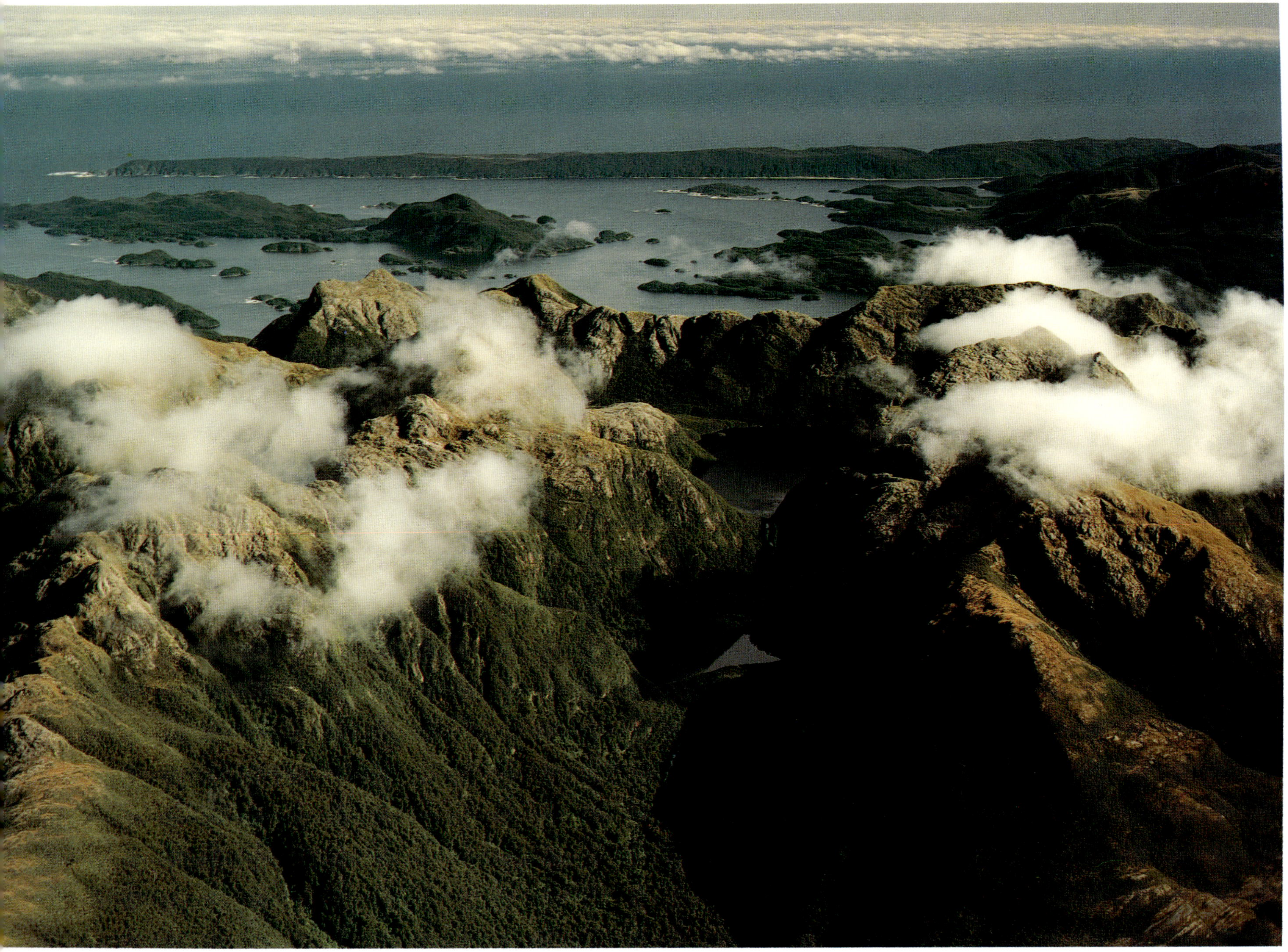

19

19 The Kakapo Range lies in the south-west corner of Fiordland and it too exhibits the cirque lakes and waterfalls typical of Fiordland, but the crests of the ridges are more rounded. To the north-west, the long flat Five Fingers Peninsula, bounding the northern side of Dusky Sound, is composed of gneiss eroded to a smooth surface during a higher sea level between glaciations of the Ice Ages, and then uplifted.

20 The outer part of Dusky Sound in the south-west of the park is a remarkable contrast with the fiords further north, for here the ice has over-ridden the ridge systems, planing them down to many islands and low spurs characterised by mammillated surfaces. This is particularly apparent in the granite rocks which make up most of the smaller islands and the southern tip (middle right) of Resolution Island.

The semi-circular cove at the foot of the foreground slopes off Mt Bradshaw is Cascade Cove, with Pickersgill Harbour and Astronomer Point beyond – all historical landmarks associated with Captain James Cook. Note how Five Fingers Peninsula is only connected to the rest of Resolution Island by a 200 m-wide isthmus of sand, and how the tree line at this latitude (46°S) has been depressed to only about 750 m above sea level.

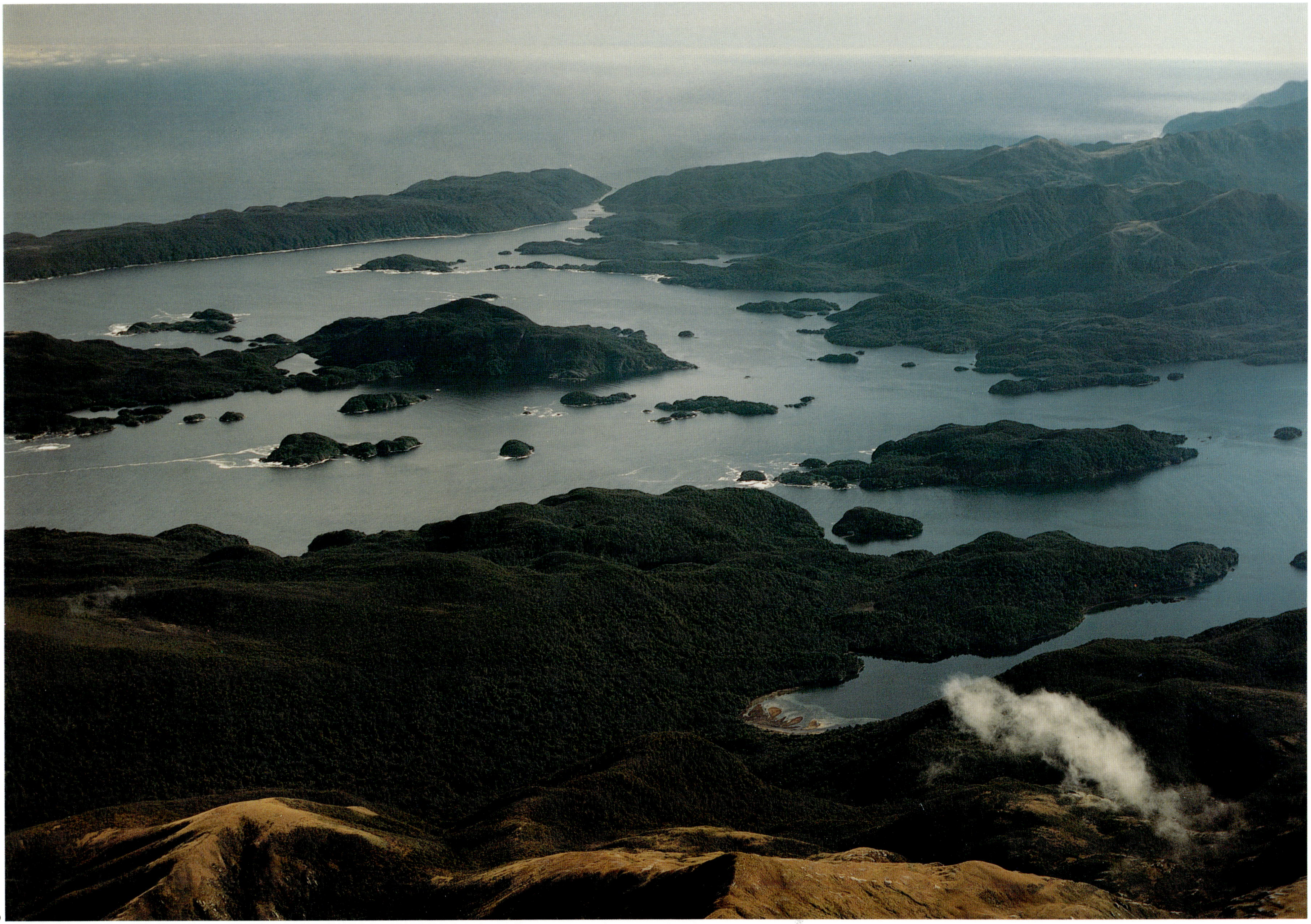

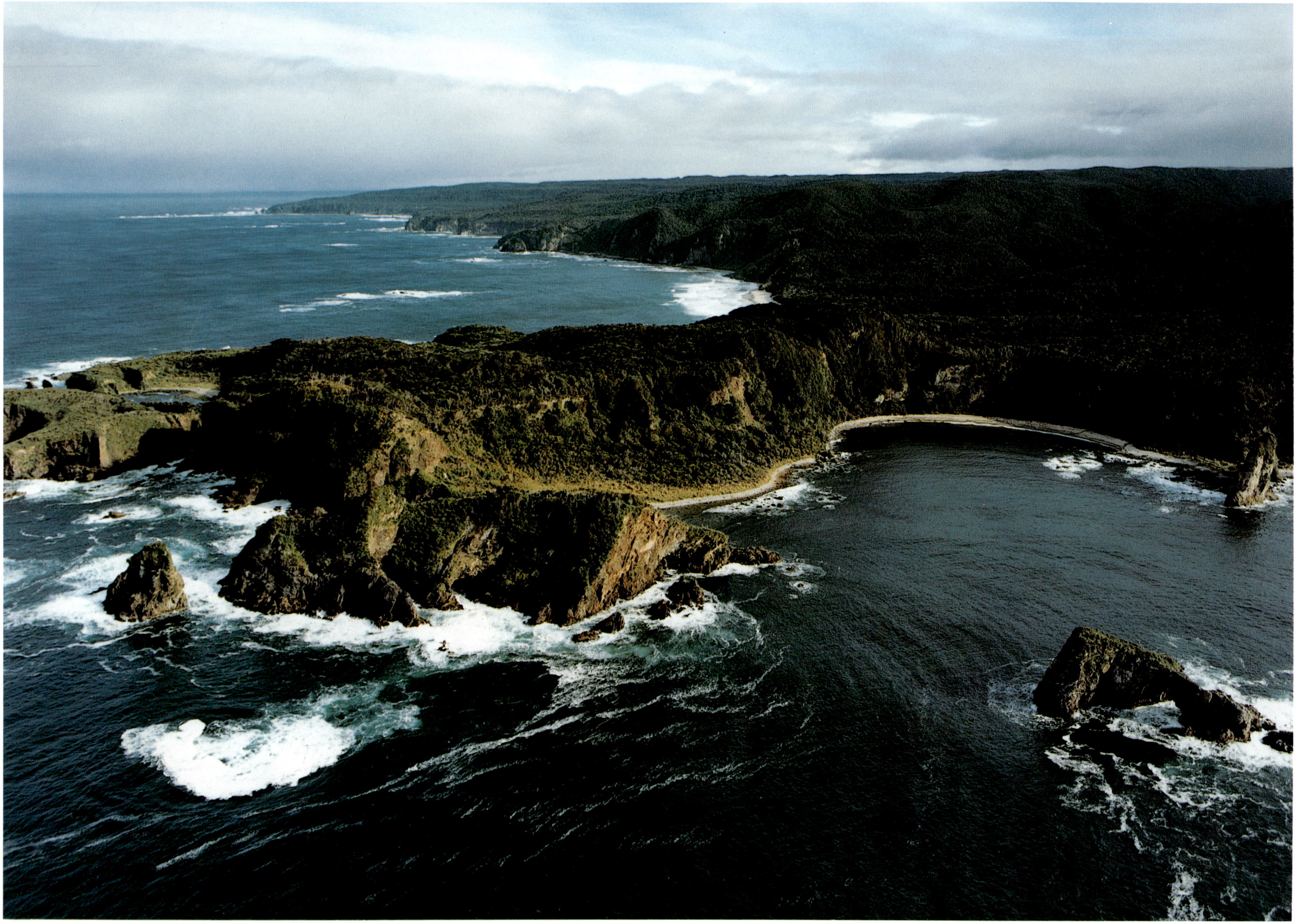

21 At Green Islets peninsula on the south coast of Fiordland, a sequence of younger Tertiary rocks – sandstone, breccia, and calcareous mudstone – overlie the older, mainly granitic rocks. Note the extensive series of uplifted marine benches along the coastline, looking westwards to Puysegur Point (see opposite page). The nearest marine bench above the cliffs to the right of the peninsula is estimated to have been cut in the basement granite and mantled with coarse, well-rounded gravels around 30 000 years ago and progressively uplifted since then.

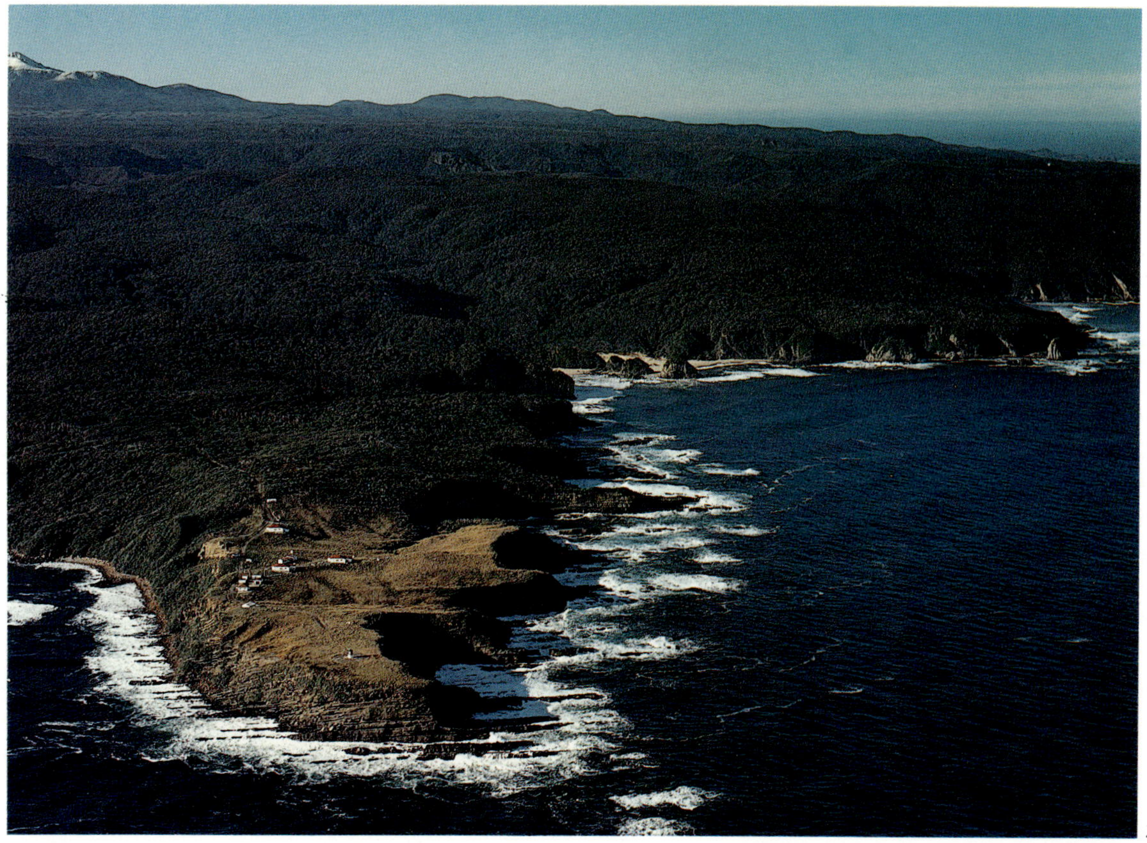
22

22 Puysegur Point (with its lighthouse and isolated settlement) is the westernmost point on the south coast of Fiordland. Wave erosion has etched out the strata of the Cretaceous sandstone and mudstone along this coastline. This view, looking eastwards, shows the flat surfaces of a remarkable flight of marine benches that extend for 50 km along this coastline as far east as the Hump Ridge. Eleven different benches have been identified and tentatively assigned ages – the lowest at 7000 years when the sea rose to its present level after the last glaciation. The oldest remnants now lie over 1000 m above sea level and up to 15 km from the present coastline. Estimates of the age of the oldest terrace range from 250 000 years to nearly one million years.

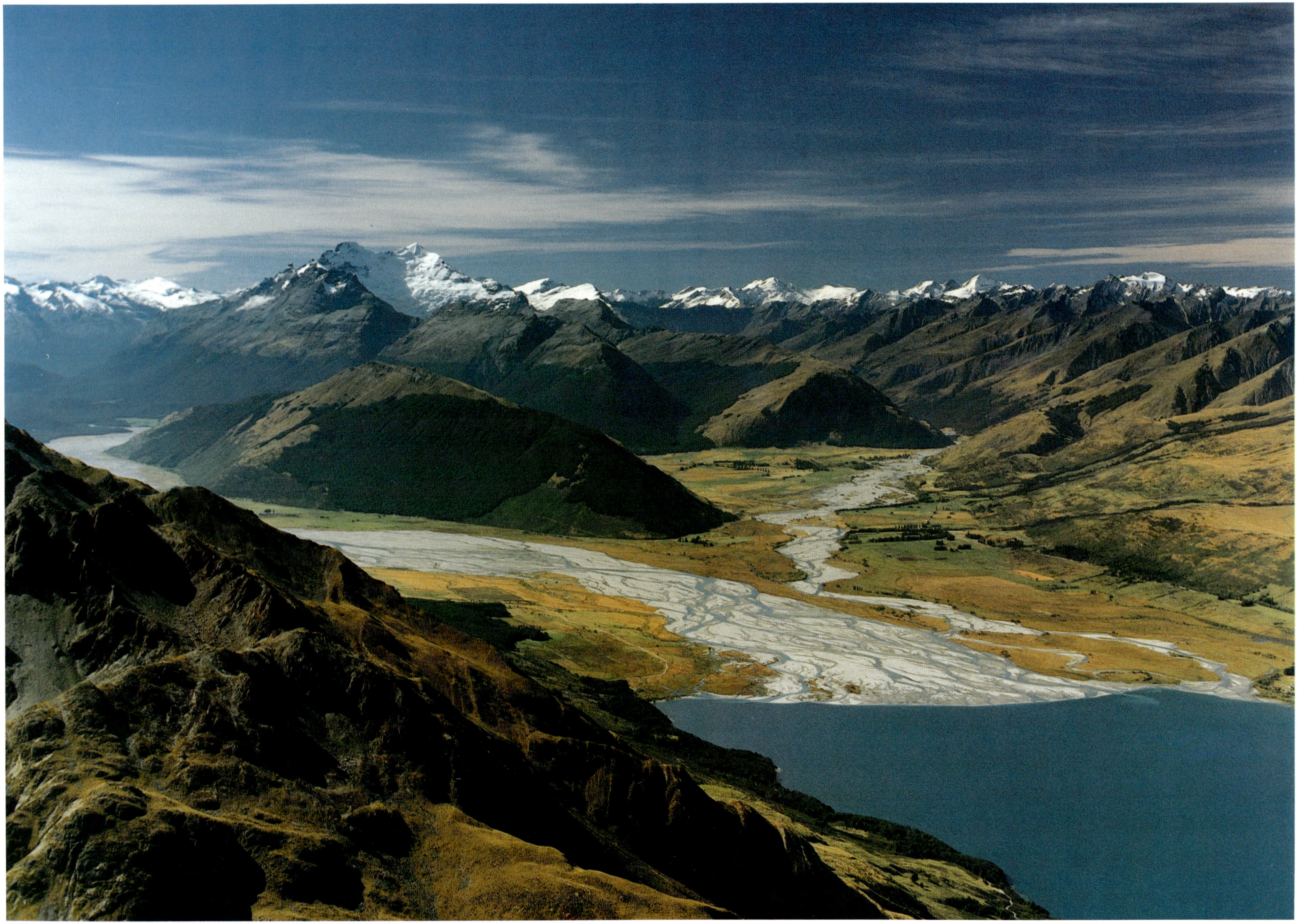

MT ASPIRING NATIONAL PARK

Mt Aspiring National Park straddles the mountainous north-western corner of Otago. There is a geological unity to the park for its rocks consist almost entirely of varieties of schist – the westernmost segment of the great arc of metamorphosed rocks which extends along the western side of the Southern Alps (see Westland National Park), through the basin and range landscapes of Central Otago, to the coast of eastern Otago. Schist rocks are slabby, and split along parallel planes to give distinctive grey or green, plate-shaped fragments that glisten in sunlight because of the flecks of mica within the rock.

In the north-west, from Jackson Bay to the Haast River, the schist rocks are truncated abruptly by the Alpine Fault. The Olivine, Haast, Selbourne and Marks Ranges stop abruptly at this major fault, the expression of a plate boundary. To the west of the fault, the coastal hills (of very old pre-Cambrian rocks) and a chain of conspicuous granite domes (such as Mt McLean) stand above the moraines, dunes, and swampy depressions of the coastal plain. South of Jackson Bay, the schists finish against the Livingstone Fault, beyond which a narrow belt of ultramafic rock has given rise to the spectacular landscapes of Red Mountain and the Little Red Hills.

GLACIAL LANDFORMS PREDOMINATE

Nearly all the landforms of the park are influenced by the intense glaciations of the latter part of the Pleistocene epoch, extending from around 200 000 to 10 000 years ago. This intense glaciation was not just confined to the park. To the east, huge glaciers carved deep troughs now filled by Lakes Wakatipu and Wanaka; to the west, the large glaciated valley of the Arawata and massive ancient moraines like those of the Cascade Plateau and Awarua Point show that the glaciers once extended beyond the present day coastline.

The orientation of most of the ranges and valleys within the park is in sharp contrast to Westland National Park, where the rivers flow more or less directly to the Tasman Sea at right angles to the Southern Alps. Here, most of the glaciated valleys follow the grain of the country, with the upper parts of the Dart, Matukituki, Joe–Arawata, and Wilkin valleys – and almost the entire lengths of the Waipara, Waiatoto, Ngatau, Burke and Wills Rivers – running parallel to the mountain chain. Only in the north-west have the Haast, Turnbull, and Okuru Rivers been able to cut a direct east-west course across the rising Alps.

Above the valleys, the crests of the mountain ranges are remarkably similar in height (2000–2500 m). Only Mt Aspiring (3027 m) and Mt Earnslaw (2819 m) stand out above the mass of peaks. There are 100 or so glacier remnants, from the tiny Mawson Glacier perched high above the Wills valley in the north-east corner of the park, to the prominent Earnslaw Glacier on the south face of the Earnslaw massif which dominates the entrance to the park from the head of Lake Wakatipu. Most of these glaciers are now only very small remnants of the ice sheets which carved this landscape. Some, like the Birley, Arawata and Liverpool Glaciers, have virtually disappeared since European explorers first named them; even major valley glaciers like the Dart and Joe are now much diminished in size, with several kilometres of moraine covering the remaining valley ice.

Only three large expanses of high altitude snowfield are left – the Bonar and Volta Glaciers surrounding Mt Aspiring, and the Olivine Ice Plateau. Although their névés appear to be little changed, the ice streams issuing from them are shrinking rapidly. The evidence for this glacial retreat can be found throughout the park, in the small stranded moraines and the exposure of unweathered rock around the terminals of retreating glaciers (e.g. the Dart and Whitbourn), and the recently formed lakes at the former glacier terminal faces in the head of valleys like the Williamson, Waipara and Waiatoto.

The imprint of the former glaciers on the landscape can be seen on all sides. In some places the ice scoured the rock, leaving a steep-sided horn – the most outstanding of which is Mt Aspiring itself. As the valley glaciers shrank, tributary ice streams were left perched on the valley sides; today, these 'hanging valleys' carry many of the tributaries of the Arawata, Waiatoto, Dart and Pyke Rivers, separated from the main valleys by waterfalls and steep gorges which have been cut since the ice retreated.

Elsewhere, the ice has gouged troughs across rock ridges leaving ice-smoothed passes (the best known being Haast Pass and Harris Saddle). Very often this ice accumulated on the shady southern side of the pass, plucking away at the rock to form steep-walled cirques below the pass (for example, the Liverpool Stream side of Arawata Saddle or Rabbit Pass at the head of the East Matukituki). These cirques now stand above rock basins excavated by ice, many of which are now filled with lakes. Prominent examples are Lakes Unknown, Nerine, Wilson and Harris in the Humboldt Mountains.

In the lower reaches of the main valleys like the Makarora and Matukituki, and on the slopes above Lakes Wakatipu and Wanaka, near-horizontal striations and benches mark the passage long ago of ice past the hill slopes; resistant bands of smoothed harder rock now protrude from the valley floors with the typical crouching shape of roche moutonnées. Most of the rock detritus produced by the huge Pleistocene glaciers has been carried beyond the park boundary. Unfortunately, therefore, the major fluvioglacial landforms lie outside the park – the deltas, braided river beds, terraces, and moraines of the lower Dart, Makarora, Matukituki and Arawata valleys.

1 At the head of Lake Wakatipu, the ice-mantled twin peaks of Mt Earnslaw (2819 m) tower above the river flats and braided streams of the delta of the Dart (left) and Rees (right) Rivers. Most of the catchments of both rivers lie within the park, behind the Mt Earnslaw massif. The distant peak of Mt Aspiring can be seen above the peaks of the Richardson Mountains along the right skyline. Note the moderately steep westward dip of the schist in the Richardson Mountains.

Huge glaciers smoothed these mountain slopes and excavated the trough now filled by Lake Wakatipu during the Pleistocene ice ages. Mt Alfred (left foreground), shaped like an upturned boat, shows the effect of parallel ice streams (of the former Dart Glacier) planing both sides of a resistant block of rock to a sharp ridge crest.

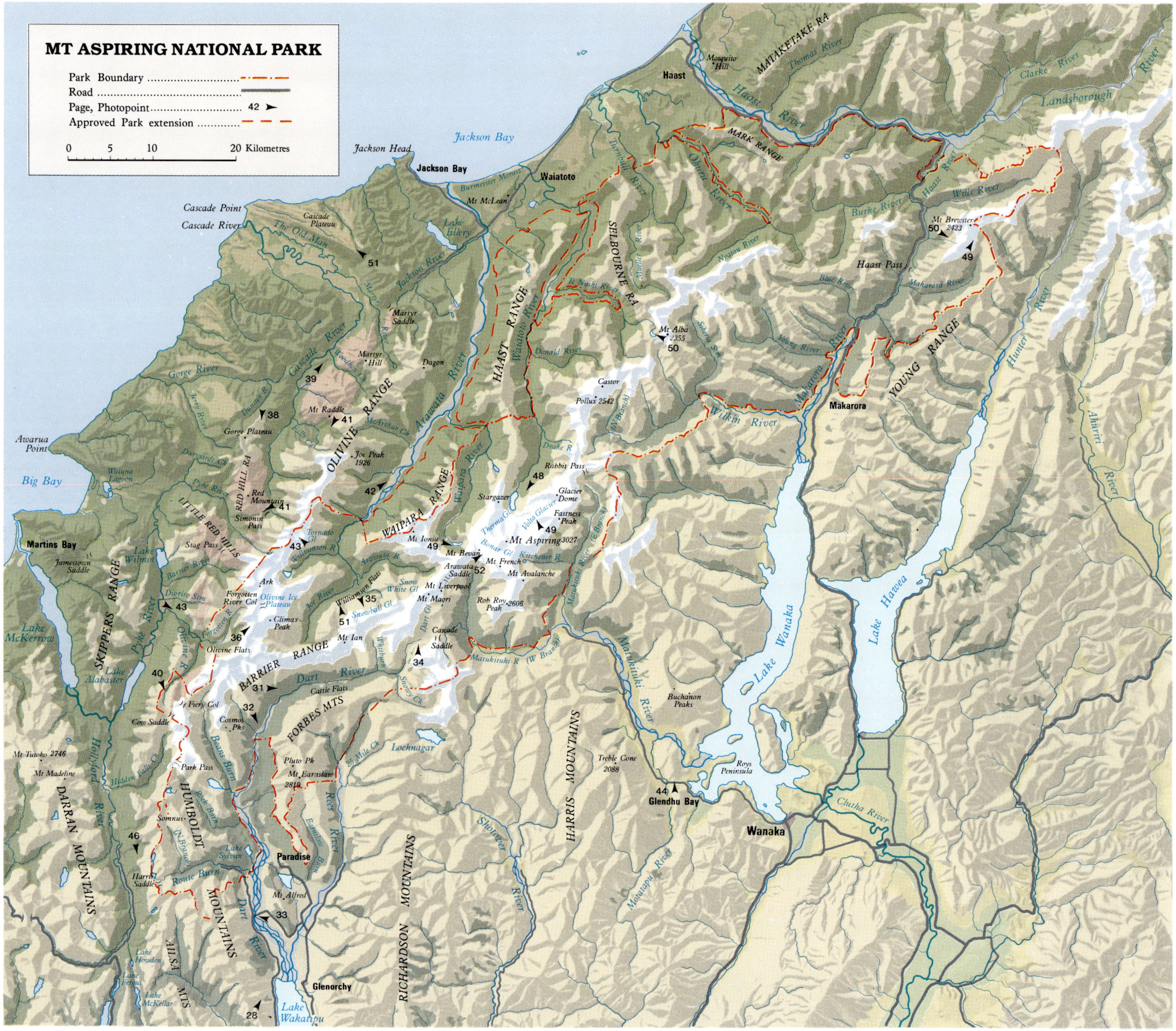
MT ASPIRING NATIONAL PARK
Park Boundary
Road
Page, Photopoint 42
Approved Park extension
0 5 10 20 Kilometres
Jackson Bay
Jackson Head
Jackson Bay
Waiatoto
Haast
Mosquito Hill
MATAKETAKE RA
Thomas River
Haast River
Clarke River
Landsborough River
MARK RANGE
Okuru River
Turnbull River
Mt McLean
Cascade Point
Cascade River
Cascade Plateau
The Old Man
Lake Ellery
51
Jackson River
Martyr Saddle
Martyr Hill
Dagon
SELBOURNE RA
HAAST RANGE
Waiatoto River
Burke River
Haast River
Wills River
Mt Brewster 2423
50
49
Haast Pass
Blue River
Makarora River
Mt Alba 2355
50
Young River
YOUNG RANGE
Hunter River
Makarora
Gorge River
Cascade River
39
Mt Raddle
41
38
Gorge Plateau
OLIVINE RANGE
Arawhata River
Castor
Pollux 2542
Wilkin River
Awarua Point
Big Bay
Joe Peak 1926
42
Waipara Range
48
Rabbit Pass
Stargazer
Glacier Dome
Fastness Peak
49
Mt Aspiring 3027
RED HILL RA
Red Mountain
41
Simonin Pass
LITTLE RED HILLS
Martins Bay
Jamestown Saddle
Lake Wilmot
Stag Pass
43
WAIPARA RANGE
Mt Ionia
49
Mt Bevan
Arawata Saddle
52
Mt French
Mt Avalanche
Matukituki River
SKIPPERS RANGE
Lake McKerrow
43
Forgotten River Col
Olivine Ice Plateau
Ark
35
Mt Liverpool
Mt Maori
Rob Roy Peak 2606
51
Climax Peak
36
Olivine Flats
Mt Ian
Cascade Saddle
34
BARRIER RANGE
Dart River
40
Lake Alabaster
31
Cattle Flats
32
Fiery Col
Cow Saddle
Cosmos Pks
FORBES MTS
Lochnagar
Matukituki R (W Branch)
Matukituki River
Buchanan Peaks
Lake Wanaka
Lake Hawea
Ahuriri River
HARRIS MOUNTAINS
Treble Cone 2088
Roys Peninsula
44
Glendhu Bay
Wanaka
Clutha River
Mt Tutoko 2746
Mt Madeline
DARRAN MOUNTAINS
Hollyford River
Park Pass
HUMBOLDT
Pluto Pk
Mt Earnslaw 2819
Rees River
Shotover River
Somnus
46
Harris Saddle
Routeburn
Lake Sylvan
Paradise
MOUNTAINS
Mt Alfred
33
RICHARDSON MOUNTAINS
Matatapu River
Dart River
AILSA MTS
Lake Howden
Lake McKellar
28
Glenorchy
Lake Wakatipu

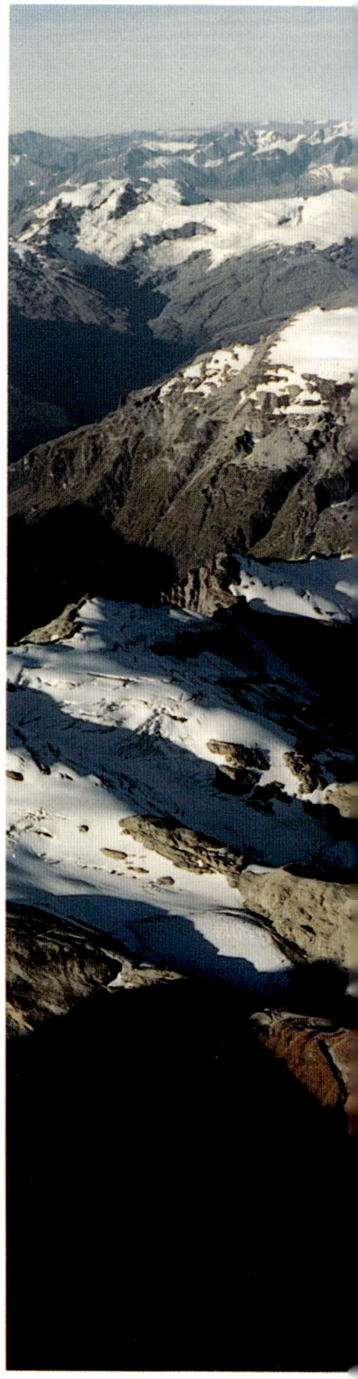

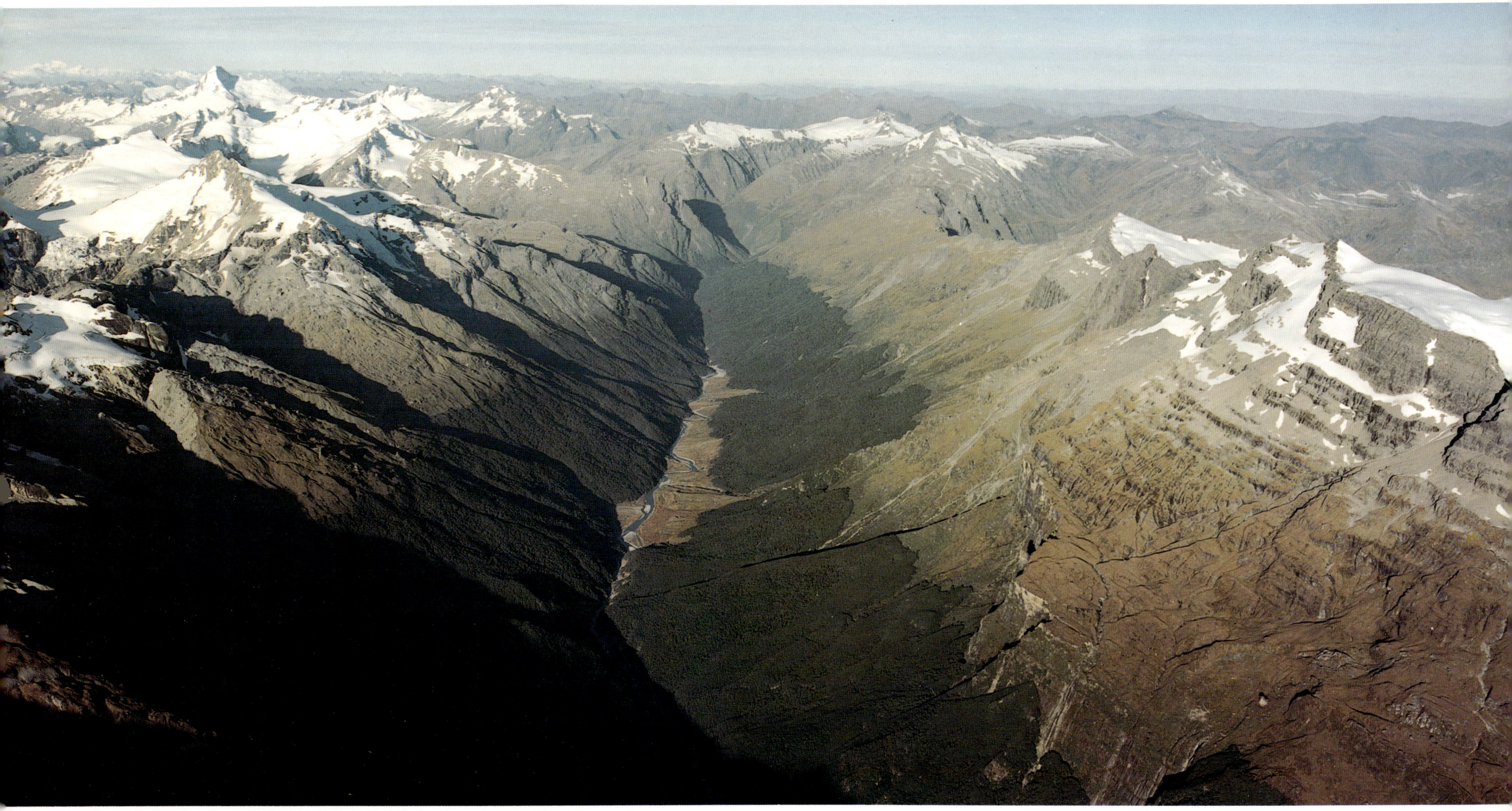

2 Cattle Flat lies between the Barrier (left) and Forbes (right) Ranges in the middle reaches of the Dart River. The 'U'-shaped glacial valley of the Dart in the upper reaches above the Snowy junction has been eroded to a 'V' shape since the retreat of the glacier. The horn of Mt Aspiring, and the high peaks of Mt Cook National Park, can be seen in the left distance. In this late summer view, the absence of snow on the north and west facing slopes is obvious. The gentle south-east dip of the schist layers in this part of the Forbes Range has resulted in a series of escarpments on the north-west (Dart) face, and small glaciers perched along the top of the dip slopes.

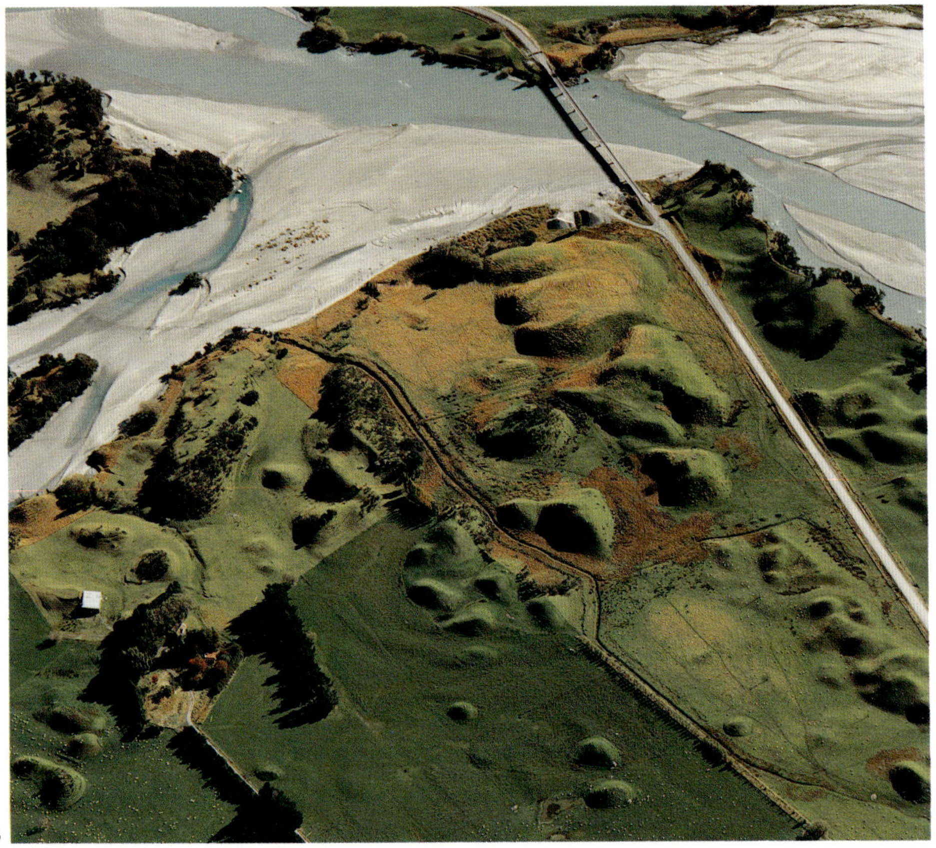

3

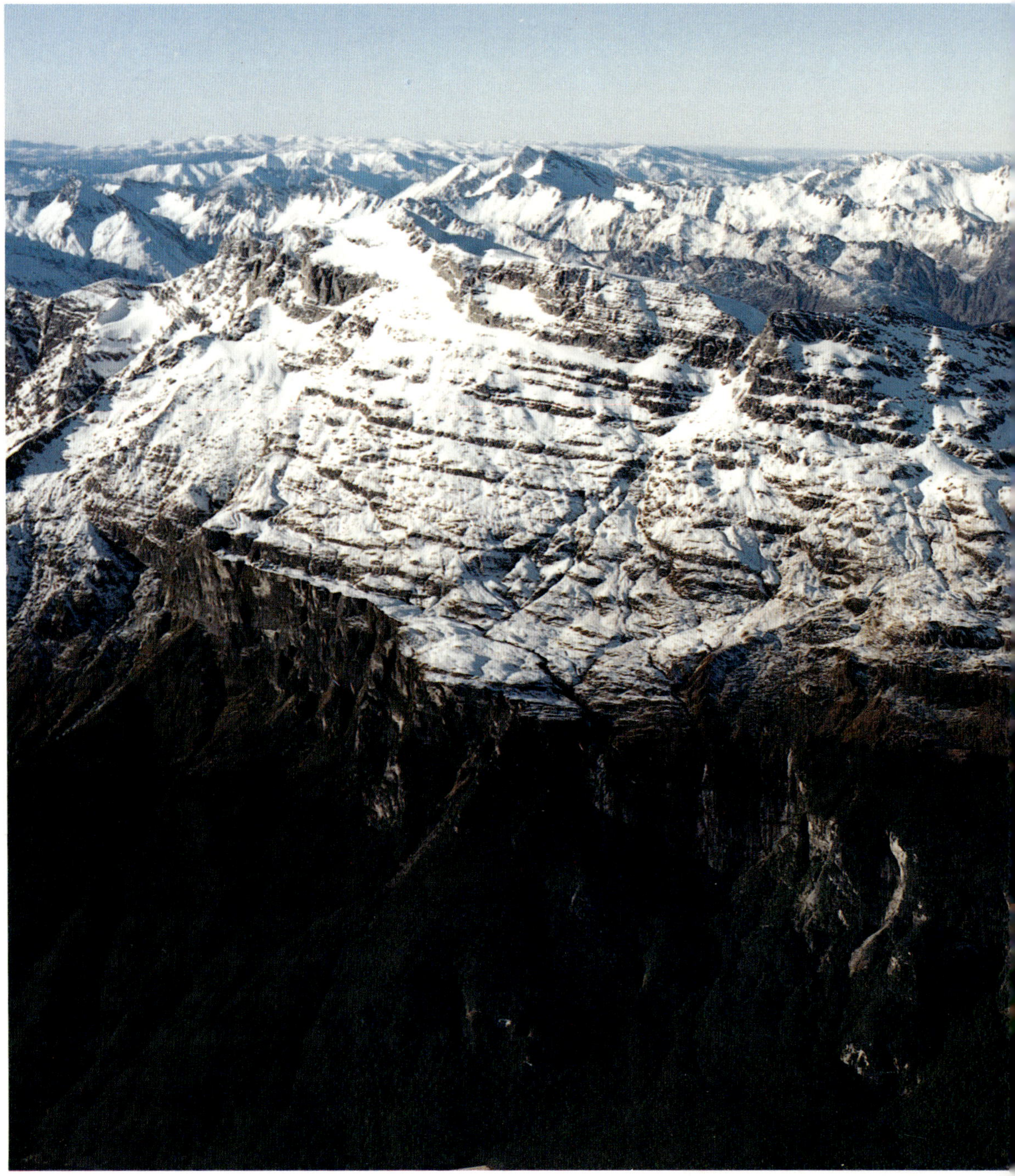

4

3 The road to the Routeburn entrance to the park passes through an interesting group of mounds known as 'the Hillocks' near the bridge over the lower Dart River. The exact nature of their glacial origin is open to conjecture. One view is that they are piles of debris from an old kamefield (an area of terraces or mounds consisting of water-laid sand and gravel of glacial origin). The irregular shapes of these lone kames were then softened with a blanket of loess.

The milky-green colour of the Dart River is due to the suspension of fine rock particles (rock flour) in the moving water.

4 From the middle reaches of the Dart valley near Dredge Flat, the north-west face of the Mt Earnslaw massif presents a striking example of gently dipping schists (a dip of about 10° to the south). Mt Alfred and Lake Wakatipu can be seen in the right distance (Fig. 1 shows the view in the opposite direction). The only significant valley floor lake within the park, Lake Sylvan, can be seen nestling among the forested glacial hillocks on the west bank of the lower Dart.

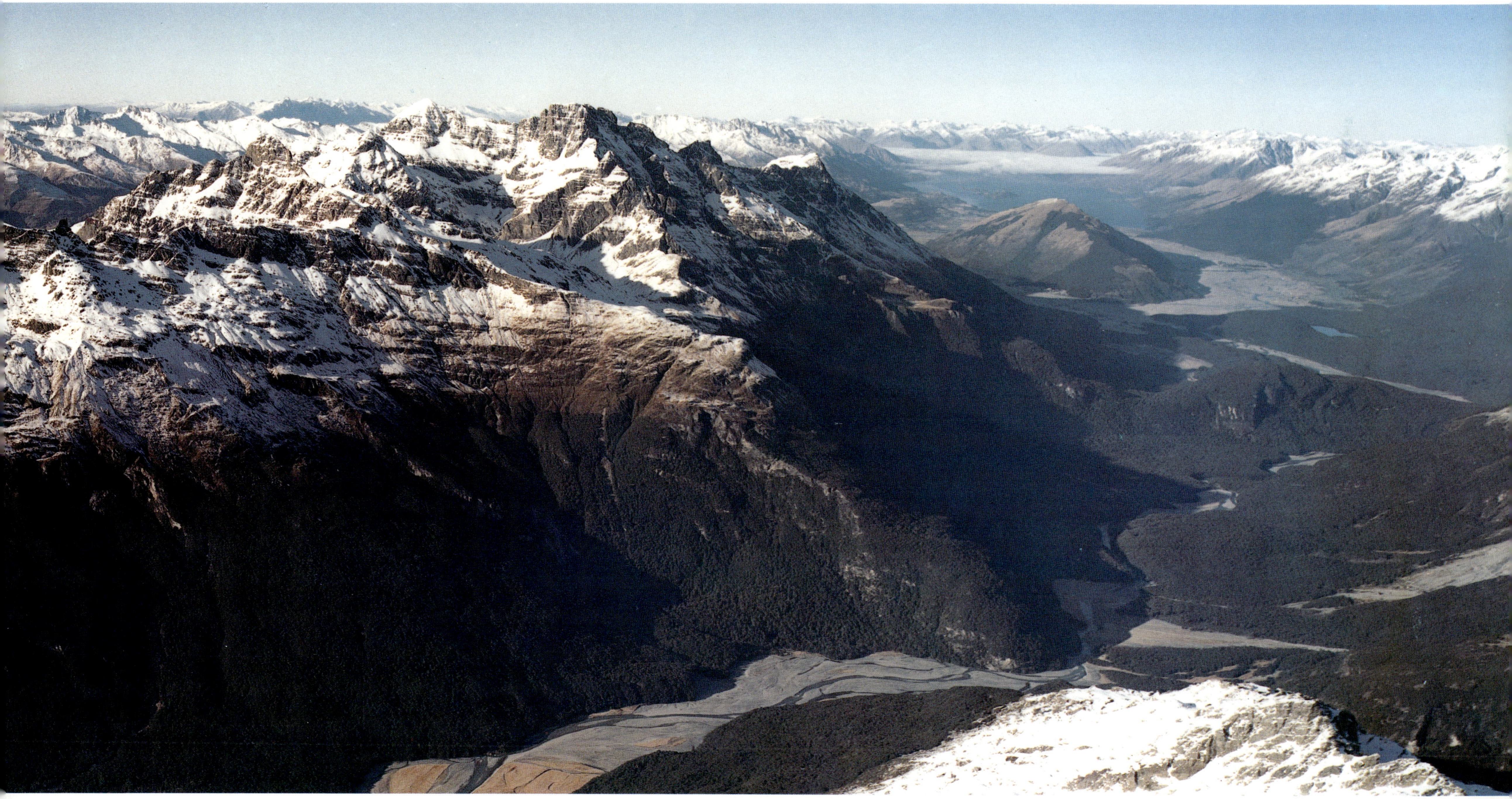

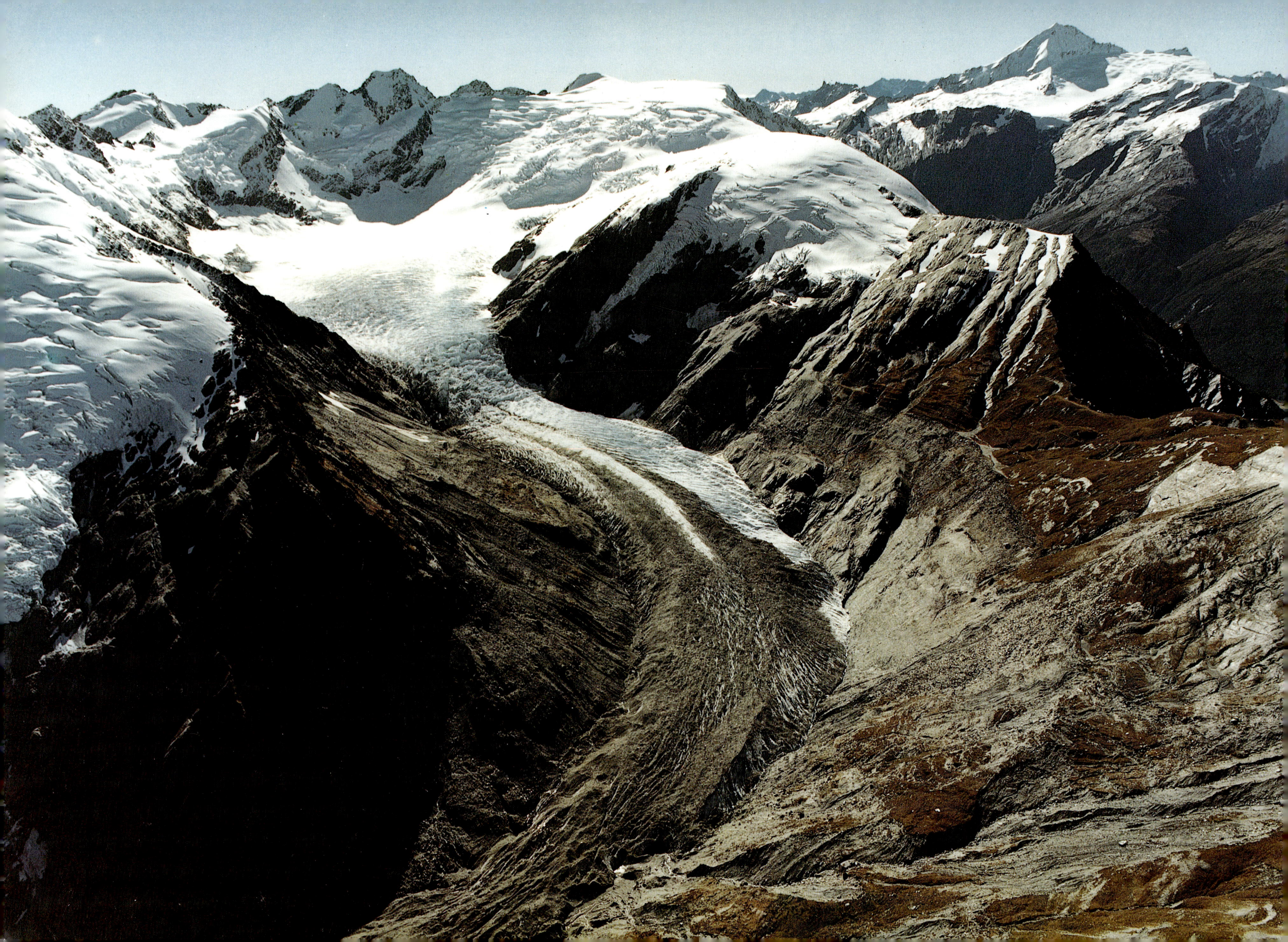

5 The Dart Glacier at the eastern end of the Barrier Range is the largest glacier feeding into the Dart River system. The terminus has retreated up-valley about 5 km since 1850, at a rate that has recently averaged 50 m a year. The surface of the glacier has dropped about 200 m over the same period, from the level marked by the prominent moraine ridge immediately below Cascade Saddle on the right. The shrinkage of this and other glaciers within the park has left many slopes unsupported, resulting in large scale slumping like that visible in the right foreground.

Mt Aspiring is the prominent peak to the north-east, with the peaks of Mt Maori, Mt Liverpool and Islington Dome around the head of the Dart névé.

6 The signs of recent glacial retreat are just as evident in the small glaciers as in the larger ones. This tongue of ice is all that remains of the south Snowball Glacier draining the Marion Plateau below Mt Ian on the northern slopes of the Snowdrift Range separating the Joe and Dart watersheds. The ice-scoured rock and lack of moraine is in contrast to valley glaciers like the Joe or Dart (Fig. 5).

6

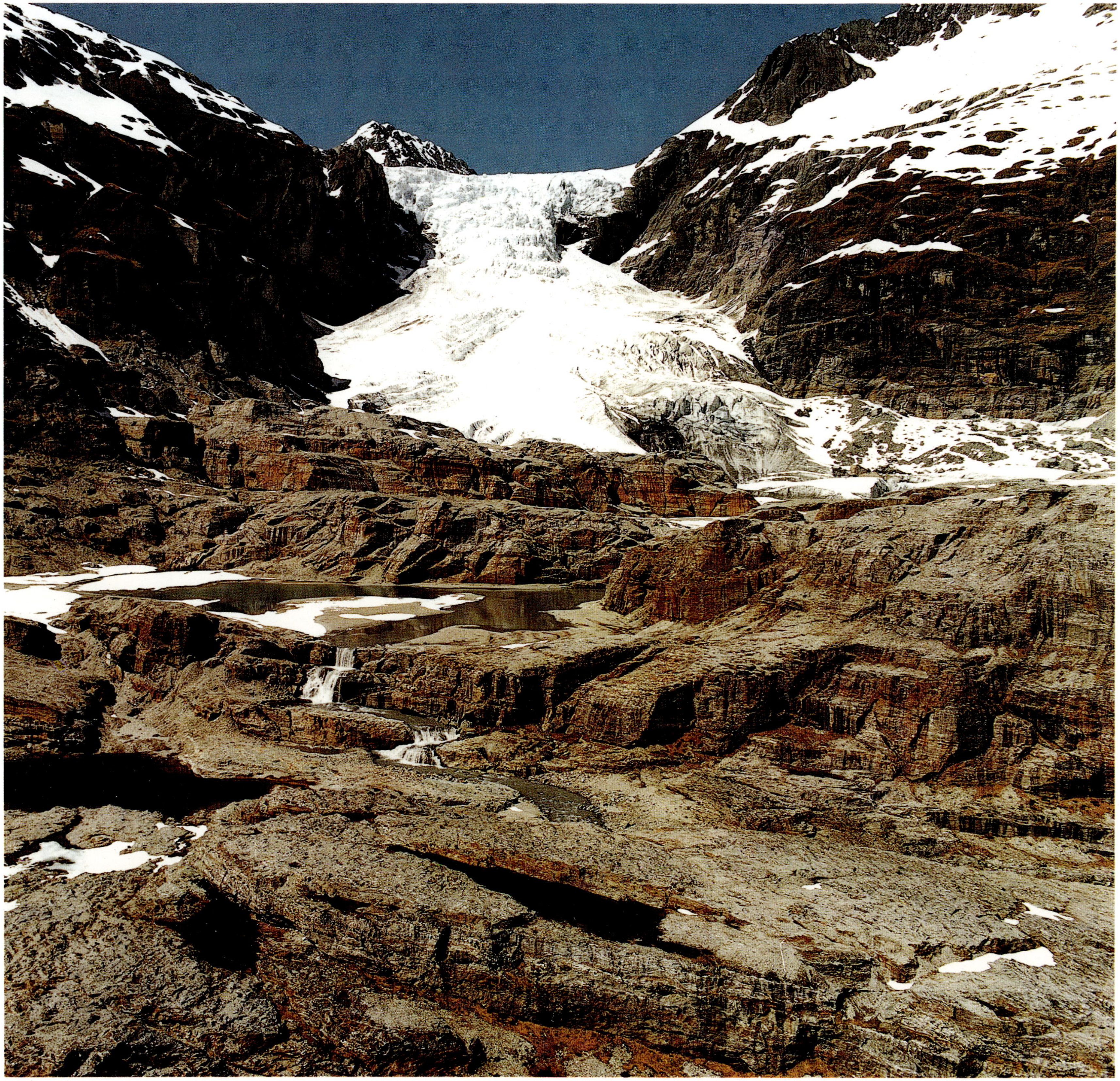

7 The Olivine Ice Plateau, at the southern end of the Olivine Range, is the névé of the Andy Glacier, one of the three major glaciers within the park (the other two being the Volta and Bonar below Mt Aspiring – right distance). At the height of the Pleistocene glaciations all the mountains in the centre of the photograph would have been buried beneath a thick ice-cap. Tongues of ice radiated out in all directions from this ice-cap, carving the hanging valleys now occupied by tributaries of the Pyke, Cascade, and Arawata Rivers. The smoothness and lack of crevasses in the Olivine Ice Plateau contrasts with the heavily-crevassed and aptly-named Thunderer Glacier on the steeper slopes of Climax Peak in the right foreground above the Joe Glacier.

Red Mountain can be seen (upper left) as well as Williamson Flats and Mt Aspiring (upper right). Note the near vertical dip to the schist on the western side of the northern Olivine Range (centre, distance; see also Figs 11 and 12).

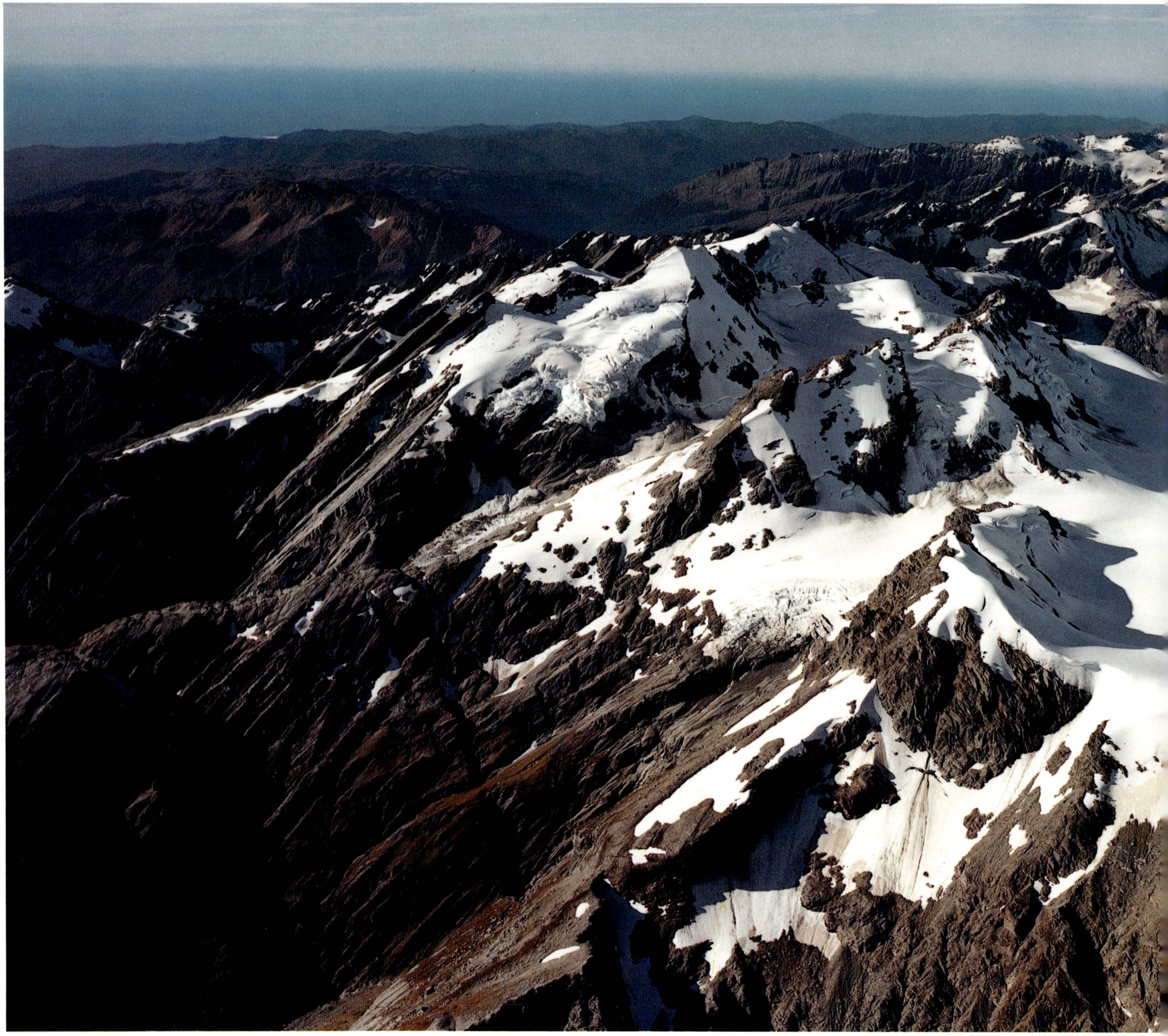

7

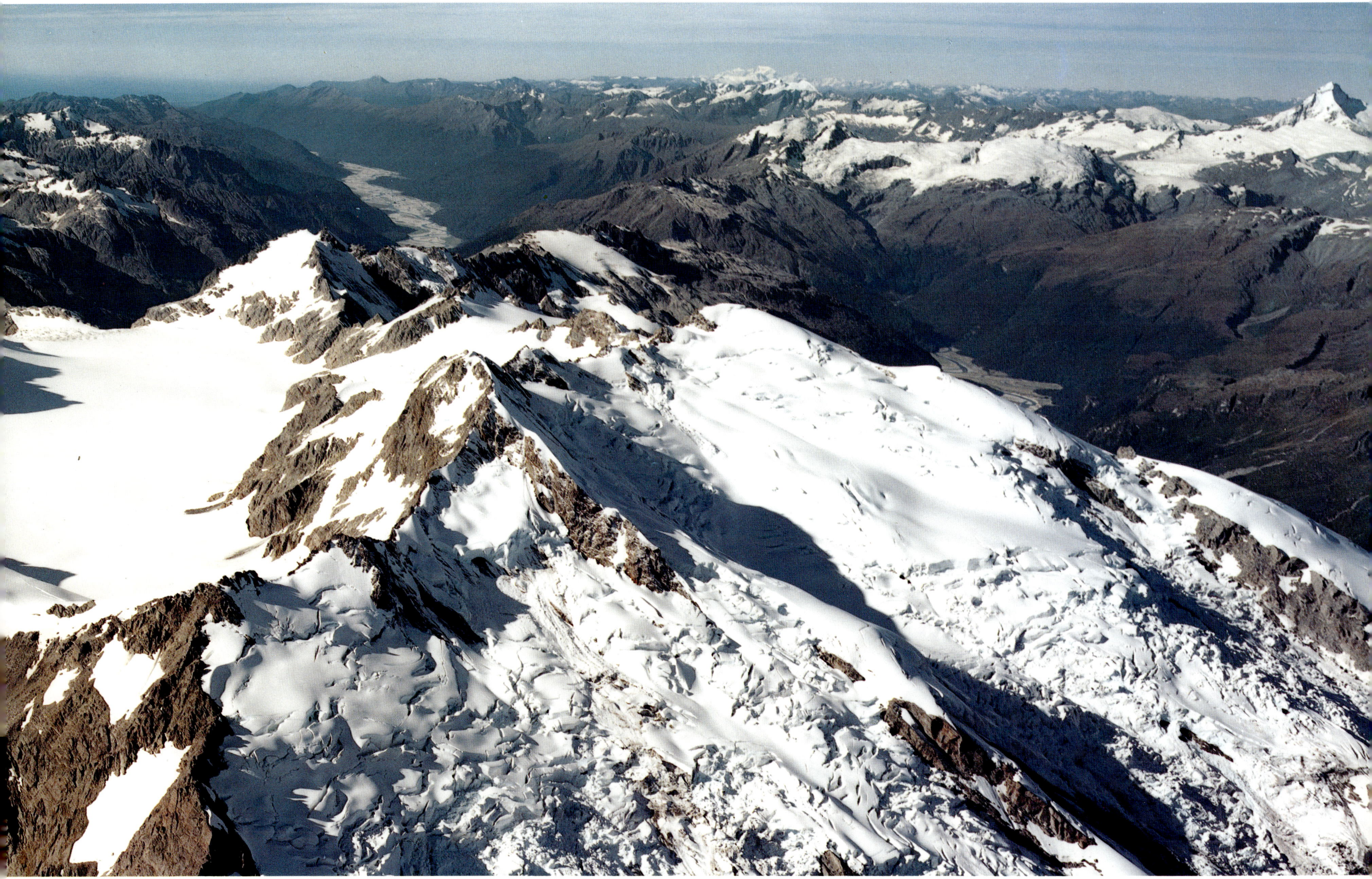

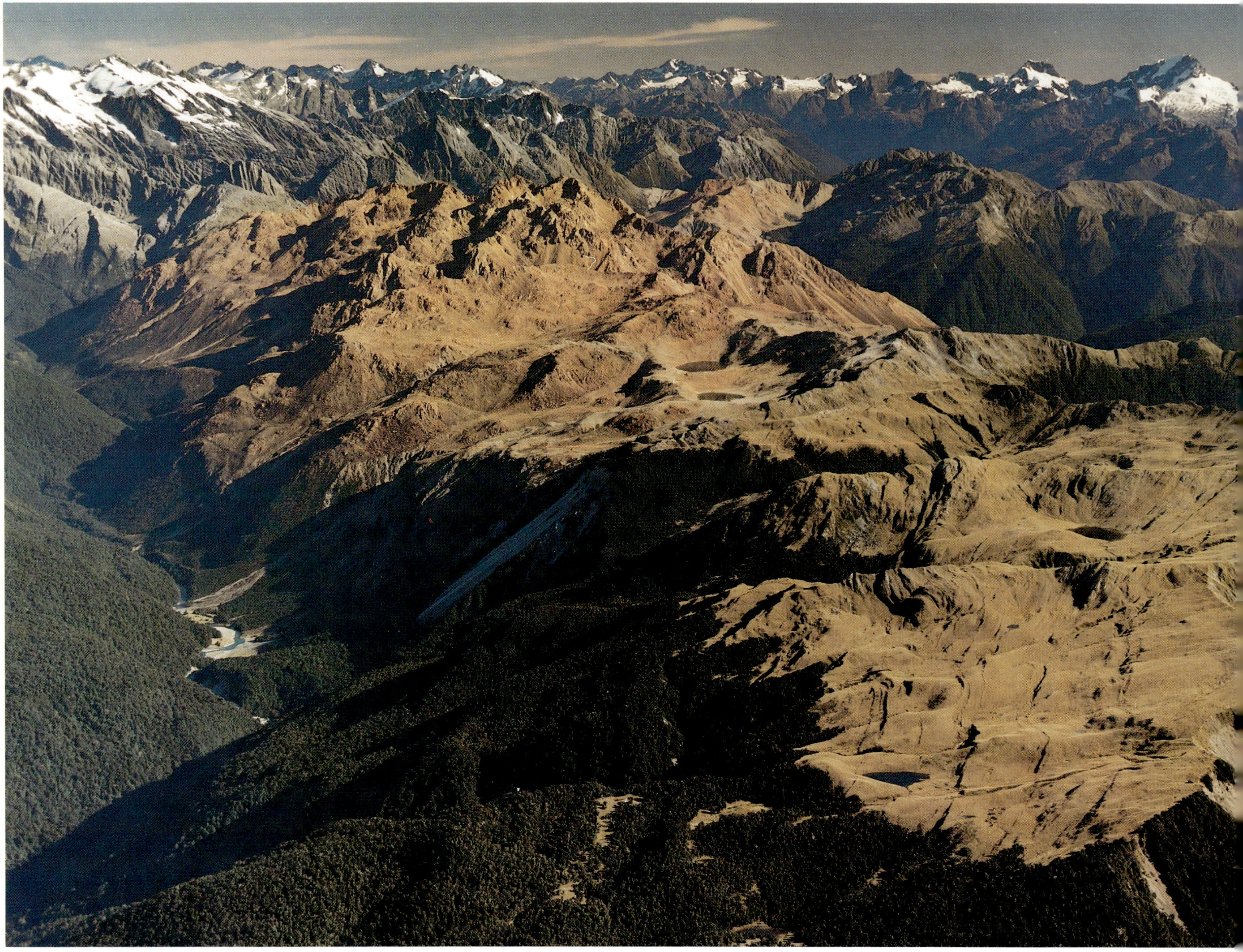

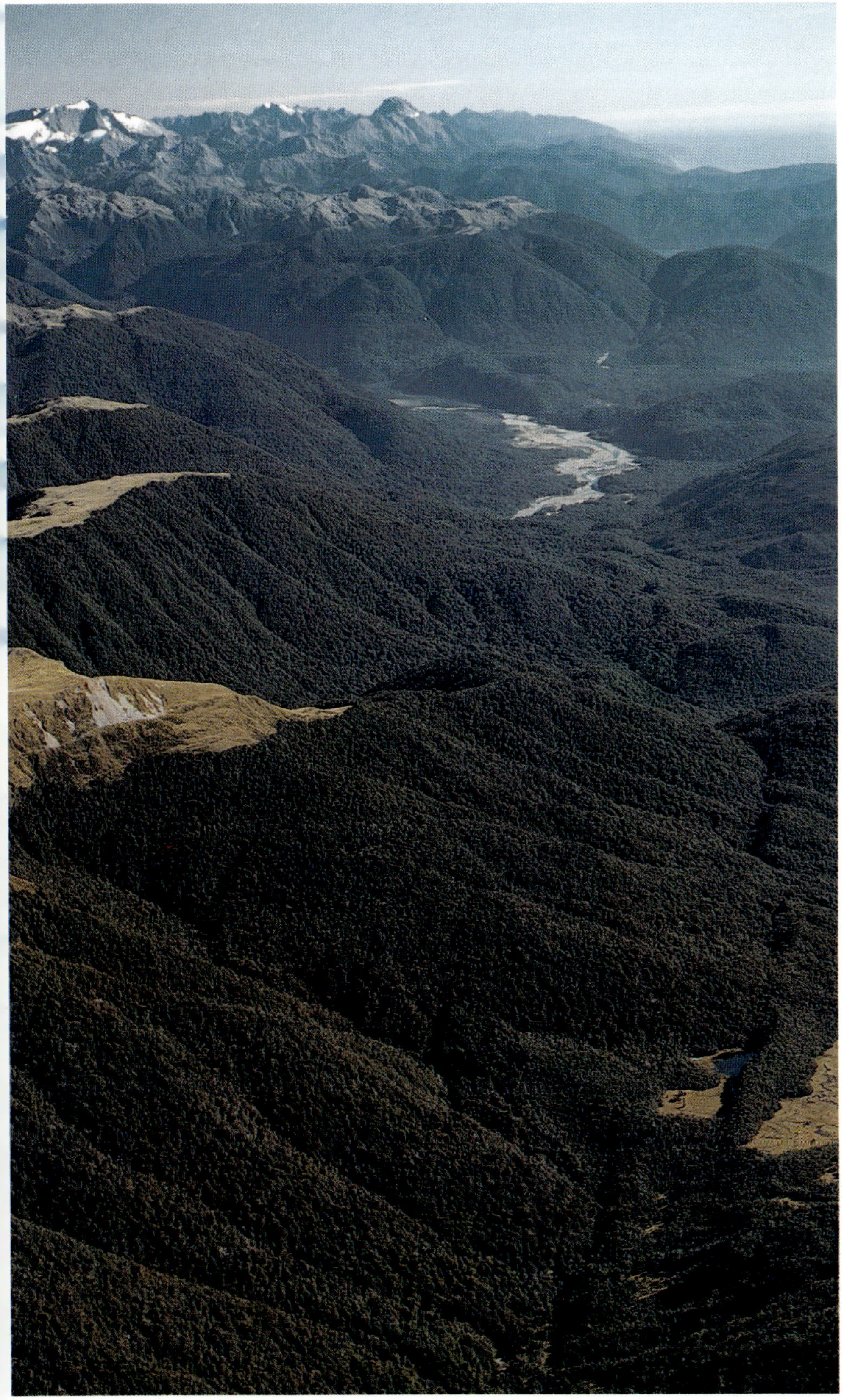

8 Looking south, across the Red Mountain and the upper Cascade River, to the peaks around the Olivine Ice Plateau (left distance), the Humboldt Range (centre, distance), and the Darran Range (right distance). The upper reaches of the Cascade River follow the Livingstone Fault, the line of contact between the schist rocks of the park and the ultramafic rocks of the Red Mountain 'mineral belt'. The main bulk of Red Mountain consists of peridotite (a rock with an assemblage of iron and magnesium silicate minerals like olivine, pyroxenes and amphiboles), and serpentinite, a rock formed by the alteration of peridotite. The iron in the peridotite and serpentinite minerals weathers to give the skin of rusty red oxides on the rocks.

The soils derived from schist on the slopes of the Olivine Range support beech forest and snow tussock. The ultramafic slopes, however, are only covered with a stunted 'serpentine scrub' on the lower talus slopes, and scattered herbs on pockets of soil at higher altitude. This sharp contrast in vegetation is due to the chemical and physical composition of the ultramafic soils. Only plants capable of tolerating high levels of soil magnesium seem to be able to colonise the ultramafic belt.

West of Red Mountain the geology again changes abruptly – to the marine sandstone, limestone and argillite of the northern part of the Red Hills Range. These sedimentary rocks are truncated by the Alpine Fault which cuts across the far right of the photograph. The fault trace runs away in a north-east to south-west direction, along the Duncan River in the foreground, to the upper Pyke River flats. Beyond the flats, the trace can be seen cutting across the northern end of the Skippers Range, across Lake McKerrow and the Kaipo hills to the entrance of Milford Sound in the distance (see Fig. 2, Fiordland, for view in opposite direction from above Lake Ronald in Fiordland National Park).

The sedimentary rocks of the northern end of the Red Hills Range around Gorge Plateau carry a remarkable series of ridge rents which run more or less parallel to the Alpine Fault.

Most of this foreground landscape lies adjacent to, but currently outside, Mt Aspiring National Park. It has been intensively prospected for minerals and is also being considered for addition to the park because of the scientific interest of its geomorphology, rock types, soils, and vegetation.

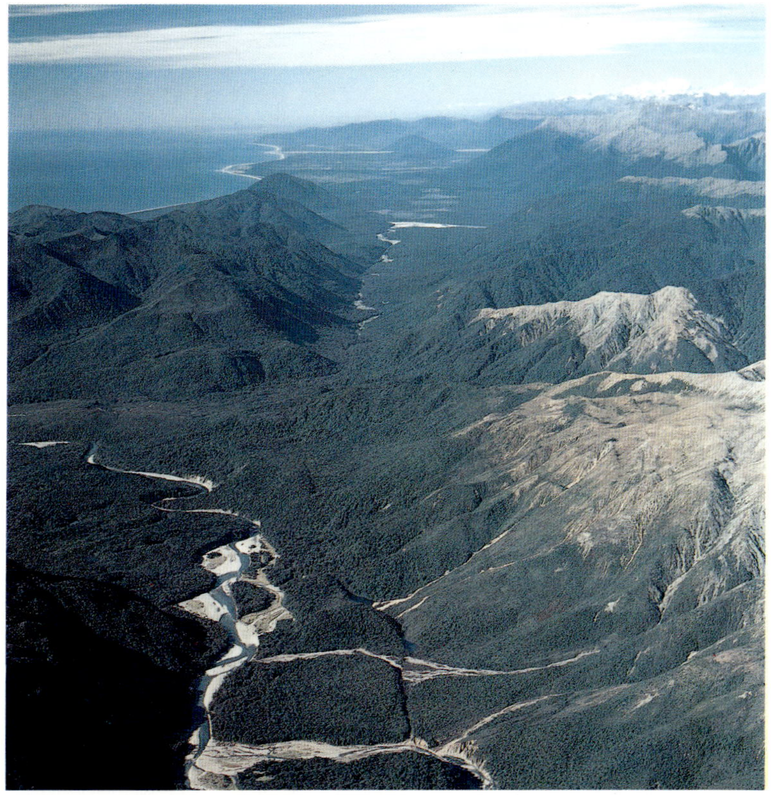

9

9 Looking north-east from above Gorge Plateau, over the middle reaches of the Cascade River (foreground) to the Jackson River (middle distance), both of which are aligned for a distance of 30 km along the Alpine Fault (for view in opposite direction, see Fig. 8).

Traces of the fault can be clearly seen cutting across the foot of Martyr Spur and two sag ponds can be seen in the trough formed by fault movement. The stunted vegetation to the right of the fault trace is 'serpentine scrub', a consequence of the toxic influence of the ultramafic rocks making up the Martyr Hill–Mt Raddle mineral belt.

10 The headwaters of the Olivine River (foreground) are separated from Hidden Falls Creek (a hanging valley tributary of the Hollyford) by Cow Saddle, immediately to the right of the prominent red slopes of ultramafic rock. This is the only area of ultramafic landscape within Mt Aspiring National Park. The lack of vegetation clearly reveals the morphology of the upper Olivine River, particularly the alluvial flats above and below the huge rockfall which has piled up in the valley floor.

10

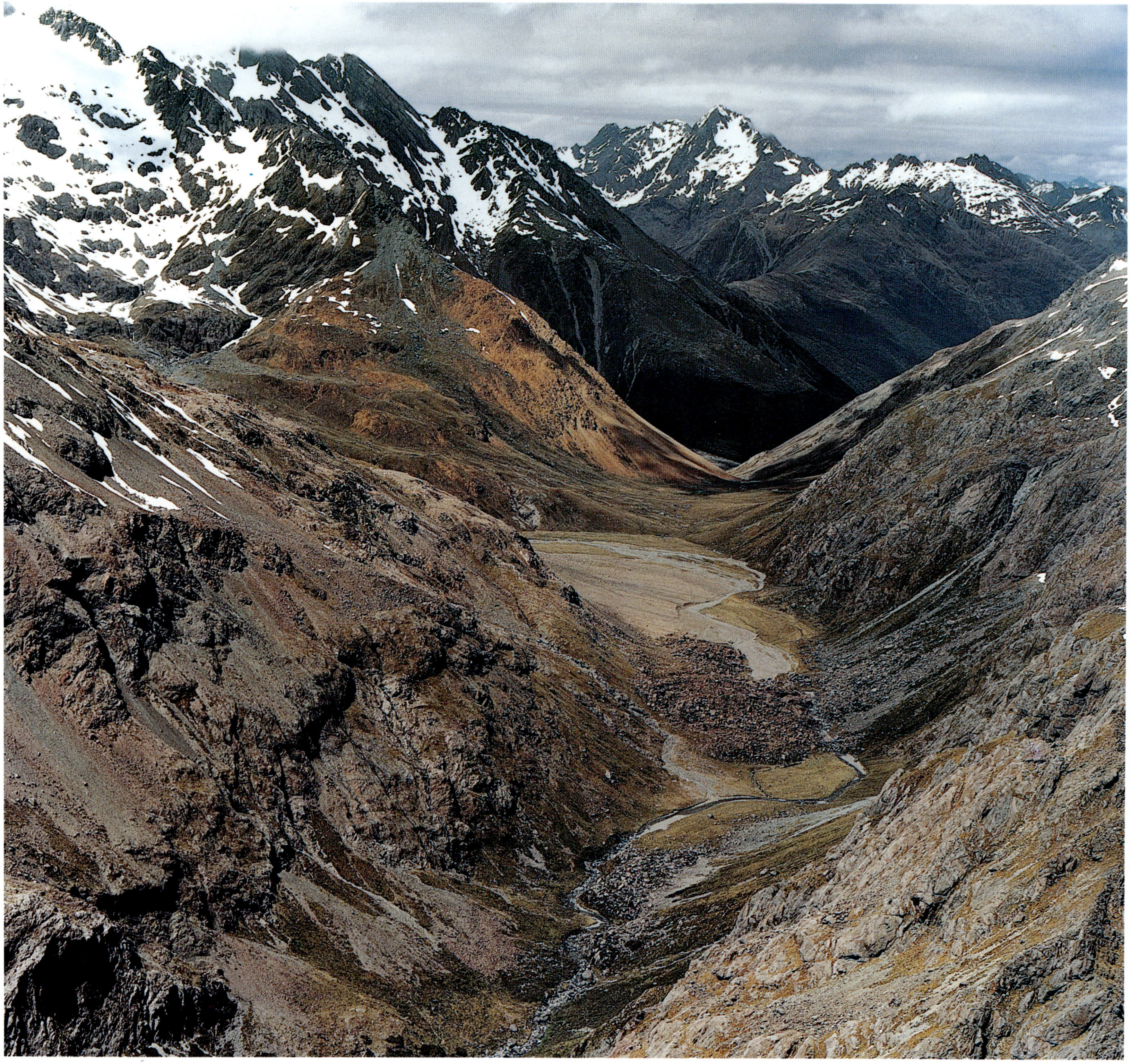

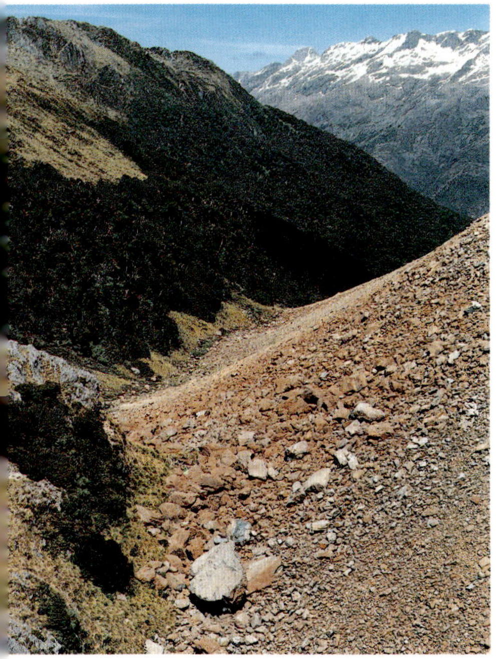

11

11 Nowhere is the effect of the underlying geology more clearly seen than at Simonin Pass, between Simonin Stream and the upper Cascade valley. At this point the Livingstone Fault separates the screes of ultramafic peridotite on the southern flank of Red Mountain from the schist rocks which make up most of the park. The true bluish-grey colour of the unoxidised serpentinite can be seen in the broken boulder in the foreground. The unfavourable physical and chemical character of the ultramafic slopes contrasts with the luxuriant silver beech forest on the soils derived from schist on the other side of the valley.

12 Looking south from above Mt Raddle, across Falls Creek to the peaks of the Olivine Range, and the Olivine Ice Plateau (left, distance) and Darran Range (right, distance). The red rocks in the right middle distance are the eastern slopes of Red Mountain, and those in the bottom right corner the northern slopes of the Mt Raddle ultramafic area. The striking curvature in the strata is the result of folding of the schist as it has been compressed against the ultramafic belt.

Note the contrast in the luxuriance of the beech forest; on the ice-scraped rocky slopes soils are very shallow and the vegetation is patchy and of low stature whereas the gentler slopes in the bottom left of the photograph carry deeper soils and dense forest.

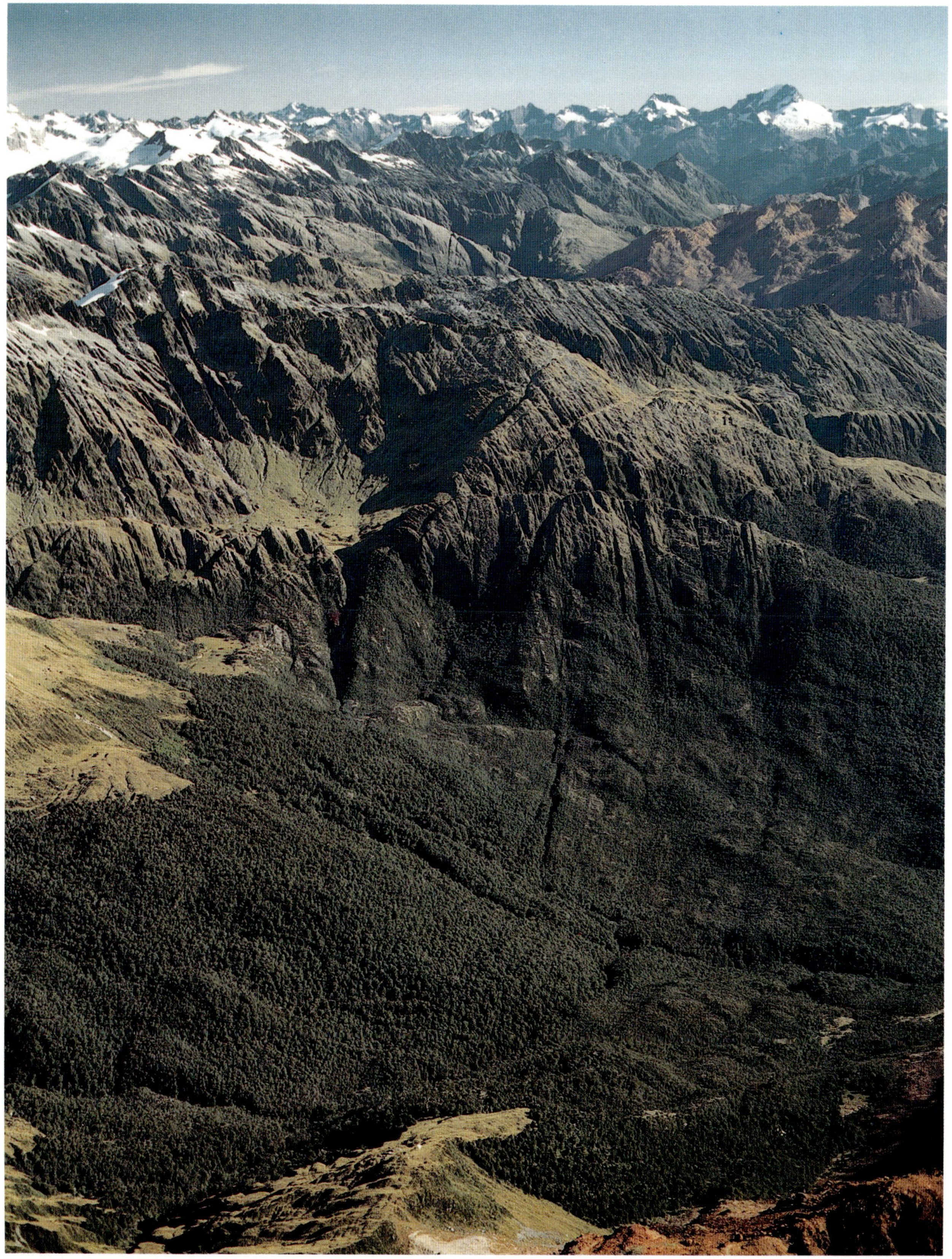

12

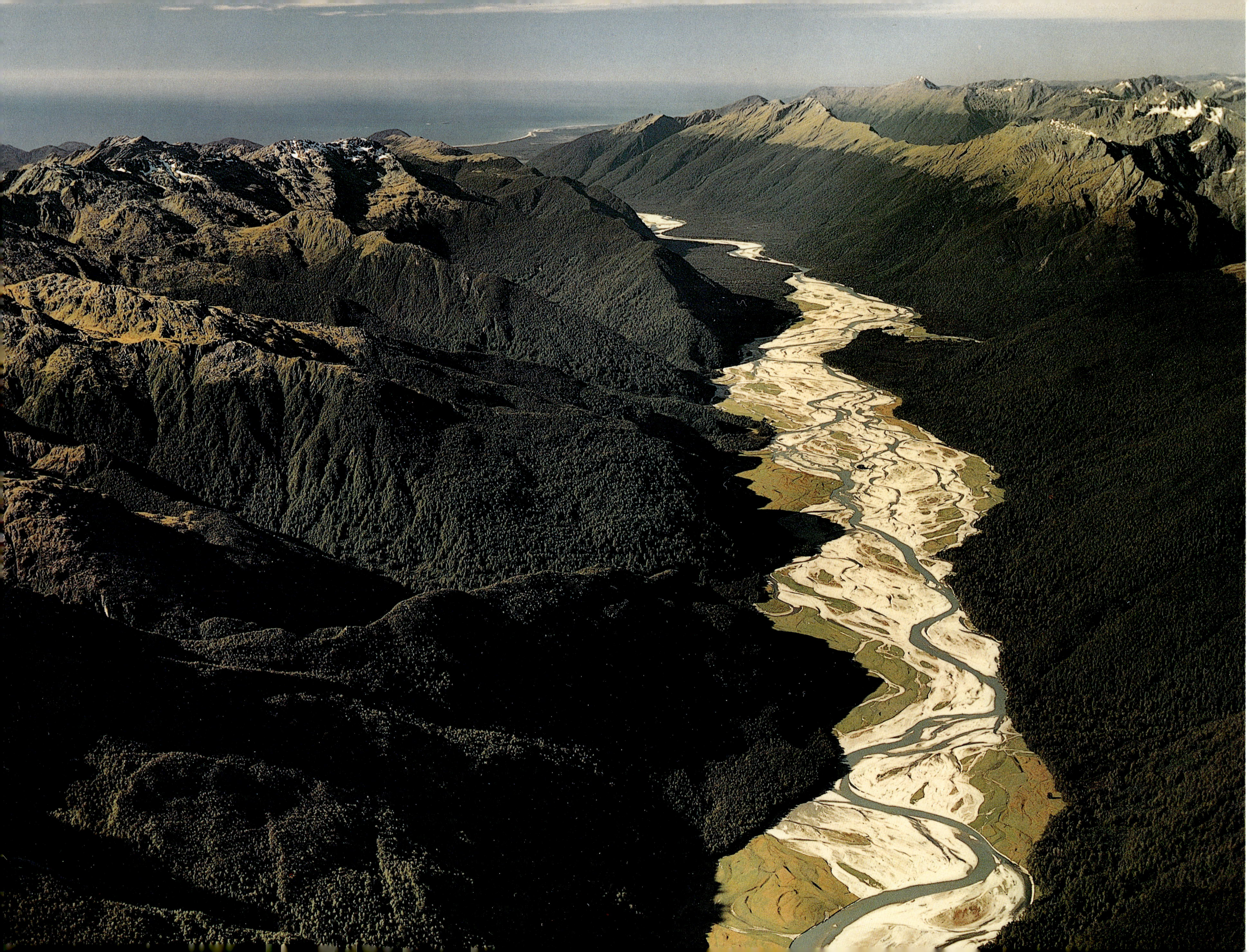

13 From the mouth of Ten Hour Gorge, where it breaks out of its confined middle reaches, the lower Arawata River drops only 80 m over a distance of 45 km to the Tasman Sea at Jackson Bay. As large quantities of alluvium have been built up on these lower flats, the river has adopted a braided character more typical of the rivers draining the eastern side of the Southern Alps. The influence of former valley glacier ice is very evident in the smooth west-facing slopes of the Waipara Range (right, foreground) and Haast Range (right, distance). In contrast, the east- and south-facing slopes of the Olivine Range (left) would have held significant areas of small tributary glaciers.

14 The Tornado Glacier, tucked under the eastern wall of the northern Olivine Range, is one of the most interesting cirque glaciers in the park. Its névé is not visible in this view looking west, for it is almost surrounded by rock walls to the right of the photograph. The icefall flows down behind the prominent rock rib on the right, collecting avalanches from the ice shelf perched on the cirque wall below Typhoon Peak. It then turns 180° and crumbles into a deep blue terminal lake, the waters of which then cascade from this hanging valley to the Williamson River 600 m below.

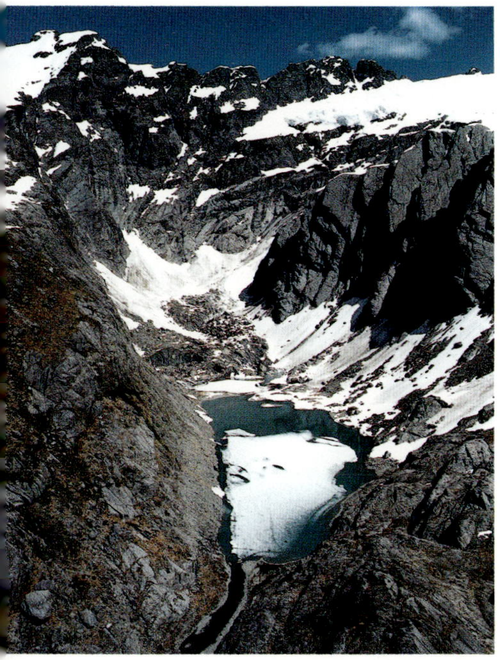

14

15 Hanging valleys are characteristic glacial landforms within Mt Aspiring National Park, particularly along the Olivine and Humboldt Ranges. This view, looking south-east towards the peaks of the Barrier Range from above the Pyke valley, shows two classic examples – the Olivine and the Forgotten. The Olivine Flats in the centre of the photograph (550 m altitude) now occupy a level reach of the former 'Olivine Glacier', and the lower Olivine Gorge (foreground) was probably once a spectacular icefall dropping to the main valley glacier which flowed through the Pyke valley. Note how the glacial ice has produced the mammillated rocky shoulders on the south side of the gorge. Beyond the Olivine Flats, the lower end of the Forgotten Flats (800 m altitude) can be just seen above the slot of the Forgotten Gorge; this hanging valley represents another even higher tributary glacier and icefall – and the highest icefield of all is the Olivine Ice Plateau (see Fig. 7) which still feeds into the Olivine watershed via the Forgotten River Icefall.

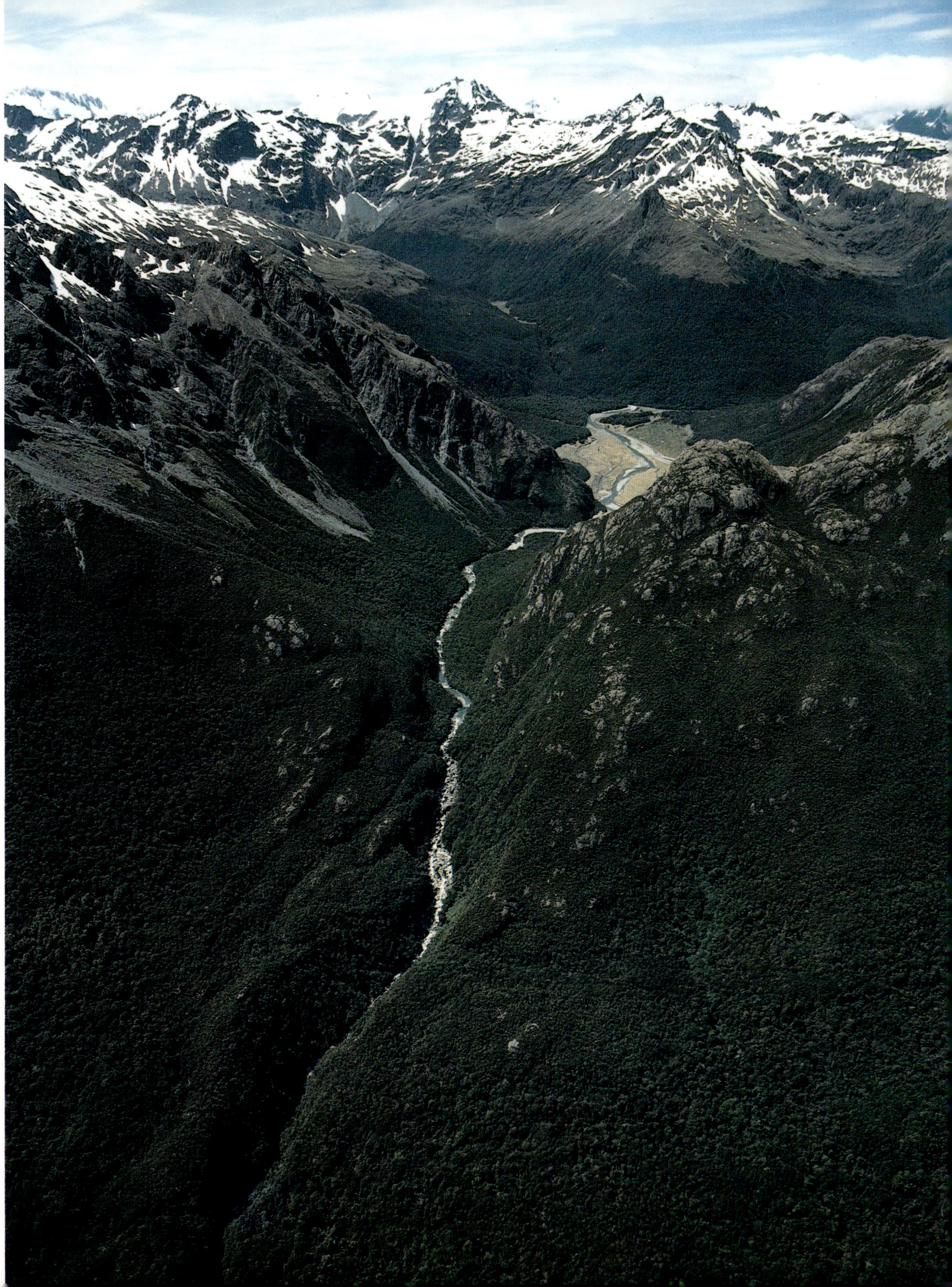

15

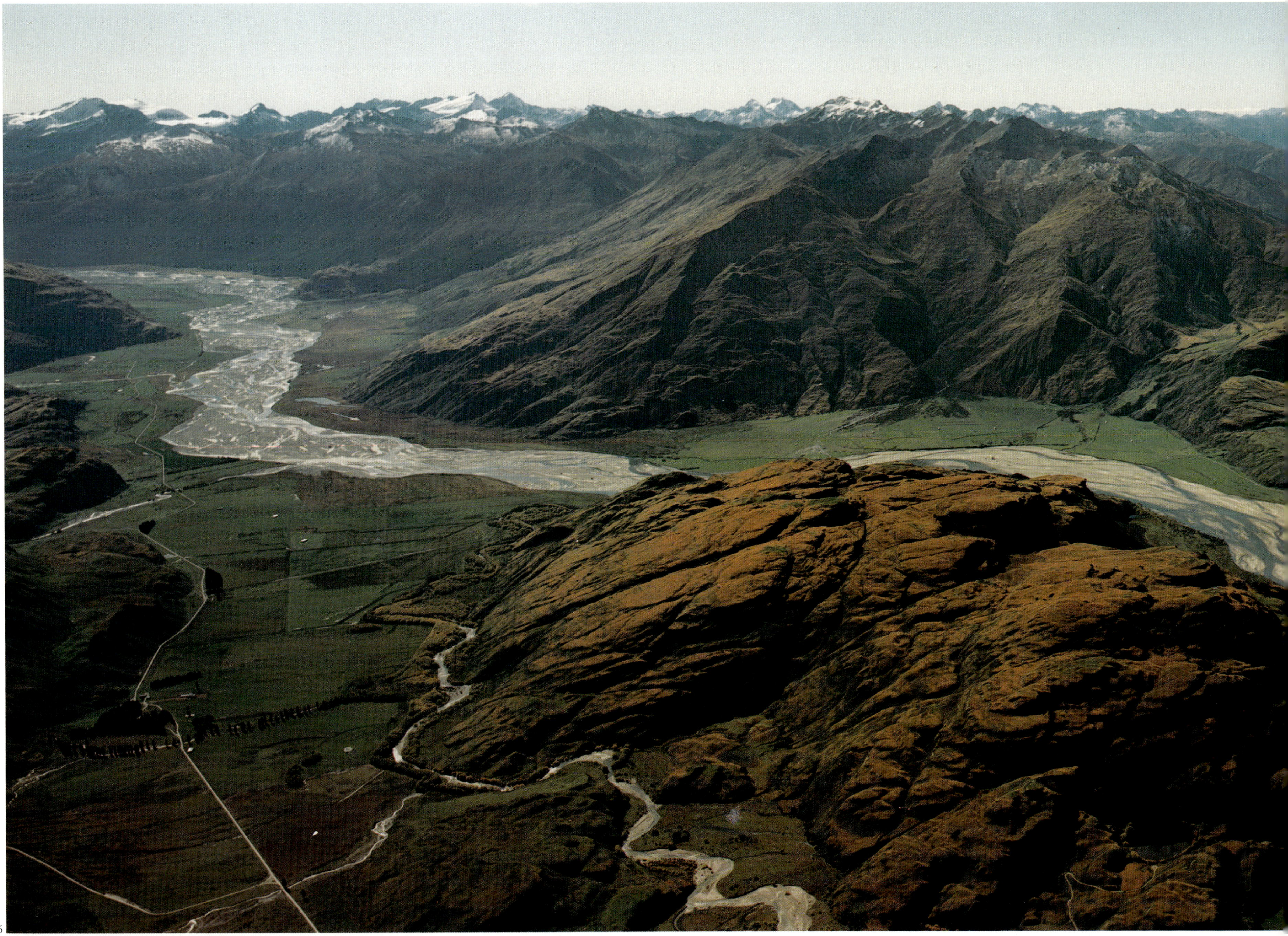

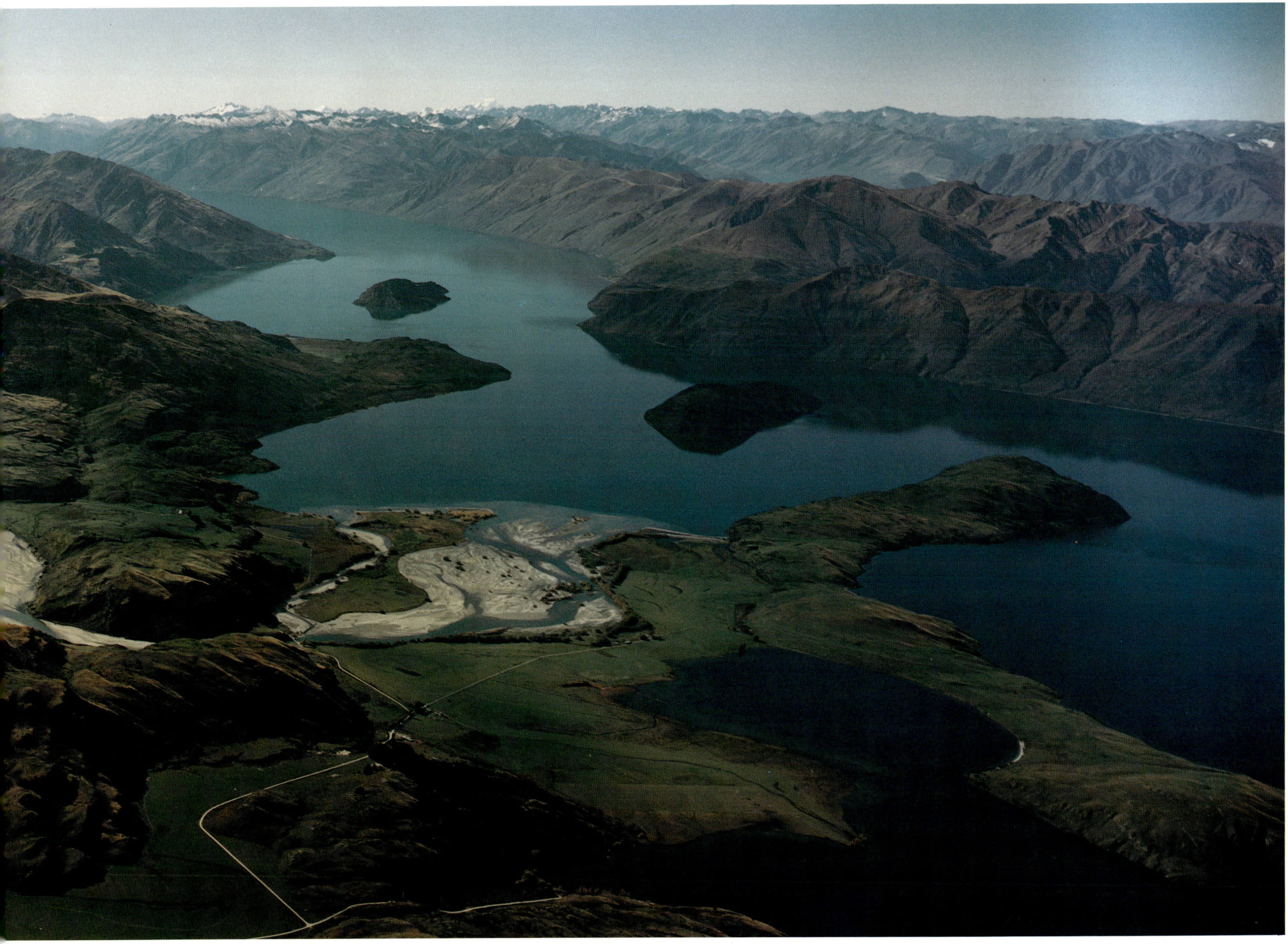

previous page

16 The ability of glacial ice to carve a landscape is superbly illustrated in this panorama looking north from above the lower reaches of the Motatapu River (foreground). The peaks of the north-eastern sector of the park are ranged along the left skyline, with the Matukituki River sweeping down from them and emptying into Lake Wanaka.

The huge slab of bedrock schist in the centre foreground is a classic example of a roche moutonnée; the upstream faces slope up gently planed to a smooth texture by the glacier ice flowing up and over the resistant rock. In contrast, the downstream faces are steep and broken, showing where the ice has plucked at the rock as it rode over it. All the surrounding slopes, especially the western slopes of the Buchanan Peaks on the opposite side of the Matukituki, show the same evidence of ice sculpting by the huge valley glacier that flowed from the park a mere 15 000 years ago. Since then, sediment carried down the Matukituki River has built a substantial delta out into the glacial trough now filled by Lake Wanaka. The two peninsulas in the bottom right were islands in the lake until these delta sediments linked them to the shore.

17 The Ailsa Mountains lie at the southern end of the park, where the Routeburn Track crosses from the Dart Valley to the Hollyford Valley (right, foreground). The Livingstone Fault runs along the eastern side of the Hollyford valley, before curving south-east through Lakes Howden and McKellar (centre, right), and the Livingstone Mountains in the distance beyond. Tongues of ice from the huge glacier that once occupied the head of the Hollyford have carved out the two prominent 'hanging valleys' in the centre right of the photograph – the Greenstone containing Lakes McKellar and Howden (only the latter draining to the Hollyford) and the Eglinton (containing Lakes Fergus and Gunn) which drains to Lake Te Anau. Lake Harris and Harris Saddle (the highest point on the Routeburn Track) are visible in the bottom left. The level of the cloud above Lake Wakatipu (left, distance) is about the height to which the valleys were once filled by glacial ice.

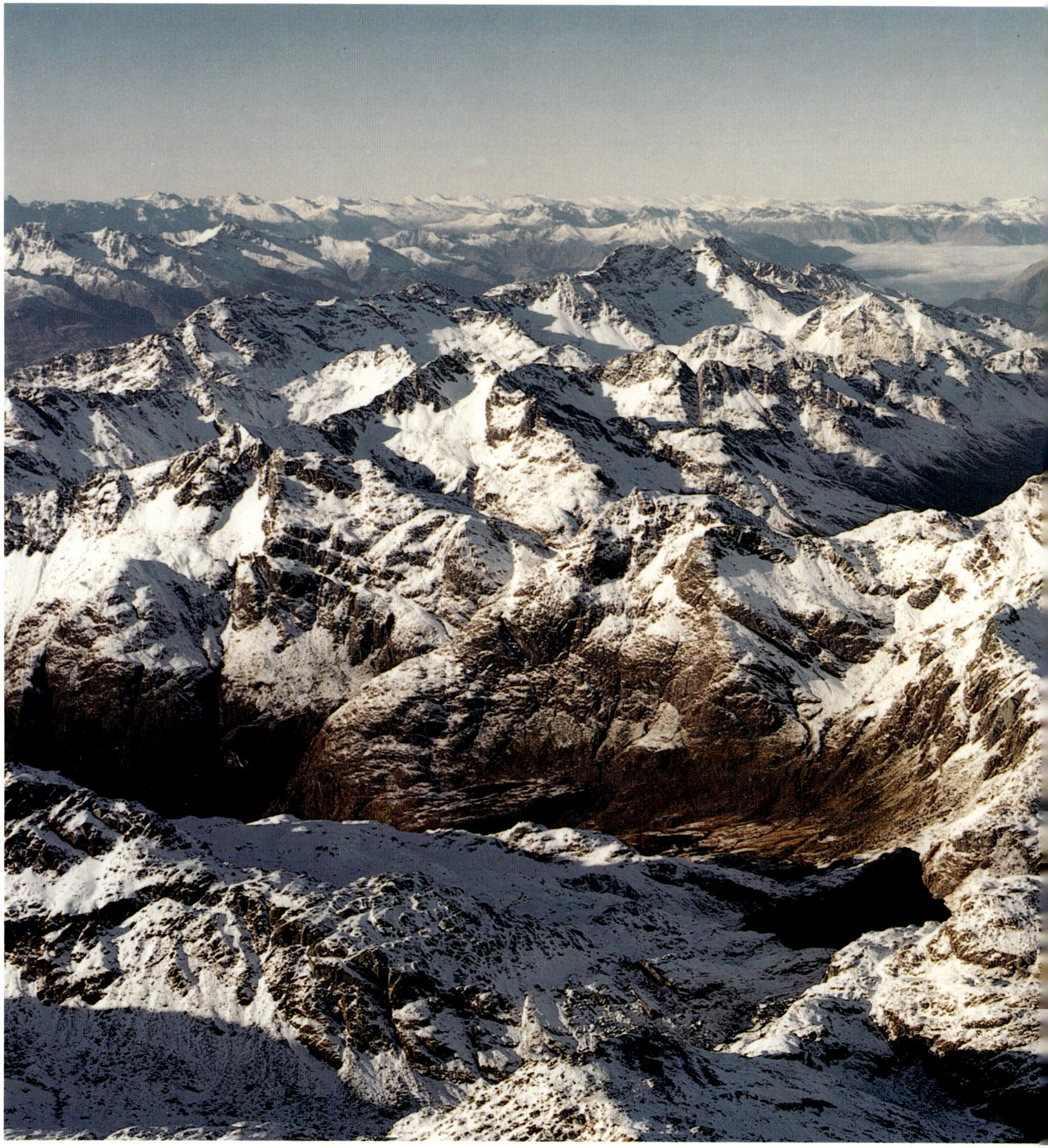

17

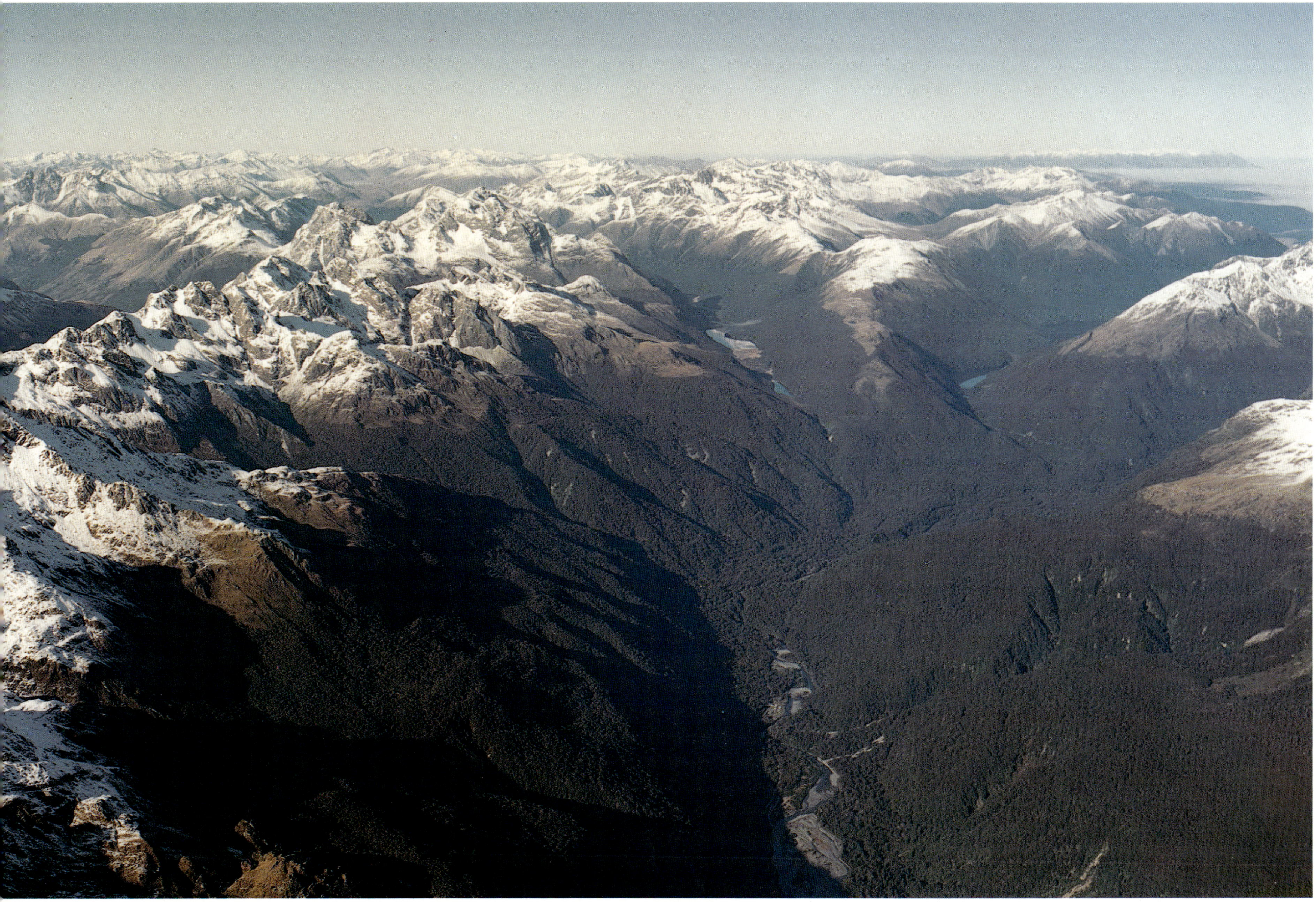

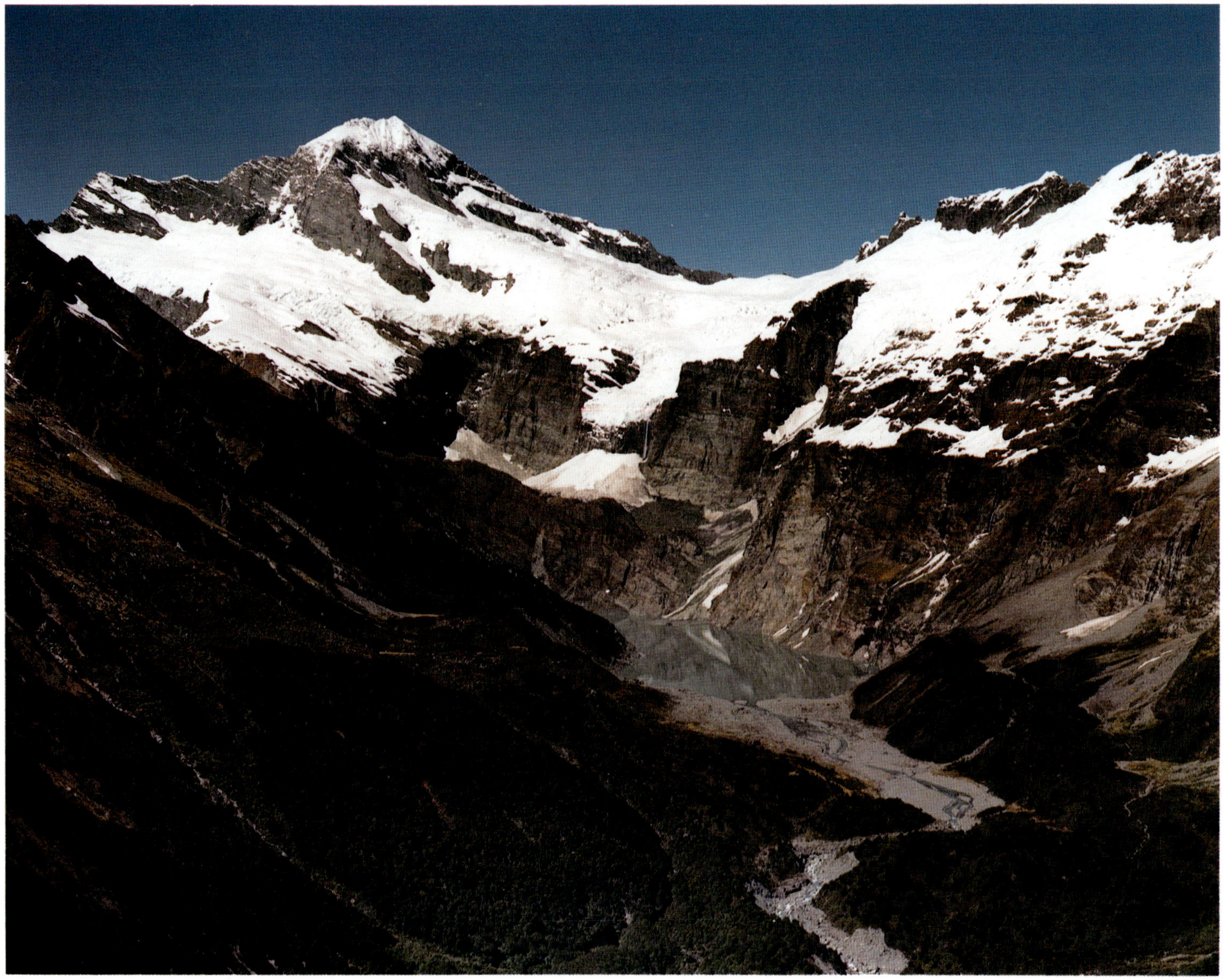

18

18 The head of the Waiatoto River, beneath the northern faces of Mt Aspiring and the cliffs of the Haast Range (right), is one of the wildest landscapes in the park. The Volta and Therma Glaciers have retreated, leaving a clear terminal lake beneath sheer rock walls. Such lakes can be quite ephemeral. With the continual deposition of rock debris they silt up and progressively develop soils and vegetation; in time, they are transformed into river flats. The lack of vegetation on the valley floor is the result of a wave of water up to 15 m high which cascaded down the valley one night in November 1978 after a huge rockfall plunged into the lake from the slopes of Mt Stargazer (right). Bush-covered lateral moraines on both sides of the river are linked by an indistinct terminal moraine. These moraines mark the position of the terminus of the Volta Glacier in the mid-nineteenth century. Since then the Waiatoto River has cut a deep rough channel through them.

19 Icebergs are sometimes a feature of glacial terminal lakes. This lake at the head of the Waipara valley catches avalanches of dirty, rock-studded ice from the Bignell – the terminal icefall of the Bonar Glacier draining the south-western slopes of Mt Aspiring.

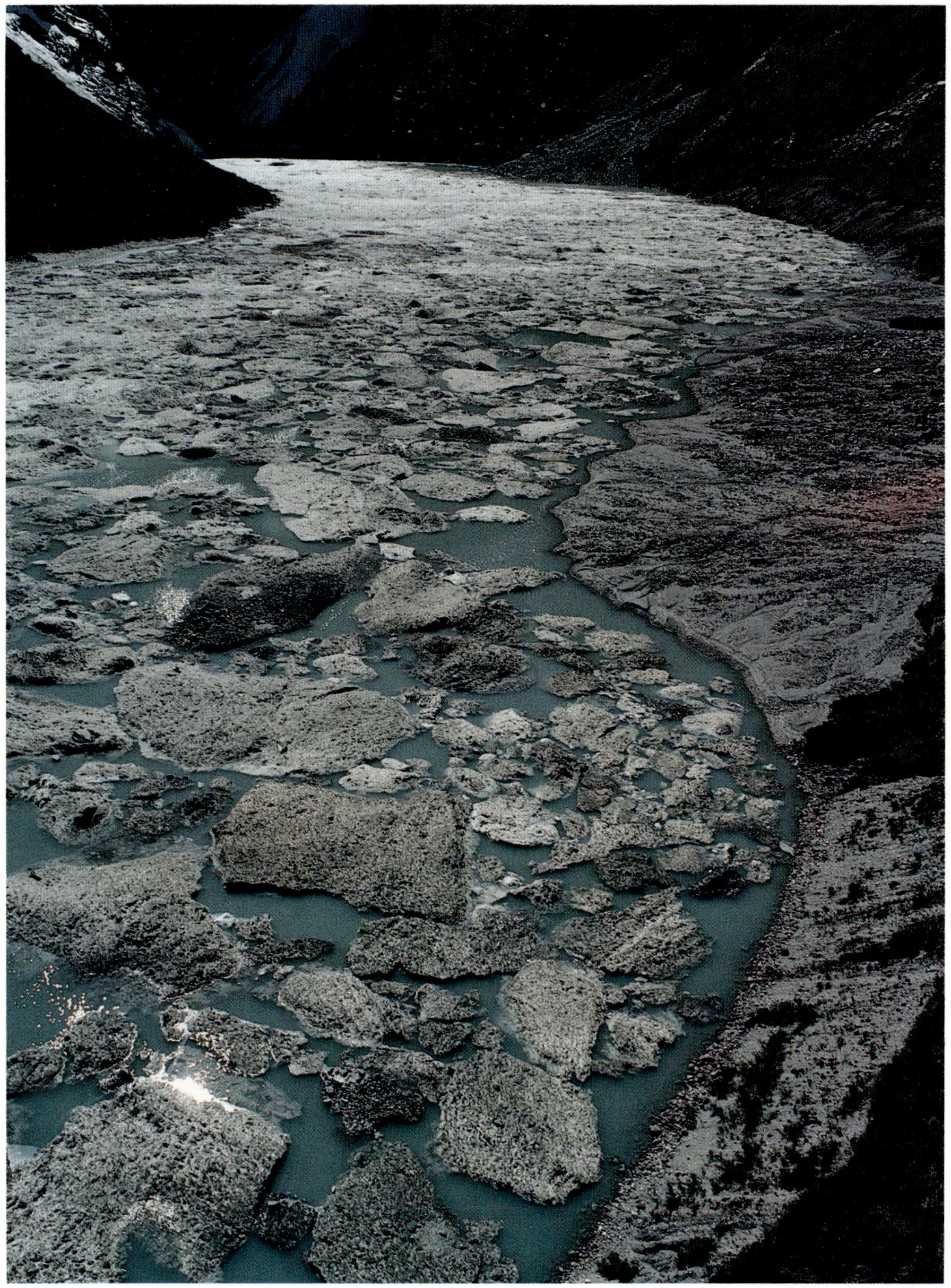

19

20 The tiny Makarora Glacier, perched on a shelf on the south-east slopes of Mt Brewster in the north-east corner of the park, is representative of the many small glaciers still surviving within the park. The curvature of the crevasses results from the higher rate of ice flow in the middle of the glacier; the jumble of ice pinnacles (seracs) on the far edge is the result of intersecting sets of crevasses.

21 Crevasse patterns in the middle reaches of the Volta Glacier north-east of Mt Aspiring show some interesting features. The small icefall in the centre of the photograph is generating bands of different coloured ice called ogives. The ogives are concave upstream, in contrast to the concave downstream crevasse pattern above the icefall. The Volta then forks into two icefalls (oriented at 180° to each other) at the extreme left of the photograph, the one at top left dropping to the Waiatoto River (see opposite page) and the one at bottom left into a cul-de-sac between Fastness Peak and Rainbow Col.

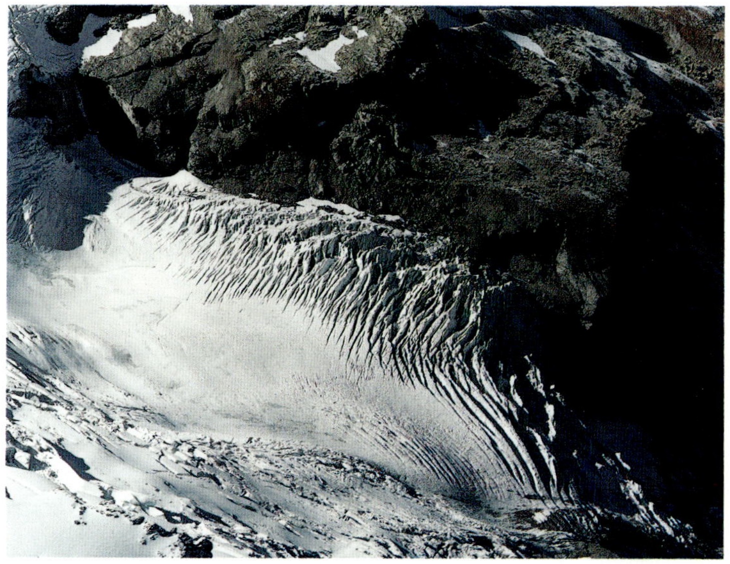

20

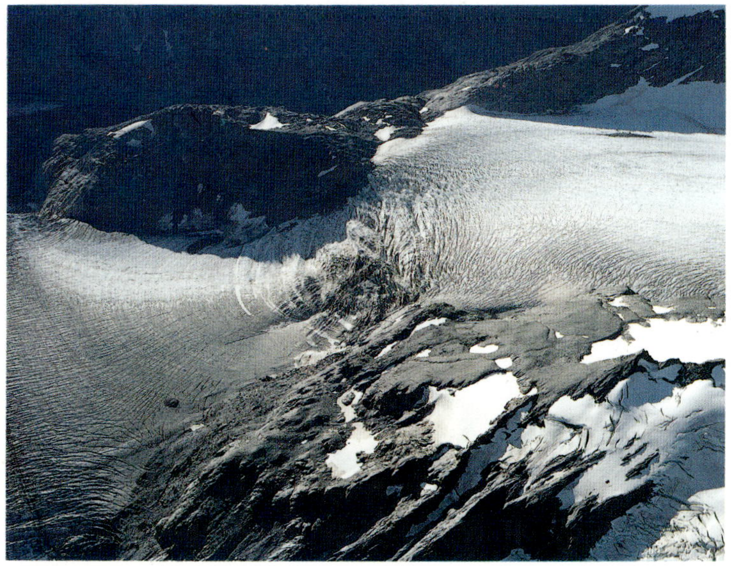

21

22 In the northern sector of the park, between the Wilkin valley and Haast Pass, the peaks are lower (generally 1800–2200 m) and there is much less permanent snow and ice. This cirque lake drains to the Te Naihi River (a major tributary of the Waiatoto) from a former cirque carved by the Axius Glacier (obscured) on the western face of Mt Alba (2355 m, foreground).

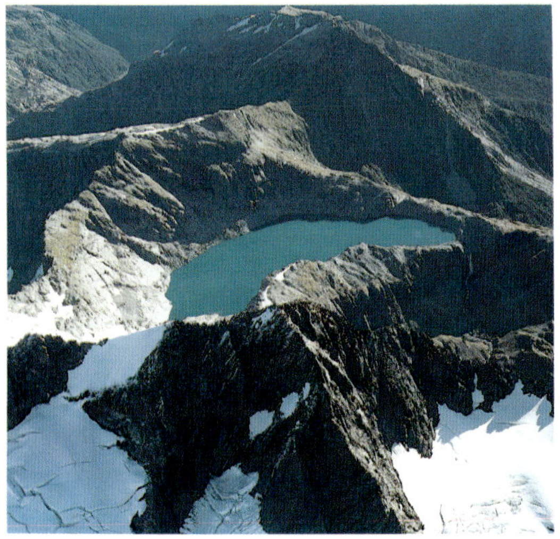

22

23 Mt Brewster (2423 m) is the most accessible major peak in Mt Aspiring National Park, lying only 5 km east of the Haast Pass highway a few kilometres upstream from the Gates of Haast bridge. The view is north-east across Pyke Creek to the drier crests of the Young Range and the peaks around the Hunter and Ahuriri valleys.

The Brewster Glacier has now lost its icefall and its névé is much reduced; it now occupies a shelf 2.5 km in length. The firn line, marking the point at which the previous season's snow has melted from the surface of the ice, can be clearly seen about 1 km above the snout of the glacier. Note the smooth, clean rocks below the lower part of the glacier, in contrast to the gullied rock face in the lower left portion of the photograph. This latter area, so dissected with drainage channels, has probably been free of ice for thousands of years compared with only a hundred or so for the rock closer to the glacier snout.

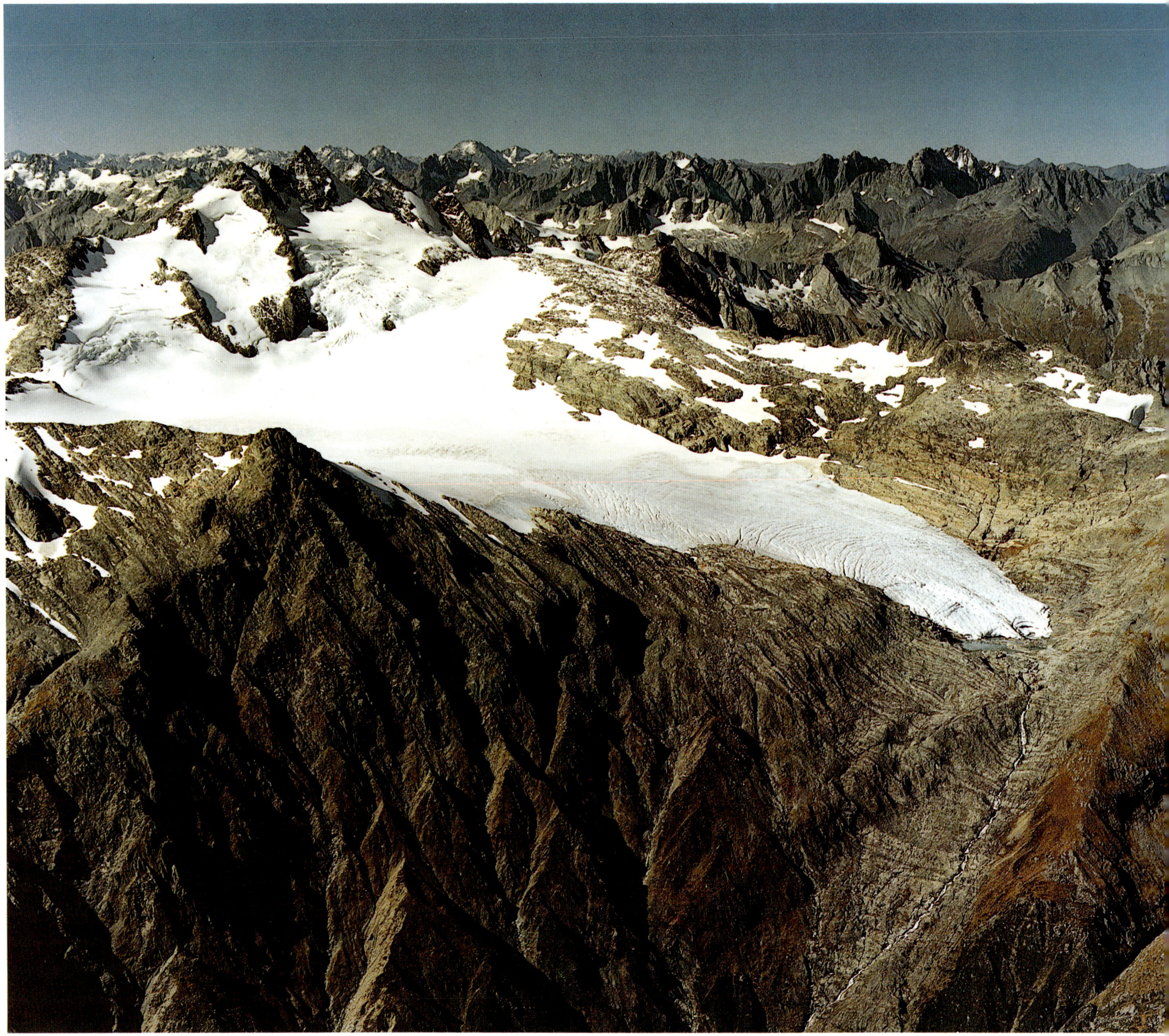

23

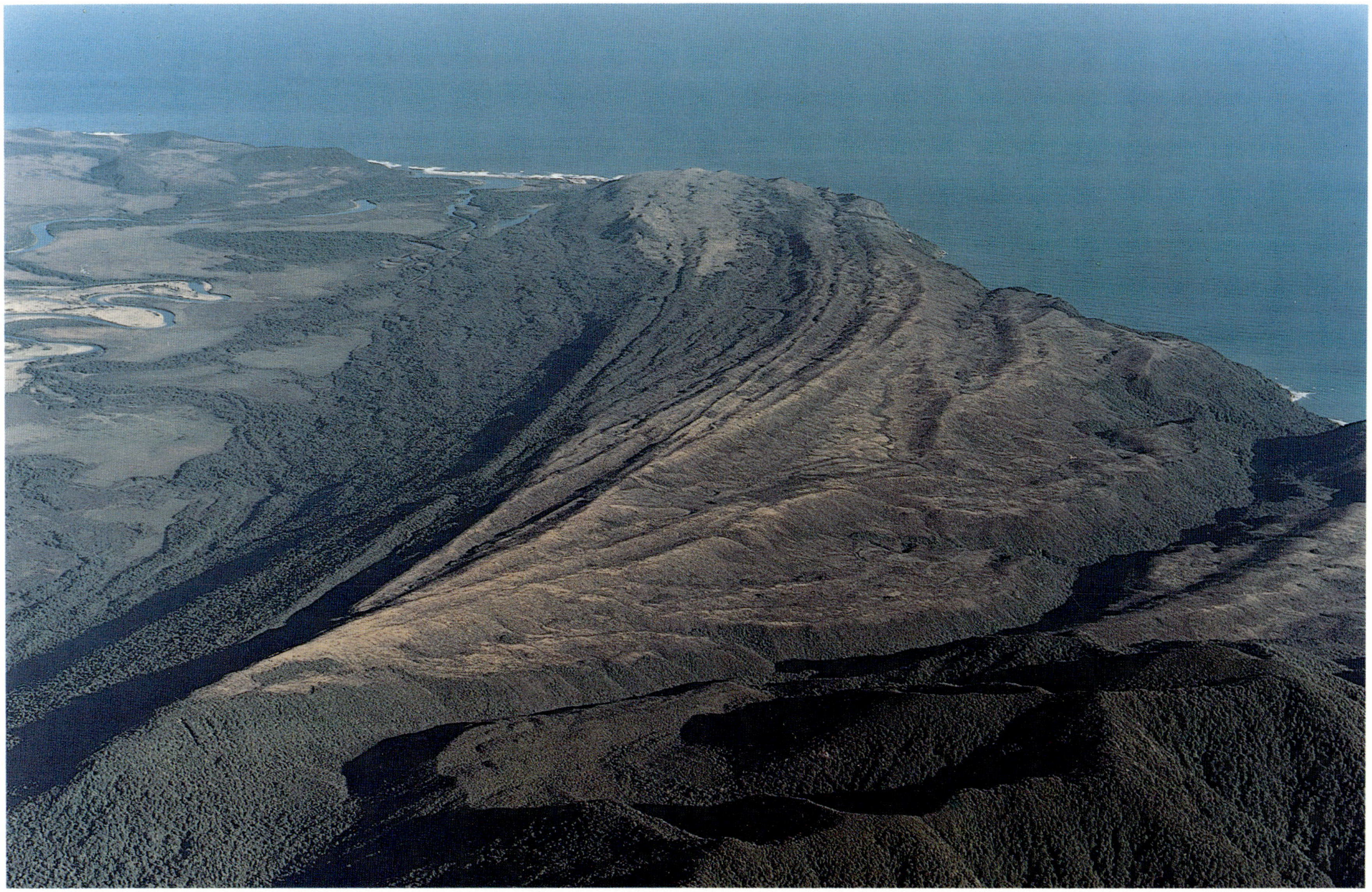

24

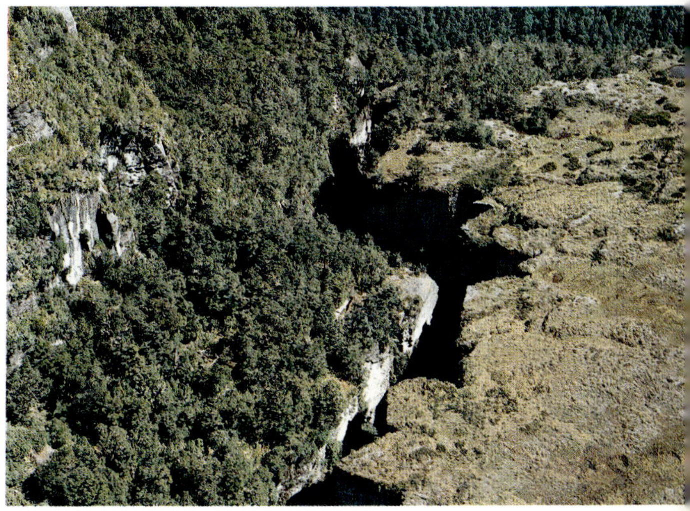

25

next page

26 Mt Aspiring (3027 m) is a classical alpine 'horn', especially when viewed from the west. This view from the south-west above the head of the West Matukituki valley shows the full extent of the Bonar Glacier before it plunges westwards into the Waipara valley. The peaks of the Haast Range (between the Waiatoto and Waipara valleys) extend northwards into the left distance, and the peaks of Mt Cook National Park can be seen 150 km to the north-east. Ice in the western and southern (in shade) cirques of the mountain has honed the north-west and south-west ridges to sharp-edged smooth arêtes. The south-east ridge (in shade), however, has been left as a ragged ridge of rock and ice pinnacles; it is appropriately named the 'Coxcomb Ridge'.

24 The Cascade Plateau between the mouth of the Cascade River (left) and Jackson Bay is a long way from the western boundary of Mt Aspiring National Park, but its relationship to glacial features within the park is as obvious as the association of the moraines of Okarito and Waikukupa with the glaciers of Westland National Park (Chapter 4).

The plateau consists of huge lateral moraine ridges, largely made up of rocks transported from the ultramafic intrusion on the western side of the northern Olivine Range (see Fig. 8). This accounts for the low vegetation on the gently sloping surface which slopes down from 400 m altitude at its eastern apex (left) to end abruptly in 250 m cliffs.

25 Slit gorges seem to be common landforms in schist mountains. One of the most spectacular is this 80 m deep cleft cut by South Snowball Creek (which drains the South Snowball Glacier, Fig. 6). From this point it plunges in shadow 500 m to join the Joe River at the head of Williamson Flats. It is easy to imagine this deep fissure being caused by an earthquake, but it is more likely to be the result of water following and eroding along the joint pattern in the schist rock. The effect of slope and soil drainage upon vegetation can be seen on the opposing sides of the cleft; the beech forest on the left cannot compete with the tussocks and bog plants which have colonised the wet flatter surface on the right.

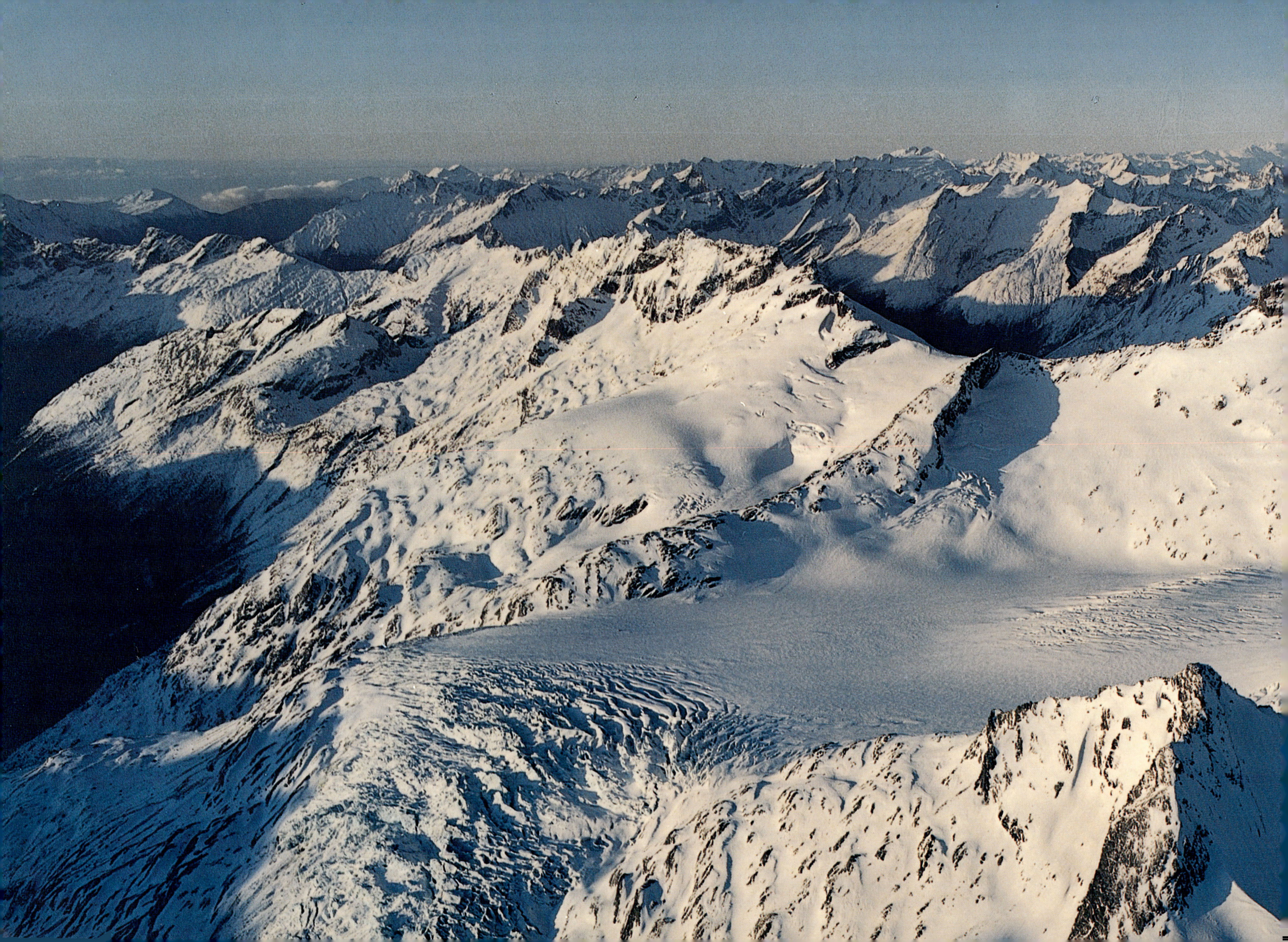

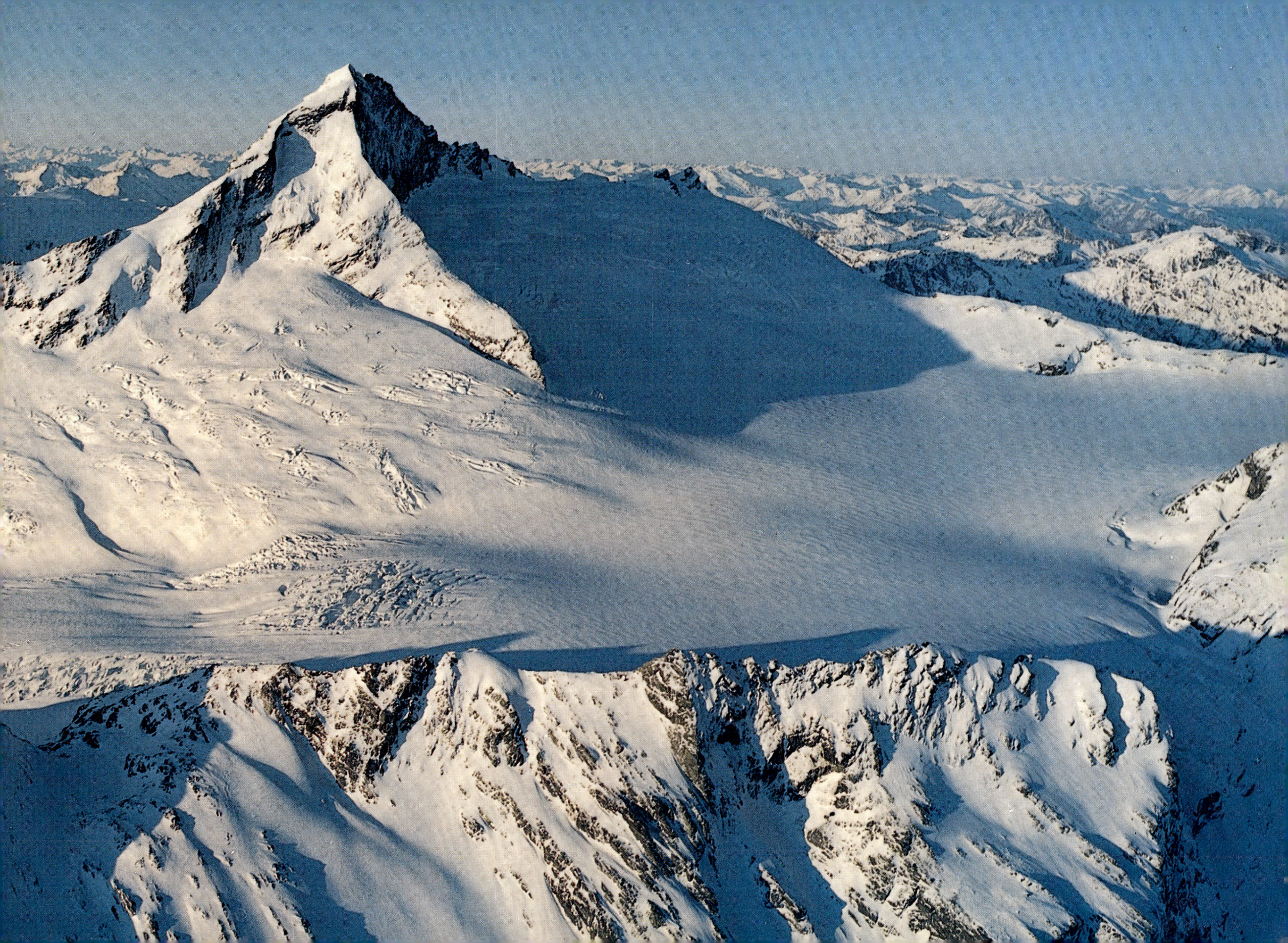

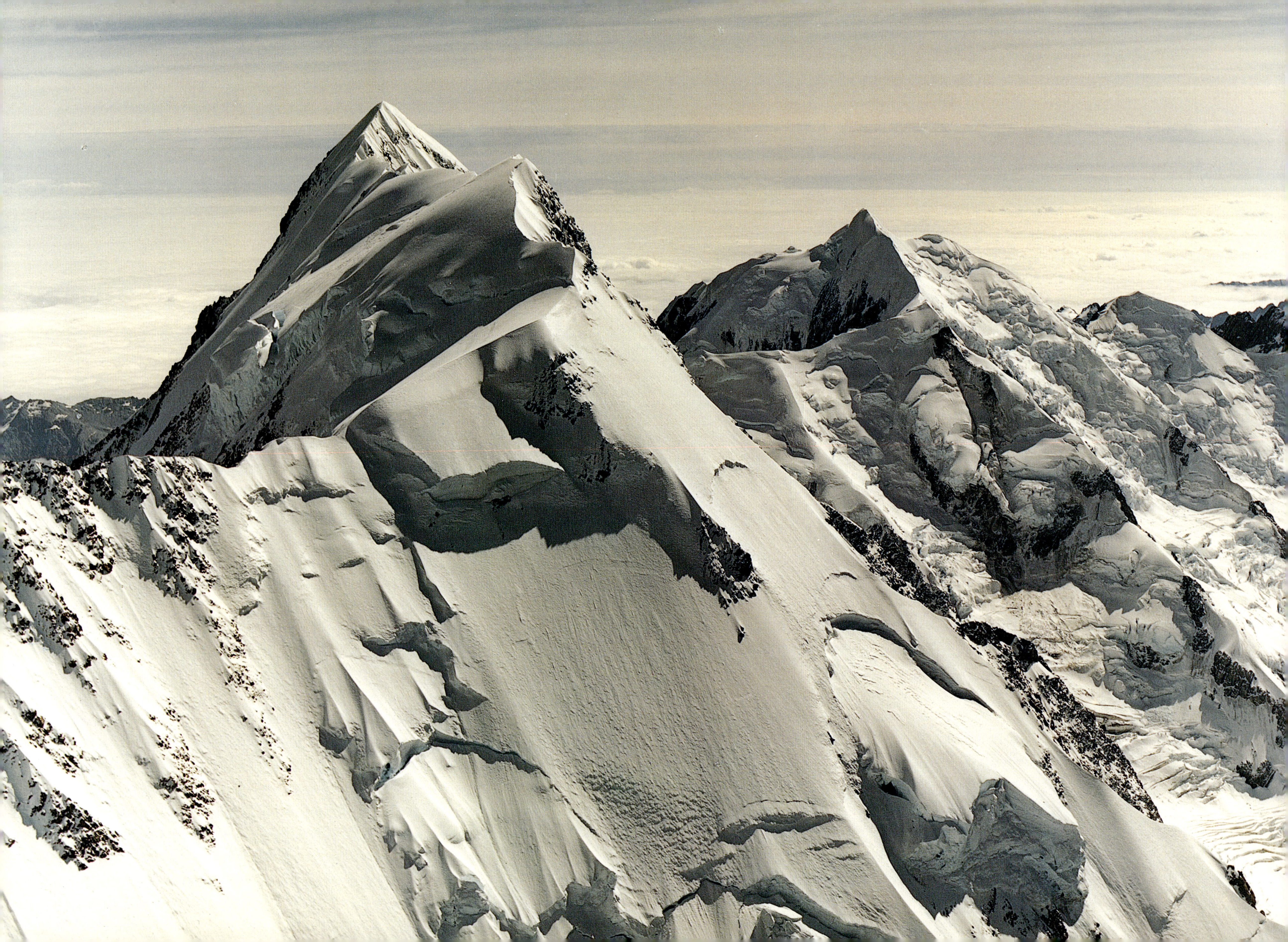

MOUNT COOK NATIONAL PARK

Mount Cook National Park is New Zealand's great alpine park. It contains 19 peaks over 3000 m in height, ranged along the main divide from Mt Sefton to Elie de Beaumont, and along the adjacent Mt Cook and Malte Brun Ranges. The park is the eastern complement of Westland National Park with which it shares the main divide as a common boundary for 40 km. Essentially, the park consists of the headwaters of two of the three great glacial lakes of the Mackenzie Basin – Lakes Pukaki and Tekapo. The waters of Lake Pukaki are a milky blue because of the large quantity of fine glacier-ground sediment ('rock flour') carried into it by the Tasman River. The Tasman drains four of the main valley glaciers within the park – the Tasman (at 29km length and an area of 100 sq. km the largest of our glaciers), Murchison, Hooker and Mueller Glaciers. The waters of Lake Tekapo are a deeper blue because the Godley River carries much less rock flour since it drains a smaller catchment with lower peaks and smaller valley glaciers (the Classen, Grey and Godley Glaciers).

The rocks of the park are almost wholly greywacke and argillite, grading into schist in the south-western corner around Mt Sefton. This greywacke and argillite was formed from sediments tens of kilometres thick, laid down between 250 and 150 million years ago. Subsequent movement along the Alpine Fault (see Chapter 4) particularly during the last five million years, has forced these sediments up as the Southern Alps. Sediments as thick as 25 km may have been uplifted but erosion has kept pace with the rate of uplift, so the mountains have probably been at about their present height throughout the Ice Ages.

During summer, a large proportion of the west-facing slopes of the Malte Brun and Liebig Ranges are snow-free, allowing a clear view of the massive folds which formed as the strata were compressed and twisted during uplift. Alternating bands of darker-coloured argillite and lighter-coloured greywacke also stand out in the steeply-dipping strata of the Liebig Range. Another distinctive geological feature is the dull reddish-brown colour of the weathered greywacke of the Malte Brun Range. Bands of bright red rock occur along the Liebig Range (see p. 69), evidence of volcanic activity which long ago provided the minerals which give these rocks their colour.

1 Ice festoons the highest summits of the Southern Alps – Mt Cook (3764 m, left) and Mt Tasman (3498 m), 3.5 km further to the north (right). Despite the steepness of the slopes, snow accumulates each winter and spring and is gradually compressed to glacier ice which almost completely covers the underlying greywacke rock. Ice cliffs across the foreground slopes indicate where huge blocks of ice have broken away, forming spectacular avalanches which periodically rake the alpine slopes of the park.

GLACIAL LANDFORMS PREDOMINATE

The landscapes in Mount Cook National Park have been carved by glacial ice which still covers 40% of the park's area. These landscapes are all younger than 20 000 years, none having survived the last glaciation. Annual precipitation is as high as 8000 mm along the main divide – mainly in the form of snow (up to 50 m on the névés of the Tasman and Hooker Glaciers). The gradient of Mt Cook National Park's glaciers is quite gentle in comparison with the glaciers of Westland National Park, which plunge down icefalls on the steep western side of the Southern Alps. For instance, the Franz Josef drops 1600 m in a distance of only 12 km from the head of its névé on the Baird Range above the Giekie Snowfield; the Tasman Glacier takes 29 km to drop the same amount of altitude from Tasman Saddle to its terminal. As a river of ice the Tasman is larger, but slower moving, than the glaciers to the west.

The rasping power of the rock embedded in the ice of a glacier is often not appreciated. It can erode the rock at the sides and base of the glacier much more rapidly than water can erode a landscape. The difference is graphically illustrated by the quantity of sediment carried by two tributaries of the Tasman River. The Jollie River (p. 59) drains the south-eastern slopes of the Liebig Range, which carry only a few small glacial remnants; its waters are discoloured only after heavy rain and carry only about 200 tonnes of sediment per sq. km of catchment annually. The Hooker River (also p. 59) carries the sediment gouged out by both the Mueller and Hooker Glaciers (which fill most of the valley floor; see pp. 60–61); its waters are always turbid and annually carry about 4000 tonnes of sediment (per sq. km of catchment) into the Tasman River, and eventually Lake Pukaki.

At the height of the last glaciation (40 000 to 30 000 years ago) the Tasman Glacier extended several kilometres beyond the southern shore of Lake Pukaki, and the depth of ice was so great that the Mt Cook village site would have been buried under 700 m of ice. Since the end of this last major glacial stage 14 000 years ago, the terminal of the glacier has retreated 60 km to its present position. Here the depth of ice is still about 200 m, hidden under a deceptively thin veneer of rock debris. In the wake of the retreating glacier, the deep trough formerly filled by ice was filled with outwash sediments (the floodplain of the Tasman River) and meltwaters (Lake Pukaki) – each to a depth of 500–1000 m.

Eventually, Lake Pukaki will disappear as it is filled by the delta of the Tasman River advancing down valley. Lake formation through ice melting at the terminal face is occurring at the present terminals of the Hooker and Tasman Glaciers. Although these lakes are forming at a rapid rate, the terminal of the Tasman Glacier has not retreated significantly during the last century. Instead, ice has melted from the surface at a dramatic rate. Late last century climbers had to clamber up over ten metres of lateral moraine onto the surface of the Tasman Glacier at its junction with the Ball Glacier; today's climbers face a difficult descent down 130 m of unstable moraine wall at the same point. In contrast, the glaciers in the Godley valley have retreated several kilometres over the same period, and three wide lakes at the terminals of the Classen, Grey and Godley Glaciers now make travel into the upper valley quite difficult.

Within the park itself post-glacial erosion has tended to obliterate most of the obvious landforms associated with the maximum extent of the last glaciation; this is not the case on the slopes above Lakes Tekapo and Pukaki where flights of old glacial benches have been preserved in a less rigorous montane (rather than alpine) environment. These parallel benches (see pp. 58,59), a series of old lateral moraines and kame terraces marking successively lower levels of glacial ice, extend up to 600 m above the lake surface at the top end and slope down to around 200–300 m above the lake surface at the southern end. Sadly, Lake Pukaki, and its magnificent glacial benches, lie outside the park; its size, glacial landforms, and uncluttered vistas of the high peaks superbly complement the alpine landforms of the park.

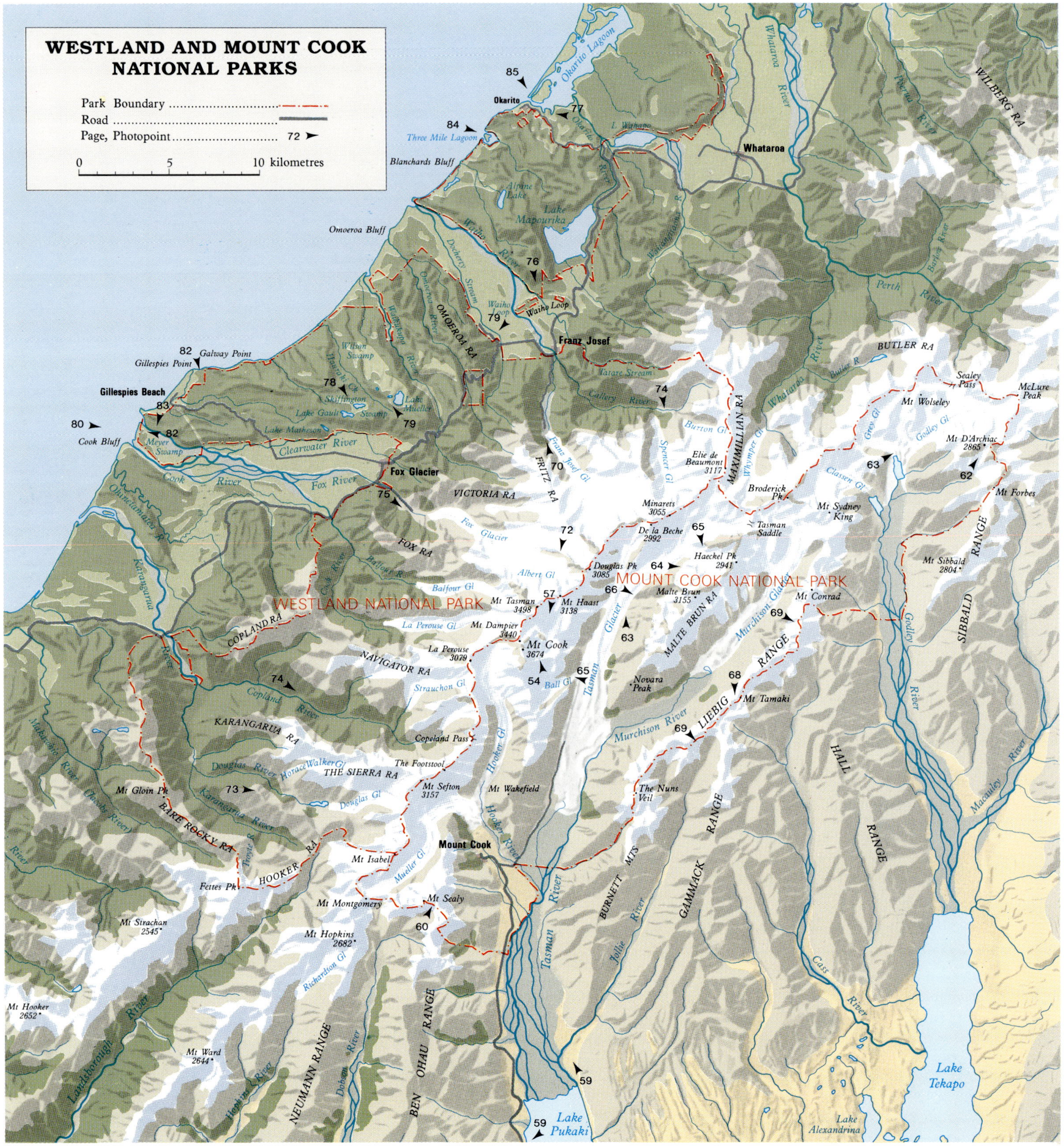

WESTLAND AND MOUNT COOK NATIONAL PARKS
Park Boundary
Road
Page, Photopoint 72
0 5 10 kilometres
WESTLAND NATIONAL PARK
MOUNT COOK NATIONAL PARK
Okarito
Okarito Lagoon
Three Mile Lagoon
Blanchards Bluff
Whataroa
Whataroa River
Perth River
WILBERG RA
Omoeroa Bluff
Lake Mapourika
Alpine Lake
Waiho River
Waiho Loop
Franz Josef
OMOEROA RA
Galway Point
Gillespies Point
Gillespies Beach
Cook Bluff
Lake Gault
Lake Matheson
Clearwater River
Fox River
Cook River
Fox Glacier
VICTORIA RA
FRITZ RA
FOX RA
Franz Josef Gl
Fox Glacier
Callery River
BUTLER RA
Butler R
Sealey Pass
McLure Peak
Mt Wolseley
Mt D'Archiac 2865
Mt Forbes
Elie de Beaumont 3117
MAXIMILIAN RA
Broderick Pk
Mt Sydney King
Minarets 3055
De la Beche 2992
Tasman Saddle
Haeckel Pk 2941
Douglas Pk 3085
Mt Tasman 3498
Mt Haast 3138
Malte Brun 3155
MALTE BRUN RA
Mt Conrad
Mt Sibbald 2804
SIBBALD RANGE
Godley River
Mt Dampier 3440
Mt Cook 3674
La Perouse 3079
La Perouse Gl
Balfour Gl
Albert Gl
NAVIGATOR RA
COPLAND RA
Copland River
Strauchon Gl
Ball Gl
Tasman Glacier
Murchison Gl
Murchison River
Novara Peak
LIEBIG RANGE
Mt Tamaki
KARANGARUA RA
Copeland Pass
The Footstool
THE SIERRA RA
Douglas River
Horace Walker Gl
Mt Gloin Pk
BARE ROCKY RA
Mt Sefton 3157
Mt Wakefield
Hooker Gl
Hooker River
Mount Cook
Mt Isabel
Mueller Gl
HOOKER RA
Fettes Pk
Mt Montgomery
Mt Sealy
Mt Strachan 2545
Mt Hopkins 2682
Richardson Gl
The Nuns Veil
BURNETT MTS
GAMMACK RANGE
HALL RANGE
Jollie River
Cass River
Macaulay River
Tasman River
Mt Hooker 2652
Landsborough River
Mt Ward 2644
NEUMANN RANGE
Dobson River
BEN OHAU RANGE
Lake Pukaki
Lake Tekapo
Lake Alexandrina

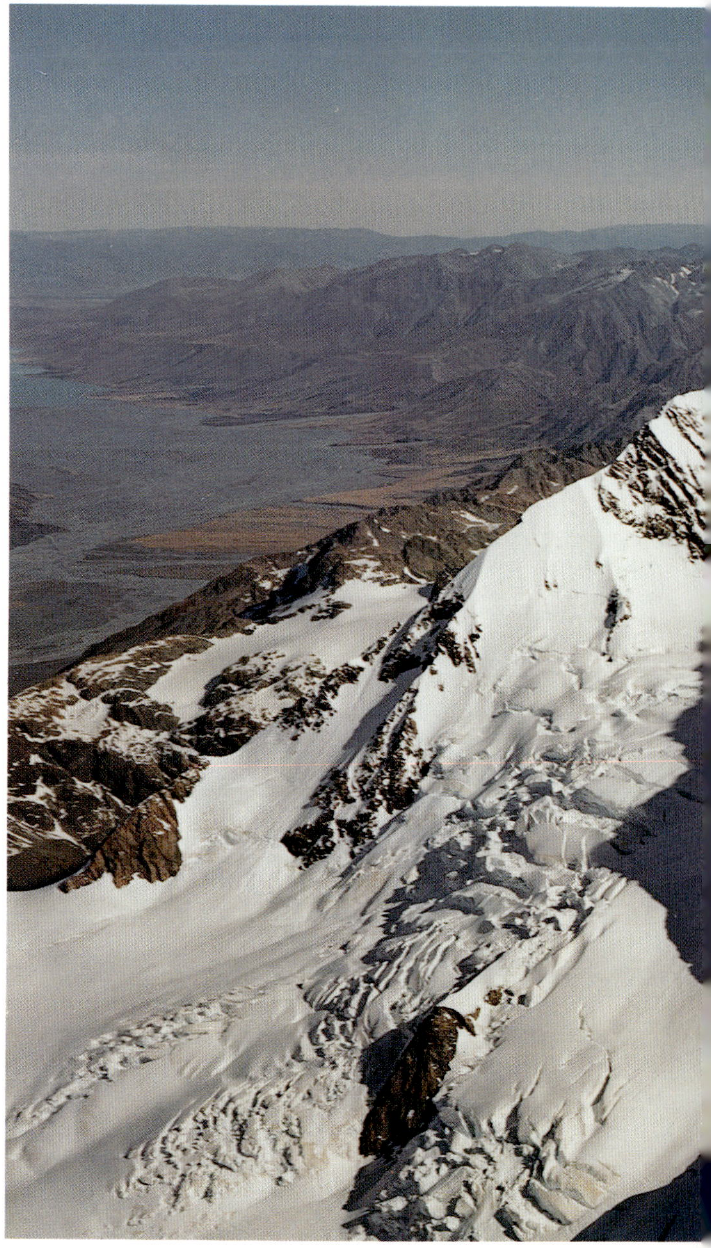

2

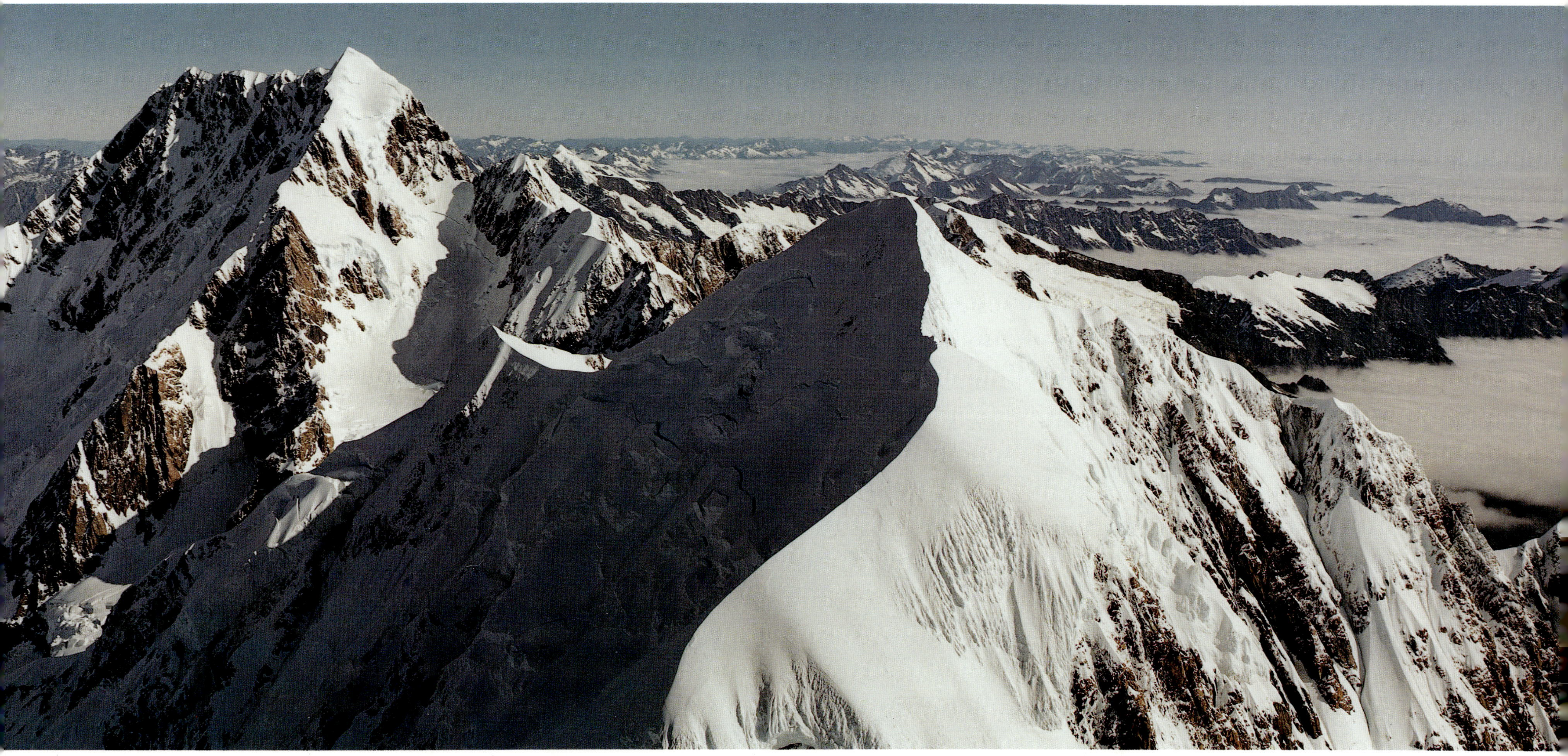

2 Afternoon sunlight highlights the snow arête curving up to the summit of Mt Tasman (foreground, right). Cloud has built up in the western valleys (Westland National Park) but the Ben Ohau Range, Tasman River and top of Lake Pukaki (left, distance) are clear. Note the crevasses and ice cliffs on the shady east faces of Mts Tasman and Cook; each face generates avalanches which plunge down to the Grand Plateau (bottom, left), the névé of the Hochstetter Glacier.

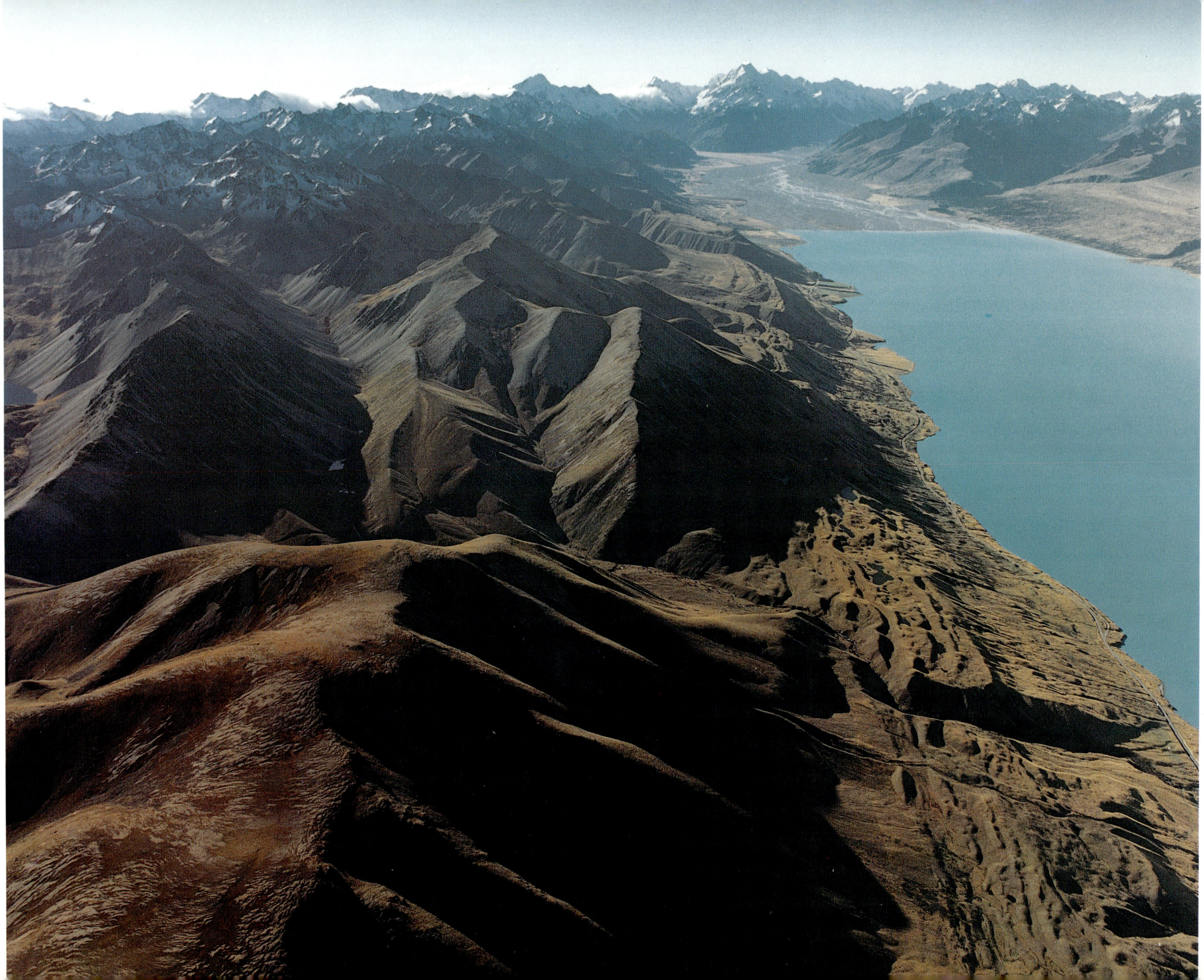

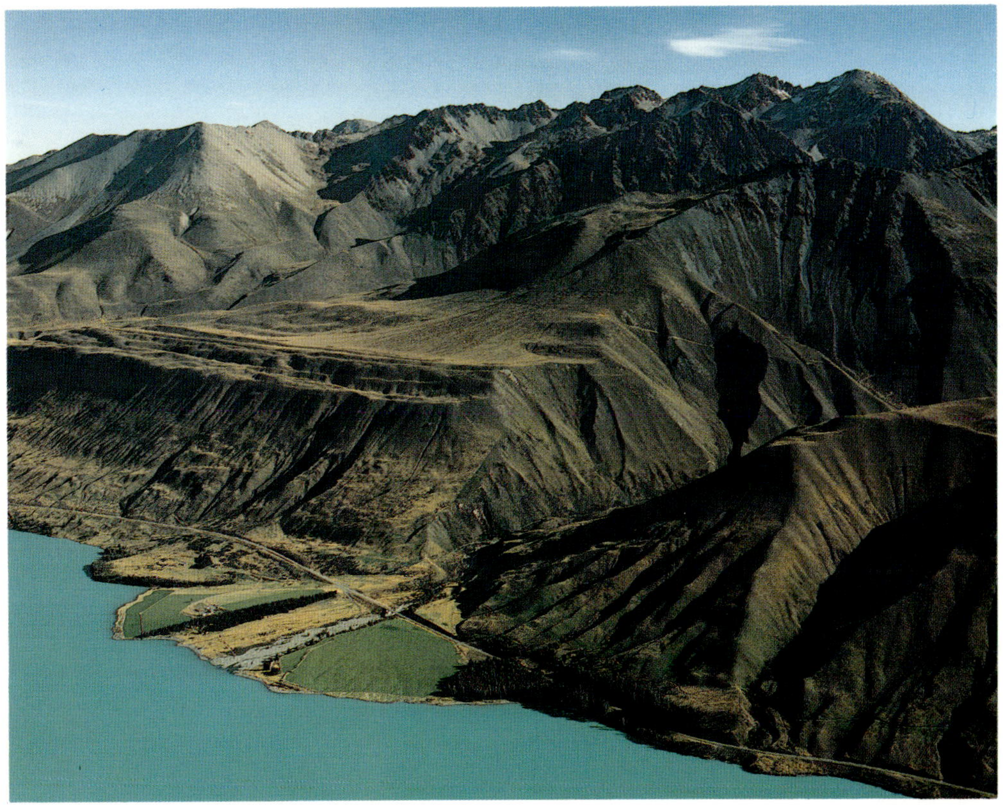

4

3 The present day glaciers of the park are mere remnants of the valley glaciers that filled the park during the Ice Ages. These glaciers flowed southward and coalesced to form a huge piedmont glacier. As these glaciers later retreated, their troughs were filled with melt waters, forming the three great glacial lakes of the Mackenzie Basin – Lakes Tekapo, Pukaki (right) and Ohau. Parallel lines of lateral moraine and kame terraces (formed by melt waters running parallel to the edge of the glacier) can be seen extending for 30 km along the western shores of Lake Pukaki (right). The lines of glacial debris mark surface levels of the glacier as its thickness of ice dropped hundreds of metres in stages; as the surface dropped the terminal retreated into the distance behind the Burnett Mountains (distance, right). Subsequent streams draining the Ben Ohau Range (such as Boundary Stream, centre) have cut down through the glacial debris en route to the lake shore.

4 The landscape around Whale Stream near the head of Lake Pukaki shows the imposition of younger alluvial landforms on older glacial landforms. The series of stepped terraces are remnants of ancient glacial levels, the highest as much as 600 m above lake level. Whale Stream has carved a deep gully and built up a small fan into the lake.

5 The magnificent sweep of the braided floodplains of the Tasman (foreground) and Hooker (centre, left) Rivers seems to extend right back into the mountainous heart of the park. The Jollie River joins the Tasman River in the bottom right of the photograph. The water of the Tasman River is a milky grey colour because of the high content of fine greywacke sediment ('rock flour'). After each glacial retreat, the fierce north-westerly winds swept up the fine silt particles of this rock flour and transported them as loess to the terraces and downlands of the Mackenzie Basin and the Canterbury Plains.

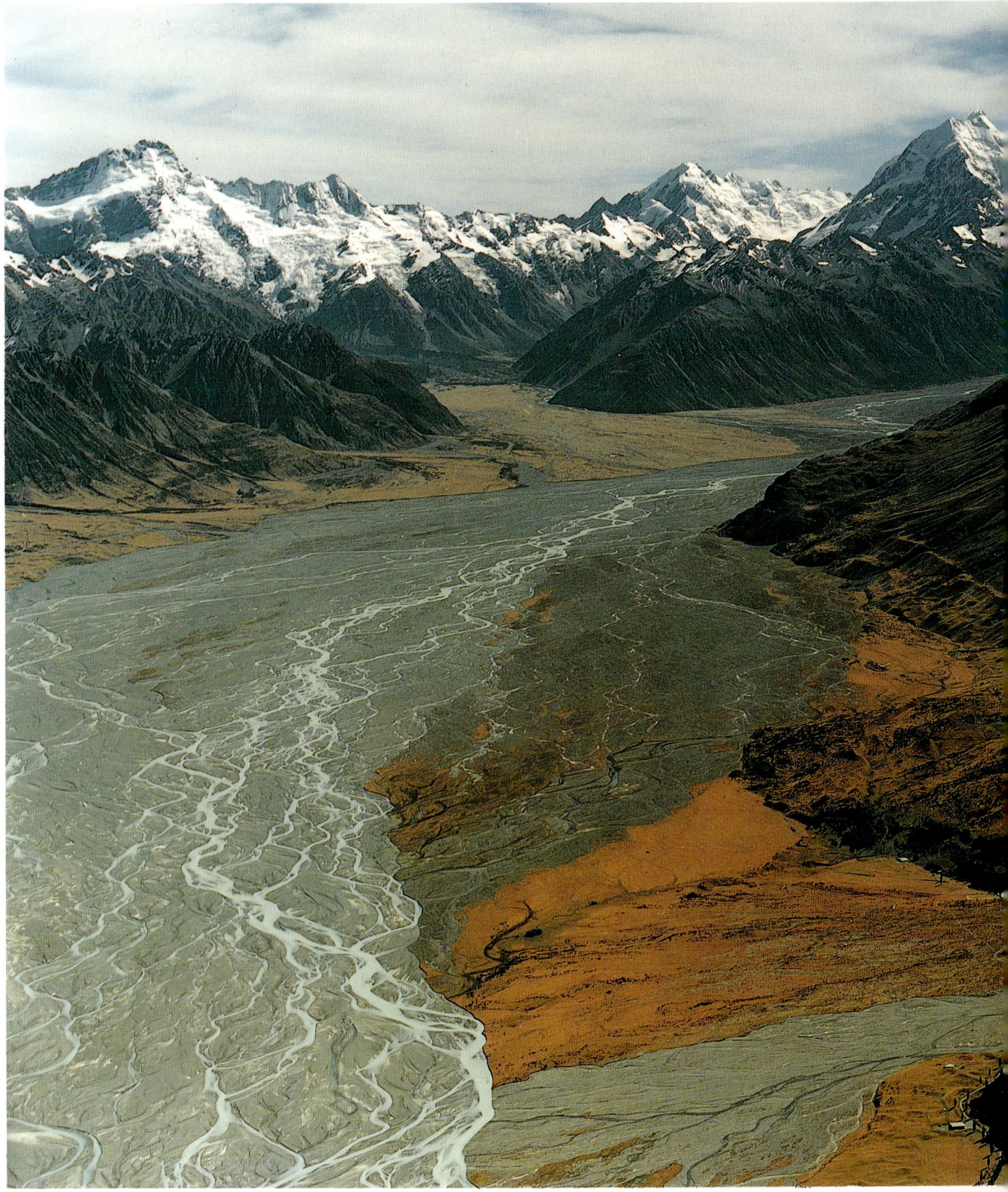

5

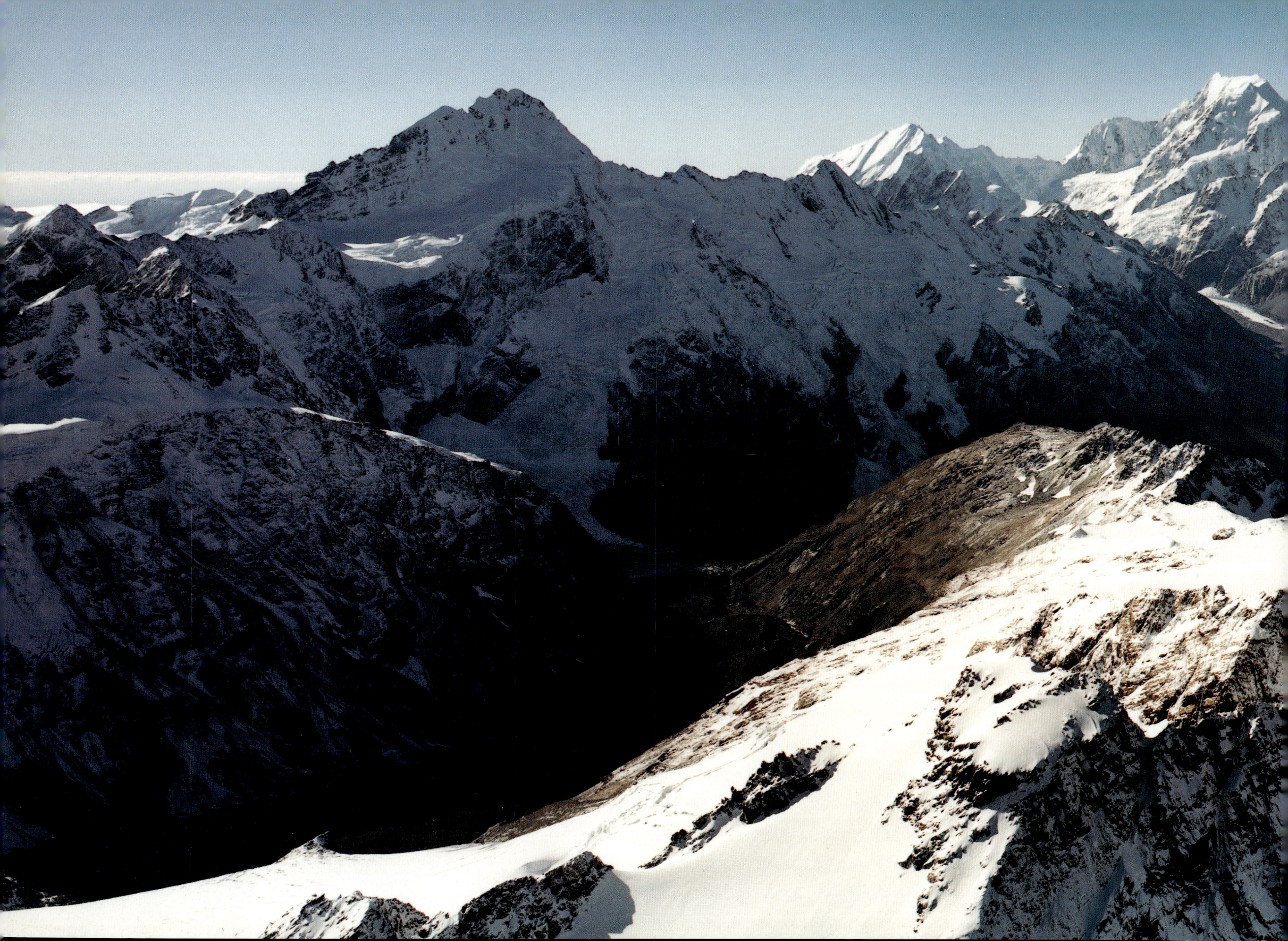

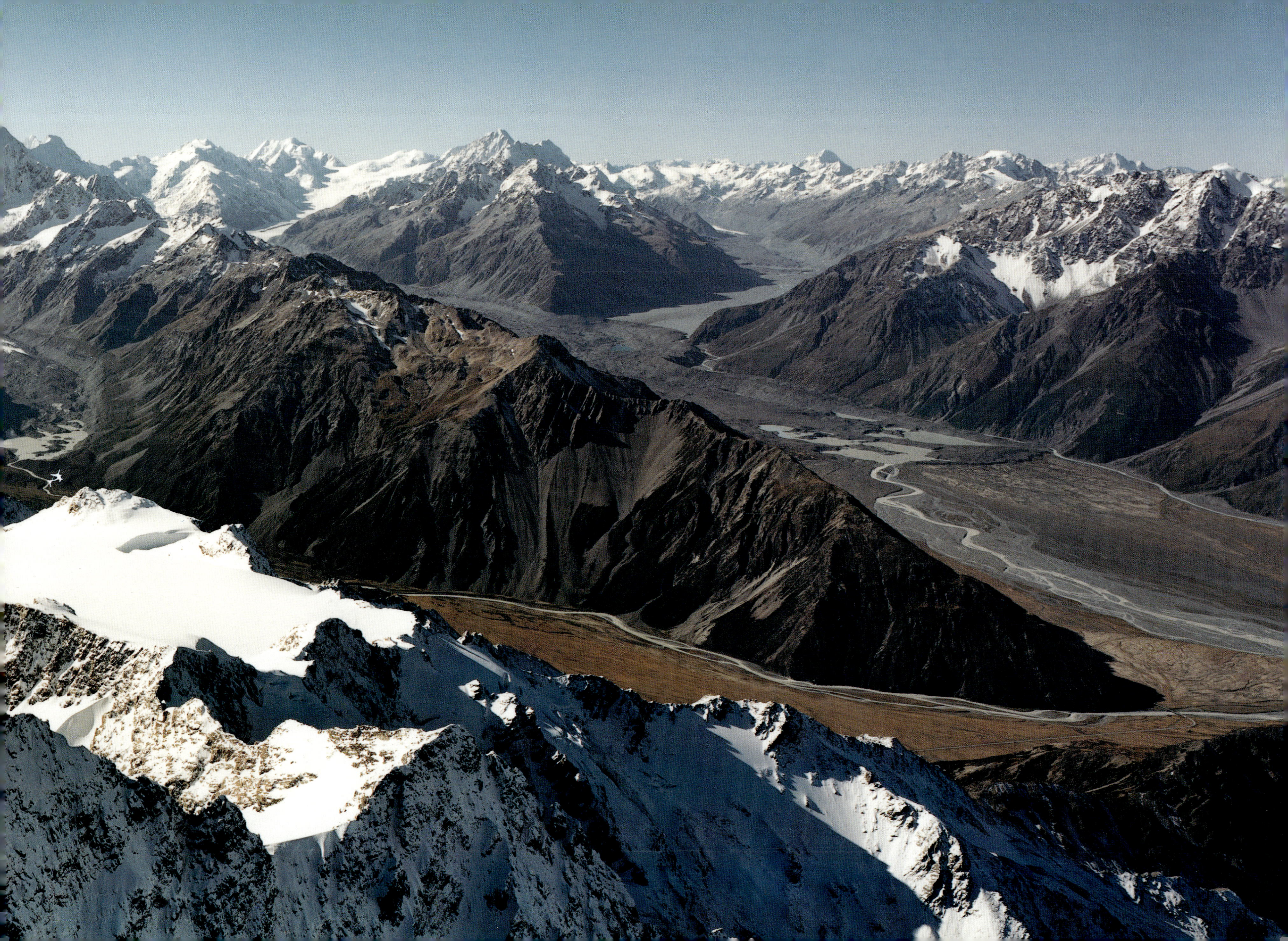

previous page

6 From above Mt Sealy in the south-west corner of Mt Cook National Park, the panorama to the north-east shows the four main valley glaciers feeding into the Tasman River and Lake Pukaki; from left to right – the Mueller, Hooker, Tasman (partly obscured) and the Murchison. Grey surface moraine covers the ice in the lower reaches of all four glaciers. Note the glacier lakes at the terminals of the Hooker and Tasman Glaciers, and how the Murchison River manages to squeeze past the eastern side of the lower Tasman Glacier. The heights of the mountains, and the distances involved (Mt Cook is 20 km away), are such that they tend to 'flatten out' the valleys. The gradients are quite significant, however; for instance, the Hooker valley drops 700 m from the top of the visible tongue of ice (centre) to the Hooker Corner road bridge at the foot of the spur at the southern end of the Mt Cook Range (right).

The most obvious skyline peaks, from left to right, are: Mts Sefton, La Perouse, Cook, the Minarets, Elie de Beaumont, Malte Brun, and D'Archiac (behind the Murchison valley). Whereas the shady south-eastern slopes are plastered with snow and ice, the sunny western faces of the drier more easterly ranges (Mt Cook, Malte Brun, and Liebig Ranges) are generally free of snow.

7 By the time the ice of the Tasman Glacier joins the ice stream from the Hochstetter Icefall (bottom, left) it is almost completely covered with rock debris – most of it coming from the slopes above the Rudolf Glacier (top, left) and the eastern slopes of the main divide (left). The sharp vegetation line on the lower slopes of the Malte Brun Range (right) shows how the surface of the glacier has dropped about 100 m through melting of the ice over the past century. Despite this graphic wastage of the Tasman Glacier, the depth of ice is still estimated to be about 600 m at this point – that is, the base of the glacier is about 100 m below the surface of Lake Pukaki 35 km downstream. Note the elevated ridge of medial ice running down the centre of the glacier, compressed by the merging of the Rudolf, Haast (centre, left) and other glaciers with the ice of the main Tasman Glacier.

The two peaks to the right of the Rudolf Glacier are De la Beche and the Minarets; Elie de Beaumont is the prominent peak at the head of the Tasman Glacier, and Hochstetter Dome the rounded dome to the right.

7

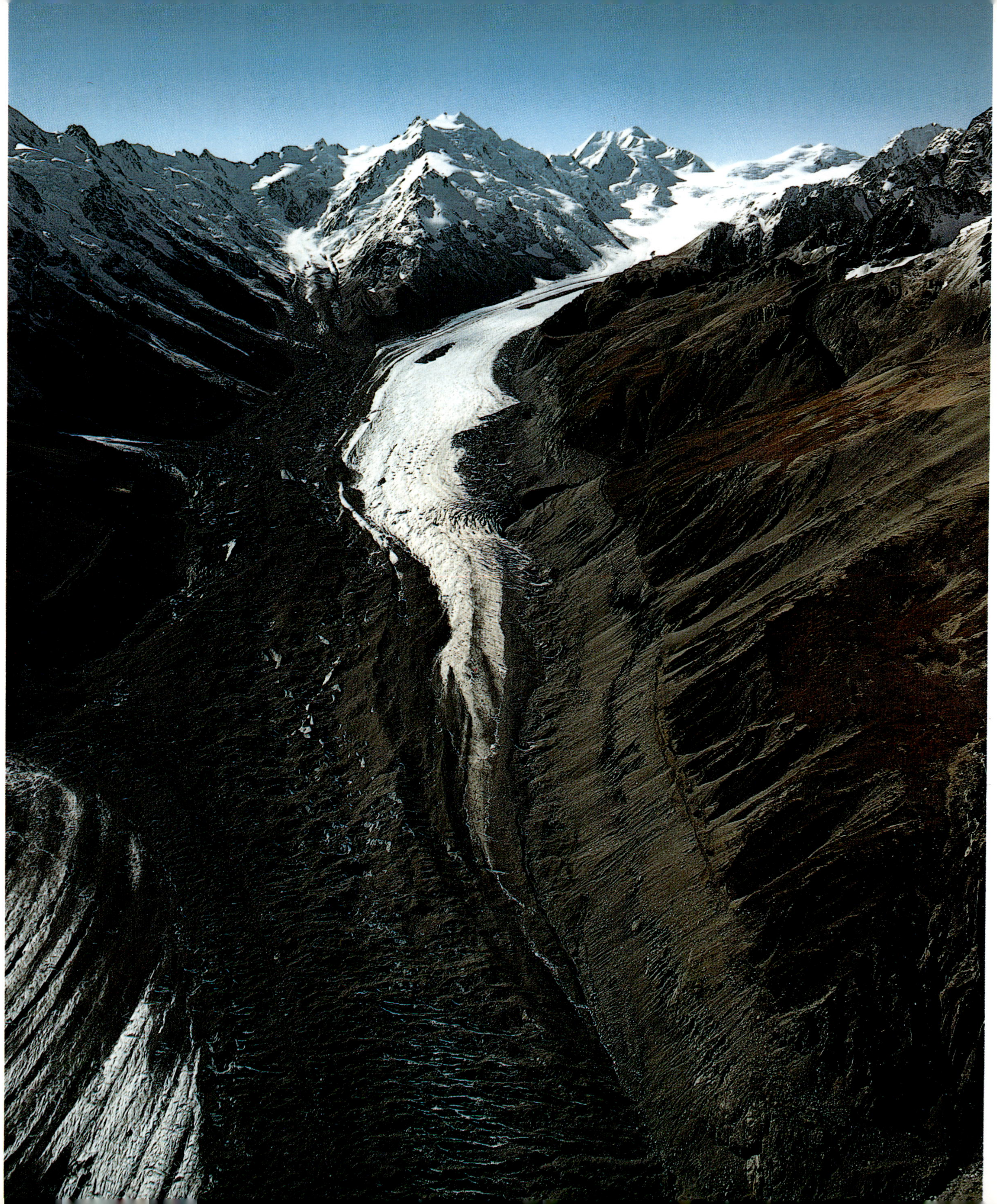

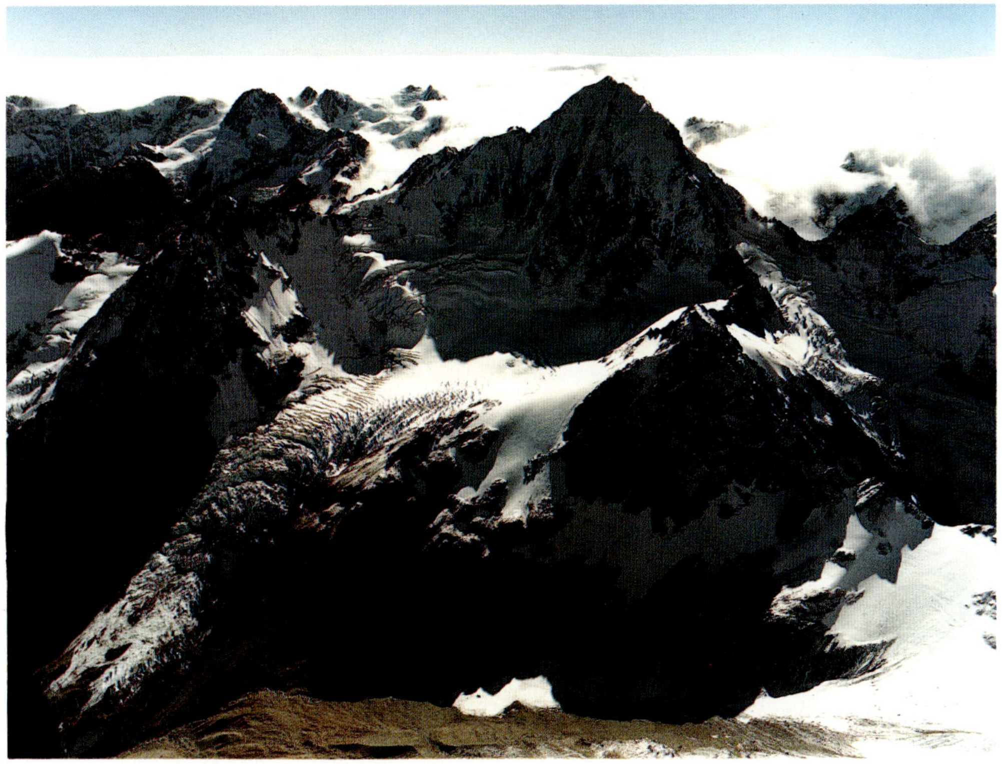

8

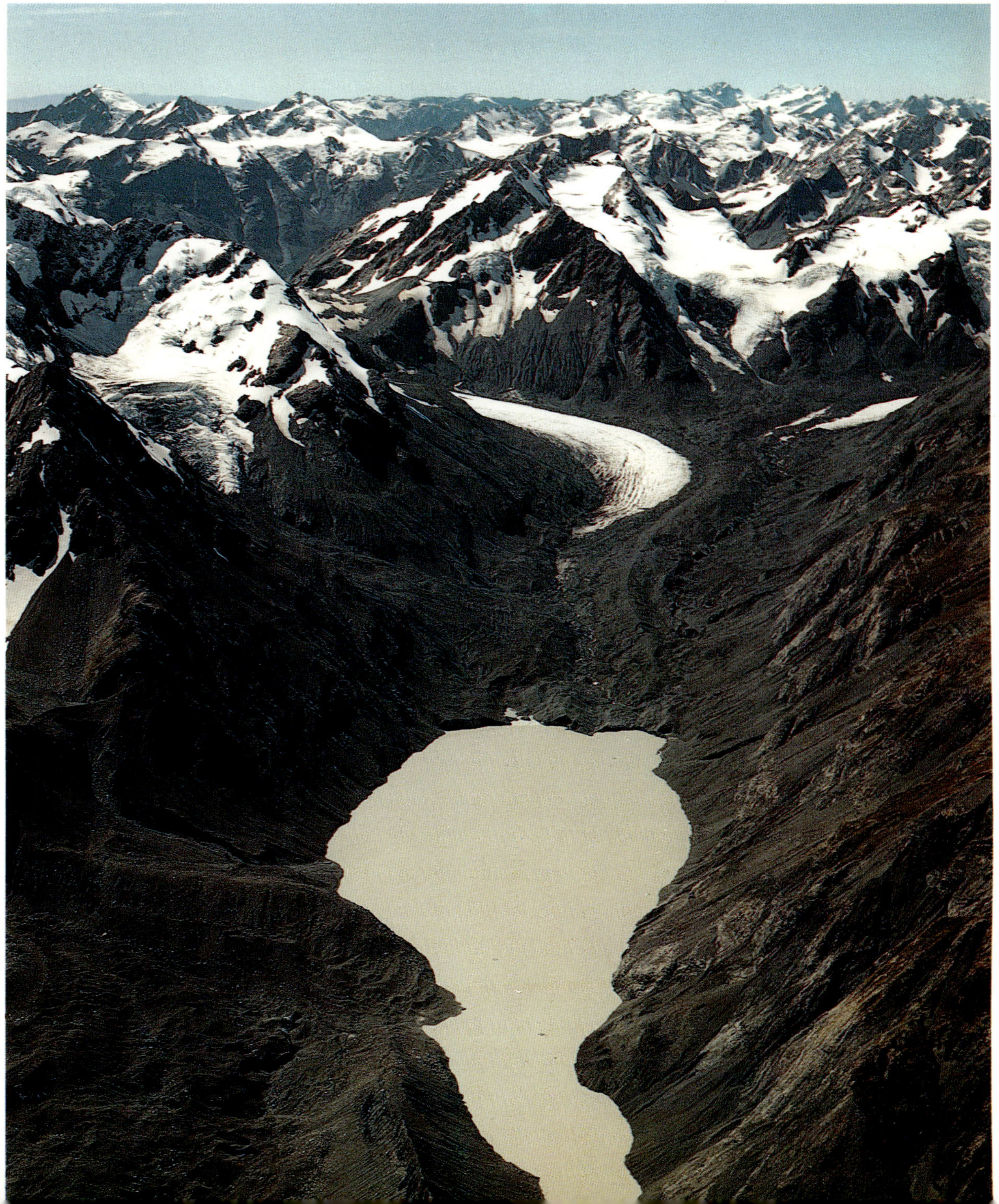

9

8 Mt D'Archiac (2865 m) stands up in the north-eastern corner of the park, where the Two Thumb Range joins the main divide . It is one of the best examples within the park of a glacial horn, a peak honed to a steep-sided pyramid by several cirque glaciers. Five glaciers – Trident, Dennistoun, South Forbes (right), Separation (foreground, left) and Fitzgerald Glaciers – ring Mt D'Archiac on all sides, providing climbers with a variety of routes to the peak.

9 The Godley Glacier (centre) has retreated at least 5 km and a large lake has formed since Julius von Haast's visit in 1862. Note the medial moraine formed by the convergence of the eastern and western branches of the Godley Glacier. A similar medial moraine (left, foreground) has been formed by the convergence of the Godley Glacier with the Grey Glacier.

The unstable moraine and scree slopes around the terminal lake make foot travel to the upper Godley valley both arduous and dangerous. The peaks to the north-east lie around the Gardens of Eden and Allah, two large névés straddling the main divide between the Rangitata and Whataroa valleys outside the park. Sealy Pass (centre, left) is the low point on the main divide beyond the prominent curve in the western branch of the Godley Glacier.

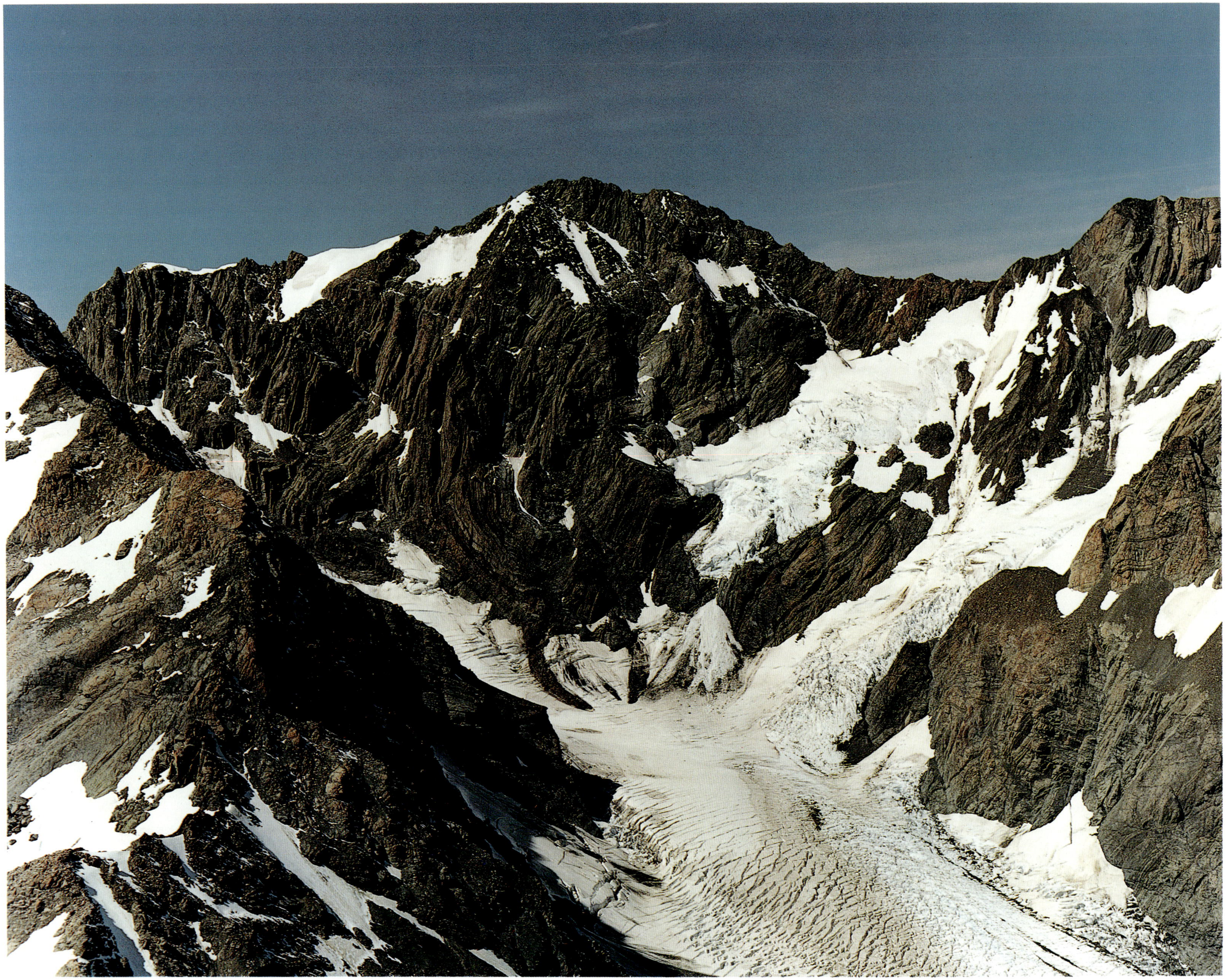

10

10 At the north-eastern end of the Malte Brun Range, the intense folding of the greywacke rocks is illustrated by the folds in the strata on the western side of Haeckel Peak (centre). During the last five million years these rocks have been uplifted 20–25 km, and erosion has exposed these spectacular structures formed many millions of years ago within the earth's crust.

11 In these high alpine areas rockfalls, such as this one off the northern slopes of Mt Darwin above the upper Tasman Glacier (see pp. 66–67) are relatively common. They contribute most of the surface rock debris that covers the middle and lower reaches of the valley glaciers.

The patches of pinkish snow (left, foreground) indicate the previous season's snowfall which has been colonised by red algae.

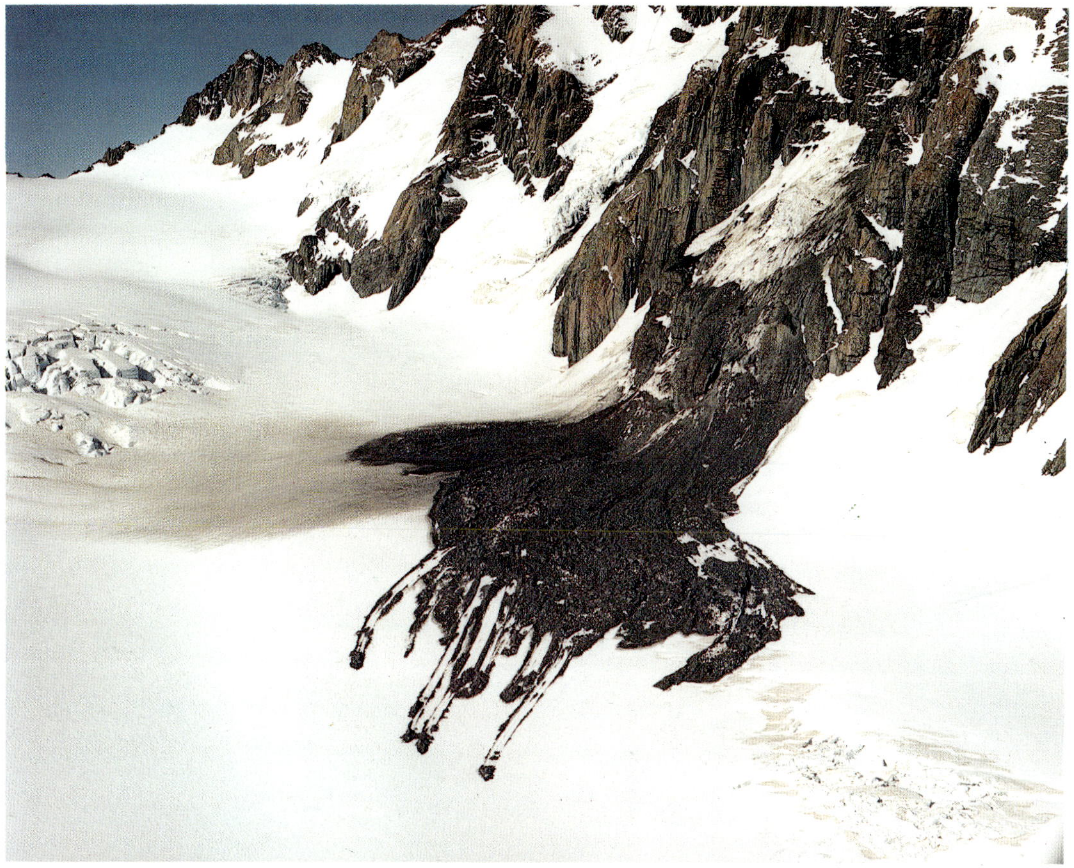

11

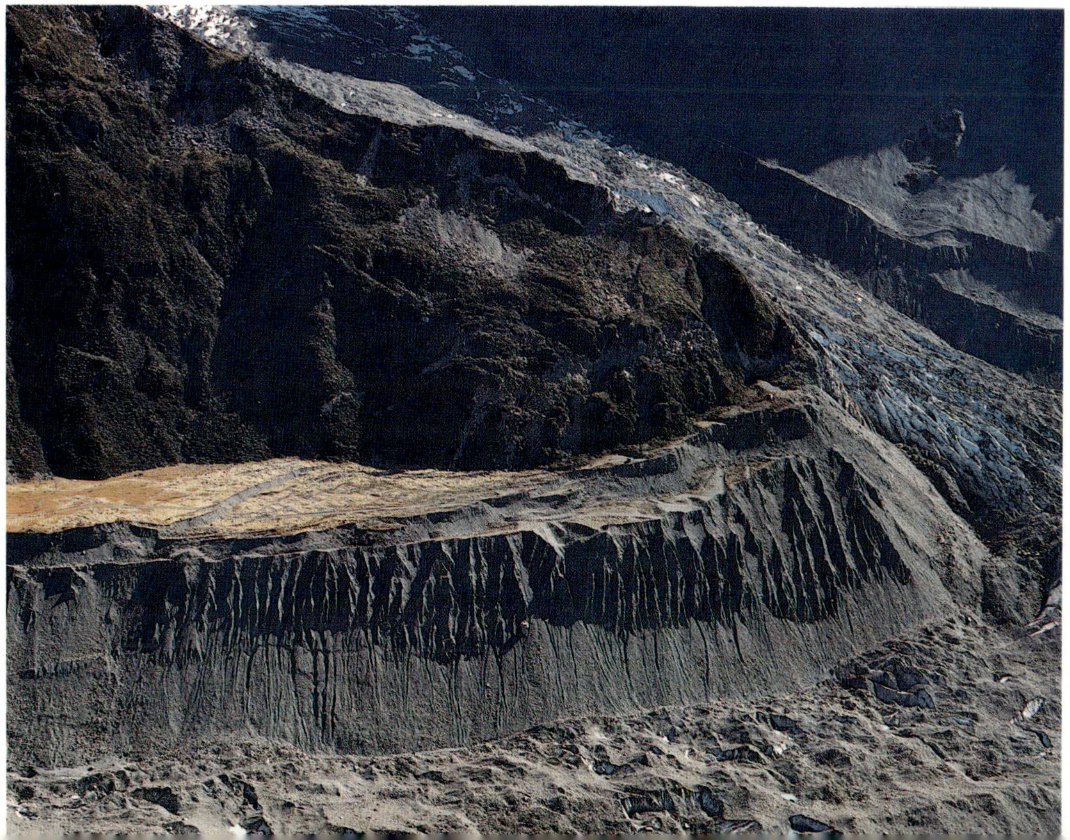

12

12 The icefall of the Ball Glacier (top, diagonal left to right) joins the main flow of the Tasman Glacier (bottom) about 10 km upstream from the present-day terminal of the Tasman. The surface of the glacier at this point acts as a huge conveyor-belt transporting a deceptively-thin (0.5–1.0 m) veneer of rock debris which has fallen onto the surface of the ice (see adjacent photograph of rockfall on the névé of the glacier). This veneer of rock, although unsightly, protects the surface of the glacier by insulating it to some extent from solar radiation, thereby slowing its melting rate.

This is the site of the historic Ball Hut. Built in 1891 it was one of the first purely recreational huts built in our national parks. From the mid 1930's until the 1960's the locality was a popular skifield, at times even hosting the New Zealand championships. Today it is a sad relic of a commercial skifield but a graphic illustration of the dynamic landforms in the vicinity of a shrinking valley glacier. The surface of the Tasman Glacier is now 130 m below the grass-covered kame terrace; a century ago a pioneer climber, the Rev W.S. Green, spoke of having to scramble up over lateral moraine onto the glacier surface at this point.

The steep moraine wall is now fluted with water-cut drainage channels. Note the cracks and fissures cutting the surface of the terrace (and the old Ball Hut Road). The shrinkage of the glacier has left the moraine wall unsupported and it is collapsing back into the valley. Several other hut sites in similar situations within the park have also had to be abandoned because of moraine collapse.

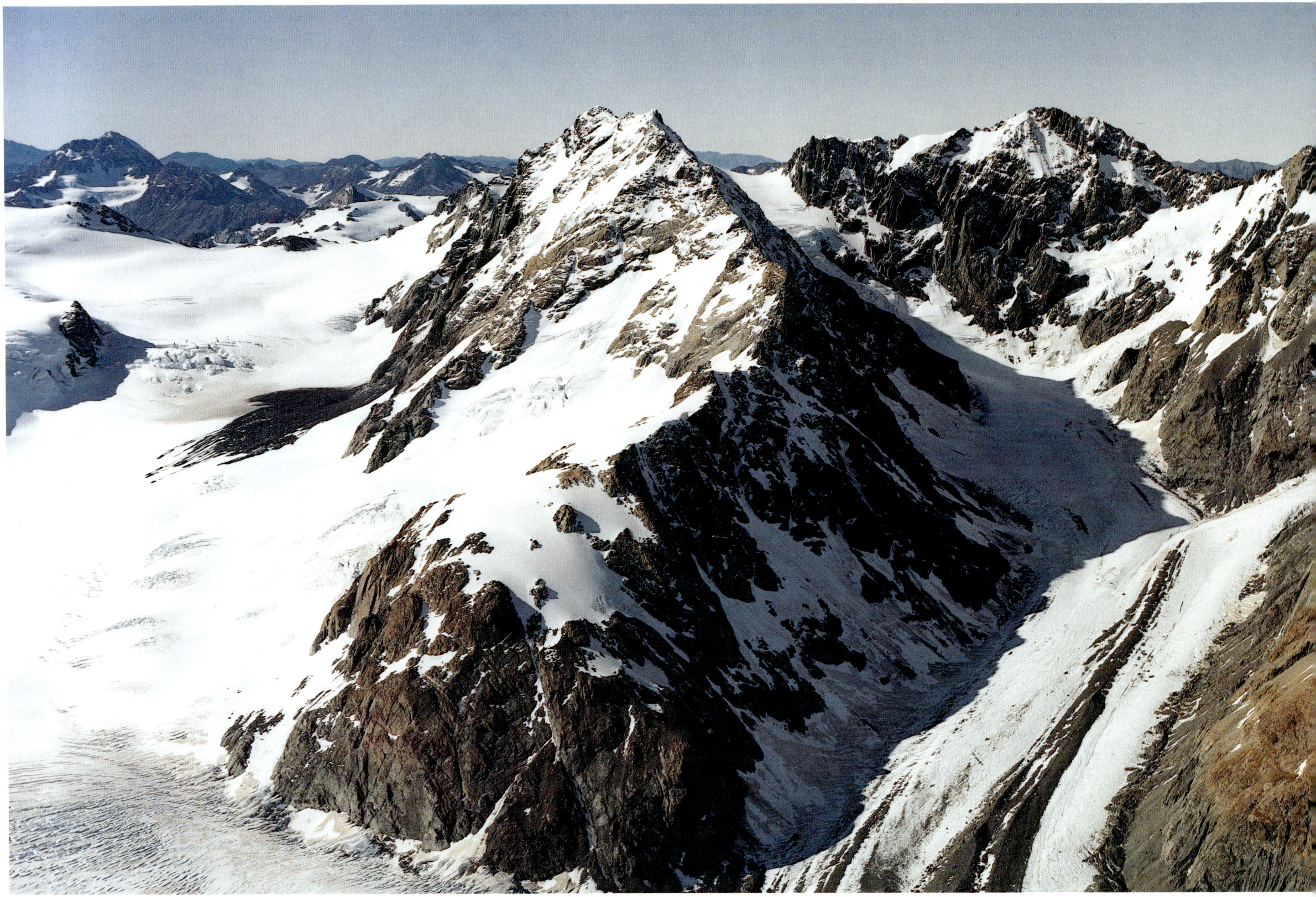

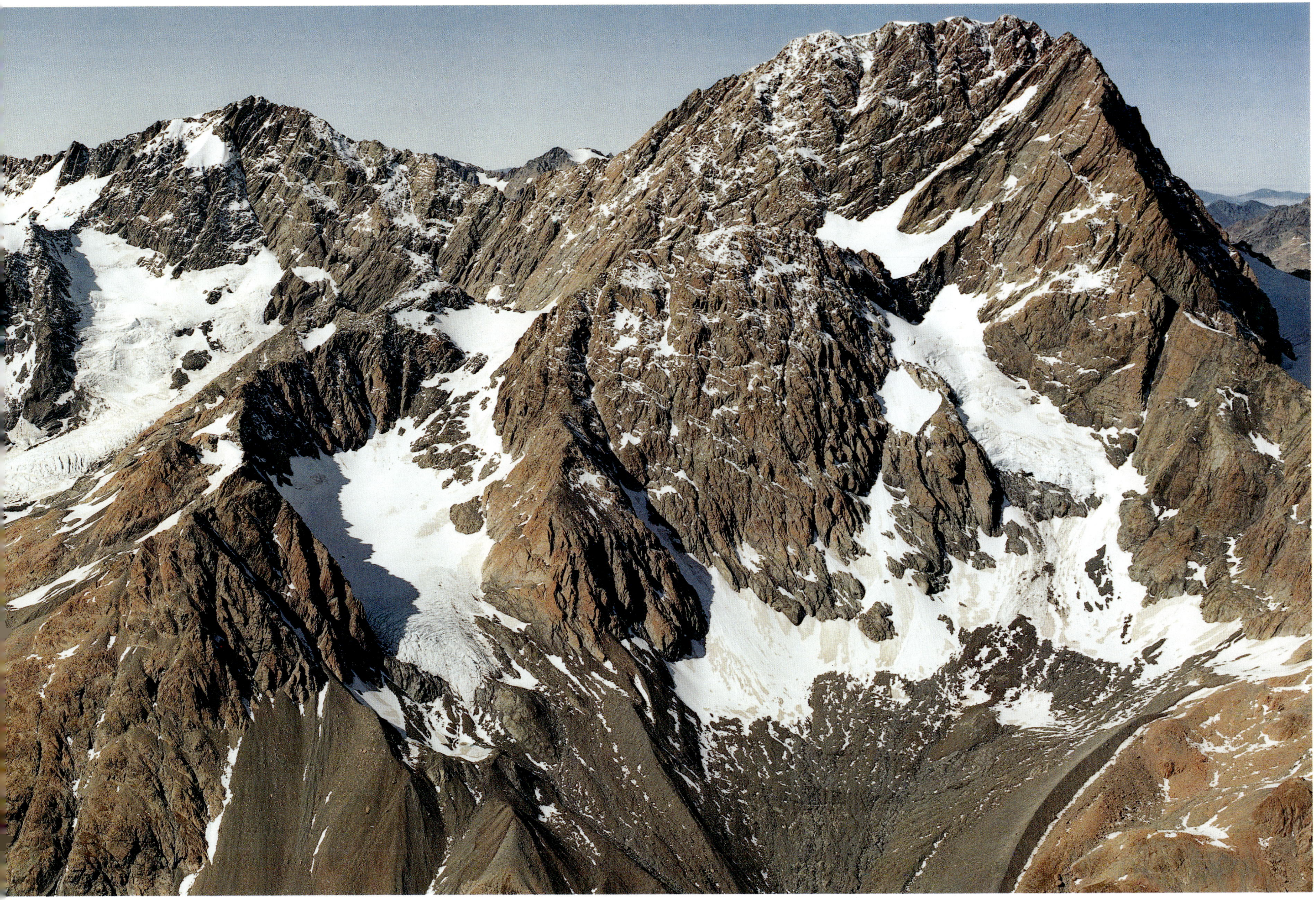

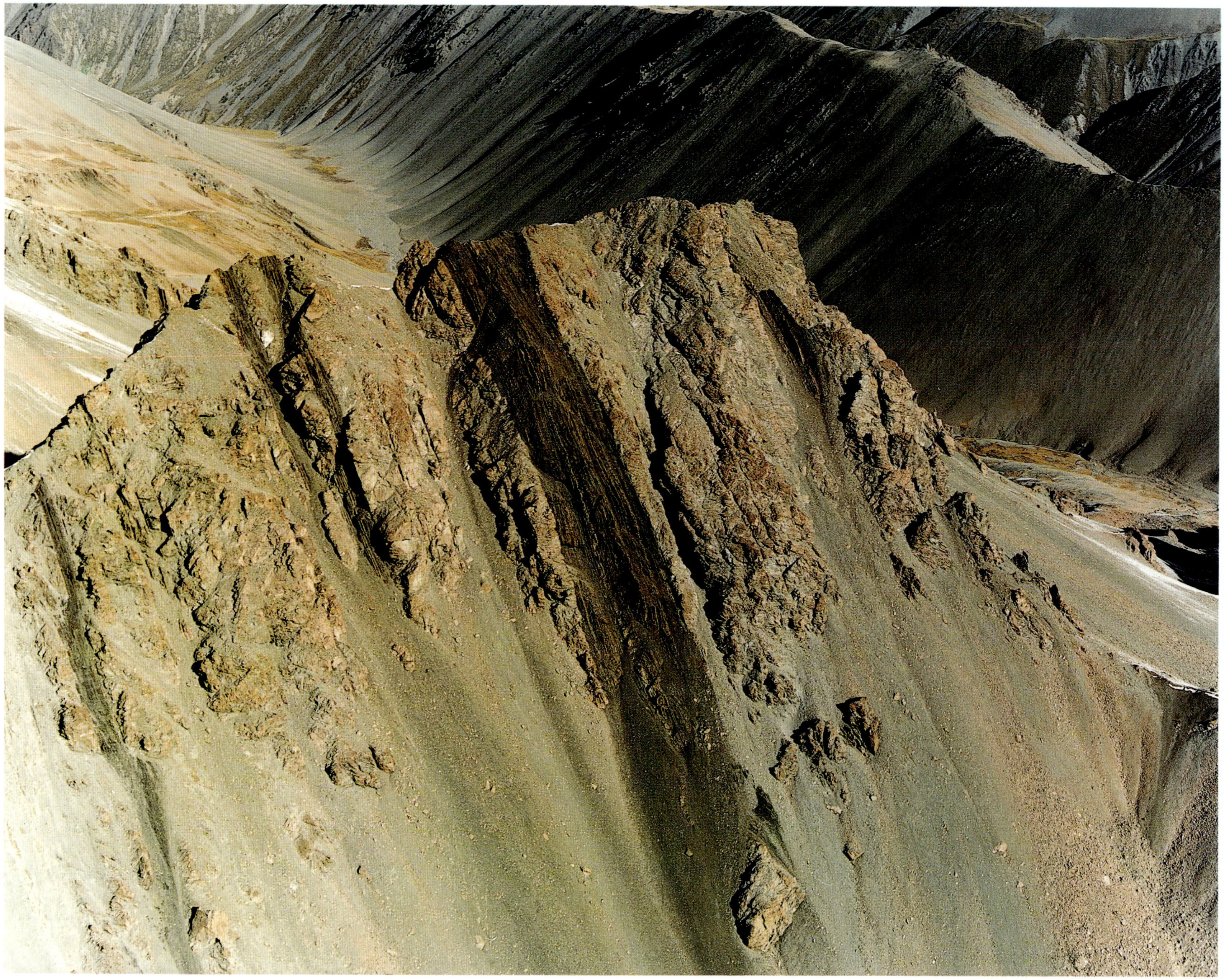

14

previous page

13 The Malte Brun Range forms the eastern side of the upper Tasman valley, its reddish rock contrasting with the snow and ice of the main divide 8 km to the west. The view, looking eastwards from above De la Beche Ridge, is dominated by the bulk of Malte Brun (3155 m) on the far right of the photograph. Tasman Saddle, laading to the head of the Murchison Glacier, is just east of the main divide at the far left. Note the large rockfall off Mt Darwin (see p. 65).

The lack of snow and ice on the range during summer reveals the steeply dipping greywacke strata. The red colour of the rock is due to the weathering of iron-containing minerals.

The firn line on the Tasman Glacier can be seen in the bottom left corner. Above this line is the accumulation zone where the white snow of the previous winter persists; below it lies the ablation (melting) zone where reddish-tinged snow (over one year old), or bare ice, is exposed. Two other glacial features stand out: the line of medial moraine on the Darwin Glacier (centre, foreground) and the two smooth ridges of lateral moraine left abandoned by the retreating Malte Brun Glacier (bottom, right).

14 The Liebig Range, on the eastern boundary of the park, lies in the rain-shadow of the main divide and the Mt Cook and Malte Brun Ranges. Screes are particularly well developed on its deglaciated slopes, and within the catchments of the Jollie and Cass Rivers to the east beyond the park boundary. The colour bands in the foreground rocks are due to alternating layers of darker siltstone (argillite) and lighter sandstone (greywacke) sediments which were deposited in the ancient marine basins where they were eventually compressed into rocks, and later tilted on end to now dip almost vertically.

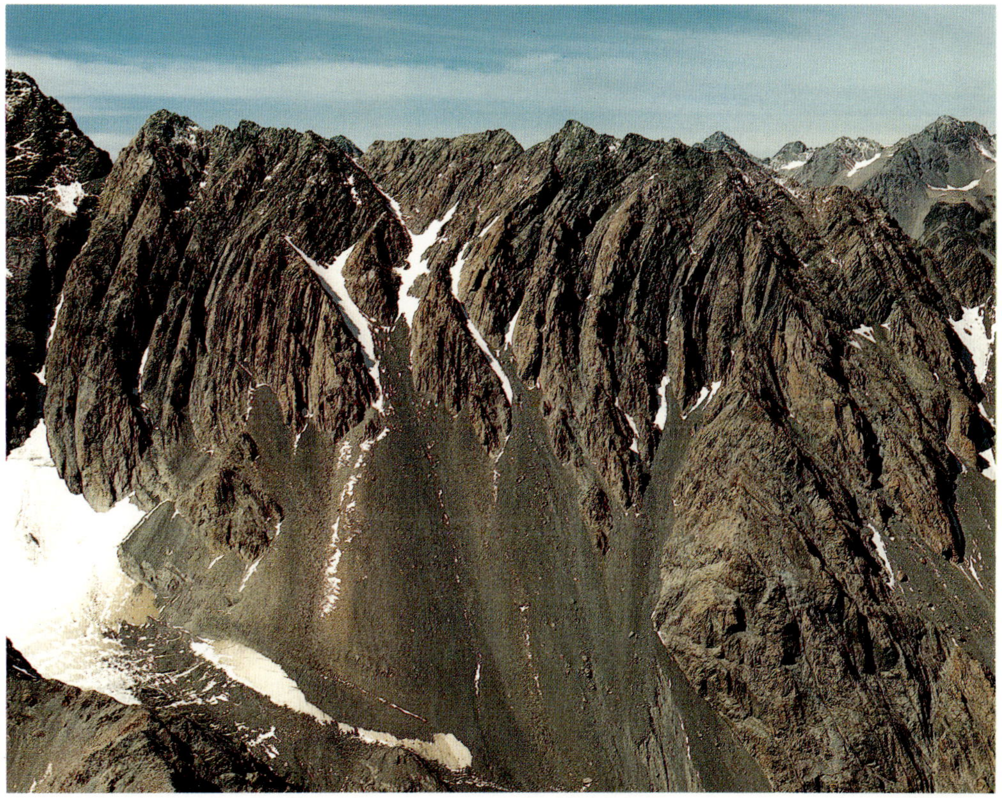

15

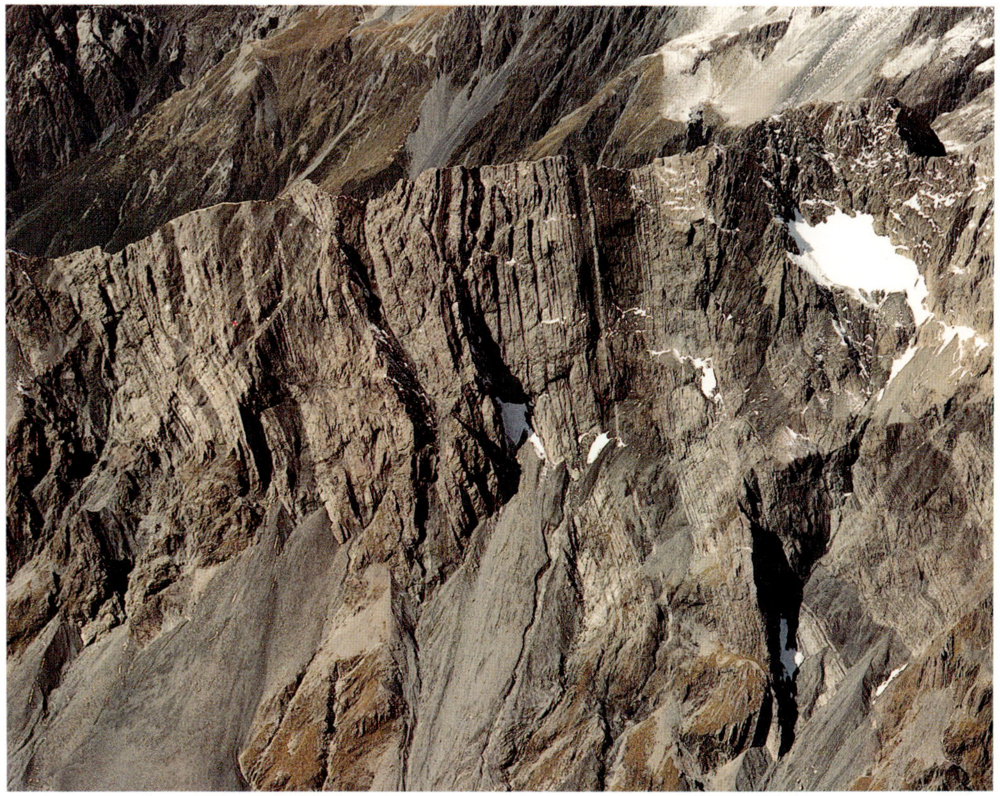

15

15 Lack of summer snow on the Malte Brun and Liebig Ranges allows a number of distinctive rock features to be appreciated:

• gently curving folds in near vertical strata.

• alternating bands of dark siltstone (argillite) and lighter sandstone (greywacke). The argillite band just left of the largest patch of snow shows offsets caused by the movement of small faults.

• a band of bright red (and less obvious green) rocks of volcanic origin are interlayered within the more usual greywacke and argillite. The rocks on the near ridge dip less steeply than the prominent vertical strata on the ridge beyond (top, right).

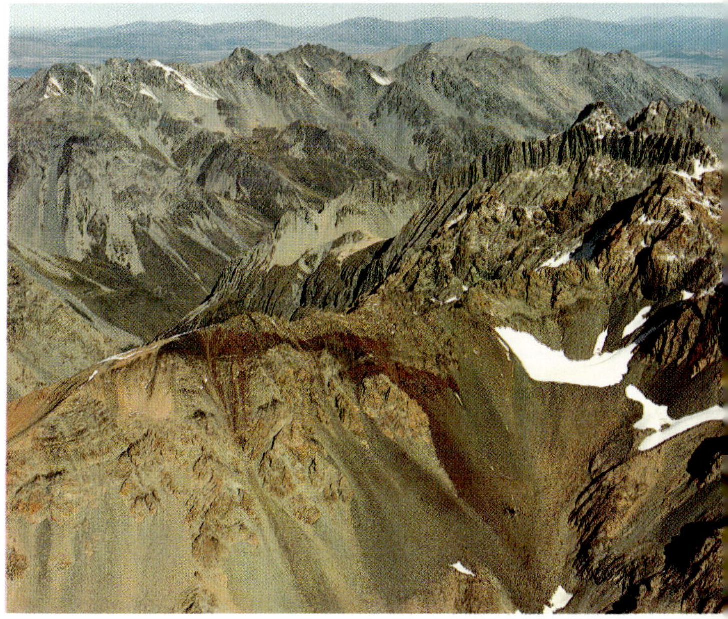

15

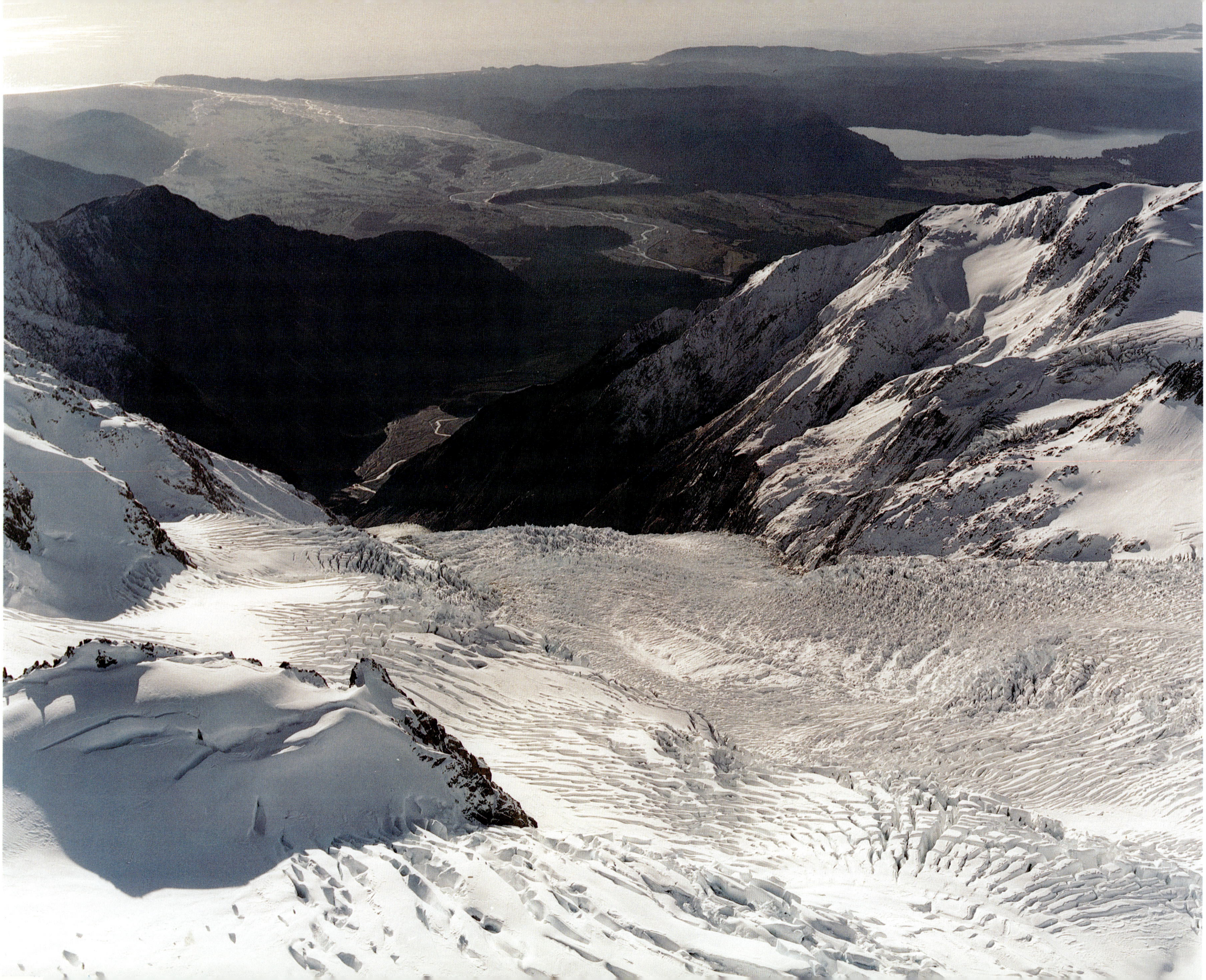

1

WESTLAND NATIONAL PARK

Westland National Park is a landscape of superlatives. A distance of only 25 km separates Mt Tasman (3498 m) from the Tasman Sea; two major glaciers extend down to the lowland forests; the park contains the full range of glacial landforms, from cirque glaciers on the high peaks to coastal lagoons now occupying long-abandoned glacial troughs. In contrast, adjacent Mt Cook National Park is truly alpine in character and does not include important glacial landforms like the high terraces and lake-filled glacial troughs, which extend out into the MacKenzie Basin. Physiographically, Westland National Park falls into two sectors: the mountains east of the Alpine Fault and the piedmont to the west.

MOUNTAINS EAST OF ALPINE FAULT

Most of the mountains within the park consist of the schist rock type, ranging from highly metamorphosed garnet schist nearest the Alpine Fault to weakly metamorphosed chlorite schist near the greywacke spine of the Southern Alps. The dramatic western wall of the Alps is the result of the extraordinarily high rate of uplift – 18 000 m since the onset of the Kaikoura Orogeny a few million years ago and a current rate estimated at 10–14 mm per year.

Sixty or so glaciers occur at higher altitudes, the largest being the Burton, Spencer, Franz Josef, Fox, Balfour, La Perouse Strauchon, Horace Walker, and Douglas. The Franz Josef and Fox have the largest névés in New Zealand and in historical time descended as ice tongues down to a mere 200 m above sea level – the realm of the lowland podocarp/hardwood forest. The rate of movement in the icefall of the Franz Josef Glacier (2–3 m per day) is one of the highest in the world. It reached almost 8 m per day during a brief advance in 1965–67; in comparison, the rate of the Tasman Glacier is only 0.6 m per day.

All glaciers except the Franz Josef and Fox have now retreated from the montane zone, leaving deeply-incised valleys now running east to west. These are now occupied by the headwaters of the major rivers of the park: the Tatare, Callery, Waikukupa, Balfour, Cook, Copland, Douglas and Karangarua. The valley walls are steep and landslides are frequent. The annual precipitation of 5000–12 000 mm on these western slopes is the highest in the country. To shed this water quickly, a unique set of vegetation communities, soils and drainage channels have evolved. The dense cover of forest (podocarp/kamahi/*Quintinia*), subalpine scrub and snow tussock tends to mask the intensive erosion which seems to be a cyclic event on these steep mountain slopes. Consequently, most of the soils on the slopes are probably only 1000–2000 years old, and the moist climate has promoted the rapid revegetation of the erosion scars.

The Alpine Fault is the transition zone between the mountains and the piedmont. It can be traced as a line across the narrow waist of the park between Franz Josef and Fox townships. The full effect of the Alpine Fault can only be appreciated from a western vantage point (for example, Okarito Trig) or from the air. As Abel Tasman recorded when he first sighted this landscape in 1642, the land to the east of the fault is truly 'uplifted high', the forested wall of the ranges rising unbroken for 1000 m.

FORESTED PIEDMONT AND COASTAL LAGOONS

Initially, Westland National Park lacked any significant lowlands. But in 1982 the southern Okarito and Waikukupa forests were added to the park after a major conservation campaign. This action extended the park to the Tasman Sea, thereby protecting not only the most outstanding lowland podocarp forest in Central Westland, but also the full range of landforms left behind when the glaciers retreated at the end of each stage of glacial advance. Vast amounts of erosion debris mantle these lowlands, and only in the 600 m high Omoeroa range between the Waiho and Omoeroa Rivers do the basement rocks (very old granite, greywacke and argillite) still stand above the glacial outwash. Elsewhere, the piedmont consists of a jumble of heavily vegetated moraine, fluvio-glacial outwash, and alluvial floodplains which can be grouped into three classes according to age.

(i) *The oldest surfaces*: the dissected Waikukupa Plateau at 300–400 m altitude between the Omoeroa River and Gillespies Point in the south, and the somewhat lower (200–300 m) moraines wedged between the Waiho River, Lake Mapourika and Okarito Lagoon in the north.

(ii) *Landforms from the last glaciation* (Otiran): lakes, moraines and outwash terraces formed between 25 000 and 14 000 years ago, remaining along the main glacial troughs. Examples are: Lake Wahapo, the moraines impounding Okarito Lagoon and Okarito Forest, the lower Waiho valley, and Lake Mapourika.

(iii) *Post-glacial Landforms*: of the Waiho and Fox/Cook valleys and the coastline. The best known of these is the Waiho Loop, a bush-covered terminal moraine of the Franz Josef Glacier, dated at 11 000–12 000 years old.

The floodplains of major rivers, like the Waiho, Cook and Waitangitaona, are notorious for their instability. Periodically over the last twenty years each of these three rivers has built up its bed and suddenly changed direction: the Waiho has several times swept away the access road to the foot of the Franz Josef Glacier; the Waitangitaona changed its course to flow into Lake Wahapo thereby killing a large area of kahikatea forest and turning the lake turbid from suspended sediments; and the Cook River changed its course through the Meyer Swamp near its mouth, again killing a large area of kahikatea forest.

The coastal lagoons – the large Okarito Lagoon and the much smaller Three-Mile, Five-Mile and Gillespies Lagoons – are also highly dynamic landforms, sometimes enclosed, sometimes open to the Tasman Sea through the breaching of the sandbar. They occupy the troughs of former glacial tongues. Now abandoned by the swift-flowing ice-fed rivers, they are generally fed by humus-stained meandering creeks and constitute important wildlife habitats in the park.

1 The Franz Josef Glacier is one of the most impressive features of Westland National Park today. Fifteen thousand years ago it extended beyond Waiho Bluff, which can be seen in the top left of the picture where the present-day Waiho River flows into the Tasman Sea. For the last 13 000 years it has inexorably retreated back into the mountain fastness of the park. When Abel Tasman sighted this 'land uplifted high' in 1642, the glacier was still within 1–2 km of the modern Franz Josef Glacier township. Climatic fluctuations during the thousands of years of retreat led to periodic advances, one of which left the arc of terminal moraine now covered in dense forest and known as the 'Waiho Loop' (in the middle distance).

Vast amounts of glacial and water-borne rock debris have been carried down from the mountains to build up the floodplain of the Waiho River. The river can be clearly seen swinging around the left of Waiho Loop while, beyond the right-hand end of the loop, Lake Mapourika nestles in a trough carved by another lobe of the Franz Josef Glacier. Okarito Lagoon can be seen in the distance.

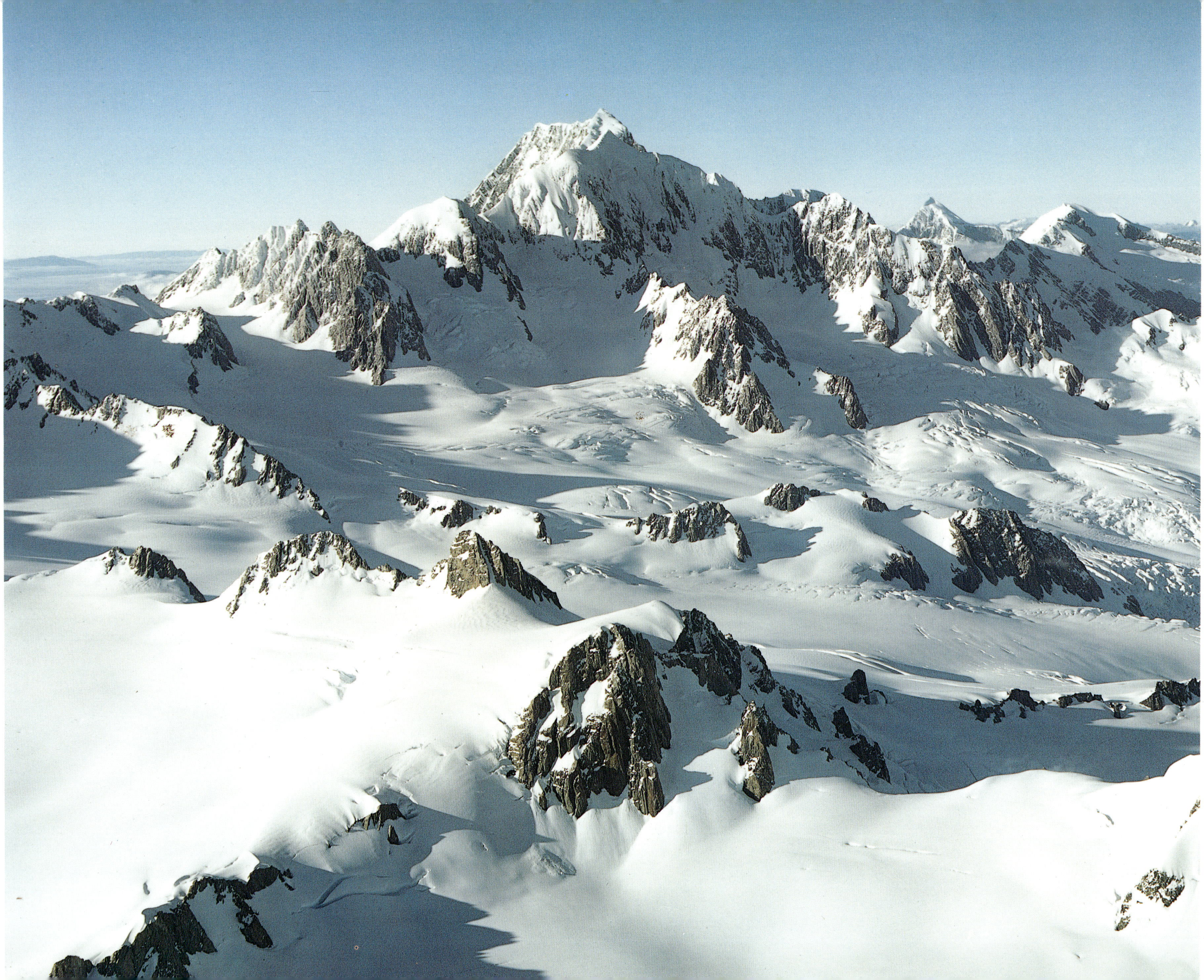

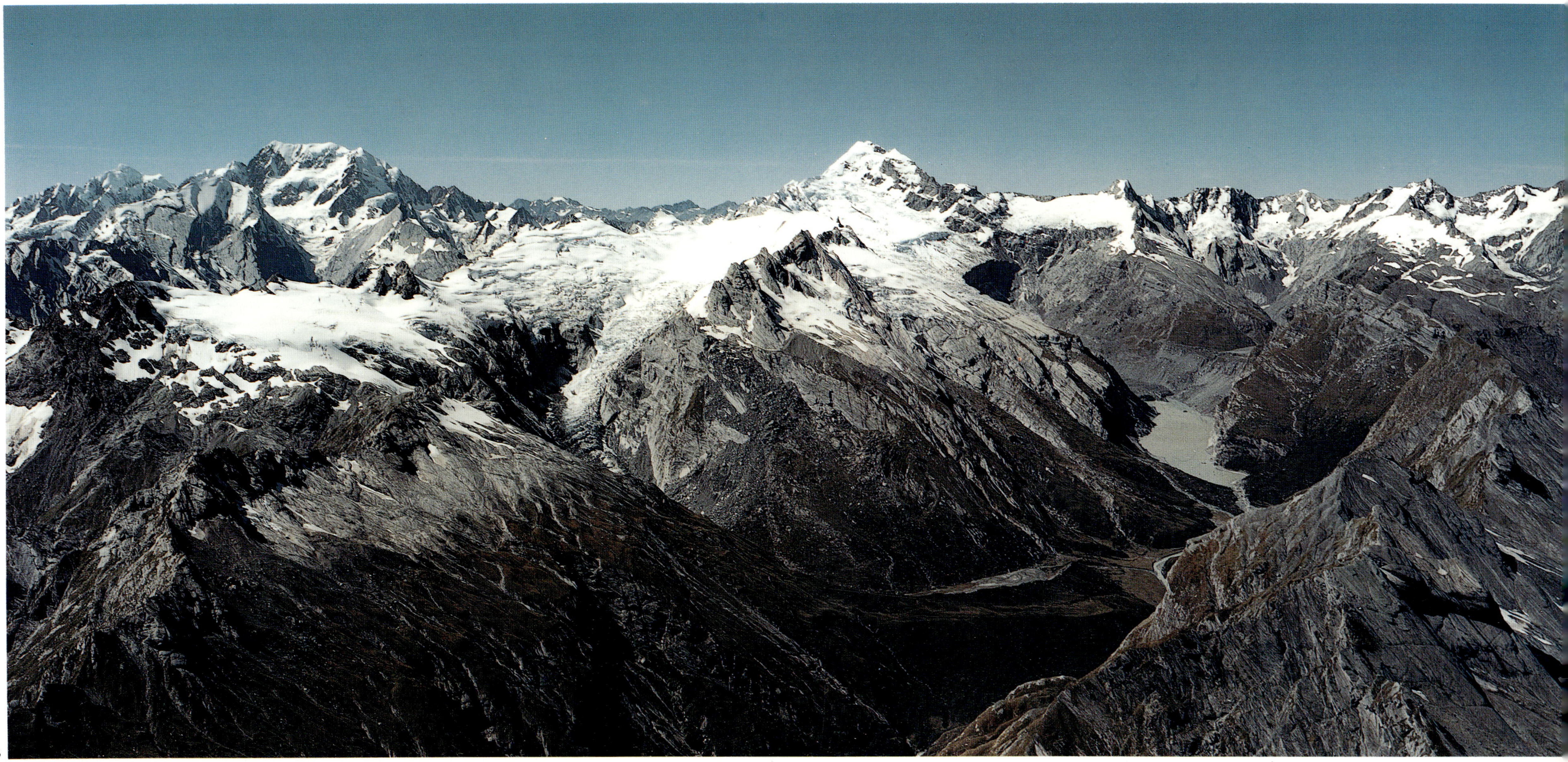

3

2 Looking south-south-west across Pioneer Ridge and the Albert Glacier (in the névé of the Fox), towards the highest peaks in New Zealand (from left to right): Mts Haast, Tasman (superimposed on the high peak of Mt Cook), Hicks, Sefton, and La Perouse.

The landforms of this highest part of the park are being influenced by present-day glaciation. Ice sculpts the steeply dipping schist to arêtes and cirques, but mostly the ice is so thick (up to 300 m) that the bedrock only shows through as a series of rocky vertebrae on the spines of ridges running westward from the main divide. Although this glacial landscape is much higher than the western frontal ranges, precipitation is lower (5000–8000 mm, much of it as snow) as is the rate of uplift (5 mm per year).

3 The Douglas valley is a tributary hanging valley in the headwaters of the Karangarua River in the south-east corner of the park. It is the remotest and wildest of the glaciated valleys, and the retreat of the Douglas (centre, right) and Horace Walker (centre, left) Glaciers has made valley access to the névés on the western side of the Mt Sefton (centre) quite difficult.

The Douglas Glacier must have been a remarkable sight when explorer Charles Douglas climbed to Douglas Pass at the head of the Hooker Range during his 1887 journey to the upper Landsborough with Gerhard Mueller. A century later, the névé breaks away along a line of magnificent ice cliffs causing avalanches to sweep continually across a rock shelf and plunge nearly 1000 m to the grey debris-covered trunk of ice in the canyon below. Access to this wild cirque from the main Douglas valley is barred by a huge terminal lake behind a moraine marking the end of one of the post-Otiran glacial advances.

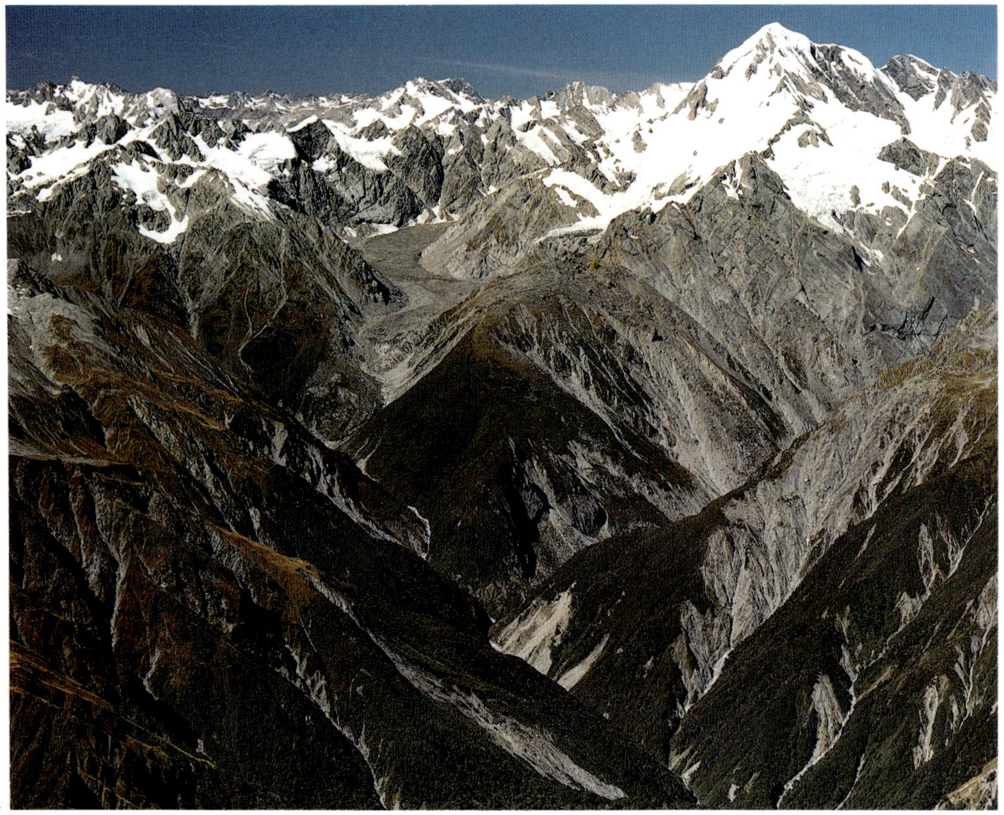

4

4 The prominent peak of Elie de Beaumont lies at the northern end of the main divide within the park. The debris-covered Burton Glacier rises on its northern slopes and can be seen curving around to the west before its drainage joins the other tributaries of the Callery River.

The foreground is typical of the mountainous landforms in this band of schist between the Alpine Fault and the glacial névés along the main divide. This is the zone of New Zealand's highest rainfall (up to 12 000 mm per year) and very high levels of erosion. These tributaries of the Callery run through V-shaped valleys, dropping steeply through gorges containing rapids and waterfalls. Rapid down-cutting by the streams leads to huge debris avalanches, especially during the frequent rain-storms from the north-west. Most of this rock debris is flushed out of these valleys and onto the piedmont floodplains. Further evidence for the youthfulness of this landform can be found in the soils on the slopes; most soils are immature, with an age of less than 2000 years. So, although erosion dominates the landscape, the high rainfall and rapid weathering of fresh rock surfaces allows the vegetation to recolonise the slopes rapidly.

5 The Copland valley is a major tributary of the Karangarua River, draining the northern slopes of the Sierra Range and the main divide to the north of Mt Sefton (right). It is an important trans-alpine route to Mt Cook National Park via Copland Pass (centre left). Welcome Flats (centre) are notable because they are the only grassy river flats in the forested upper reaches of the gorged valleys in the park. They are also famous for their hot pools, one of several groups scattered along the western side of the Southern Alps.

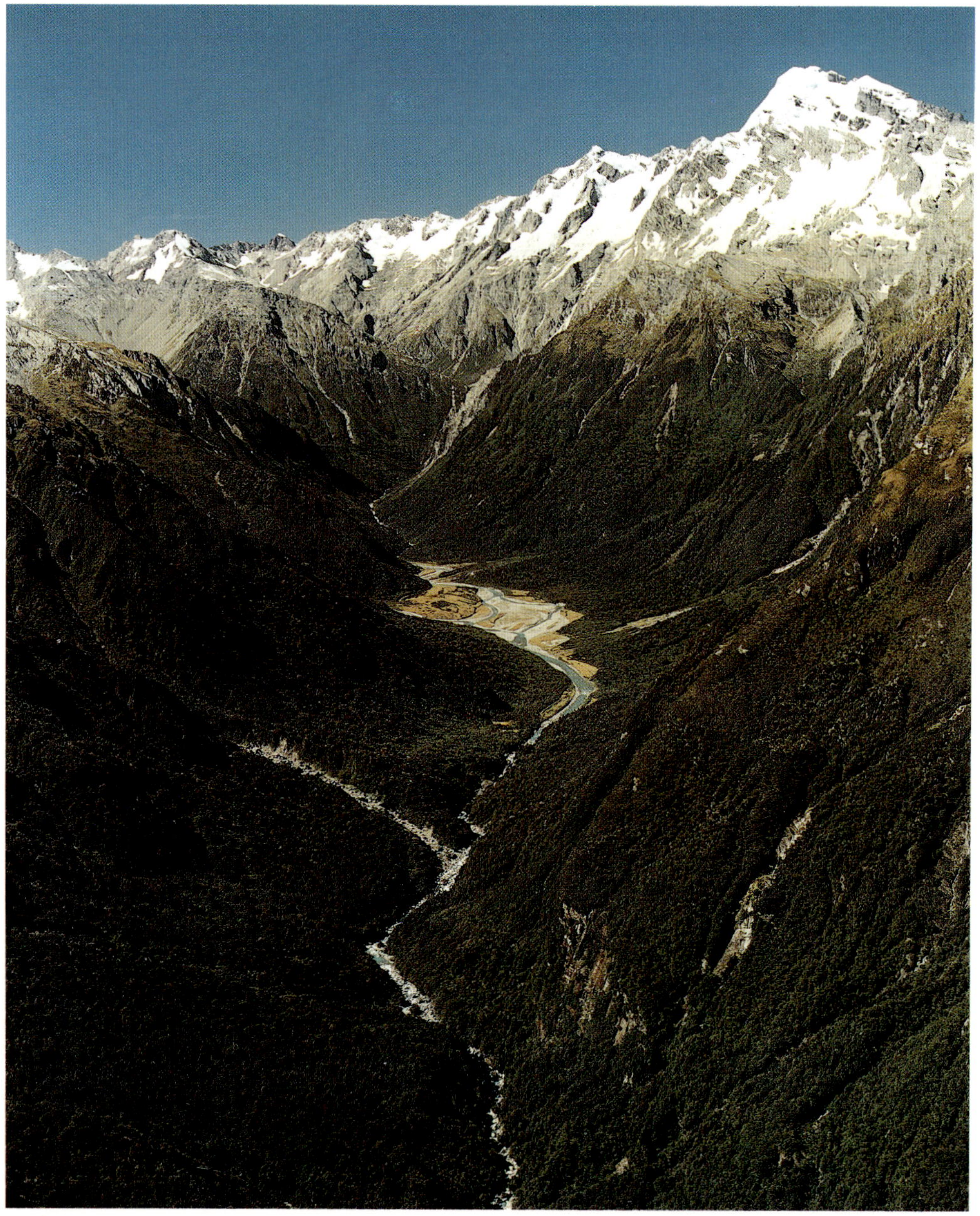

5

6 The Fox Glacier drains 2000 ha of snowfields on the northern side of Mt Tasman (centre) and descends to an altitude of 300 m. In contrast to the Franz Josef Glacier, it still has a significant amount of ice buried under outwash gravels beyond the surface terminal. Consequently, kettlehole lakes are a feature of the floor of the Fox valley.

Cone Rock (500 m) is the prominent roche moutonnée on the western side of the bend where the valley swings from west to north; only 250 years ago the ice flowed around both sides of Cone Rock. Beyond the terminal of the glacier (just obscured by shadow) the fresh rock faces show different stages of vegetation recolonisation. The whole slope is gradually slumping as the ice withdraws and no longer props up the toe of the slope.

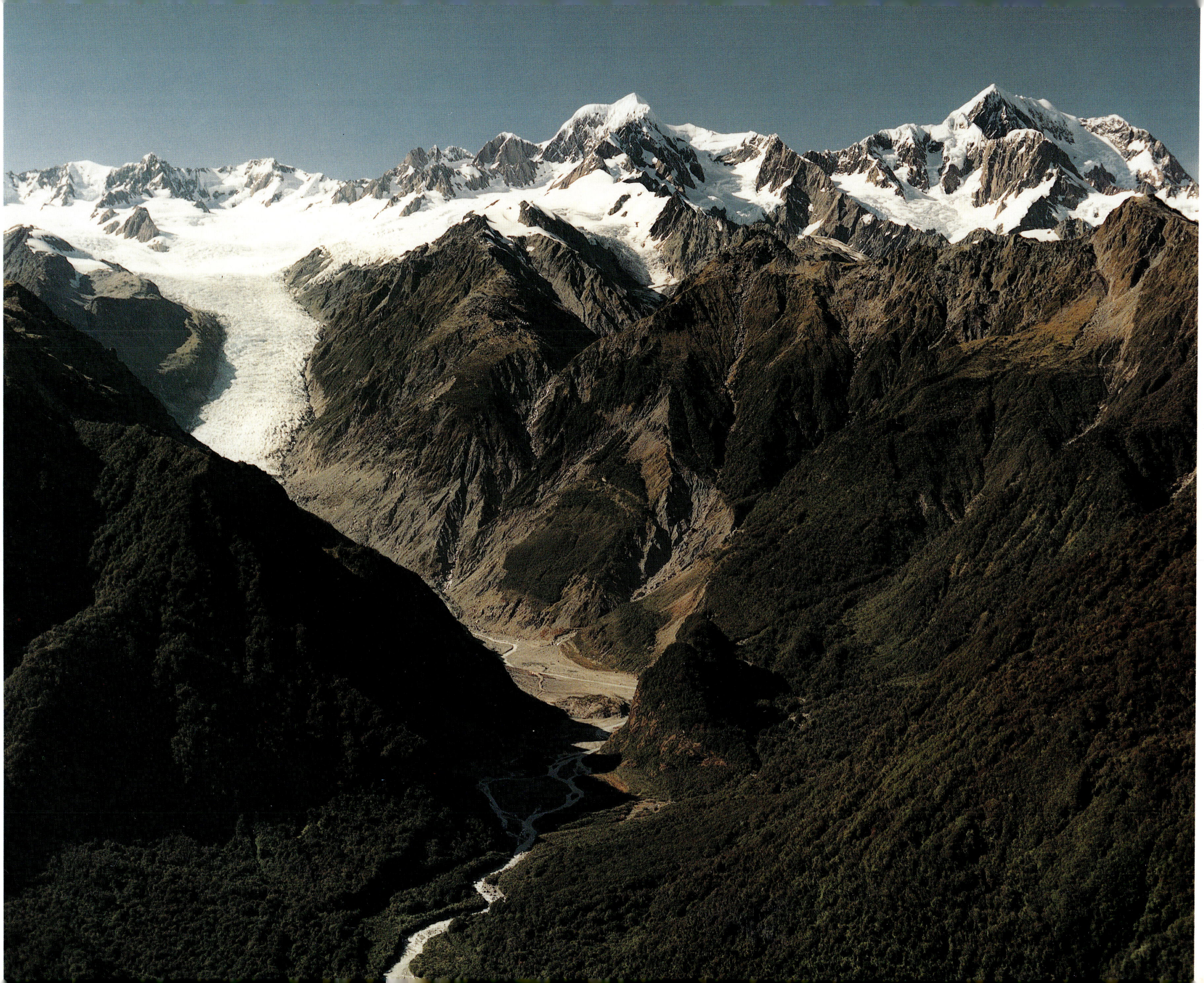

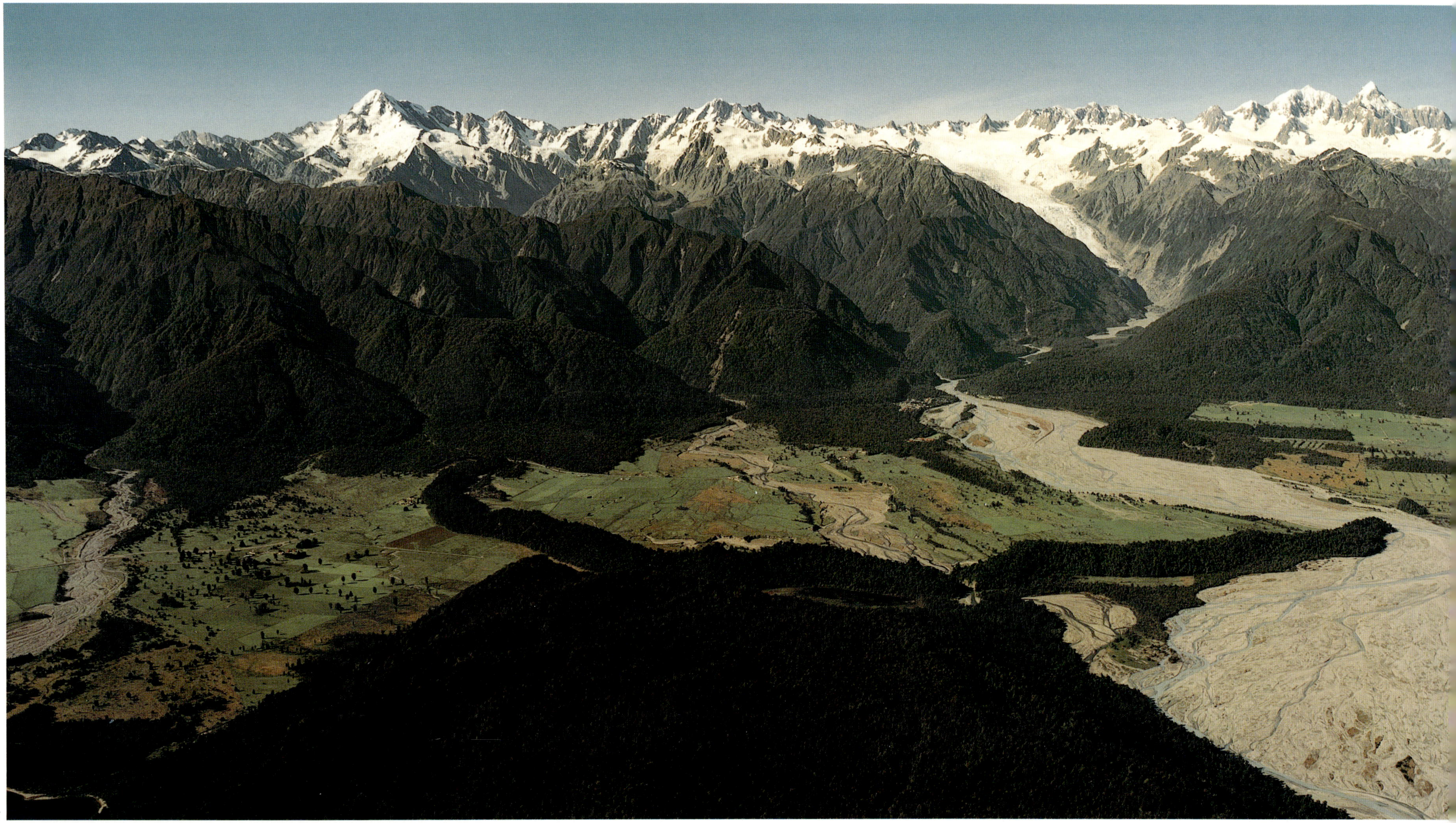

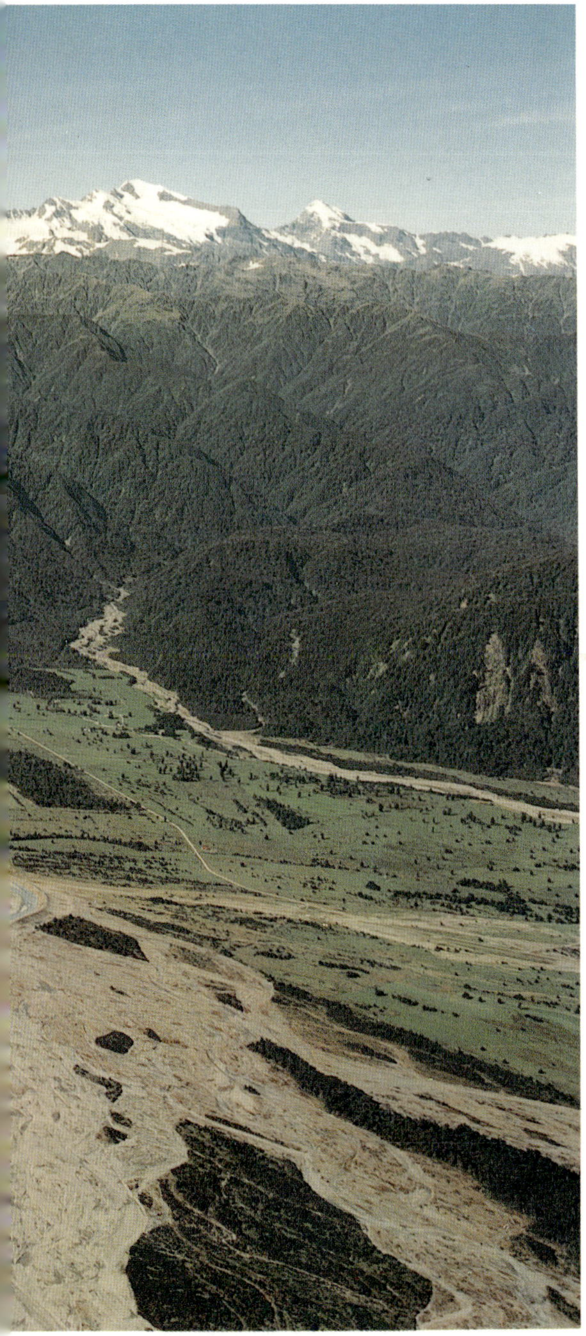

7 From State Highway 6 the Waiho Loop is hardly noticed, a bush-covered ridge to be skirted at its eastern end. In the air, however, it stands out as one of the most interesting landforms in the park, a superbly preserved 11–12 000 year old terminal moraine of the Franz Josef Glacier extending for 5 km as a 60 m high arc across the eastern side of the Waiho valley (see Fig. 1 for the view in the opposite direction). The loop is the largest moraine marking a temporary advance during the overall post-Otiran glacial retreat; less well-preserved moraines can be found closer to the glacier, indicating further brief advances estimated at 5000, 2500, 1500, 350, 240 and 150 years ago. Studies of the vegetation and the degree of soil development on these different-aged surfaces indicate a rapid plant succession. Scattered mats of scabweed (*Raoulia* spp.) and moss appear on the gravels within a year or two of glacial recession; an open shrubland of nitrogen-fixing native broom and tutu within fifty years; a dense low forest of hardwoods (*Olearia*, *Senecio*, *Schefflera*, rata and kamahi) in 150–200 years; and a tall podocarp forest after 1000–5000 years. By this time the soil has become podzolised and lost most of its available phosphorus and other important nutrients.

The trace of the Alpine Fault can be seen cutting across the foot of the frontal ranges, and farmlands (outside the park) have been developed on the freer-draining soils on the low-angle fans of the four water-courses in the photograph. These are (left to right): Potters Creek, Tatare Stream, Waiho River and Docherty Creek.

8

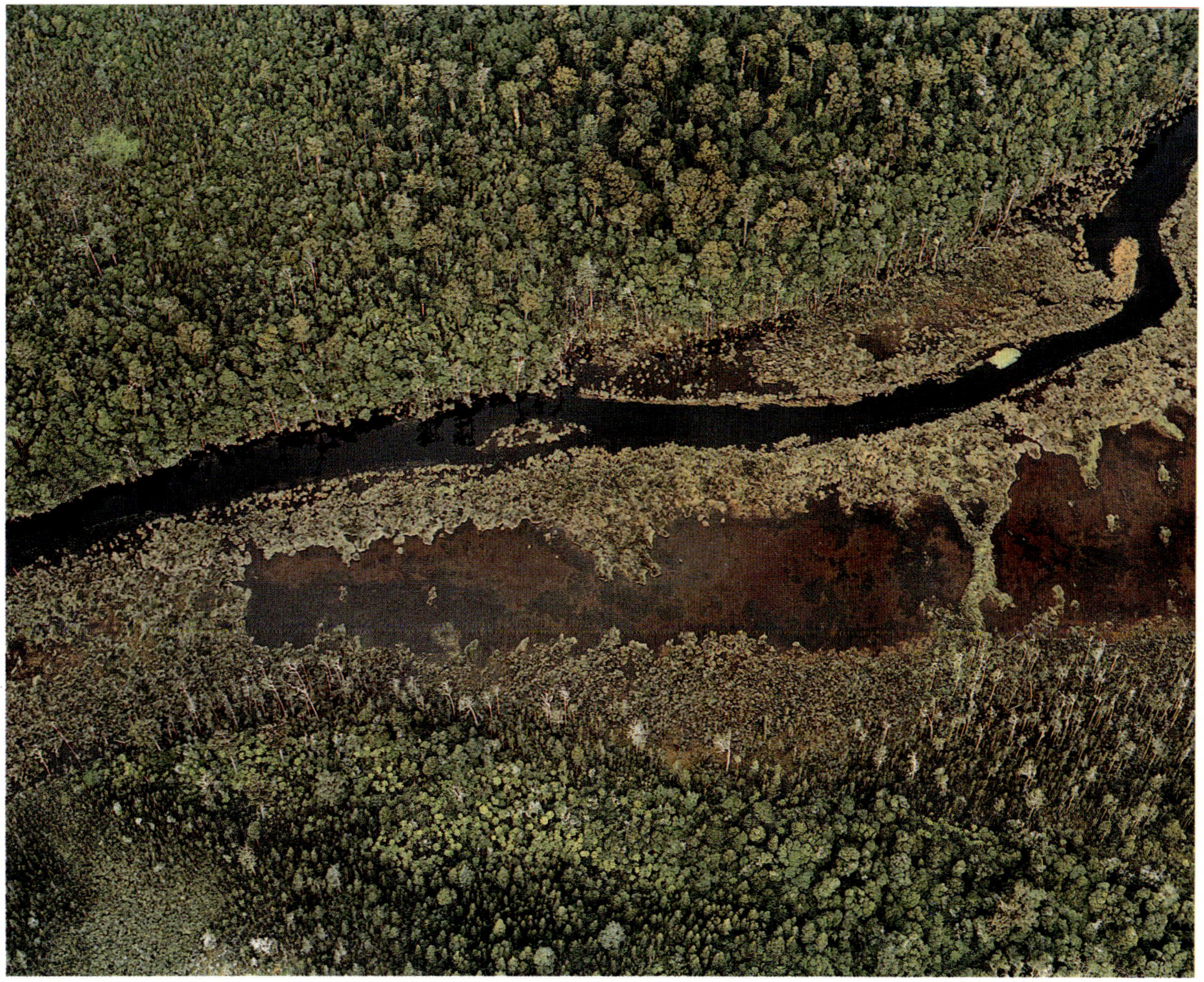

8 Water is ubiquitous in Westland National Park, and topography can influence the height of the water table and thereby determine the survival of vegetation communities. The creek is dark brown from the humus leached from the peaty soils; the floating mat of sedge will eventually consolidate and allow vegetation at the water margin to take root. A fringe of tall spindly kahikatea marks where drainage improves slightly at the toe of the moraines. The slopes of the moraines are better drained and covered in dense podocarp/hardwood forest.

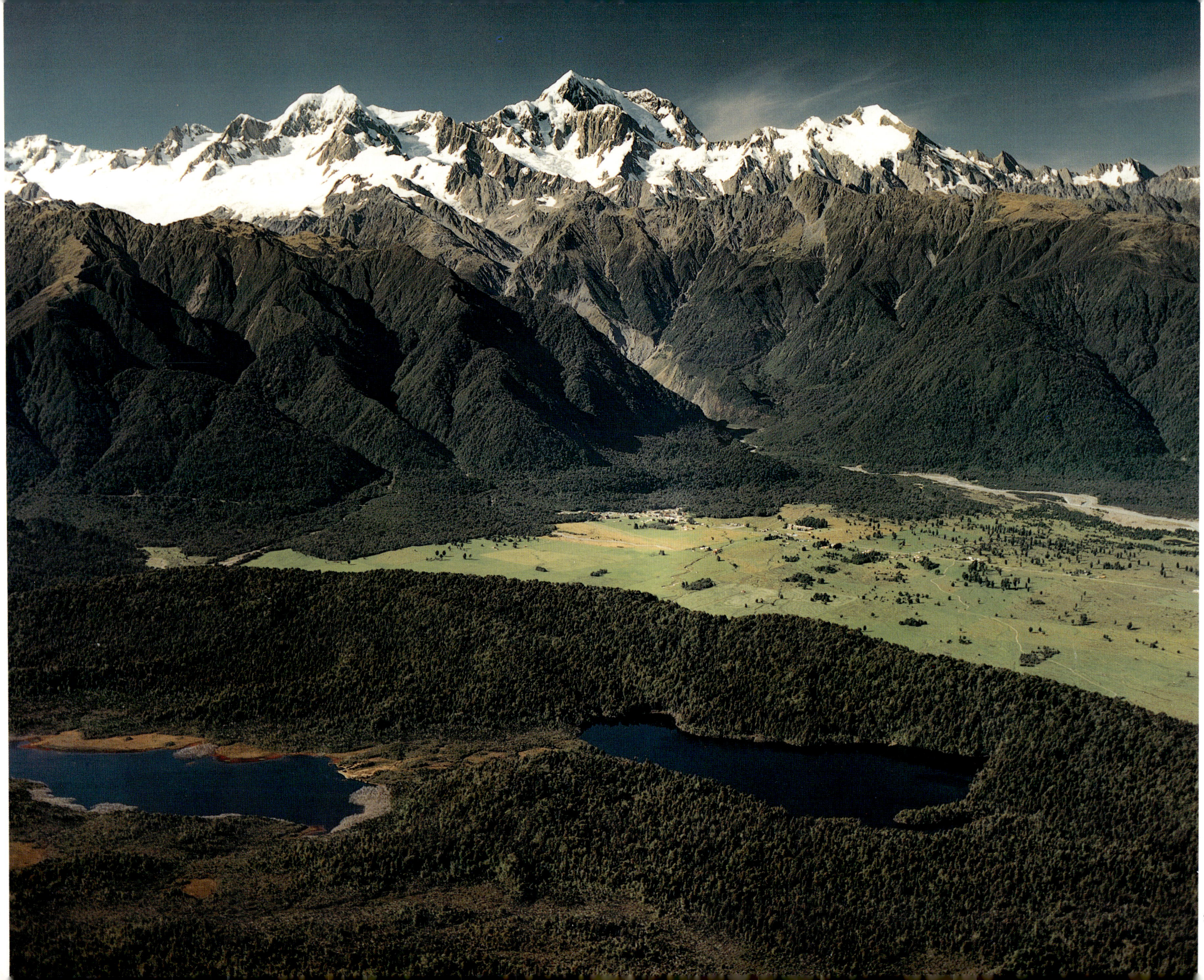

9 The topographic contrast between the Waikukupa piedmont and the Southern Alps can be appreciated in this view looking south-east across the Fox Flats. The icefall of the Fox Glacier is hidden behind the bush-covered ridges but some of the névé can be seen below Mt Tasman in the top left. Mt Cook (3764 m), the highest point in New Zealand, is the peak in the centre and La Perouse the peak to the right.

Skiffington Swamp (left) and Lake Gault (right) are two of the wetlands and lakes that now occupy kettleholes and depressions on this old stable piedmont surface 300 m above the alluvial flats beneath.

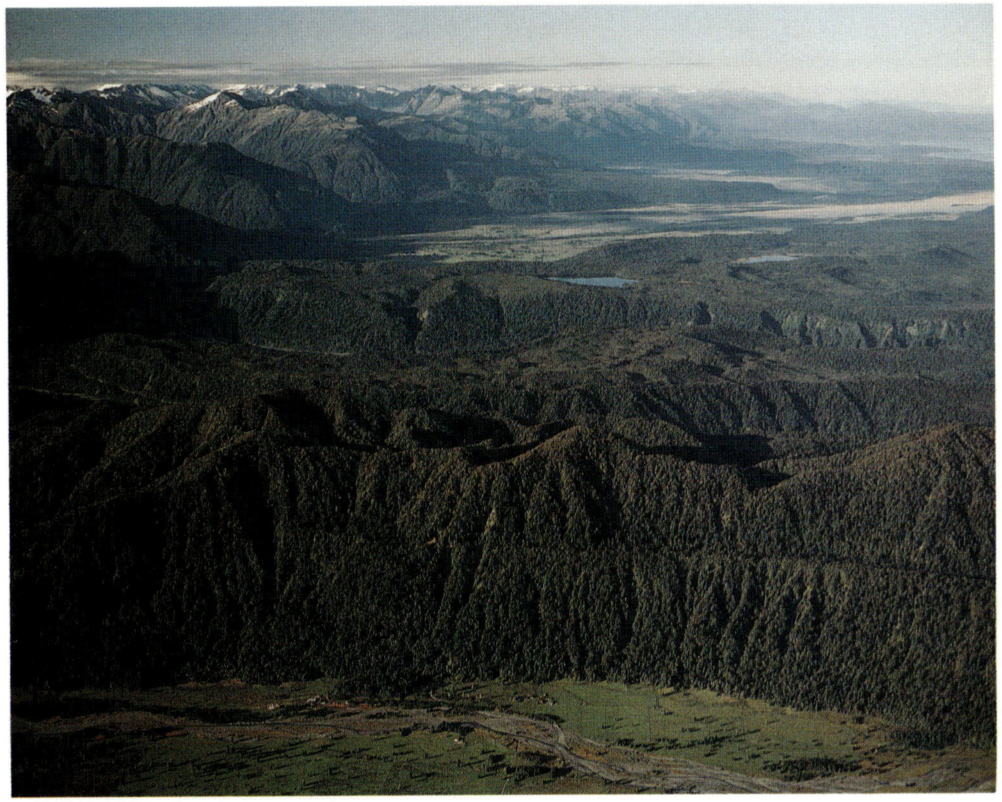

10

10 Looking south-west from the floodplain of the Waiho River, across Docherty Creek and the undulating summits of the Omoeroa Range, to the old glacial outwash of Waikukupa forest and the flats of the Fox and Cook Rivers. This view, parallel with the Alpine Fault on the left, contains most of the variety of landforms in the forested piedmont: a line of lateral moraine of late Otiran age stranded on the Waiho face of the Omoeroa Range; the hard, old basement rocks of the Omoeroa Range, which probably survived as islands when ice covered the piedmont; the gently sloping outwash surfaces between the Omoeroa River and the Waikukupa plateau running from Lake Mueller (middle, distance) to Gillespies Point on the coast. This is one of the oldest landforms in the park (probably associated with the older part of the Otiran or even the Waimean Glaciation 30 000–70 000 years ago).

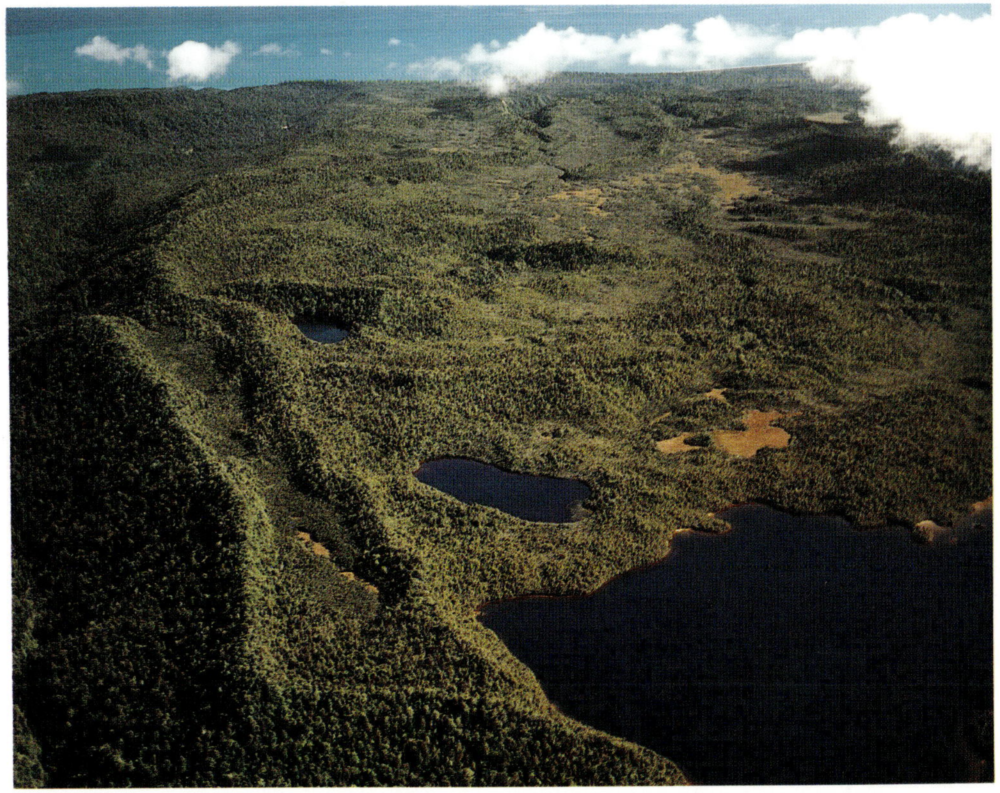

11

11 The high outwash surface of the Waikukupa piedmont, between the Omoeroa River in the north and Hauraki Creek (extreme left) in the south, is one of the oldest landforms of glacial origin in the park. In this view looking north-west across Lake Mueller to the Tasman Sea, two parallel lines of lateral moraine mark the edges of ancient glacial advances, probably 30 000–70 000 years ago.

The vegetation and soils on this undulating plateau (250–450 m altitude) reflect its great age and poor drainage. The soils are extremely leached and are therefore acidic and infertile gley podzols. Rimu/rata/kamahi forest can be seen on the more elevated and better drained spurs, but the high water-tables in the depressions (like Wilson Swamp in the distance) can only be tolerated by low herbs, grasses, and ferns – red tussock, wire-rush, and umbrella fern. Around the margins of these natural pakihis there is a colourful mosaic of shrubby trees, usually *Dacrydium* species such as pink pine and silver pine, manuka, celery pine and kaikawaka (mountain cedar).

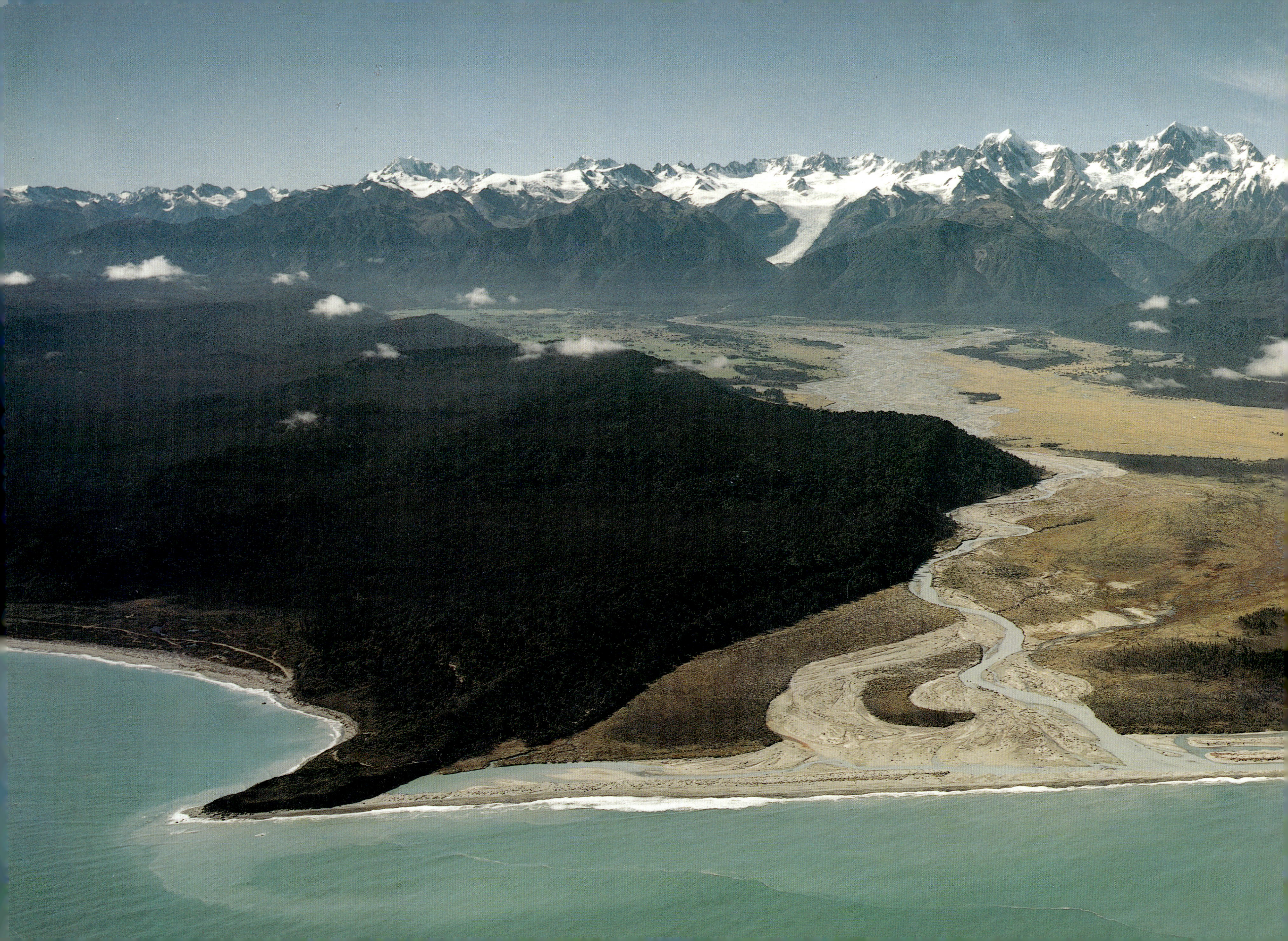

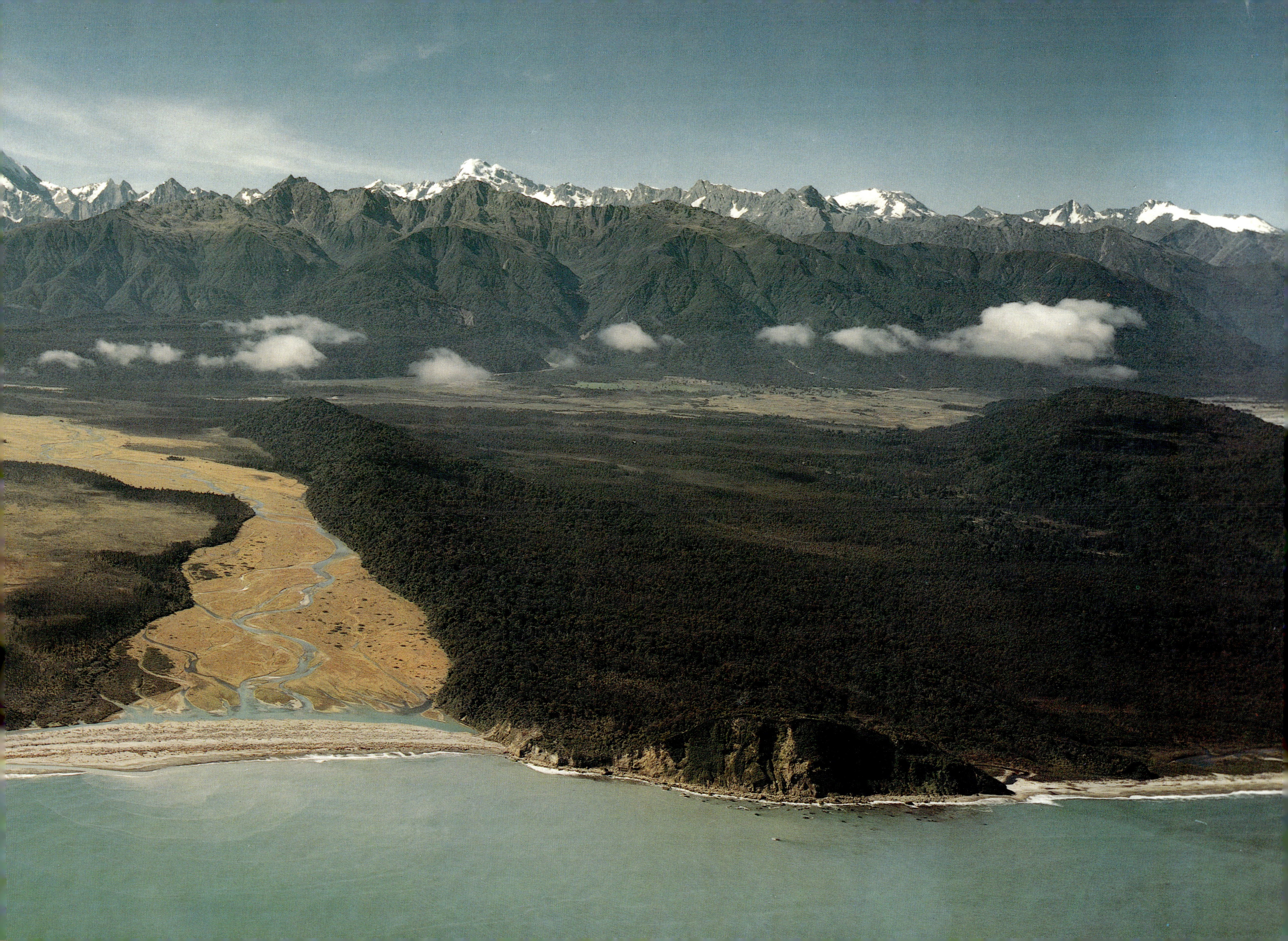

previous page

12 This view of the Southern Alps and the piedmont (from the mouth of the Cook River) shows the full range of glaciated landscapes that make up Westland National Park. Lines of moraine are silhouetted in the forests behind Gillespies Beach (left) and in the Ohinetamatea catchment (right). The floodplain of the Cook River is confined between two prominent lateral moraines which terminate in Otorokua Point (left) and Cook Bluff (right).

The Cook River has now abandoned its former more southerly outlet and captured the former bed of the Clearwater River which once meandered through the Meyer Swamp. The destructive impact of such a natural phenomenon is shown in detail in Figs 14 and 15.

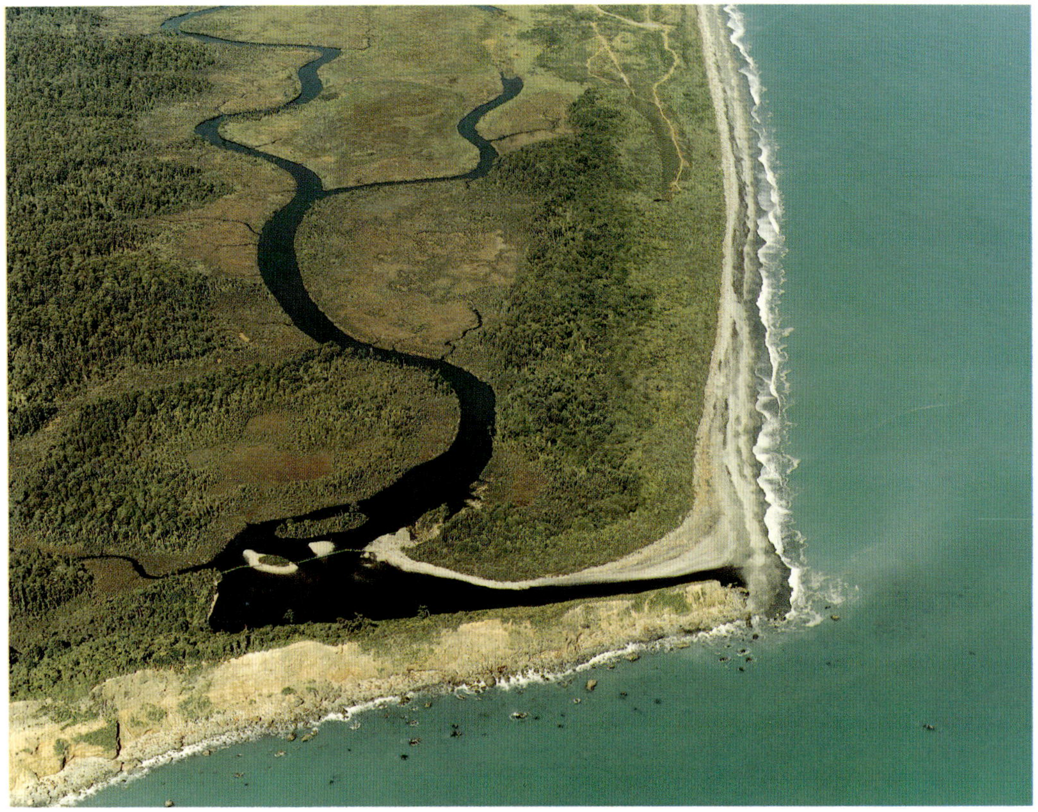

13

13 This coastal wetland at Gillespies Beach has been formed by the impounding of the Waikowhai Stream behind the foredune, and (in the foreground) the arm of wave-eroded lateral moraine running down to Gillespies Point. The shape of this landform is similar to the mouth of the Cook River, but it is much older because of its more stable situation. Note that the mouth of the lagoon is currently closed by a sandbar. The workings of the former Gillespies Beach gold dredge can be seen at the top right.

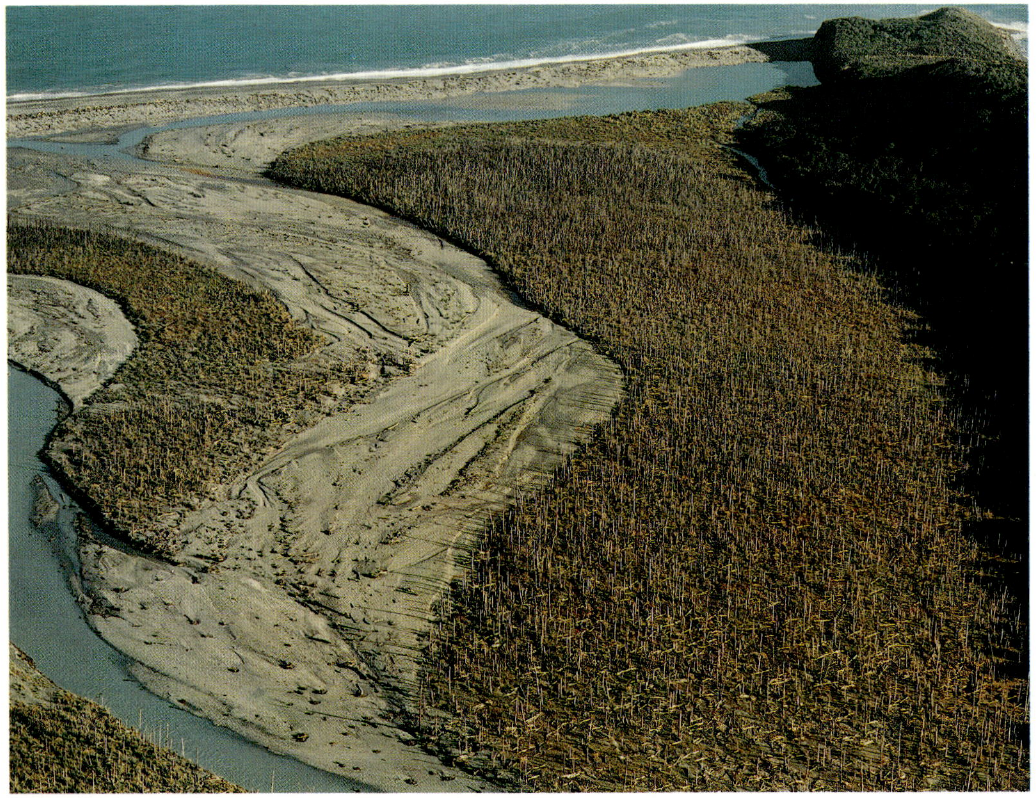

14

14 An abrupt change in direction by the Cook River has caused the destruction of this kahikatea forest on the lower part of the river's floodplain. Glacial silts have been deposited throughout the forest, and the watertable has possibly been modified. If the new river channel stabilises for some years the cycle will begin again. Kahikatea forest requires fertile soils, which are usually only found on youthful landscapes because of the way in which nutrients are leached from the soil, particularly in areas of high rainfall such as the West Coast. So the periodic rejuvenation of floodplain soils by the addition of fresh mineral material, while destructive in the short term, ultimately leads to the perpetuation of this rare forest community, which has unfortunately been cleared for farmlands throughout most of New Zealand.

In this sense of soil and vegetation rejuvenation through natural catastrophe, the floodplains of the piedmont and the steep slopes of the mountain valleys are very similar, although their terrain could hardly be more different.

15 The mouth of the Cook River marks the southern extent of the coastline within Westland National Park. This view looks south-west across Cook Bluff, the Ohinetamatea and Karangarua River mouths, to the swamps and forests behind Bruce Bay. The stability of the floodplain around Bullock Creek contrasts with the mobility of the floodplain around the turbid glacier-fed Cook River in the foreground.

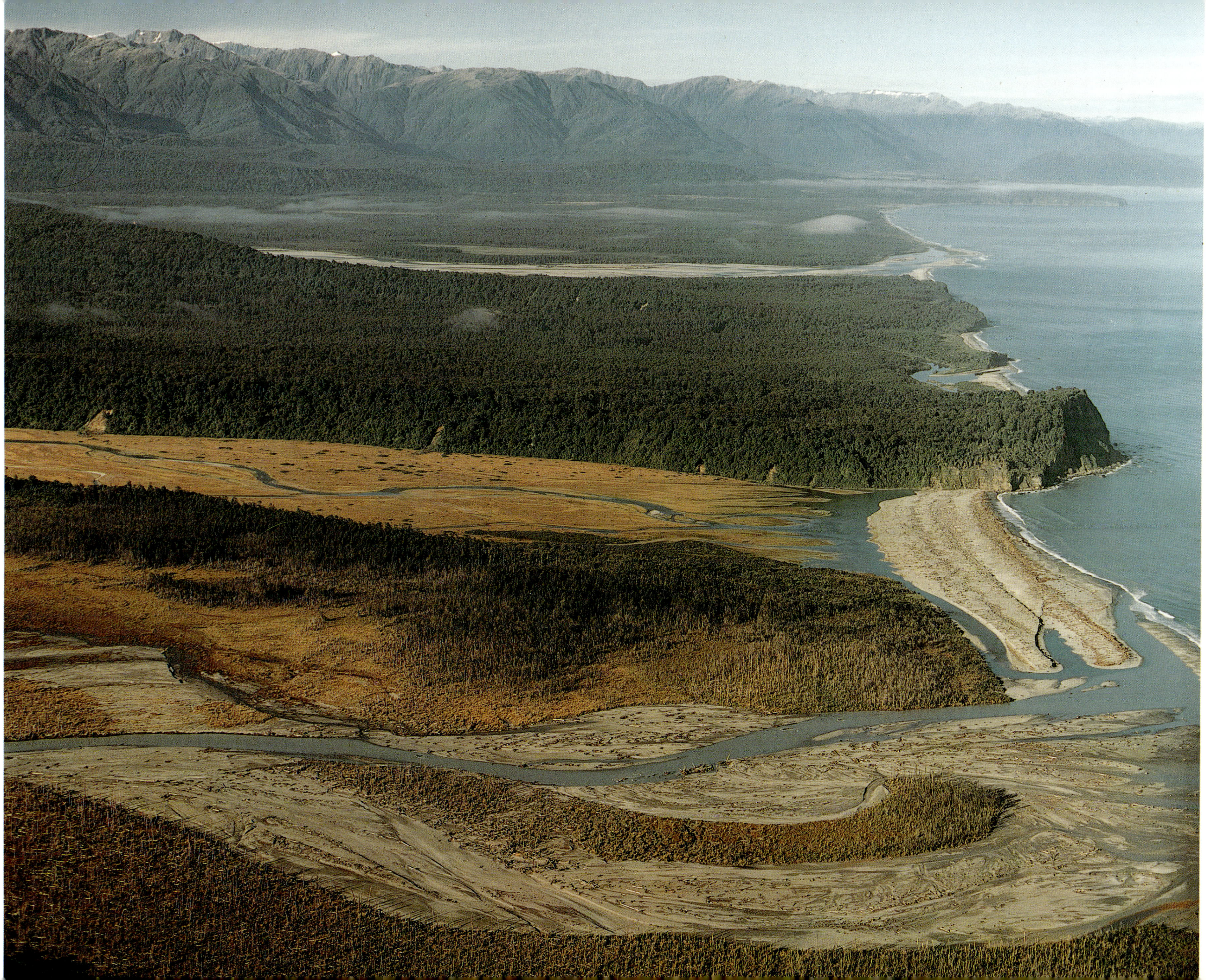

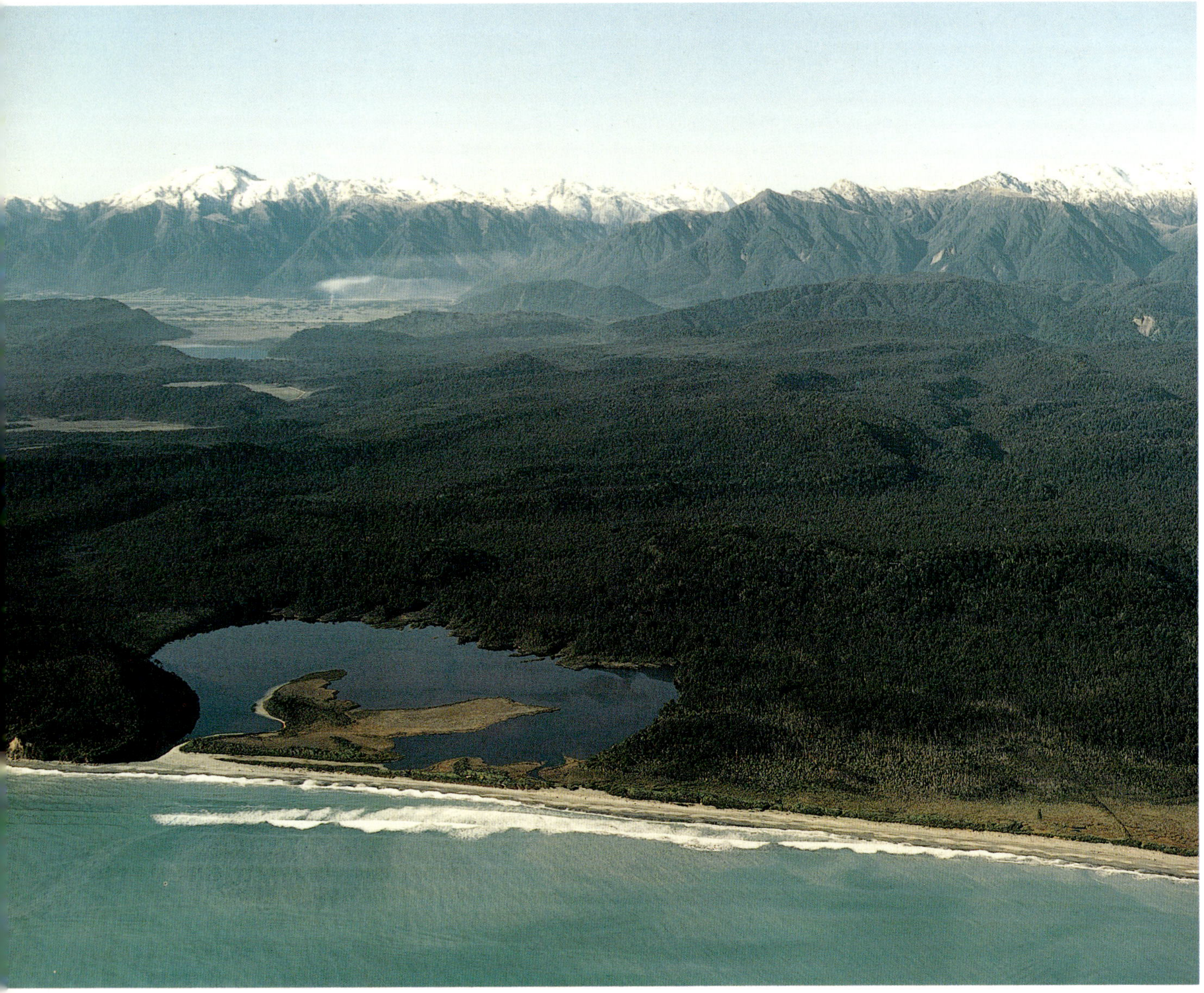

16

16 Three-Mile Lagoon actually lies 3 km south-west of Okarito village, nestled in an old glacial trough among the moraines which snake their way through Okarito forest.

Lake Wahapo and smoke from the Whataroa sawmill can be seen in the distance to the east.

17 Okarito Lagoon is the largest of the coastal lagoons in the vicinity of the park. This panorama looks south-east across the forested piedmont and natural pakihis within Okarito forest to Lake Mapourika and the main divide around Franz Josef Glacier. The main drainage channel flows like an artery through the lagoon, to empty into the Tasman Sea beside the vulnerable village of Okarito sited on a corner of the young floodplain.

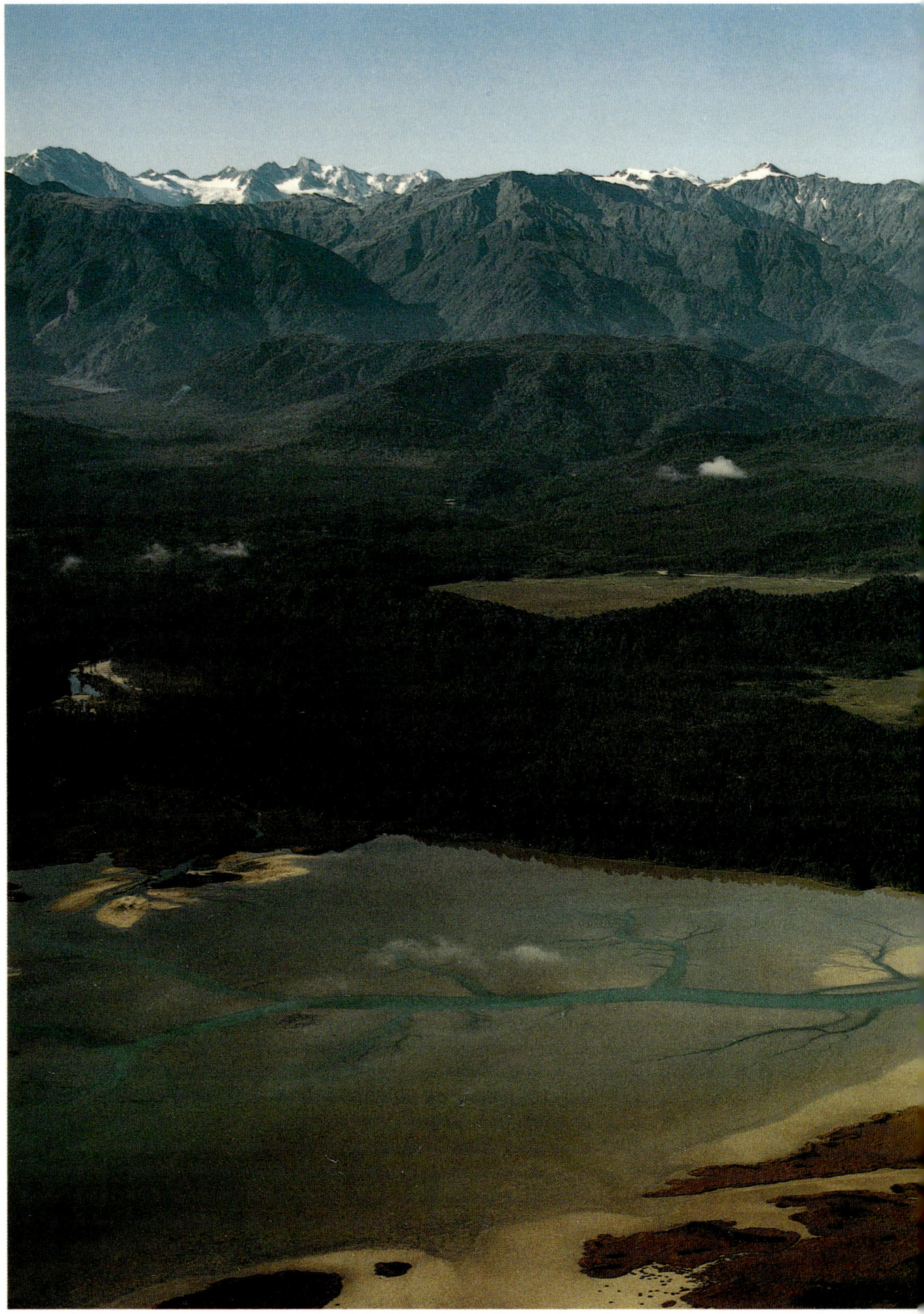

17

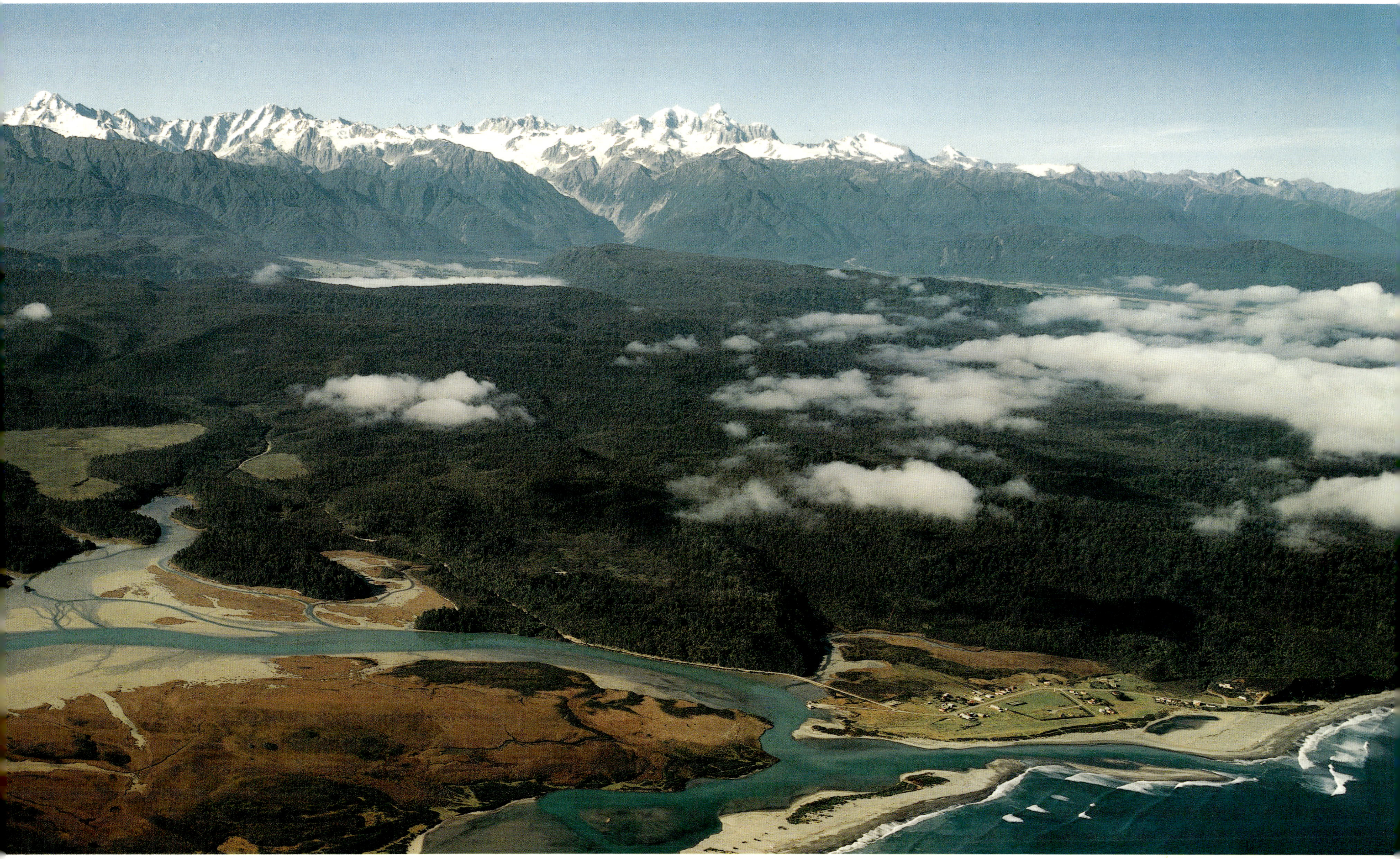

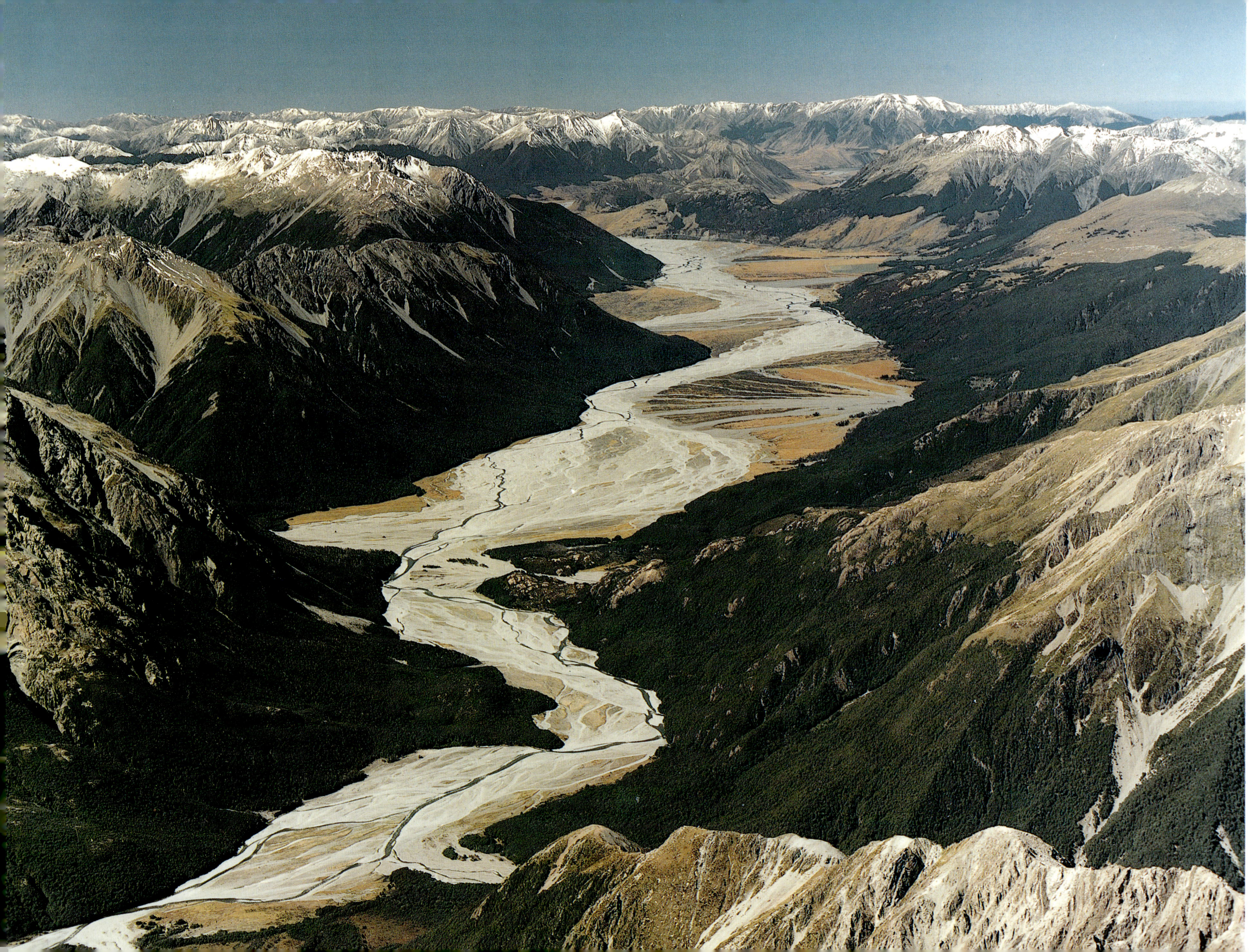

1

ARTHUR'S PASS NATIONAL PARK

Arthur's Pass National Park was the first national park to be formally set aside in the South Island (1929). It was established to protect the accessible mountainous landscapes around the road over Arthur's Pass and the Midland Railway link to the West Coast (via the Bealey and Otira valleys and the Otira tunnel). The park is compact, its boundaries are topographically distinct, and it is geologically simple (all Torlesse greywacke/argillite save for a small sliver of semi-schist in the Kelly Range in the far west). Geographically, it extends from the upper catchment of the Waimakariri River on the eastern side of the main divide to, on the western side, the southern tributaries of the Taramakau River between Harpers Pass and the Kelly Range. Consequently, it straddles the divide, reserving a representative cross-section of landforms and vegetation across this portion of the Southern Alps.

The Taramakau River, which forms the northern boundary of the park, flows east to west along the crush zone of the Hope Fault. This fault, a major splinter of the Alpine Fault, cuts right across the greywacke mountains to the Hurunui valley, Hanmer, and eventually Kaikoura on the east coast.

Between the Taramakau and Waimakariri valleys, on opposite boundaries of the park, the tributary rivers are orientated north/south, even though they flow in opposite directions. On the relief-shaded map on p. 88 the Taipo/upper Waimakariri, Otira/Bealey, Deception/Mingha, Otehake (west branch)/Edwards, Otehake (east branch)/Hawdon, Poulter, and Cox/Esk show this parallel orientation. This parallel 'grain of the land' is also apparent in the valleys and ranges of Nelson Lakes National Park (Chapter 7).

GREYWACKE, GLACIERS AND GRAVEL

The evolution of landforms in Arthur's Pass National Park followed a similar pattern to the other two alpine parks of greywacke rock (Mt Cook and Nelson Lakes). The massive uplift of the rocks (about 18 000 m in the last 2 million years) was counterbalanced by erosion to keep the mountain crests at around their present height (1700–2300 m), extensive glaciation took place during the Pleistocene, and scree and alluvial landforms developed in the valleys since the end of the Ice Ages. The same sharp decrease in the rainfall gradient occurs as in the other parks straddling the main divide; annual precipitation is over 8000 mm on the western slopes above Otira but is down to 1500 mm at the Waimakariri between Bealey and Cass. Consequently, sediment discharge to the Taramakau is much higher than to the Waimakariri and the rainforests of the western slopes are much more luxuriant and diverse than the simple, open, mountain beech forests of the Waimakariri and Poulter valleys.

Arthur's Pass National Park lacks the great glaciers of Mt Cook but they have not yet disappeared altogether (as has happened at Nelson Lakes). Only about ten remain, a few (like the Crow Glacier) around the best-known peak in the park, Mt Rolleston (2271 m), and the rest on the south-eastern side of the ridges enclosing the White River, the westernmost tributary of the Waimakariri River. The two largest – the White and Marmaduke Dixon Glaciers – are each less than 1 sq. km in area. Small as most of the glaciers are (less than 0.5 sq. km) they are the northern-most glaciers in the South Island.

Unlike Nelson Lakes National Park, there are very few cirque lakes in the park; the three good examples occur below Mts Franklin and Oates on the Aicken Range. In fact, lakes are not a feature of the park at all. The only two valley lakes are non-glacial in origin; Lake Kaurapataka adjacent to the Taramakau valley lies behind debris flows in a depression probably formed by movement on the Kelly Fault and Lake Minchin (in the upper Poulter catchment) was formed by a huge rockslide off the Snow Cup Range.

Swarms of ridge rents are distinctive landform features that are very apparent from the air. They are particularly evident on both sides of the Otira valley, the Kelly Range and the ridge to the west of Dome peak near the Bealey/Waimakariri junction. The rents, which are usually parallel and generally no more than one kilometre long, were formed by earthquakes and often act as a zone of weakness leading to subsequent rockslides and rock avalanches.

Trampers will be familiar with most of the spectacular rock avalanches throughout the park: one off the Poulter Range formed a transient lake in Thompson Stream; Casey Hut in the Poulter and Hawdon Hut are sited on them; one lies opposite Crow Hut in the upper Crow valley; and the most remarkable of all fills the topmost 3 km of the west branch of the Otehake River below Falling Mountain (see pp. 94–95). Motorists should be able to recognise another huge rockfall, for they travel over it between Deaths Corner and Candy Bend at the head of the Otira Gorge.

Although the park has recently been extended to include the Cox valley, the extension unfortunately did not include the excellent set of moraine hummocks, the Mounds of Misery, on the outwash surface where the Cox River turns south-west to become the east branch of the Poulter. At present there is very little distinctive moraine topography protected within the park and accessible to the public, save the small moraine ridges left by the Otira Glacier as it retreated across Arthur's Pass itself. There are superb alluvial landforms within the park (such as the classical fan of Jordan Stream), but most of the spectacular glacial and alluvial landforms around Lake Coleridge (pp. 92–93) and within the Waimakariri valley (such as the former lake beaches, roche moutonnées, and glacial lakes near Cass, pp. 89–90) lie outside the park, although they warrant no less protection.

1 The Waimakariri River is the largest river in the park. It rises in the west sector between the main divide and Arthur's Pass, then flows eastwards along the southern boundary to join the Poulter River (centre, distance), its major tributary which drains the eastern part of the park. The glacial landforms of the Waimakariri valley have been modified significantly in the 14 000–18 000 years since the Waimakariri Glacier began to retreat from its last major terminus at the junction with the Esk River another 40 km down valley from this point. Ice-smoothed slopes are still evident on the south side of the valley and two roches moutonnées can be seen at the mouth of the Anti-Crow River (centre), but the valley is now full of post-glacial deposits. These include the braided bed of the river as it continues to build up its floodplain, and the classic example of a low-angle fan where the Jordan Stream spills out onto the southern side of the valley (centre). The forested concave slopes slightly upstream of and opposite the Jordan fan are another depositional feature – rock screes which stabilised long ago and have since become vegetated.

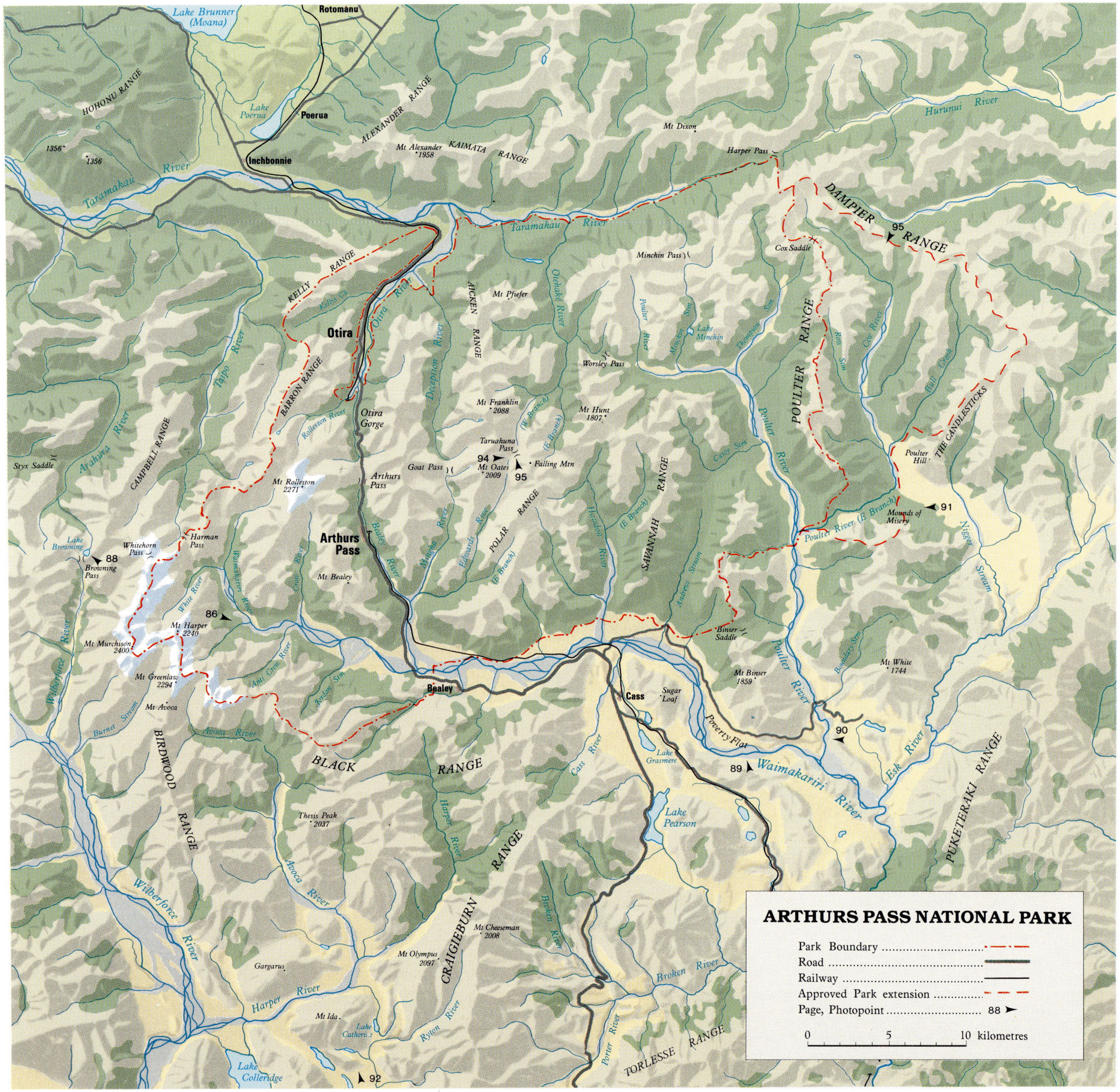
ARTHURS PASS NATIONAL PARK
Park Boundary
Road
Railway
Approved Park extension
Page, Photopoint
88
0
5
10
kilometres
Lake Brunner (Moana)
Rotomanu
HOHONU RANGE
Lake Poerua
Poerua
ALEXANDER RANGE
Inchbonnie
Mt Alexander 1958
KAIMATA RANGE
Mt Dixon
Harper Pass
Hurunui River
Taramakau River
DAMPIER RANGE
Cox Saddle
Minchin Pass
KELLY RANGE
Otira
Mt Pfeifer
JACKEN RANGE
Otehake River
Lake Minchin
POULTER RANGE
Worsley Pass
BARRON RANGE
Taipo River
Otira Gorge
Mt Franklin 2088
Mt Hunt 1807
THE CANDLESTICKS
Poulter Hill
Styx Saddle
Arahura River
CAMPBELL RANGE
Taruahuna Pass
Mt Oates 2009
Falling Mtn
Goat Pass
Arthurs Pass
Mt Rollesston 2271
SAVANNAH RANGE
Poulter River
Mounds of Misery
Poulter River (E Branch)
Harman Pass
Whitehorn Pass
Lake Browning
Browning Pass
Arthurs Pass
POLAR RANGE
Mt Bealey
Mt Harper 2240
Mt Murchison 2400
Binser Saddle
Mt Greenlaw 2294
Mt Avoca
Bealey
Cass
Sugar Loaf
Mt Binser 1859
Mt White 1744
Poverty Flat
BLACK RANGE
RANGE
BIRDWOOD RANGE
Lake Grasmere
Waimakariri River
Esk River
PUKETERAKI RANGE
Thesis Peak 2037
Lake Pearson
Wilberforce River
Avoca River
CRAIGIEBURN RANGE
Mt Cheeseman 2008
Mt Olympus 2097
Gargarus
Broken River
Harper River
Mt Ida
Lake Coleridge
TORLESSE RANGE
Porter River
Ryton River
86
88
89
90
91
92
94
95

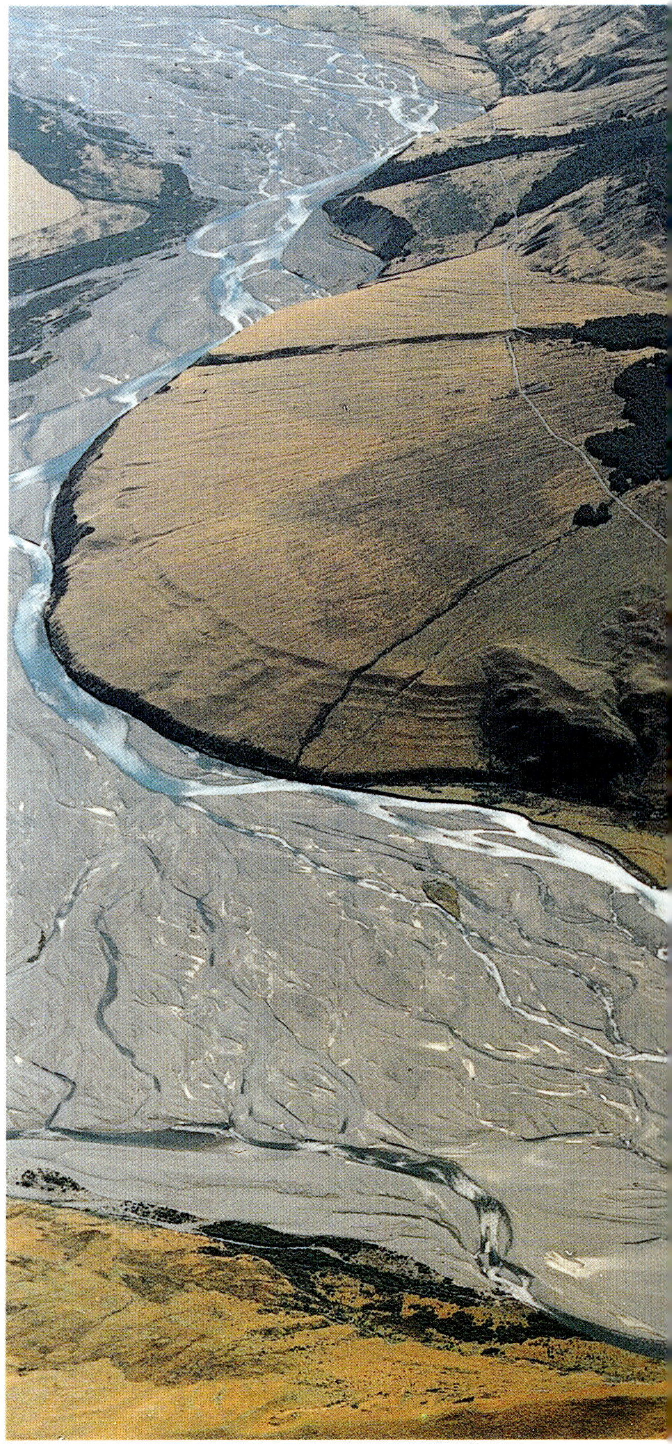

2

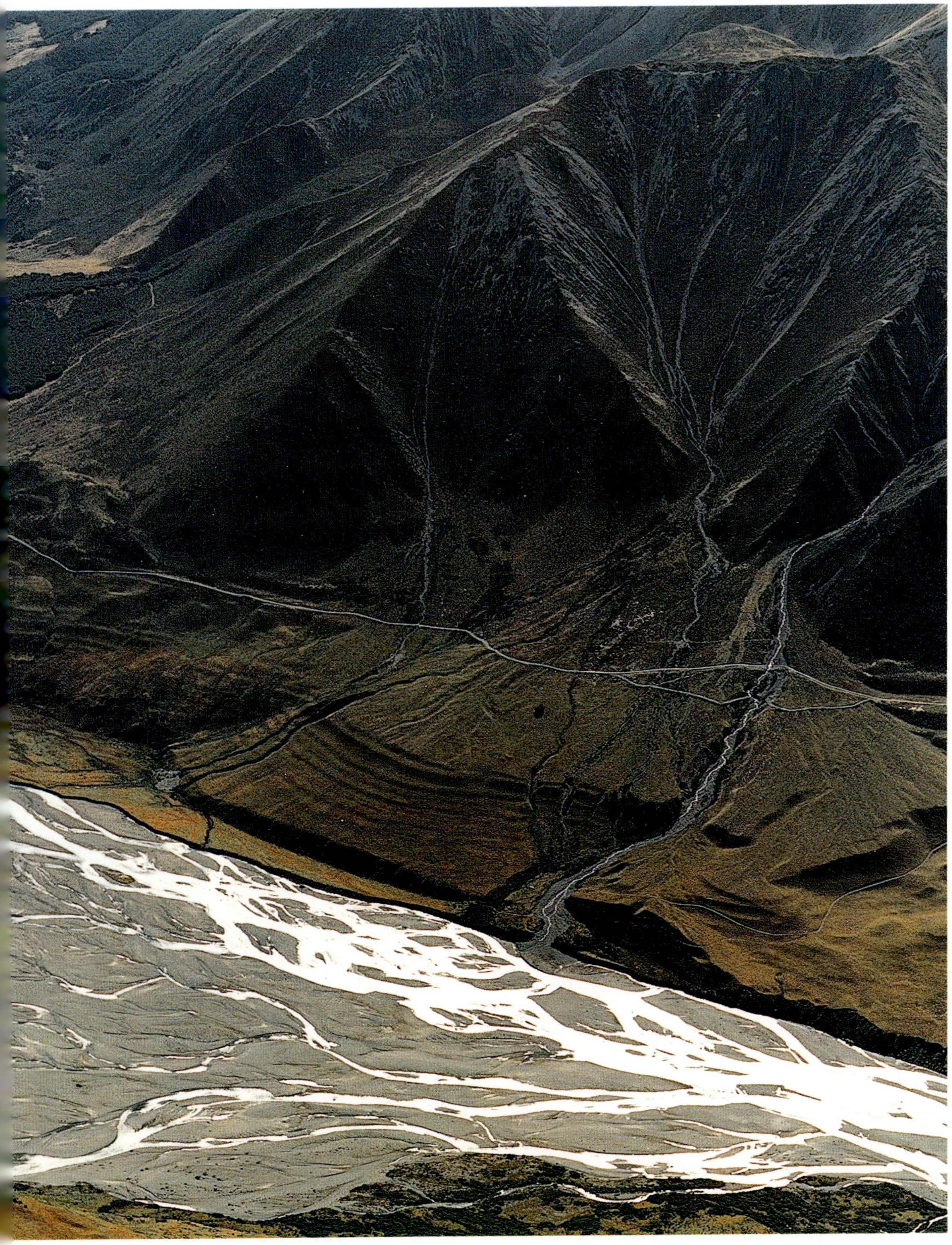

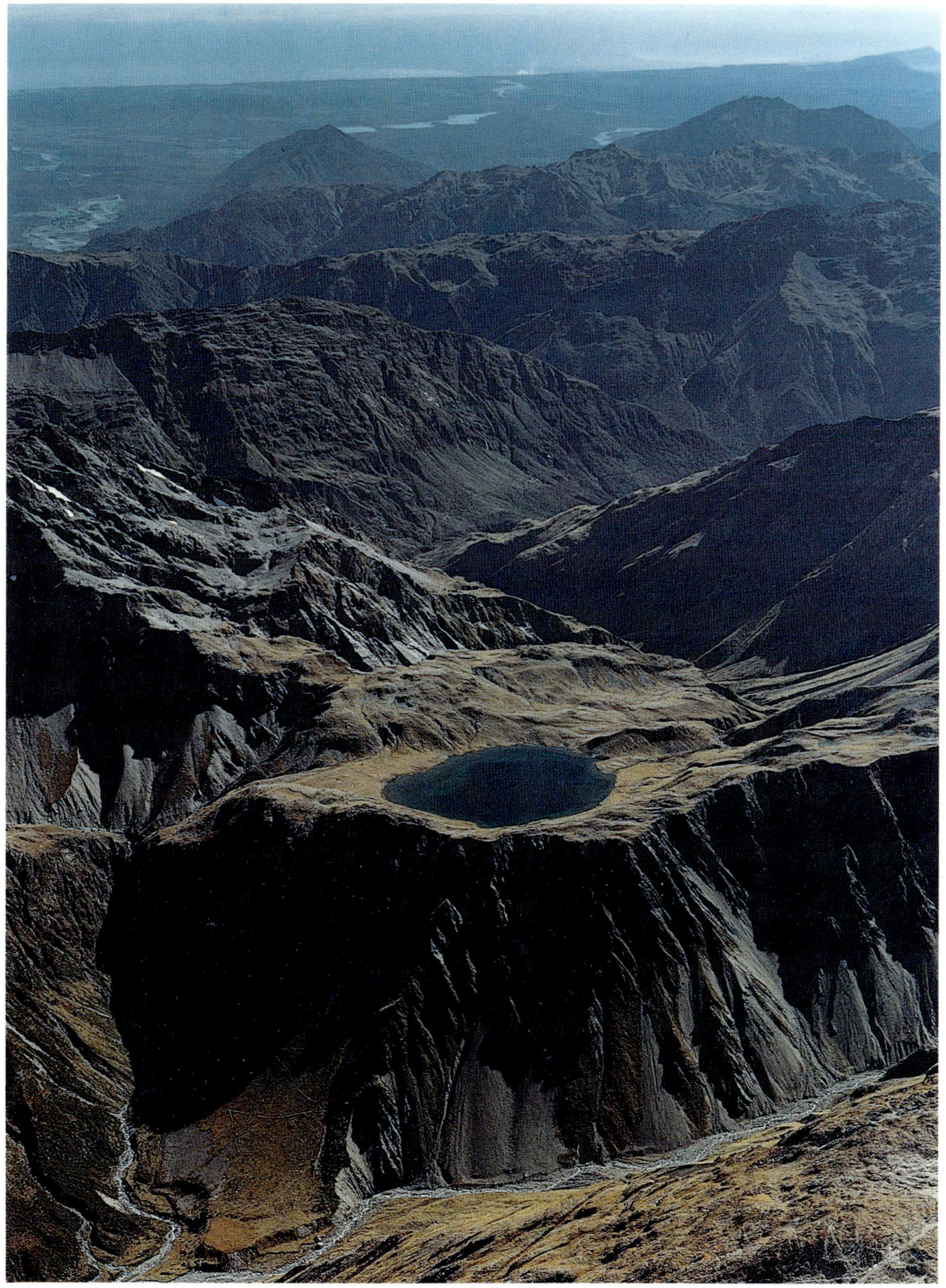

3

2 Immediately east of Cass, the northern banks of the braided Waimakariri River show interesting post-glacial features. Greywacke rock debris eroded from the slopes of Mt Binser has spread out as two fans on either side of a remnant of moraine from the last glaciation (centre). Other rockslides or avalanche deposits appear to have dammed the river downstream forming a lake as the fans were built up. As the lake outlet cut down, lake levels dropped in stages exposing at least nine different shore levels on the outer edge of the fans.

3 Lake Browning lies just below Browning Pass (1400 m), a low-altitude pass on the main divide just west of Mt Davie in the western-most corner of the park. The headwaters of the Wilberforce River (foreground) give access, via a historic zig-zag miners' track up the steep escarpment, to the pass and the Arahura River which drains Lake Browning and flows through deep gorges to the West Coast (distance). Faint recent fault traces and ridge rents can be seen in the foreground slopes below the camera.

The orientation of the upper Wilberforce and the Arahura/Harman River (centre) may be partially fault-controlled, since they are parallel to the Taramakau River (Hope Fault) but no fault has yet been identified.

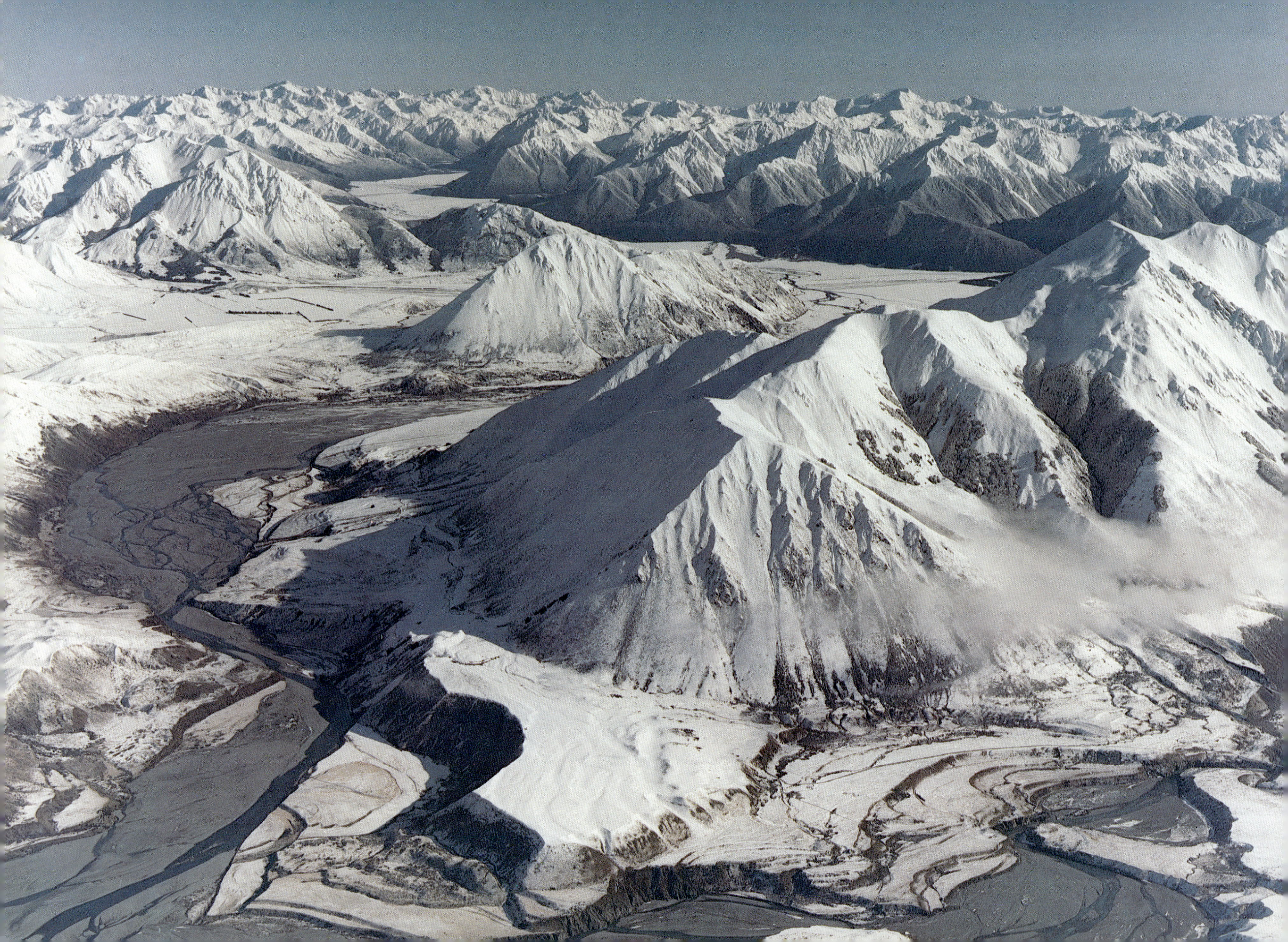

4 Winter snows can give greater relief to the glacial and alluvial landforms of the park. This view, looking west up the Waimakariri River from its junction with the Poulter River (foreground, right), is the opposite of that shown in Fig. 1. The peaks of the park lie along the skyline and the northern side of the Waimakariri River. The fans and old lake beaches around Poverty Flat can be seen, centre left (see also Fig. 2).

During the height of the Ice Ages, tongues of the Waimakariri Glacier would have taken a more direct route towards the camera, forming the low saddles on the Black Range behind Cass and the troughs now filled by Lakes Sarah and Grasmere (centre, left). The roche moutonnée (centre) is Cass Hill/Sugar Loaf; this block of bedrock greywacke has been honed to a conical shape by ice streams passing it on both sides. The prominent snow-covered terrace in the centre foreground is a remnant of the outwash surface deposited during the last glaciation; the rivers have downcut into this glacial till leaving it as a high terrace above younger alluvial terraces which step down to the present floodplain of the rivers.

5 The Mounds of Misery (foreground) lie at the western end of a broad glacial outwash surface dating back to the last glaciation. They lie on the eastern periphery of the park and are an excellent example of hummocky moraine preserved as the lobe of the Poulter Glacier gently retreated and the Cox River (centre right) downcut its way to the south-west to join the Poulter River (centre left). The mounds are now perched 150 m above the bed of the Cox River.

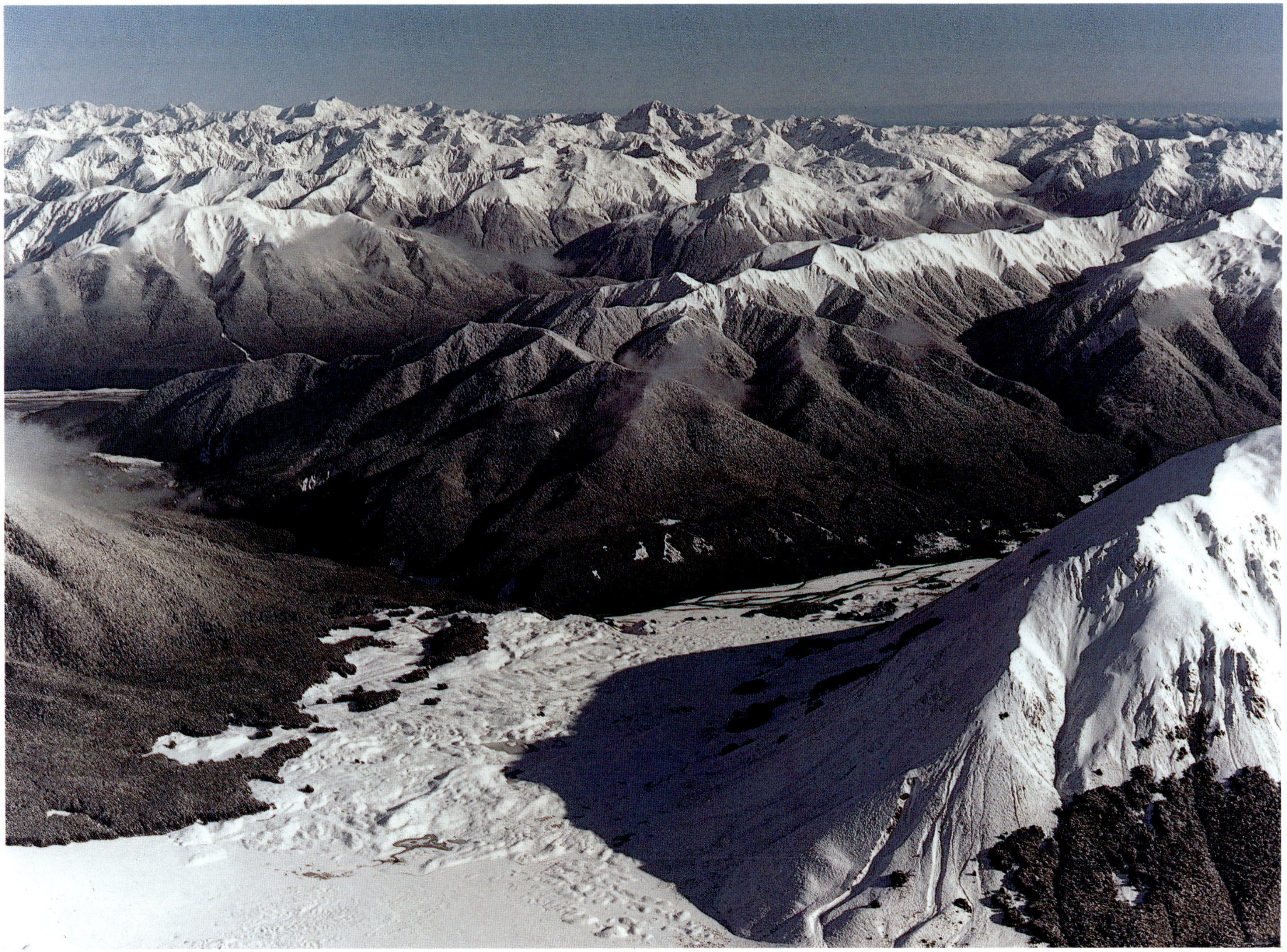

5

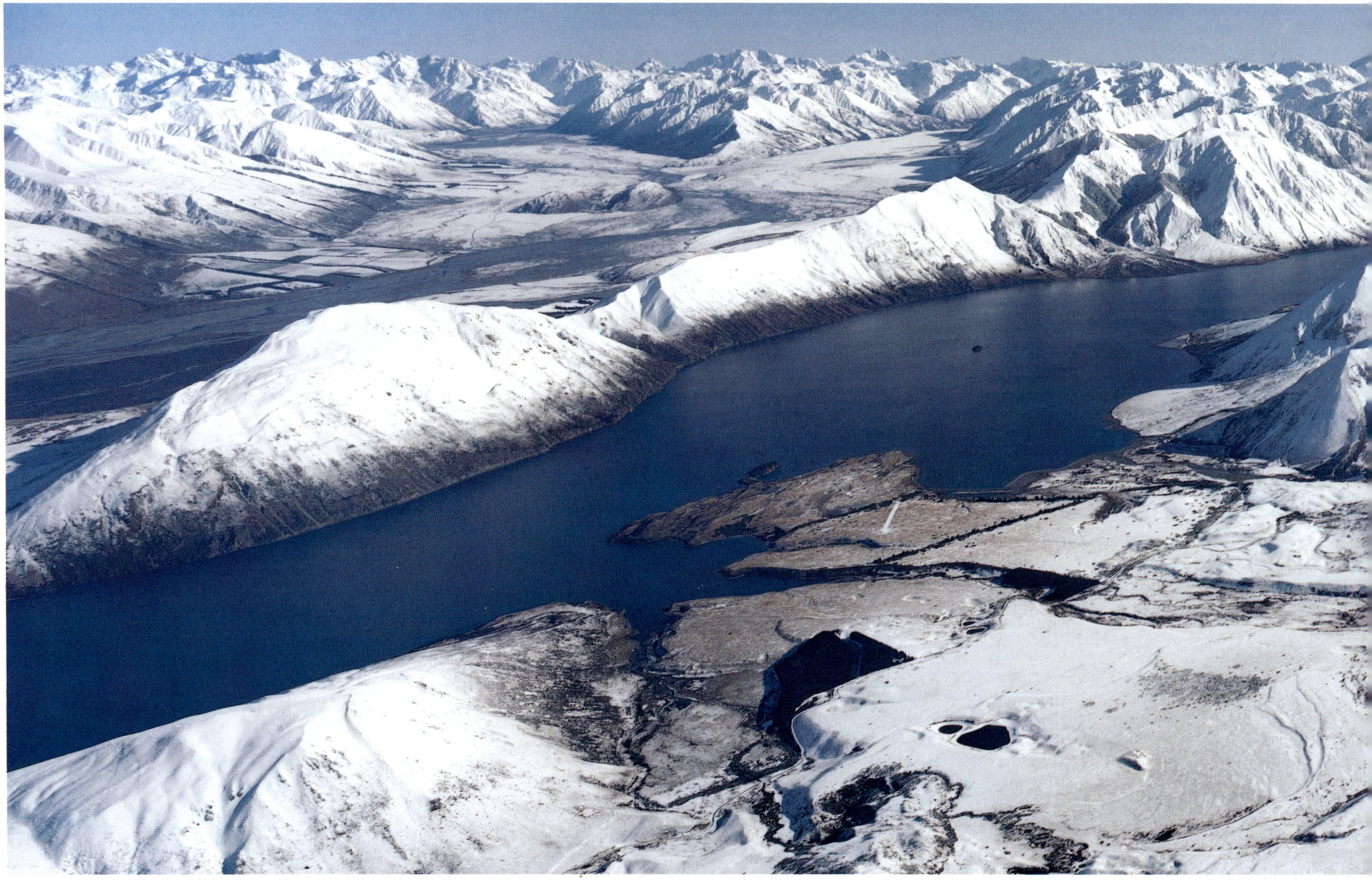

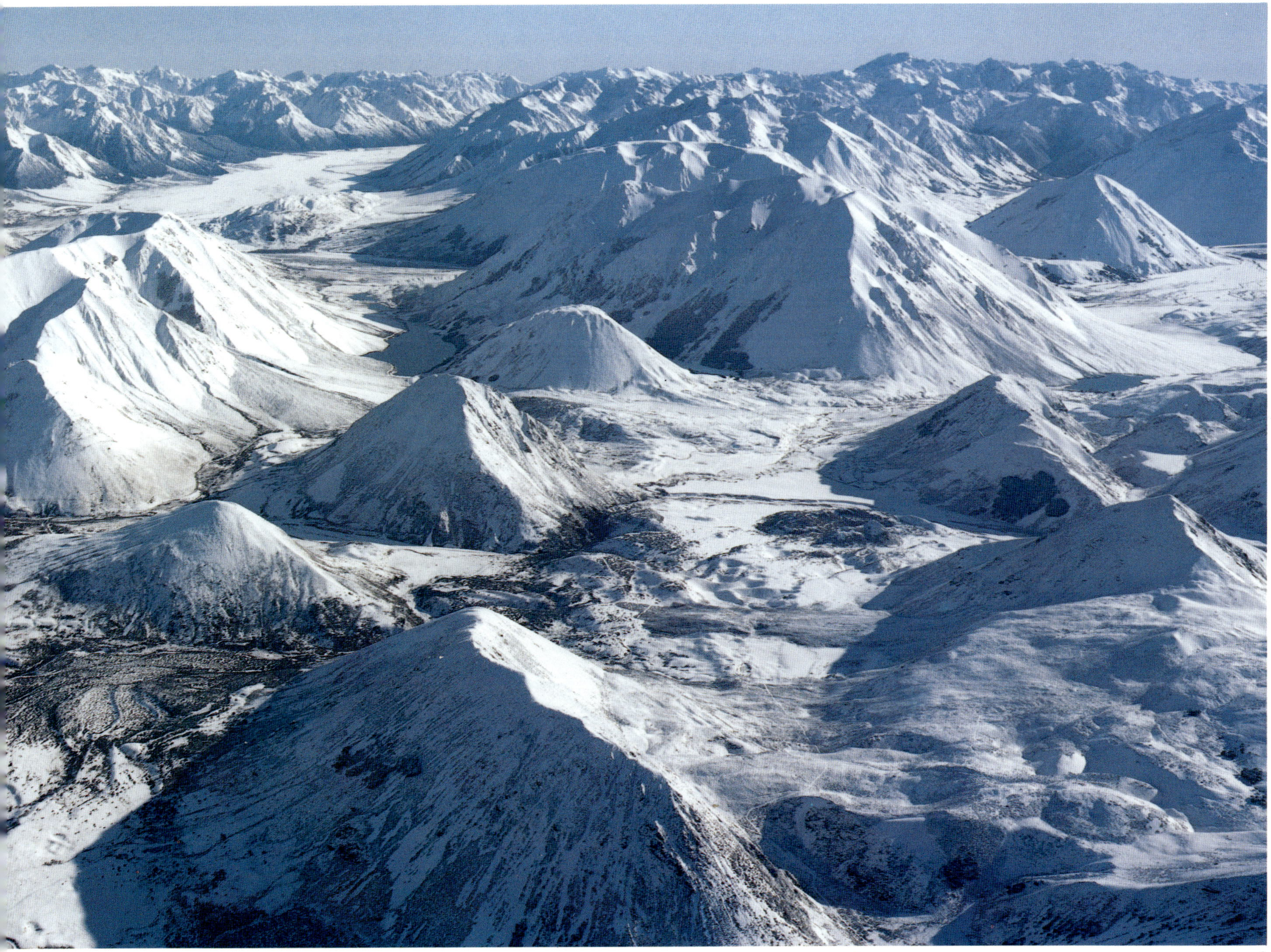

6

6 Lake Coleridge occupies a trough carved by the huge glacier that flowed down the Wilberforce valley (centre, distance) from the peaks at the western end of the park (skyline, right). In this view looking north-west, the Harper and Avoca Rivers (right, distance) flow into the Wilberforce from the Black and Craigieburn Ranges. The broad glaciated sweep of the Rakaia valley can be seen in the far left beyond Lake Coleridge; it is joined by the Mathais River just above a prominent roche moutonnée (Double Hill).

The whole panorama is a superb example of a landscape which has retained the landforms marking its glacial origin. The ridges and conical hills on either side of the lake consist of bedrock greywacke planed to a 'hogback' or 'razor-backed' shape by a maze of ice streams. The broad troughs between the ridges and isolated hills are occupied by many small lakes or filled with glacial outwash, the higher outwash surfaces predating the last glaciation. An interesting feature of this landscape is the reversal of drainage from the Coleridge trough. The Wilberforce River no longer flows through Lake Coleridge but has cut down between Mts Algidus and Oakden (centre, distance) to join the Rakaia; the natural outlet from Lake Coleridge is now 'upstream' into the Wilberforce River at this point.

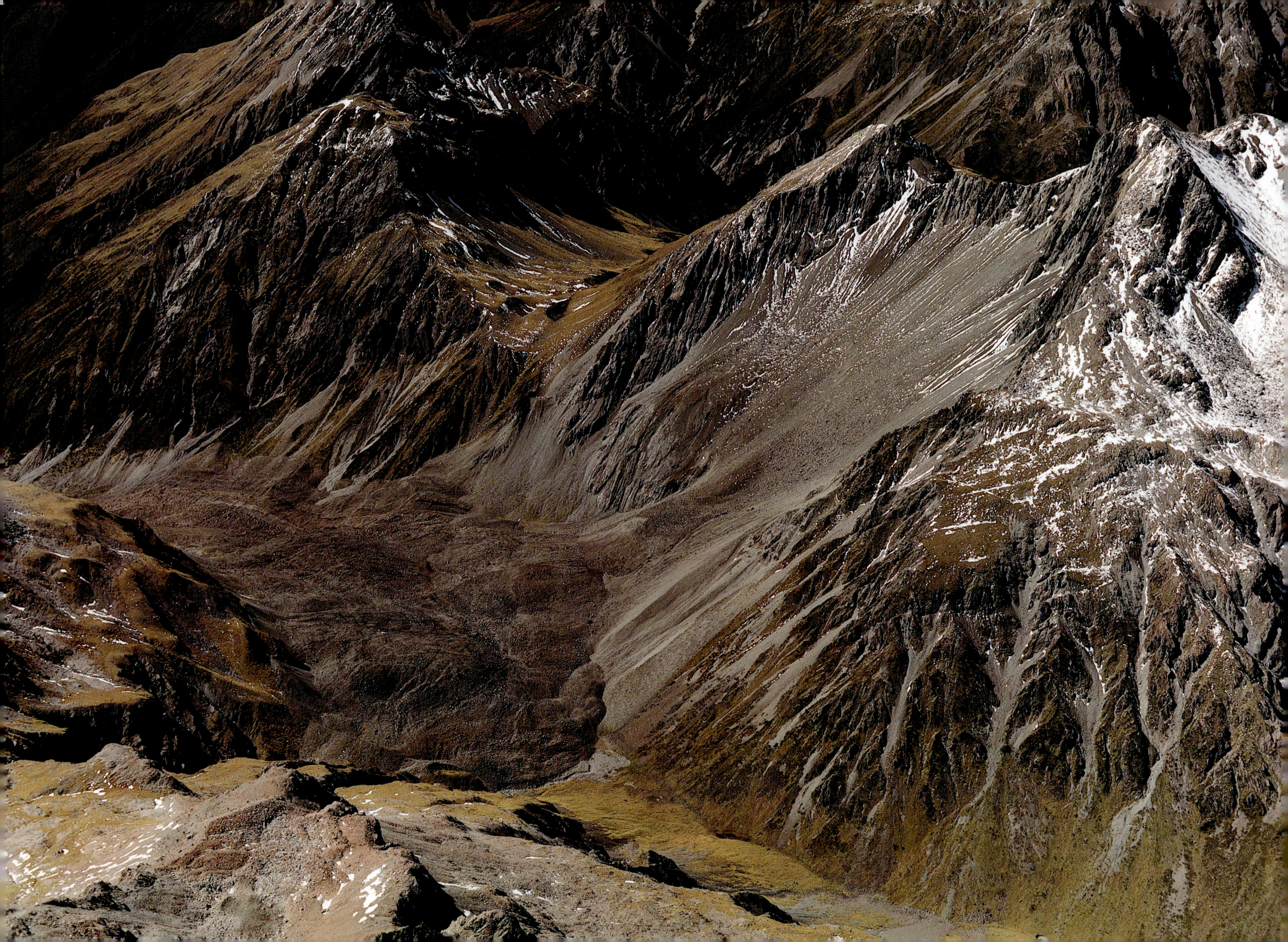

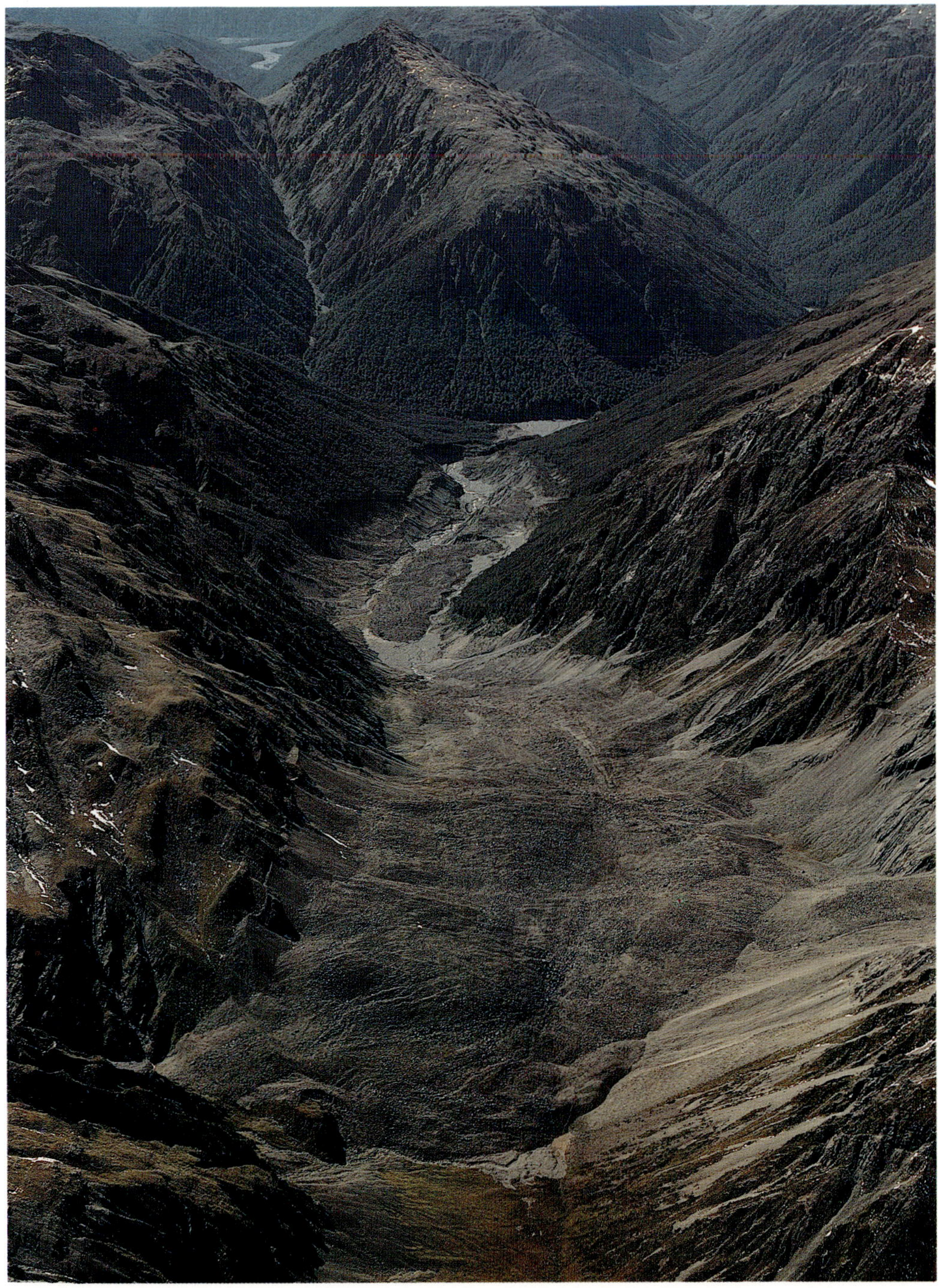

8

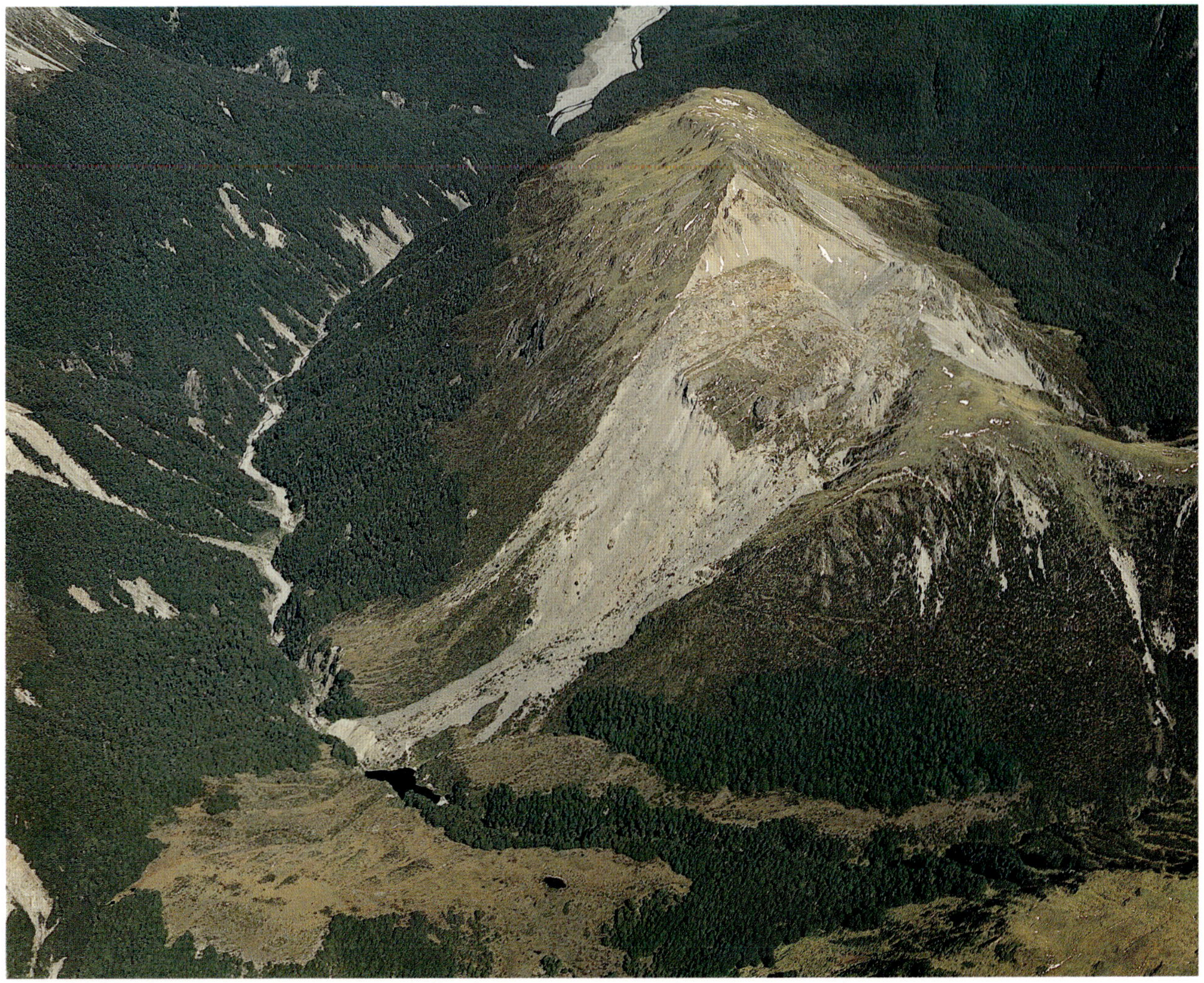

9

8 The debris from the rock avalanche off Falling Mountain travelled 3 km down the valley of the west branch of the Otehake River. Note the rock arête at the left hand margin of the avalanche, marking where it climbed more than 100 m up the opposite side of the valley.

Even after sixty years there are still no significant signs of revegetation of the avalanche debris. Note the active fault trace across the spur in the distance.

9 A rock avalanche off a spur of the Dampier Range in the north-east corner of the park has formed a small lake in Ellis Stream, a tributary of the Cox River. Roche Pass, a low saddle with the south branch of the Hurunui River, is in the foreground. Note that the top part of the collapsing spur has only slumped partway downslope and is still perched above the avalanche track. Many other recent slope failures can be seen downstream, all contributing rock debris to the bed of the Cox River.

7 Rock avalanches are a feature of the landscape of Arthur's Pass National Park. This one, on the north-western slopes of Falling Mountain, is the most recent of a series of very large rockfalls which have occurred since the end of the last glaciation. An earthquake in 1929 catapulted an estimated 60 million cubic metres of greywacke rock into the head of the west branch of the Otehake River. This view is north-east across Taruahuna Pass towards Tarn Col leading to the east branch of the Otehake River.

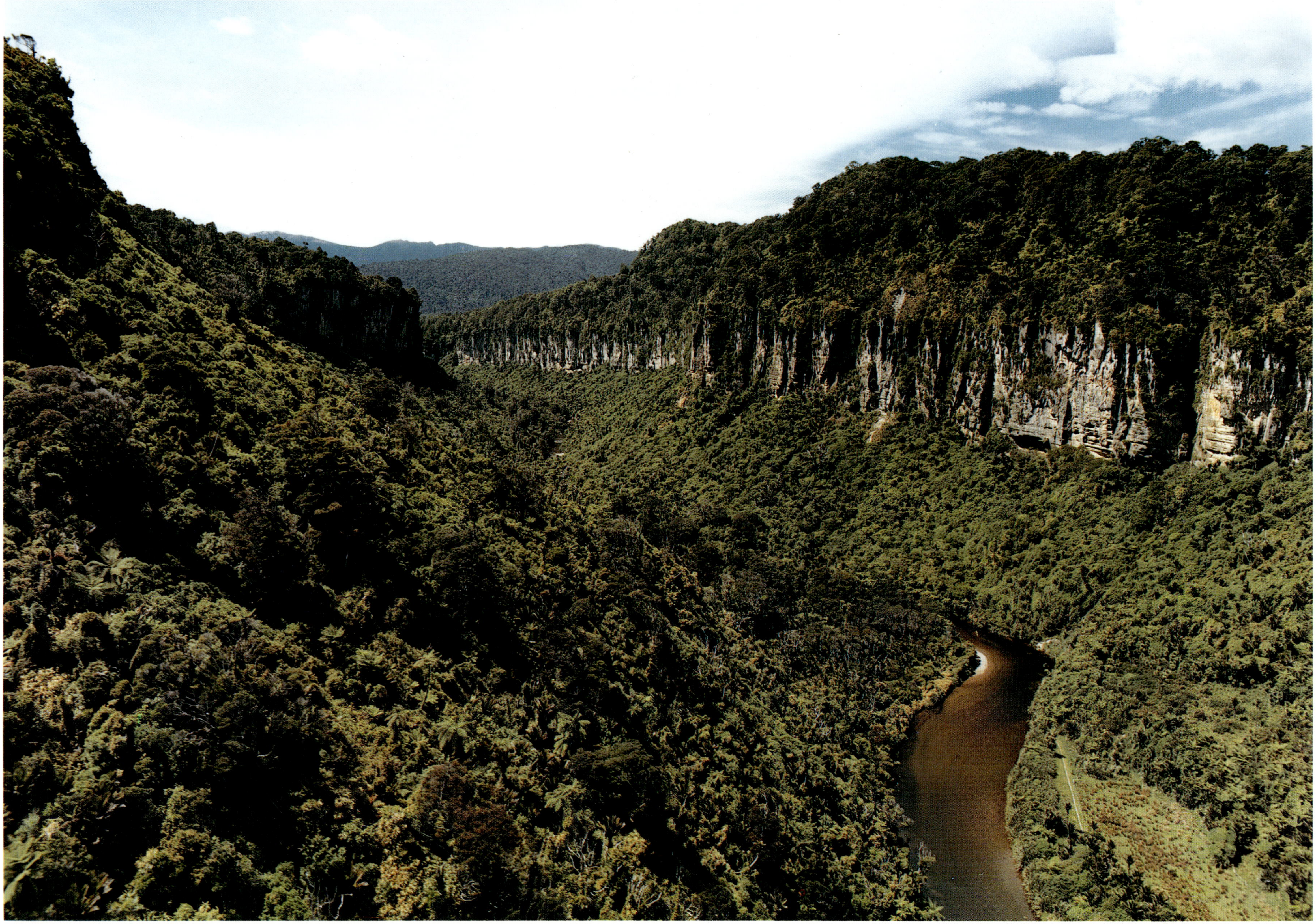

1

PAPAROA NATIONAL PARK

Paparoa National Park is New Zealand's newest national park. It covers the slopes and lowlands on the western side of the Paparoa Range on the West Coast, between the Tiropahi River in the north and the Punakaiki River in the south. An additional outlier is the catchment around the Ananui (Metro) Cave north of the Tiropahi. The Paparoa Range is 65 km long, an uplifted block of granite and gneiss rock separated from the higher ranges futher inland by the broad depressions of the Inangahua and Grey Rivers. Until the early 1970s, the area was largely unknown to the public except for the blowholes and 'pancake rocks' of Dolomite Point. Subsequently the western Paparoas became the centre of a major conservation controversy over proposals to log the lowland forests. After fourteen years of investigation and public debate the area was designated our twelfth national park on 5 December 1987 – a significant event in New Zealand's National Park Centennial Year.

Within an area of only 30 000 ha, Paparoa National Park has a magnificent diversity of landforms. There are crags and cirques along the spine of the Paparoa Range; dense forests and pakihis on the marine and alluvial terraces of the lowlands; limestone canyons and extensive cave networks; and a highly scenic coastline of cliffs, marine benches and rocky headlands. It is the first modern national park, its boundaries chosen so that the ecosystems included are scientifically representative of the landscapes on the western slopes of the Paparoa Range.

THE COASTLINE AND KARST PLATEAU

For 20 km State Highway 6 hugs the foot of a series of 300–400 m-high sheer limestone cliffs, as it threads its way from the saddle above the Tiropahi River to Razorback Point. On the seaward side of the road, the coastline is a spectacular series of headlands, reefs, small islands, coves and pebbly beaches. At Dolomite Point the limestone has been sculpted into one of New Zealand's most famous landforms – the chasms, pipes and platy formations known as the Pancake Rocks (pp. 100–101). Elsewhere the rocks are calcareous mudstone eroded to other weird shapes – like the stacks around Seal Island and the overhanging stepped Miko Cliffs at Perpendicular Point. Just south of Perpendicular Point the Truman Track descends a marine bench to give access to several small, semi-circular coves (pp. 98–99). Here, several small streams draining the flax swamps on this marine bench pour over the lip of low cliffs onto pebbly beaches fronting wave-cut alcoves and caves.

The traveller can be easily captivated by this fascinating coastline and pass by, oblivious of the secrets held in the karst plateau hundreds of metres above, beyond the high limestone cliffs. The plateau is the 4–5 km-wide western edge of a band of Oligocene-aged limestone lying in a trough known as the 'Barrytown Syncline'. As this limestone plateau was uplifted, the four main rivers in the park were still able to maintain their westerly course, carving deep canyons across the plateau (from north to south: Fox River, Bullock Creek, Porarari River and Punakaiki River). Only the mouths of these spectacular canyons can be seen from the coastal highway, but from the air their size is quickly appreciated (pp. 102, 104). So, too, is the intricate surface pattern of the karst plateau – short razor-backed, bush-covered ribs of limestone enclosing small streams which disappear underground through sinkholes (dolines). This karst plateau is seen to best advantage north of the Fox River; Cave Creek North disappears into a cave at the foot of a 65 m sheer cliff and enters the Fox River cave systems.

Within the canyons there are several impressive alcoves, particularly the 'Ballroom Overhang' in the Fox. The most interesting karst feature, however, is the underground capture of Bullock Creek. In normal flow conditions the river disappears underground at the head of its impressive canyon and resurges into Cave Creek (a tributary of the Porarari River) 1.3 km to the south. From the air, the impressive Bullock Creek canyon is an enigma – its floor covered with luxuriant rata/rimu/hardwood forest but lacking any flowing water except during high floods when the cave system fills to capacity and flood waters overflow into the surface channel.

THE BARRYTOWN SYNCLINE

The Barrytown Syncline is an ancient 3 km-wide trough, lying between the karst plateau and the eastern ranges. This trough was formed by folding of the limestone and overlying sandstones and mudstone; subsequent erosion removed the sandstone and mudstone, leaving a depression partly filled with gravels eroded from the Paparoa Range during the Ice Ages. Most of the trough is covered with dense podocarp/beech/hardwood forest but, at the northern boundary of the park around the Tiropahi River, the forest gives way to pakihi. The pakihis occur on the Tiropahi terraces, the highest member of a remarkable set of six marine terraces which range from sea level near Charleston to an upper height of 190–200 m altitude in the middle reaches of the Awakiri, Waitakere (Nile) and Tiropahi Rivers (p. 107).

WESTERN SLOPES OF THE PAPAROA RANGE

Limestone crops out again on the eastern side of the trough, in a band through which the rivers have cut deep gorges. In the upper reaches of the Porarari River, a block of Hawks Crag Breccia has been eroded to a weird cluster of rounded outcrops known as the Lone Hand (p. 109). Further south, a remarkable 300 m-high escarpment forms a 3 km-long arc around the head of the Punakaiki valley (p. 108). At this southern end of the park the smoother summits reflect the underlying coal measures and sandstone which dip gently to the east but terminate in a spectacular ridge crest escarpment on the western edge. North of this point lies the jagged spine of the Paparoa Range, the eastern skyline of the park. Despite its relatively low altitude and proximity to the sea this rarely visited mountain crest shows the influence of glaciation on the hard granitic and gneissic rocks. The similarities between the crest of the Paparoa Range and northern Fiordland, 430 km to the south-west, are quite striking. Closely related rock types attest to lateral movement of the two massifs along the Alpine Fault; the almost incessant rain of similar superhumid ocean climates and glaciation during the Ice Ages has produced within Paparoa National Park a landscape of rampart-shaped accordant summits, cirques, and U-shaped valley heads – a Fiordland in miniature.

1 The lower gorge of the Porarari River is one of four impressive canyons carved in the Oligocene-aged limestone of the karst plateau in the western, coastal part of Paparoa National Park. A segment of the Paparoa Range (around White Knight, 1224 m) can be seen on the eastern skyline. A feature of the gorge is the continuous line of talus slopes, running from the base of the cliffs to the river's edge. The soils on these slopes are among the most fertile in the park but, as yet, they lack the tall forest which has developed on the most stable sites (such as the surface of the karst plateau above the cliffs).

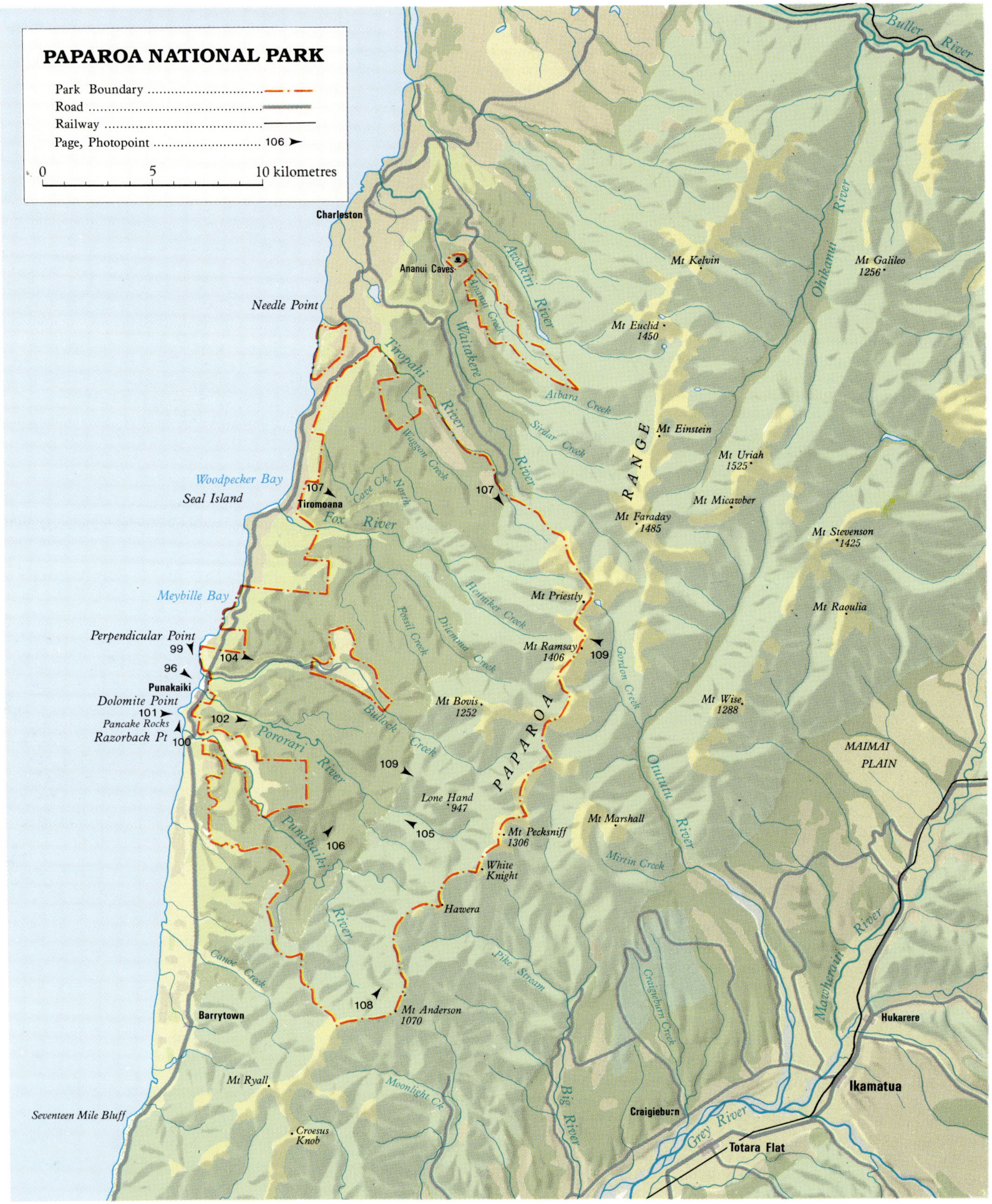
PAPAROA NATIONAL PARK
Park Boundary
Road
Railway
Page, Photopoint 106
0
5
10 kilometres
Buller River
Charleston
Ananui Caves
Needle Point
Waitakere River
Tiropahi River
Mt Kelvin
Mt Galileo 1256
Ohikanui River
Mt Euclid 1450
Atbara Creek
Sirdar Creek
Mt Einstein
RANGE
Mt Uriah 1525
Mt Micawber
Mt Faraday 1485
Mt Stevenson 1425
Woodpecker Bay
Seal Island
107
Tiromoana
Fox River
Meybille Bay
Mt Priestly
Mt Raoulia
Perpendicular Point
99
96
104
Mt Ramsay 1406
109
Gordon Creek
Punakaiki
Dolomite Point
101
Pancake Rocks
Razorback Pt
100
102
Porarari River
Bullock Creek
Mt Bovis 1252
Mt Wise 1288
MAIMAI PLAIN
PAPAROA
Lone Hand 947
105
106
Punakaiki River
Mt Pecksniff 1306
Mt Marshall
Mirtin Creek
Otututu River
White Knight
Hawera
Pike Stream
Canoe Creek
108
Mt Anderson 1070
Barrytown
Craigieburn Creek
Mawheraiti River
Hukarere
Mt Ryall
Moonlight Ck
Big River
Ikamatua
Craigieburn
Grey River
Totara Flat
Seventeen Mile Bluff
Croesus Knob

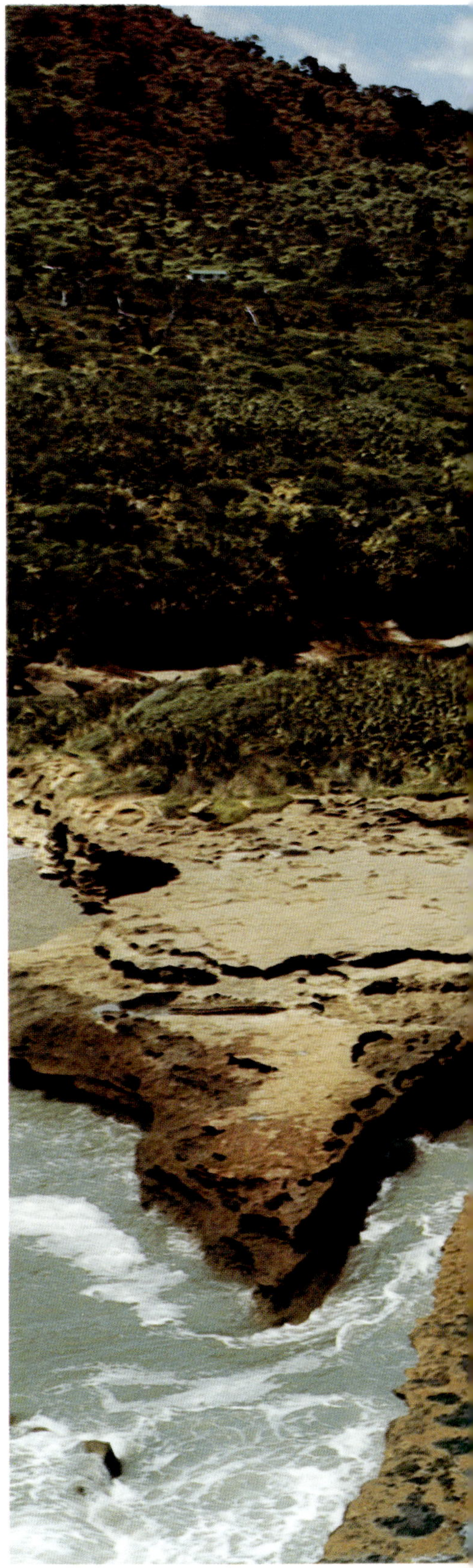

2

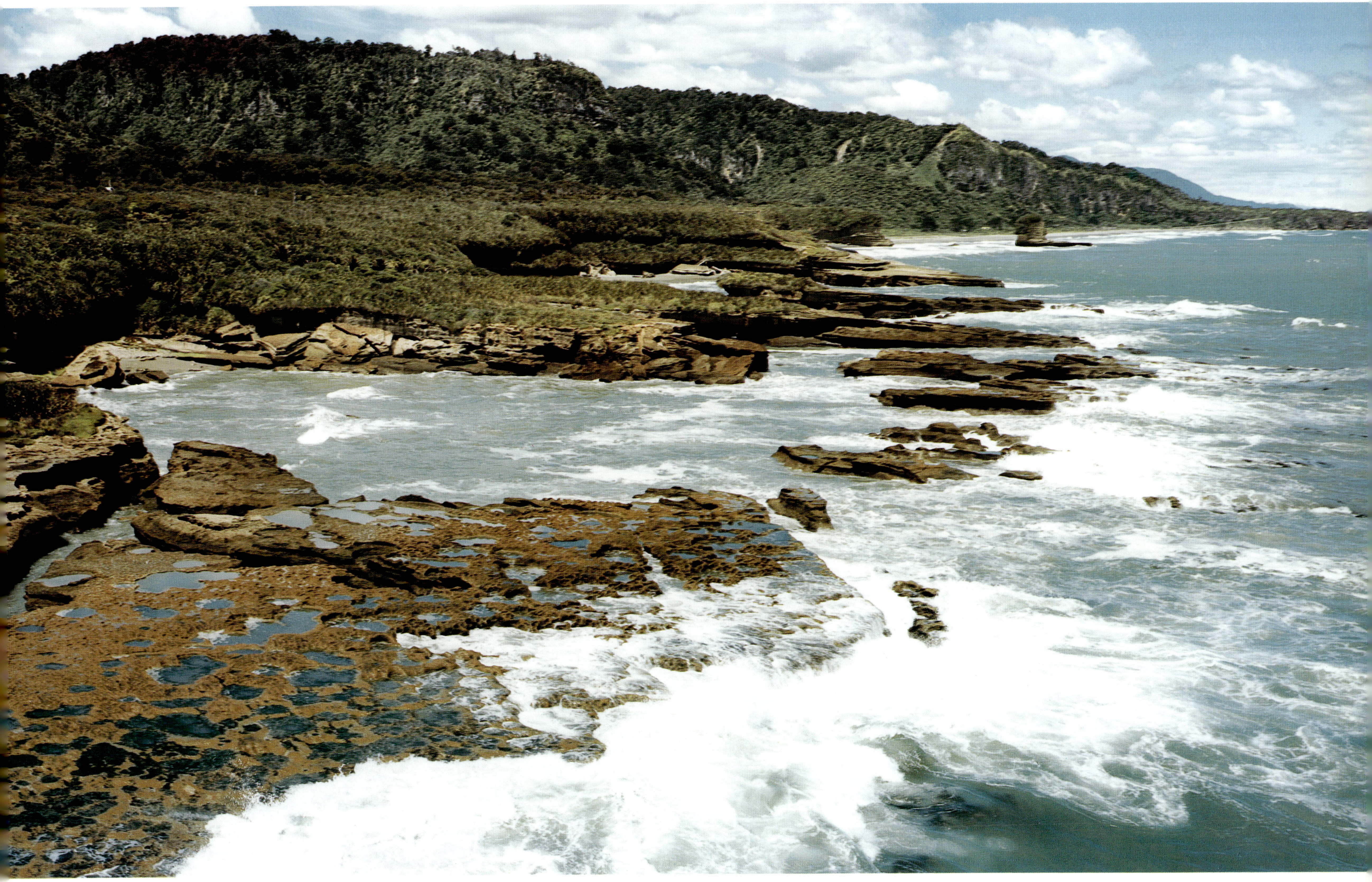

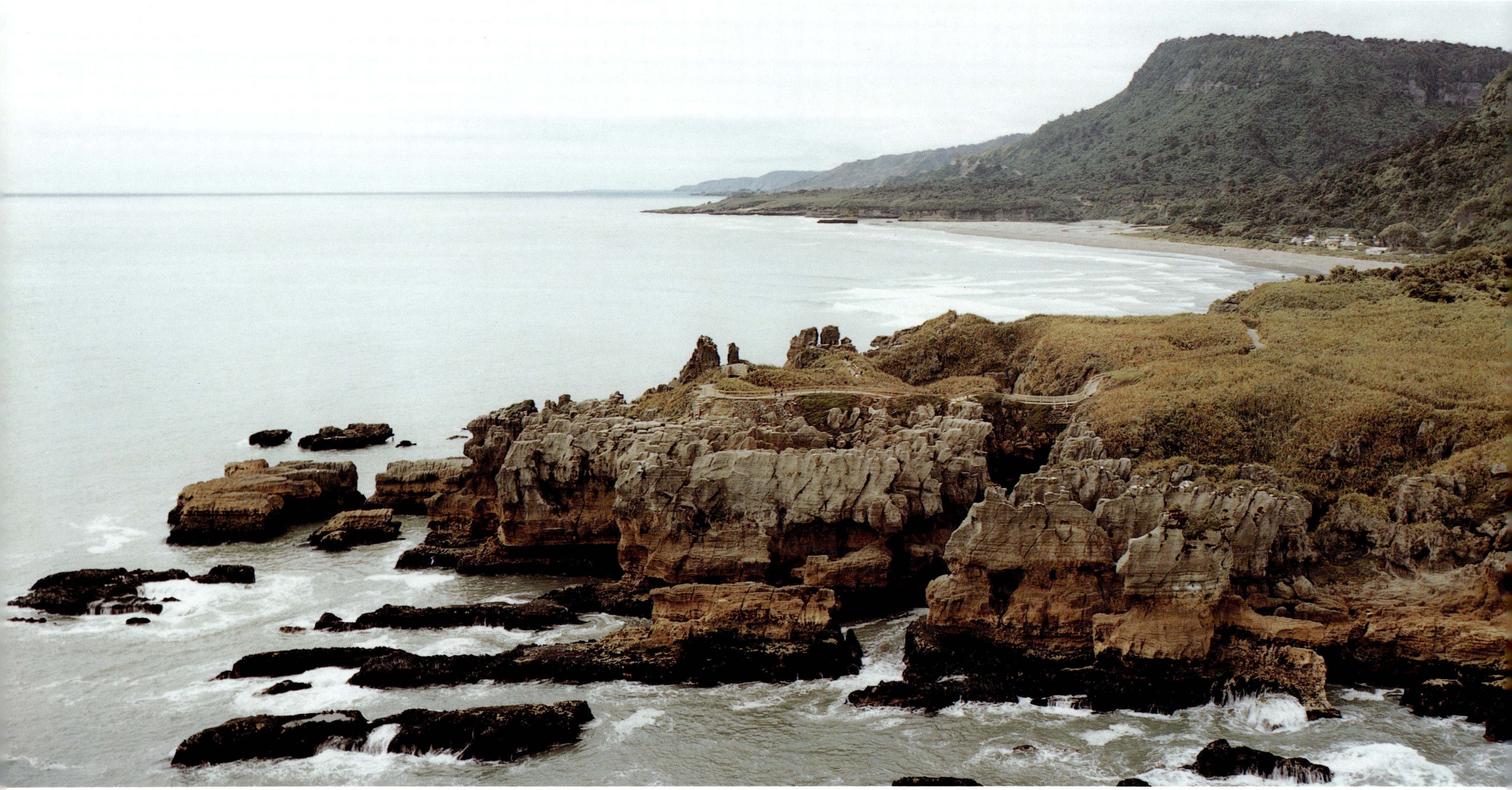

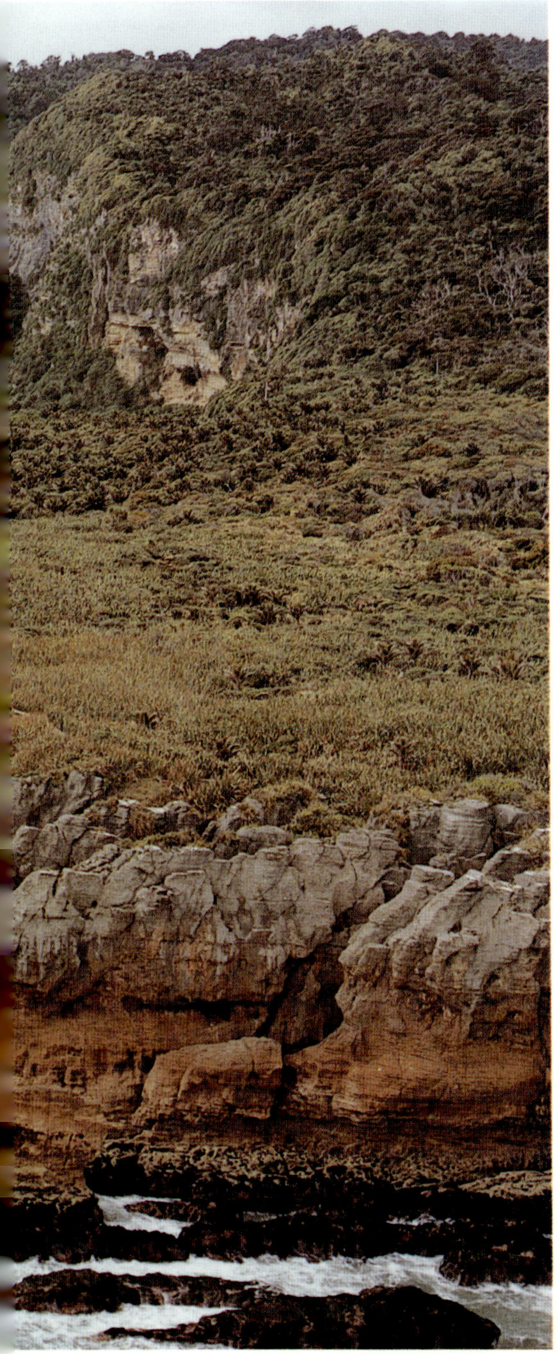

3

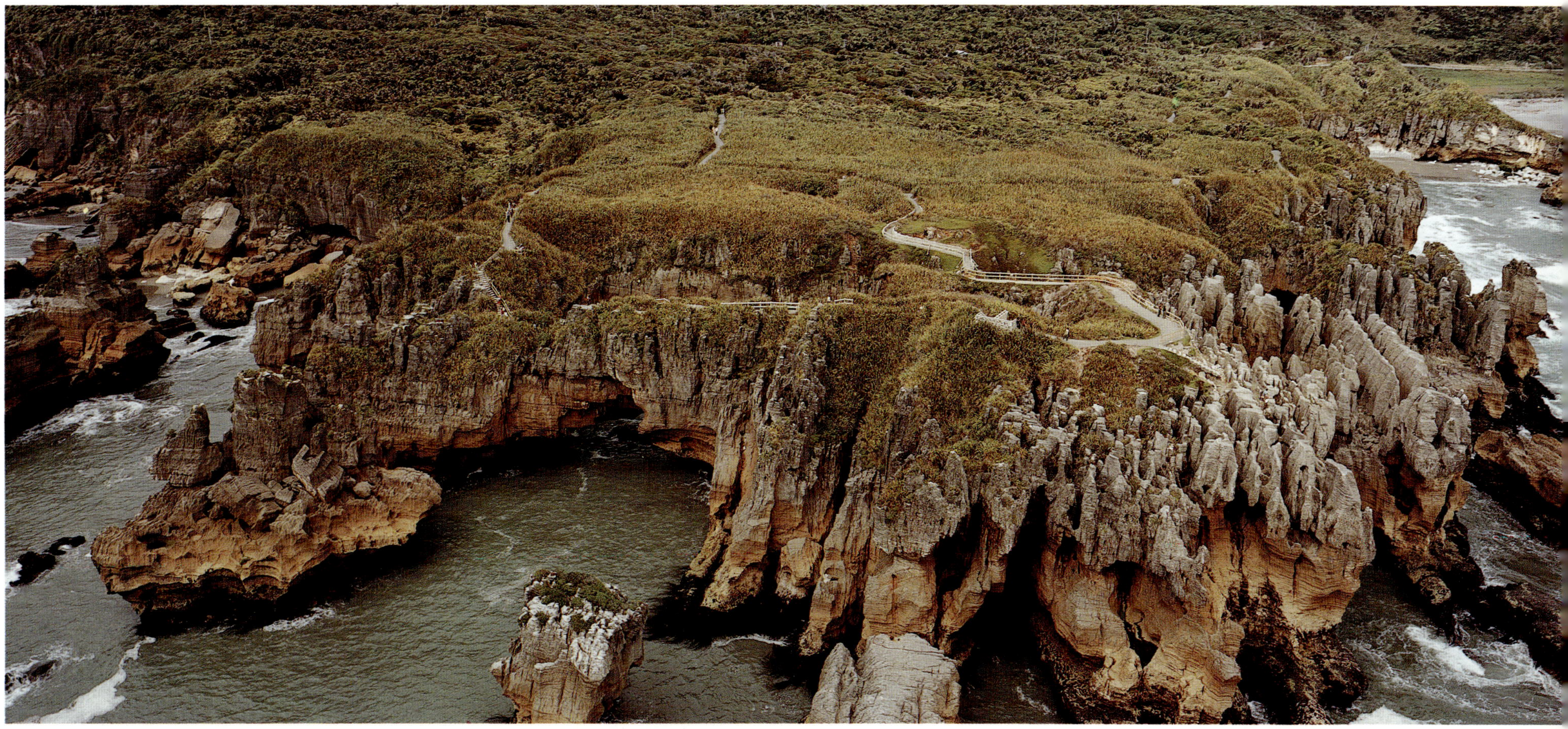

4

previous page

2 The popular Truman Track descends to a coastline consisting of a series of small semi-circular bays (centre) cut into gently-sloping uplifted marine terrace. Dolomite Point can be seen at the southern end of the bay (top, right).

The reefs in the foreground consist of Eocene and Oligocene calcareous sandstone, which is older than and underlies the limestone seen at Dolomite Point and in the background cliffs. The platforms at sea level have become pitted through wave erosion, the softer parts of the rocks dissolving away.

3 The Oligocene limestone making up the Pancake Rocks is covered with a thin deposit of terrace gravels and sands which support peaty soils and a dense flax bog. Acidic waters were leached through into the limestone, etching it into its characteristisc ramparts and spires by dissolving the calcium carbonate around tunnels formed beneath the surface. The 'pancake' layers are probably the result of accelerated erosion of clay-rich layers spaced a few centimetres apart in the limestone.

The prevailing north-west winds drive waves into the limestone causing geyser-like eruptions through chimneys ('blowholes') in the rock.

4 The Pancake Rocks of Dolomite Point are one of the most interesting landforms in the park, and a major West Coast tourist attraction. Like so many other geographical features with geological names, the point is misnamed because it does not contain any dolomite; in fact, there is no dolomite on the West Coast. This view, looking northwards to Perpendicular Point shows how the chasms and tunnels have been cut in a marine terrace uplifted 35 m above present-day sea level. Former beach gravels on this terrace can be seen in places along the track to the blowholes.

5 At the upstream end of the lower Porarari Gorge, the limestone cliffs give way abruptly and the river traveller enters a broad heavily-forested trough between the Paparoa Range (distance) and the coastal limestone plateau (see Fig. 8).

Tall forest (northern rata, rimu and red and hard beech) has established itself on the plateau above the escarpment and scattered rata can be seen on the banks of the river. In contrast, the bright-green talus slopes at the foot of the escarpment have a profuse cover of low broadleaf trees (mahoe, *Quintinia*, toro, kamahi), nikau palms and black mamaku tree ferns. The higher fertility of the soils and the youth of the talus slopes are probably the cause of this pronounced difference in vegetation.

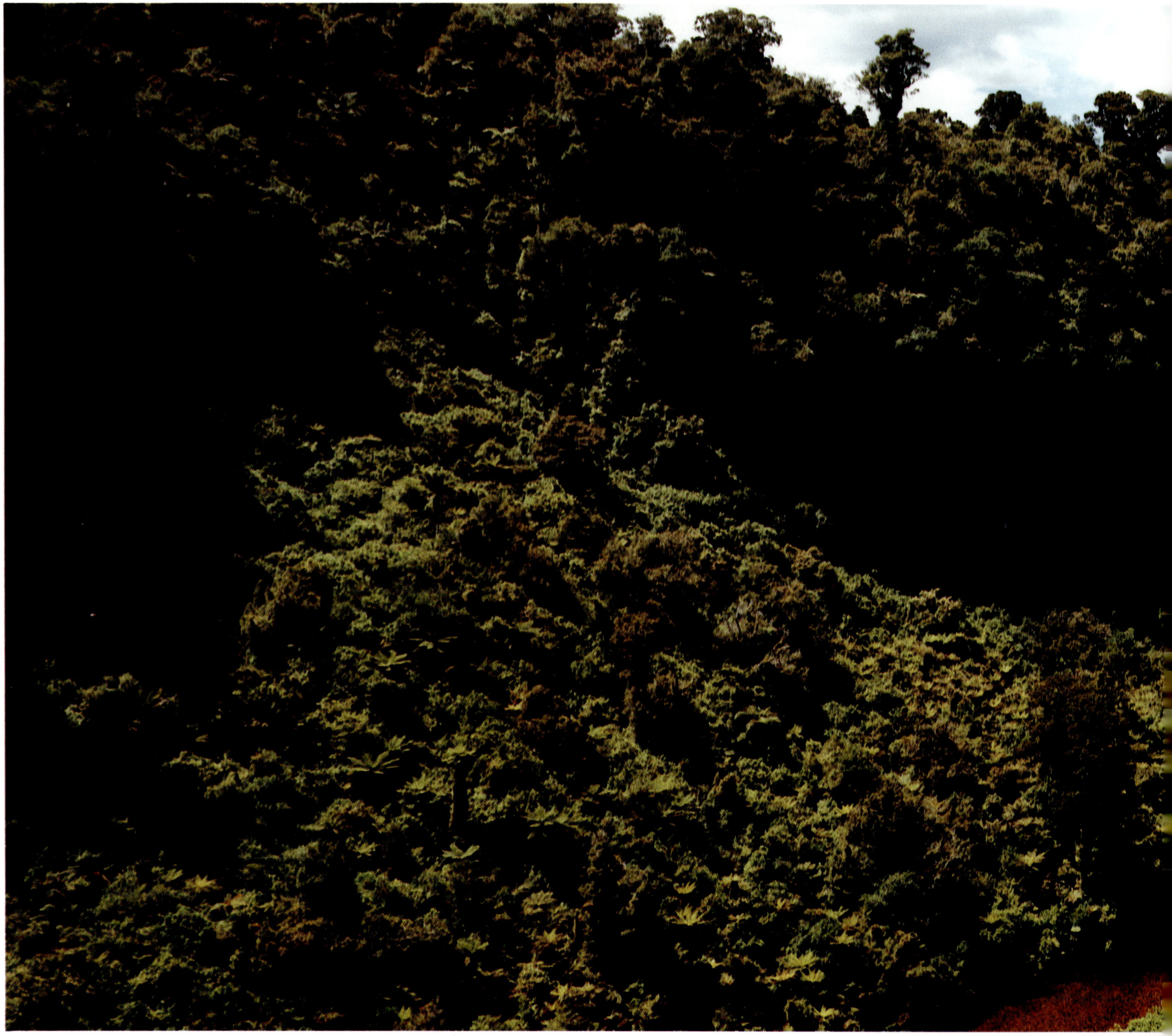

5

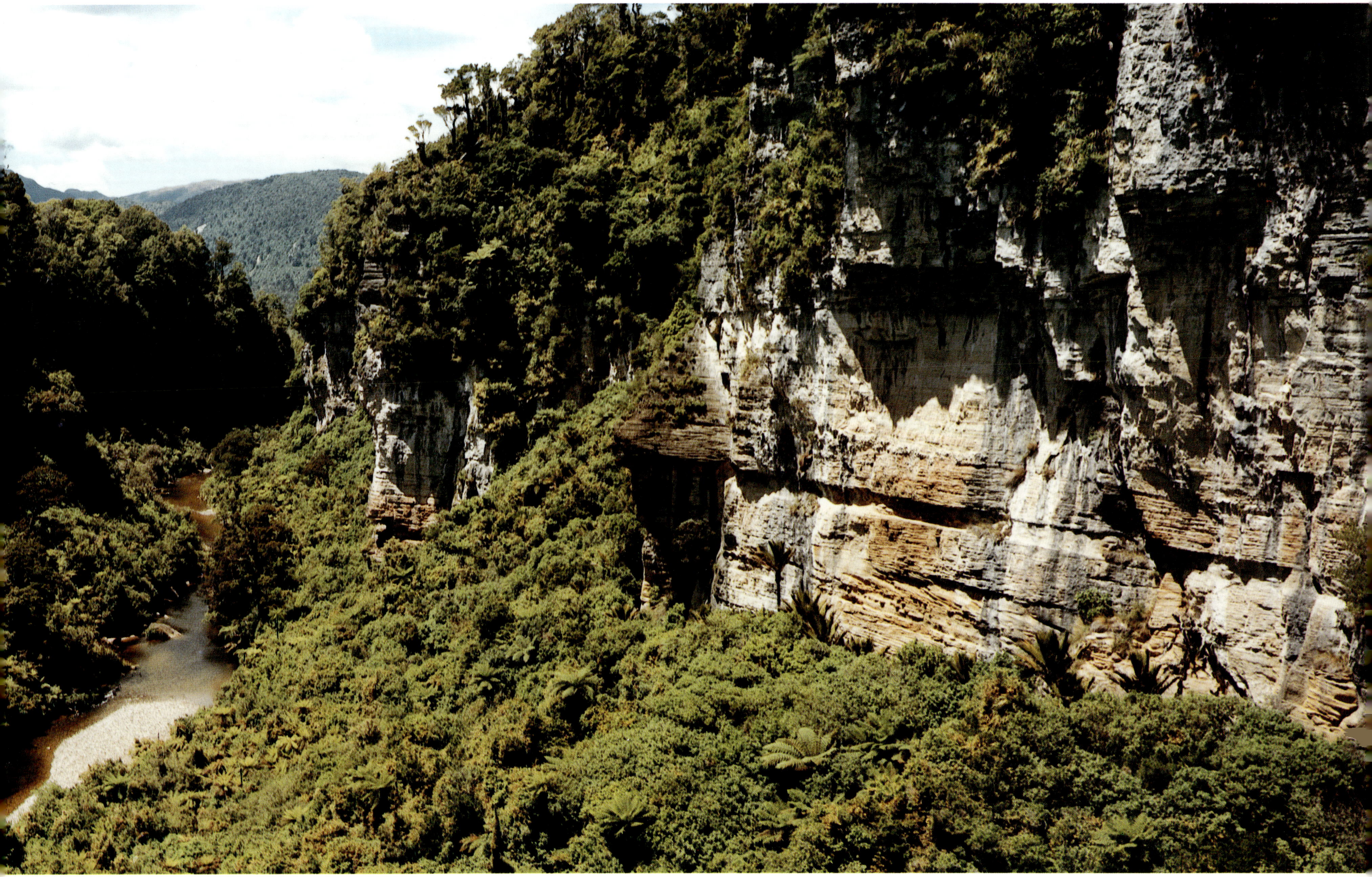

6 The canyon of Bullock Creek cuts a wide swathe through the coastal limestone plateau of the park. The heavily forested surface of the plateau exhibits typical karst features – a maze of short blind valleys and sinkholes (such as those in Fig. 9). The farmed alluvial flats lie within the Paparoa syncline (see opposite page), and the eastern boundary of the park extends along the Paparoa Range, from Mt Priestly (top, left; 1392 m) to Mt Pecksniff (top, right; 1306 m).

In normal conditions, Bullock Creek no longer flows down the canyon, for its waters swirl underground at the western end of the farmland, leaving a dry gravel-bed downstream. The waters resurge from a cavern 1.3 km to the south (centre, right) as Cave Creek, a major tributary of the Porarari River.

This underground river capture is a polje system, another classic karst feature. The lack of water is deceptive, however, for in heavy rains the underground caverns rapidly fill with water and then the stream overflows into its former bed, flooding the wetland at the head of the canyon before surging down the narrow streambed (bottom, right).

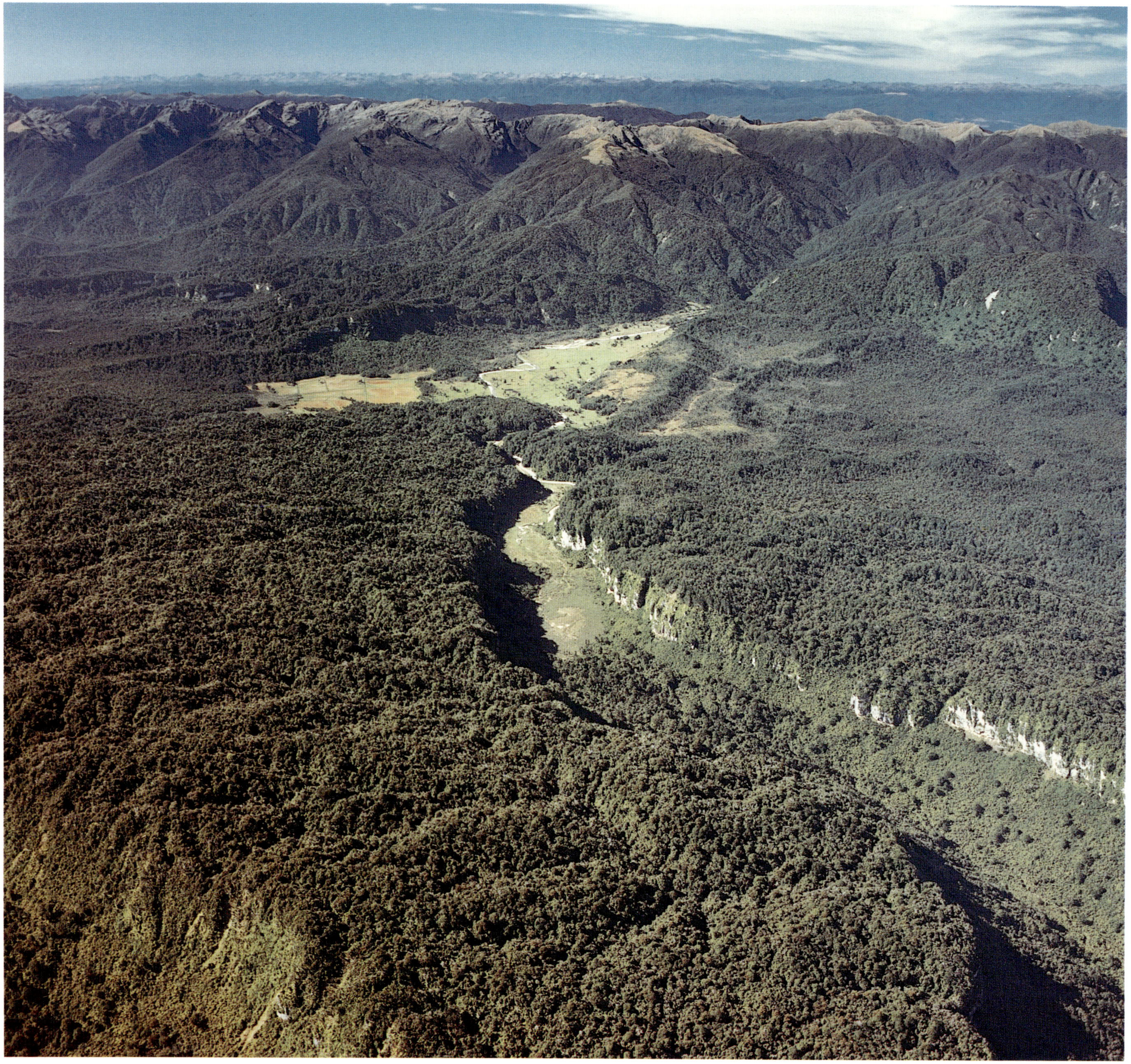

6

7 This westerly view shows the lowland landforms of Paparoa National Park, from the Punakaiki River canyon (centre, left) to that of Bullock Creek (top, right). The limestone can be seen cropping out on either side of the Barrytown Syncline, the depression cutting across the landscape from left to right. The westernmost outcrop is the coastal plateau with its river canyons (distance); the easternmost outcrop can be seen in the centre (foreground), where the Porarari River cuts through its upper gorge and emerges into the trough (syncline) filled with relatively soft mudstone and river terrace alluvium.

7

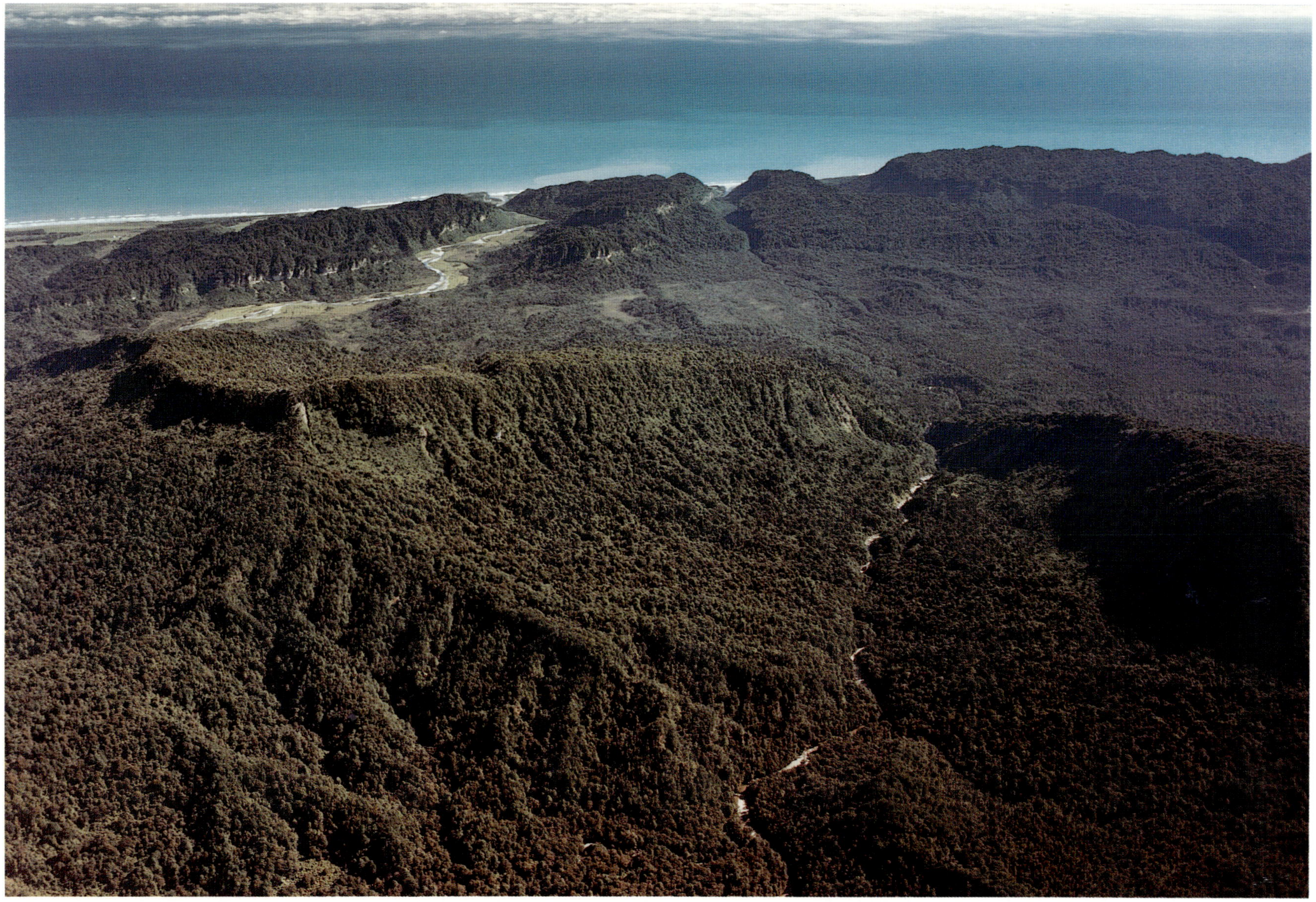

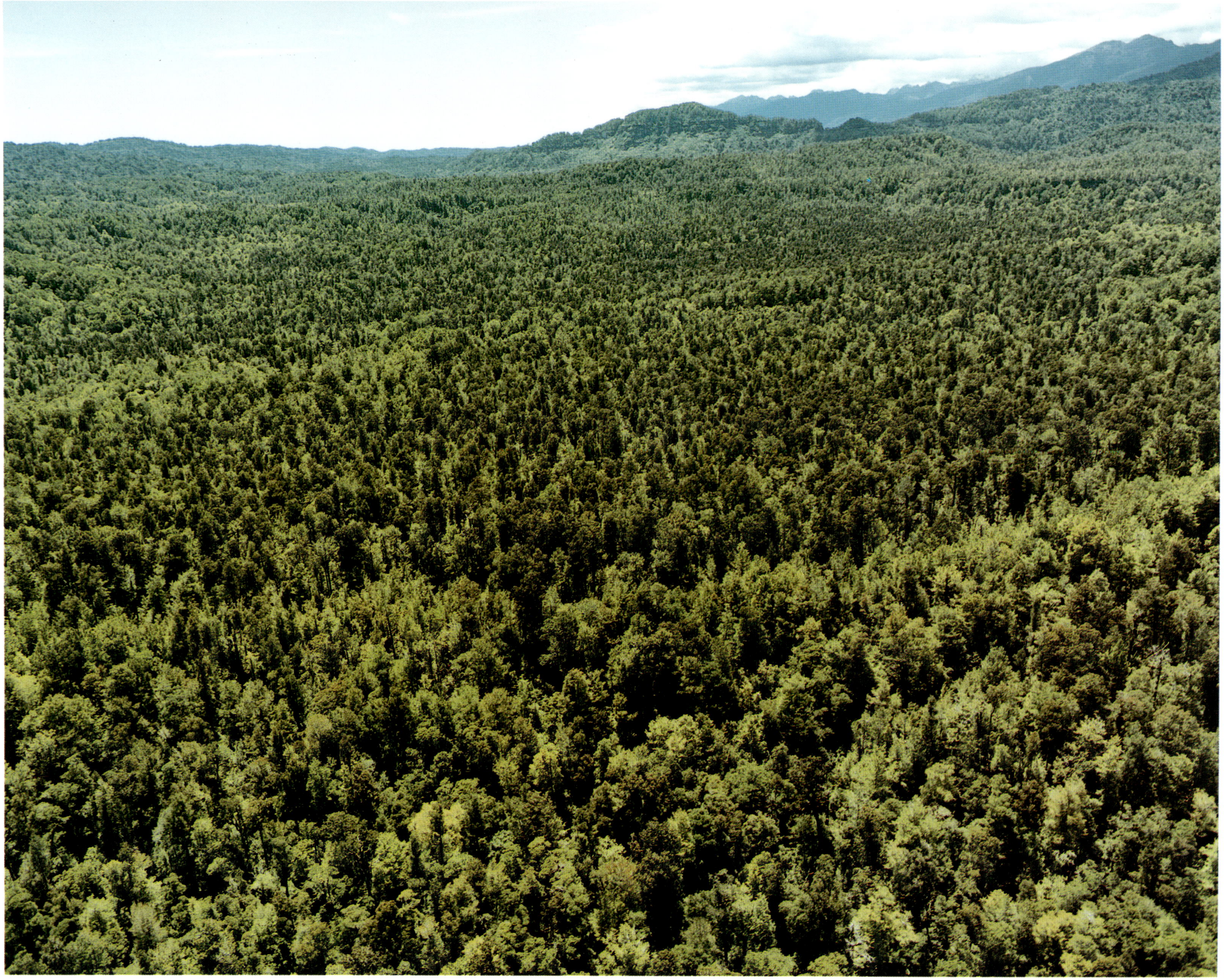

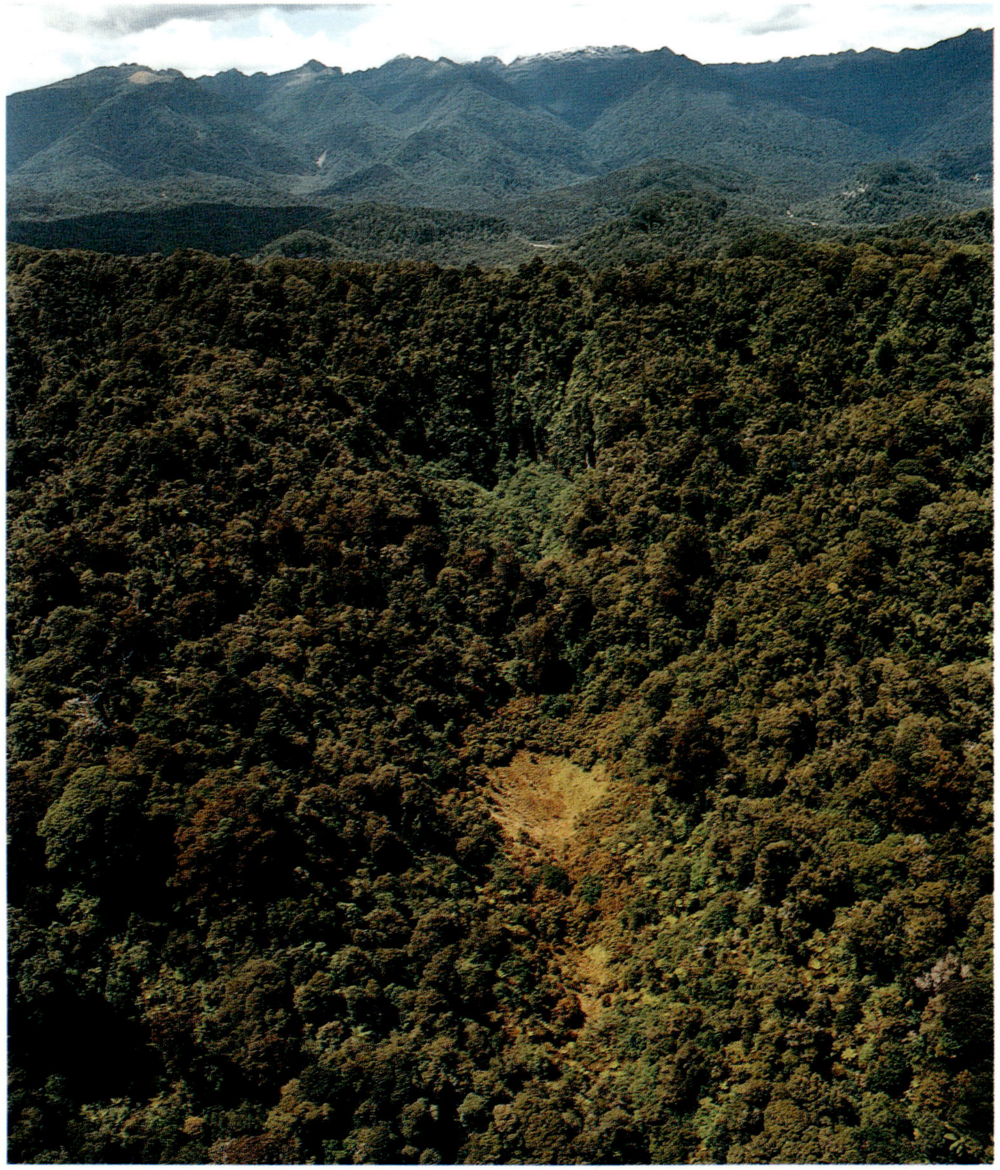

9

8 The Barrytown Syncline is a 3 km-wide trough running north-east/south-west and lying between the coastal limestone plateau and the limestone band running along the foot of the western slopes of the Paparoa Range (top, right). This is the most extensive tract of lowland forest (podocarp/beech/broadleaf) in the park. Rimu and miro are the most common of the podocarps and the other common large trees are red beech and silver beech (the latter on colder, wetter sites).

9 The surface of the coastal karst plateau is densely forested and pockmarked with sinkholes (dolines). This group occur on the northern side of the Fox River canyon near where Cave Creek North disappears underground. The vegetation around the doline in the foreground shows evidence of temperature inversion, for the floor of the depression carries grasses, hard ferns and shrubs typical of a 'frost hollow'.

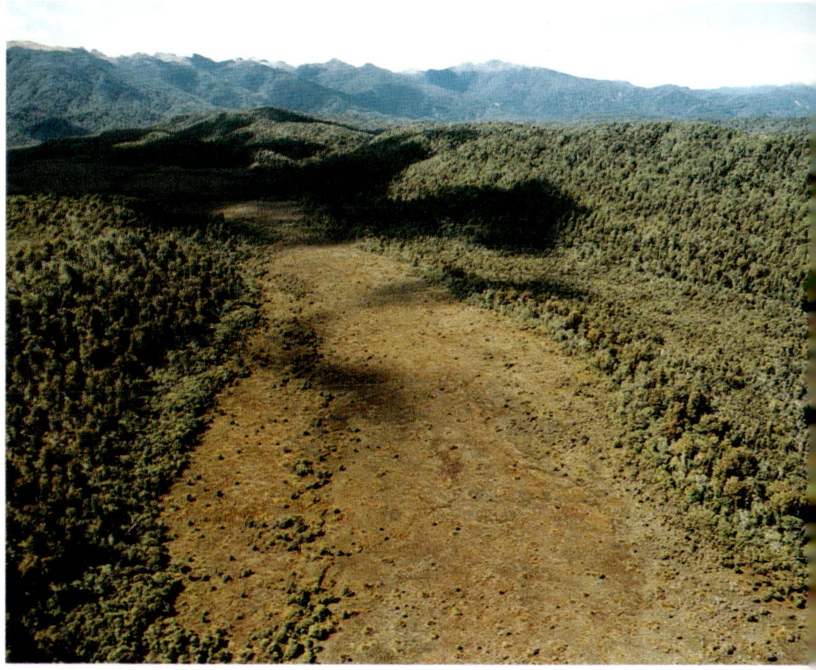

10

10 The best examples of terraced landforms lie around the middle reaches of the Tiropahi River at the northern end of the park. Three different terraces, between 100 m and 190 m above sea level, mark ancient river levels formed during Quaternary inter-glacial times. These old terraces are much broader than could have been formed by the present-day Tiropahi River. They are evidence that the headwaters of the Fox River probably flowed this way but were later captured, to flow down their present course through the Fox canyon.

The terraces consist of sandy gravels, and soils formed in these materials have become podzolised, with characteristic cemented subsoils, poor drainage, high acidity and low fertility. Fires have also contributed to the formation of pakihis on the gently-sloping terrace surfaces. The pakihi vegetation consists of manuka scrub, sedges and ferns; hardier podocarps (rimu, silver pine, yellow-silver pine) and mountain beech can be seen as a fringe around the pakihi.

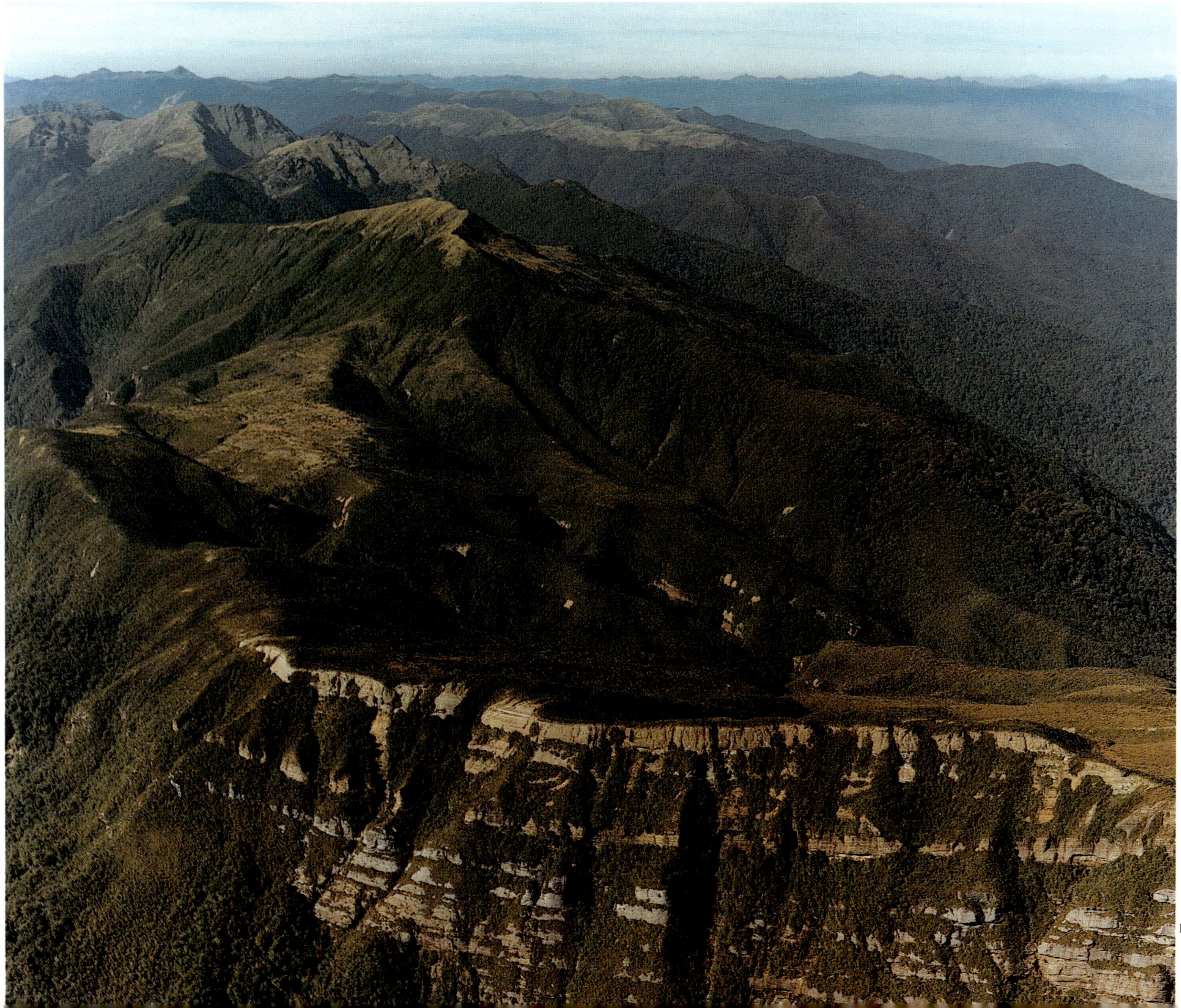

11 An impressive escarpment in the head of the Punakaiki River shows alternating bands of coal measures and mudstone, capped by a thick layer of marine sandstone. The formation dips to the east into the Pike Stream, a tributary of the Grey River (top, right); it contains thick seams of highly bituminous coal (the 'Pike River Coalfield').

The escarpment lies in the south-east corner of the park and part of the Paparoa Range (the eastern boundary of the park) can be seen extending to the north-east as far as Mt Pecksniff (top, left).

11

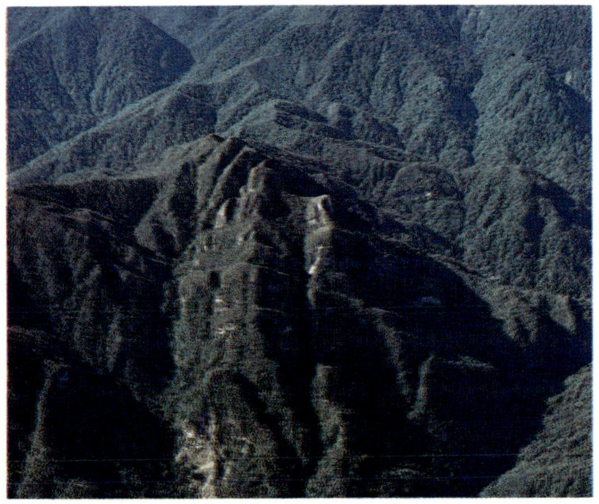

12

12 The Lone Hand, in the upper reaches of the Porarari River, is a prominent outcrop of Hawks Crag breccia (consisting of fragments of granite and sandstone in a sandy matrix) which has a distinctive, rugged outcrop pattern. This formation is of historical interest because of prospecting interest in its patchy uranium mineralisation. Note the stunted scrubby vegetation on the outcrop.

13 Gneiss rock, formed over 100 million years ago, makes up the spine of the Paparoa Range which forms the eastern boundary of the park. These hard rocks have been glaciated and the mountains exhibit glacial features like couloirs, cirques and U-shaped headwaters to the valleys draining the crest of the range. To the west, across the syncline, the Fox River canyon can be seen cutting through the coastal limestone plateau (see Fig. 6 for opposite view).

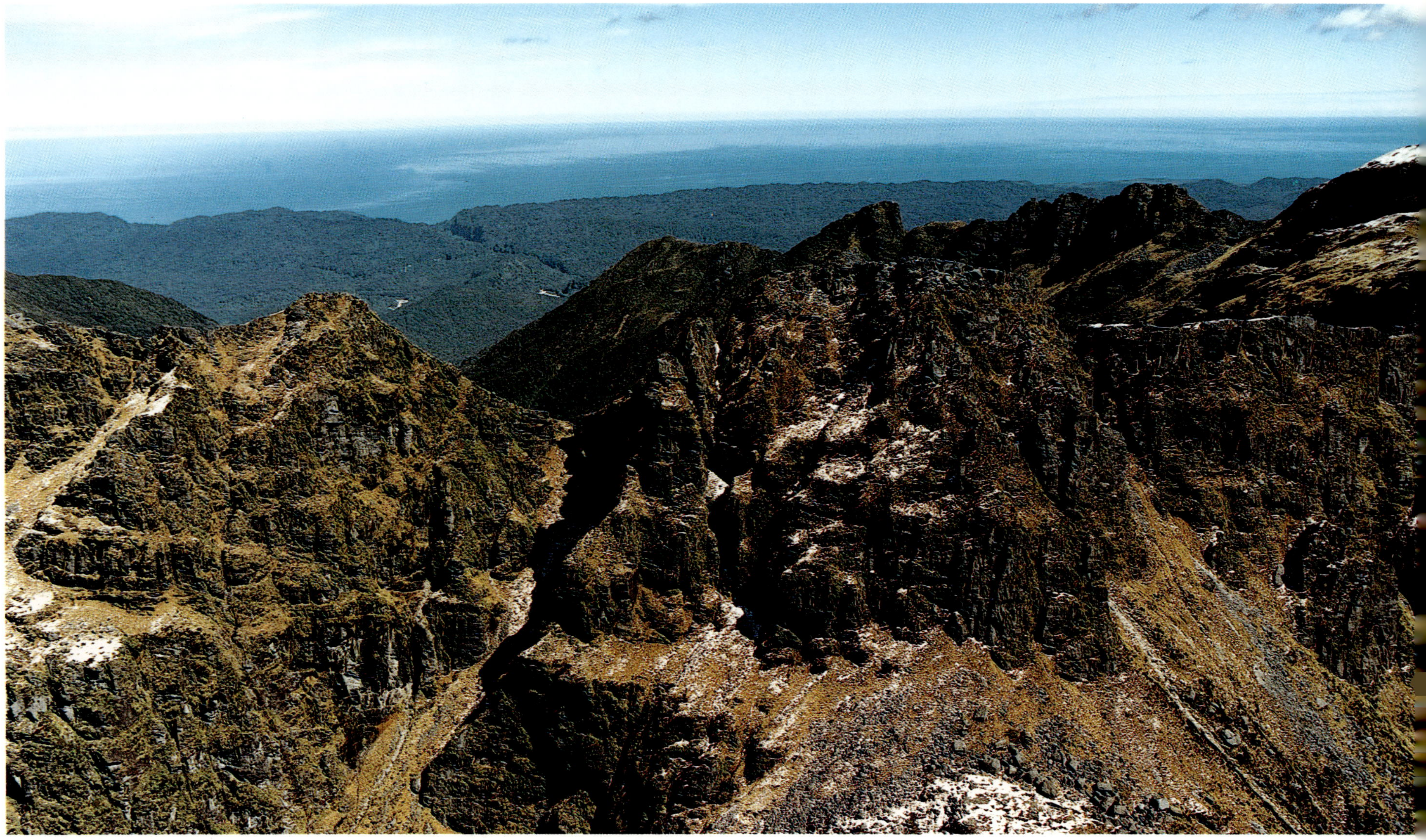

13

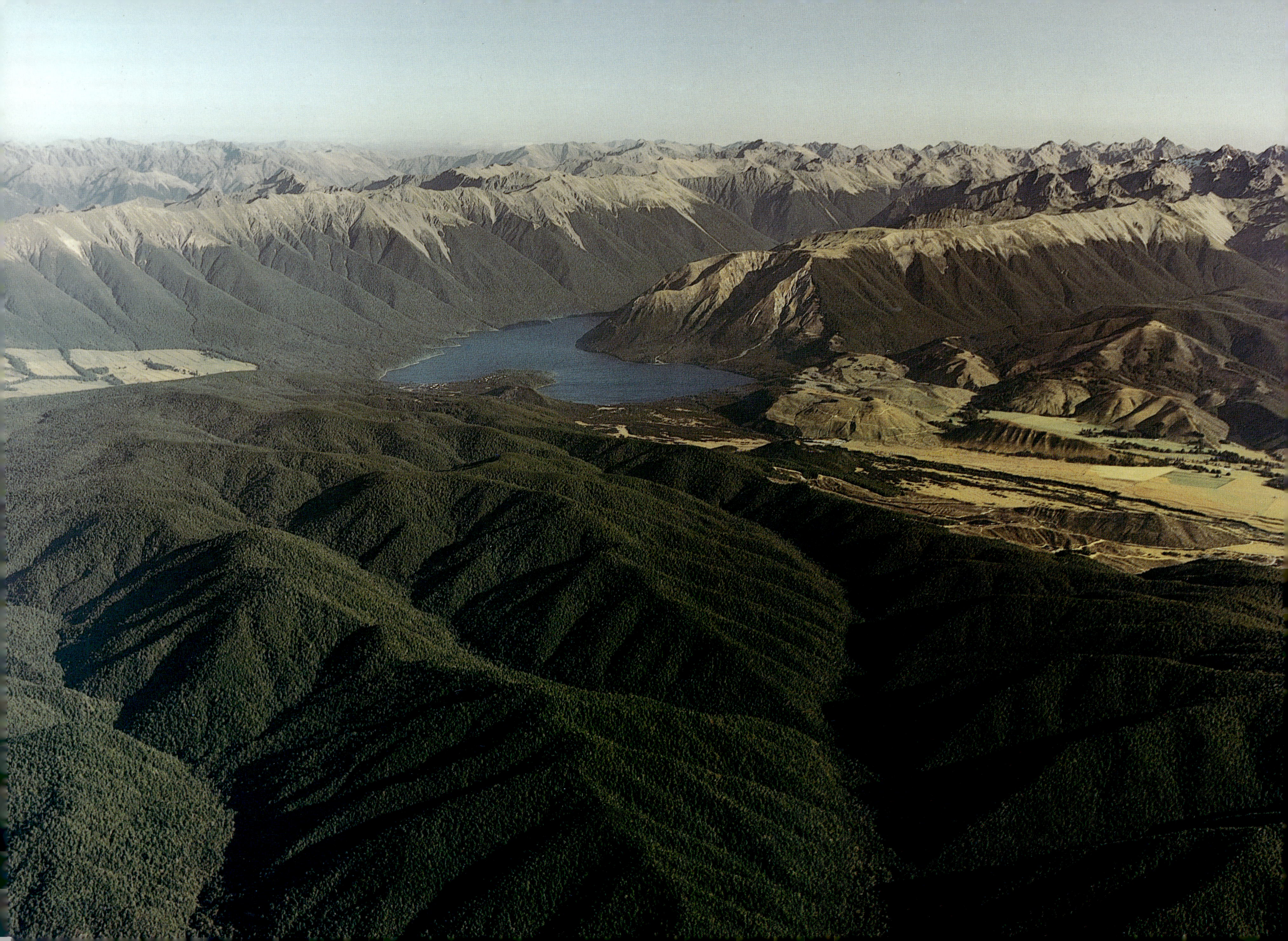

NELSON LAKES NATIONAL PARK

The name 'Nelson Lakes' refers to the two glacial troughs filled by Lakes Rotoiti and Rotoroa. The lakes lie on the north-western boundary of the park, easily accessible from the north via the Wairau and Motupiko valleys and the low Tophouse Saddle on the main divide. The lakes are significant features of the park but it is in fact dominated by mountains – a 75 km-long band of them, culminating in the Spenser Mountains north of the Lewis Pass highway. These mountains are remarkable for their symmetry, as their crests are uniform at 2200–2300 m altitude. They form a wedge 15–20 km wide between the main divide and the path of the Alpine Fault running along their western edge. The ranges are drained by five parallel tributaries of the westward-flowing Buller River, the Travers, Sabine, D'Urville, Matakitaki and Glenroy Rivers – all of which flow south to north until they cross the Alpine Fault.

The park's mountains were created by the rapid uplift of the rocks on the south-eastern side of the Alpine Fault, the most important structural feature of this northern part of the South Island. This uplift continues today, resulting in further erosion and the infilling of the river valleys draining the mountains. The Alpine Fault runs along the western flanks of the Spenser Mountains; the middle reaches of the Glenroy River flow along it, and it truncates all the parallel ranges of the north-east in a series of low points – Station Creek, Mole Saddle, Speargrass Saddle, and Tophouse Saddle.

The landscapes within the park are not fully representative of the range of ecosystems which have evolved in these greywacke mountains, because the park is confined to the wetter western slopes of the main divide. The eastward-draining Wairau, Clarence and Waiau catchments are excluded, and the bed and shoreline of Lake Tennyson is the only formally protected landform within the eastern rainshadow ecosystems. This emphasis upon mountains is indicative of the earlier pre-1981 style of national park – areas usually selected on scenic or recreational, rather than scientific, grounds.

The park encompasses few of the western glacial outwash surfaces, the deposits of the Ice Age glaciers that shaped the mountains of the park. This landscape of low dissected hills, high terraces and moraines lies to the west of the Alpine Fault: the vast deposits of Moutere Gravel; the undulating Porika surface between the headwaters of the upper Motupiko River and Lake Rotoroa; and the moraines of the late Pleistocene glaciations which are so well preserved in the Tophouse locality, the Howard valley, and the Matakitaki valley where it turns sharply to the west at the junction with Mole Stream.

WANING IMPRINT OF THE GLACIERS

There are no glaciers, or significant permanent snowfields within the park. Yet their imprint is very evident in the overall shape of the land; ice filled the five major tributaries of the Buller to a height of hundreds of metres above the present valley floors, carving them into a classic 'U'-shape and gouging out the troughs now filled by the lakes. Spurs were truncated as the ice planed off their lower limbs; excellent examples can be seen on the western slopes of the St Arnaud Range above Lake Rotoiti (opposite page) or the slopes of Mt Cann above the Glenroy River (p. 119). Hanging valleys with cirques in their heads range along the shady south-eastern slopes of the Travers Range. A huge rockfall impounds Lake Constance in the cirque in the head of the west branch of the Sabine River and scores of small alpine tarns fill the remarkably regular series of cirque basins at the head of the south-eastern slopes of Robert Ridge (including Angelus Basin) and the St Arnaud Range. These basins form popular winter ski fields.

To the summer visitor the impression gained from the air, or from a high vantage point, is one of a maze of grey scree-covered peaks above steep forest slopes and narrow valleys. The geology of the park is very uniform – the early Mesozoic greywackes (metamorphosed to schist in the south-west).

It is the characteristic jointing pattern of the greywacke rock (allowing water to enter, then freeze, fragmenting the rock) which has led to the proliferation of screes that so dominate the landscape above treeline. Indeed, the rocky peaks stand like derelict spires above an apron of fallen masonry. While it has been too easy in the past to attribute this rock erosion on a grand scale to the influence of human and wild animal interference, the causes are more complex and to a large extent natural. Earthquakes (such as the one which dammed Lake Constance, p. 117) and the melting of glaciers have contributed, by causing slumping and ridge rents (p. 115). Since the retreat of the glaciers, there has also been a steady process of valley modification. Rivers have down-cut, transforming the profile of the valley from a 'U' into a 'V' shape; rock debris has accumulated as fans and been washed down valley to form prominent deltas, not only in the two major lakes but also in the smaller Lakes Constance and Tennyson. Most of the screes are still perched above treeline and are not actively contributing to the sediment load of the rivers, but those that have broken through to the valley floor spill out as debris fans which further soften the steep walls of the formerly-glacial valleys.

Nelson Lakes National Park has many similarities to its Canterbury neighbour, Arthur's Pass National Park (Chapter 5). Neither park can be considered as spectacular as the great southern parks, but together they protect the range of glacial and post-glacial landforms in the greywacke mountains of the main divide in the northern half of the South Island.

1 Lake Rotoiti lies at the northern end of Nelson Lakes National Park. It is the smaller of the two lakes (the other is Lake Rotoroa to the west) from which the park takes its name. This view, looking south from near the junction of the Rainy River and Prospector Creek, shows the abrupt change in relief between the hinterland of steep greywacke mountains and the more rounded landscape of huge piles of gravel on this side of the lake outlet. The boundary between the two landscapes is the Alpine Fault, which runs along Speargrass Creek at the foot of Robert Ridge (top right, and Fig. 2) across the lake and up the Black Valley Stream (the cleared land at the foot of the St Arnaud Range, top left). Note the smooth triangular bush-covered faces of the truncated spurs on the north-west facing slopes, especially the St Arnaud Range – the effect of ice filling the valleys during glaciations. These glaciations bulldozed up huge quantities of rock debris as moraines, some of which was subsequently washed out onto the plains by melt waters. The forest-covered 'herringbone' spurs in the foreground are part of the oldest outwash deposits – the Moutere Gravel of early Pleistocene age. Later deposits, representing five major glacial advances during the late Pleistocene, can be identified in the cleared country around the upper part of the Buller valley (centre, right).

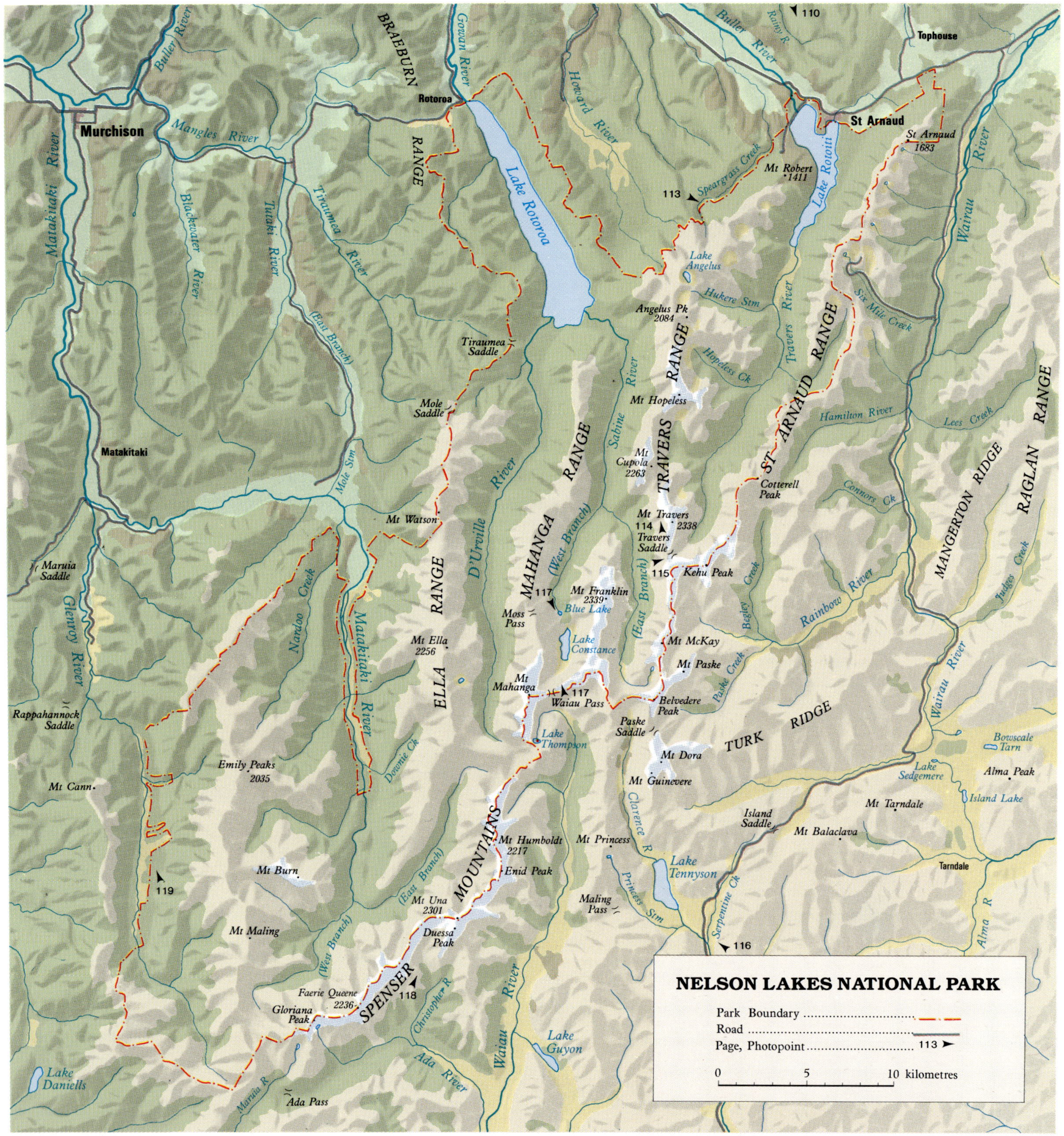

2 The north-east trending Alpine Fault follows Speargrass Creek (foreground), across Lake Rotoiti, through Tophouse Saddle (one of the lowest points on the main divide), and down the Wairau valley (centre, distance). The north-eastern boundary of the park approximately follows this faultline, from Tophouse Saddle to Mole Saddle between the D'Urville and Matakitaki Rivers. There are numerous instances of ground displacement along this fault; one of them can be seen in the foreground, where the western side of a terminal moraine has been pushed up.

The headwaters of Speargrass Creek illustrate the mix of glacial and post-glacial erosional landforms that make up the park. Screes of greywacke detritus from the north-western slopes of Robert Ridge (centre, left) have partly covered moraines in the head of the stream. This summer view to the south-east shows the Angelus Ridge and the scree-covered peaks around the St Arnaud Range and Turk Ridge in the upper Wairau; none of these mountains are high enough to carry permanent snowfields.

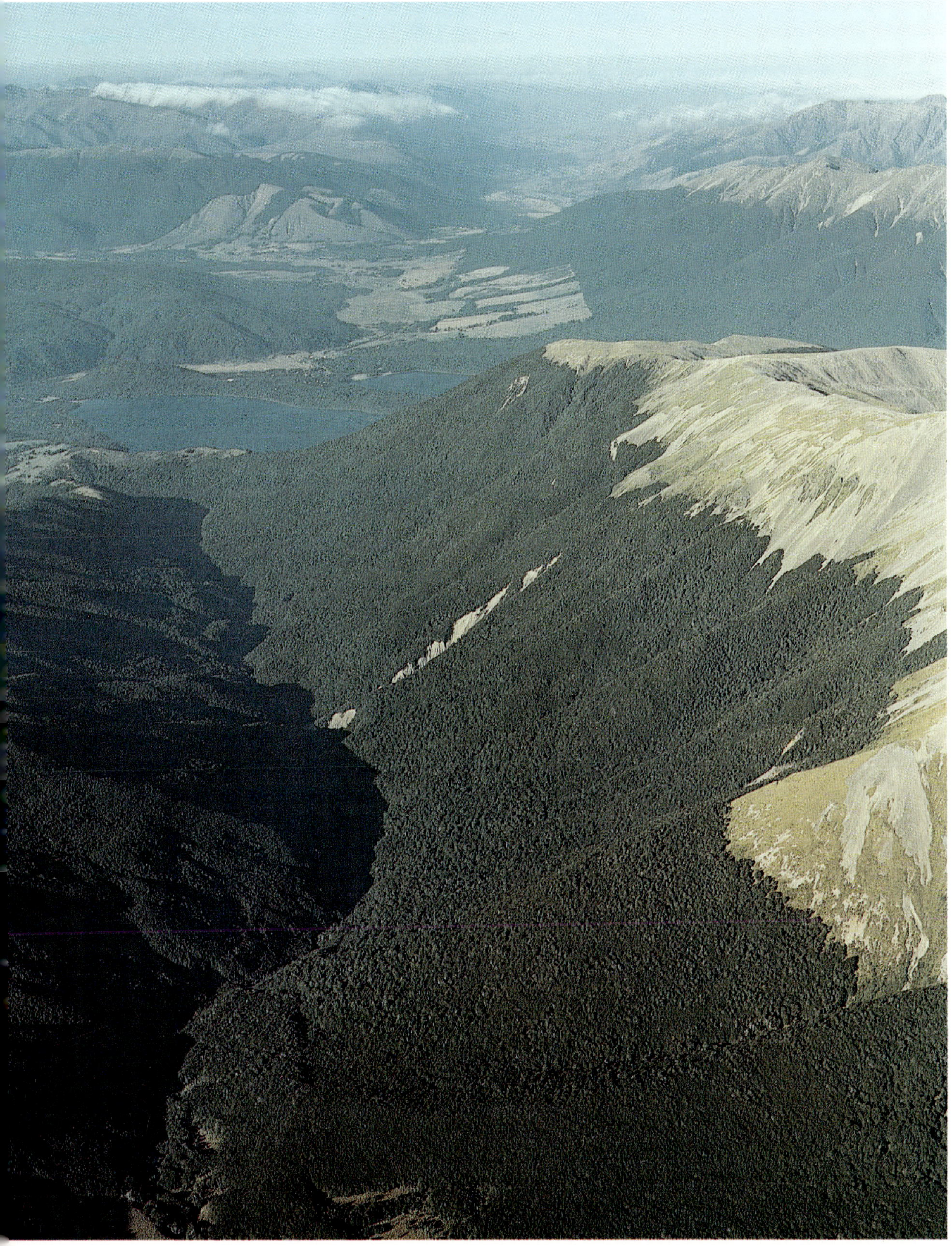

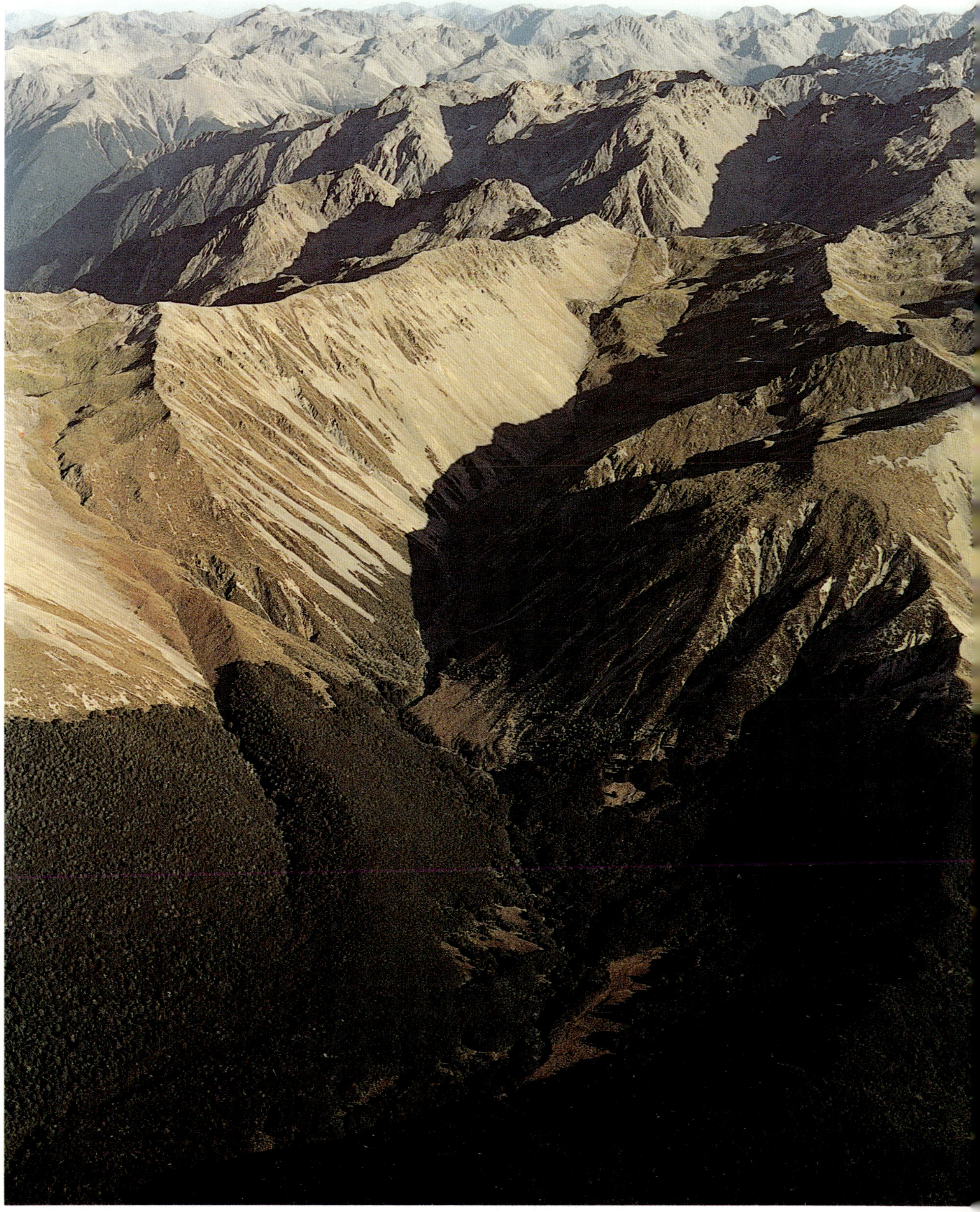

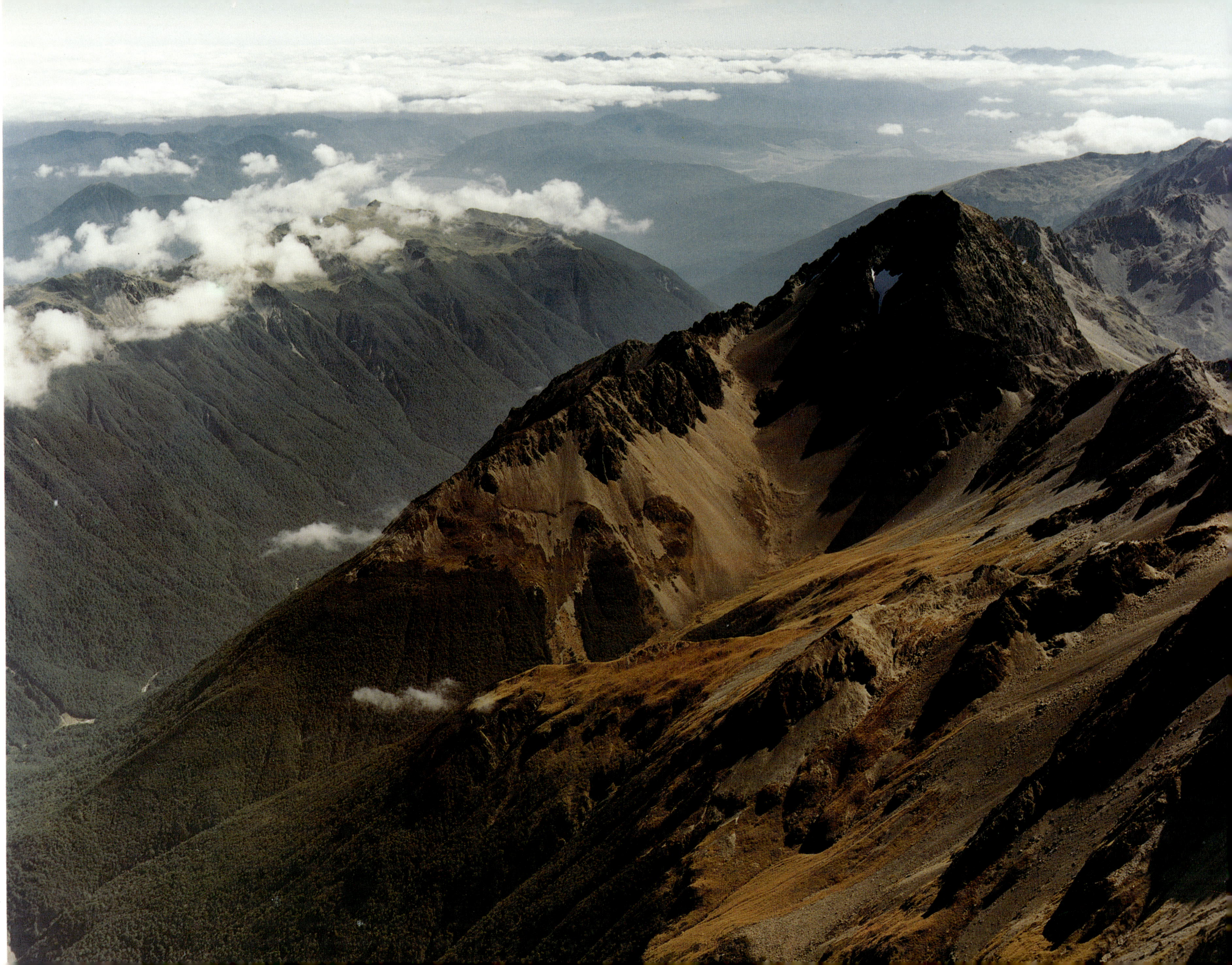

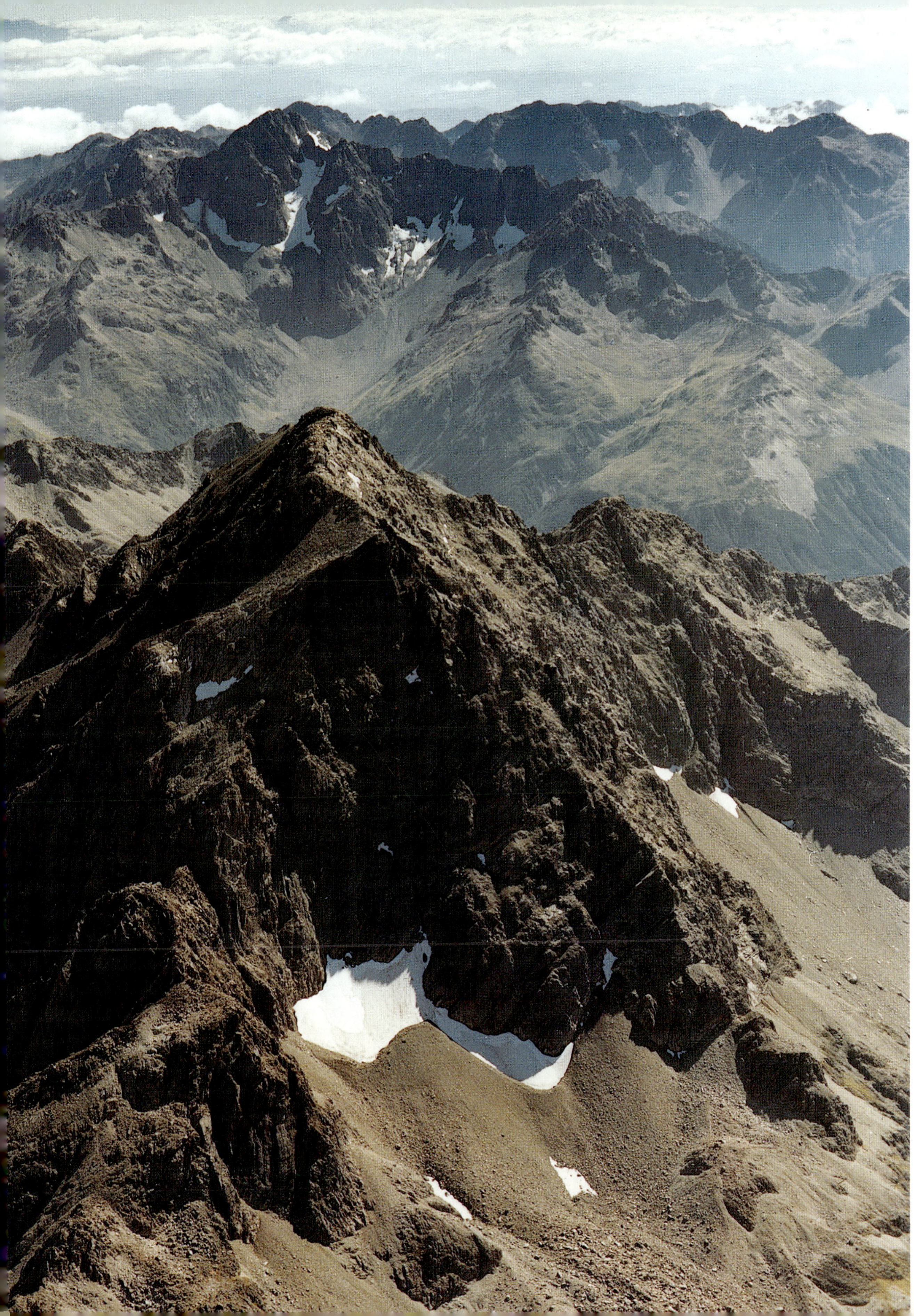

3

3 Mt Travers (2338 m, right foreground) is the highest peak on the Travers Range which extends from Travers Saddle to the north through Mt Cupola (centre) and Mt Hopeless (right distance). The Sabine River (left) flows to Lake Rotoroa which is partly obscured by the scattered clouds over the Mahanga Range. Steeply-dipping greywacke forming the peaks is continually fretted away by freeze/thaw activity which leads to extensive scree slopes.

4 The head of the Travers valley is a particularly good example of a glacier-carved U-shaped valley. In this view, looking eastwards from Travers Saddle across Begley Saddle on the St Arnaud Range, a prominent tussock-covered bench on the eastern side of the valley marks an earlier glacier level. Greywacke screes extend down onto the edge of this bench. The older and more stable screes are a reddish-purple tinge from lichens which are gradually colonising them. Below the bench, beech forest has colonised the steeper lower slopes of the valley which were probably carved in the last glaciation.

Tarns and small mounds of moraine are scattered over Travers Saddle (foreground). The small escarpment (running across the western slope below the saddle) is a very good example of a ridge rent, formed by the partial collapse under gravity of this part of the mountain slope.

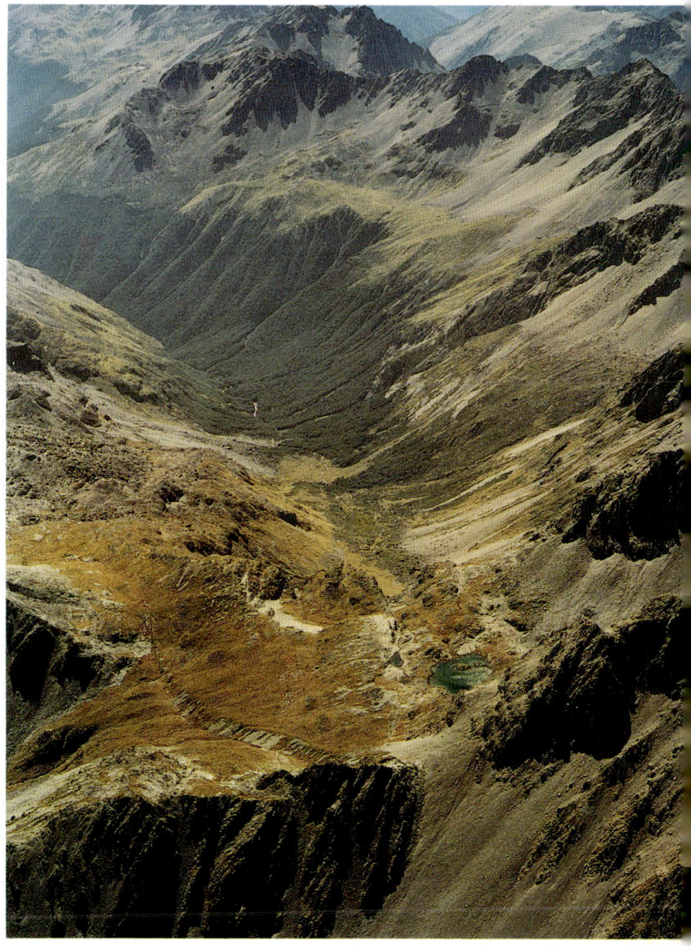

4

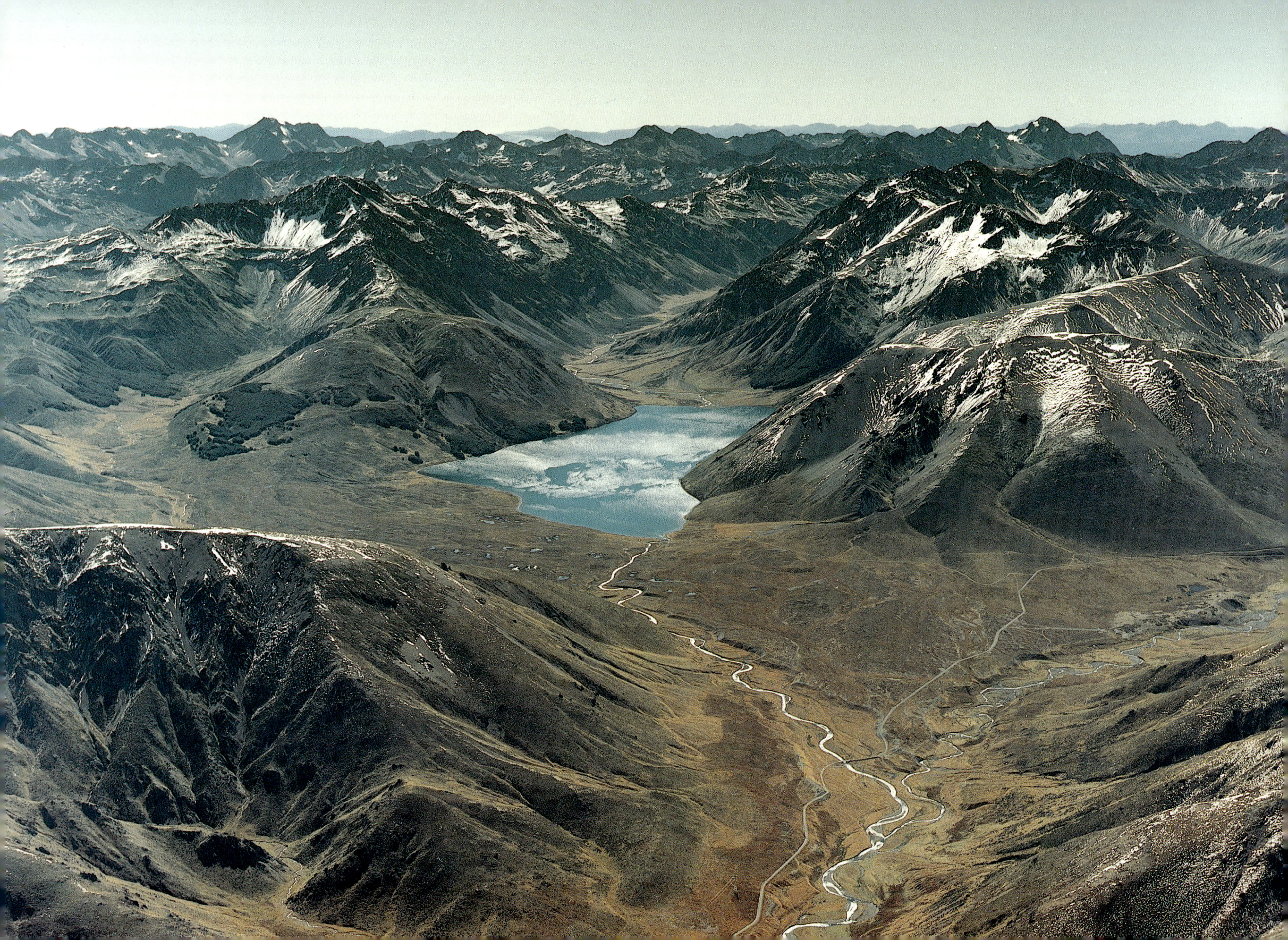

5 Lake Tennyson, in the headwaters of the Clarence River (foreground), lies on the eastern margin of Nelson Lakes National Park.

The ragged, greywacke peaks of the park are ranged along the skyline, from Mt Ella (left, distance) to Mts Franklin and Travers (right, distance). The foreground slopes of the St James Range (left) and the Crimea Range (right) are much gentler and the summits are smoother, probably because uplift has not been as rapid as further north and west. The Awatere Fault which branches off the Alpine Fault trends south-west to north-east across the centre of this landscape. Erosion from this and other small faults has produced the valleys extending from Princess Stream (centre, left) to Serpentine Creek (centre, right).

The low, broad terminal moraine impounding Lake Tennyson is studded with dozens of small tarns, the kettleholes left by the melting of blocks of ice as the 'Clarence Glacier' retreated. The upper Clarence valley (above the lake) and the slopes of Princess Stream show signs of post-glacial modification of 'U'-shaped glacial valleys as screes and slumping of the slopes tend to convert the valleys to a 'V' profile. Because this eastern landscape is in the rainshadow of the main divide, the glacial geomorphology around Lake Tennyson (annual precipitation less than 1400 mm) has not been greatly modified by water erosion. By comparison with the wet forested Glenroy valley (Fig. 9) on the western side of the park where annual precipitation is 3000–4000 mm, the deforested landscape here is only weakly dissected; there is no evidence of recent build-up of sediment on the old floodplain of the Clarence River.

6 Blue Lake (foreground) and Lake Constance lie in the headwaters of the west branch of the Sabine River. Lake Constance, at 1300 m altitude, is impounded behind a natural dam caused by a huge rockfall from the eastern slopes of Franklin Ridge (left); the lake drains underground to a spring which is just visible in the bush to the right of the top of Blue Lake. Note the rock debris in the streambeds coming down from the slopes of the Mahanga Range (right) and spreading around both sides of the dam.

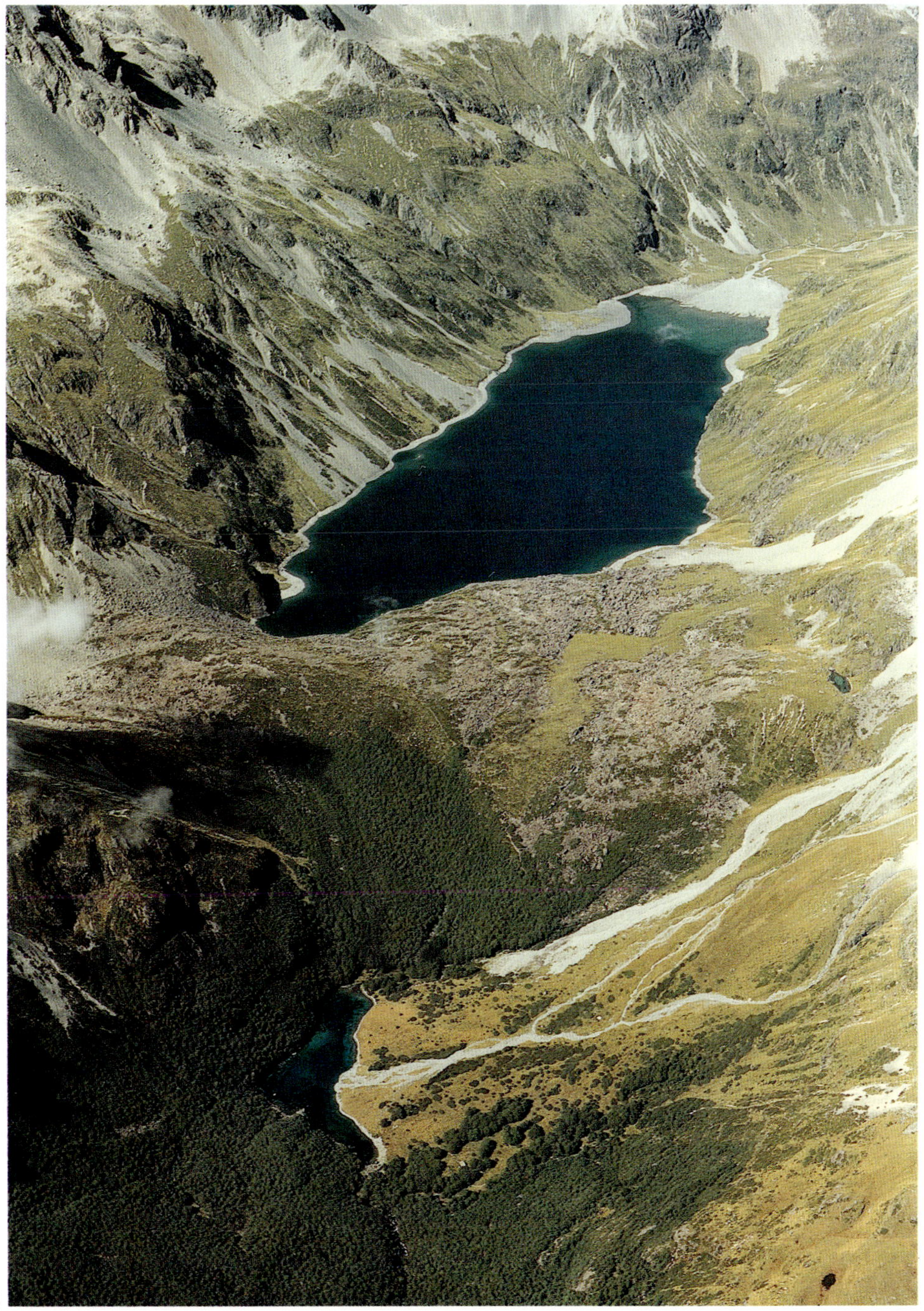

6

7 Three lake levels can be seen in this opposite view looking north-north-east into the head of the west branch of the Sabine River. The alpine tarn in the foreground is tucked in a cirque under the crest of the main divide; the other two lakes are Lake Constance impounded behind the rock dam and the lower end of Blue Lake. The Mahanga Range on the skyline is a watershed with the D'Urville valley. The head of Lake Constance is being infilled by fan deposits and a small delta.

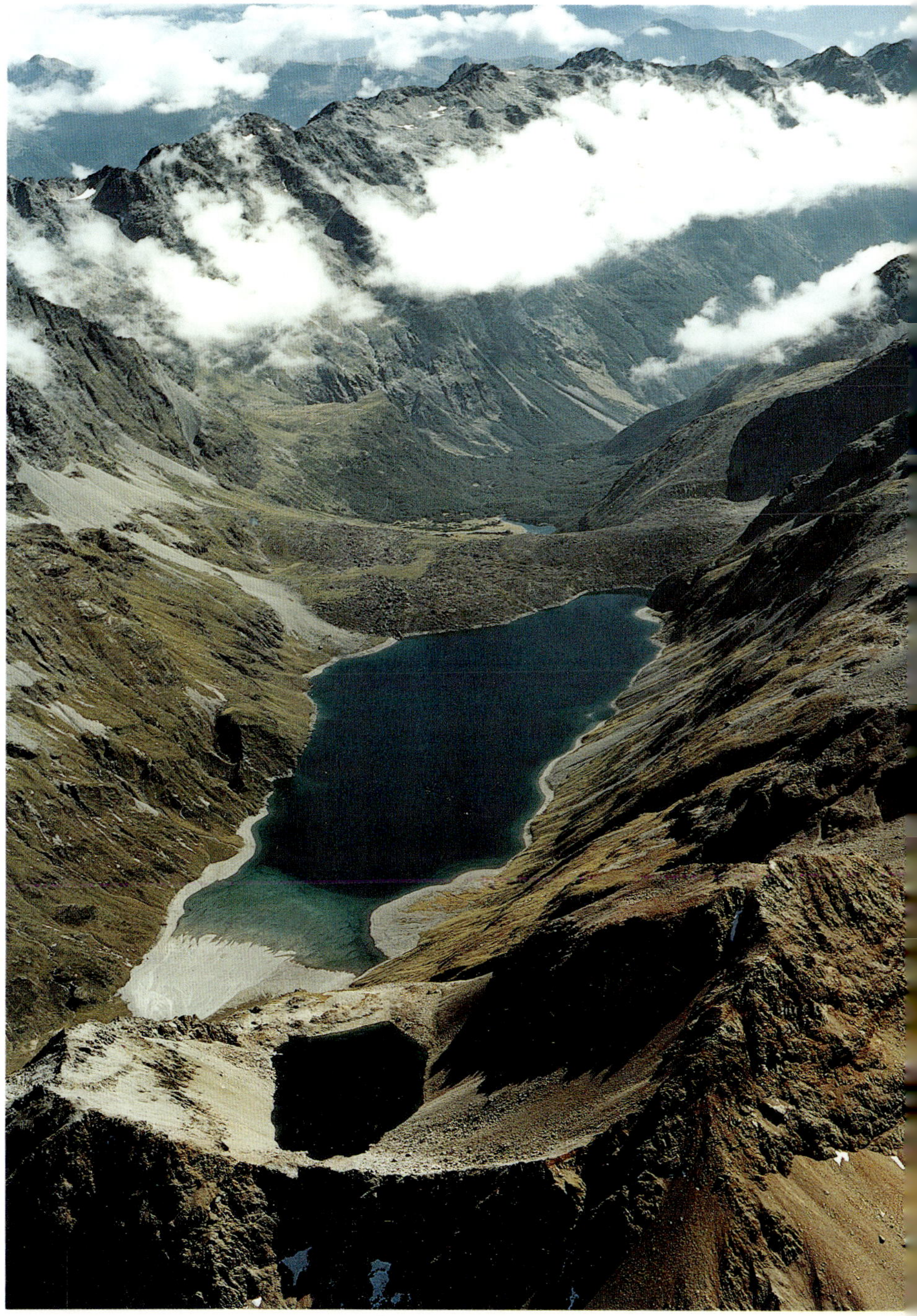

7

9 The Glenroy River in the south-western corner of the park flows northwards along the Alpine Fault. The fault separates the more resistant (to erosion) diorite rocks of the Rotoroa Igneous Complex (such as Mt Cann, centre left) from the schist making up the slopes on the eastern side of the valley. The wide valley floor and the triangular shape of the truncated spurs on both sides of the valley are the result of past glaciations. Contrast the dissection pattern in the two different rock types; the steep diorite slopes carry deep and narrow gullies, whereas the less resistant schist slopes are much more dissected. Erosion of the schist slopes has given rise to a series of coalescing low-angle fans which have pushed the Glenroy River westward against the igneous rocks. These fans are now largely inactive and, except for the beds of the two streams and the floodplain of the river, are covered in beech forest.

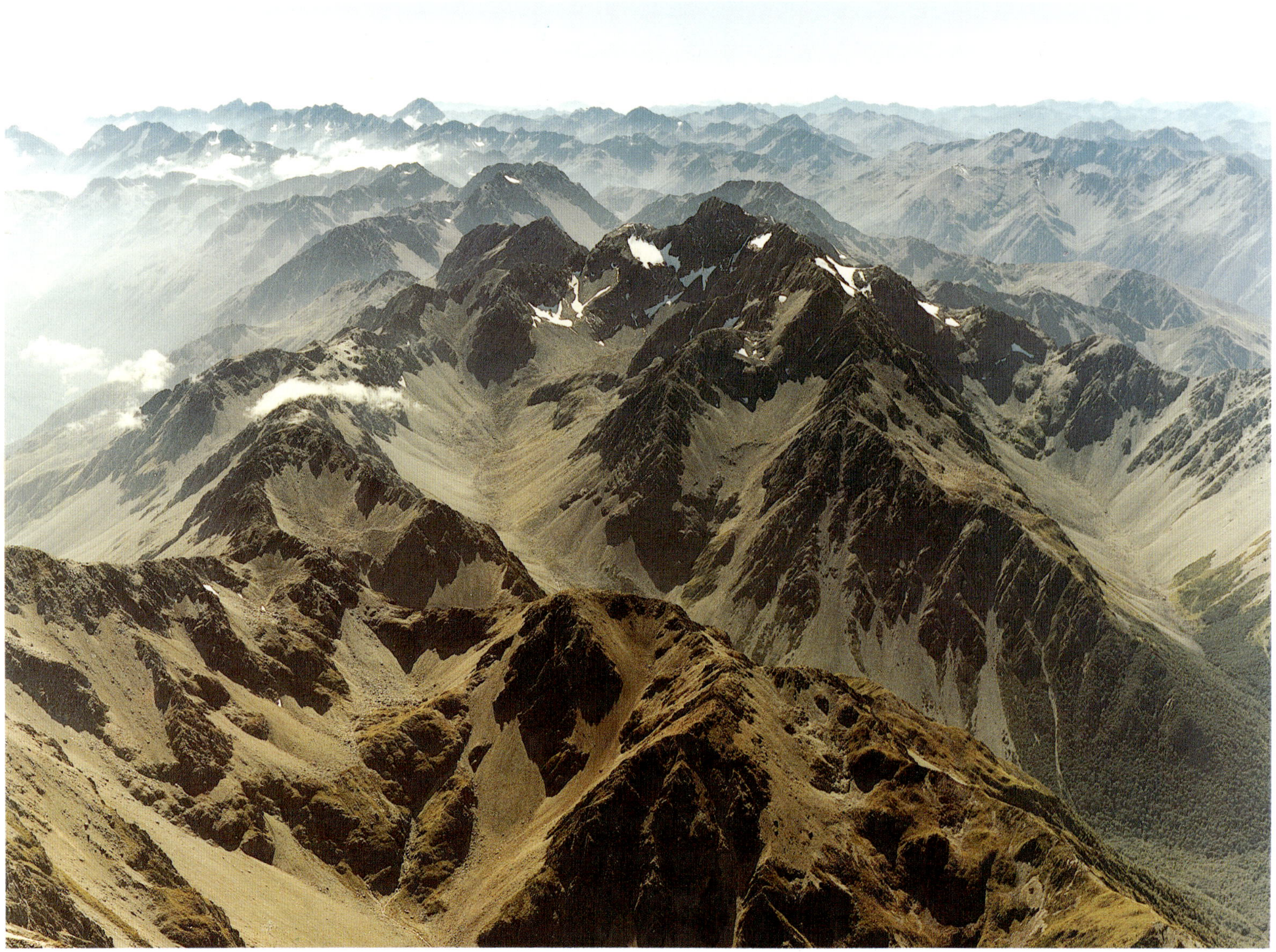

8

8 The Spenser Mountains, at the southern end of Nelson Lakes National Park, form the Main Divide between the Matakitaki (left) and Waiau (right) Rivers. In this view across the headwaters of the Christopher River and Mt Una, the maze of 2200–2300 m high peaks extend north-eastwards to the skyline ridges of the Travers and St Arnaud Ranges. The glacial landforms have been largely modified by greywacke detritus derived from the crumbling peaks; this detritus has filled the cirque basins and U-shaped valleys with screes which are inhospitable for the growth of most subalpine plants.

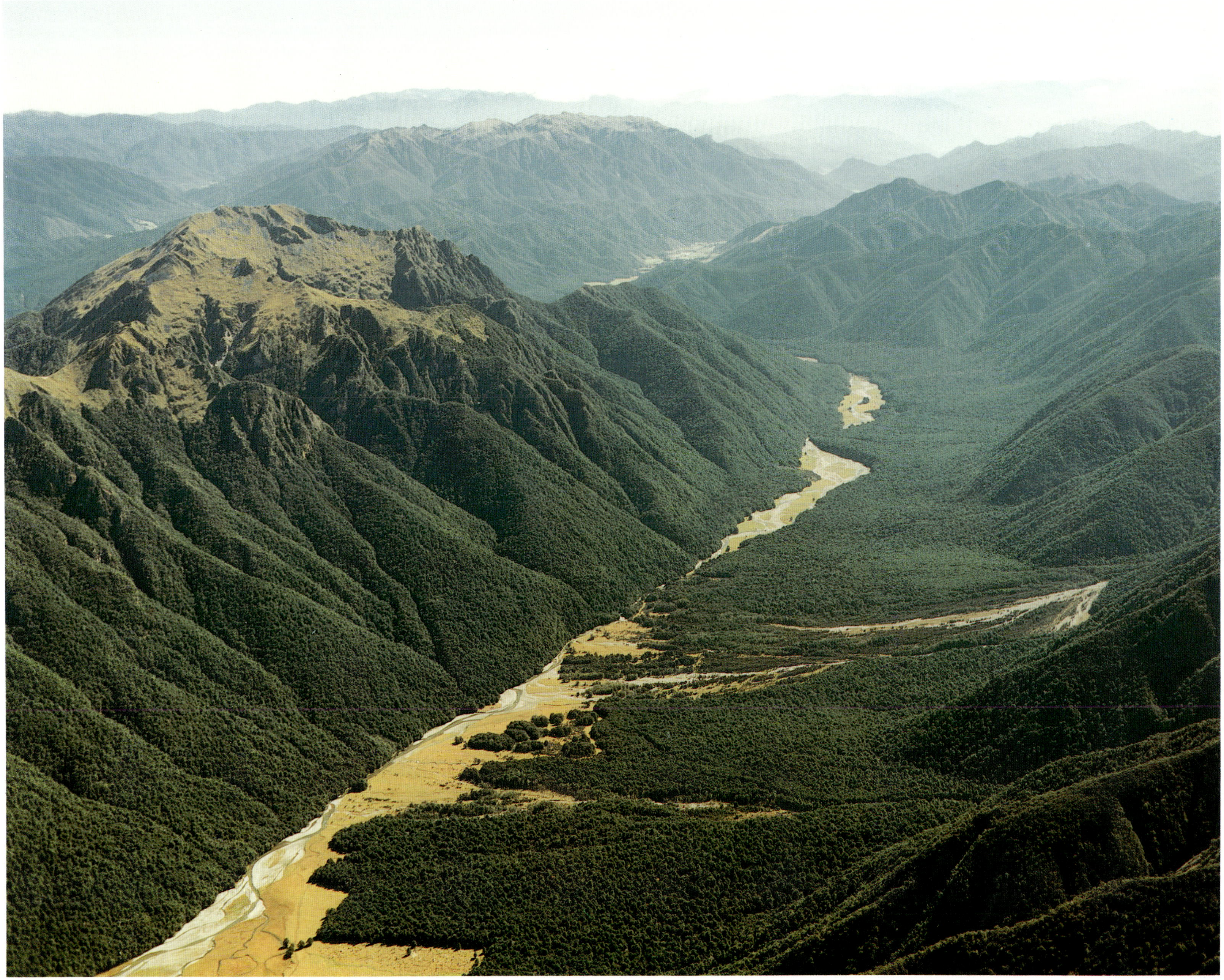

9

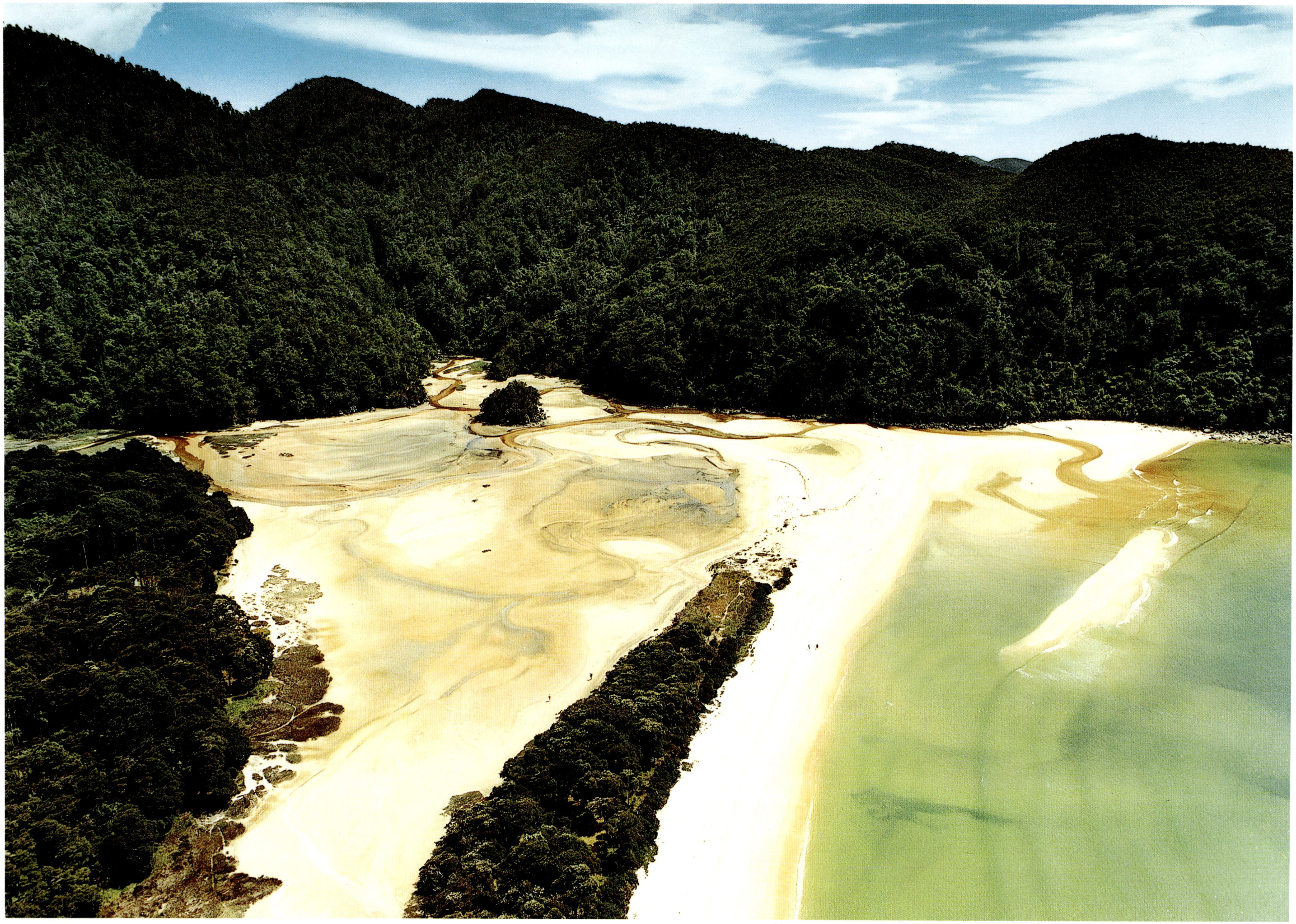

1

ABEL TASMAN NATIONAL PARK

Abel Tasman National Park is New Zealand's smallest national park (22 500 ha), but it contains some remarkable contrasts in geology and landforms. The park extends across the northern part of the Pikikiruna Range, a rugged hilly promontory which separates Tasman Bay from Golden Bay in north-west Nelson.

There are three main rock types within the park. The coastal zone and interior in the north and east consist of Lower Cretaceous age granite. In the west and south-west, the tableland is made up of Ordovician age marble, and Devonian age diorite and gabbro around Mts Pisgah and Evans.

COASTAL ZONE

The granite has weathered to create a distinctive coastline of rocky headlands alternating with sandy beaches. Granite weathers differentially, with the rocks breaking down along joints, leading to the formation of rectangular blocks. These blocks then have their corners rounded and cracks widened through further weathering. The process leads to a variety of landforms, including:

- The huge vertical joints at Separation Point.
- Wave-cut platforms around a pedestal of more resistant rock. An excellent example is Pinnacle Island off Sandfly Bay. The regular wetting and drying of the rock by the tides accelerates the fracture of the granite just above low tide mark; the rock above this point is continually fretted away, leaving a steep-sided pedestal above the platform.
- Distinctive landmarks such as Cottage Loaf Rock or Split Apple Rock, caused by the rounding off of the rectangular blocks of granite.

On the north-western coastline softer limestone (Oligocene age) has been eroded to leave steep cliffs dropping straight to the waters edge without the rock platforms so characteristic of the granite. Best known examples are the Tata Islands off Abel Tasman Point, and Taupo Point north of Wainui Inlet.

The popular beaches of the park often occur on the curving landward end of the series of semi-circular bays which indent the coastline. Some of these bays, such as Torrent Bay, Bark Bay, Awaroa Inlet and Wainui Inlet, were caused by the sea flooding the lower parts of the former valleys (particularly if the whole mass of granite was gradually tilted to the east). Some bays, especially Wainui and Awaroa Inlets and Bark and Sandfly Bays, have prominent sand spits across their mouths. The sand comes from the granite hinterland as well as the coastal zone itself. Quartz tends to dominate in the whiter beaches and feldspars in the attractive golden beaches.

The characteristic sand spits in the park are formed by the deposition of sand in the deltas of the streams, together with the very pronounced direction of the currents along the coastline. In addition, the tidal range along the park's coastline is one of the highest in New Zealand (3–4 m), so there is plenty of wave energy to lift the sand into suspension and produce a 'longshore drift'. The variety of coastal sand landforms is intriguing : Awaroa Inlet has an intricate network of bars and spits including a succession of beach ridges; the outlet of Falls River in Sandfly Bay seems to oscillate regularly from one end of the spit to the other; and longshore drift has joined the limestone 'island' of Taupo Point to the northern coastline by a short tombolo – another type of sand spit which, in this case provides a neck of dry land.

RUGGED INTERIOR

To the west and south of the coastal zone, the granite hinterland rises sharply through the rugged interior to a tableland at 800–1000 m altitude. There is a pronounced parallel grain to much of the landscape, with most of the streams between Marahau and Awaroa Inlet running north-west to south-east and following small faults or fracture zones in the granite.

Further to the west, around the northern and eastern rim of the summit tableland, rise the main rivers of the park – Wainui, Awapoto, Awaroa, Falls, Torrent, and Marahau. These rivers have followed the route of least resistance, plunging through rapids and waterfalls in a series of gorges notorious for their difficulty of navigation. Just as on the coast, the cascading water has helped weather the granite into a fantastic jumble of huge smooth boulders and steep-walled pools.

One particularly interesting landscape in the granite part of the tableland is Moa Park, a narrow, forest-fringed tussock enclave in the head of Table Creek, a tributary of Awaroa River. With its vegetation and highly leached acidic and infertile soils, Moa Park resembles the larger moorlands of the Gouland Downs and Mt Arthur Tablelands in North-west Nelson Forest Park.

KARST LANDSCAPE OF THE TABLELAND

In the south-west corner of the park, the granite suddenly gives way to marble. The result is one of the most interesting landforms in our national park system – the karst landscape of the Canaan basin and the Takaka Hill highway over the southern end of the Pikikiruna Range.

Most streams on this part of the tableland disappear into sinkholes like Harwoods Hole (at 176 m the deepest vertical shaft in the country). Further south around the Takaka Hill, many of the streams resurge 500 m below in an entirely different catchment, the north branch of the Riwaka River in Riwaka Scenic Reserve. The waters of the Gorge River resurgence are also linked (via the underground drainage of the Takaka River) to the famous Waikoropupu Springs 4 km to the west of Takaka township. With the recent discoveries of the full extent of the huge Nettlebed Cave system on the Arthur Range south of the tableland, it is apparent that the band of marble mountains culminating in Abel Tasman National Park may contain the oldest, longest and deepest caves in New Zealand.

1 Bark Bay is a perfect example, in miniature, of the sandy bays along the granite coastline of Abel Tasman National Park. Streams draining the steep hinterland have carried down grains of quartz and other more resistant minerals, and wave action has eroded much of the coastal granite to sand-sized particles. The long-shore drift of the sea has fashioned this sand into sand spits and a shallow estuary, through which the brown humus-stained Huffam Stream meanders at low tide to the northern end of the bay. Further evidence for the long-shore drift can be seen in the series of shallow sand bars in the water (bottom, right).

The vegetation reflects both the environment and the impact of human activity. Salt marsh plants occur around the shallow fringe of the estuary and tall kanuka forest on the spit and the sheltered flats at bottom left. The forest in the gully slopes at the head of the bay is a mixture of black, hard and silver beech, but the devastating effect of previous fires can be seen in the regenerating forest on the drier ridges.

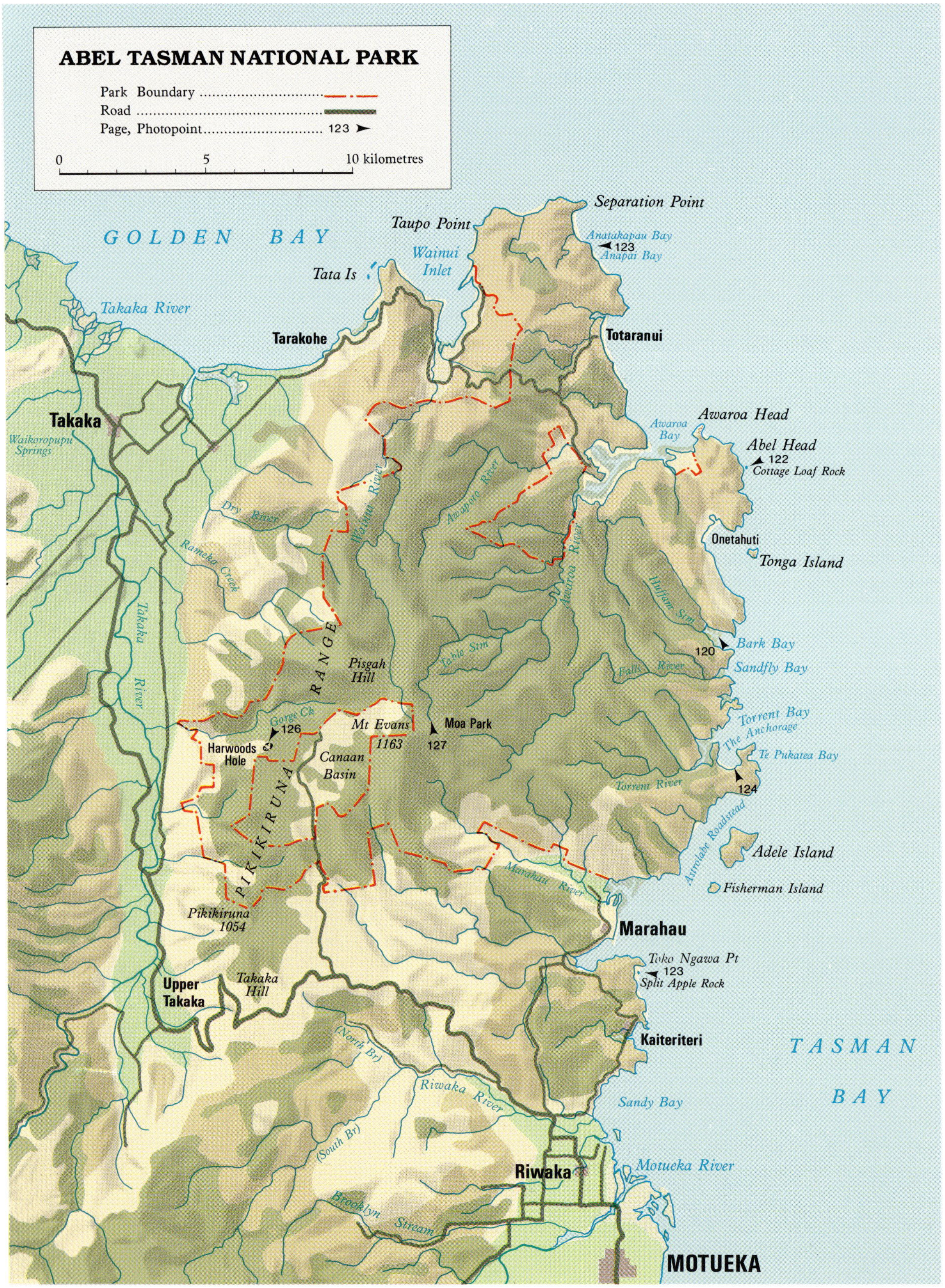

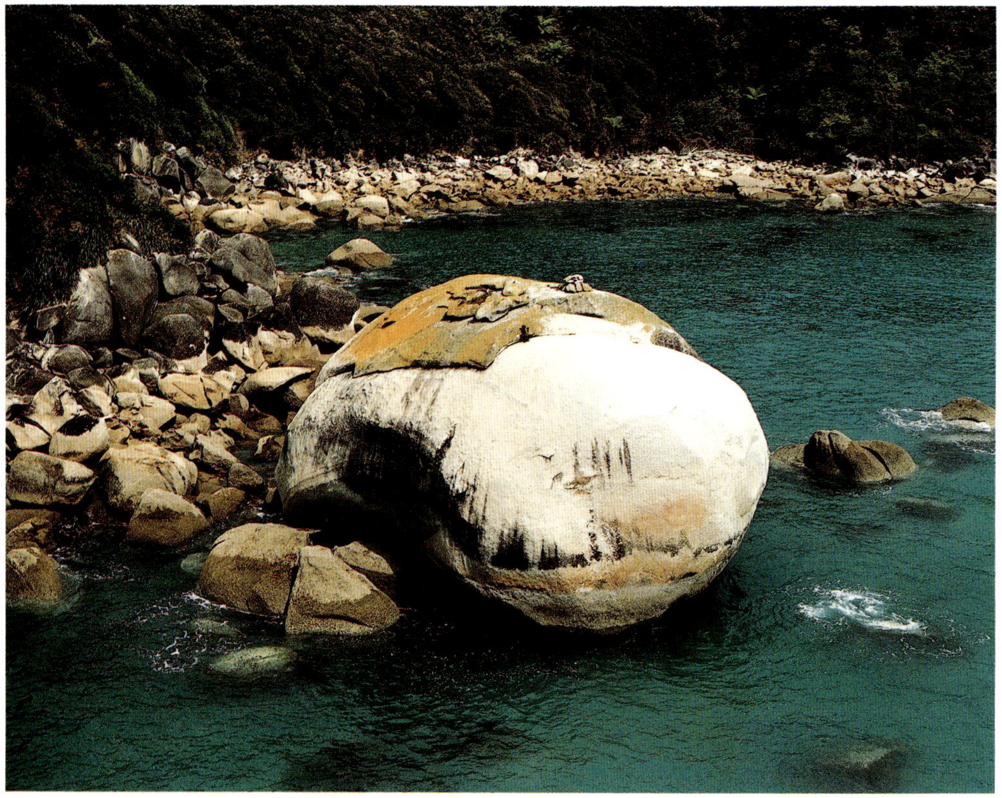

2

2 Cottage Loaf Rock, near Abel Head, is one of the distinctive landmarks of the coastline. This huge rock well demonstrates the process of 'exfoliation', whereby an outer shell of granite cracks and weathers, and then flakes away leaving a fresh, smooth, generally rounded surface. The cap of yellow lichen-covered rock is a remnant of an older surface of the rock which has yet to flake away. Note the lack of any *in situ* granite; here wave action has reduced the coastal granite to boulders.

3 The coastline of Abel Tasman National Park is a succession of rocky headlands and sandy beaches; Anatakapau Bay and its headlands (near Separation Point) are typical examples. A prominent set of vertical joints can be seen in the granite of the headland extending out towards the viewer. The combined effects of sun, rain and wind enlarge these cracks along the joints in the rock. The ebb and flow of the tides accelerates the weathering leaving a pedestal of sunbleached and salt-encrusted rock above high-water mark and a darker wave-cut platform below.

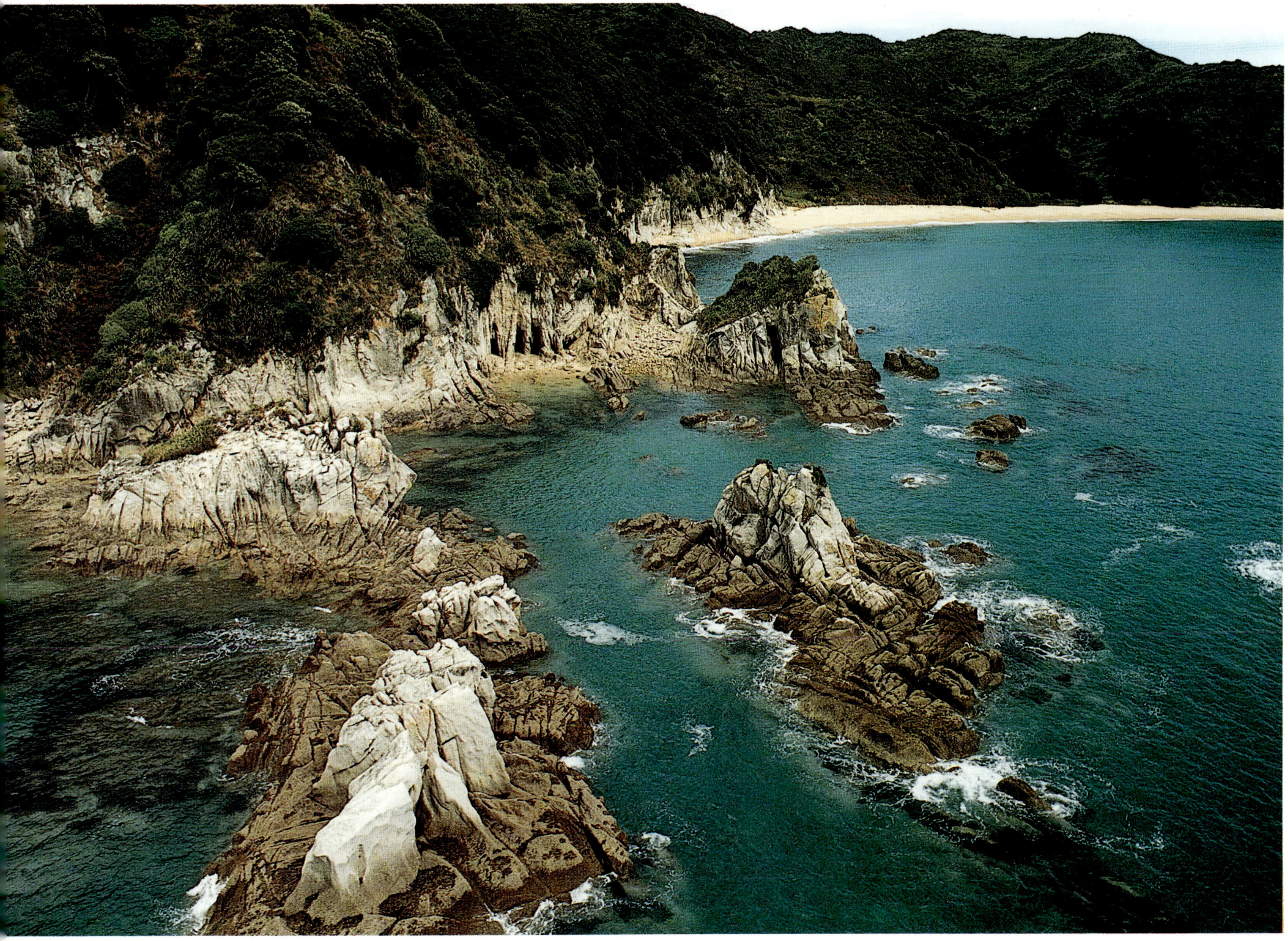

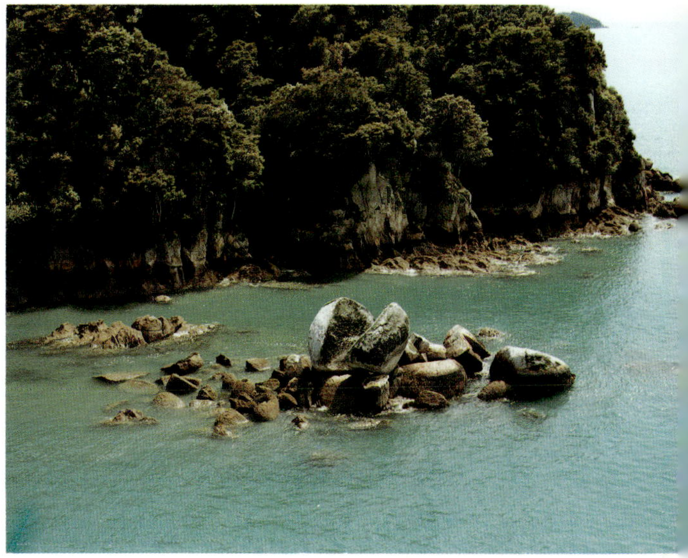

4

4 Split Apple Rock off Toko Ngawa Point near the southern end of the park is a well-known coastal feature in Tasman Bay. Exfoliation has given rise to a group of near-spherical rocks, the largest of which has subsequently split in two along a joint in the granite. Note the wavecut platform and weathered cliffs beyond Split Apple Rock.

next page

5 Looking across Anchorage Bay towards Torrent Bay and the indented coastline of the park extending north towards Totaranui and Separation Point. The settlement of Torrent Bay is partly obscured behind the headland on the left centre and in the distance Pinnacle Island and Tonga Island. Te Pukatea Bay is at bottom right.

The vegetation is a mosaic of the original forest in the moister gullies and some coastal cliffs, but the ravages of fires (from pre-European times to the present) have left their imprint on this landscape. Beech (black, hard and silver), kamahi and rimu predominate in the forest, and manuka/kanuka forest is attempting to recolonise the burnt ridges.

3

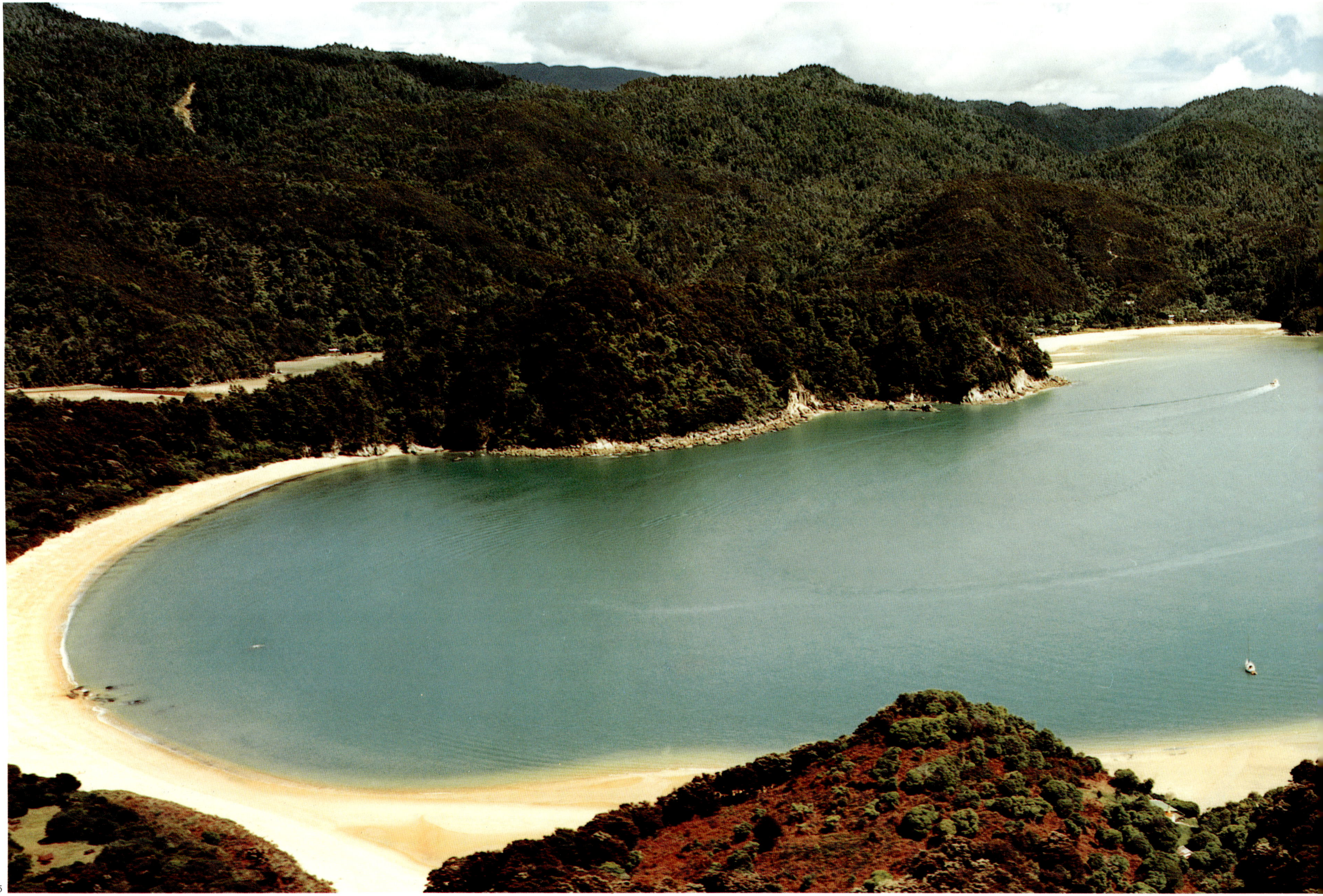

5

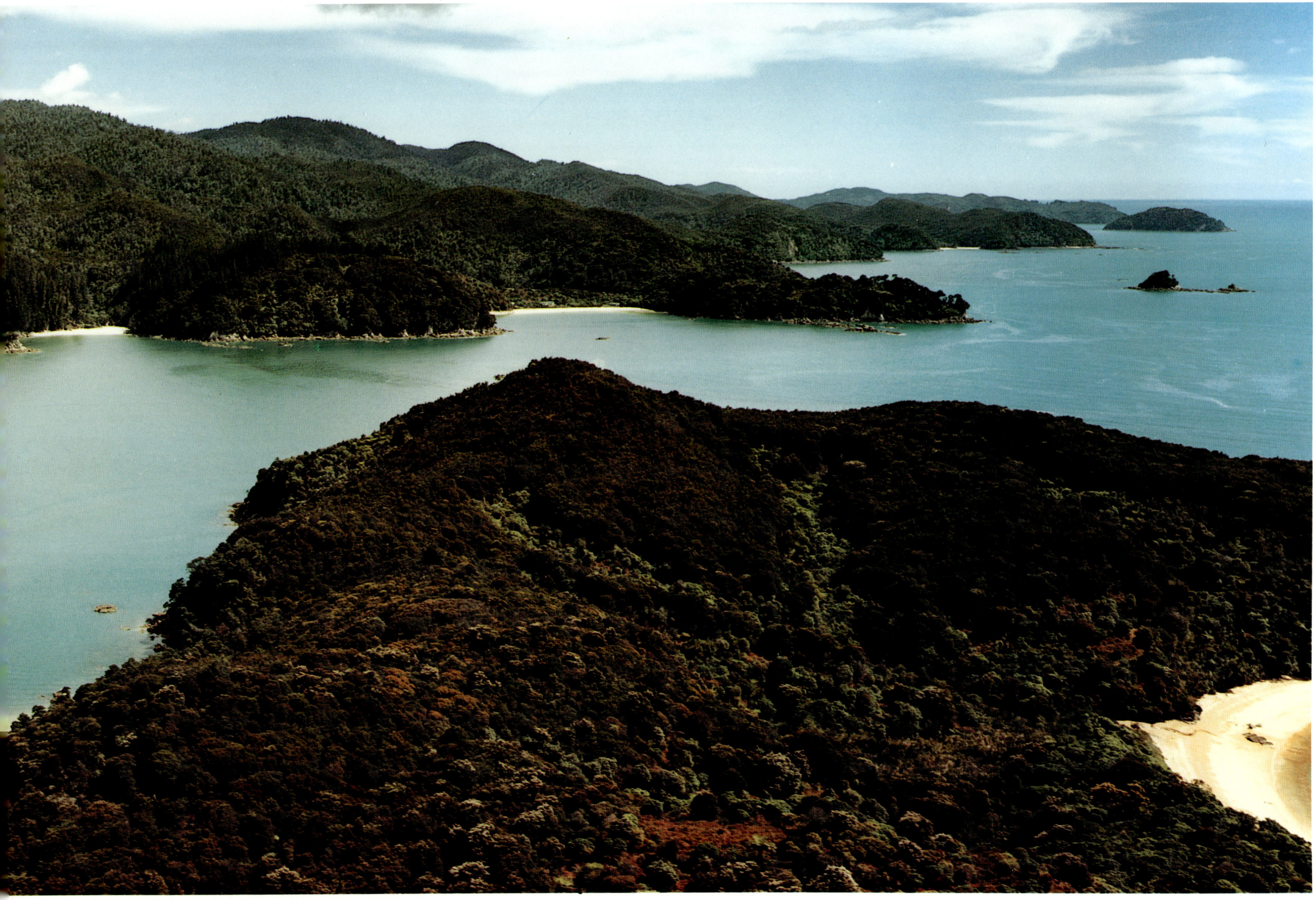

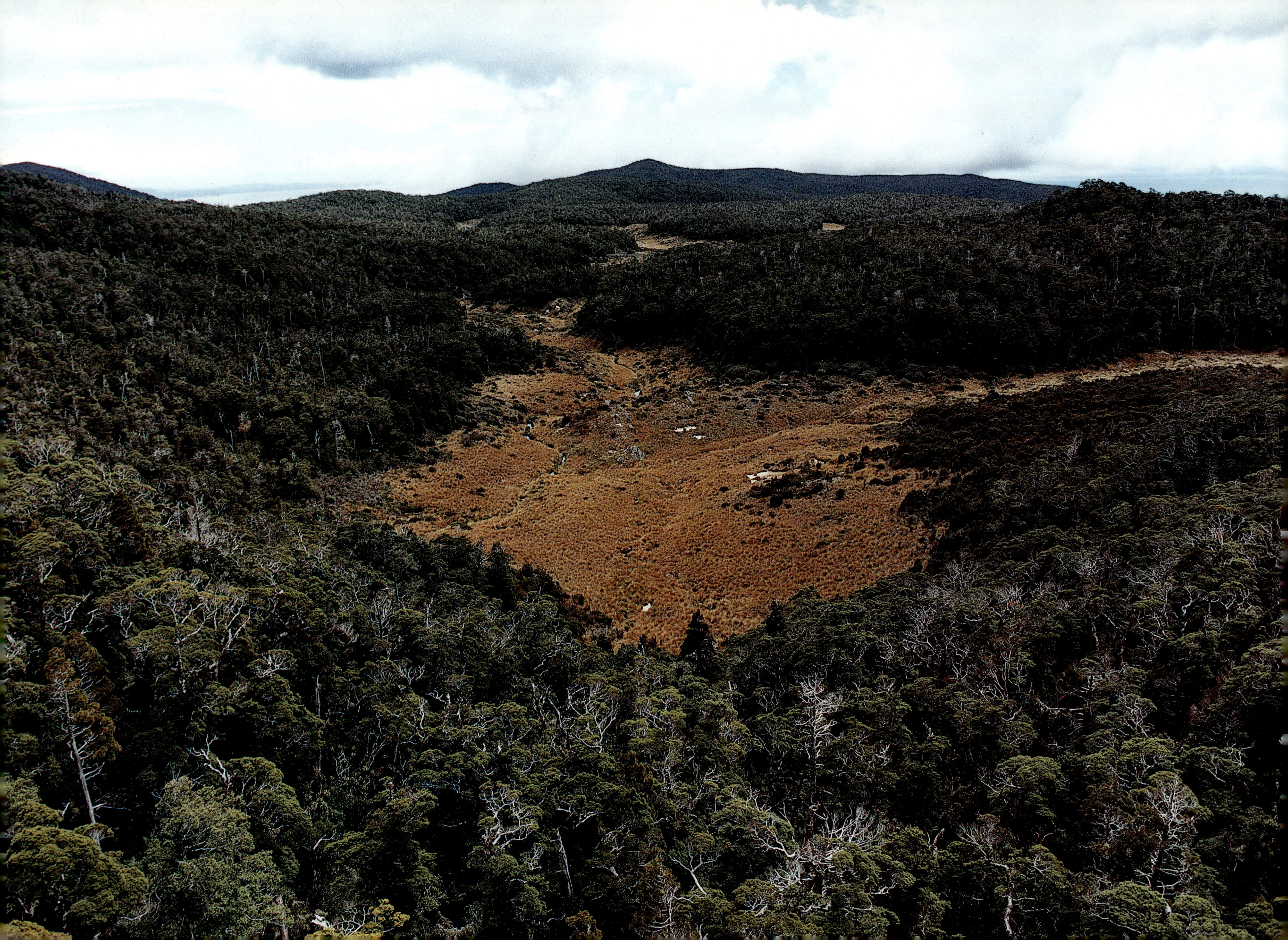

6 Moa Park, a 2 km-long enclave of red tussock in the head of Table Creek, is one of the most interesting landscapes on the undulating granite tableland in the south-west of the park. The accordant summits of the low ridges, seen in this view looking north, reinforce the belief that the tableland is an old peneplain. The shallow soils of the tableland are strongly leached and therefore acidic and infertile; generally they are covered in a mixed forest of red, silver and mountain beech, and the occasional mountain cedar and southern rata. In Moa Park, however, the combined effect of high water-table and the accumulation of cold air in the valley has led to a subalpine environment at only 1000 m altitude (i.e. 300–400 m lower than the regional treeline). Unlike so much of the coastal vegetation, fires are not considered to have caused the clearing, although a local fire may have induced the patch of manuka on the right centre.

7 Harwoods Hole lies on the western edge of the tableland and just west of the Canaan basin at an altitude of 800 m. It is the largest of the numerous sinkholes in this karst landscape, and marks the place where a former stream once plunged deep into the subterranean passages worn in the marble.

The 176 m drop from Harwoods Hole into Starlight Cave is the deepest vertical drop in any New Zealand cave. This is now a largely dry cave system as surface streams found deeper routes through the marble, to resurge as Gorge Creek far below near the Takaka River at the foot of the Pikikiruna Escarpment.

The grey marble on the right-hand-side of the hole shows karren features – fluted ribs of rock, honed to a sharp edge by rivulets of water gradually wearing a regular pattern of grooves.

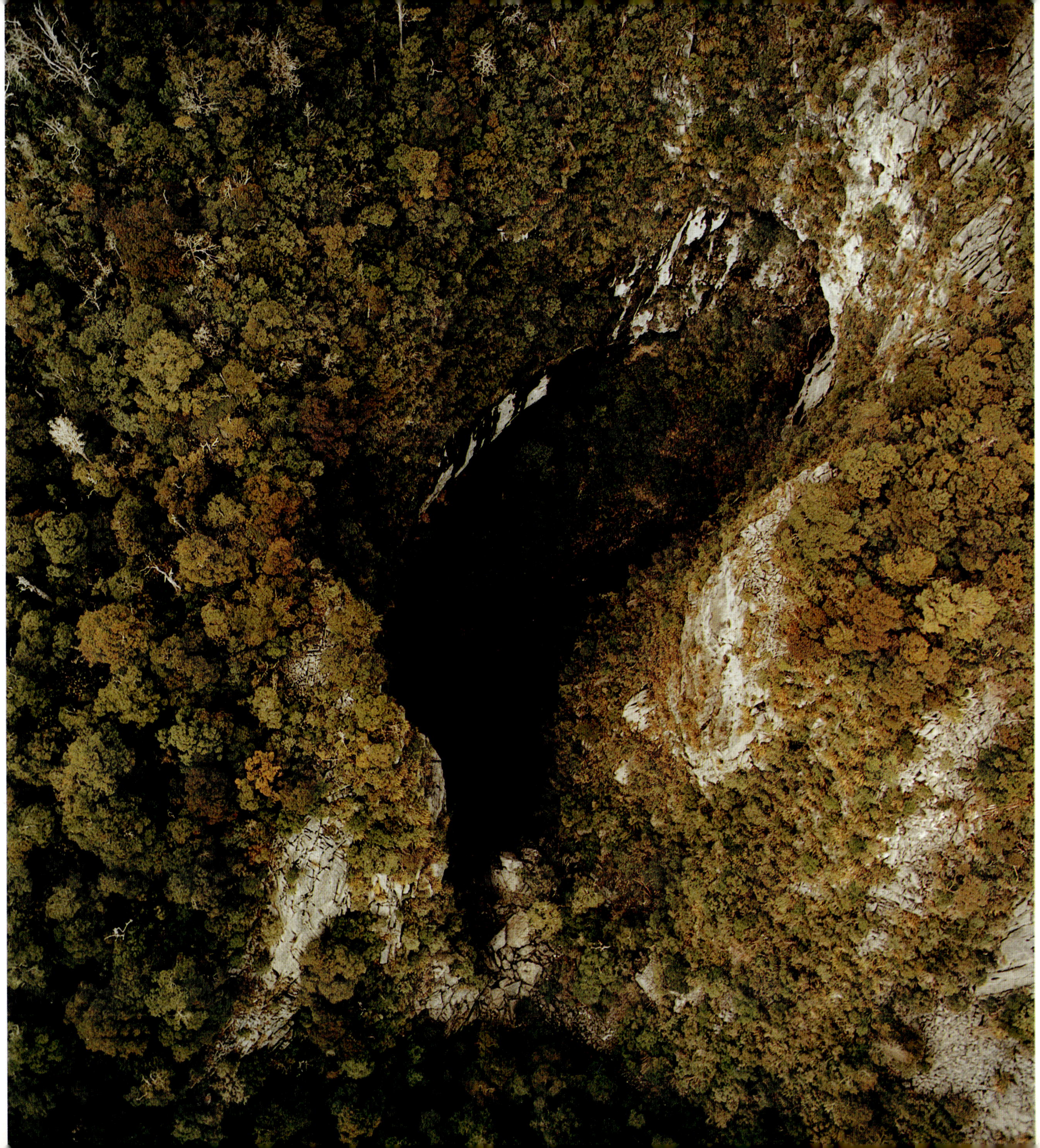

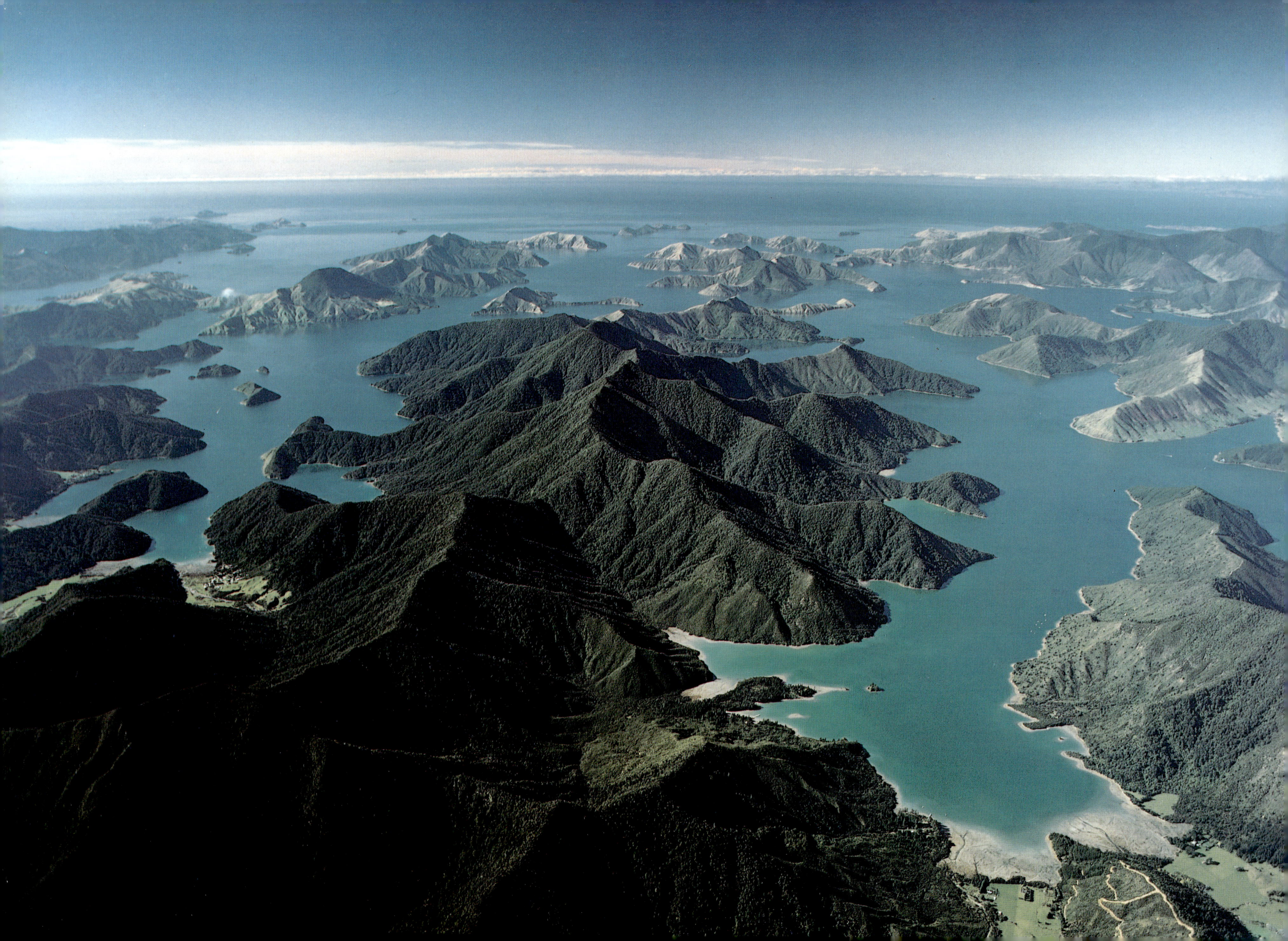

MARLBOROUGH SOUNDS MARITIME PARK

The Marlborough Sounds at the north-eastern tip of the South Island are a fascinating maze of steep hills threaded by waterways. Although they lack the size and scenic grandeur of Fiordland at the opposite end of the island, in many ways their landscapes are just as distinctive. The intricacy of the coastline of the Marlborough Sounds is unique within New Zealand. Whereas all the mountainous areas described in this book are being uplifted by huge forces associated with the movements of the Pacific and Indian–Australian plates in relation to each other, the hills around the Sounds are gradually sinking into the sea.

Prior to European settlement most of the hills were covered in podocarp/hardwood forest which merged into beech forest at higher altitudes and on less preferred sites hard beech on the dry ridges, red beech above 500 m and silver beech in the highest, wettest areas (generally above 700 m). Over two-thirds of this indigenous forest cover (especially below 500 m altitude) was cleared between 1880 and 1920, for timber and to establish pastoral farming. Because of the isolation, steep topography, infertile clay soils, and the lack of fresh water much of this farming failed. Subsequently, many areas of reverting farmland were established in exotic forests. As the indigenous forests dwindled, pressure grew to protect the widely scattered surviving remnants. Over the years more than 50 000 ha in over 100 reserves were set aside. In 1973 these were amalgamated with 900 km of foreshore reserve (a 20 m wide strip above high tide mark) to constitute the Marlborough Sounds Maritime Park.

A DROWNED VALLEY LANDSCAPE

The Marlborough Sounds are aptly described as a 'drowned valley' landscape, caused by the tilting to the north-east of the whole block of land between the Wairau valley in the south-east and the Moutere Depression (Waimea Plains and Tasman Bay) in the west. So, as the Bryant and Richmond Ranges are rising, the hills around the Sounds are being tipped towards the depths of Cook Strait.

The rocks of the Marlborough Sounds match those already described for the western boundary of Mt Aspiring National Park (see pp. 38–39). Greywacke and argillite make up the central part of the Sounds but over large areas (particularly in the east) they are metamorphosed to low grade schist. In the west, running from Croisilles Harbour to D'Urville Island, lies the northern end of the 'Nelson Mineral Belt', a band of mafic and ultramafic rocks of early Permian age (280 million years ago). At that time these rocks adjoined identical rocks in the Red Mountain locality of north-west Otago but have been wrenched apart by nearly 500 km of horizontal movement along the Alpine Fault. This great fault extends into the Wairau valley and forms the south-eastern margin of the crustal block that contains the Marlborough Sounds. The tilting probably began about 5 million years ago at the onset of a great mountain-building episode known as the 'Kaikoura Orogeny'.

The landforms of the Sounds were influenced by the cold climate of the Ice Ages, but they were not close enough to the main mountains axis (or high enough) to be glaciated. Lower sea levels during glacial stages exposed most of the floors of the Sounds. The lack of vegetation on the hill slopes in this periglacial climate accelerated the development of the screes through frost weathering. Today the hillsides are generally steep and smooth without deep gullies (see p. 131) and fossil screes, consisting of weakly-weathered rock debris up to 10 m thick, are widespread, particularly above 300 m altitude. Below 200 m, the slopes were not significantly rejuvenated by the deposition of rock debris during the last glaciation, and here strongly-weathered soils cover what is probably a remnant of an older landscape that was deeply weathered during the warmer interglacials.

There are some marked differences between the 'inner' and 'outer' Sounds. The coastline of the outer Sounds is exposed to constant erosion by the waves of Cook Strait which have formed high cliffs (p. 135). This dramatic transition in both water turbulence and ruggedness of landscape is easily witnessed during the passage of the inter-island ferries from the turbulent waters of Cook Strait to the relative calm of Tory Channel (p. 135).

In accepting the 'drowned valley' origin of the landscape it is easy to assume that the ancient rivers in the valleys originally flowed north-eastwards, simply because both Pelorus and Queen Charlotte Sounds seem to open out as Cook Strait is approached. A close examination of the map (p. 130) shows that this may not be so; Kenepuru Sound, Tory Channel and East Bay widen towards the south-west. Some sea-floor depth measurements suggest that these ancient valleys did drain to the south-west – probably into the Wairau valley via the Kaituna River (and present-day Havelock, see p. 134) or the Tuamarina River.

1 Marlborough Sounds Maritime Park is not a contiguous landmass like most of the national parks. It consists of over 100 discrete reserves – including virtually all the forested landscape in this view north-eastwards across Pelorus Sound; the two major arms of the Sound in the foreground are Tennyson Inlet (left) and Nydia Bay (right). The park also includes many of the islands (such as the Chetwodes, Maud Island, and Titi Island, all visible in this photograph and each an important wildlife reserve) and about 900 km of a foreshore reserve consisting of a 20 m-wide strip above high tide mark. Most of the farmed landscape and exotic forests are in private ownership.

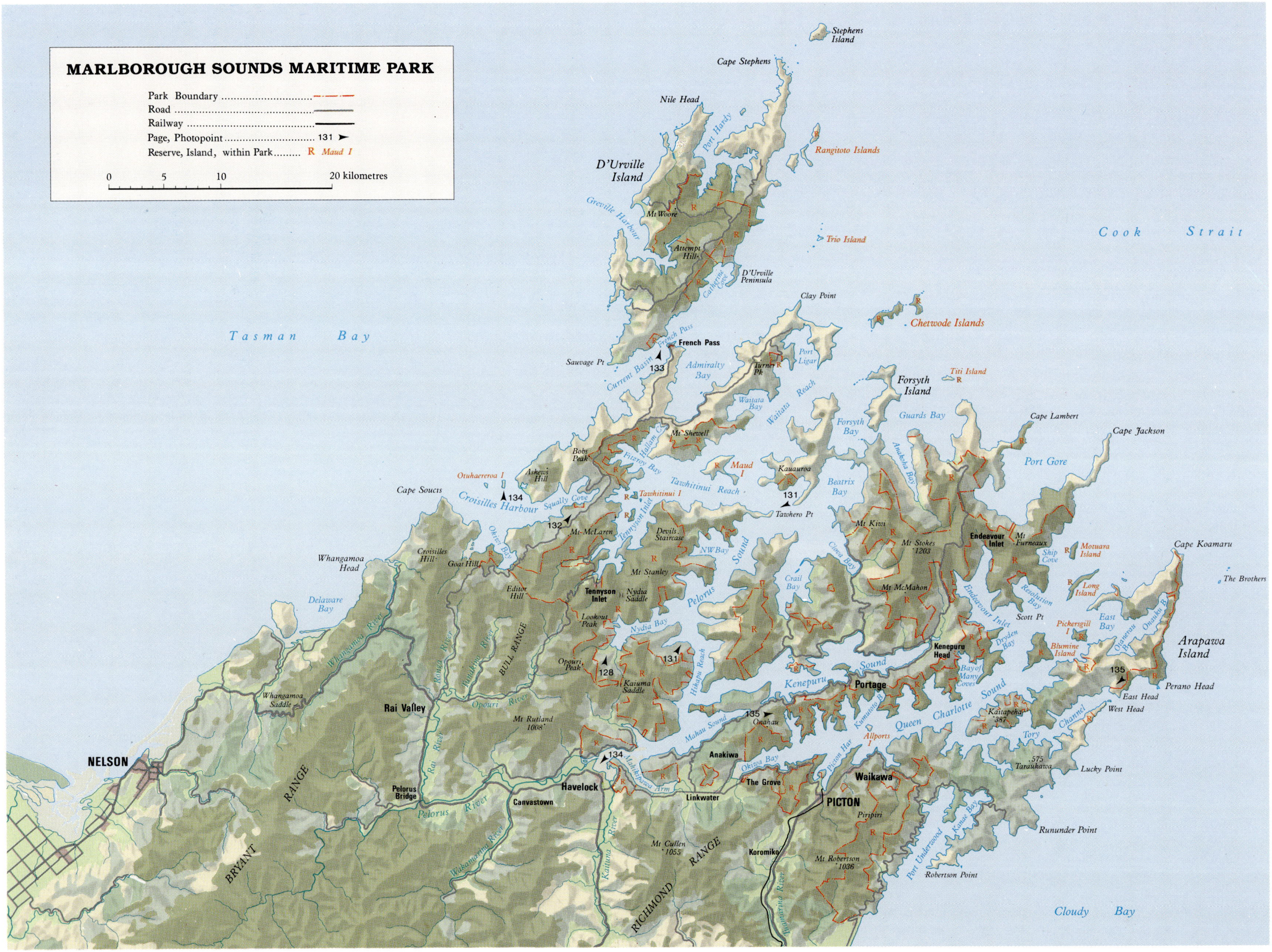
MARLBOROUGH SOUNDS MARITIME PARK
Park Boundary
Road
Railway
Page, Photopoint 131
Reserve, Island, within Park R Maud I
0 5 10 20 kilometres
Stephens Island
Cape Stephens
Nile Head
Port Hardy
Rangitoto Islands
D'Urville Island
Greville Harbour
Mt Moore
Attempt Hill
Trio Island
Catherine Cove
D'Urville Peninsula
Cook Strait
Clay Point
Chetwode Islands
Tasman Bay
French Pass
Sauvage Pt
Current Basin
133
Admiralty Bay
Turner Pk
Port Ligar
Titi Island
Forsyth Island
Waitata Bay
Waitata Reach
Forsyth Bay
Guards Bay
Cape Lambert
Cape Jackson
Port Gore
Mt Shewell
Bobs Peak
Askews Hill
Maud I
Kauauroa
Otuhaereroa I
Tawhitinui Reach
Beatrix Bay
Cape Soucis
Croisilles Harbour
134
Squally Cove
Tawhitinui I
131
Tawhero Pt
132
Mt McLaren
Tennyson Inlet
Devils Staircase
Mt Kiwi
Mt Stokes 1203
Endeavour Inlet
Mt Furneaux
Motuara Island
Ship Cove
Cape Koamaru
The Brothers
Whangamoa Head
Croisilles Hill
Goat Hill
Okiwi Bay
NW Bay
Mt Stanley
Crail Bay
Clova Bay
Mt McMahon
Long Island
Resolution Bay
Delaware Bay
Editor Hill
Tennyson Inlet
Nydia Saddle
Pelorus Sound
Endeavour Inlet
Scott Pt
East Bay
Pickersgill I
Blumine Island
Arapawa Island
Lookout Peak
Nydia Bay
Kenepuru Head
Dryden Bay
BULL RANGE
Opouri Peak
128
131
Kaiuma Saddle
Hikapu Reach
Kenepuru Sound
Portage
Bay of Many Coves
135
Perano Head
East Head
West Head
Whangamoa River
Whangamoa Saddle
Rai Valley
Opouri River
Mt Rutland 1008
135 Onahau
Mahau Sound
Queen Charlotte Sound
Kaitapeha 387
Tory Channel
NELSON
Anakiwa
Allports I
Okiwa Bay
Picton Har
134
Havelock
Mahakipawa Arm
The Grove
Waikawa
Tarakawa 575
Lucky Point
RANGE
Pelorus Bridge
Rai River
Pelorus River
Canvastown
Linkwater
PICTON
Piripiri
Runanga Point
Kaituna River
Mt Cullen 1055
RANGE
Koromiko
Mt Robertson 1036
Port Underwood
Robertson Point
BRYANT
RICHMOND
Cloudy Bay

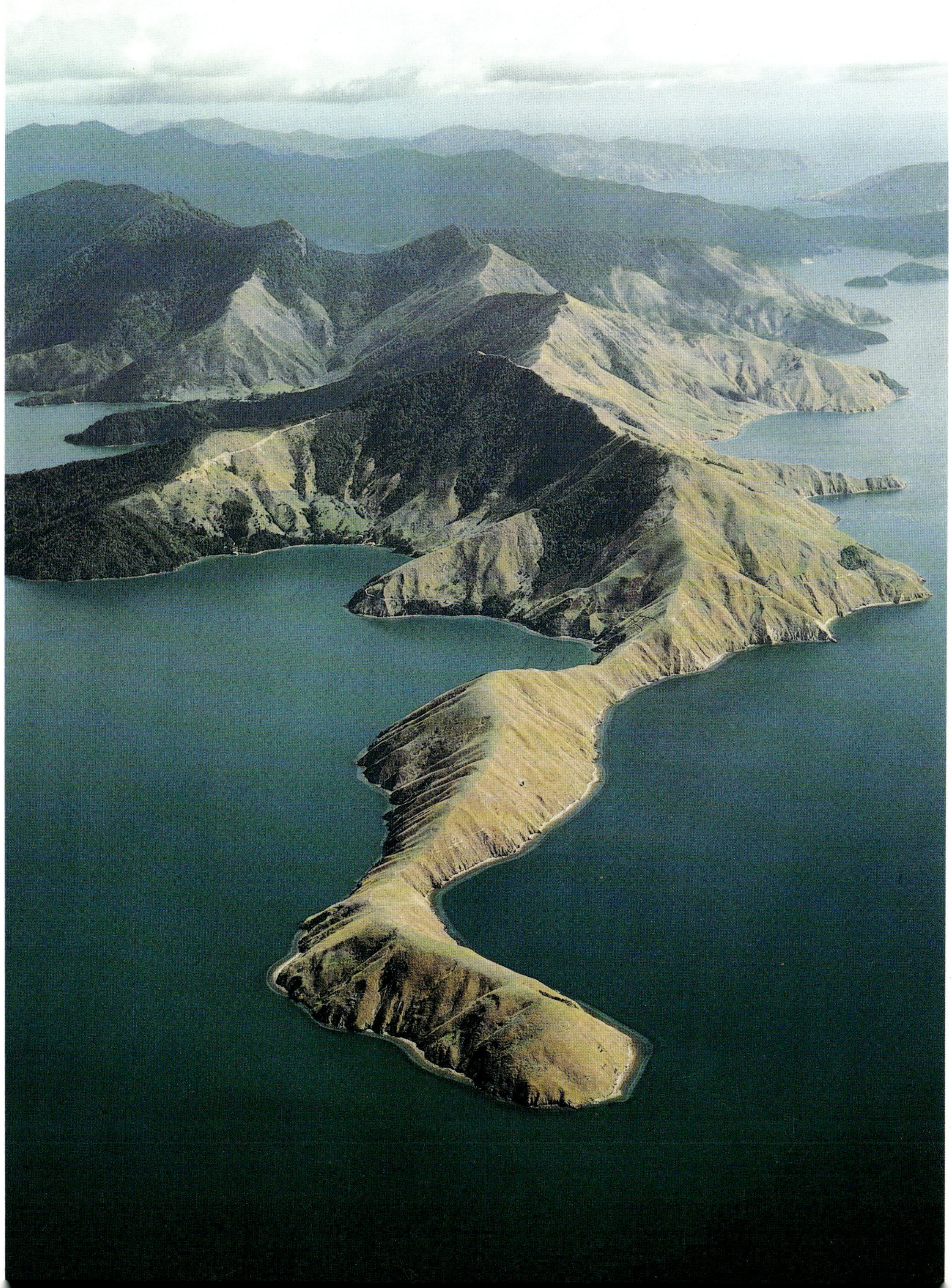

2

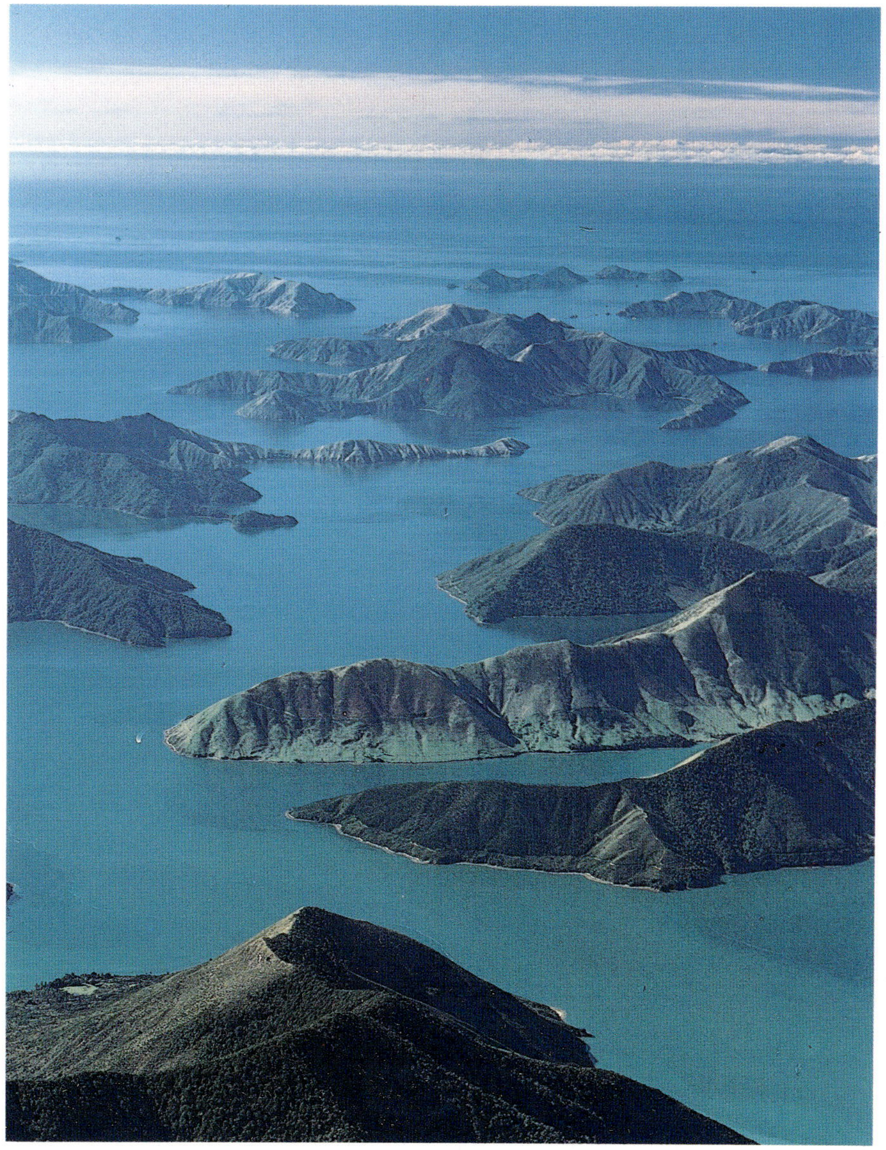

2

2 The 'drowned valley' topography of the Marlborough Sounds is very apparent in these views of former valley spurs whose crests jut out as long narrow spines into Pelorus Sound (left photo). The distinctive east–west trending peninsula terminating in Tawero Point (centre distance) is pictured end on in the right hand photograph.

The Marlborough Sounds were not affected by the ice of the last glaciation but there is plenty of evidence of widespread frost-weathering ('peri-glaciation') in the steep-sided ridges and the presence of fossil screes (up to 10 m thick), particularly on the higher slopes.

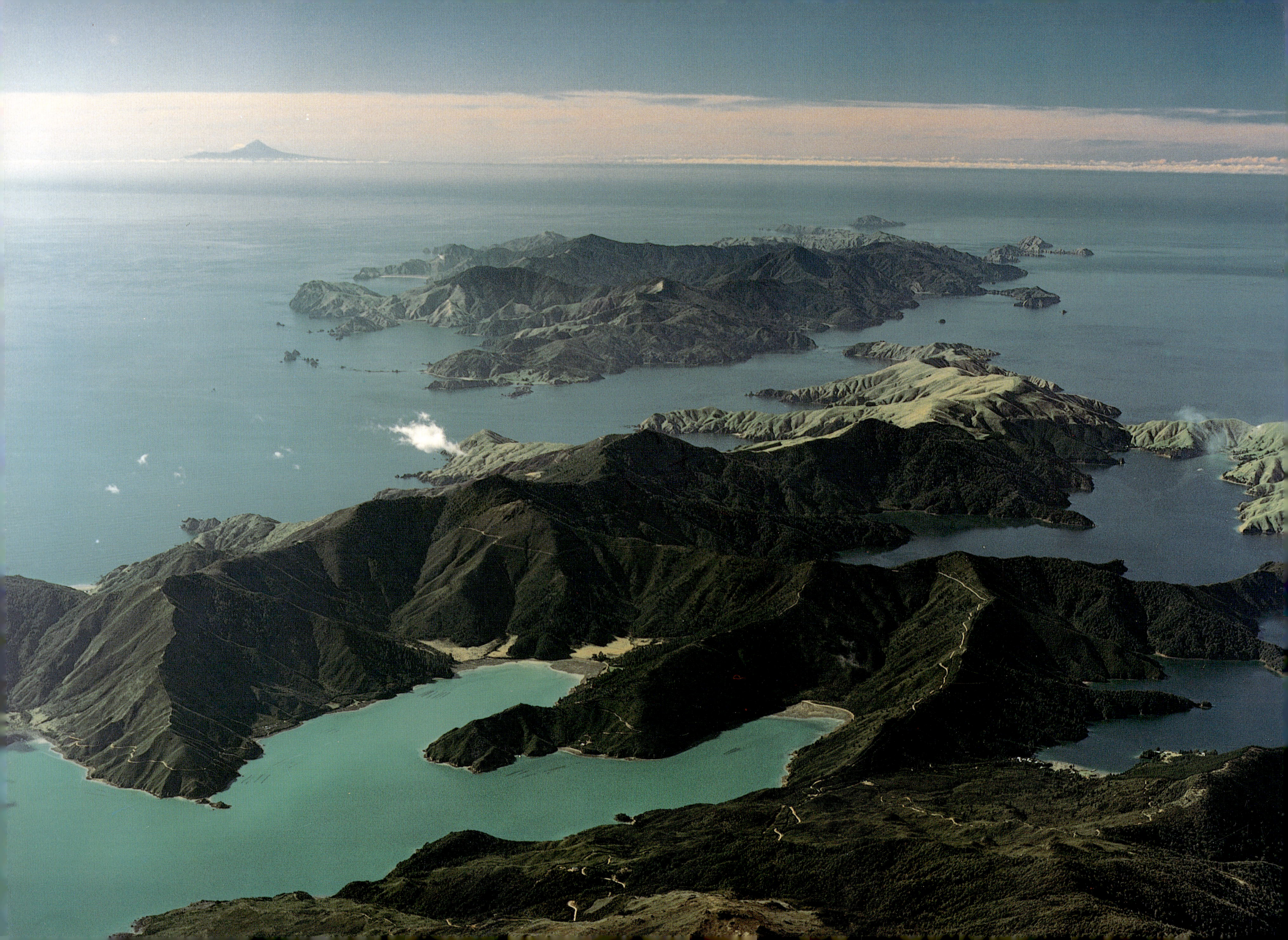

3 D'Urville Island (middle distance), and beyond it the important wildlife sanctuary of Stephens Island, are the northernmost part of the Marlborough Sounds. Geologically, D'Urville Island and the hills around Squally Cove in Croisilles Harbour (bottom left) and Fitzroy and Elaine Bays (right) are very different than the rest of the park, for they contain the northernmost outcrops of the 'mineral belt'(Fig. 3, Fiordland and Fig. 8, Mt Aspiring). The characteristic bare, red, weathering outcrops and associated stunted 'serpentine scrub' occur in the hummocky topography in the left foreground.

The siltstone blocks caught up in the mineral belt were altered to a very hard, tough rock (a type of dark grey argillite) that was worked by the Maori into adzes. At least twelve quarry sites occur on D'Urville Island and adjacent to Croisilles Harbour. These adzes were widely traded by the Maori people throughout Aotearoa.

The volcanic cone of Mt Taranaki, in Egmont National Park (Chapter 10), dominates the horizon 200 km to the north in the North Island.

4 D'Urville Island (left) is only just an island. At French Pass the former ridgeline is barely submerged, and the tide can be seen surging across the reef from Admiralty Bay into the aptly named Current Basin (foregound). Cook Strait and parts of the Marlborough Sounds experience the strongest tidal flows in New Zealand and the intricate nature of the Sounds results in very complex tidal patterns. Nowhere in the Sounds are tidal forces resulting from converging currents more dramatically expressed than at French Pass where the tide can cause a flow of 7 knots.

The Trio Islands, another wildlife sanctuary, can be seen in the top right.

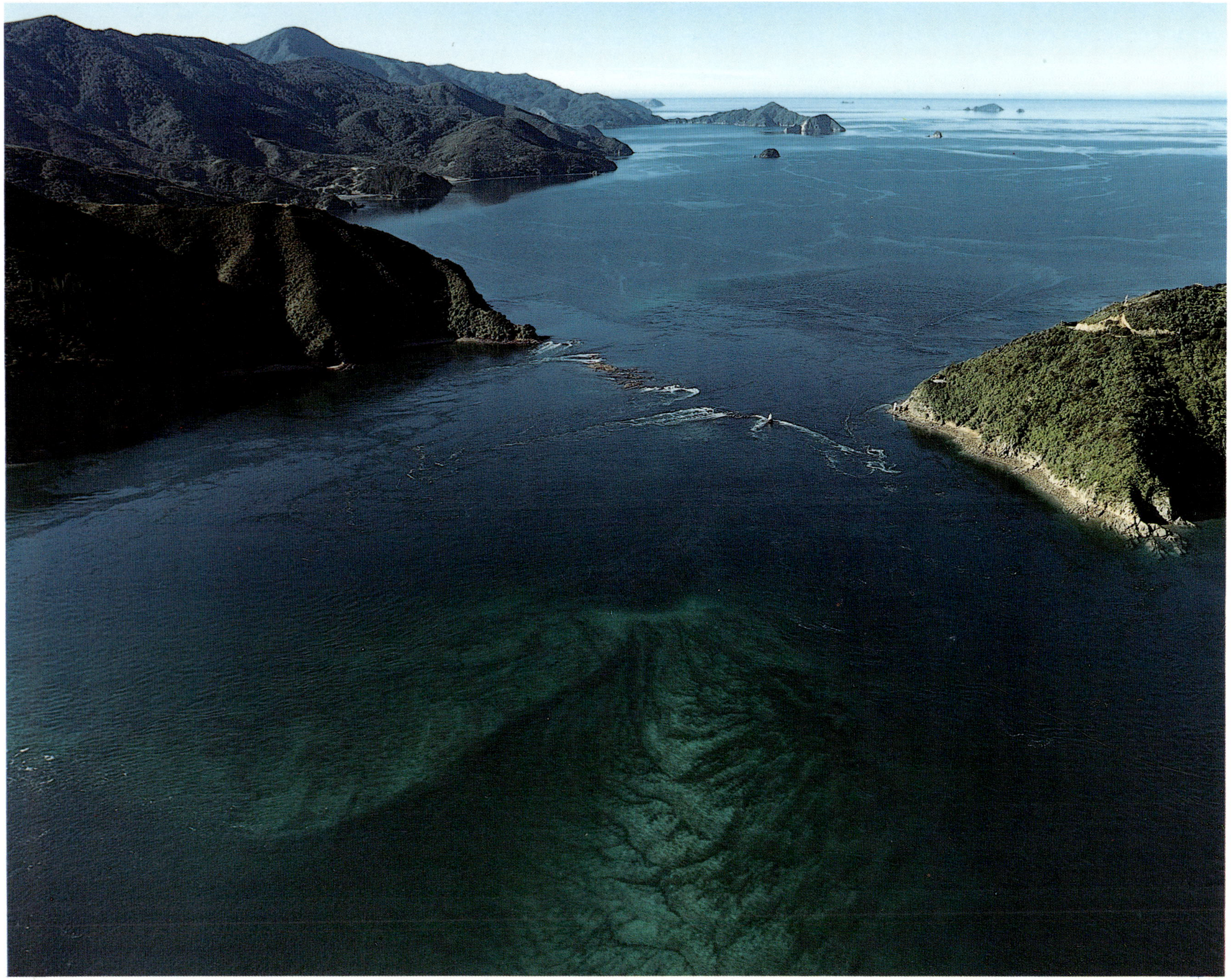

4

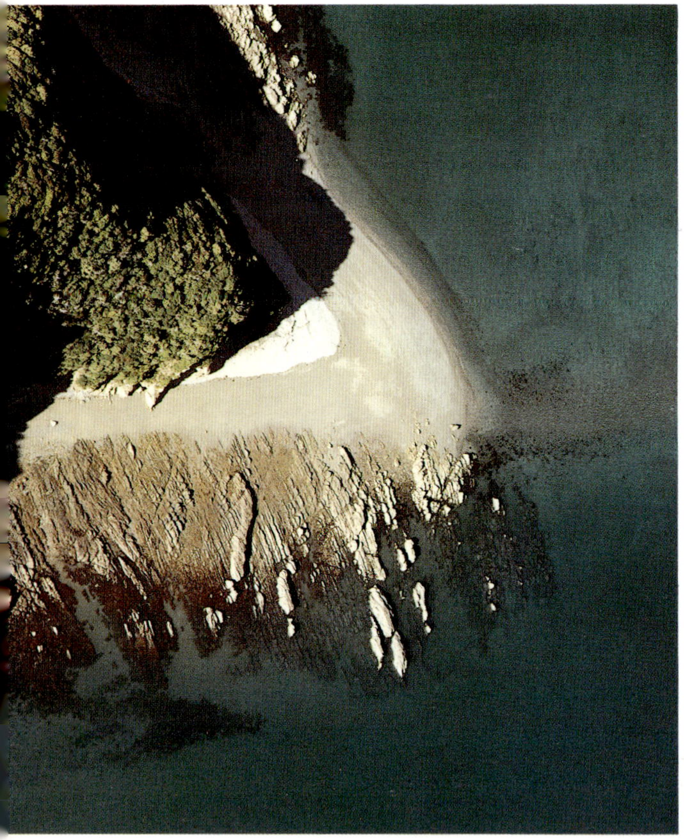

5

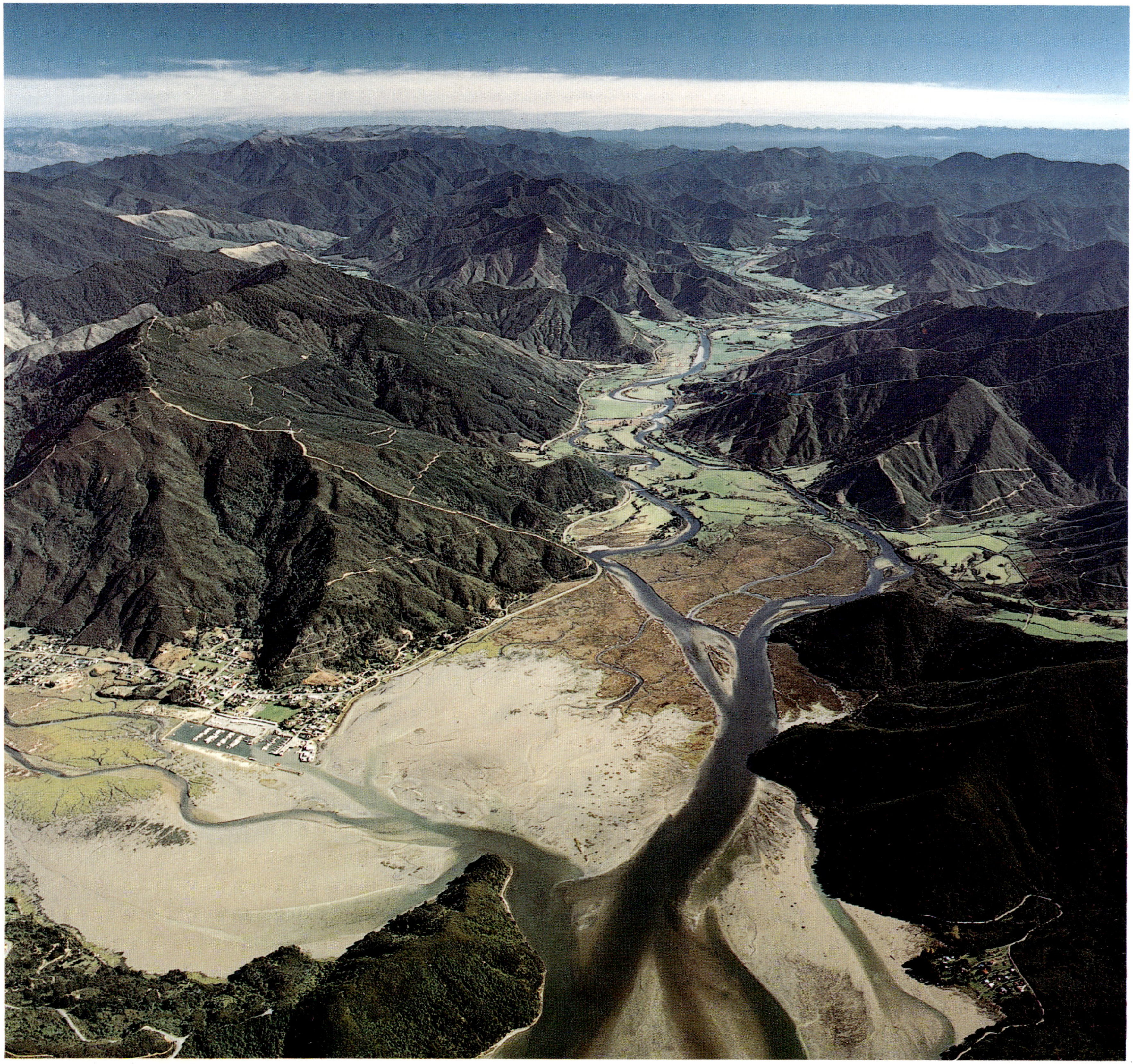

6

5 A vertical view of steeply dipping sandstone/siltstone beds forming the shore platform on the south-east corner of Otuhaereroa Island at the entrance to Croisilles Harbour. Small faults cut diagonally across the parallel strata.

6 The resort and fishing port of Havelock lies on the southern edge of the Pelorus River estuary at the head of Pelorus Sound. Infilling of the Sound with alluvium eroded from these ranges has formed the fertile flats of the lower Pelorus valley. There is evidence that the Pelorus River once flowed to the Wairau valley in the east via the present-day Kaituna valley in the bottom left of the photograph.

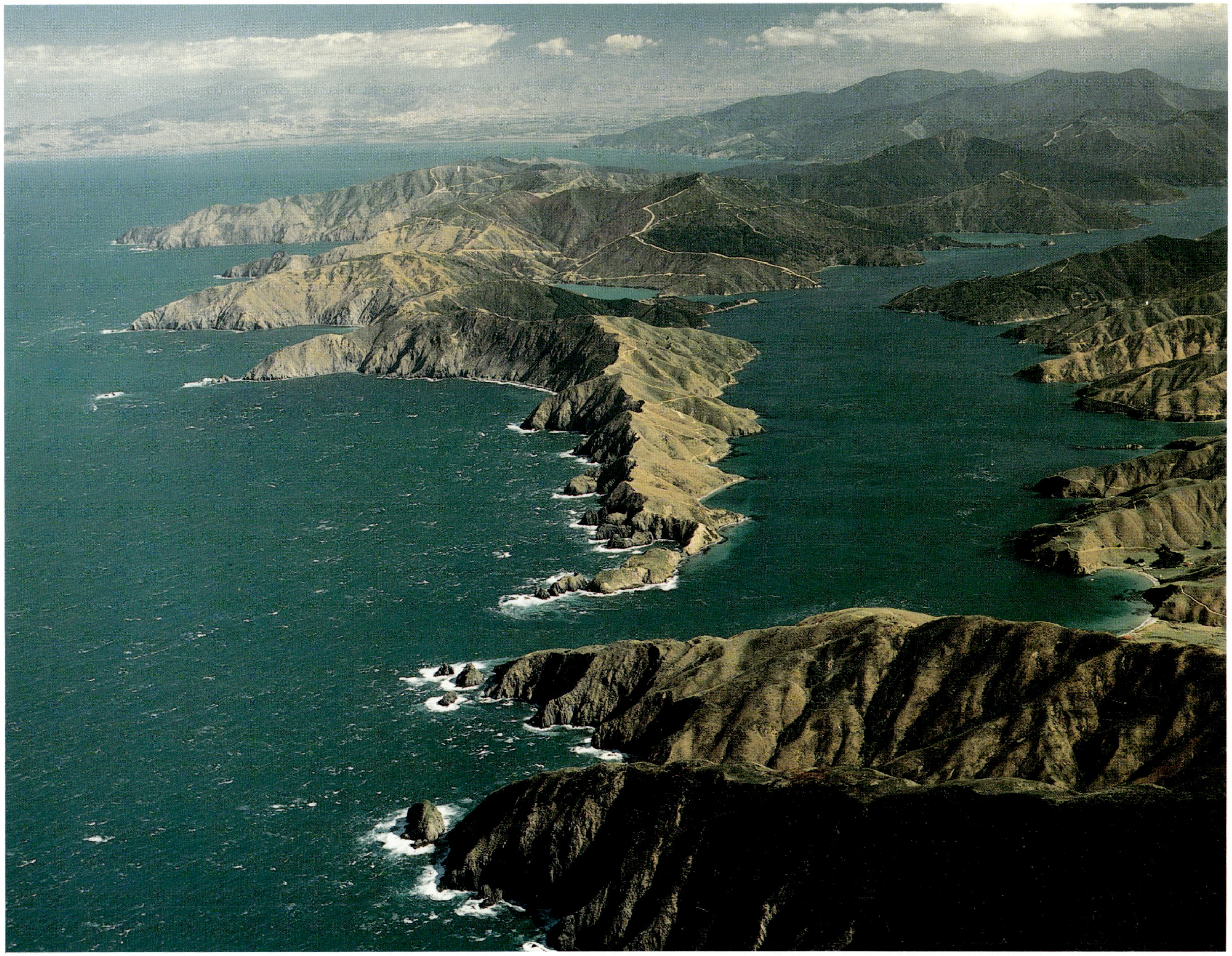

7

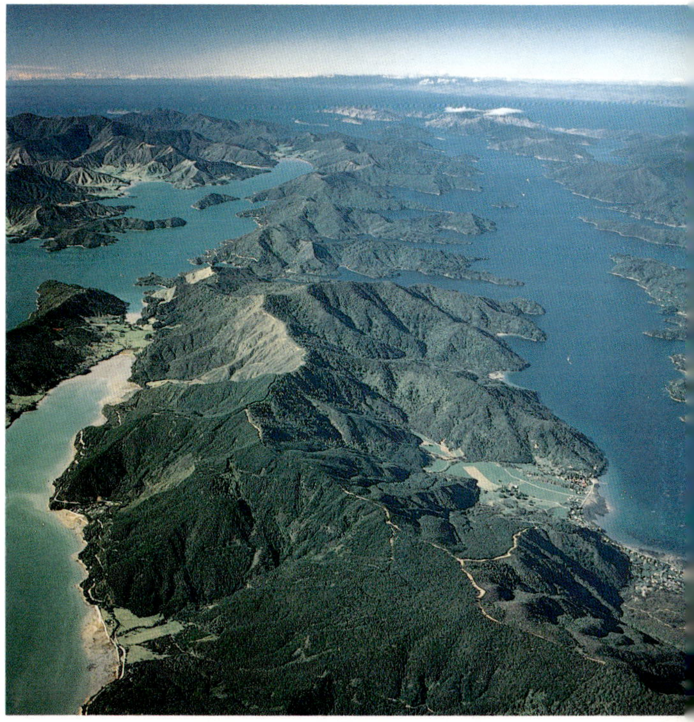

8

7 Tory Channel (right) is an alternative and historically important entrance to Queen Charlotte Sound. The most conspicuous landscape features of the outer edge of the Marlborough Sounds are the wave-eroded sea cliffs and the wind-swept pastures and shrublands.

8 The parallel ENE-trending Kenepuru Sound (left) and Queen Charlotte Sound (right) are probably fault-controlled. Although Queen Charlotte Sound discharges to Cook Strait (distance), Kenepuru Sound is land-locked in this direction and, instead, joins the head of Pelorus Sound near Havelock (see opposite page). The floors of both sounds slope towards the camera and this feature suggests that the ancient valley systems in this eastern part of the Sounds may have drained to the south-west.

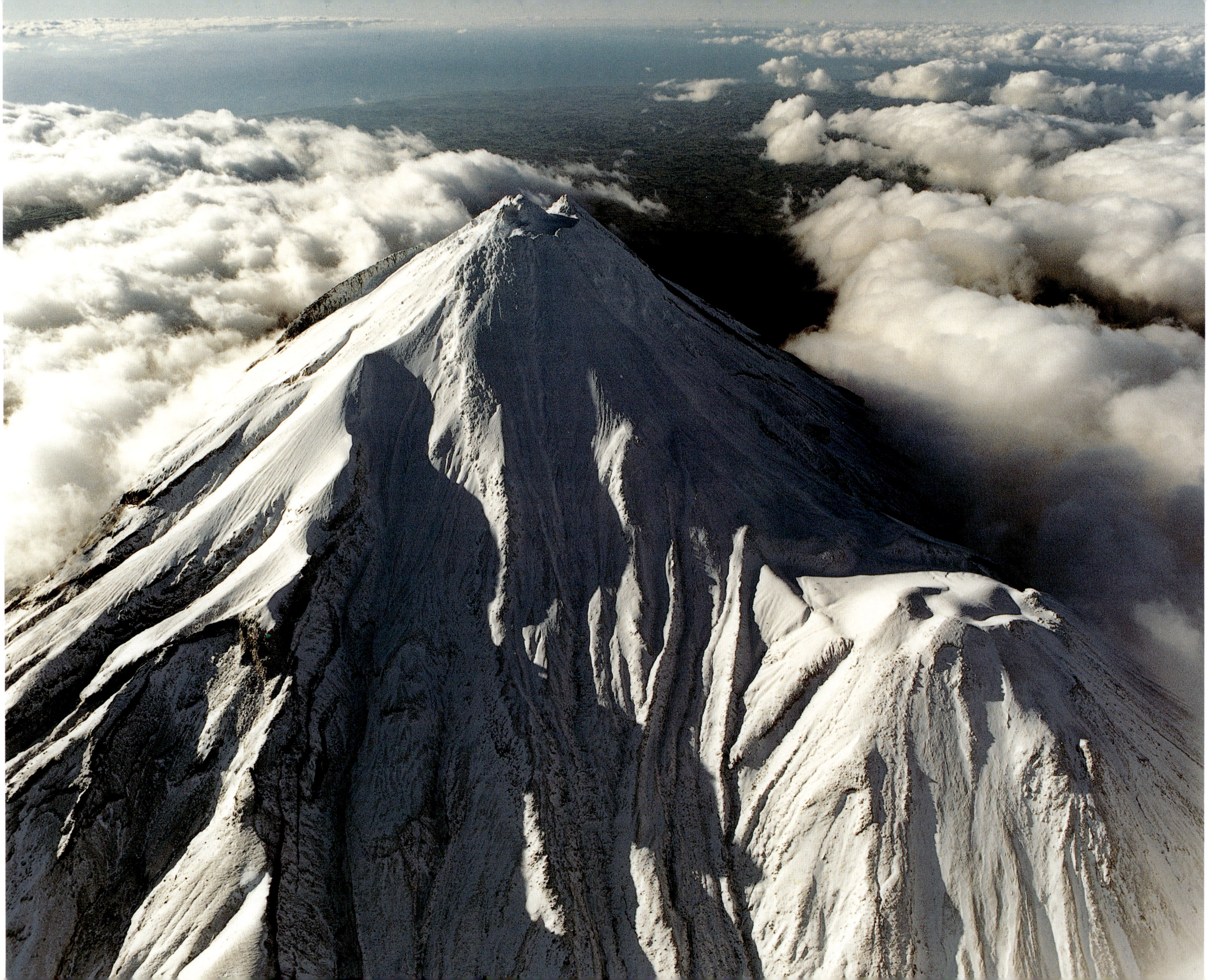

1

EGMONT NATIONAL PARK

Egmont National Park has the simplest landform structure of New Zealand's national parks. Its area of 33 500 ha is made up of the cone and ringplain of the dormant volcano, Mt Taranaki or Mt Egmont, and its volcanic forebears, Pouakai and Patuha (the Kaitake Range). When the park was set aside in October 1900, it was described just as 'land comprised with a circle having a radius of six miles, and a centre on the summit of Mt Egmont' – that is, the mountain slopes above the contour lines at 400–500 m on Mts Taranaki and Pouakai, and 200 m on the Kaitake Range.

ORIGIN OF THE VOLCANIC LANDFORMS

Although Mt Taranaki dominates the park today, it is only the most recent of a series of andesitic volcanoes that have developed in western Taranaki during the past 2 million years. The oldest volcanic remnants lie off New Plymouth to the north – the Sugar Loaf Islands and Paritutu, a group of resistant lava spines and domes from an ancient volcano which has long since been eroded away by the sea. By 600 000 years ago, volcanic activity had moved 15 km south-west to the heavily forested deeply eroded stump of a volcano that was once probably as large as Mt Taranaki. Most of the ringplain of this Kaitake volcano was subsequently buried by lahars and tephra from a newer volcano, Pouakai, which formed 10 km to the south-east around 250 000 years ago.

The Pouakai ringplain only survives as a surface feature in the north (from Oakura to Inglewood), and in the south-east between Stratford and Eltham; elsewhere it has been covered by volcanic debris flows from Mt Taranaki which began to form over 100 000 years ago. Where the old Pouakai ringplain remains, it has been smoothed through the accumulation over a long period of airfall tephra from Mt Taranaki; its streams (such as the Oakura River) are more deeply incised because of the greater age of the surface. Because the Mt Taranaki ringplain is younger, it is much easier to recognise each major episode of cone collapse or erosion that has shaped it.

1 The dormant volcanic cone of Mt Taranaki (2518 m) is the central feature of Egmont National Park. This winter view of the south-western sector shows the parasitic cone of Fanthams Peak (lower right) and the fluted slopes of the main peak – a consequence of both erosion and the periodic deposition of tongues of lava.

The 'amphitheatre' largely in shadow between Fanthams Peak and Bobs Ridge (left, in sunlight) was the source of a major lahar which 7000 years ago flowed to the coastline around Opunake depositing volcanic mud and rocks over 120 sq. km of the Mt Taranaki ringplain.

The summit is not part of the crater wall (like Sharks Tooth in sunlight on the right), but lava which cooled rapidly when extruded around 300 years ago, and formed a dome (called a tholoid) rather than flowing out of the crater.

EROSION RESHAPES THE CONE OF MT TARANAKI

Although Mt Taranaki looks like a very simple volcanic landform, it is not made up of layer upon layer of lava, like the great basaltic lava volcanoes of Hawaii or even our own miniature shield volcano, Rangitoto. Instead, the andesite has been erupted in a variety of forms – solid pyroclastic rocks and ash from explosions as well as thick tongues of molten but rather viscous lava from non-explosive eruptions. The explosive deposits are collectively termed tephras, so the steep cone of volcanic material that developed consisted of highly-erodible mixed layers of lava and tephra.

The present-day shape of Mt Taranaki is the sum total of the two countervailing forces of deposition (of fresh volcanic material) and erosion (of this same material) on the slopes over the last 100 000 or so years. Erosion plays a particularly important part here because the slopes of Mt Taranaki are probably the wettest locality in the North Island; annual precipitation at the Dawson Falls, East Egmont and North Egmont roadends (900–1300 m altitude) is as high as 6500–7500 mm, and probably reaches 8000 mm at around 2000 m altitude. By contrast, the north-western slopes at the same altitude on Mt Ruapehu (around Whakapapa Village) receive much less rainfall (2500–3000 mm). The intensity of the rainfall on Mt Taranaki almost rivals that of the wettest section of the Southern Alps (Chapter 4); Dawson Falls has been known to receive as much rain in two days (845 mm) as Dunedin usually gets in a year; or in a month, more rain (1700 mm) than New Plymouth usually gets in a year!

The rain-storms tend to wash out the finer tephras, ultimately creating ravines, undercutting the slope, and causing more resistant lava-capped sections to collapse and form local debris flows. These rarely travel more than 15 km from their source. Some of the volcano's spectacular collapses, however, may have been triggered by eruptions which sent huge debris avalanches and waves of lahars (highly mobile volcanic mudflows) out across the ringplain. The largest of these volcanic avalanche and mudflow deposits covered areas up to 200 square kilometres and reached the present day west Taranaki coastline.

The rolling ringplain on the eastern (Stratford) side of Mt Taranaki consists of lahars which occurred between 20 000 and 50 000 years ago and have subsequently been covered with moderately thick airfall tephra. The northern and western slopes, however, have collapsed regularly in series of four major debris avalanche and lahar episodes estimated at 30–35 000 years (Opunake), 23 000 years (Pungarehu), 12–16 000 years (Warea), and 7000 years (Opua). It is these debris flows which have produced west Taranaki's distinctive topography.

A major phase of cone-building began around 20 000 years ago and remnants of these older lava flows are preserved as lava-capped ridges (such as West Ridge) or prominent isolated landmarks, such as Humphries Castle and Warwick Castle. During the later stages of the cone-building a series of lava domes were formed at different points on the volcano (The Dome, Skinner Hill and the Beehives, as well as within the main summit crater). These domes are the result of highly viscous lava forming 'blisters' over vents, rather than flowing down the slope as lava flows.

The most recent evidence of the collapse of the slopes of Mt Taranaki can be seen in the north-western sector. Over 3500 years ago local debris flows blocked the upper Stony River and formed the Ahukawakawa Swamp in the basin between Taranaki and Pouakai . Previously, Stony River flowed around the south side of the Dome, but the debris blocked this channel and forced the river to cut its way through the lava on the north side of the lava dome; Bells Falls was formed in the process. Over the last 500 years at least fourteen major debris flows have occurred, most of them in this part of the park. The most spectacular are the Maero Debris Flows between Skinner Hill and Kahui Hill, where the tree line has been depressed by 300 m, and Pyramid, Turehu and Maero Streams have carved narrow gullies in the smooth surfaces of the unconsolidated volcanic debris.

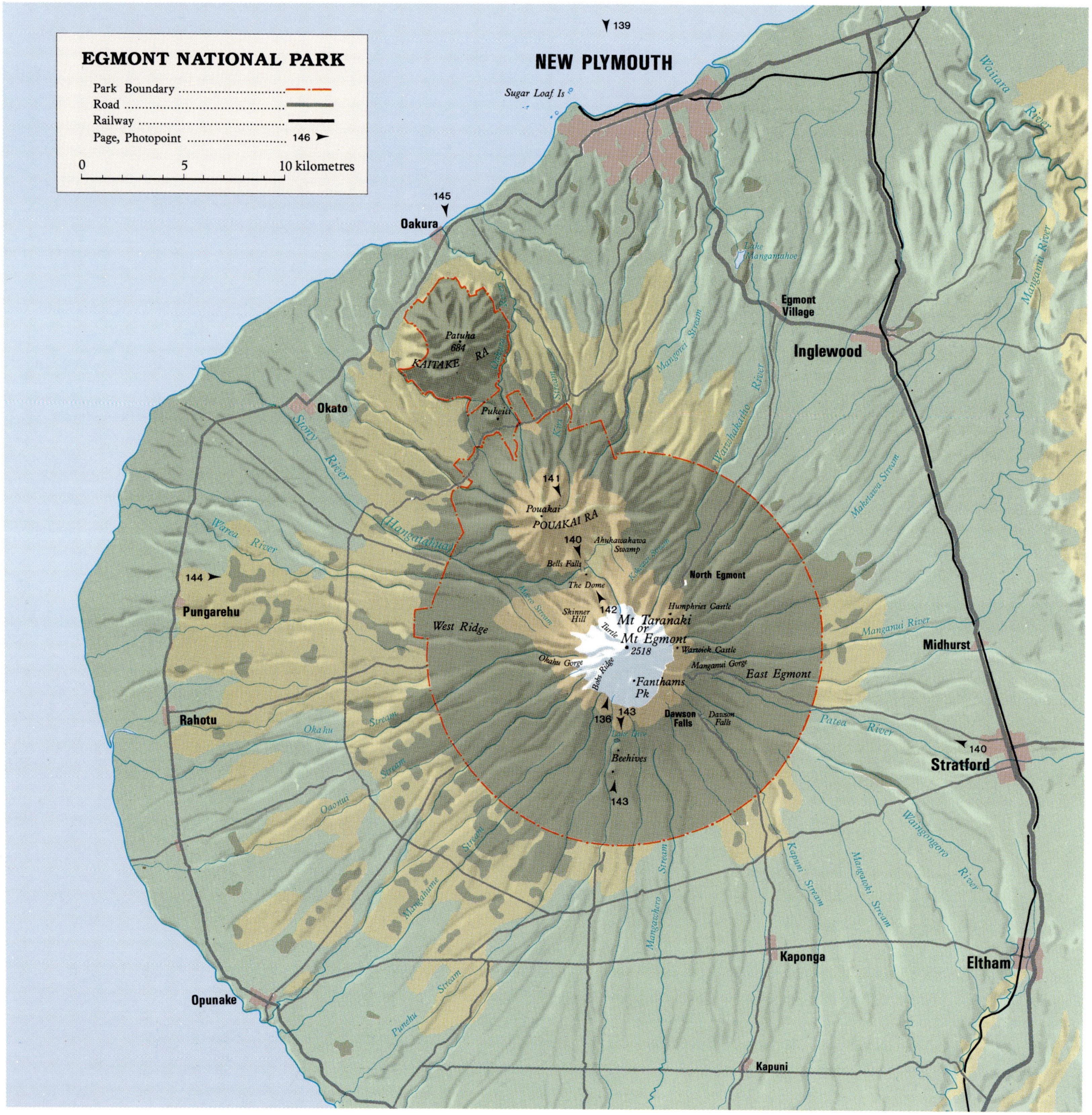
EGMONT NATIONAL PARK
Park Boundary
Road
Railway
Page, Photopoint 146
0 5 10 kilometres
139
NEW PLYMOUTH
Sugar Loaf Is
145
Oakura
Waitara River
Lake Mangamahoe
Manganui River
Egmont Village
Inglewood
Patuha 684
KAITAKE RA
Pukeiti
Okato
Stony River
Mangorei Stream
Waiwhakaiho River
Maketawa Stream
141
Pouakai
POUAKAI RA
140
Ahukawakawa Swamp
Bells Falls
Warea River
Hangatahua
144
North Egmont
The Dome
142
Skinner Hill
Humphries Castle
Pungarehu
West Ridge
Mt Taranaki or Mt Egmont
2518
Turtle
Warwick Castle
Manganui Gorge
Manganui River
Midhurst
Okahu Gorge
Bobs Ridge
Fanthams Pk
East Egmont
143
136
Dawson Falls
Dawson Falls
Rahotu
Okahu
Stream
Patea River
140
Stratford
Beehives
143
Oaonui
Stream
Waingongoro River
Kapuni Stream
Mangatoki Stream
Mangahume
Mangawhero Stream
Kaponga
Eltham
Opunake
Punehu Stream
Kapuni

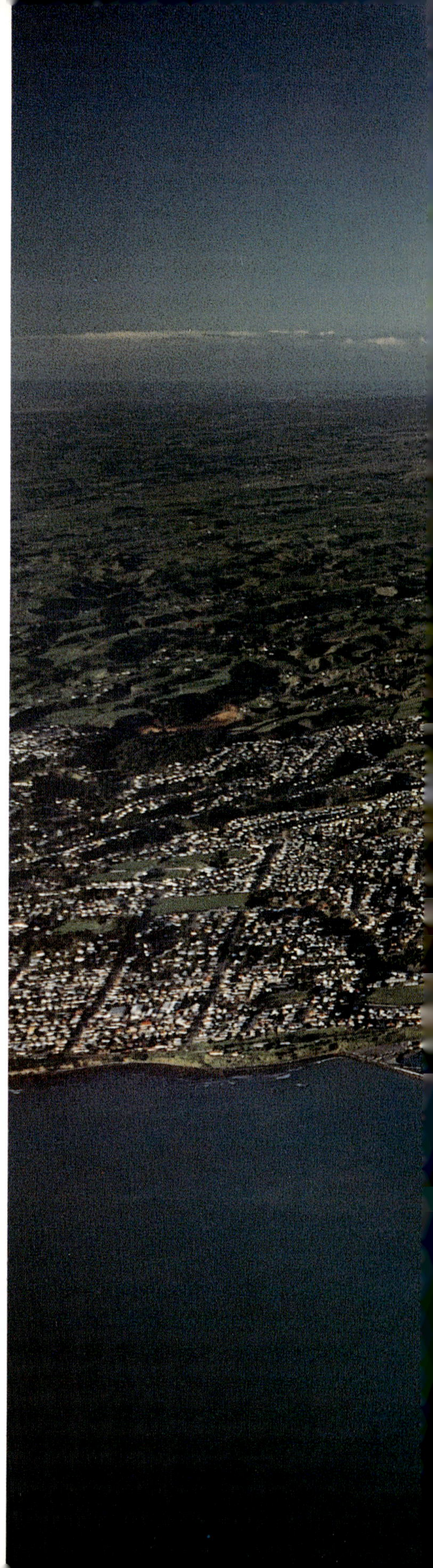

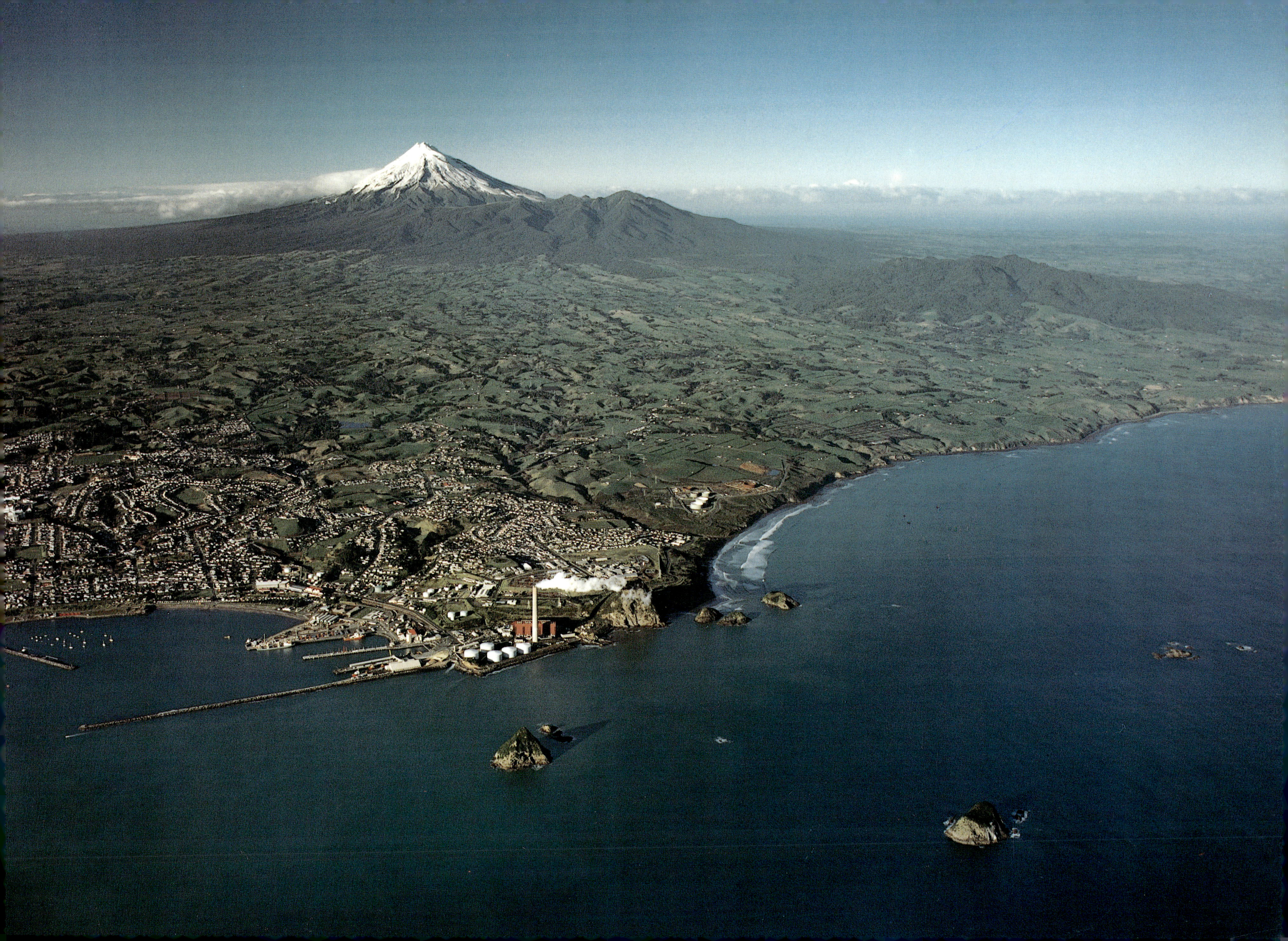

previous page

2 In the last 1.75 million years the site of volcanic activity in Taranaki has shifted west and south from the Sugar Loaf Islands (foreground) and the New Plymouth landmark of Paritutu. Smoke from the power station chimney partially obscures Paritutu, which is considered to be the erosion-resistant residual lava plug that once filled the vent of a volcano. Nearly 600 000 years ago activity shifted to the Kaitake Range (far right) and subsequently in a south-easterly direction to the Pouakai Range and Mt Taranaki (centre, distance).

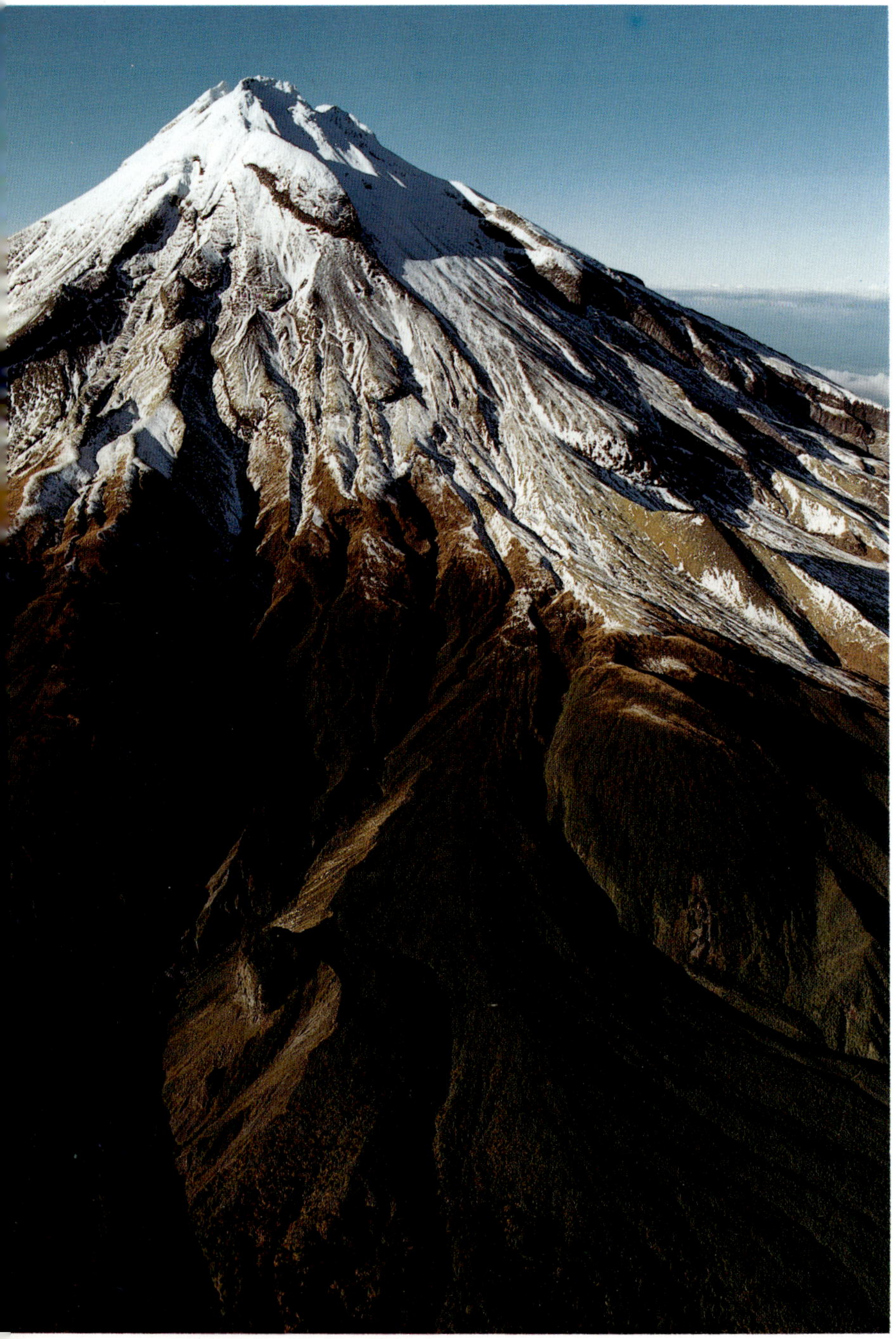

3

3 The north-western slopes of Mt Taranaki illustrate the twin forces of erosion and lava eruption that have shaped the volcano. Remnants of older lava flows (such as the 'Turtle', near the top centre) now perch precariously on the steep slopes, so extensive has the collapse of the outer lava and tephra shell been over the last 10 000 years. Before the present cone was built, the slopes of a former cone collapsed and flowed out to the west, depositing the Pungarehu Formation (Fig. 8).

The prominent almond-shaped bulge (Skinner Hill, centre right) is a relatively young (3000–7000 years) lava dome where lava has cooled over a vent outside the main crater. Most of the dark vegetation on the lower slopes is a dense subalpine shrubland of leatherwood, mountain five-finger and inaka, and a forest canopy can only be seen at the bottom of the photograph. Over the last 500 years, several huge hot and cold flows of debris (known as the Maero Debris Flows) have depressed the tree line here by 300 m compared with other sides of the volcano. The debris flows can be clearly seen running down each side of Skinner Hill.

4 The northern slopes of Mt Taranaki present a dramatic sight 8 km distant from above the summit of the Pouakai Range. No other sector of the volcano shows the ravages of erosion more clearly – from the lahars that impounded the headwaters of Stony River (Hangatahua) to form the Ahukawakawa Swamp (centre), westwards across the deeply-gullied Maero Debris Flows to the skyline cliffs of West Ridge.

There is a superficial resemblance between the red tussock/subalpine scrub of the tops of the Pouakai Range in the foreground and the facing slopes of Mt Taranaki. The tussocklands of the Pouakai tops, however, are poorly drained and carry a number of relatively common subalpine plants absent from or rare on Mt Taranaki.

4

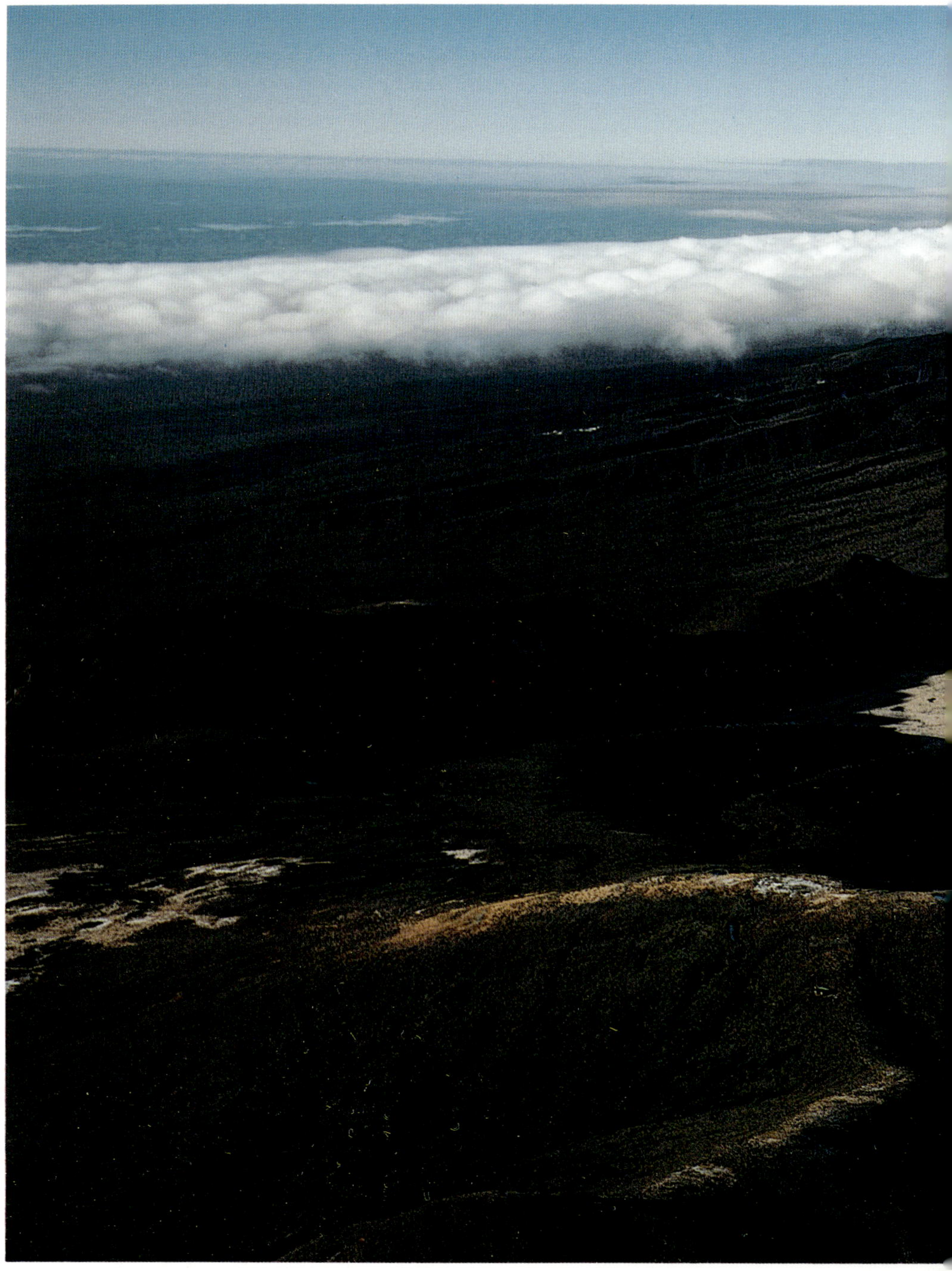

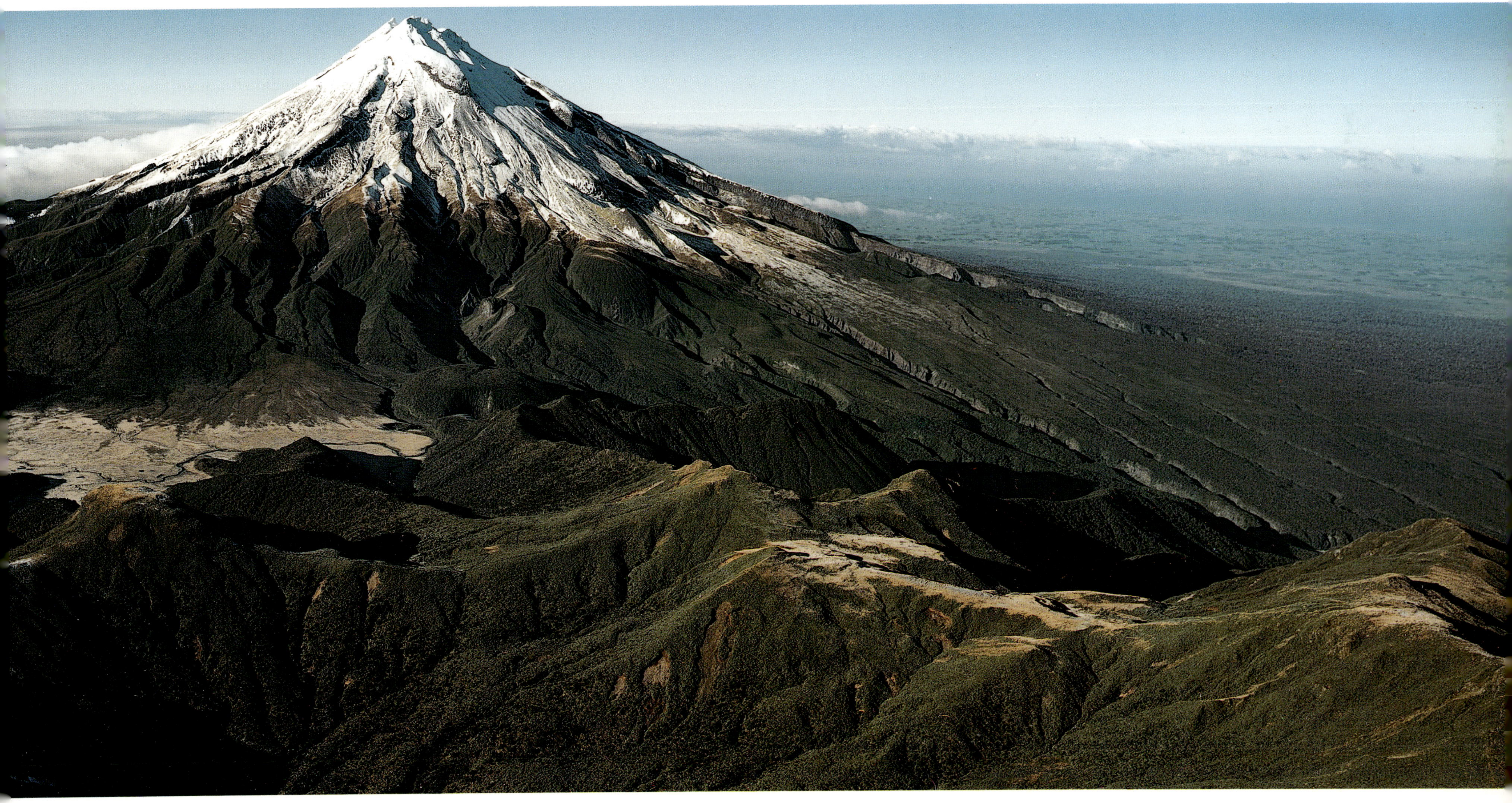

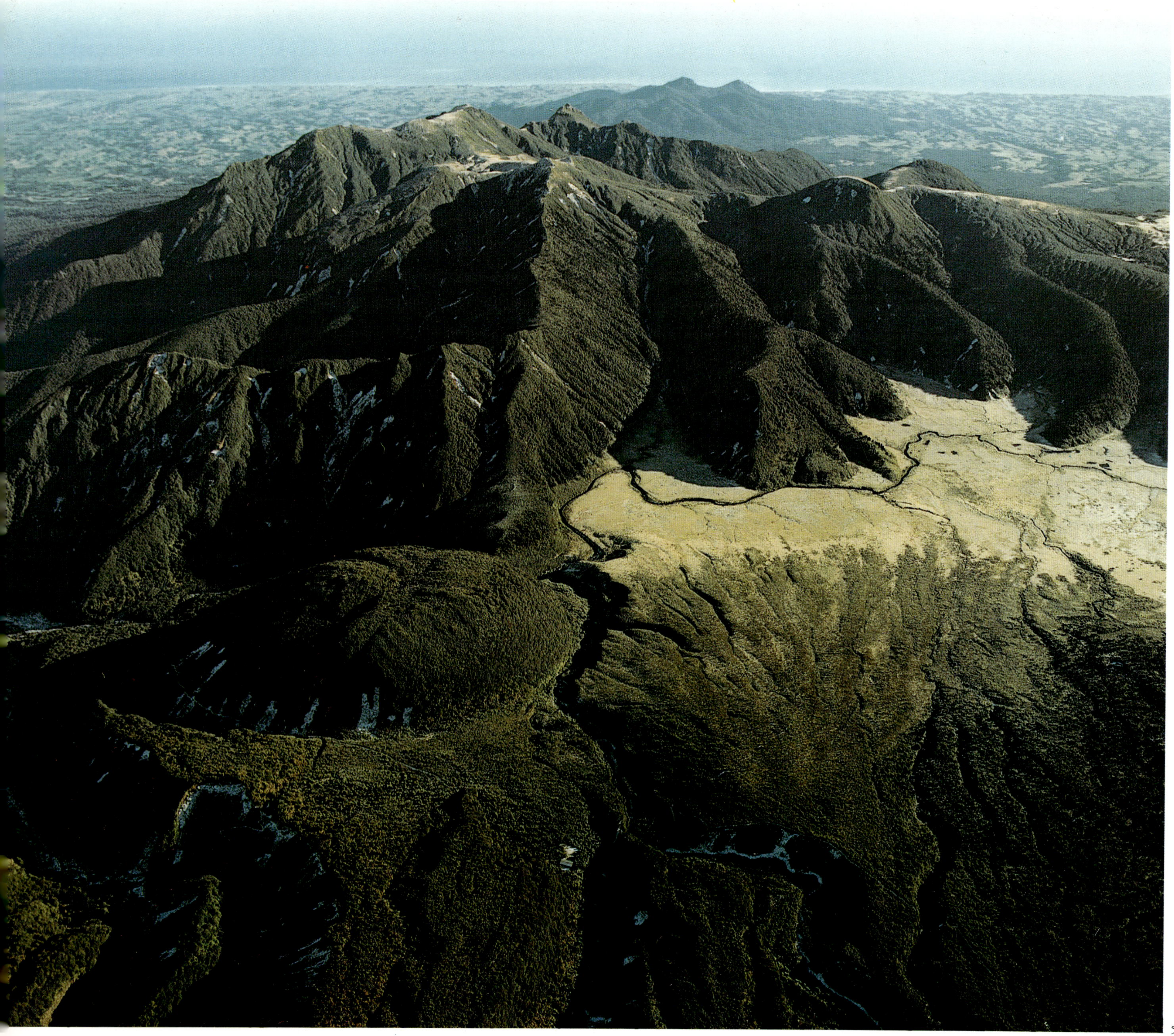

5 Ahukawakawa Swamp is one of the most interesting landforms within the park. It is tucked at 920 m altitude between the northern slopes of Mt Taranaki and the dissected spurs of the Pouakai Range (centre distance); the forested skyline of the Kaitake Range can be seen in the distance. The swamp owes its origin, sometime between 7000 and 3500 years ago, to two events: one was depositional (the welling up of lava forming a new cumulodome, The Dome, seen in the centre left) and the other erosional (the series of debris flows which poured down around The Dome). Debris from these flows can be clearly seen as a fan extending into the swamp from the bottom right of the photograph. As this volcanic debris filled the former bed of Stony River, the river was forced across to the northern side of The Dome, where it cut its way through the lava and formed Bells Falls in the process.

Ahukawakawa Swamp is a large montane wetland covering nearly 270 ha, with peaty soils (containing layers of tephras) and a rich and diverse flora of nearly 260 species of higher plants. Its vegetation reduces in size as the drainage deteriorates, from kaikawaka/kamahi forest on the toe of the Pouakai Range spurs, to red tussockland containing areas of *Carex* spp./*Schoenus pauciflorus* sedgeland, and a groundcover of sphagnum on the wettest and most acidic sites.

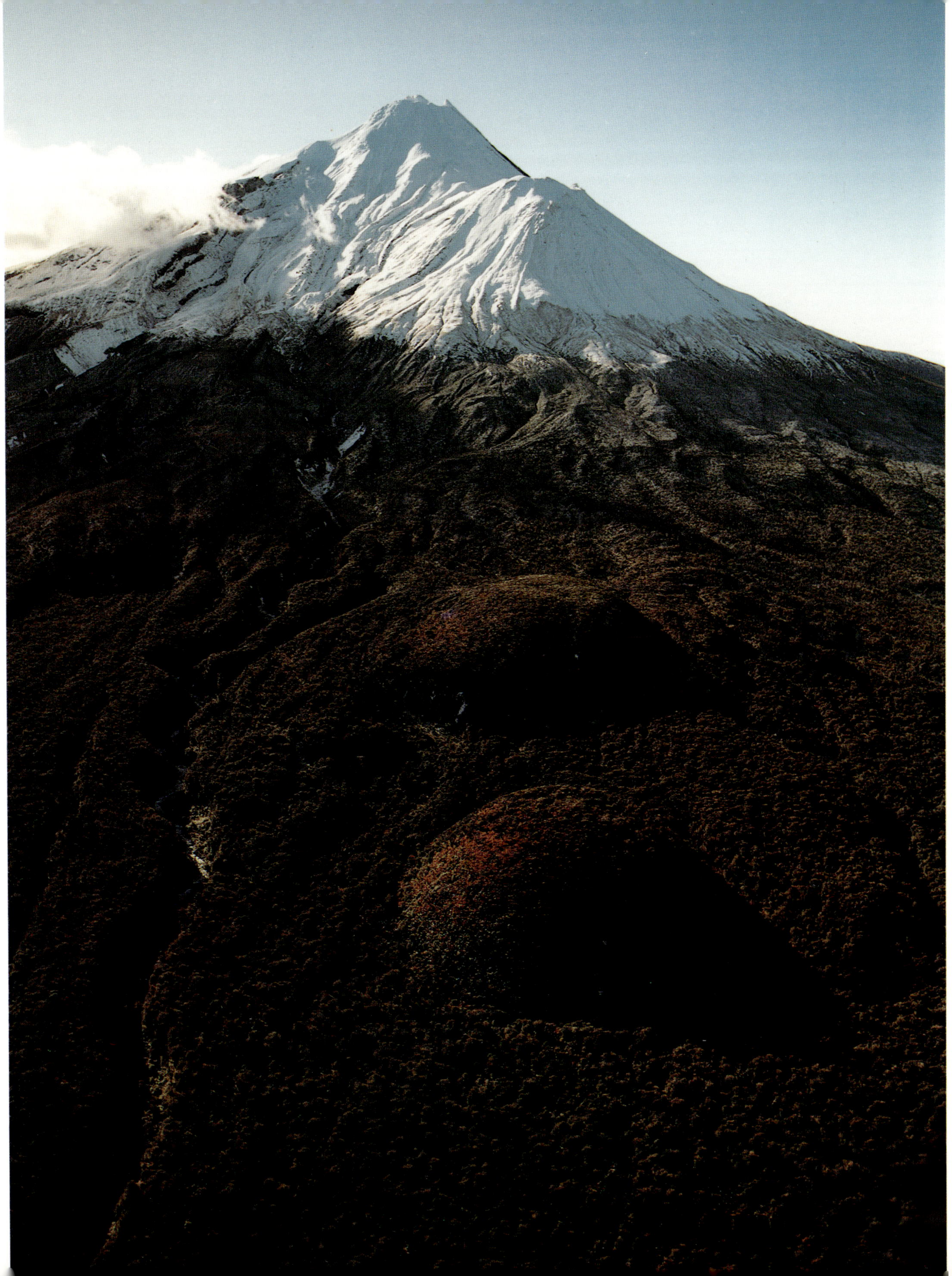

6

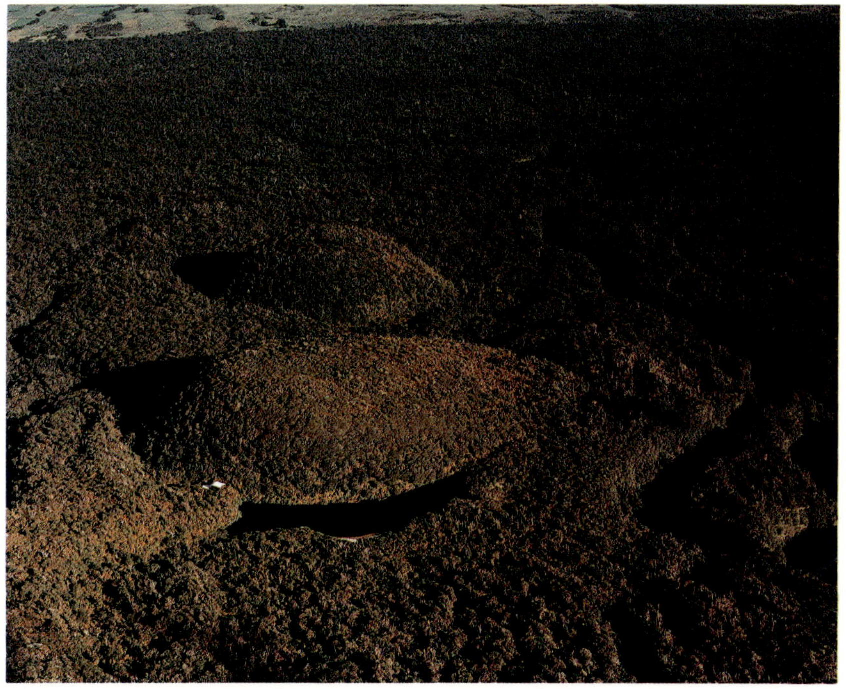

7

6 Two distinctive lava domes, the Beehives, occur at 870 m and 950 m altitude on the southern slopes of Fanthams Peak. Technically called cumulodomes, they were formed between 7000 and 3000 years ago when viscous lava cooled over two subsidiary vents, before it could flow downslope.

The incised bed of Punehu Stream, on the western side of the Beehives, is typical of the course of the fifty or so streams that radiate out from Mt Taranaki. The stream is deeply entrenched in its upper reaches but much less so by the time it reaches the ringplain at the park boundary.

7 Tiny Lake Dive, the only real lake feature of the park, nestles behind the upper Beehive. The position of the lava dome, and later debris flows which piled up around it, have had the effect of ponding the local surface drainage.

The northern and western slopes of the Beehives show differences in vegetation from the surrounding kamahi/mountain totara forest. Goat browsing on the sunny western faces has eliminated palatable plants such as mountain five-finger; this has been replaced with *Pseudowintera colorata* which imparts the reddish-orange colour to the vegetation. Salt in the prevailing westerly winds also has a major effect, and is probably responsible for the large number of dead mountain cedar trees which can be seen in the photograph.

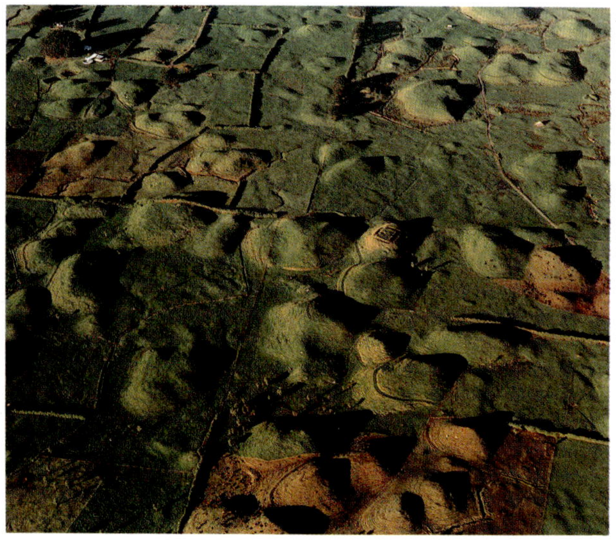

9

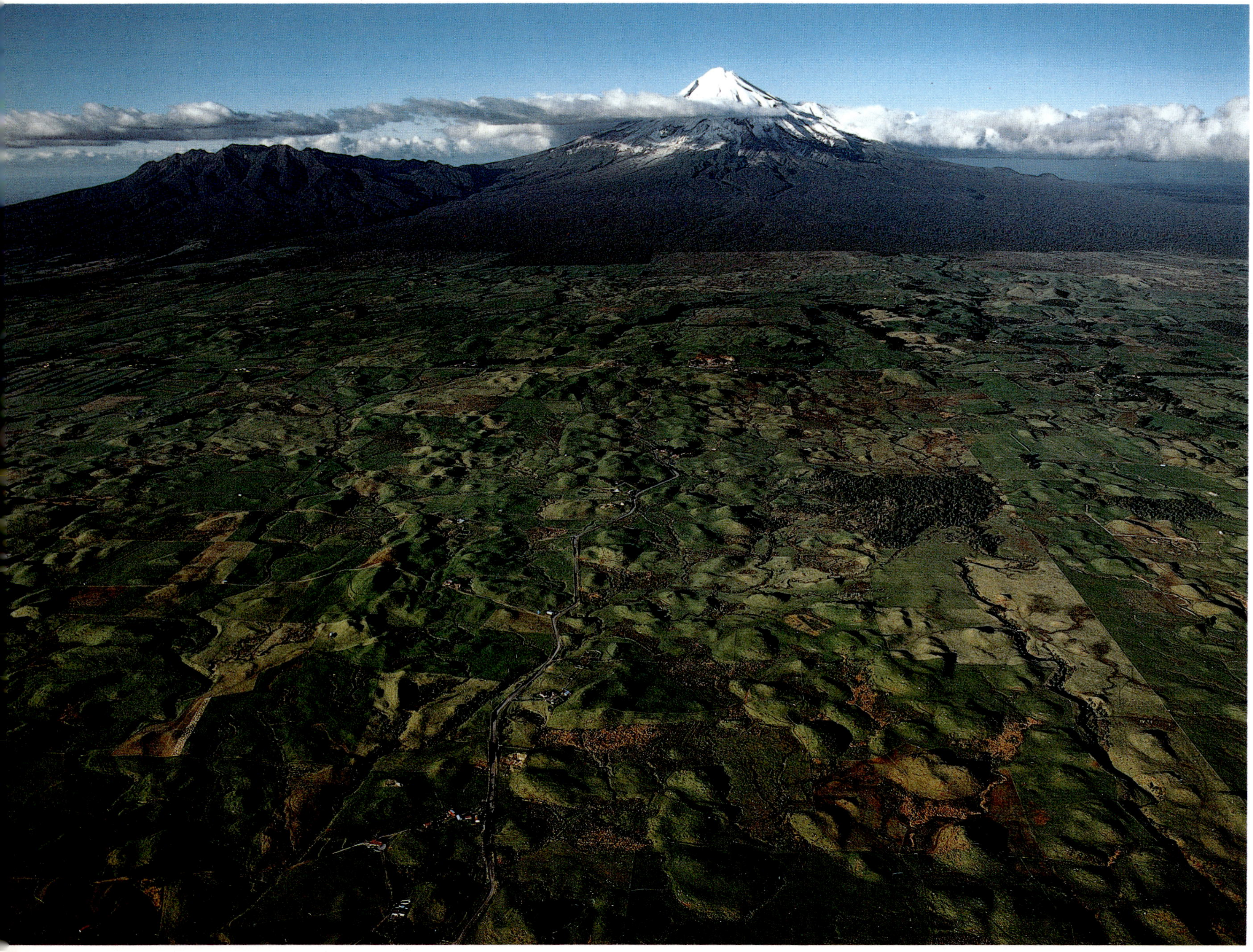

8

8 For 30 km from Okato to Opunake, the surface of the western sector of the Mt Taranaki ringplain is covered by three widespread debris avalanche deposits. The oldest of these is the Pungarehu Formation (estimated at 23 000 years old) pictured here with Mt Taranaki and the Pouakai Range (left) in the background. Characteristic of this formation are the thousands of mounds which dimple the ringplain, now clearly visible since the removal of the forest.

9 The debris avalanche mounds vary from cones to flattened hemispheres. They consist of stones and boulders covered with a layer of volcanic ash (airfall from subsequent eruptions) which varies in depth from 60 cm near the coast to over 2 m at the park boundary. Weathering of the deposits has caused some cementation of the rock debris, which, coupled with the closed basins between the mounds, has impeded soil drainage in the lower-lying areas.

The remains of a Maori fortification can be seen on the summit of one of the mounds (centre).

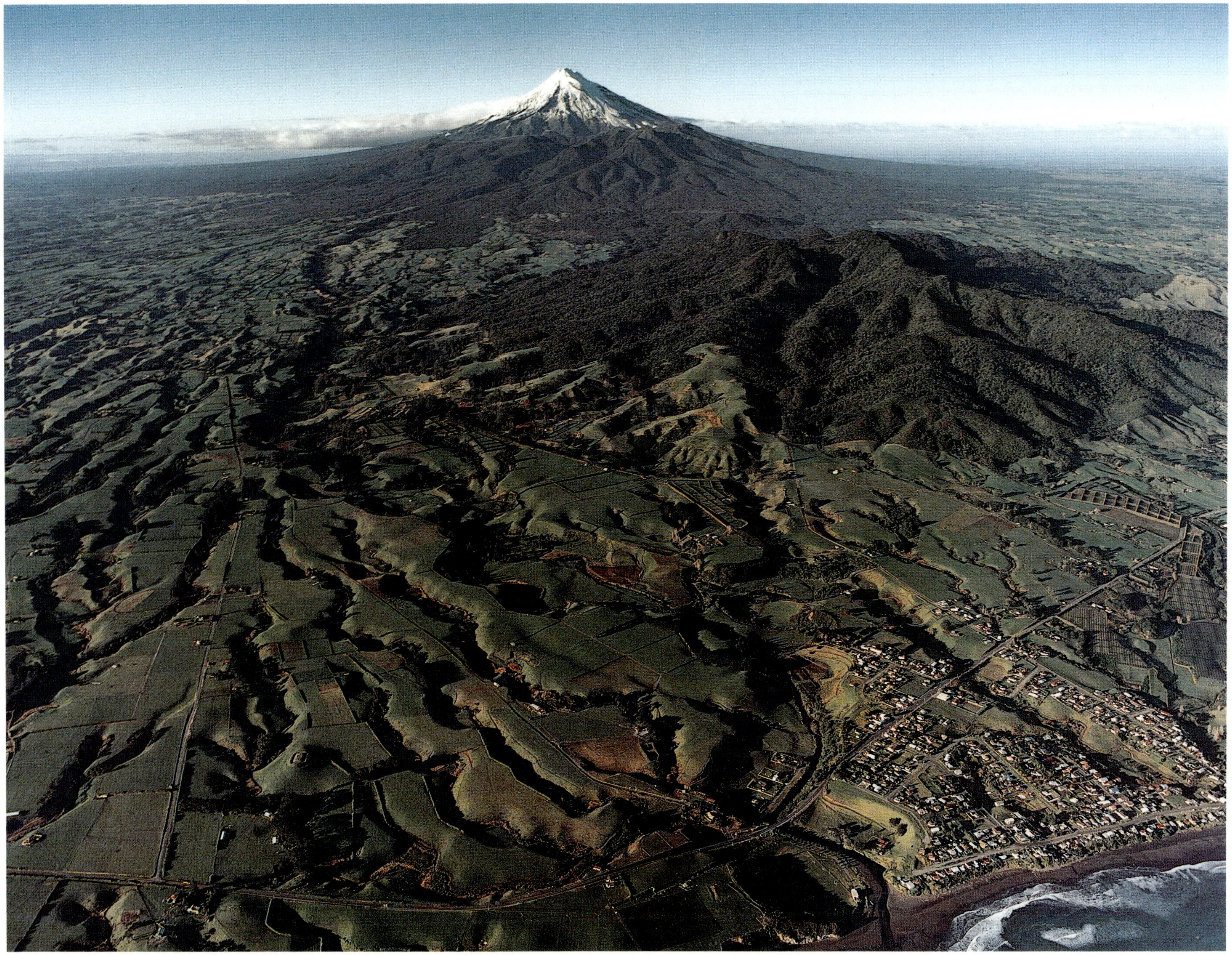

10

10 From above the town of Oakura on the north Taranaki coast, the line of volcanic activity can be seen running south-east from the 600 000 year-old deeply eroded cone of Patuha in the Kaitake Range (foreground) to Mt Taranaki on the skyline. Mt Taranaki's symmetrical concave slopes are typical of a strato-volcano: a steep central cone built up by layers of lava and tephra from which a gently sloping ringplain has developed through erosion over tens of thousands of years.

The extensive debris avalanches and lahars from the northern slopes of Mt Taranaki did not reach this coastline between New Plymouth and the mouth of the Stony River because they were blocked by the bulk of Pouakai. Consequently, the old Pouakai ringplain remains as the main landform (left and foreground), its surface smoothed by thick additions of airfall volcanic ash and dissected by the Oakura River (outlet, bottom right) and other streams.

11 From Stratford in the east, the snow-covered cone of Mt Taranaki appears to float high above its apron of forest. The circular boundary of the park (9.6 km radius from the summit of the cone) can be easily appreciated from this vantage point.

The debris avalanche mounds, so prevalent on the western sector of Mt Taranaki's ringplain (Figs 8 and 9), are absent from the east. Here, watery lahars, instead of creating mounds, formed a level surface now thickly mantled with a series of coarse tephras. The youngest of these are collectively termed the Stratford Ash and have been erupted since 7000 years ago.

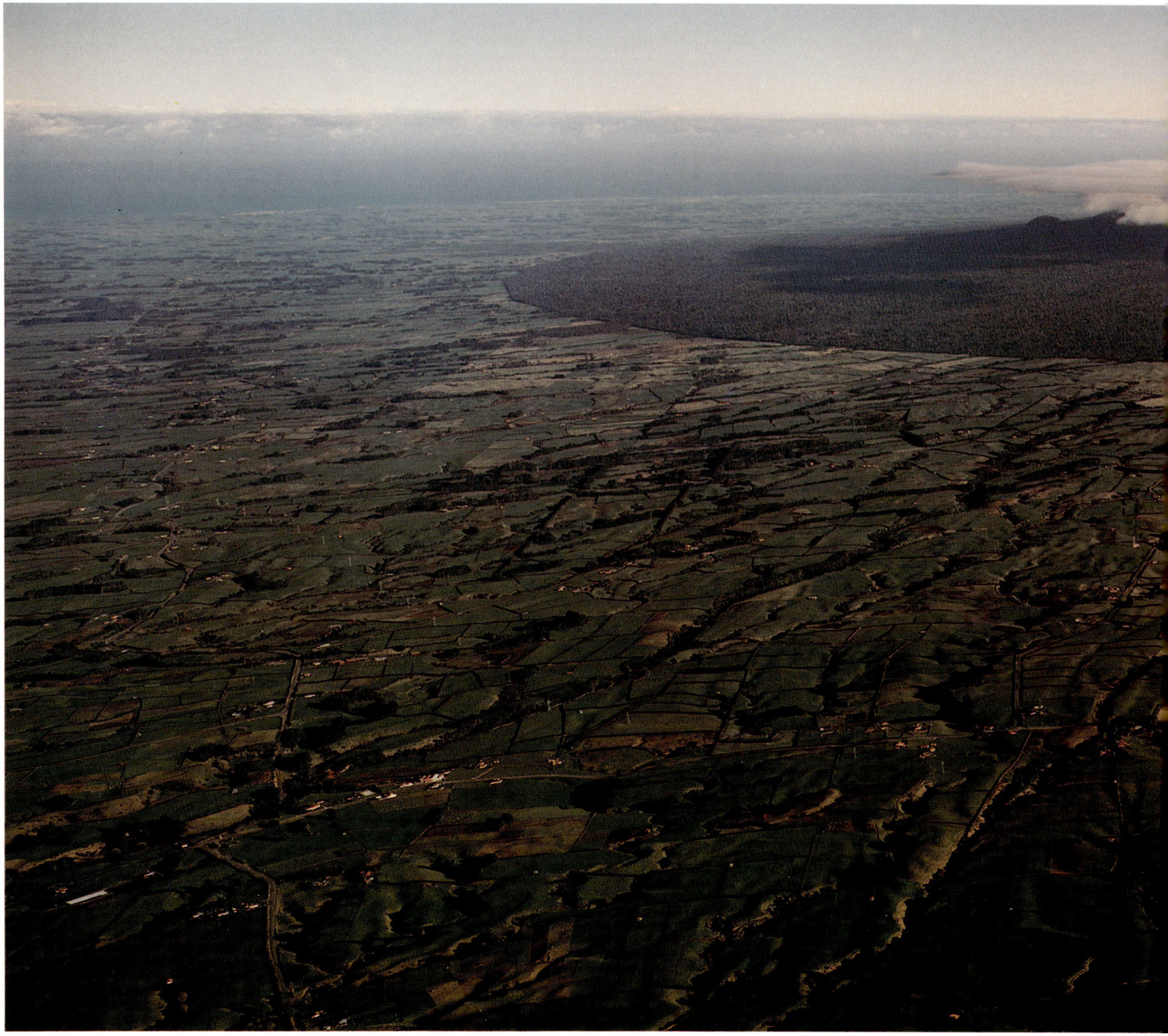

11

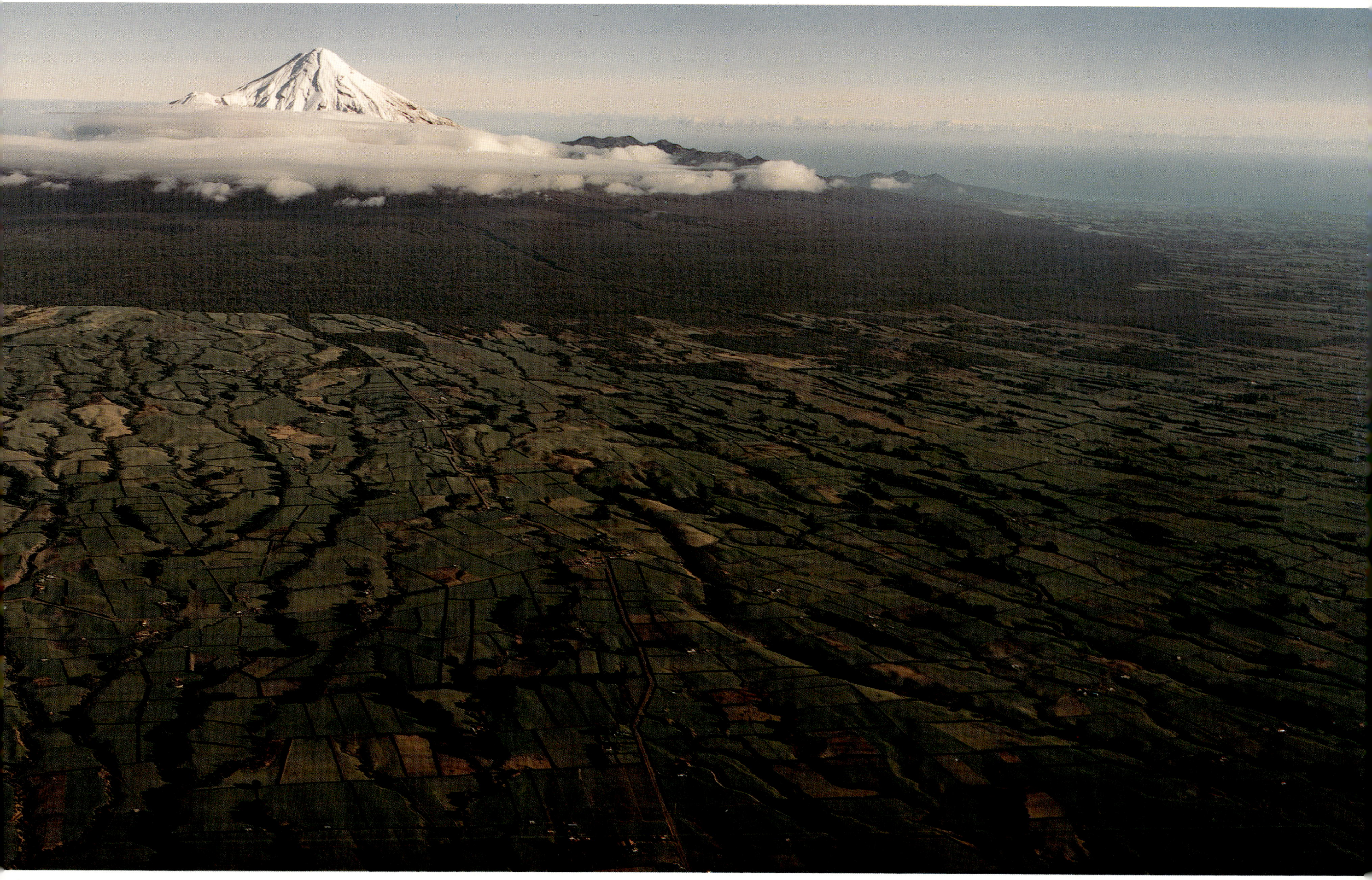

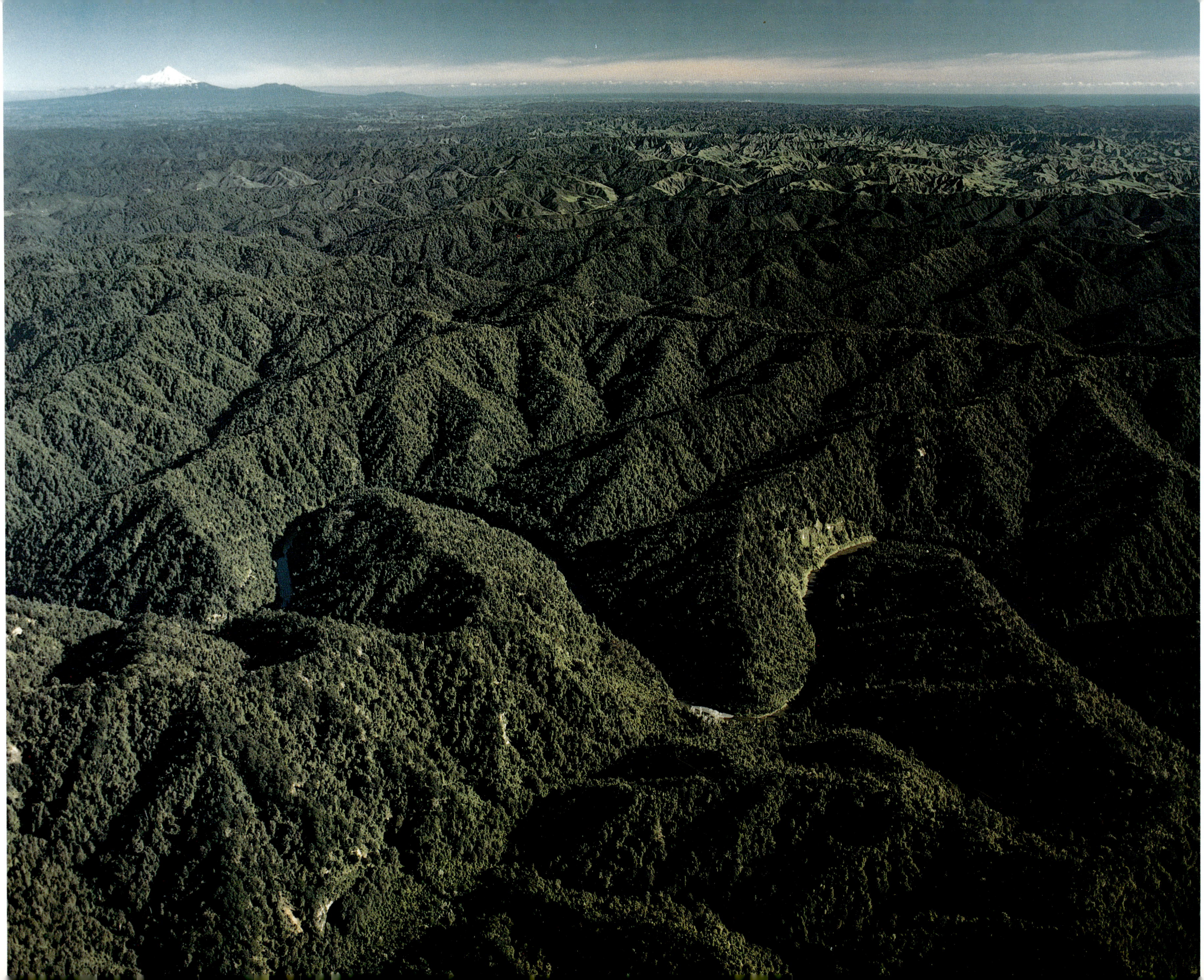

1

WHANGANUI NATIONAL PARK

Whanganui National Park is very different from the rest of New Zealand's national parks. It has no alpine areas or volcanoes; there are no coastal headlands and beaches, lakes, glaciers or braided rivers. Instead, the park has only one feature which dominates its rugged, densely-forested landscapes – the entrenched Wanganui River. The river weaves a tortuous route for 170 km through the three separate sections of the park, from Te Maire 15 km below Taumarunui to Atene 30 km from Wanganui city (see map, p. 150). Virtually the entire 74 000 hectares of the park lie within the Wanganui catchment, so the river is an artery conducting the flow of energy through the park. It collects the waters from the western slopes of the volcanoes at the southern end of the Taupo Volcanic Zone (Chapter 12); historically, it was the access route to the interior, not only for the Maori people but also for European settlers prior to the completion of the North Island Main Trunk Railway in the early part of this century. Today, the river is still the main route through the park, popular with canoeists, jet-boaters and other tourist craft because of its scenery, ease of navigation, and deep historic and cultural significance to Maori and Pakeha alike.

LANDFORMS OF THE WANGANUI BASIN

From the late-Tertiary to mid-Quaternary period, the Wanganui locality was a sea-floor basin. Over millions of years a depth of thousands of metres of sediment had collected in this basin, eroded from a huge arc of higher land extending around the volcanoes of Taranaki and Tongariro, to the Ruahine Ranges, and the mountains of north-west Nelson in the south. Gradually, this basin was uplifted and the sea retreated to the south-west, leaving a flat surface of soft weakly-folded sediments which dips gently to the south. Most of these soft rocks are mudstones ('papa') with occasional bands of sandstone, dating from early Quaternary near the coastline, to Pliocene in the southern part of the park, to late Miocene north of the Tangahoe locality. This is the only substantial area of soft sedimentary rocks (except for the Miocene mudstone/sandstone around Lake Waikaremoana, p. 175) within New Zealand's national parks.

The soft sediments of the Wanganui basin are easily eroded. The relatively homogenous rock types and lack of faults allows gullies and streams to develop almost at random. Two very characteristic landform features have emerged – a dendritic drainage system and a maturely dissected landscape in which all valley slopes lie at the same angle (see p. 151). A dendritic drainage network is shaped like the branches of a tree, all gradually feeding in to the trunk (the channel of the Wanganui itself); this is in marked contrast to the symmetry of the radial drainage pattern on the ringplains of the volcanoes of Egmont and Tongariro National Parks which flank Whanganui National Park (compare the maps on pp. 138, 150 and 156).

The water quality of the two volcanic parks contrast with that of Whanganui National Park. The streams draining the volcanoes are swift rapidly-flowing and generally clear; they rise rapidly during heavy rain but the volcanic debris swept along in their floodwaters is coarse (generally sand or gravel), and soon settles out around the margins of the volcanic ringplain forming characteristic aggrading streambeds (such as Punehu Stream in Egmont National Park, p. 143). Where the rivers draining the western slopes of Tongariro National Park (the upper Wanganui, Whakapapa, Manganui-a-te-ao, and Mangawhero) pass into the 'papa country' their waters quickly become turbid from the silt- and clay-sized sediments eroded from the soft mudstone. These fine suspended sediments account for the muddy colour of the eastern tributaries of the Wanganui – like the Ongarue, Ohura, Tangarakau and Whangamomona Rivers.

The soft nature of the sedimentary rocks has allowed the Wanganui River to develop a gentle gradient; although there are over 200 named rapids between Taumarunui and Pipiriki, most of them have a vertical drop of less than 1 metre. Rock hazards are almost non-existent below the junction with the Retaruke River and, instead, the river traveller is hemmed in by sheer papa walls and the lack of beaches. In the lower reaches of the Wanganui River, approaching Atene, river terraces again become a prominent feature of the landscape. From the air, most of the ridge crests are of similar altitude and it is possible to appreciate how they were once parts of an ancient uplifted marine surface which has been almost destroyed by the down-cutting of the major streams and the extension of gullies as they progressively eat their way back towards their interfluves (a process termed 'headward erosion', well illustrated on p. 151). Below Atene, at the southern end of the park, the great marine terraces of the Quaternary period step down to the Wanganui coastline. Each major terrace marks high sea level during the fluctuating cold and warm stages of the so-called Ice Ages. These remarkable terraces provide an uninterrupted record of marine deposition in New Zealand from the late Pliocene to the present day. Perhaps it is not an idle hope that, one day, representative segments of these marine terraces may be given more formal protection. With the sedimentary landforms of the hinterland in Whanganui National Park, they are an outstanding example of landforms representing the depositional geological processes in New Zealand over the last 25 million years.

1 Whanganui National Park is a very rugged elongated national park, based on the middle reaches of the Wanganui River. At this point, just above Otaihanga reach (centre, left), the river is over 150 km from its mouth but it is still only 70 m above sea level. As the Wanganui basin has been gradaully lifted, the river has had little difficulty in cutting down through the soft mudstone ('papa') and sandstone. The gradient of the Wanganui River is, therefore, so gentle that it was navigated as the main route to the Tongariro volcanoes and Lake Taupo for both Maori and nineteenth-century European travellers.

The volcanic cone of Mt Taranaki (Fig. 10, Egmont) can be seen 80 km to the west, as well as the sea within the North Taranaki Bight, 50 km to the north-west (top, right).

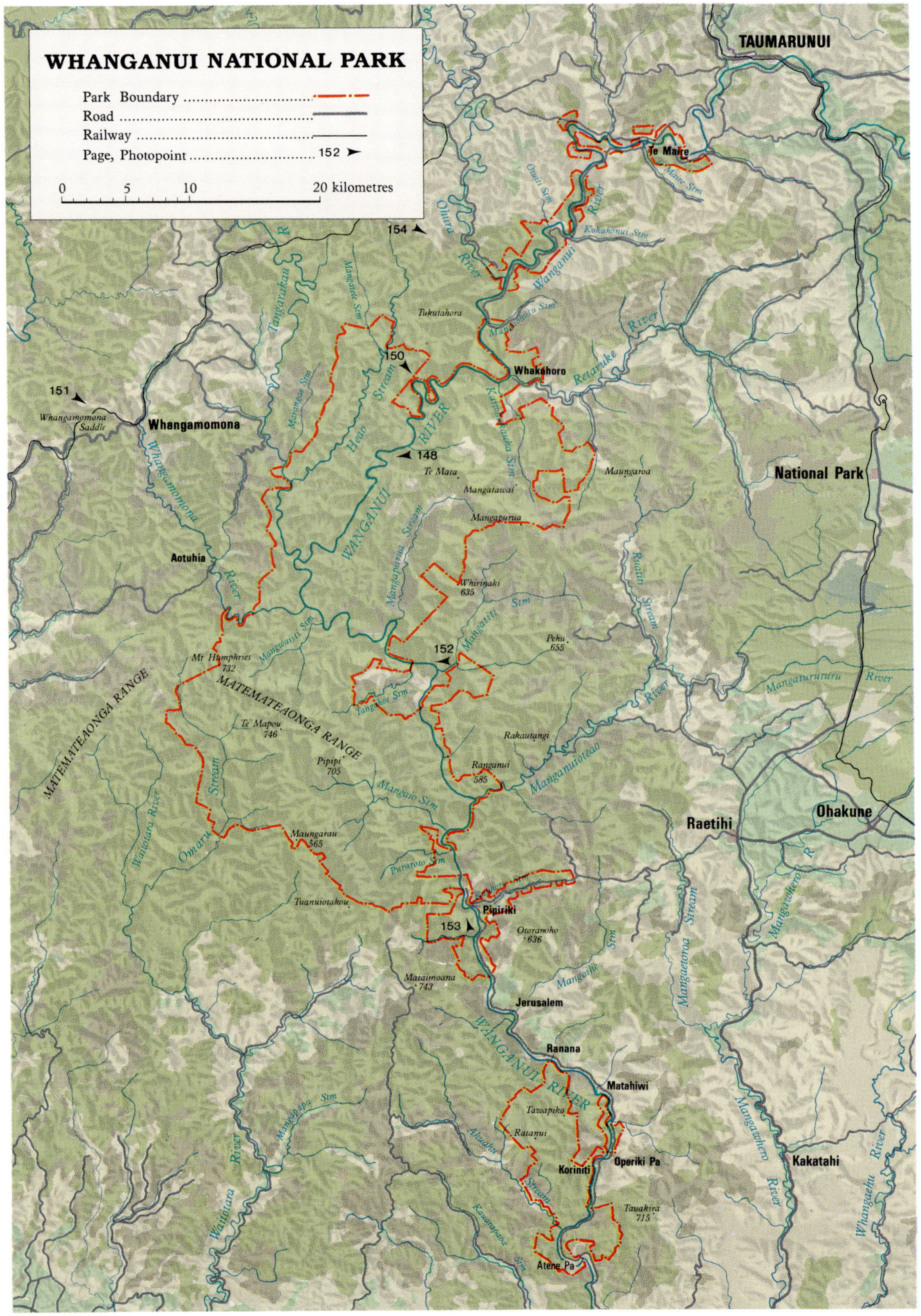

2 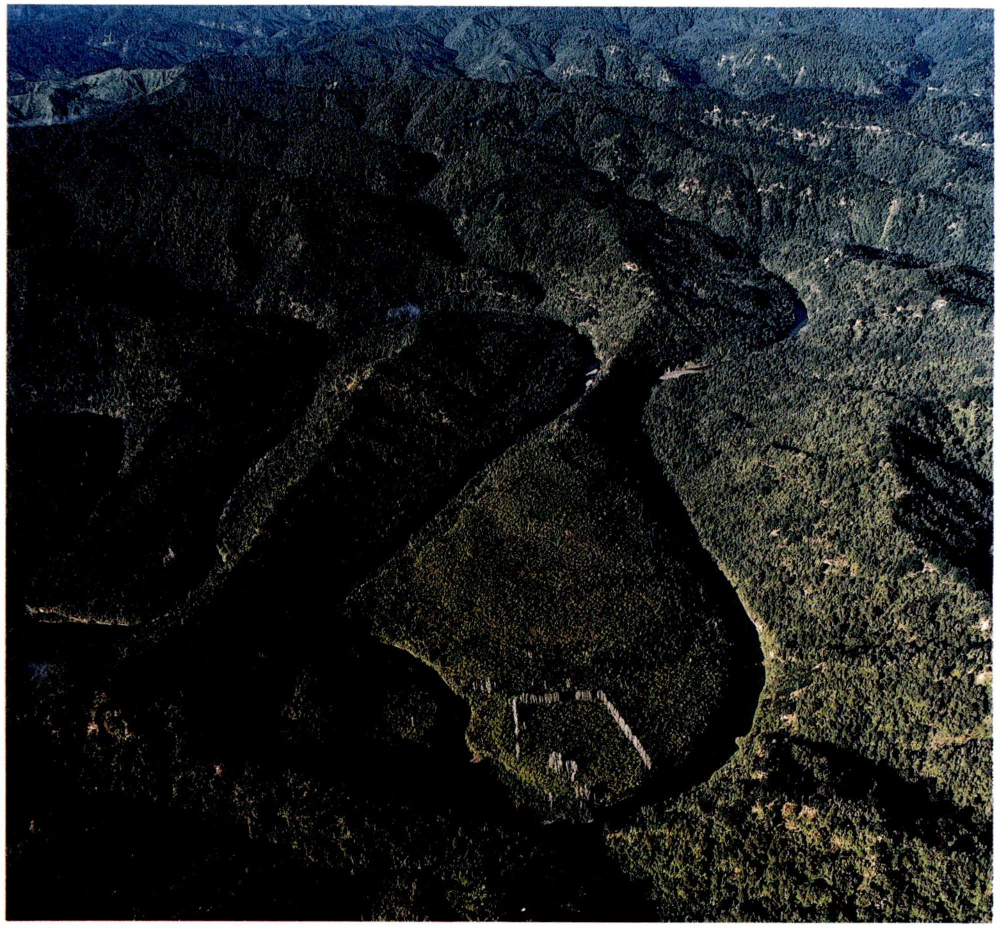

2 A few kilometres below its junction with the Retaruke River, the Wanganui River has cut a series of regular, flowing curves as it begins to meander from one side of its valley to the other. As the river matures, these meanders become more pronounced and the river can almost double back on itself. Eventually the stream may break through the neck, shortening the river's course and leaving a cut-off meander. These horseshoe-shaped ponds are often called 'ox-bow lakes', which eventually fill up with sediment and peat to become swamps. The Atene ox-bow at the southern end of the park is a very good example of a cutoff meander.

3 The Wanganui River flows from left to right in the middle distance as it drains the vast sedimentary basin between the hill country of east Taranaki (foreground) and the volcanic uplands around Mt Ruapehu and Tongariro National Park in the distance (see Chapter 12). The Stratford–Okahukura Railway can be seen in the foreground on the northern side of Whangamomona Saddle.

Clearance of forest from the hills has revealed the distinctive erosional landforms which have developed in the soft mudstone. Note the smooth surfaces to most of the spur crests and the regular-spaced gullies on sides of the spurs. Many of these gullies are eroding towards their head, eventually producing a razor-backed crest to the spur.

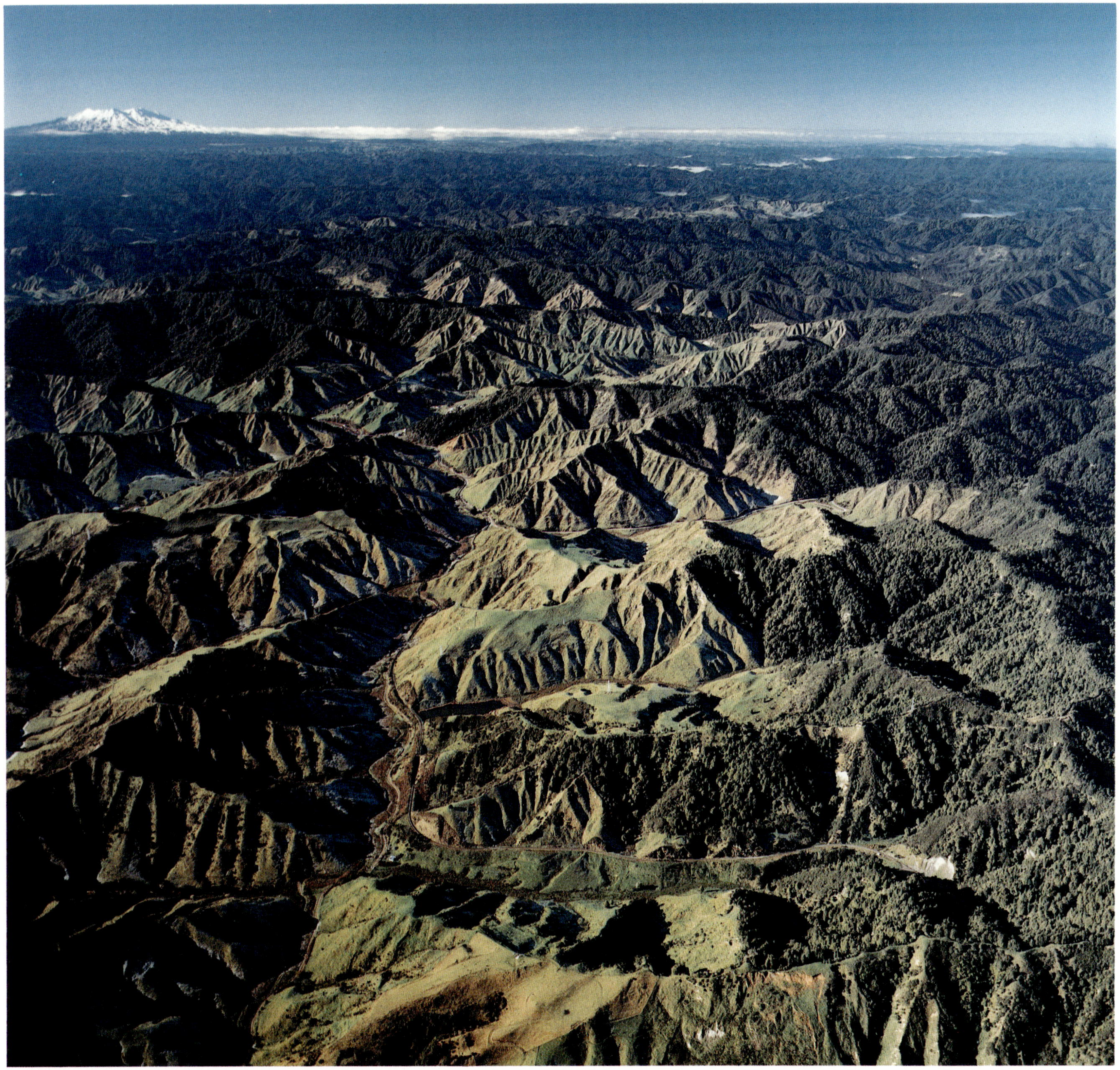

3

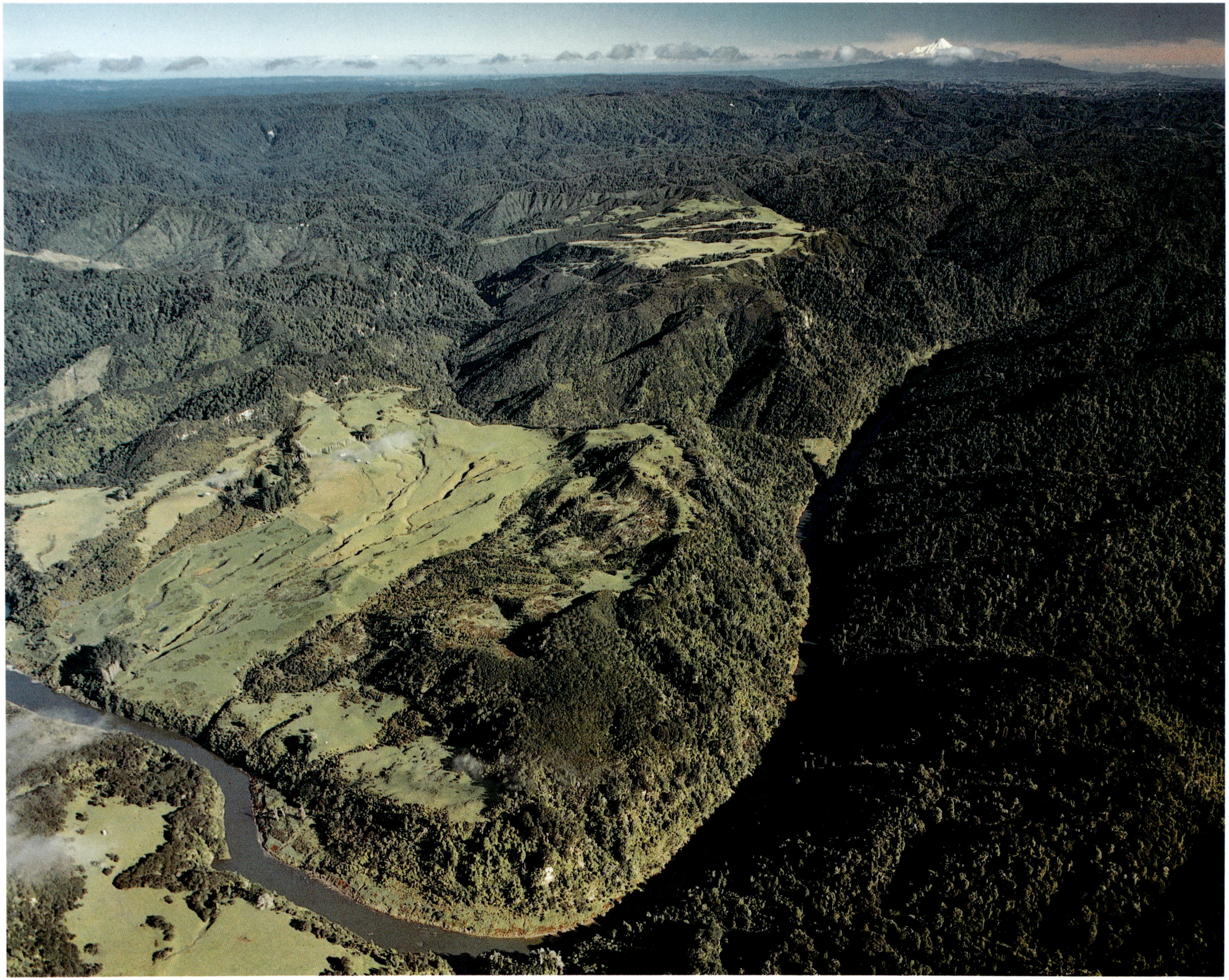

4

4 Just below the Tangahoe Stream (centre) the Wanganui River makes a very pronounced turn to the south. The smooth crests of the densely-forested Matemateaonga Range can be seen in the middle distance to the west.

In contrast to the dissected east Taranaki hill country shown in Fig. 3, this landscape appears more subdued with broader summits whose heights are fairly constant at 500–700 m altitude. These accordant summits are probably the remnants of the surfaces of very old marine terraces. The drainage pattern in this sedimentary landscape is deeply incised and very irregular (termed a 'dendritic stream pattern' because of its resemblance to the branches of a tree). Contrast this pattern with the near-perfect radial drainage pattern on the ringplain of volcanoes like Mt Taranaki in the distance.

5 The lack of significant rapids in the graded channel of the Wanganui River can be appreciated from this view upstream from Pipiriki. Note the absence of any floodplain, although by this stage a discontinuous series of terrace remnants occur about 40 m above the river.

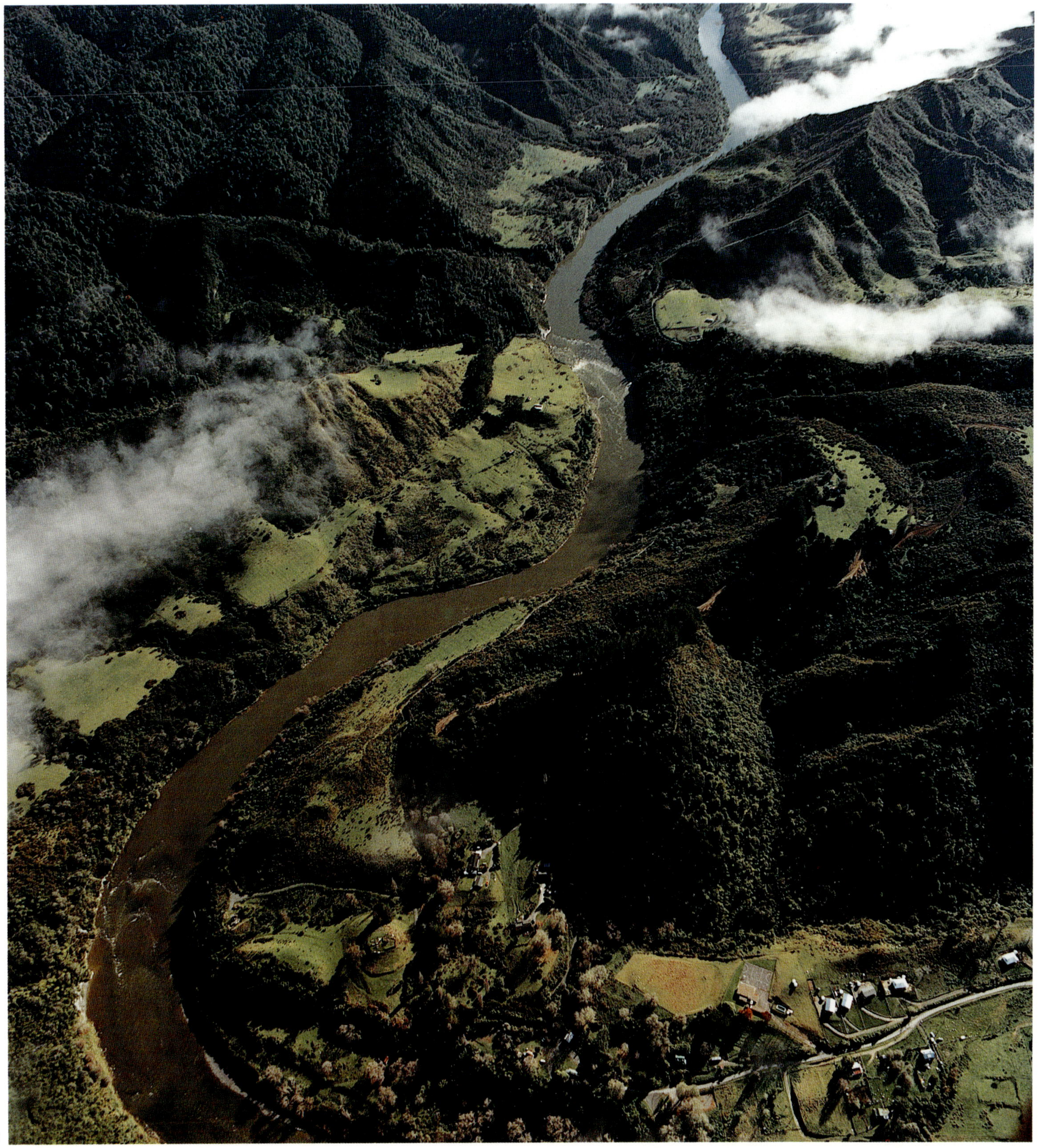

5

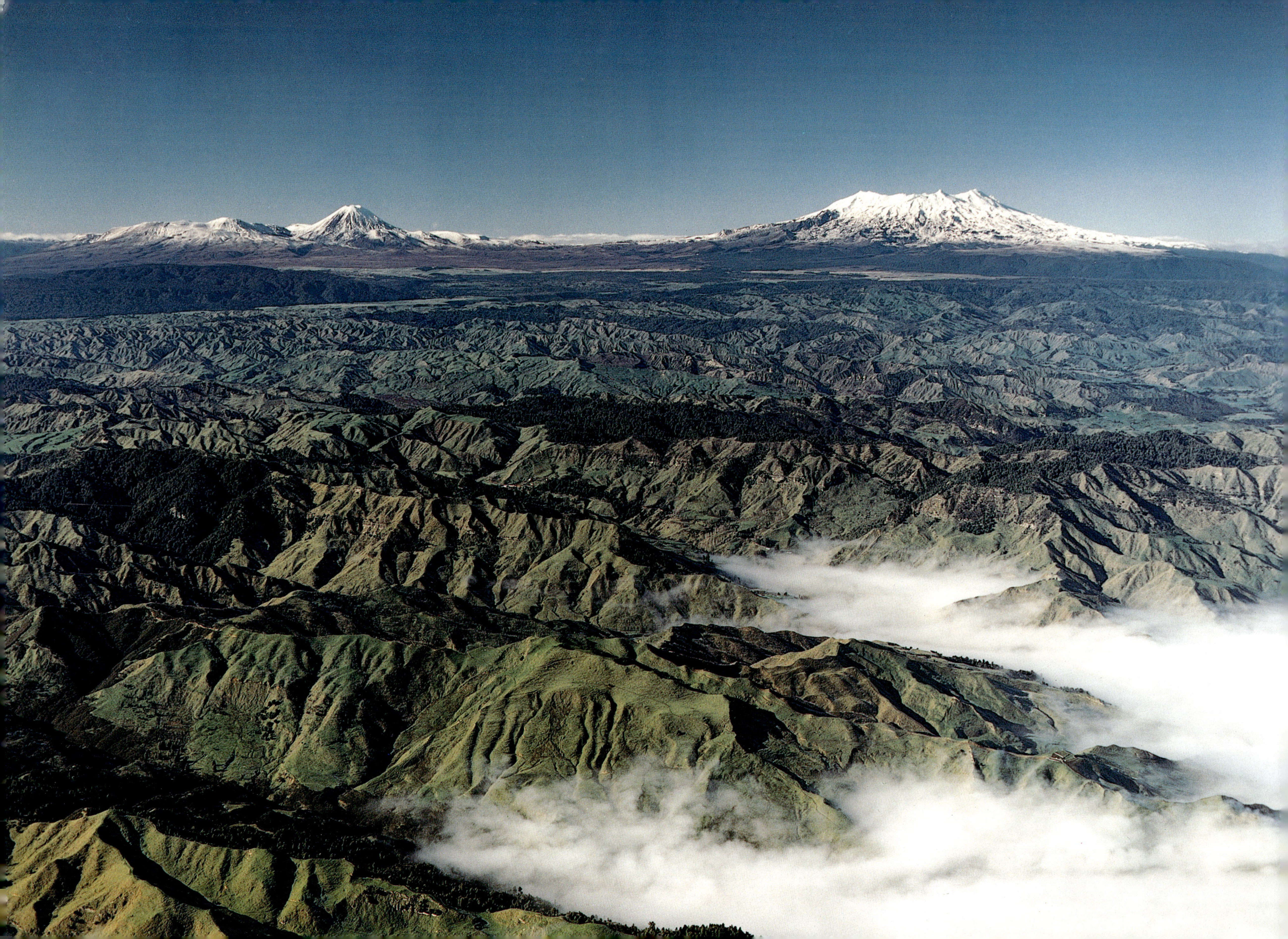

TONGARIRO NATIONAL PARK

Tongariro National Park is New Zealand's premier national park – the best known and the most visited. Its volcanic landscape is the scenic highlight of any road or rail journey between Wellington and Auckland and in winter its skifields attract skiers from the entire North Island. It is also New Zealand's oldest national park – in an administrative rather than a geological sense, for the centennial of the gifting by the Ngati Tuwharetoa people of this the first national park was celebrated on 23 September 1987. In geological terms Tongariro and Egmont National Parks contain the youngest rock types in our national park system.

TAUPO VOLCANIC ZONE

Tongariro National Park stands at the south-western end of a massive rift zone which runs north-east through Lake Taupo, past Rotorua to White Island in the Bay of Plenty. Known as the Taupo Volcanic Zone, this rift is an active part of a long chain of volcanoes extending northwards along the edge of the Pacific Plate through the Kermadec Islands and Tonga to Samoa. The central part of the Taupo Volcanic Zone (Lakes Rotorua, Okataina and Taupo) is characterised by explosive eruptions of highly viscous rhyolitic pumice, whereas the volcanoes of the Tongariro National Park are andesitic in composition and their eruptions are usually less violent.

VOLCANOES OF THE PARK

The largest (albeit lowest) of the volcanoes is Tongariro, from which the park takes its name; it is a sprawling composite volcano pockmarked with as many as eight recognisable craters and major vents. Its huge size (100 sq. km) and complexity is generally not appreciated by the passer-by, for Mts Ruapehu and Ngauruhoe are much more imposing peaks. Mts Tongariro and Ruapehu were active as long as 250 000 years ago. Tongariro is a rather quiescent volcano now. Eruptions from the upper Te Mari Crater in 1896–97 spread significant amounts of volcanic ash to the east; ash was also erupted from Red Crater in 1896, and again in 1926. Today, vulcanism is only evident at the surface in three small thermal areas – the fumaroles and warm ground at Red Crater, Te Mari Crater, and Ketetahi Hot Springs on the northern flanks of North Crater.

Mt Ruapehu is another huge and complex volcano, its 3 km-long summit made up of five craters and six main peaks – Tahurangi, Te Heu Heu, Paretetaitonga, Girdlestone, Mitre and Pyramid Peak – all with permanent snowfields. Ruapehu still carries the only glaciers within the park, although they are now greatly reduced in size. Its present active vent is filled by a warm lake, Crater Lake, whose colour changes dramatically according to the presence or absence of volcanic activity below.

The peak of most interest to the amateur vulcanologist is Mt Ngauruhoe. Its present steep-sided symmetrical cone is only 2500 years old, it is generally active, and the climb to the rim of the active vent on the summit is relatively easy. Both Ruapehu and Ngauruhoe have erupted spectacularly within the memory of most adults – Ruapehu in 1945 (a major eruption), 1969 and 1975; and Ngauruhoe in 1949, 1954 (a major eruption), 1974 and 1975. Each eruption produced lava or tephra to further build up each cone or mantle the surrounding landscape. The 1969 and 1975 eruptions on Mt Ruapehu produced lahars which flowed into the Whakapapa skifield area, damaging facilities – a timely reminder of the inevitable risks involved in recreation on an active volcano.

Many of the lava flows are more apparent from the air than on the ground, particularly where their vegetation cover is different from the rest of the landscape. The huge Rangataua lava flows extend for 14 km down the south-west slopes of Mt Ruapehu; they are more than 10 000 years old and dense silver and red beech forest tends to mask their subtle outlines. The Oturere valley lava flow, on the other hand, is only sparsely vegetated even though it was erupted more than 2500 years ago; the transverse ripples of jagged dark lava stand out along the 8 km length of the flow from the Red Crater of Tongariro. Perhaps the most striking example from the air is the relatively young (450 years) lava flow from the upper Te Mari crater; the sombre purple colour of the lava still shows through a sparse cover of mountain toatoa and manuka.

IMPRINT OF ICE AGE GLACIERS

Of the three main peaks, only Tongariro still carries easily recognisable landforms of glacial origin. The Mangatepopo, Makahikatoa, Waihohonu, Oturere, and Mangahouhounui valleys all used to carry glaciers which radiated out from Tongariro and a former larger volcano around the vent now occupied by Ngauruhoe. These glaciers were up to 5 km long and gouged out the broad troughs now flanked by ridges of lateral moraine in the upper reaches of the valleys. Unfortunately, there are no surviving terminal moraines to match the Waiho Loop of Westland National Park (see pp. 76–77).

Of the other two peaks, Ngauruhoe is too young and volcanic activity and erosion seem to have obliterated most of the moraines around Ruapehu. The Waihianoa valley, draining the south-eastern slopes, is probably the best preserved example of a glacier-shaped valley on Mt Ruapehu.

EFFECT OF TAUPO ERUPTION

The most devastating eruption in the vicinity of the park in post-glacial times emanated from the north-east corner of present-day Lake Taupo – the great Taupo Eruption of 1800 years ago. Rhyolitic pumice (up to 50 m thick along the eastern shores of Lake Taupo) covered large sections of the central and eastern parts of the North Island. An enormous hot pyroclastic flow devastated two-thirds of the vegetation around the volcanic peaks, except where it was sheltered on the lee slopes – the southern sides of the Kakaramea–Tihia–Pihanga volcanoes, Hauhungatahi, and Ruapehu. Taupo pumice deposits within the park were up to 30 cm thick, but have been eroded from the steeper areas and unstable sites like the gravelfields of the Rangipo 'Desert' in the rainshadow on the eastern side of Mt Ruapehu.

1 The position of the volcanic peaks of Tongariro National Park on the central 'roof' of the North Island is well illustrated in this photograph looking east-south-east from near the junction of the Wanganui River with the Ohura River. The three volcanoes (left to right: Tongariro, Ngauruhoe, Ruapehu) have built up relatively smooth, gently-sloping aprons called ringplains. The western sectors of these ringplains (middle distance) give way abruptly to a very different, non-volcanic rock type – the softer, easily-eroded late Tertiary sediments that make up the dissected upper Wanganui hill country. All the streams draining this landscape eventually flow into the Wanganui River within Whanganui National Park (Chapter 11).

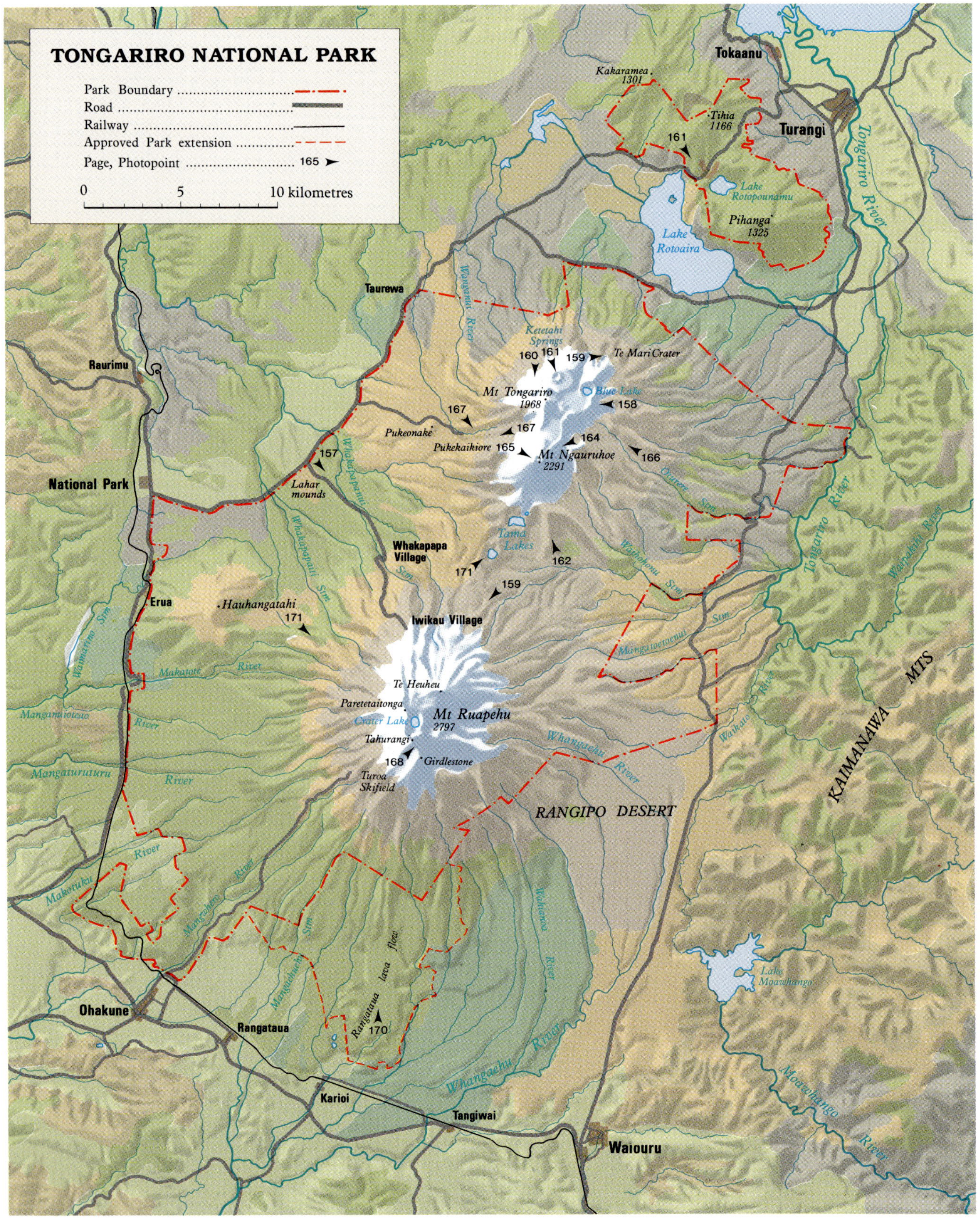
TONGARIRO NATIONAL PARK
Park Boundary
Road
Railway
Approved Park extension
Page, Photopoint 165
0 5 10 kilometres
Tokaanu
Kakaramea 1301
Tihia 1166
Turangi
Tongariro River
161
Lake Rotopounamu
Lake Rotoaira
Pihanga 1325
Taurewa
Whanganui River
Ketetahi Springs
160 161 159
Te Mari Crater
Raurimu
Mt Tongariro 1968
Blue Lake
158
167
Pukeonake
167
Pukekaikiore 165
164
Mt Ngauruhoe 2291
166
157
Lahar mounds
National Park
Whakapapanui
Whakapapaiti Stm
Oturere Stm
Tama Lakes
Whakapapa Village
162
171
159
Waihohonu Stm
Erua
Hauhangatahi
171
Iwikau Village
Mangatoetoenui Stm
Waimarino Stm
Makatote River
Te Heuheu
Paretetaitonga
Manganuiateao River
Crater Lake
Mt Ruapehu 2797
Tahurangi
168
Girdlestone
Turoa Skifield
Whangaehu River
Waikato Stm
KAIMANAWA MTS
Mangaturuturu River
RANGIPO DESERT
Tongariro River
Waipakihi River
Makotuku River
Mangawhero River
Mangaehuehu Stm
Rangataua lava flow
Wahianoa River
Lake Moawhango
Ohakune
Rangataua
170
Whangaehu River
Karioi
Tangiwai
Waiouru
Moawhango River

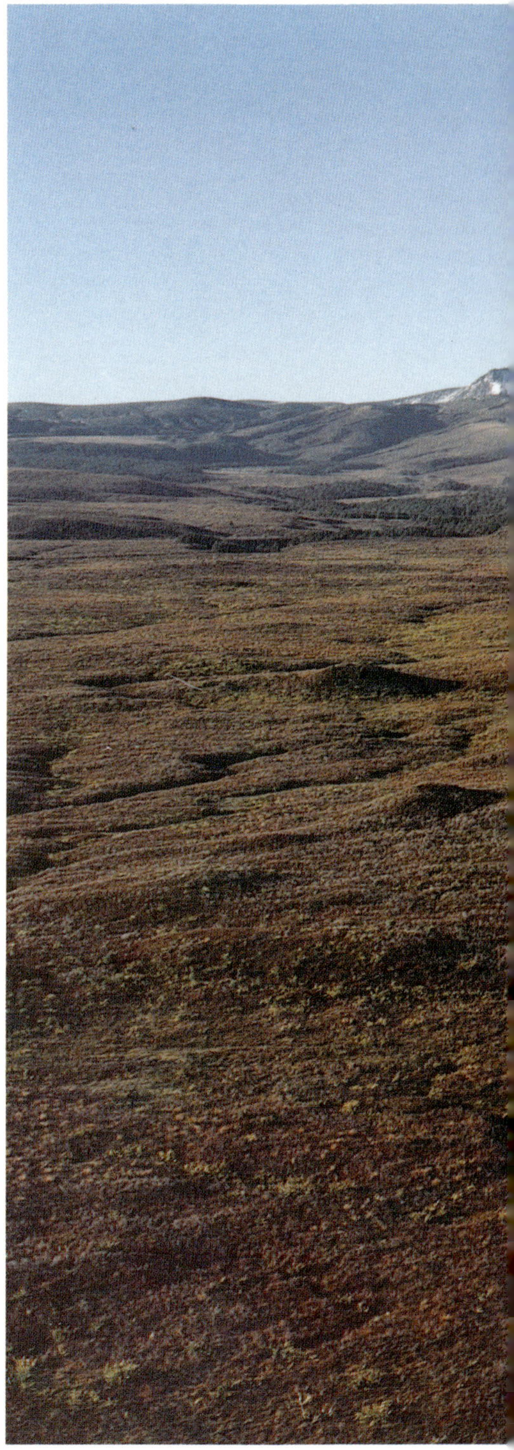

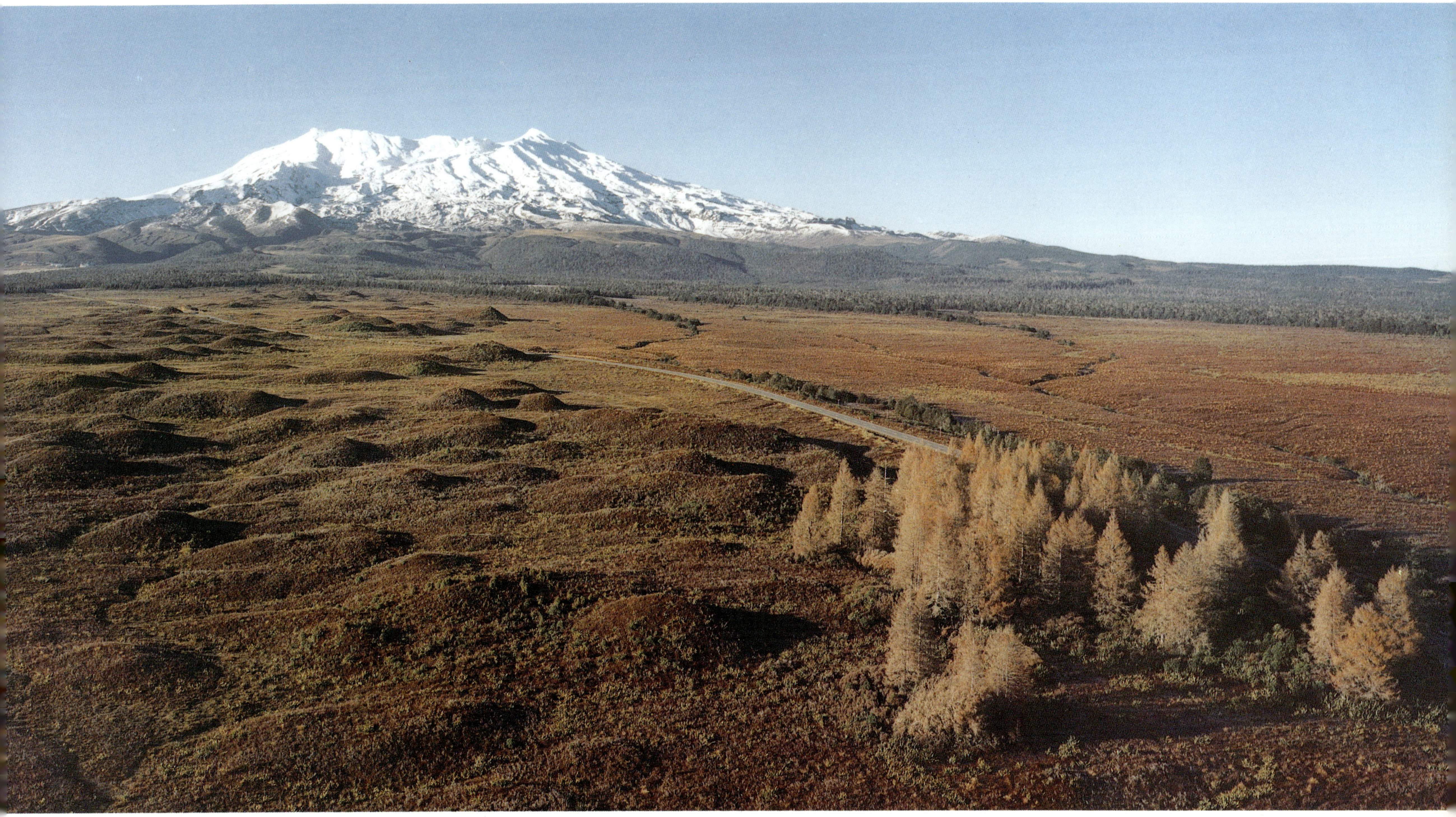

2 Among the more interesting landforms of the park are the small conical hills termed 'lahar mounds' far out on the north-western sector of the ringplain of Mt Ruapehu (seen here from the junction of State Highways 47 and 48). These mounds form the surface of a debris avalanche which occurred when a portion of the cone of Mt Ruapehu collapsed 9500 years ago and slid out onto the ringplain. This collapse would have been similar to that which occurred on Mt St Helens volcano in the United States in May 1980.

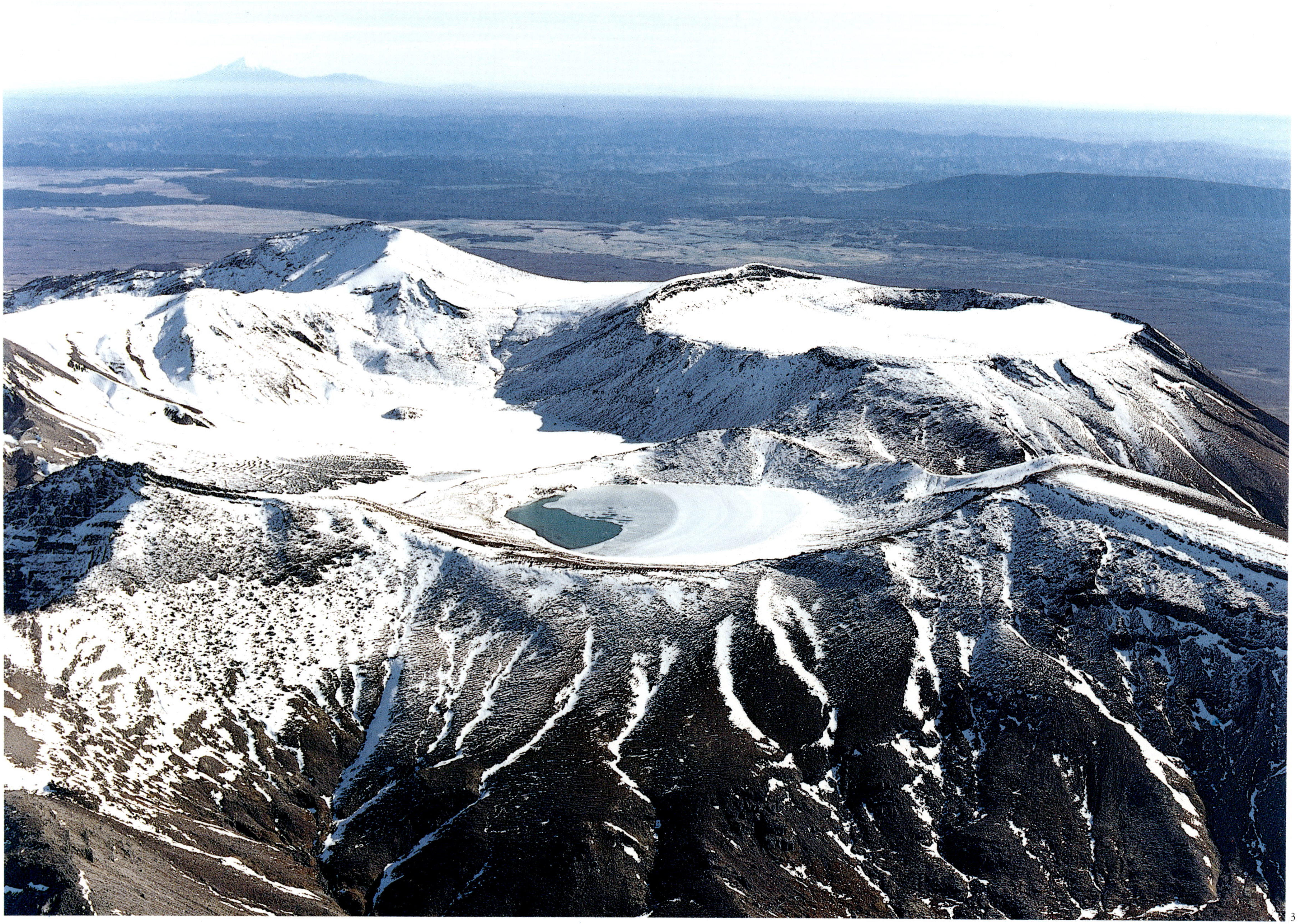

3

3 The composite nature of Mt Tongariro can be appreciated in this view westwards across the Central Crater and the summit peak (1967 m) towards Mt Taranaki (Chapter 10). The crater in the foreground is Blue Lake Crater (with the lake almost completely frozen over); the symmetrical crater beyond and to the right is North Crater, filled by a solidified lava lake. The construction of this complex volcano has been underway for at least 250 000 years. Today, it consists of five major volcanic vents (Central, North, Blue Lake, Red and South Craters) and three subsidary vents on the flanks (upper and lower Te Mari and Oturere).

4 The Te Mari Craters on the north-eastern flanks of Mt Tongariro are examples of younger subsidiary vents. The lower Te Mari Crater is 400 m wide and 100 m deep; it is quite symmetrical except for a breach of its southern rim by material ejected from the upper crater late last century. The andesitic lava flow in the right foreground was produced about 450 years ago from a vent near the present-day upper Te Mari Crater. It can still be traced for 5 km down through the surrounding scrub and forest, as the lava surface has been only slowly colonised by a patchy low forest of mountain toatoa and manuka.

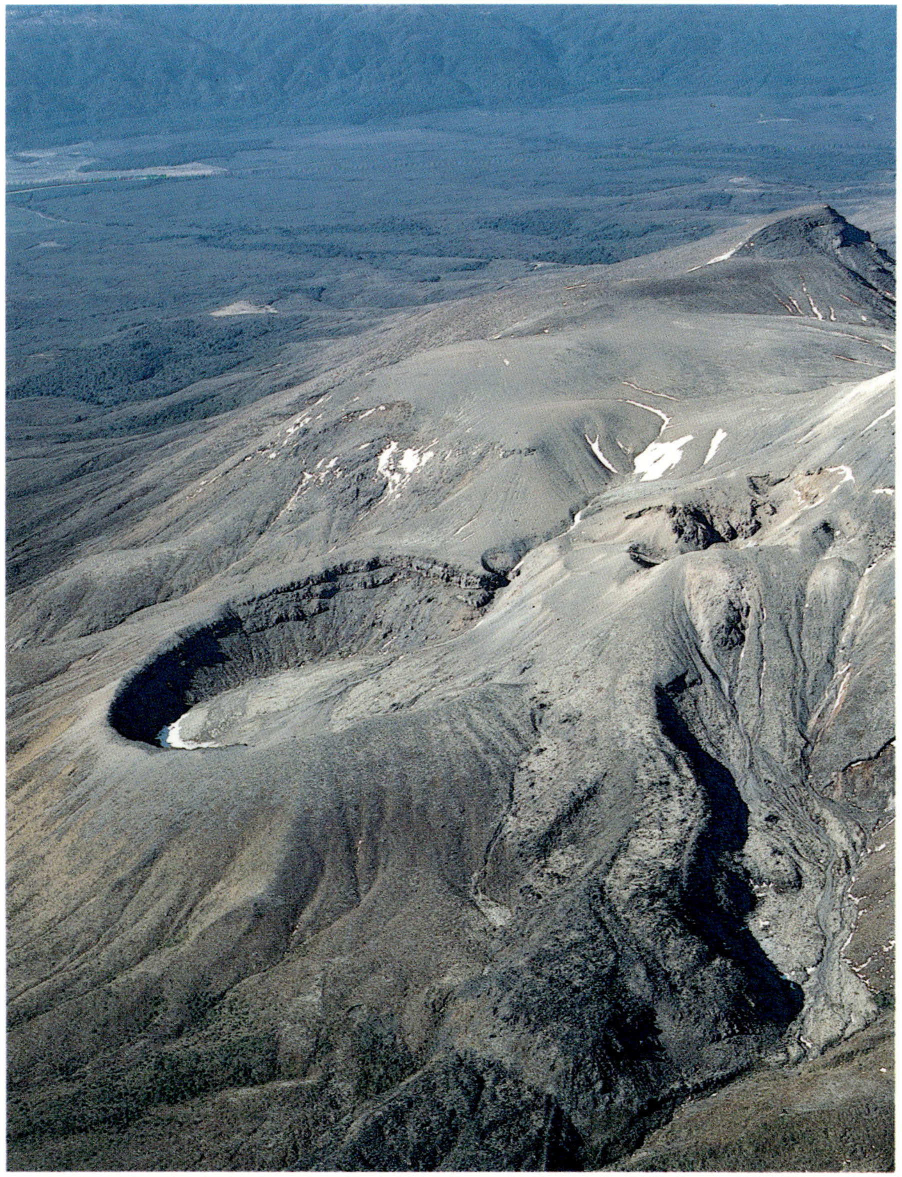
4

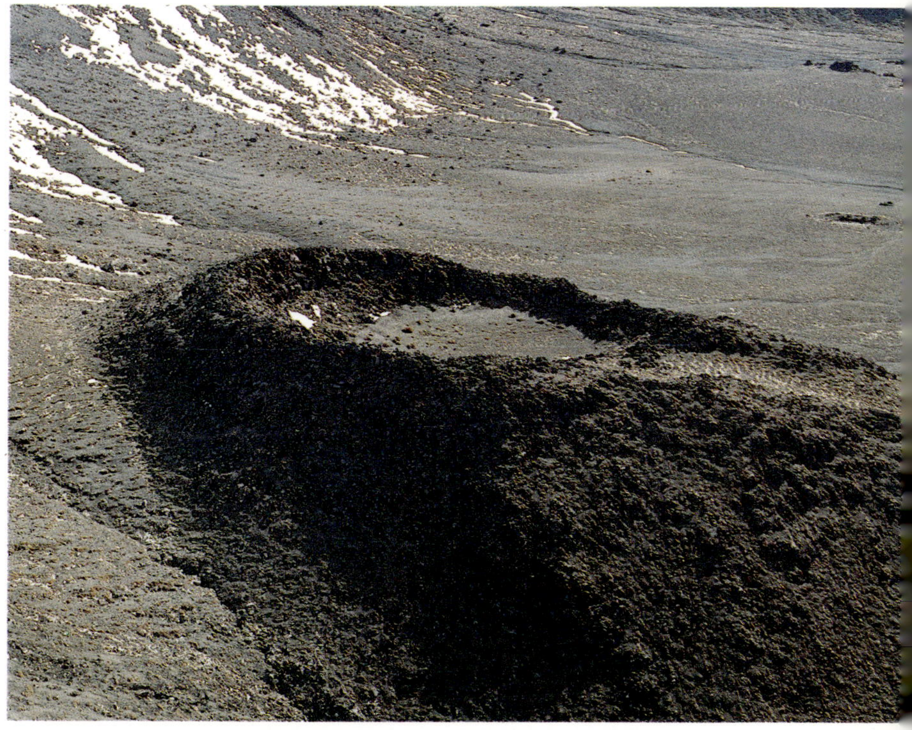
5

5 This small 100 m-wide cone marks a subsidiary vent on the lower north-eastern slopes of Mt Ruapehu, about 3 km south-south-west of the Lower Tama Lake. Lava flows breached the northern rim of the cone (right) 5000 to 10 000 years ago and flowed 2–3 km into the head of the Waihohonu valley where they are well preserved today under red tussock. The Whakapapa–Waihohonu track passes along the foot of this young lava flow.

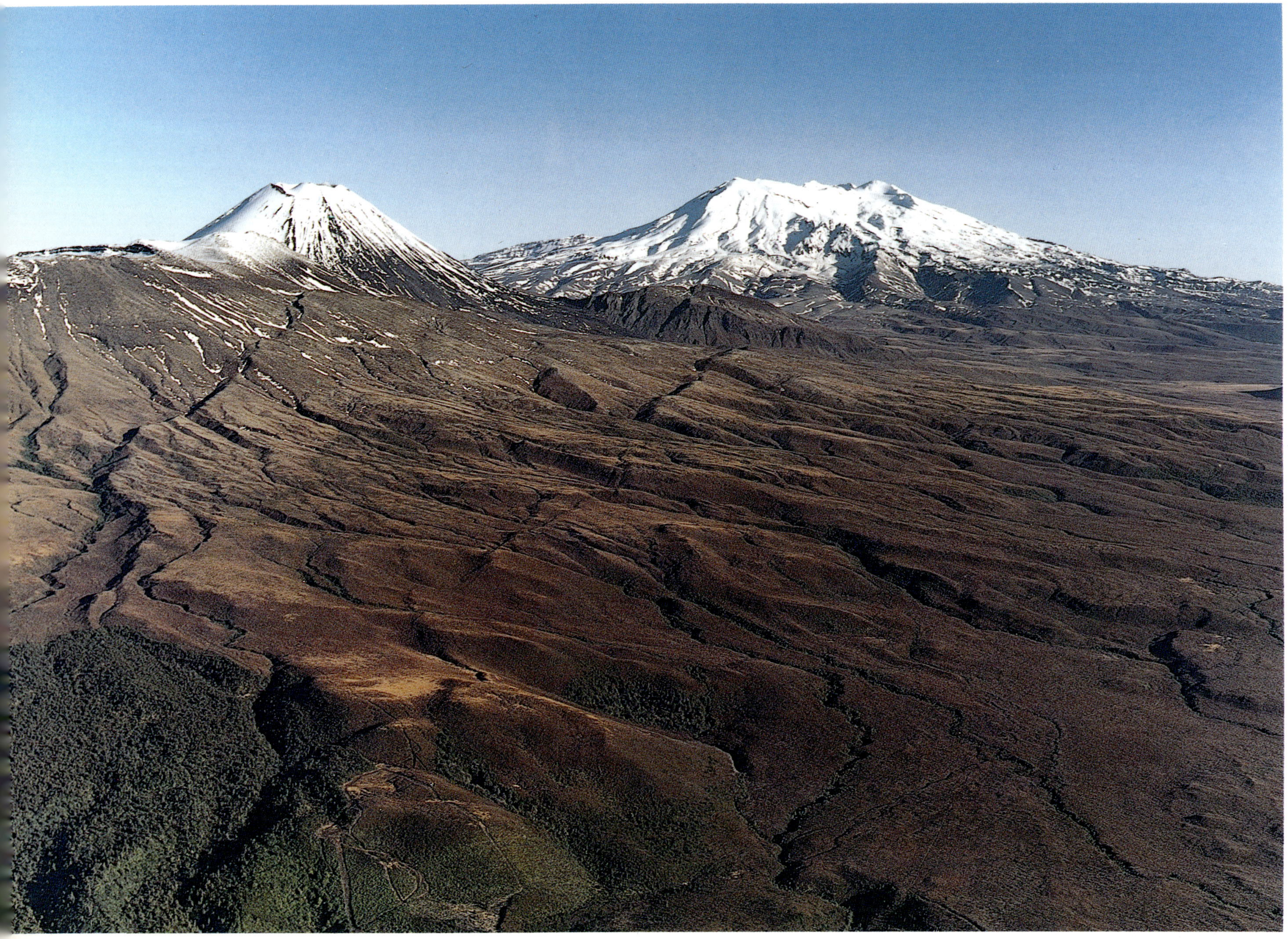

6

6 Mts Ruapehu and Ngauruhoe lie to the south-west in this view across the north-western slopes of Mt Tongariro. Ketetahi Hot Springs, a major site of thermal activity, can be seen as a cloud of steam on the extreme left on the upper outer slopes of North Crater. Two parallel fault traces can be seen running north-north-east/south-south-west across the slopes of Tongariro in the foreground; movement has occurred along these faults since the Taupo eruption 1800 years ago.

7 Mt Pihanga (1325 m) is one of three northern volcanoes – Kakaramea, Tihia and Pihanga – separated from the rest of the park by the depression occupied by Lake Rotoaira (bottom, right). Lake Rotopounamu (centre) nestles in a basin formed by a series of smaller younger volcanic cones on the north-western slopes of Mt Pihanga. This basin is oriented north-east/south-west in line with the volcanic cones of the Tongariro massif to the south, and it may have been formed simply through down-faulting, rather than being an explosion crater.

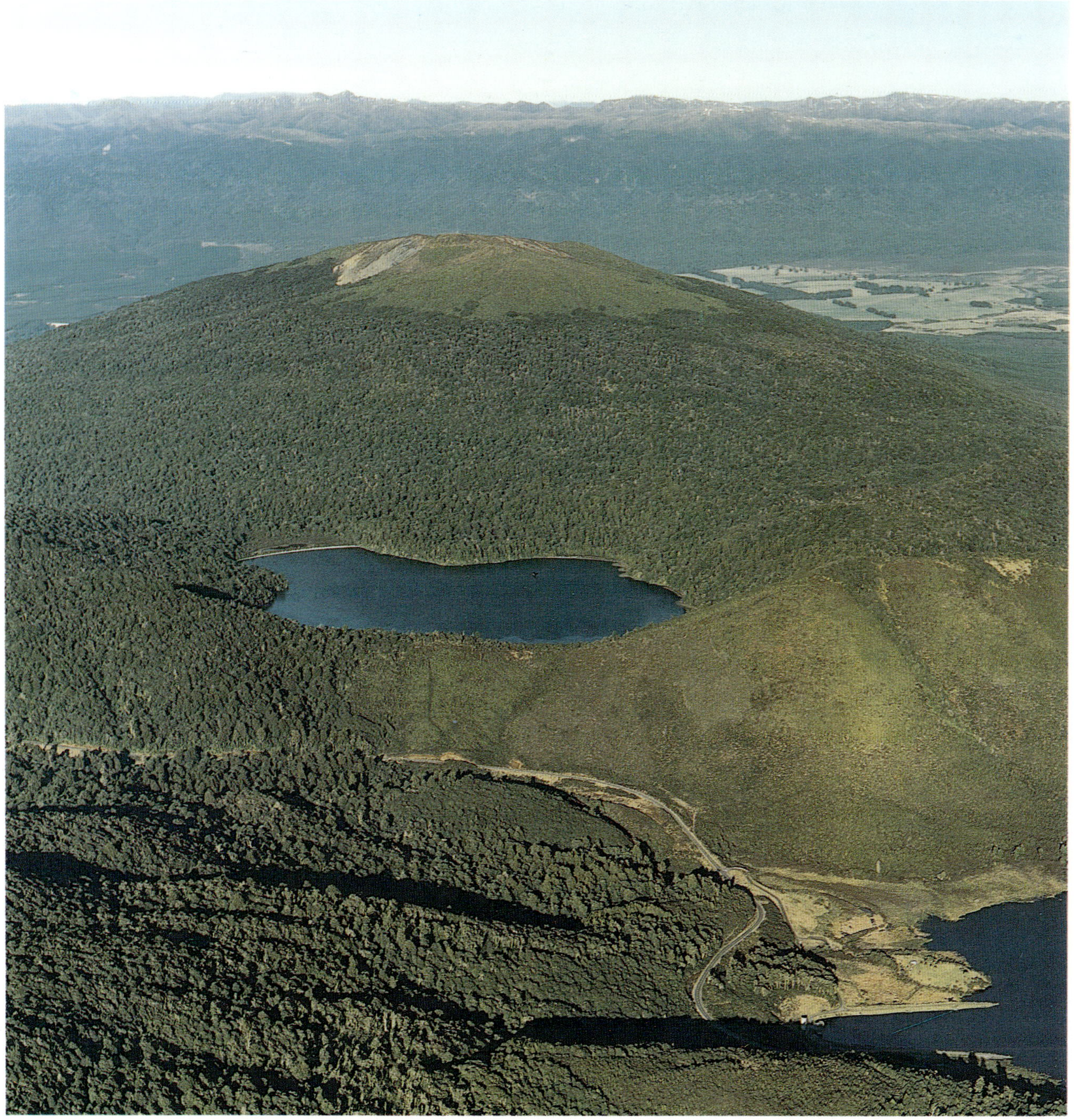

7

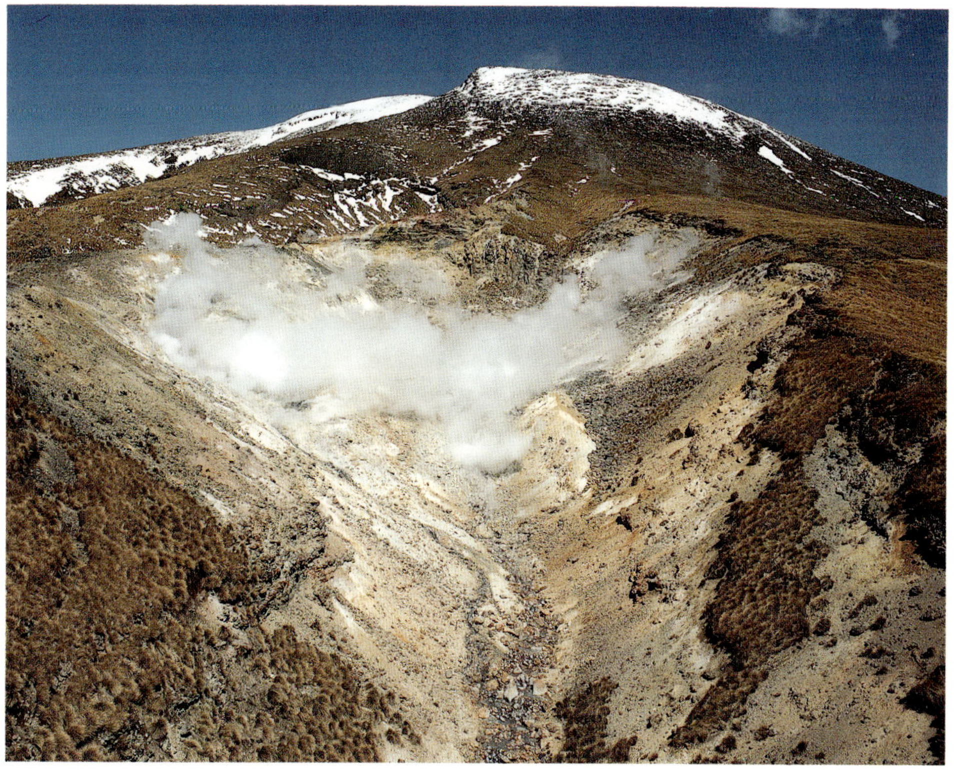

8

8 Ketetahi Hot Springs, at 1400 m altitude on the northern slopes of Mt Tongariro, lie in an enclave of land retained by the Ngati Tuwharetoa people. More than forty fumaroles with numerous mudpools and boiling springs can be found in this 30 ha basin in the head of Mangatipua Stream. The waters have high levels of acids or mineral salts of boron, sulphur, magnesium, calcium and iron. Yet life can survive in this harsh hydrothermal environment, for colourful red and blue-green algae grow in the hot waters.

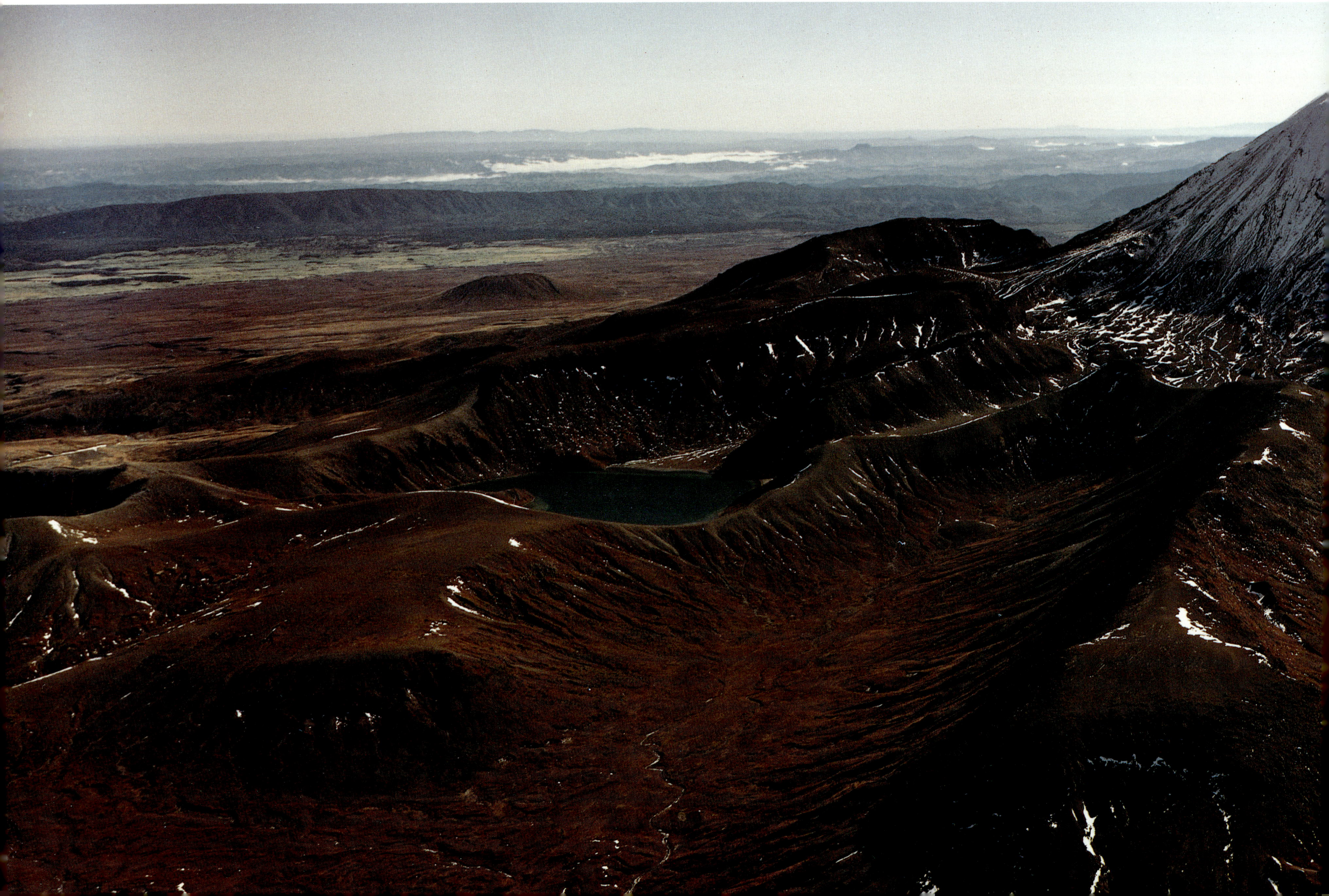

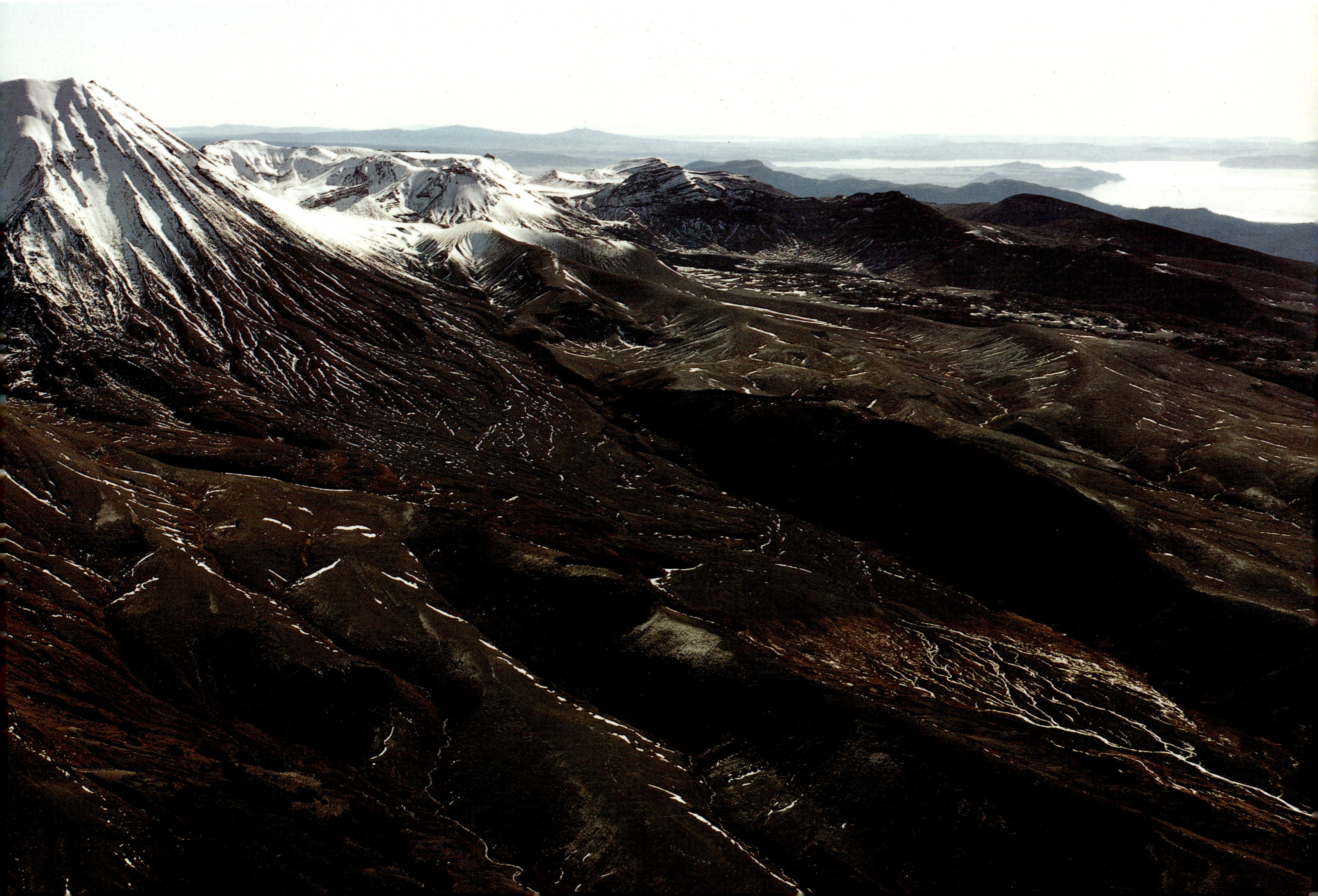

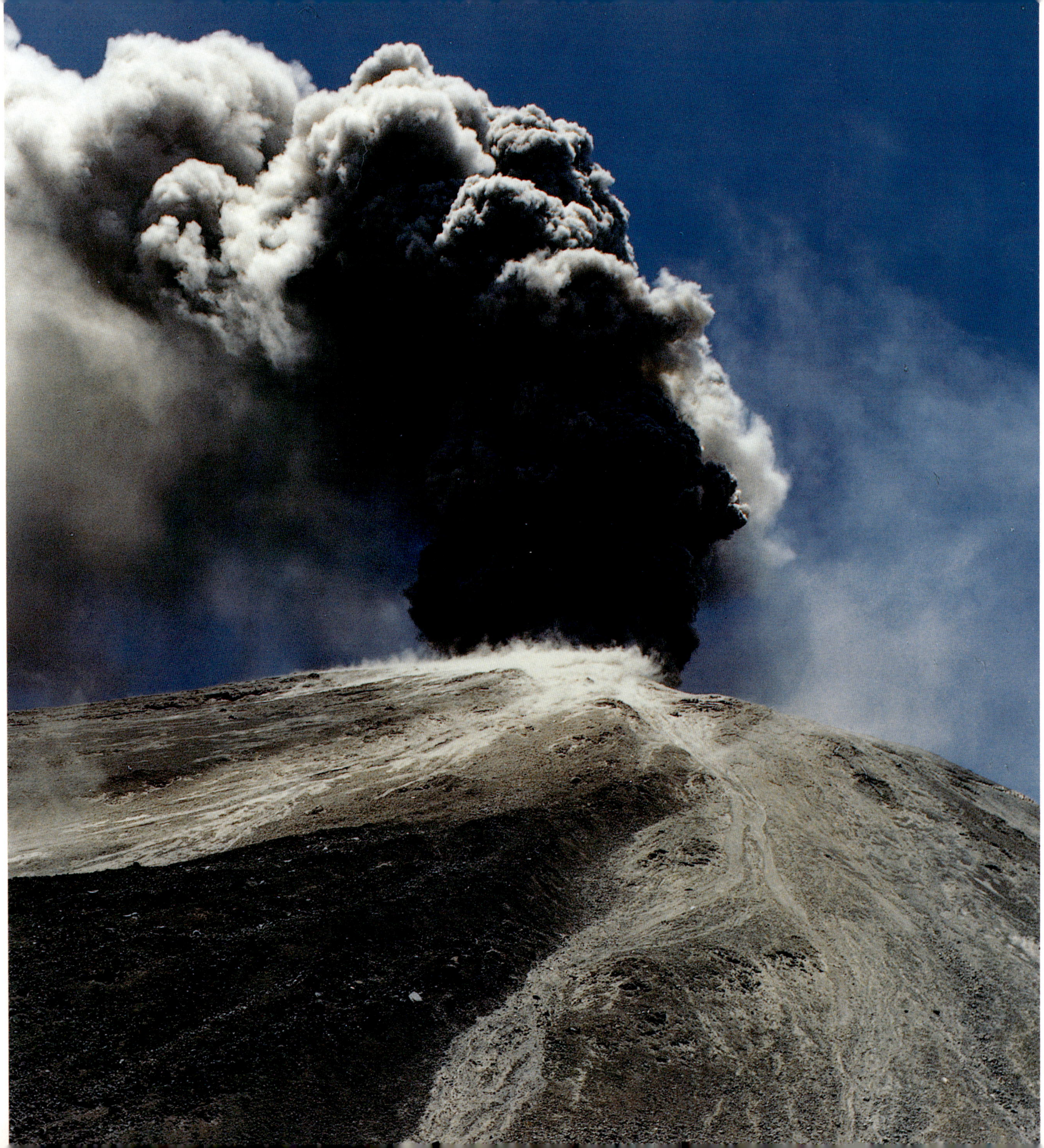

previous page

9 The full sweep of the deforested landscape around Mts Ngauruhoe and Tongariro is evident in this panorama looking north-north-west from near the historic Waihohonu Hut. From left to right, the Mangatepopo, Waihohonu and Oturere Streams radiate out from the volcanoes, their once-glaciated headwaters now filled with lava flows and lahars. The ridges separating these valleys are probably remnants of older, eroded cones that predated Ngauruhoe. Prominent landmarks to the west are Upper Tama Lake, Pukekaikiore, and the outlying scoria cone of Pukeonake. Lake Taupo, site of the huge Taupo eruption 1800 years ago, can be seen in the distance to the north.

10 Mt Ngauruhoe in eruption, 26 January 1974. The column of tephra during this eruption contained mainly ash which rose several kilometres above the summit. Whereas the 1954 eruption produced lava-fountaining and flows of the strombolian type, the 1974–75 eruptions were of the vulcanian type – more explosive, with cooler, more viscous lava often thrown up to 3 km from the vent. During this type of eruption portions of the column periodically collapsed, generating avalanches of scoria and hot gas down the flanks of the cone.

11 Mt Ngauruhoe (2287 m) is the youngest and most symmetrical of the three volcanic peaks in the park. The present cone is probably only 2500 years old and is still being built.

The summit has a 'cone-in-cone' structure; the inner cone was formed during the eruptions in 1954 and it remained largely intact during the 1974–75 eruptions. It is termed a 'spatter cone' from the incandescent blobs of lava which fell back from the eruption to build a 60 m high rim around the vent – just like the miniature vents in boiling mudpools in the hydrothermal areas in the Taupo Volcanic Zone. This photograph, looking south-eastwards into the northern headwaters of Waihohonu Stream, was taken in July 1984.

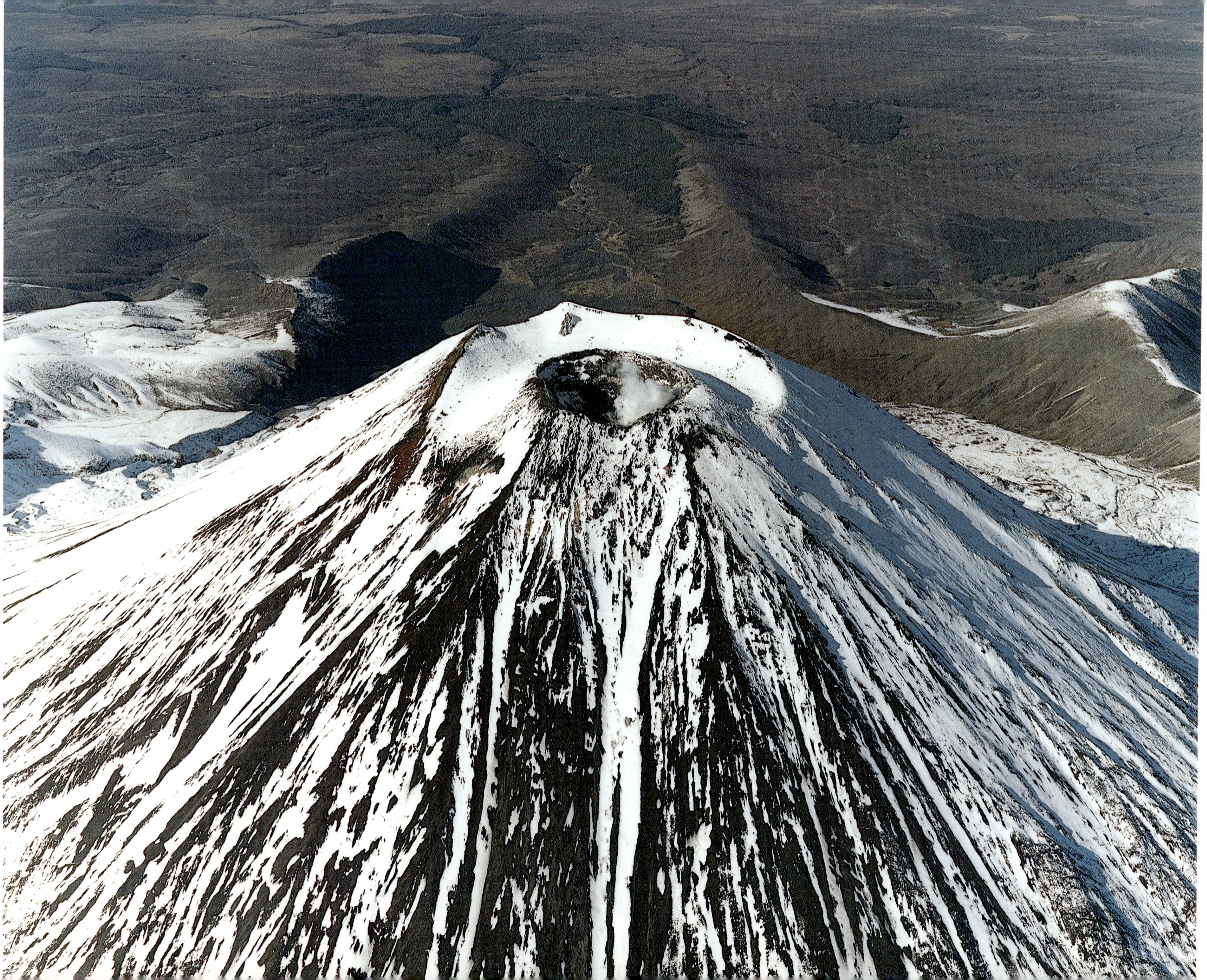

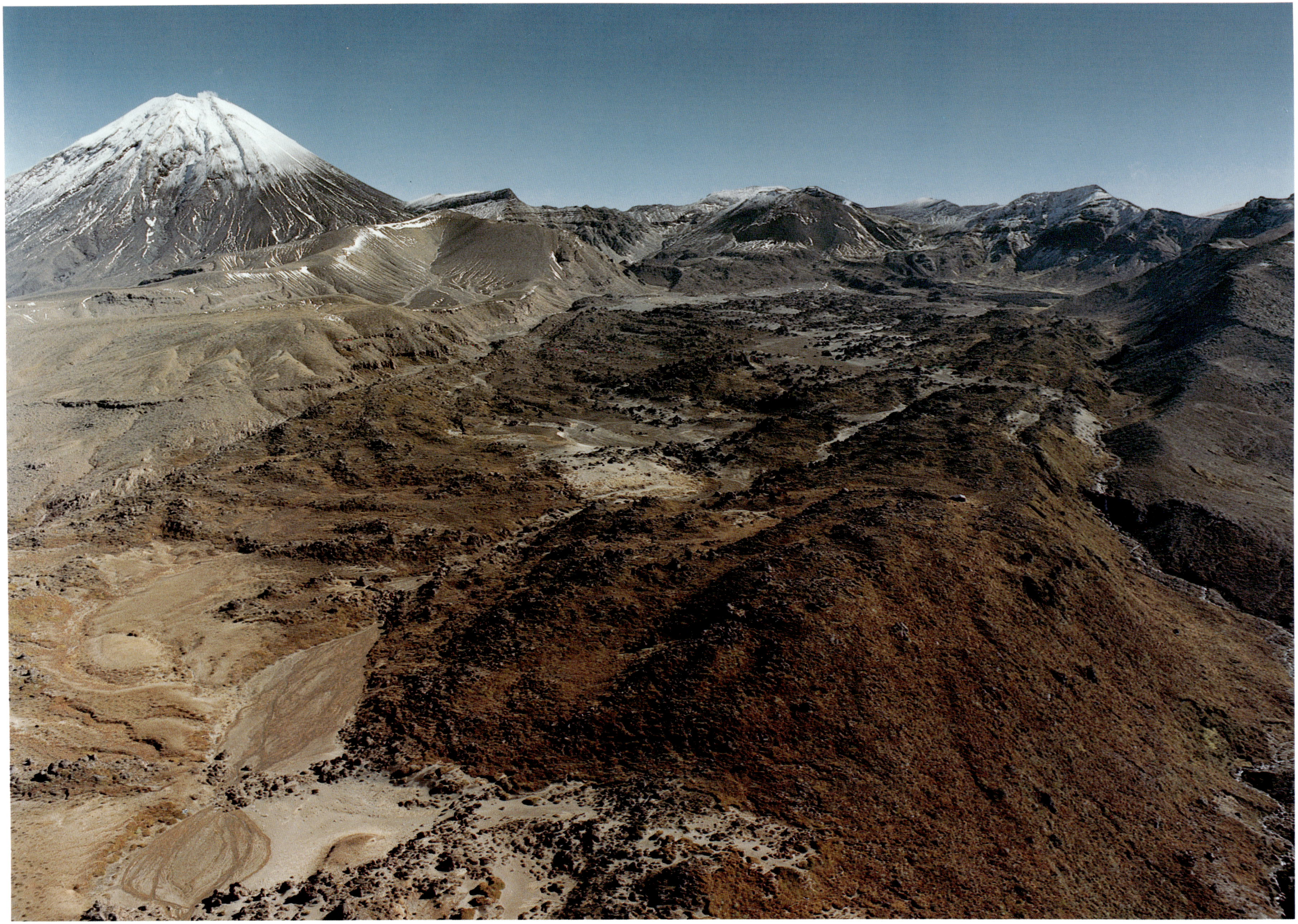

12

12 During the Ice Ages a glacier carved the Oturere valley from the south-eastern slopes of Mt Tongariro; now its place has been taken by large lava flows which were probably erupted from Red Crater between 10 000 and 2500 years ago. The lava flows are 7 km long and up to 1 km wide, with transverse ridges on the surface indicating the direction of flow – just like crevasses in a glacier. Oturere Hut, on the Waihohonu–Ketetahi track across Mt Tongariro, can be seen on the lava flow on the southern side of Oturere Stream in the centre right of the photograph.

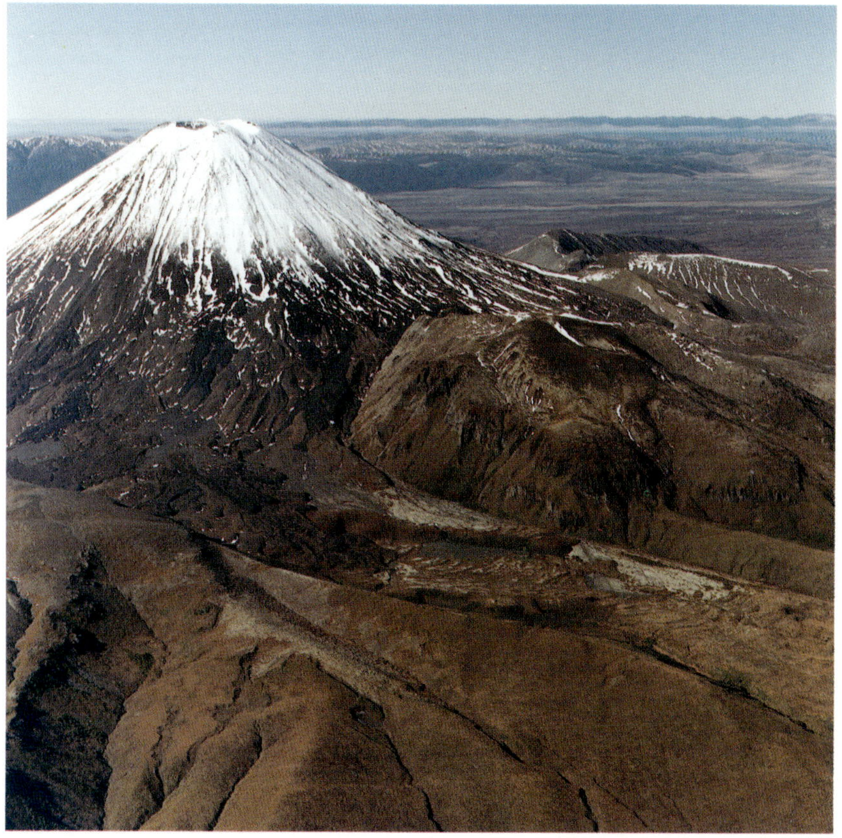

13

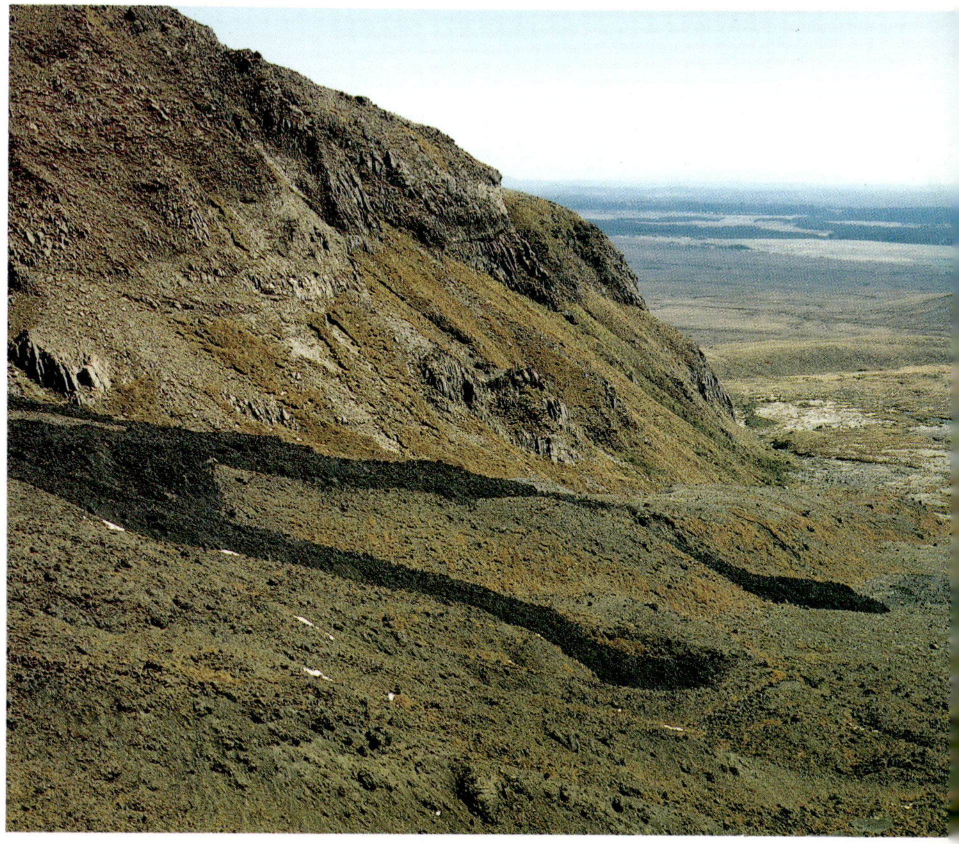

14

13 The Mangatepopo valley drains the western side of Mt Ngauruhoe, and its outlier Pukekaikiore (centre right). The valley serves as the usual walking route to the slopes of Ngauruhoe and the South Crater of Tongariro and en route the traveller passes landforms of both glacial and volcanic origin. The two ridges enclosing the valley (bottom right) show signs of ice smoothing, and the head of the valley has been filled with a mixture of more recent lahars and lava flows from the slopes of Ngauruhoe. The origin of Pukekaikiore is a matter of debate: it may be the eroded remnant of an older larger volcano, or it may be a cumulodome (a dome of viscous lava which has bulged up without revealing an eruptive vent).

14 In the head of the Mangatepopo valley below the cliffs of Pukekaikiore, the amateur can roughly date the different lava flows from Mt Ngauruhoe by their colour and vegetation. The two black andesitic lava flows date from the 1954 eruption; they are of the rough surface type (aa) and are insufficiently weathered yet for soil development. Consequently, they have only mosses and lichens on them. The older surrounding lava flows carry a patchy cover of bristle tussock, mountain inaka and subalpine herbs, depending on the degree of development of rudimentary soils – sands weathered from the lava or pockets of airfall tephra.

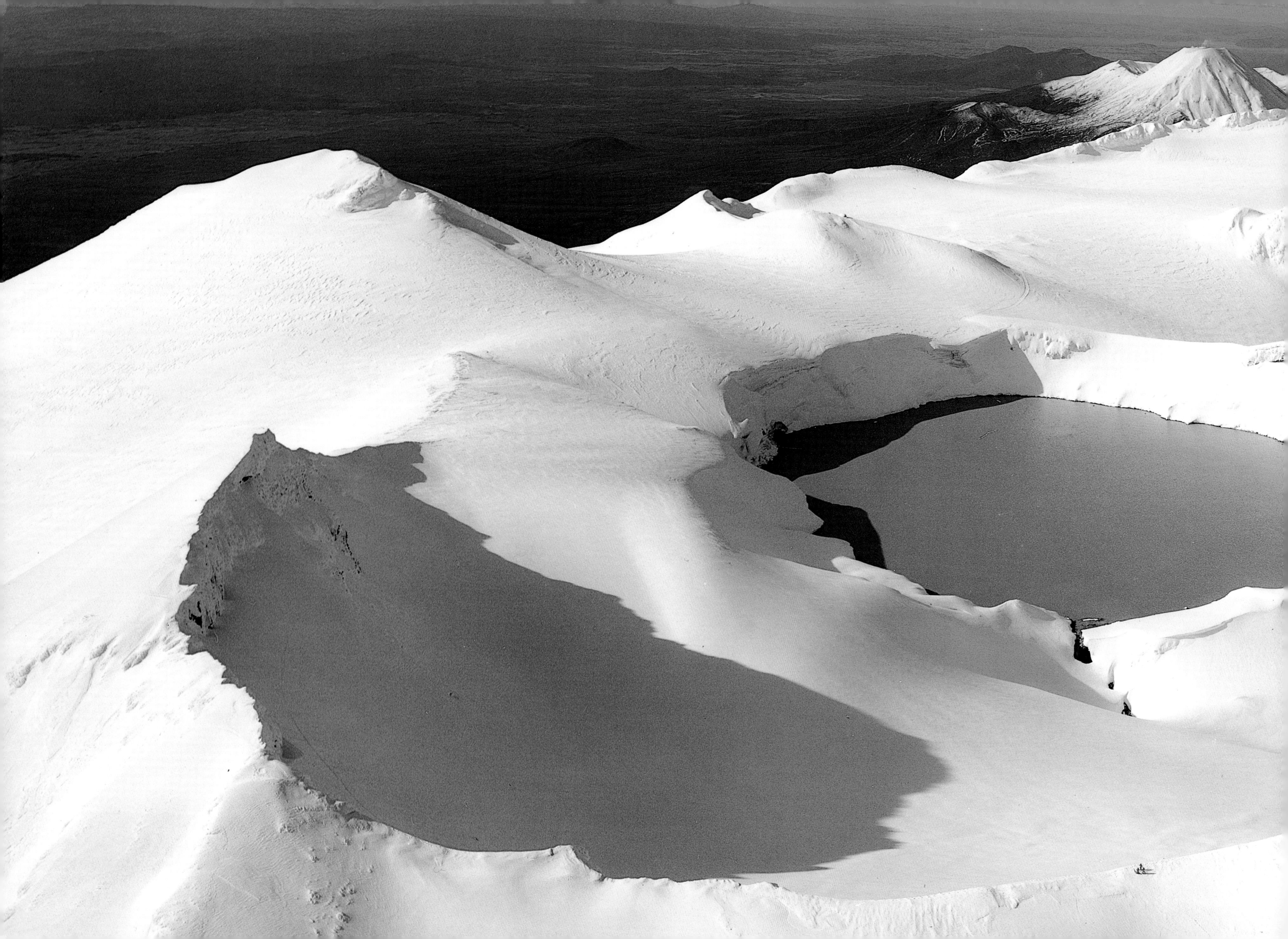

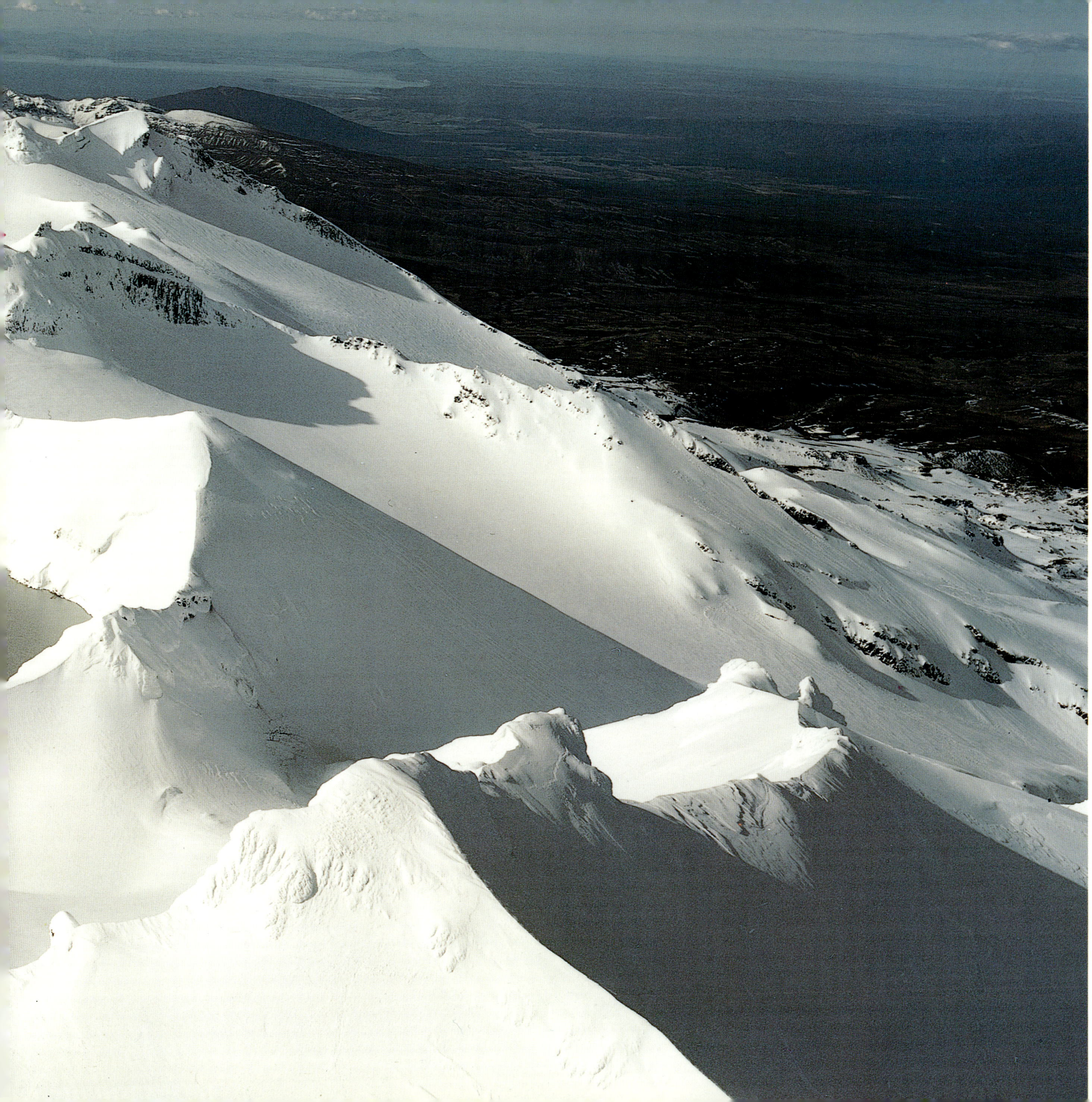

15 Mt Ruapehu is a composite volcano like Mt Tongariro, although the four separate summit craters and vents are not all as well preserved. This view north-east along the line of volcanoes shows the shadow of the summit peak (Tahurangi, 2797 m) spreading across the West Crater and its hot, acidic Crater Lake. All historical activity on Mt Ruapehu has been confined to this crater, where fifty-four eruptions have been recorded since 1950.

The colour of the water in Crater Lake ranges from blue/green during quiet phases to a metallic grey when volcanic activity produces suspended solids in the water. Crater Lake periodically drains to the Whangaehu River through an ice cave. In December 1953, collapse of an unstable snow and rock barrier across the cave precipitated 8 m of lake water into the river, forming a lahar which swept 30 km before carrying away the Tangiwai railway bridge and express train with a loss of 151 lives.

15

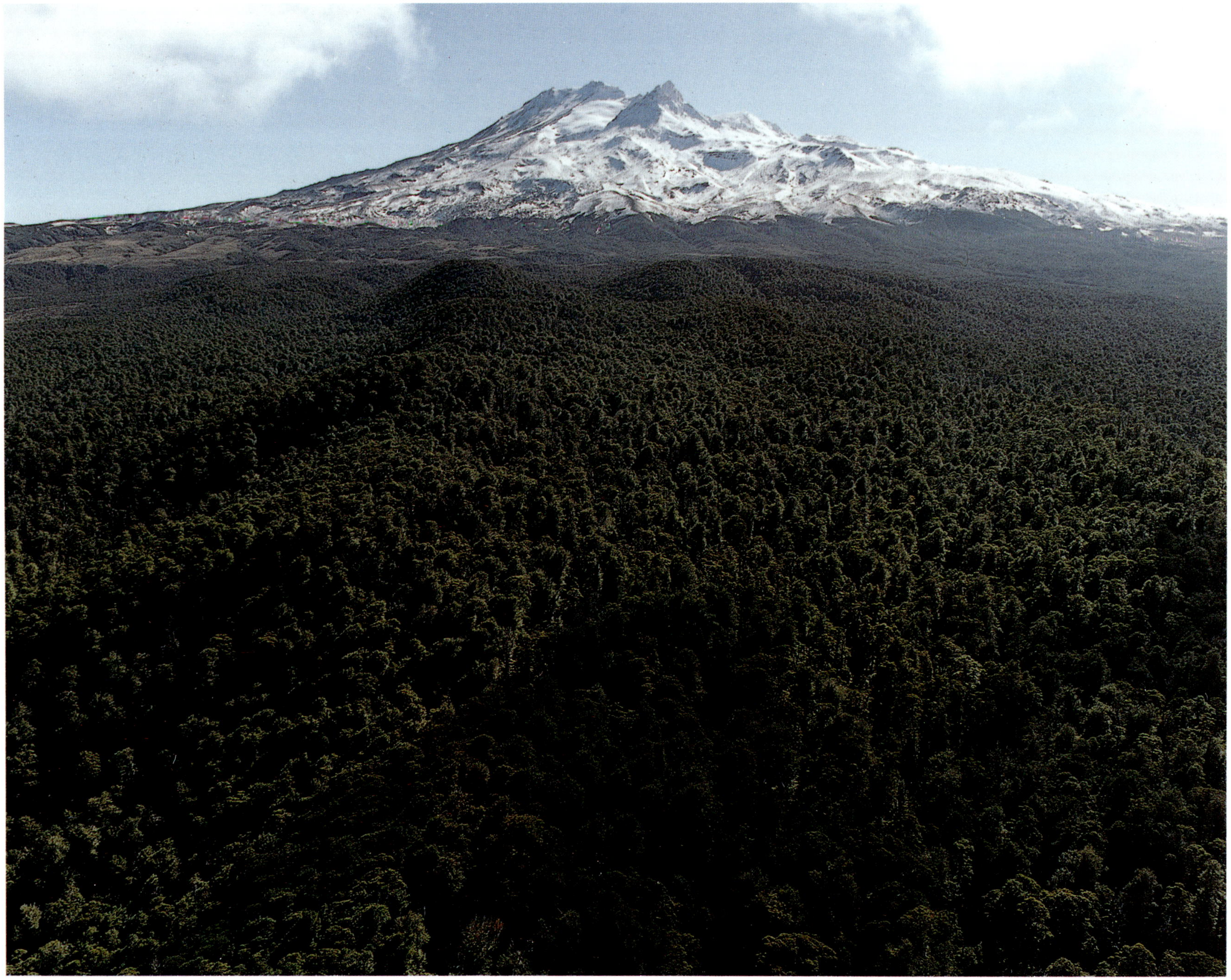

16 The southern slopes of Mt Ruapehu contain the largest of the lava flows within the park – the 14 km long and 4 km wide Rangataua flows estimated (from both glacial and tephra evidence) to be 10 000–20 000 years old. The flows originated at a small vent below Girdlestone Peak, the jagged outlier peak to the right of the summit in this photograph. The surface of the lava flows is masked by a dense mature silver and red beech forest from 1200 m altitude down to 700 m altitude near Karioi.

The mature forest on the southern and south-western slopes of Mt Ruapehu contrasts with the low stature of the vegetation around the rest of the southern group of volcanoes. These forests, in the lee of Hauhungatahi and Ruapehu, were sheltered from the hot pyroclastic flow of pumice from the Taupo eruption vent which burnt most of the existing forest 1800 years ago.

17 The Tama Lakes nestle in the broad saddle between Mt Ruapehu and Mt Ngauruhoe (top left). They occupy explosion craters which formed around 10 000 years ago when magma rising to the surface came into contact with groundwater. The Upper Tama Lake (1315 m) appears to occupy two adjacent craters, whereas the Lower Tama Lake (1240 m) in the foreground occupies a single circular crater. A fan of sediment is building up in the delta of the stream flowing into the north-western corner of the lower lake; neither lake has any surface outlet.

18 The forest cover on the western slopes of Mt Ruapehu is patchy, the beech forest sometimes appearing as 'islands' within red tussocklands and wetlands. The area has probably been swept with fires in earlier times and forest re-establishment inhibited because of the bogginess of much of the landscape. Drainage is often impeded where there is a sharp change in soil texture, as can occur when a coarse tephra (such as Taupo Pumice) lies on finer tephras (such as the Tongariro Ashes).

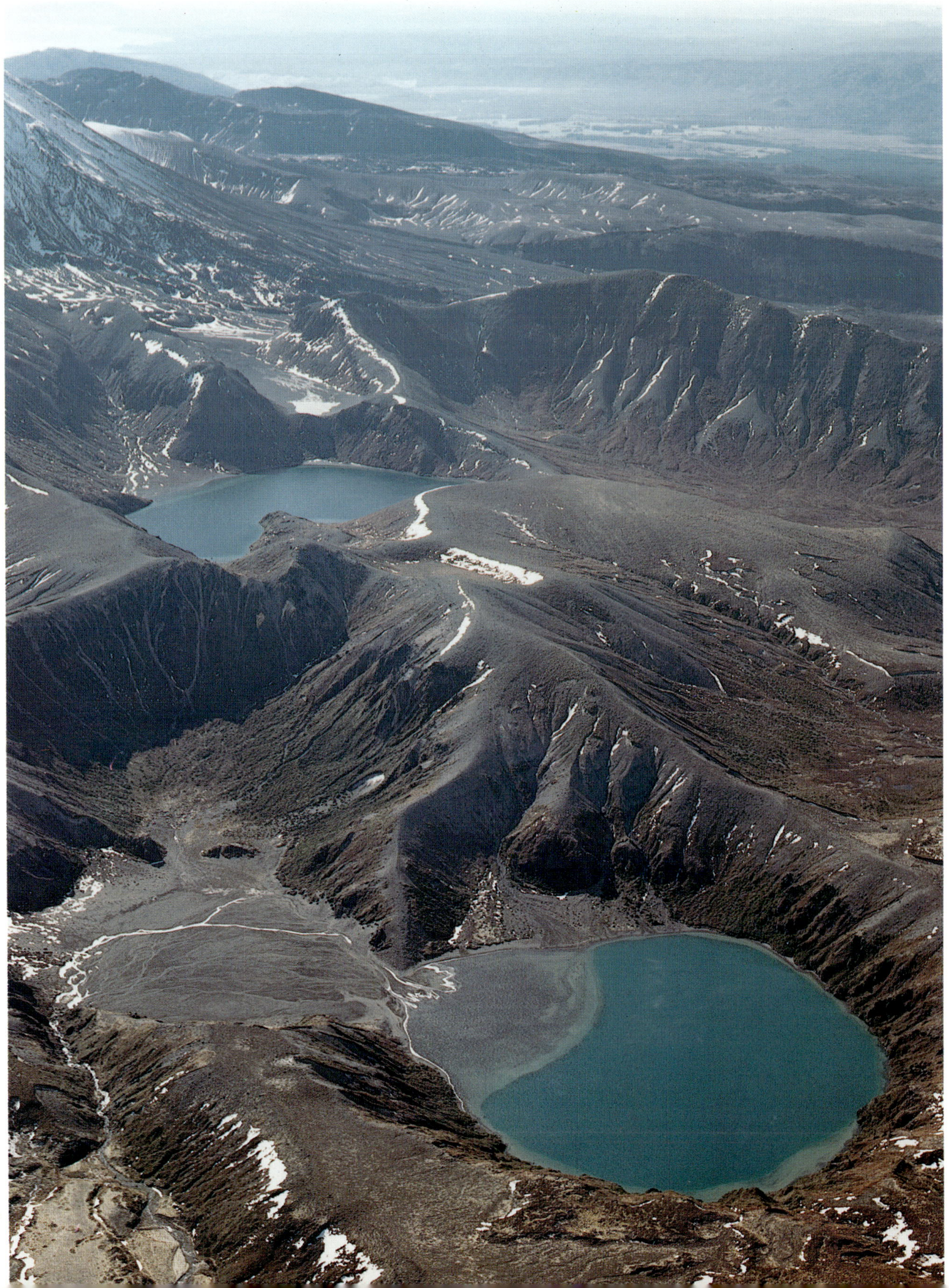

17

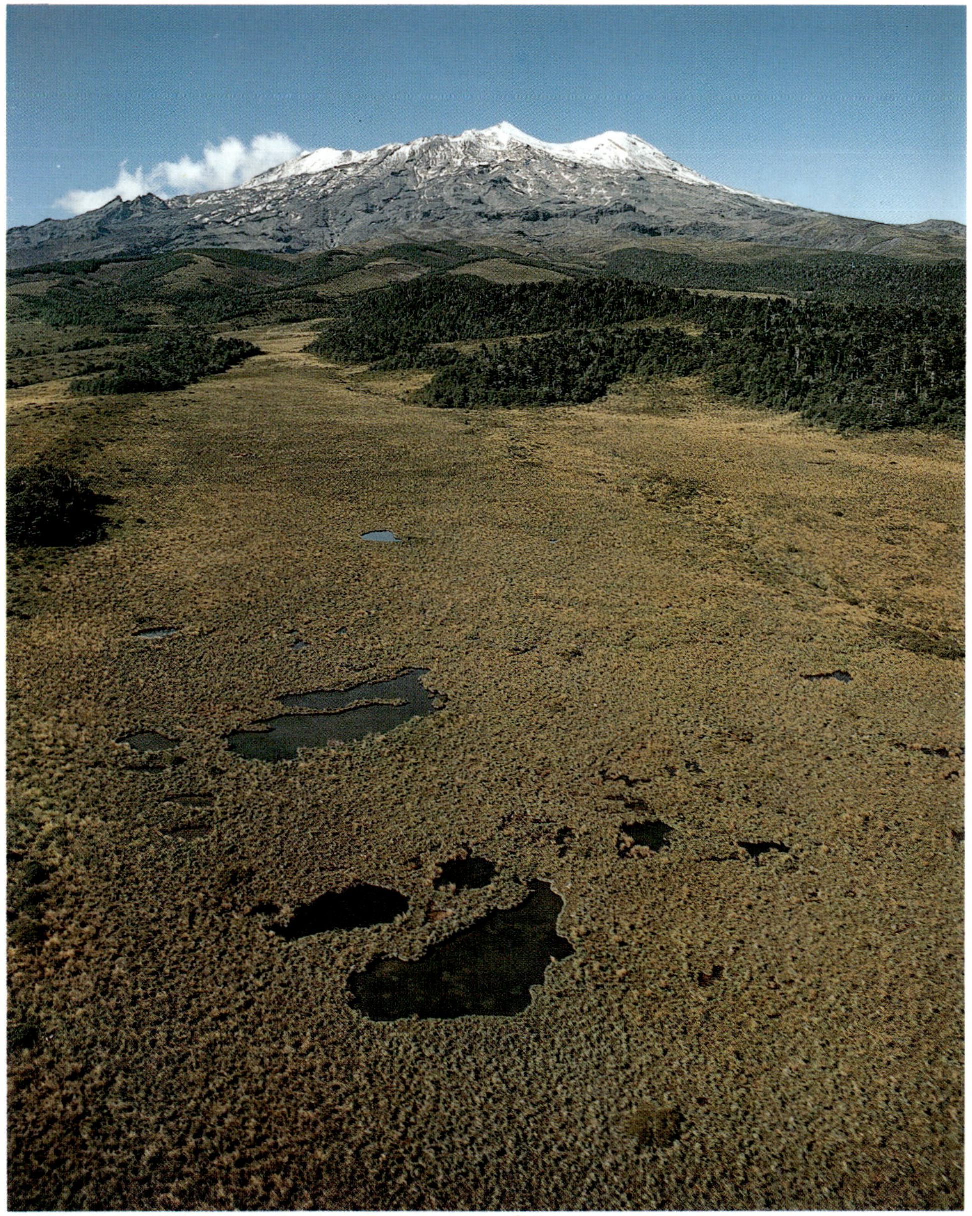

18

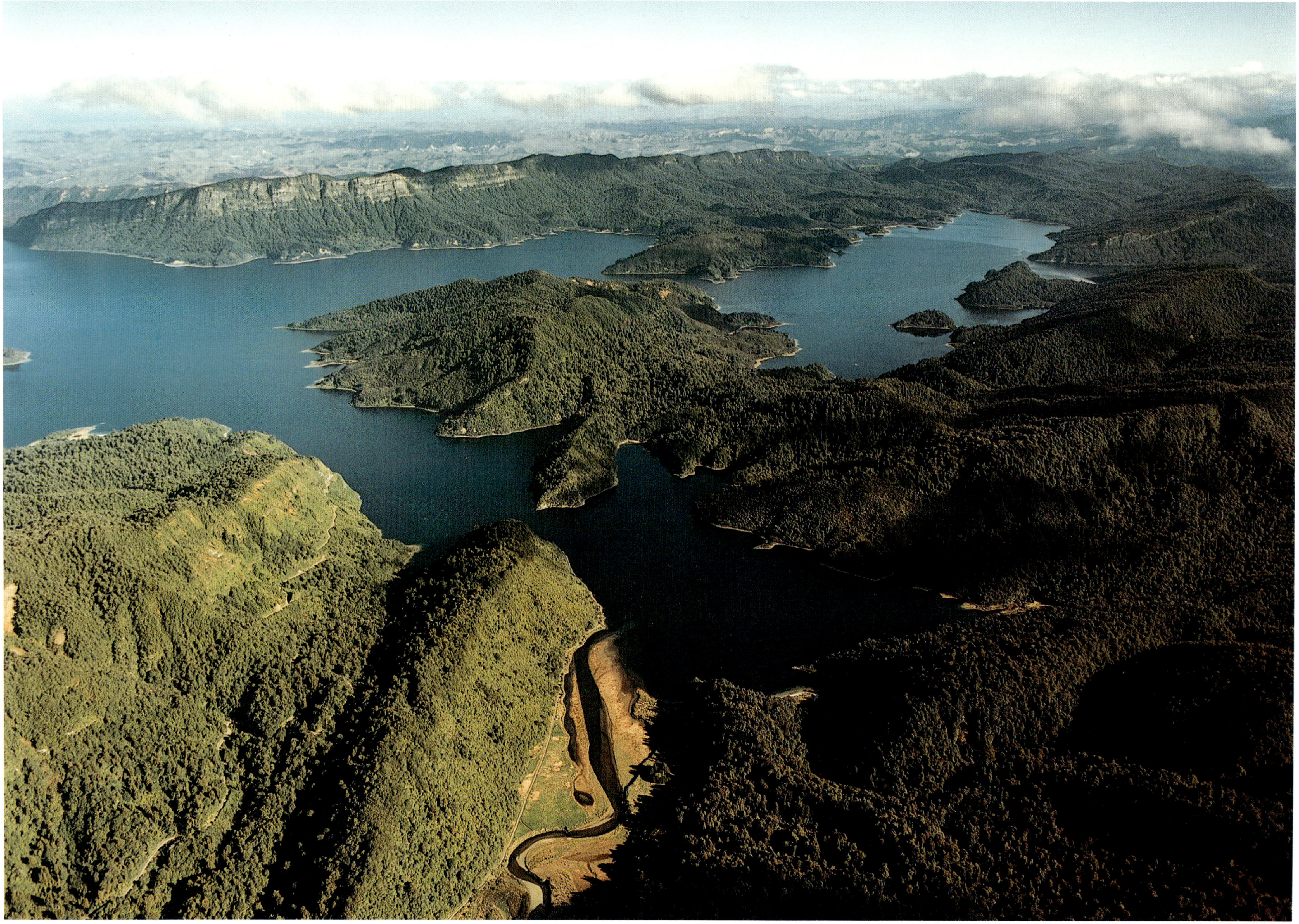

UREWERA NATIONAL PARK

Urewera National Park lies high in a remote and rugged part of the North Island. It straddles the heavily forested Huiarau and Ikawhenua Ranges. These are part of the 700 km-long axial greywacke range of the North Island, running from the Rimutaka Range near Cook Strait to the Raukumara Range in the East Cape.

With an area of 213 000 ha, Urewera is New Zealand's third largest national park, and its size is accentuated by the uniformity of landforms and horizons which confront the visitor. State Highway 38 (between Murupara and Wairoa) provides vistas of forested ridges and escarpments, with no open tops and few broad valleys; Lake Waikaremoana alone relieves the road traveller's sense of confinement within an endless hallway of enormous trees. This roadside impression is largely correct, for Urewera is one of New Zealand's most densely-forested national parks, the ridge crests are all about the same height (1100–1300 m), and the two highest points, Manuoha (1403 m) and Maungapohatu (1366 m), barely rise above the tree line.

From the air, however, an interesting topographic pattern to the park can be quickly appreciated. Virtually all the major ridges and valleys are parallel, running north-north-east to south-south-west in the southern sector and north-south in the northern sector inland from Whakatane. Western and northern valleys, such as the Parahaki Stream headwaters of the Waiau River, and the Whirinaki, Waikare, Tauranga/Waimana and Whakatane Rivers, tend to follow faultlines between the parallel blocks of greywacke and argillite which make up the ridges. Most of these faults do not appear to be very active now.

Geologically, there are two main sectors of the park:

• In the north and west, Mesozoic rocks (the Urewera greywackes and Cretaceous sediments, including minor areas of volcanic rocks).

• In the south and east, Tertiary sedimentary rocks around the upper rim of the Wairoa Basin.

There is a small area of Quaternary volcanics in the west (the Te Whaiti ignimbrite), but this rock type is of more significance farther west in the adjoining Whirinaki Forest Park.

The entire area has been mantled with at least eight major tephras in the last 20 000 years. Four of these can be found on the more stable sites – an old rhyolitic tephra (probably Whakatane Ash), the Waimihia Ash (3500 years old), Taupo Pumice (1800 years old) and the Kaharoa Ash (660 years old). Subsequent erosion has stripped all or some of these tephras from the steeper slopes, so the soil pattern can be quite variable.

The forest varies according to the climate and the depth of soil-forming tephras. As a generalisation the forests below 700 m on the Huiarau Range and around Lake Waikaremoana comprise northern rata/rimu/tawa; at higher altitudes, red and silver beech begin to dominate. Rimu rarely survives above 900 m altitude, and the solitude of the mist-shrouded summit ridges is left to a tight-canopied forest of gnarled and moss-covered silver beech – like so many other wet, exposed ridge tops from the Tararua Range to Fiordland.

LANDFORM CONTRASTS

The landforms in the older, harder sandstones, greywackes and argillites of the north and west differ markedly from those in the younger, softer sediments of the east around Lake Waikaremoana. The north is characterised by the parallel alignment of the ridges. Many of the streams draining the greywacke sector of the park (along the Ikawhenua Range and the western side of the Huiarau Range) are deeply incised in gorges. The steep slopes of these ranges carry many rockfalls and landslides, probably triggered by earthquakes and rainstorms.

The softer Tertiary sediments (generally alternating mudstones and sandstones) of the Wairoa Basin were uplifted two million years ago. The western margin (which now cuts across the south-eastern sector of the park) is curved up like the rim of a saucer. The edge of the rim is a series of spectacular ridges and bluffs around Lake Waikaremoana – Panekiri Bluff, the Ngamoko–Matakuhia Range and Haowhenua Ridge. Lake Waikaremoana owes its origin to a massive landslide of these Tertiary sediments, probably triggered by an earthquake. Around 2000 years ago, the south-western slopes of the Ngamoko Range slid into the valley of the Waikaretaheke River, damming the lake which slowly drained underground through the debris dam to a series of springs and seepages. The age of the landslide has been estimated through analysis of the tephra layers on the surface of the slump debris around lakelets near Miromiro and Kaitawa.

Further landslides along the basin edges between Mt Manuoha and the Ngamoko Range have given rise to the most visually interesting landscape within the park. The centrepiece is island-studded Lake Waikareiti and its surrounding lakelets and wetlands, such as Kaipo Lagoon. This colourful mosaic of wetlands and forested knolls is referred to locally as 'the tundra', and is the habitat of a number of subalpine plants normally only found 400 m higher above bushline on Mt Manuoha. The surrounding red/silver beech forest generally gives way abruptly to a shrubland fringe of bog pine and celery pine, and then a variety of mosses and rushes in the centre of the natural clearings. The reasons for this vegetation community, unique to this corner of the park, are probably a combination of severe local climate and wet, unfavourable soil conditions.

Another feature of this south-eastern sector of the park is a number of spectacular waterfalls – Papakorito, Momakahi and Te Tangiotehinerau Falls on the Aniwaniwa Stream close to the national park headquarters, Mokau Falls, and the Takapou-o-Hinewai Cascades on Hopuruahine Stream. All are within two minutes walk of the road. More remote but just as notable are Korokoro Falls in the Wairaumoana arm of Lake Waikaremoana and Waitangi Falls on the Ruakituri River. Most of these waterfalls have a characteristic veil-like shape from the water flowing over a broad sill of hard sandstone after the water has eroded away any softer mudstone downstream.

1 The deeply indented shores of Lake Waikaremoana can be appreciated in this view looking south across the mouth of the Hopuruahine Stream where it enters the Whanganui Inlet. The Waikaremoana Fault, one of many north-north-east trending faults within the park, is responsible for the orientation and steepness of the north-western face of Haowhenua Ridge in the centre foreground; the same fault runs up the valley of the Hopuruahine Stream and along the western side of the escarpment of Maungapohatu (see Fig. 9).

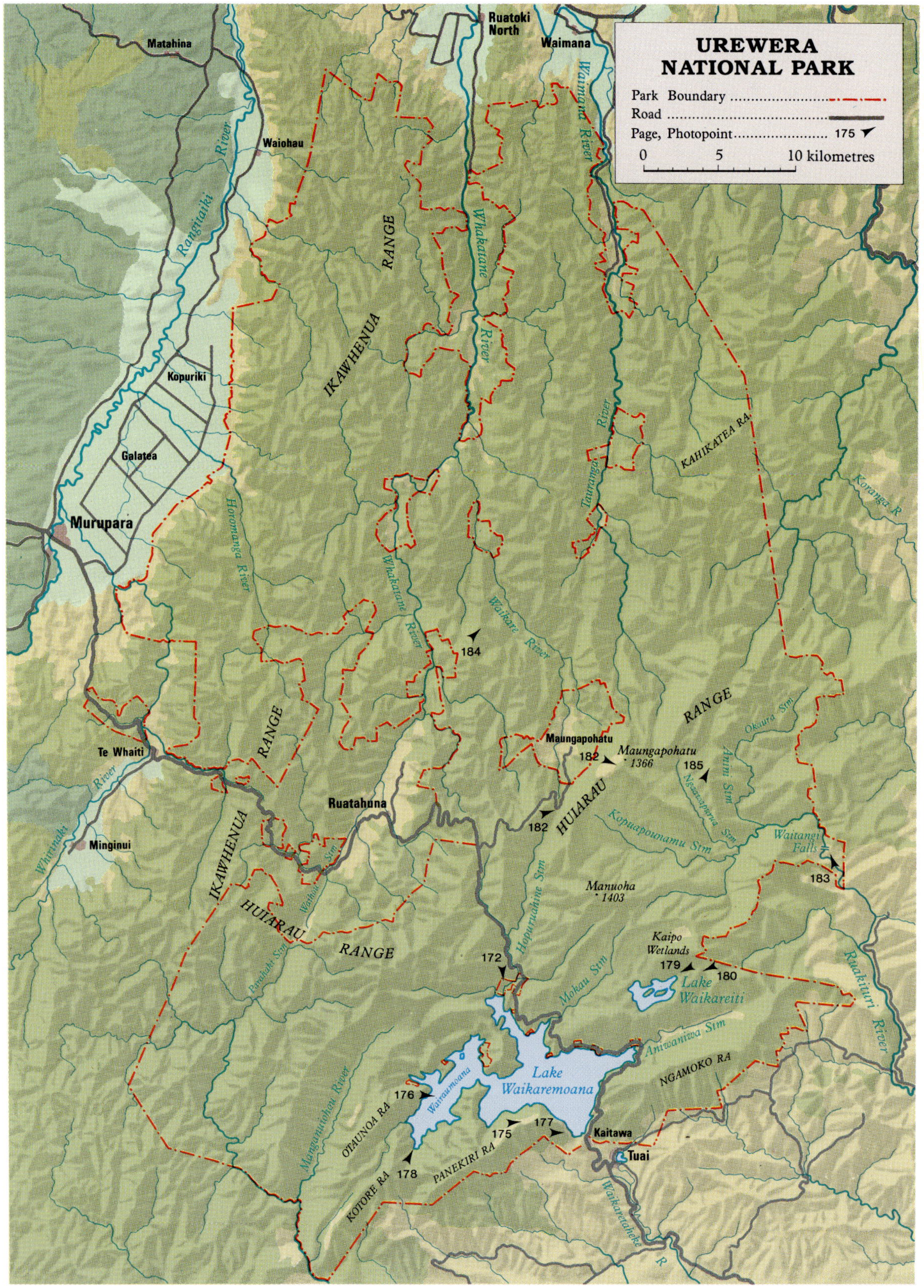

2 Panekiri Bluff towers above the southern shores of Lake Waikaremoana. It is an outstanding example of the escarpment of the tilted blocks of alternating Miocene-aged sandstone and mudstone which make up the eastern part of the park. The sandstone bluff in the foreground exhibits the layers of sediments laid down in shallow seas about ten million years ago, then gradually compressed and subsequently uplifted as the western margin of the Wairoa Basin. To the right of the escarpment the tilted surfaces of the blocks which make up the Panekiri Range (and the Ngamoko Range in the background) can be seen sloping down to the Wairoa Basin in the south-east.

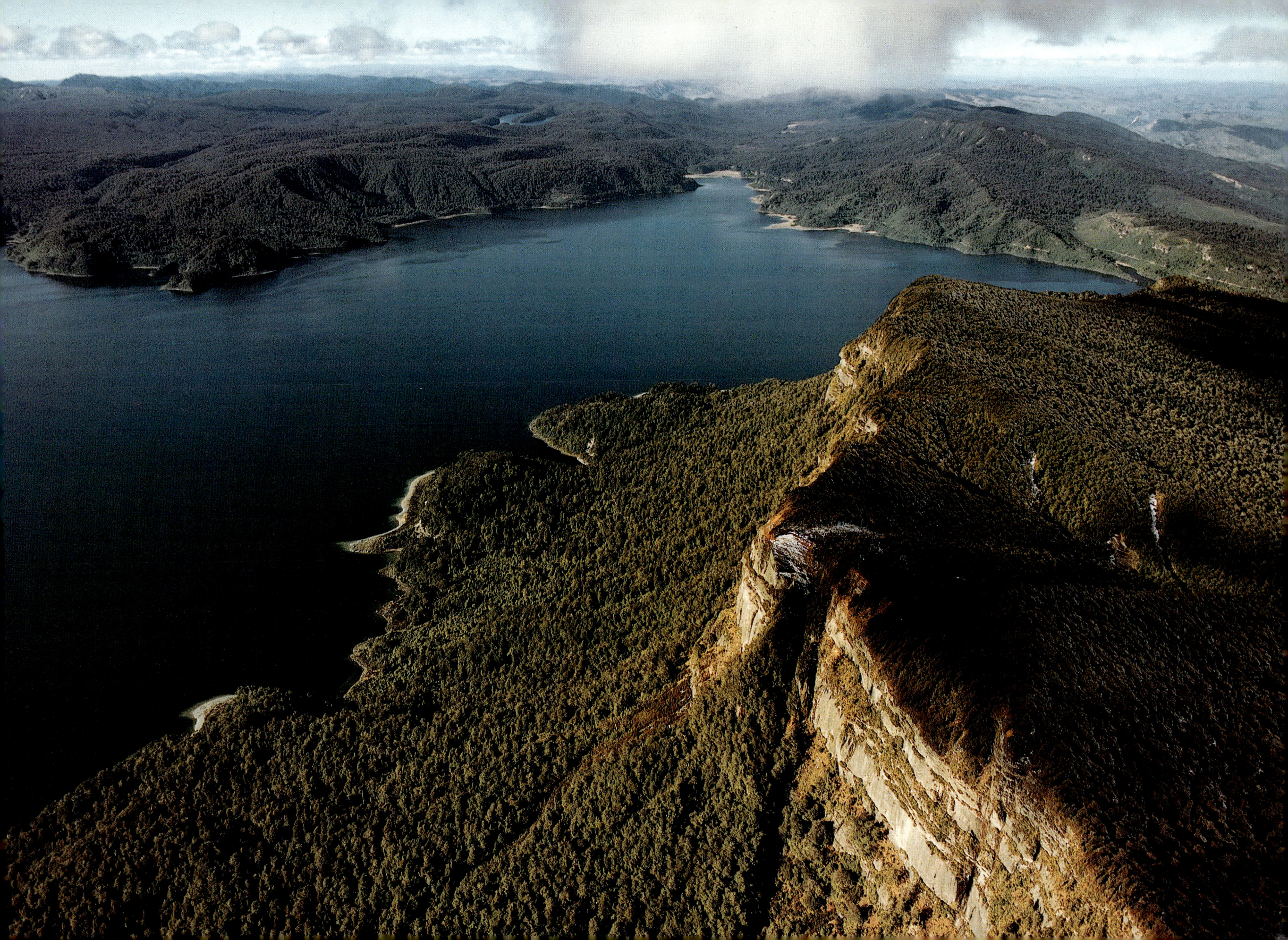

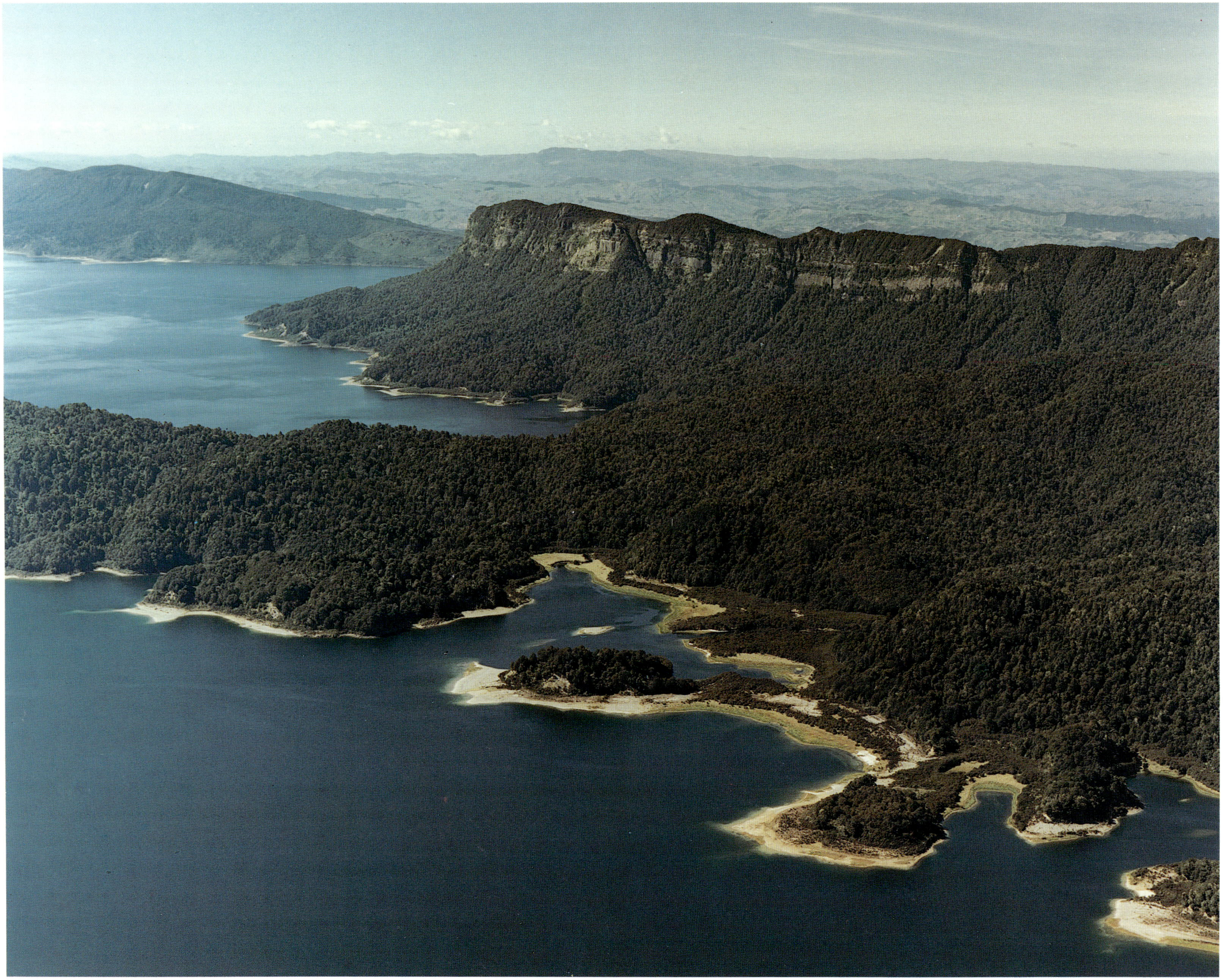

3 Lake Waikaremoana occupies the former upper catchment of the Waikaretaheke River which was blocked by a huge landslide, probably as the result of a major earthquake about 2000 years ago. The lake is perched at 585 m above sea level with its surrounding ranges, such as Panekiri in the middle distance, rising to 1200 m. The Waikaretaheke River flows through the deforested hill country in the distance; this hill country consists of Tertiary sediments which become progressively younger towards the coast.

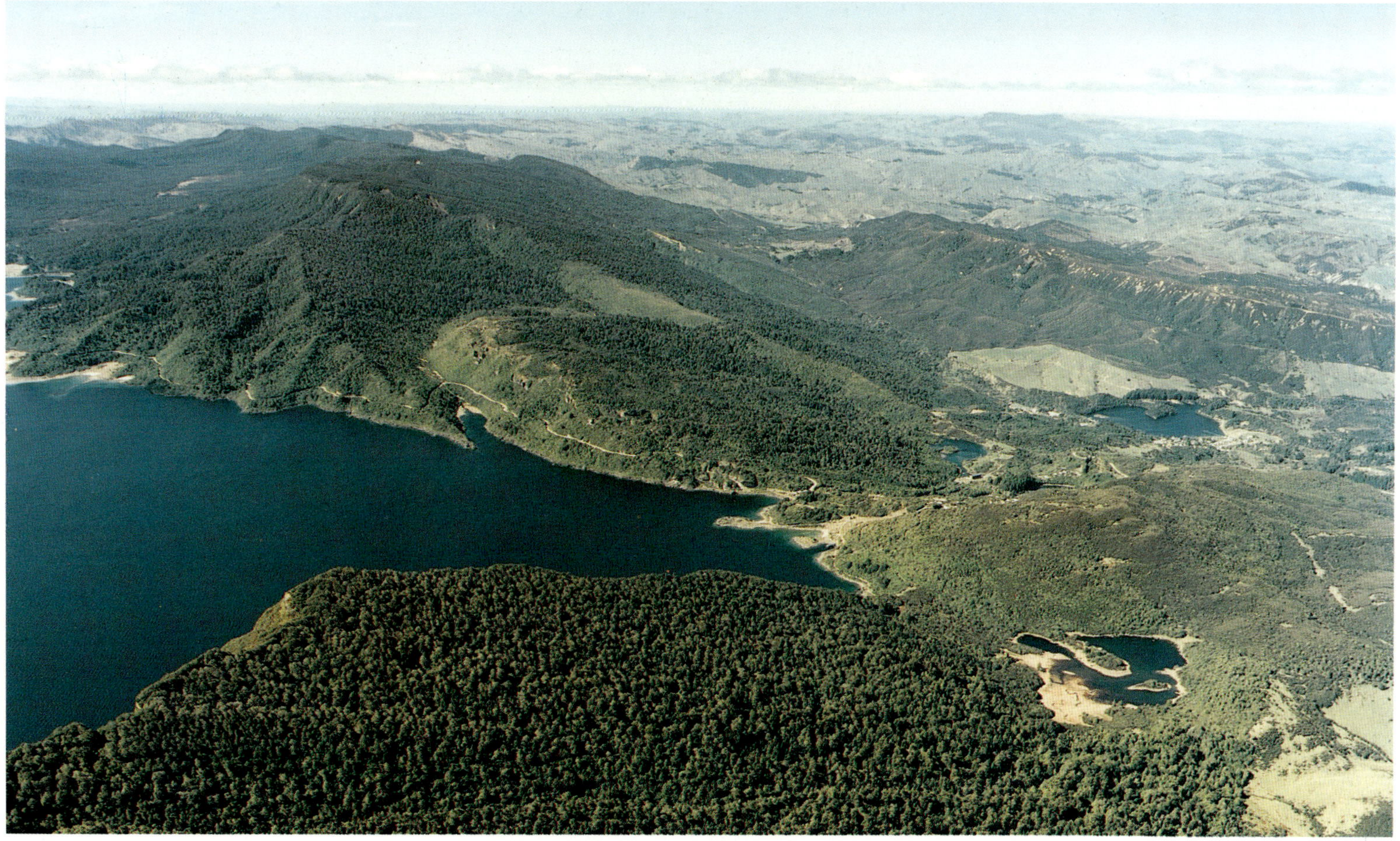

4

4 The huge landslide which dammed the Waikaretaheke River to form Lake Waikaremoana can be seen in the centre of this photograph, looking north-east across the underground outlet at Kaitawa. A wedge of sandstone and siltstone, nearly 3 km long, slid down in a south-westerly direction from the western end of the Ngamoko Range. To the right of the outlet, the hummocky landscape, pockmarked with several shallow lakes, is a jumbled mass of debris from the landslide.

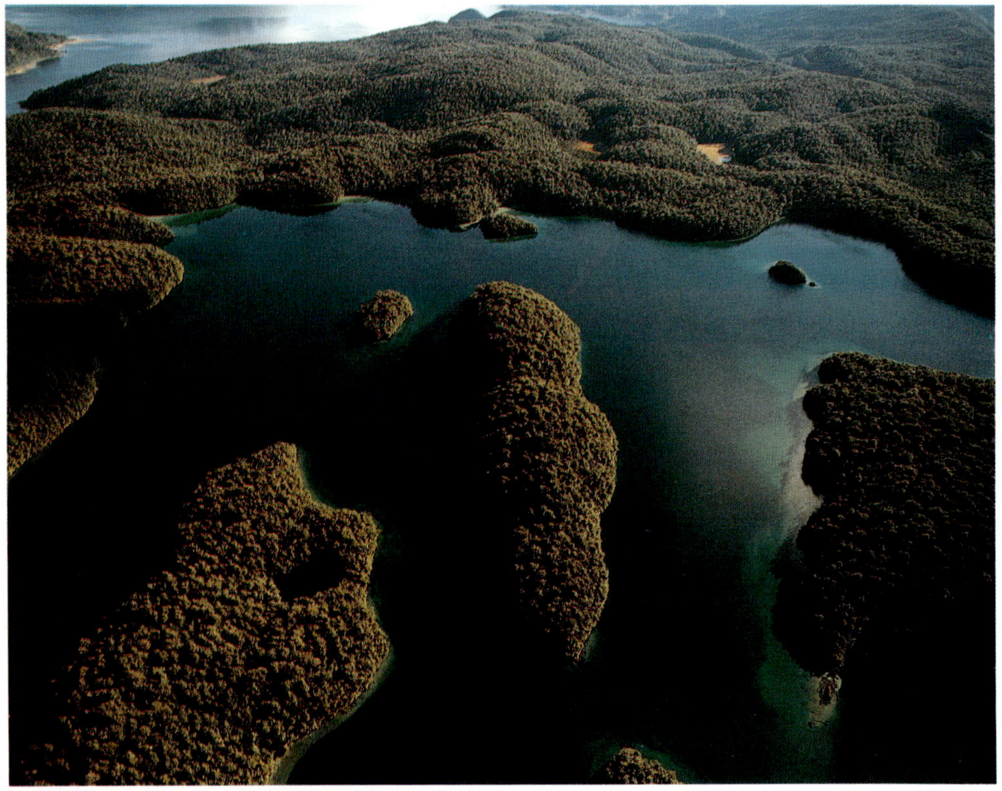

6

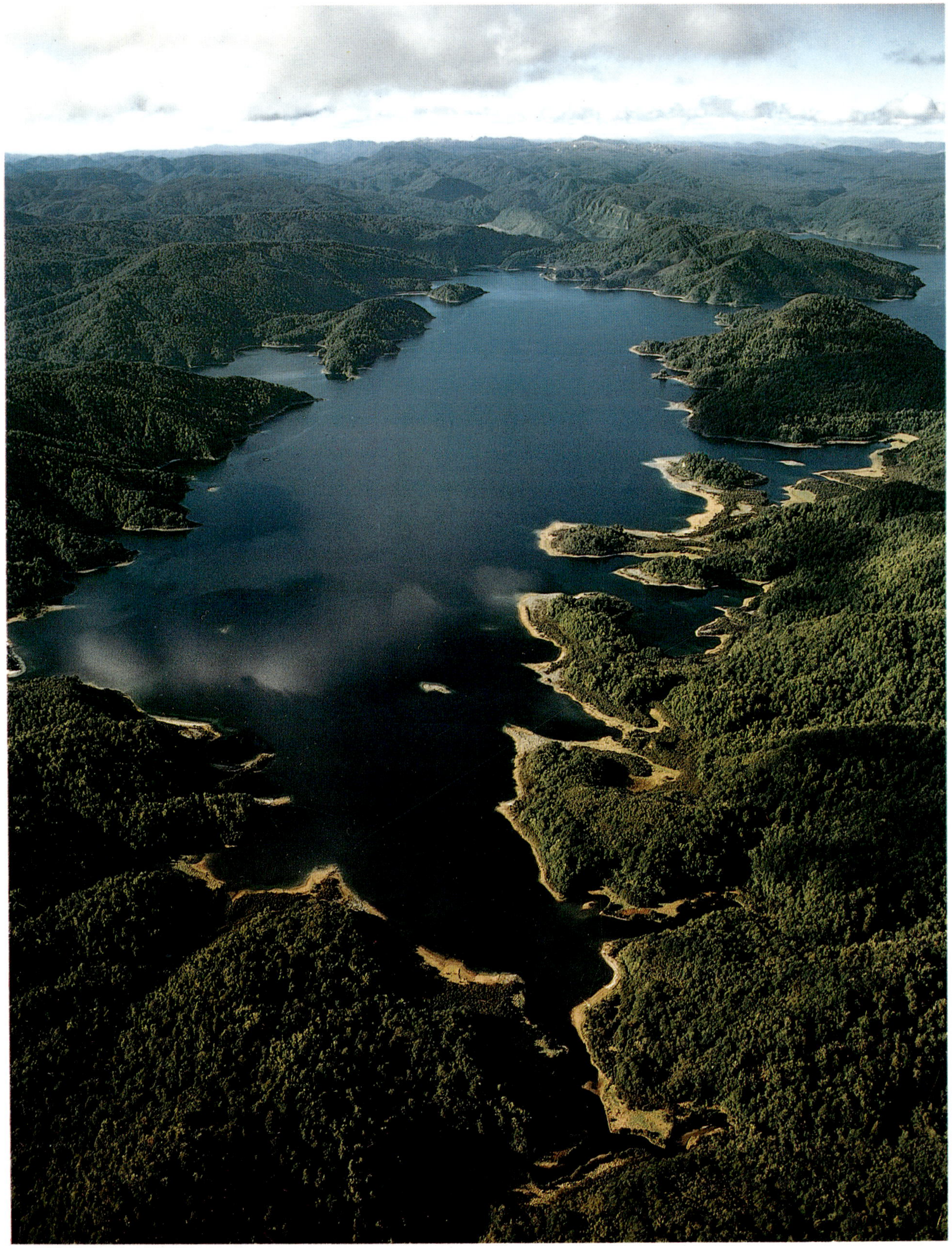

5

5 The eastern shores of the Wairaumoana arm of Lake Waikaremoana have prominent beaches, clearly exposed since the level of the lake was lowered in 1946 when the outflow was harnessed for the generation of hydroelectricity. Beaches are particularly prominent on the eastern shores of the arm, where the Tertiary sediments are softer and susceptible to erosion from the waves driven onto this shore by the prevailing westerly winds.

6 Lake Waikareiti, one of the gems of Urewera National Park, nestles among the undulating folds of a heavily forested subdued basin 300 m above Lake Waikaremoana. The lake is dotted with six islands, the largest of them (Rahui) even enclosing a small lake. There is no obvious stream draining the lake and its origin is likely to be similar to that of Lake Waikaremoana – landslides associated with earthquakes. At this altitude the forest canopy is dominated by red and silver beech, rimu having reached its altitudinal limit.

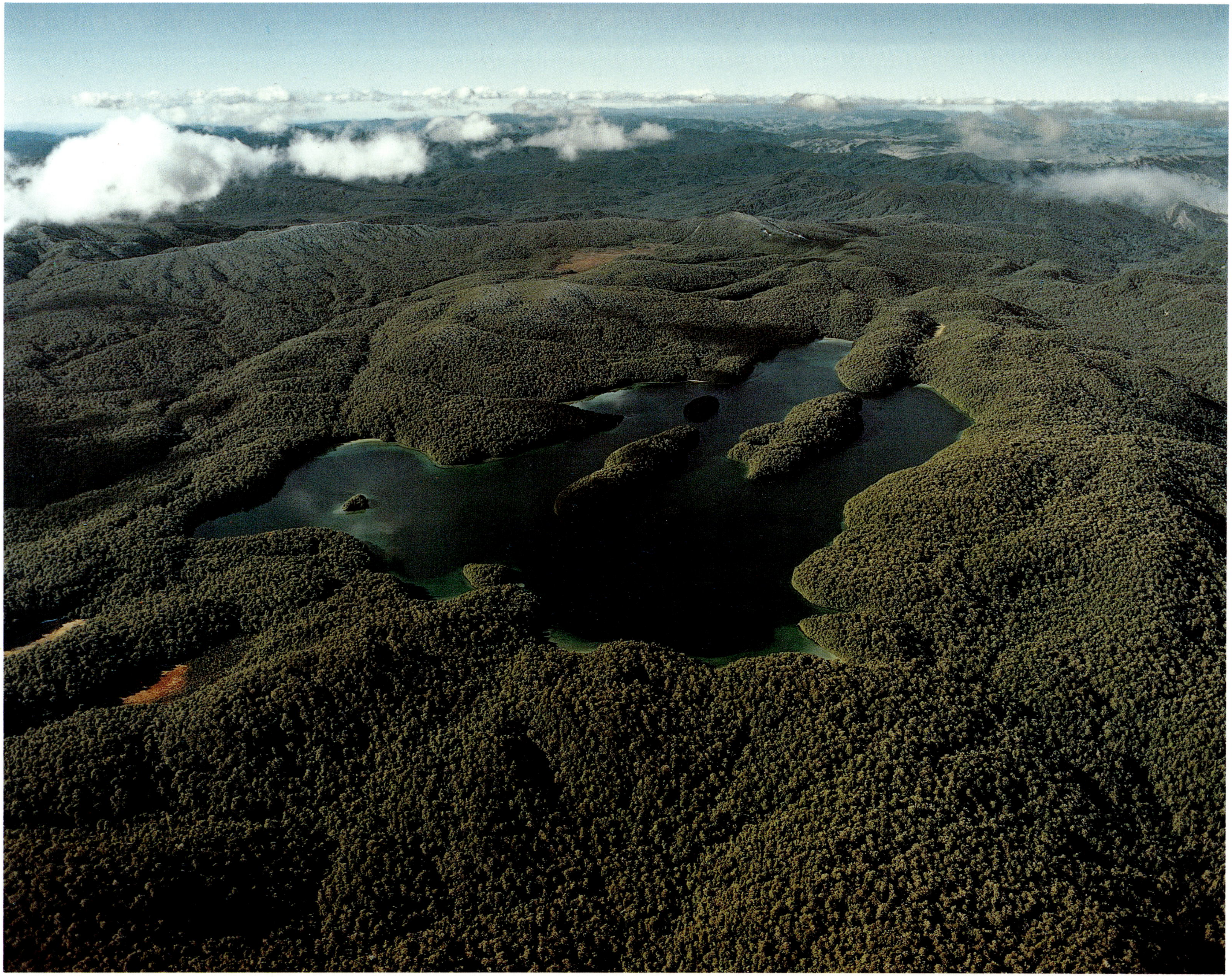

6

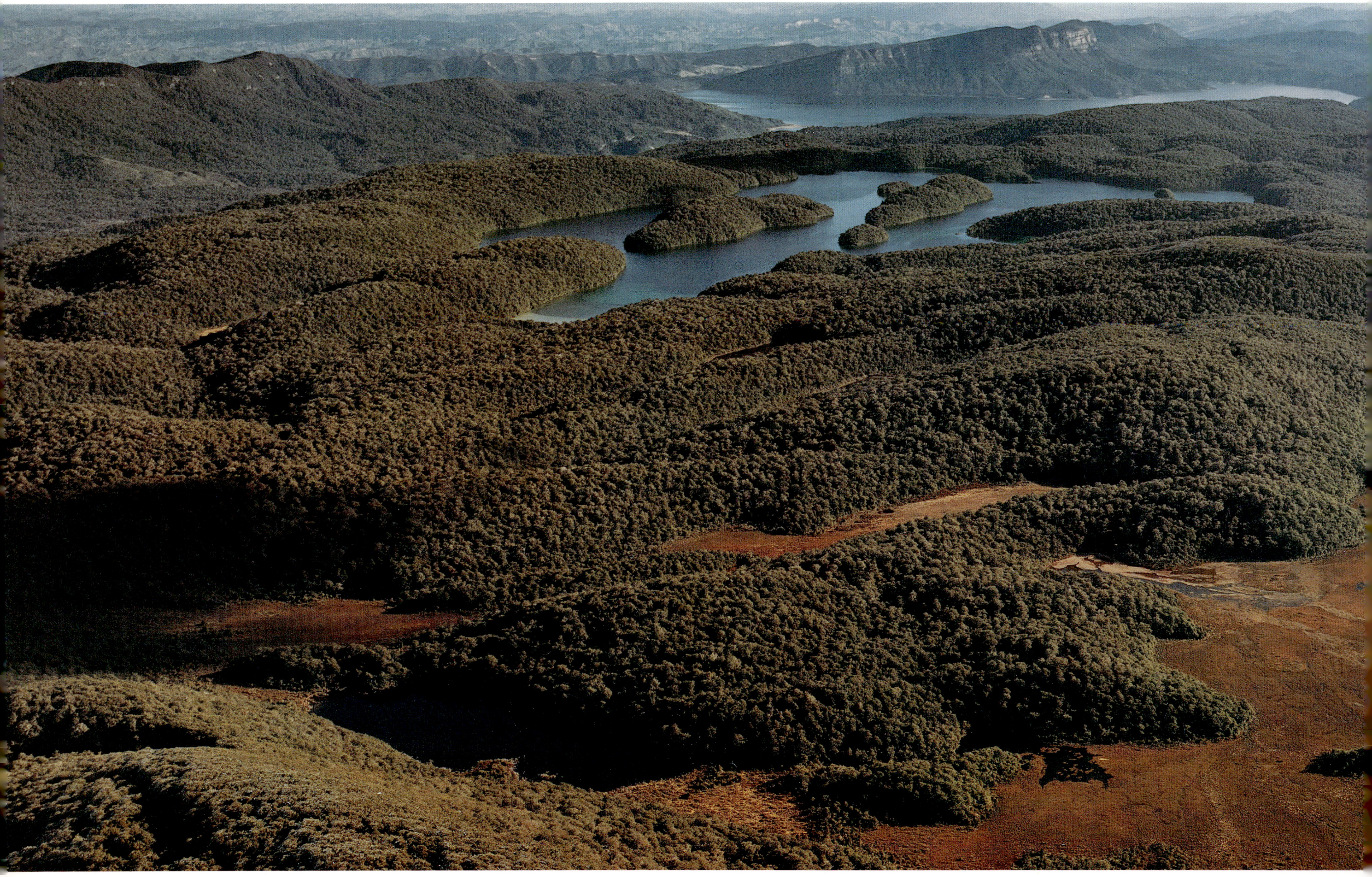

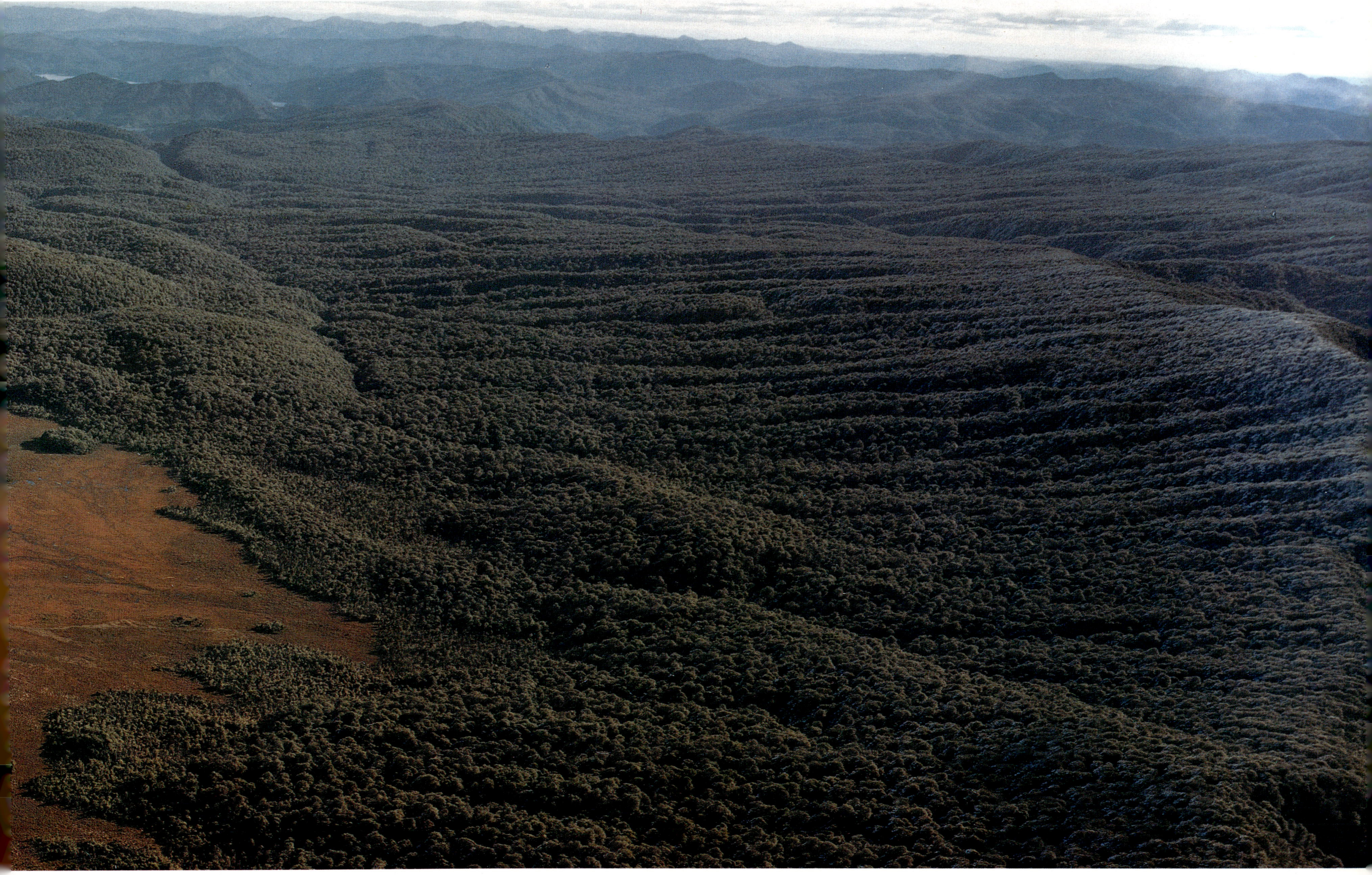

previous page

7 This panorama looking south-west from the head of Kaipo Stream reveals one of the most unusual landscapes in the park. The bold escarpments of the Ngamoko Range and Panekiri Bluff along the eastern skyline contrast with the gentle undulations around Lake Waikareiti and the 'tundra' clearings and wetlands in the foreground. To the right, the regular spacing of the streams draining the slopes of the Kaipo and Mokau valleys probably reflects the homogenous nature of the underlying rocks.

The 'tundra' wetlands are something of an enigma, with vegetation communities unique to this corner of the park. Their origin is not clear but impeded soil drainage seems a common factor, giving the tundras a superficial resemblance to the 'pakihis' of Westland National Park. Peat has formed in places and many of the plants normally occur in the subalpine zone (such as the summit of Mt Manuoha). The wetlands are bordered by rushes, then transitional zones of mosses and herbs and a fringe of *Dacrydium* and *Phyllocladus* shrubland, which merges into the tall red and silver beech forest on the surrounding ridges.

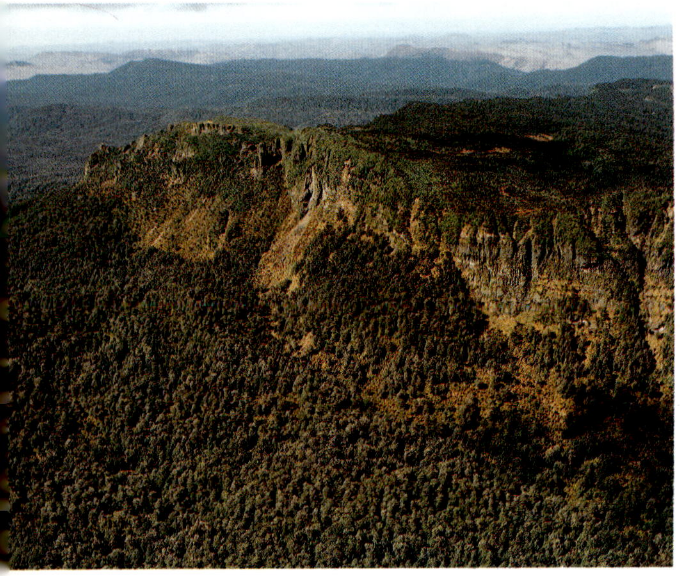

8

8 Maungapohatu (1366 m) is one of only two higher points in the park which manage to clear the bushline (the other is Mt Manuoha, 1403 m). Subalpine shrubland covers the crest while the steep talus slopes below the sandstone cliffs carry beech forest on the more stable sites and shrubland on the young scree slopes.

Maungapohatu is a mountain sacred to the Tuhoe people and to followers of the messianic Maori leader Rua Kenana.

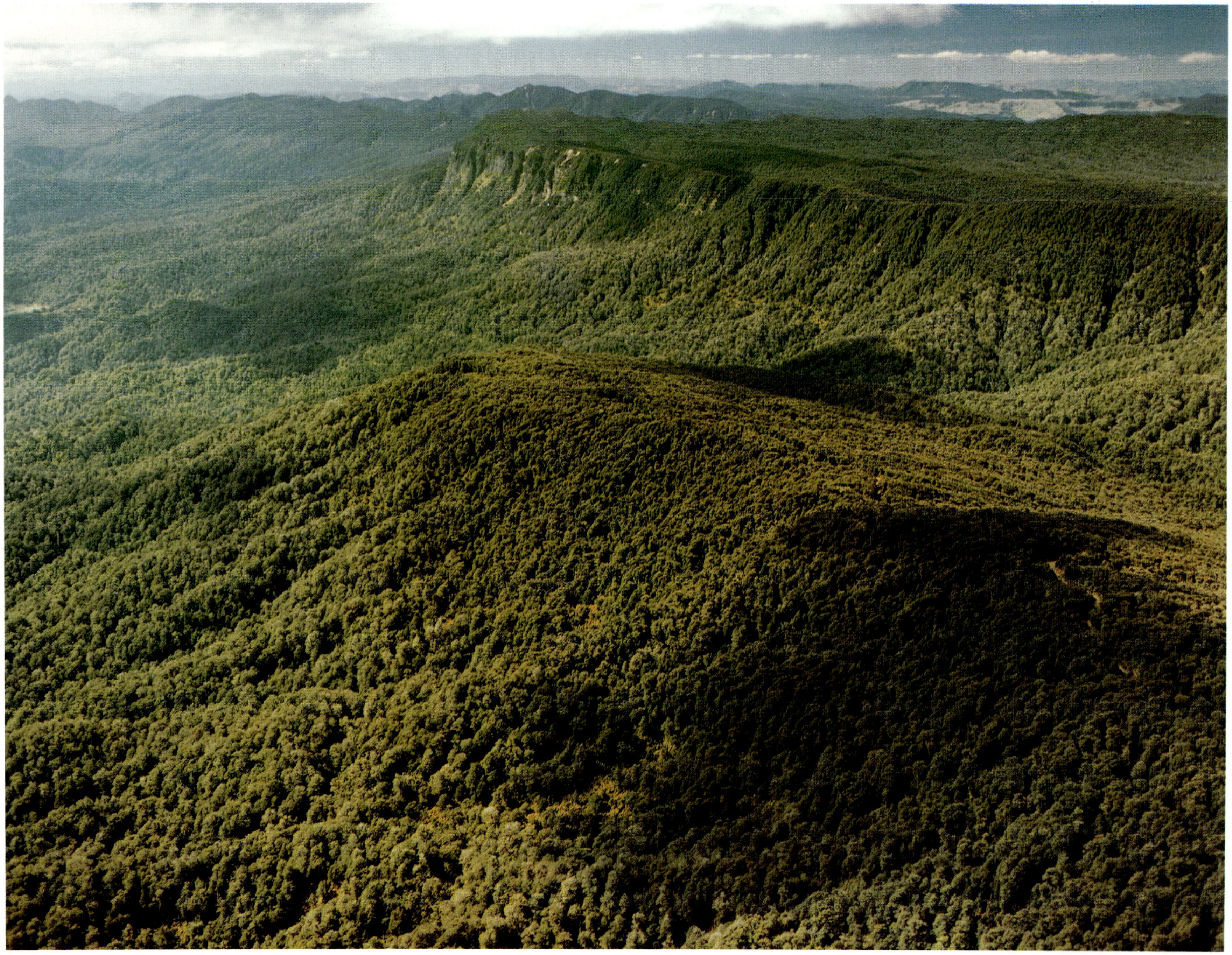

9

9 The north-western rim of the Tertiary sediments in the eastern part of the park can be seen in this view looking north-east towards Maungapohatu. This escarpment is also the watershed of the Huiarau Range, with drainage from the slopes in the foreground entering the north-flowing Whakatane River, and the valleys beyond Maungapohatu draining into the east-flowing Ruakituri River. The escarpment lies just east of, and parallel to, the Waikaremoana Fault which here separates the Tertiary sediments from the greywackes in the western and northern parts of the park.

10 Waitangi Falls on the Ruakituri River on the eastern boundary of the park is one of many spectacular waterfalls formed by rivers and streams flowing over sills of sandstone which remain after softer mudstones have been eroded away. Other falls, such as Papakorito, Aniwaniwa, and Korokoro, all have a similar origin, and the typical shape of a wide cascade sometimes broken into several tongues.

10

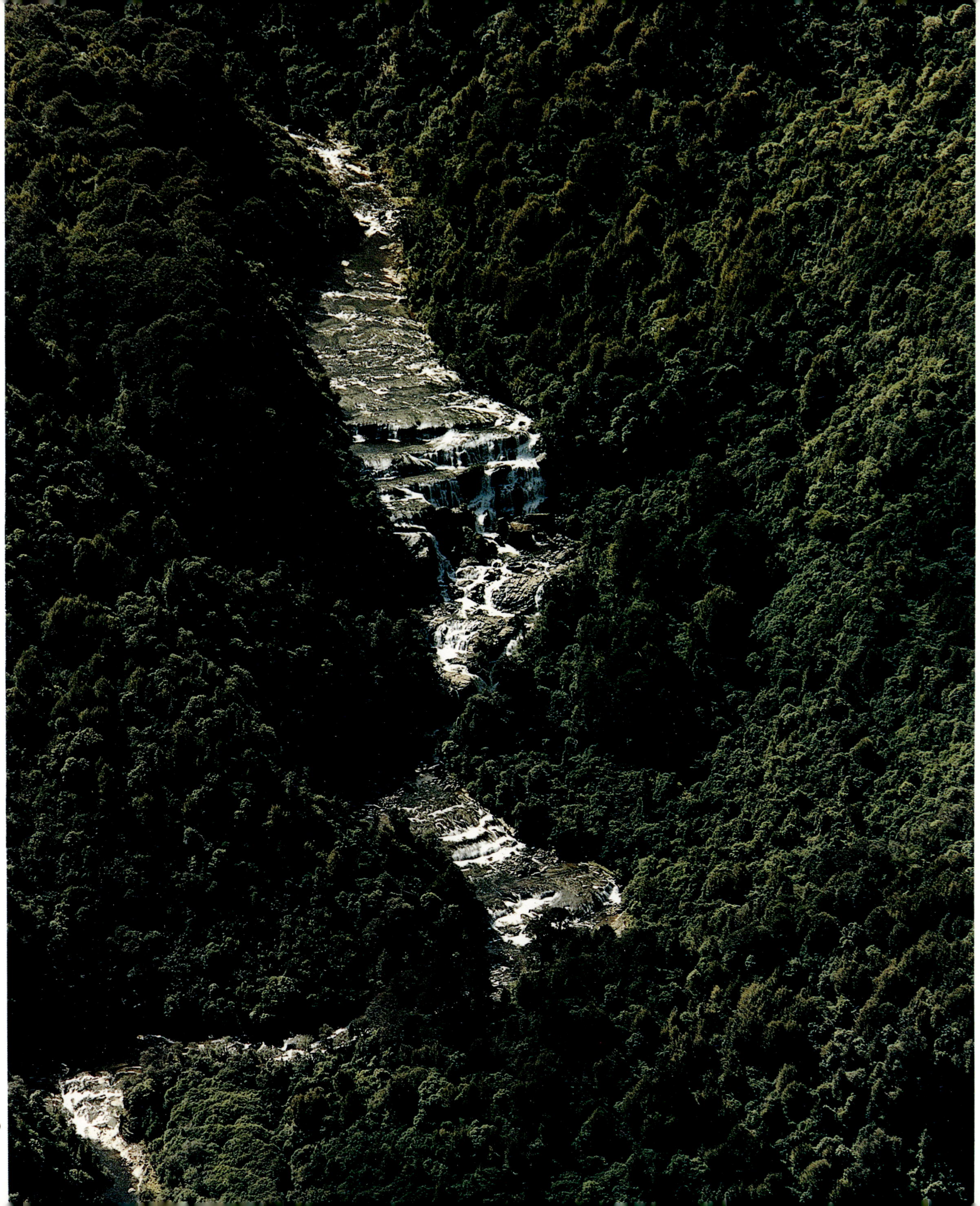

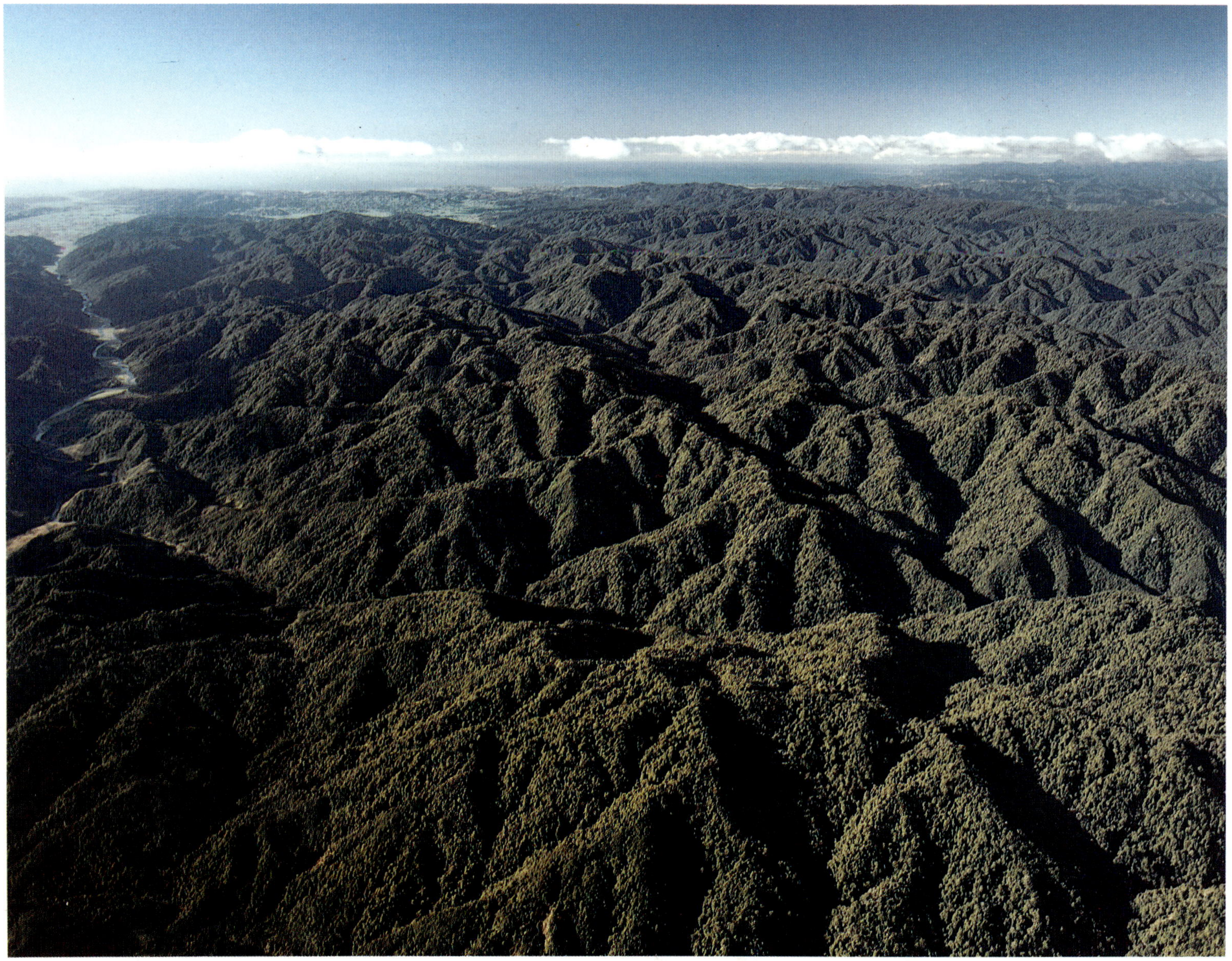

11

11 A feature of the northern part of the park is the finely dissected nature of the landscape and the parallel alignment of the north- to north-north-east–oriented greywacke ridges. Most of the rivers flow north-north-east – south-south-west along the Te Whaiti, Whakatane, Waimana, Waikaremoana, and Kahunui Faults. Here, near the middle reaches of the Whakatane and Tauranga Rivers, the Mesozoic rocks are harder than the Tertiary rocks around Lake Waikaremoana. (Contrast the pattern of dissection with that around Lake Waikareiti and Kaipo Stream, Fig. 7).

12 Looking north-north-east along the parallel ridges in the headwaters of the Ruakituri River. The old Gisborne–Ruatahuna Stock Track (known as Rua's Track) lies off the bottom of the photograph, the headwaters of Anini Stream to the left and Okaura Stream to the right. The early Cretaceous greywacke basement rocks on the right have been piled up like a concertina against the thicker and more resistant late Cretaceous sandstones on the left, producing these classic strike ridges.

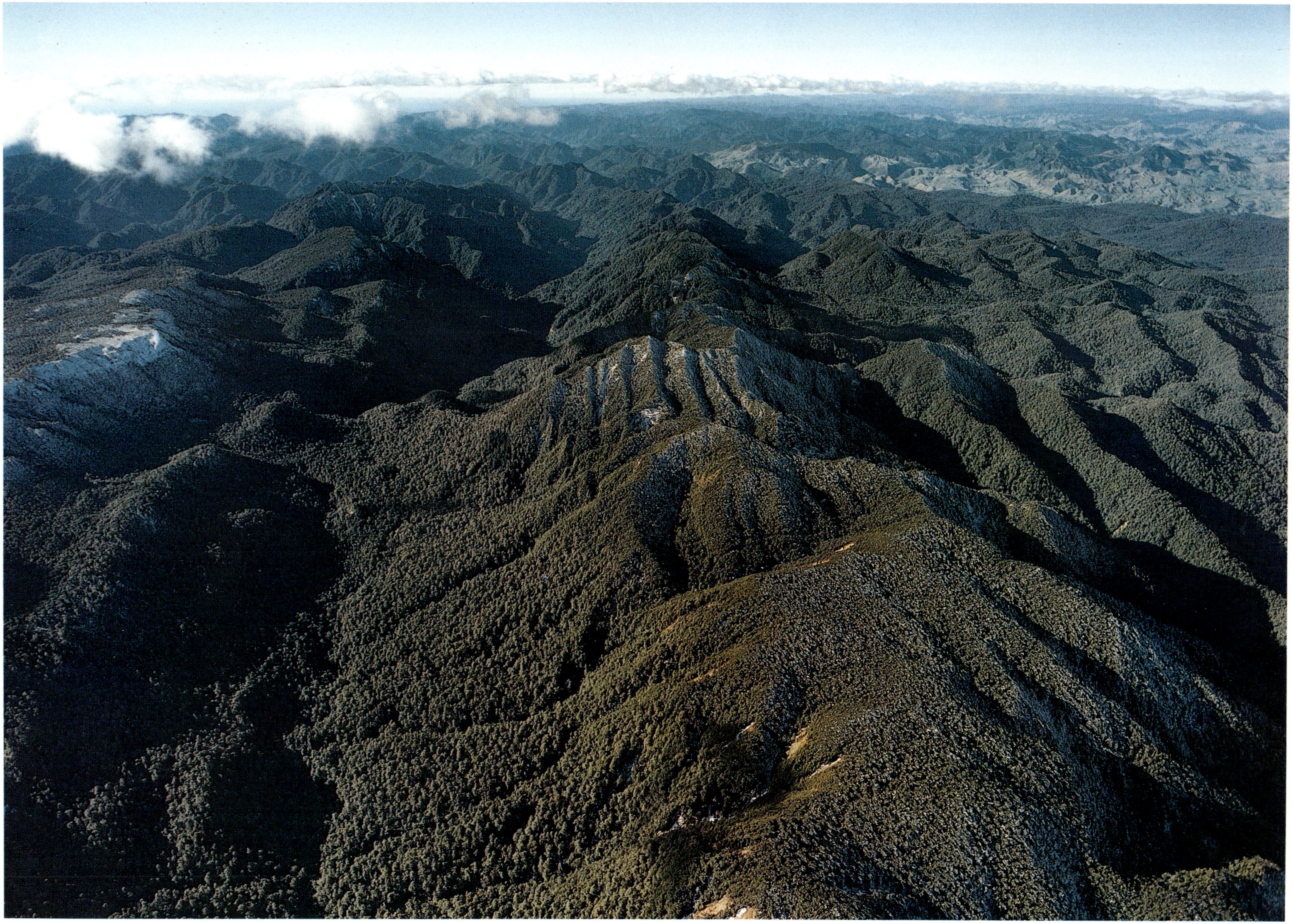

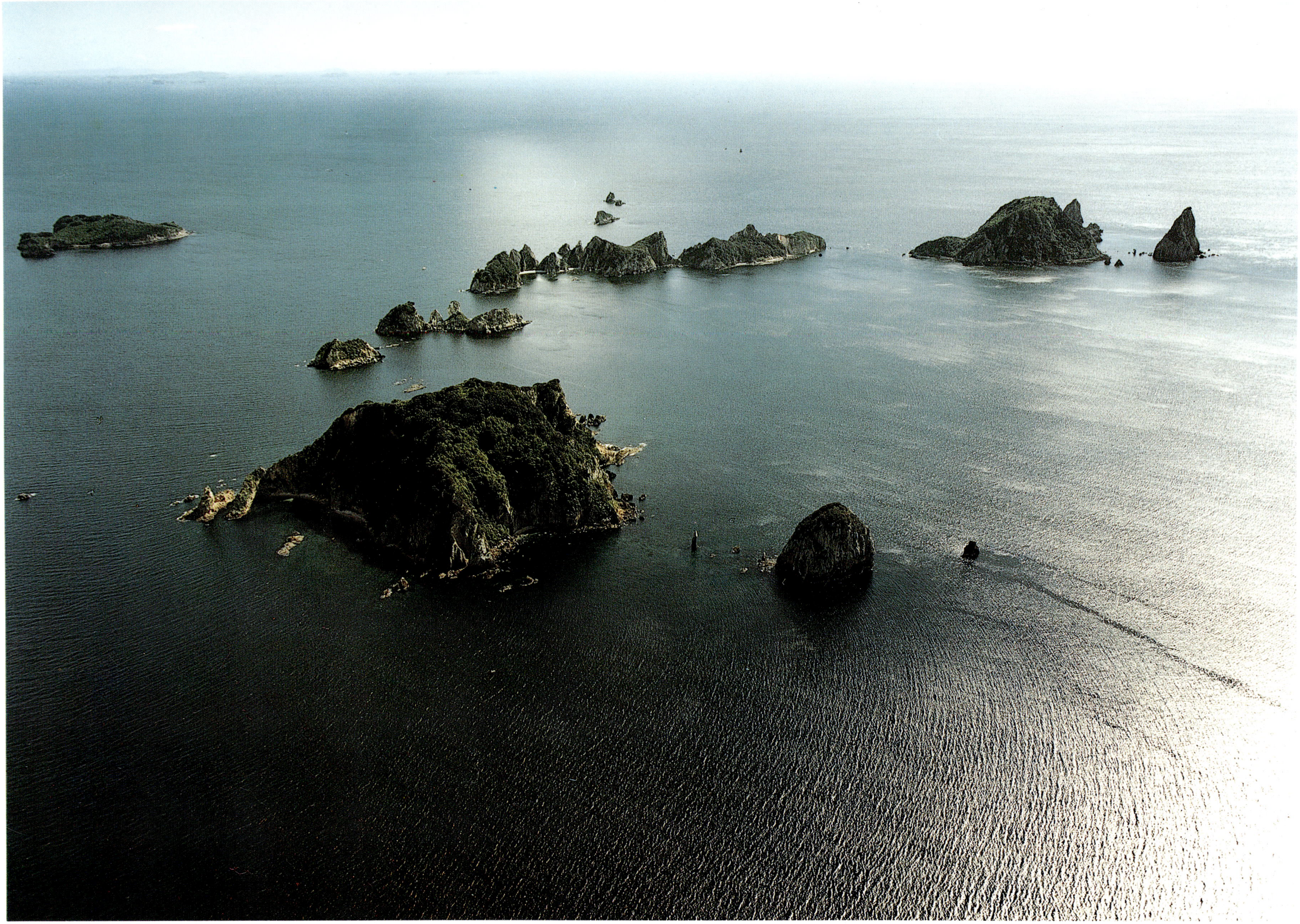

1

MARITIME PARKS OF THE NORTH

No account of the landforms of New Zealand's parks is complete without the islands, headlands, beaches and estuaries that are protected as maritime parks around the Coromandel, Auckland and Northland coastline. Unlike the large national parks with their contiguous landforms, these maritime parks consist of a wide variety of rock types and landforms, protected in a large number of relatively small reserves dispersed around a coastline of thousands of kilometres. The largest group are the islands off the Coromandel coastline and within the Hauraki Gulf; these make up the Hauraki Gulf Maritime Park. Further north lie the islands and headlands around the Bay of Islands and Whangaroa Harbour – the Bay of Islands Maritime and Historic Park. In the far north, at the tip of the huge tombolo of the Aupouri Peninsula, lies a group of reserves from Cape Maria van Diemen to North Cape which are in the process of being amalgamated into a new park entity – the Te Paki Conservation Park.

HAURAKI GULF MARITIME PARK

The park consists of twenty-seven islands or island groups, extending from the jagged spires of the Aldermen Islands in the Bay of Plenty to the Poor Knights Islands, 200 km away off the Northland coastline north-east of Whangarei. The outer Gulf islands (such as Little Barrier, Poor Knights, Cuvier, Aldermen) are all of inestimable importance as sanctuaries for rare and endangered wildlife; they are all classified as Nature Reserves and public access is controlled. The inner Gulf islands (such as Rangitoto, Motutapu, Motuihe, Tiritiri Matangi, Kawau) are a mixture of Scenic, Recreation and Scientific Reserves where public use is encouraged.

Geologically, the islands fall into two main groups:

- The volcanic islands, their geological composition ranging widely from rhyolite (Aldermen, Poor Knights), through andesite (Taranga, Little Barrier), to basalt (Browns, Rangitoto). These volcanic islands span a wide range of ages, from Rangitoto whose lava flows are probably less than 1000 years old tothe deeply weathered Miocene-aged andesites of Taranga and rhyolites of the Poor Knights. Cuvier and Coppermine Islands are different again, plutonic in origin rather than volcanic, consisting of early Miocene diorites and granodiorites.
- The sedimentary rock islands – fragments of the basement greywacke and sandstone rocks which make up most of eastern Northland and the Hunua Ranges west of the Firth of Thames. Some of these islands consist mainly of basement Mesozoic greywacke (Rakino, Kawau, western Marotere) and others are still partly or largely covered with a cap of Tertiary sandstone (Motuihe, Motutapu, Tiritiri Matangi, Motuora).

On some of the younger volcanic islands, the landforms are clearly related to the rock type. Youthful Rangitoto is obviously a volcano, and even Little Barrier (1 to 4 million years old) is still recognisable as a rugged, deeply eroded andesitic volcano. For other volcanic islands the landform origins are more complex. In the Aldermen group, the prominently-jointed rhyolite of several intrusive domes has been breached to form a fantastic cluster of jagged pinnacles; the much older rhyolite of the Poor Knights Islands has been eroded into an entirely different shape, with an undulating summit plateau surrounded by vertical cliffs descending far below sea level. The remarkable cliffs and underwater caves of the Poor Knights were probably carved during periods of low sea level in the glacial stages of the Ice Ages, for the Poor Knights are considered to be the only islands of the gulf that were in sufficiently deep water to remain as islands when sea levels dropped over 100 m at the height of the last glaciation (18 000–20 000 years ago). The undulating summit plateau is evidence of an uplifted former marine bench, indicating that this eastern Northland coastline has been gradually rising.

The sedimentary rock islands are lower in altitude (50–200 m) and of more subdued topography. They generally have well-developed wave-cut platforms (especially in the Miocene sandstone islands such as Motuihe and Motutapu), whereas the volcanic islands tend to lack a fringing underwater shelf.

THE BAY OF ISLANDS PARK

There is more landform unity to the Bay of Islands Maritime and Historic Park. It includes both volcanic and sedimentary rock landscapes, but the volcanic element is much less obvious than in Hauraki Gulf Maritime Park. Basaltic lavas flowed into the Kerikeri and Waitangi river valleys where the well-known Rainbow and Haruru Falls are popular scenic features; around the Whangaroa Harbour, Miocene-aged andesitic breccia has created a spectacular craggy landscape. Greywacke forms most of the coastline in the park, with rocky headlands extending south from Cape Brett through Whangamumu and Whangaruru to Mimiwhangata Bay. The Cavalli Islands, and most of the islands in the Bay of Islands itself, consist of very old, deeply weathered greywacke. The soils are clay-textured and the intense weathering of this subdued landscape is indicated by the red subsoils in places such as Red Head on Okahu Island.

TE PAKI AND THE FAR NORTH

The northern tip of the Aupouri Peninsula is one of New Zealand's truly outstanding indigenous landscapes. Its scale and grandeur are in keeping with its significance to the Maori people as the spiritual departure point for the ancestral homeland of Hawaiki. Ninety Mile Beach is the south-western edge of the longest tombolo in New Zealand – an 80 km long ribbon of sand linking the volcanic remnants around Te Paki to the rest of Northland. The fingers of Parengarenga Harbour reach back towards the great sand dunes (120 m high) behind Ninety Mile Beach and the complex of Cretaceous volcanic rocks and Miocene sandstones around Te Paki and Te Hapua. The volcanic outcrops (Scott Point, Cape Maria van Diemen, Cape Reinga and Hooper Point) act as rocky anchors linking together the sweeping sandy beaches of the far north. Between North Cape and Kerr Point lie the reddish-purple Surville Cliffs, the 200 m high northernmost point in New Zealand. This is North Cape Scientific Reserve, the remnant of an ancient intrusion of ultramafic rock, containing a number of specially adapted plants confined to this tiny remote corner of the North Island.

1 The Aldermen Islands lie 20 km off the Coromandel Coast near Tairua, at the south-eastern limit of Hauraki Gulf Maritime Park. They are the jagged remnants of a volcanic complex of rhyolite domes, ignimbrites and pyroclastic flows probably erupted during Pliocene times (2–5 million years ago) along the eastern Coromandel Peninsula. Despite their isolation and difficult access they traditionally attracted Maori mutton-birding parties. Today, they are protected as an important wildlife sanctuary.

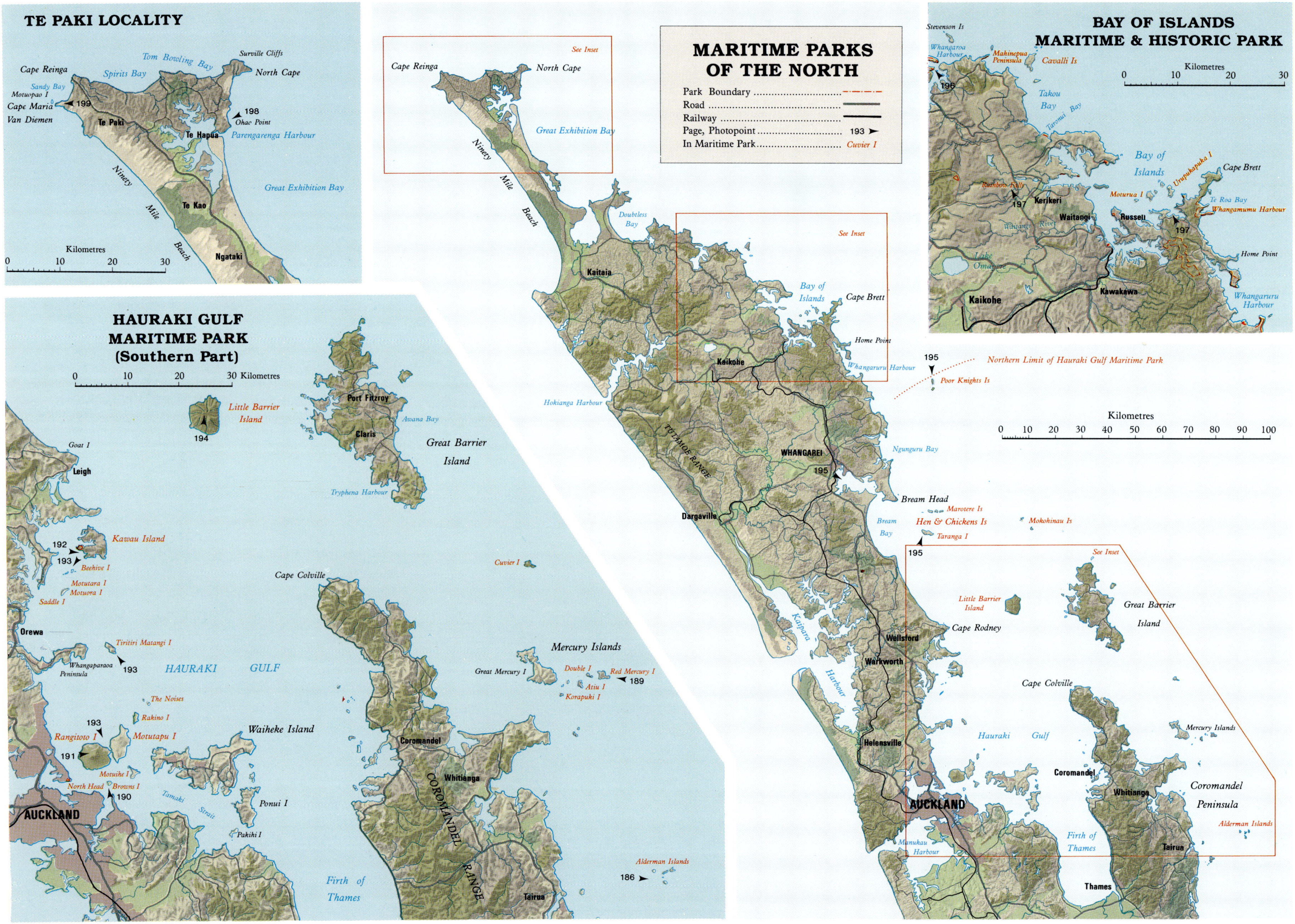
MARITIME PARKS OF THE NORTH
Park Boundary
Road
Railway
Page, Photopoint 193
In Maritime Park Cuvier I
TE PAKI LOCALITY
Cape Reinga
Sandy Bay
Motuopao I
Cape Maria Van Diemen
199
Spirits Bay
Tom Bowling Bay
Surville Cliffs
North Cape
198
Ohao Point
Te Paki
Te Hapua
Parengarenga Harbour
Ninety Mile Beach
Te Kao
Great Exhibition Bay
Ngataki
Kilometres
0 10 20 30
HAURAKI GULF MARITIME PARK (Southern Part)
0 10 20 30 Kilometres
Little Barrier Island
194
Port Fitzroy
Claris
Awana Bay
Great Barrier Island
Tryphena Harbour
Goat I
Leigh
Kawau Island
192
193
Beehive I
Motutara I
Motuora I
Saddle I
Cape Colville
Cuvier I
Orewa
Tiritiri Matangi I
Whangaparaoa Peninsula
193
HAURAKI GULF
Mercury Islands
Great Mercury I
Double I
Red Mercury I
189
Atiu I
Korapuki I
The Noises
Rakino I
193
Rangitoto I
Motutapu I
Waiheke Island
Coromandel
191
Motuihe I
North Head
Browns I
190
Whitianga
AUCKLAND
Tamaki Strait
Ponui I
Pakihi I
COROMANDEL RANGE
Alderman Islands
186
Firth of Thames
Tairua
See Inset
Cape Reinga
North Cape
Great Exhibition Bay
Ninety Mile Beach
Doubtless Bay
Kaitaia
Bay of Islands
Cape Brett
Home Point
Kaikohe
Whangaruru Harbour
Hokianga Harbour
TUTAMOE RANGE
WHANGAREI
195
Ngunguru Bay
Bream Head
Marotere Is
Hen & Chickens Is
Mokohinau Is
Bream Bay
Taranga I
Dargaville
195
195
Northern Limit of Hauraki Gulf Maritime Park
Poor Knights Is
Kilometres
0 10 20 30 40 50 60 70 80 90 100
Little Barrier Island
Great Barrier Island
Cape Rodney
Wellsford
Kaipara Harbour
Warkworth
Cape Colville
Mercury Islands
Hauraki Gulf
Helensville
Coromandel
Whitianga
Coromandel Peninsula
AUCKLAND
Manukau Harbour
Firth of Thames
Alderman Islands
Tairua
Thames
BAY OF ISLANDS MARITIME & HISTORIC PARK
Kilometres
0 10 20 30
Stevenson Is
Whangaroa Harbour
Mahinepua Peninsula
Cavalli Is
196
Takou Bay
Taronui Bay
Bay of Islands
Urupukapuka I
Cape Brett
Rainbow Falls
197
Kerikeri
Moturua I
Te Roa Bay
Whangamumu Harbour
Waitangi
Russell
197
Waitangi River
Lake Omapere
Home Point
Kaikohe
Kawakawa
Whangaruru Harbour

2 Red Mercury Island lies 30 km north-east of Whitianga on the Coromandel Peninsula. The island is the easternmost of the seven island Mercury Islands group, all of volcanic origin; the others can be seen in this view looking westwards – Double Island (centre); Stanley, Middle, Green and Korapuki Islands (centre left); and Great Mercury Island (centre, distance).

Red Mercury is a mixture of Pliocene-aged basalt flows cut by a shallow basalt intrusion, evident in the 100 m-high cliffs in the foreground. By contrast, the distant 200 m-high white cliffs on the north-eastern coast of Great Mercury consist of rhyolitic rock.

Red Mercury gets its name from the red weathering of the scoria that occurs between some of the flows; this was quarried by the early Maori as a red colouring. The undulating summit plateau was once covered with forest but this was burnt off during the long period of Maori occupation. The vegetation is now a shrubland dominated by mapou (*Myrsine australis*) with emergent pohutukawa (the darker green trees, particularly evident around the cliffs). All of the Mercury Islands (except Great Mercury which is privately owned) are Nature Reserves and major wildlife sanctuaries.

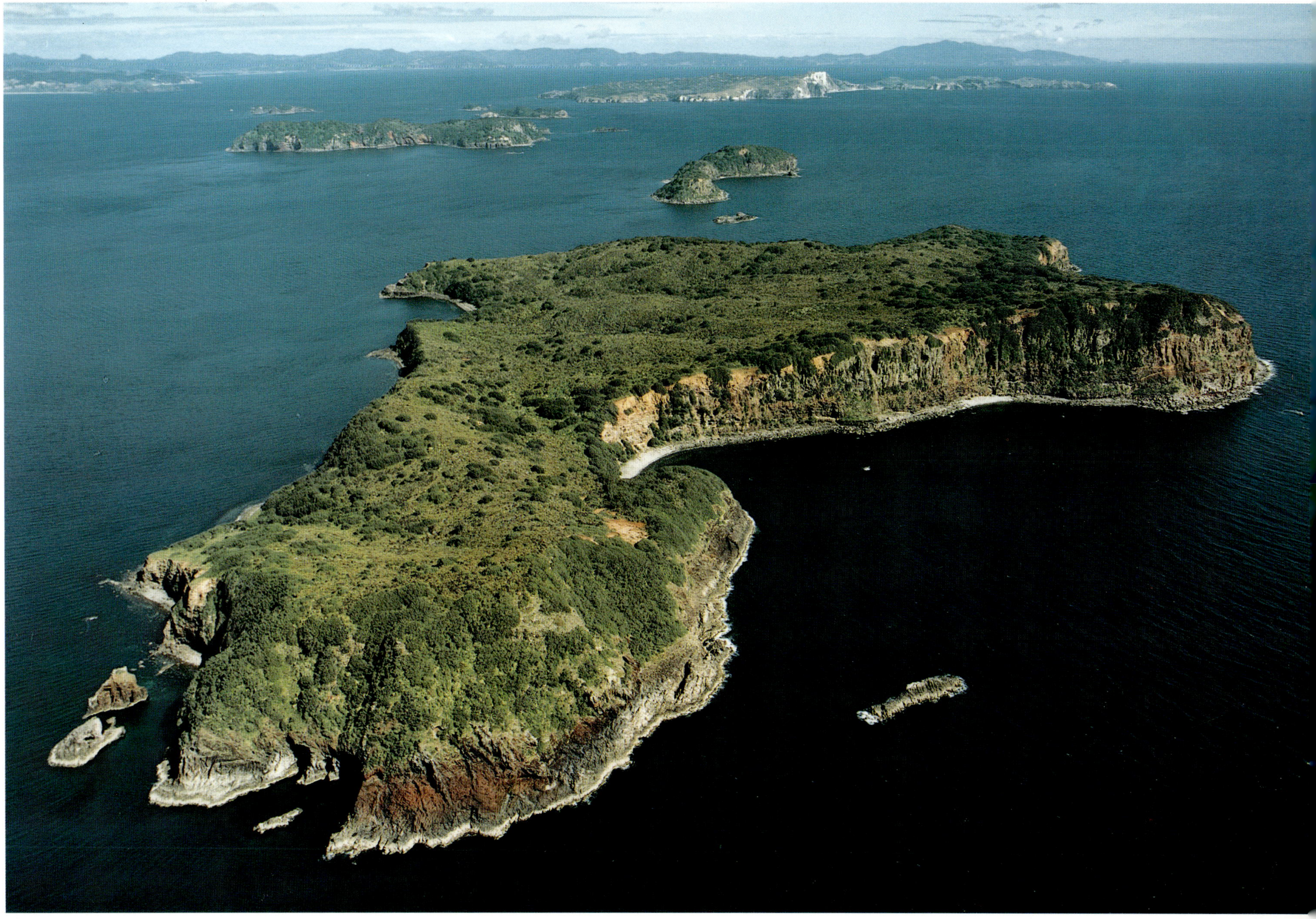

2

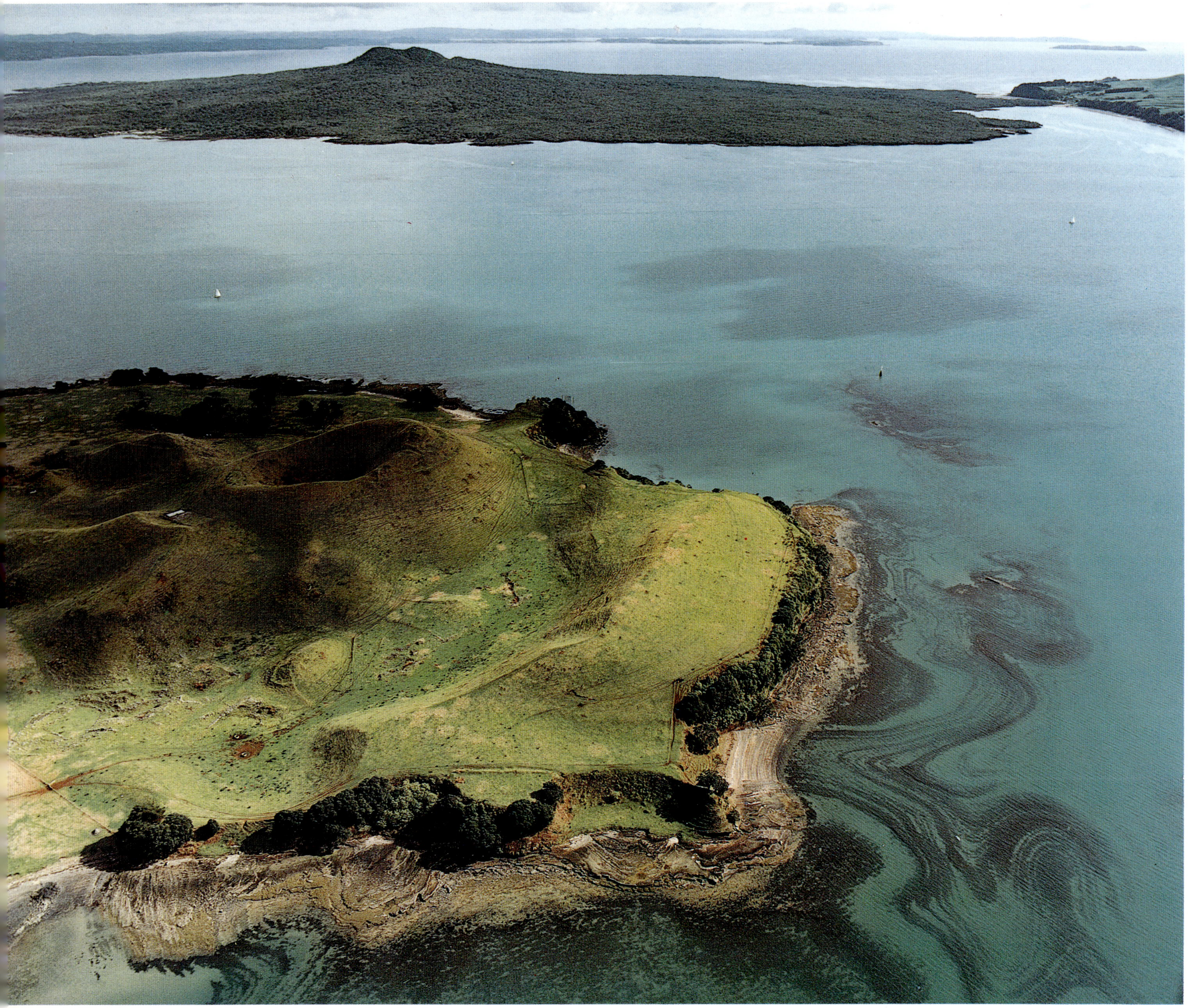

3 Browns Island (foreground) and Rangitoto Island (background) are two of the best known inner islands of Hauraki Gulf Maritime Park. Both consist of Auckland basalt, and are two of a series of volcanoes built from basaltic lava flows and scoria during the late Quaternary. The obvious feature of Browns Island is its central crater; in contrast Rangitoto Island has the classic, gently sloping lava apron of a typical shield volcano. Whereas Browns Island was probably active 10 000–15 000 years ago, Rangitoto Island began to emerge at the entrance to the Waitemata Harbour a mere 1000 years ago. The strata in the cliffs and offshore underwater rocks are bedded ash and scoria erupted from the crater.

Three pa sites can be seen on Browns Island: a hill pa on the right of the crater rim, a small coastal headland pa beyond the crater, and the ditch of a small clifftop pa in the foreground.

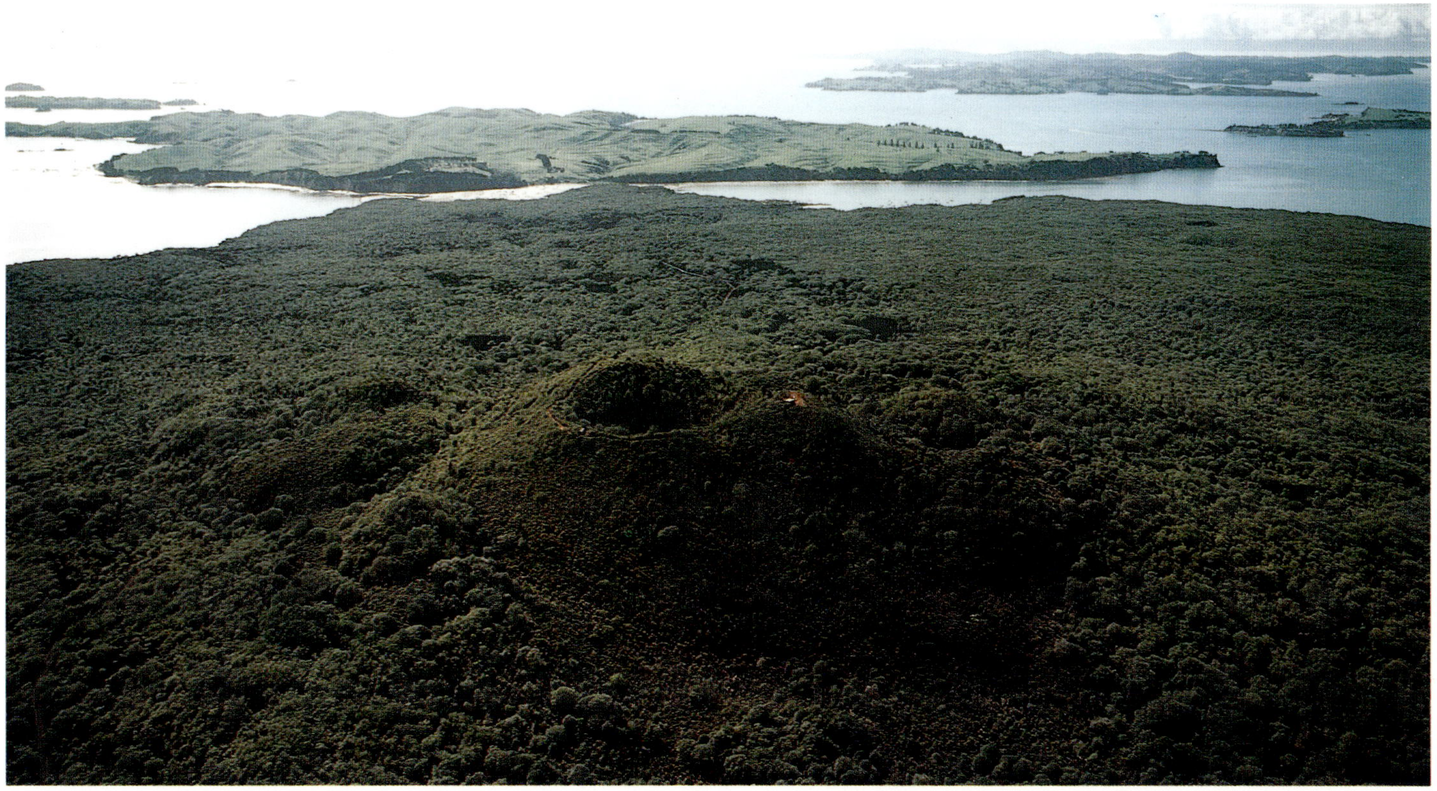

4

4 Rangitoto Island is the youngest of the more than fifty basaltic volcanoes that occur on and around the Auckland isthmus. The small 500 m-wide cinder cone on the summit looks quite incongruous perched above the 6 km-wide lava apron. The steep slope of the cone is due to scoria particles coming to rest at the angle of repose (like the typical andesitic cones of Mts Ngauruhoe and Taranaki), whereas the basalt lava was so mobile that it kept flowing outwards.

Differences in soil formation and moisture retention probably account for the contrast between the scrub on the cone (mainly manuka, mingimingi and mapou) and the pohutukawa forest on the lava flows. Motutapu Island is the grassy island beyond, with Motuihe and Waiheke Islands in the right distance.

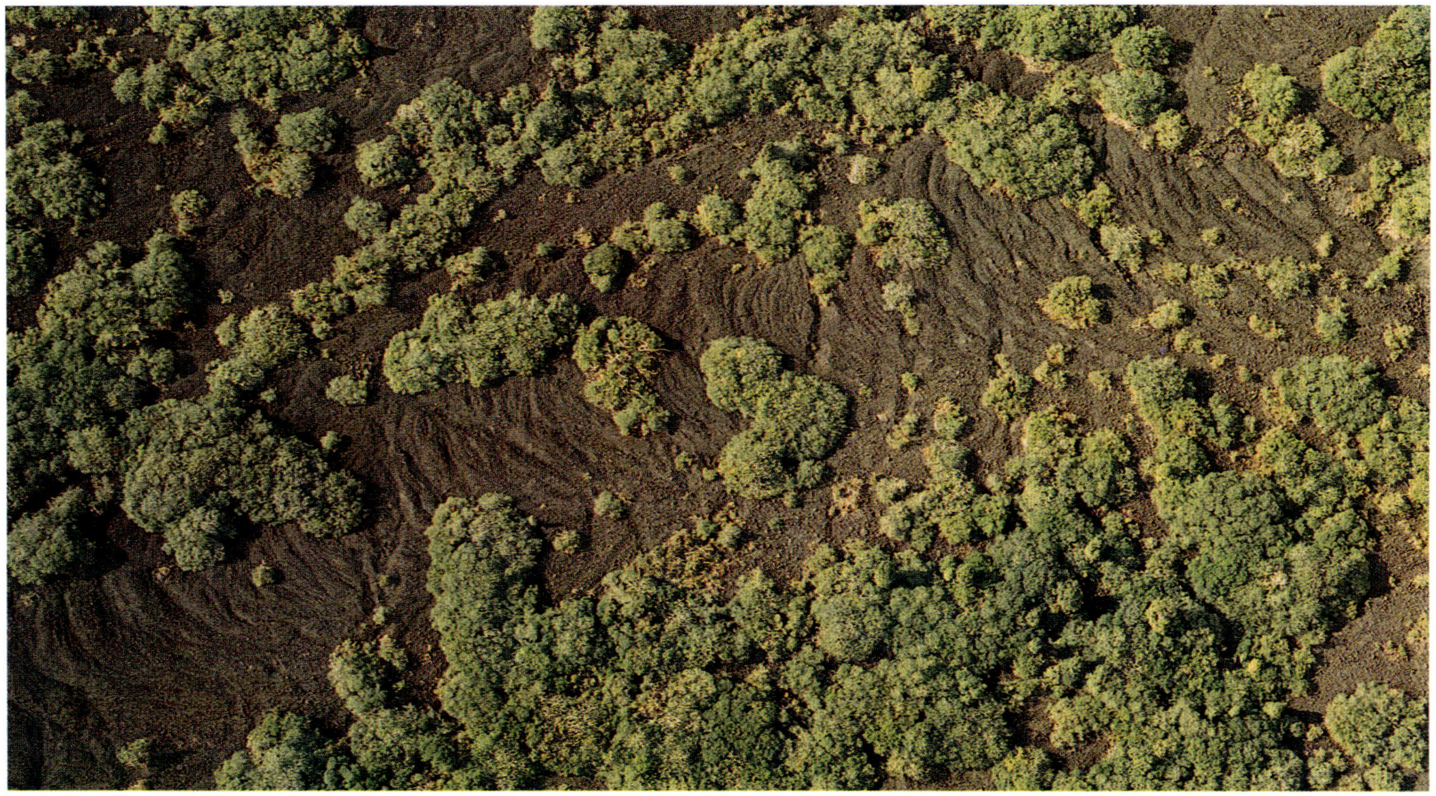

5

5 The basaltic lava flows of Rangitoto are mostly of the rough-surfaced (aa) type; on sunny days the surface temperature of the lava can reach 70°C. There are no streams or tarns, and soils are rudimentary in the extreme (usually only a sandy humus which accumulates in the fissures in the rock). The direction of lava flow is indicated by the convex down-slope shape of the flow ridges (right to left).

Despite the inhospitality of the young lava flows, Rangitoto Island supports a diverse flora of 200 indigenous plants and another 200 exotic plants. This diversity is probably the result of a combination of humid climate and the high fertility of the soil materials that eventually weather from the basalt. The cover of pohutukawa (*Metrosideros excelsa*) forest is discontinuous and is probably related to the availability of moisture.

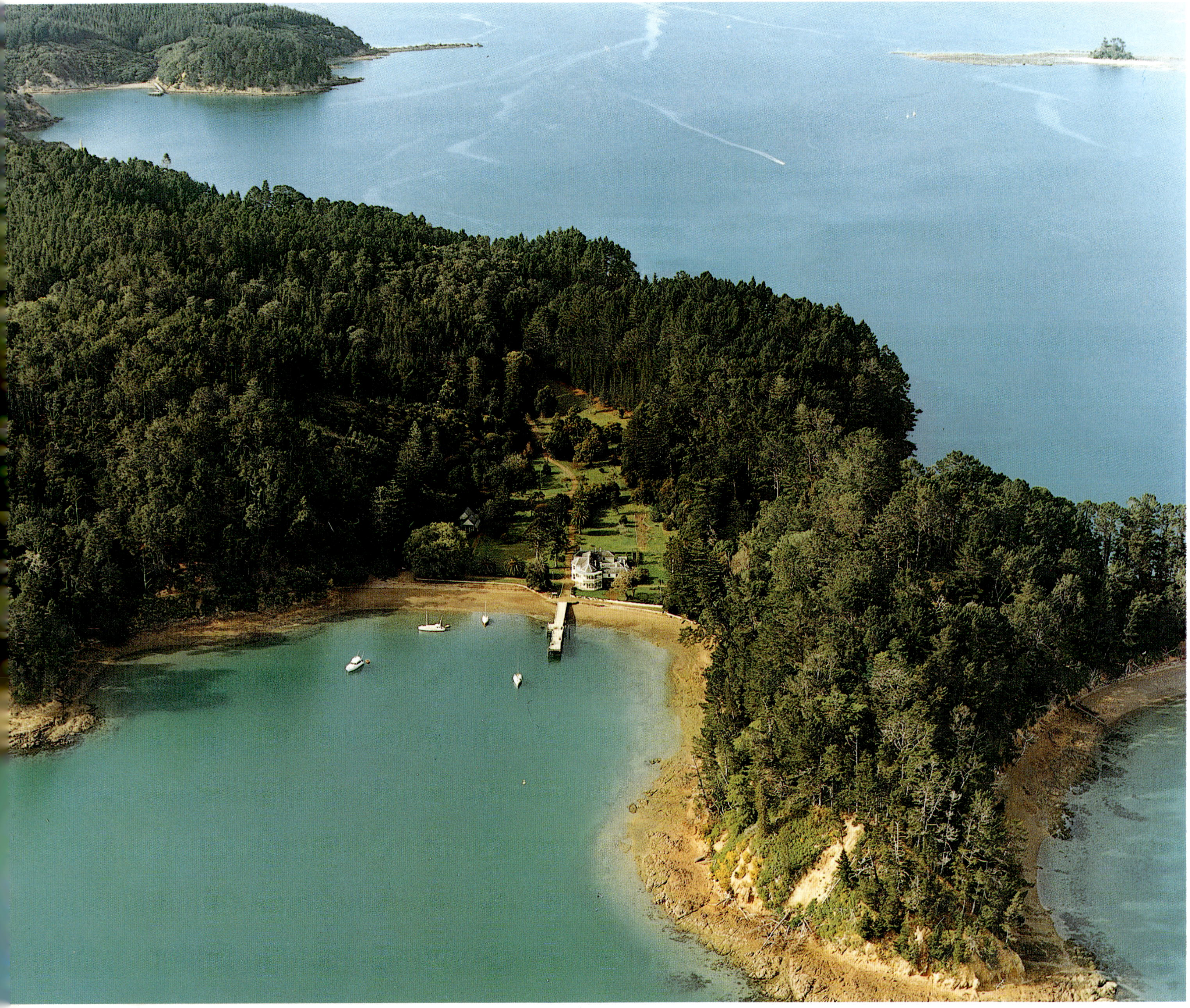

6 Kawau Island, only 8 km off the Rodney coast near Warkworth, is one of the more accessible islands of Hauraki Gulf Maritime Park. This view south-east across Mansion House Bay (towards Beehive Island, top right) shows Governor George Grey's restored mansion house, now a recreational and historic focal point of the park.

The wavecut platform has exposed the weathered basement rocks of early Mesozoic greywacke; in places the island still carries patches of Miocene sandstone, where it has not been eroded away to expose the greywacke. Copper occurs in reefs which extend below sea level in the greywacke. This ore was successfully mined in the past and the chimney of the mine pumphouse in South Cove can just be seen in the top left corner.

7 Tiny Beehive Island, 1 km off the south-west corner of Kawau Island, is one of the curiosities of Hauraki Gulf Maritime Park. The greys and browns of the alternating Miocene sandstone and mudstone strata provide a sharp contrast to the dazzling white shells which have accumulated above high water mark around the upright stack.

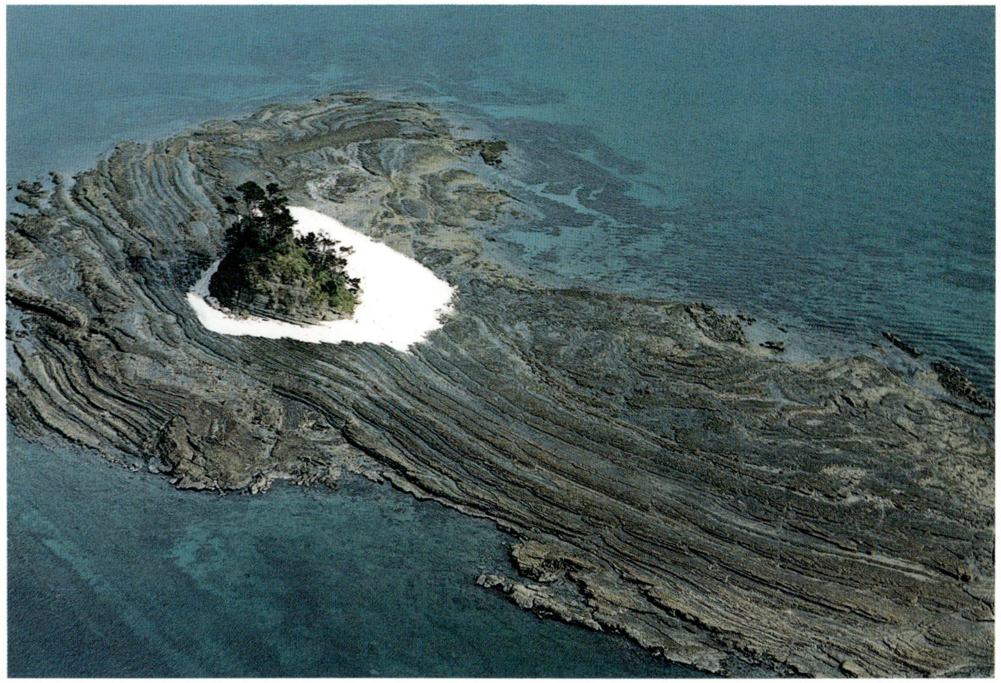

7

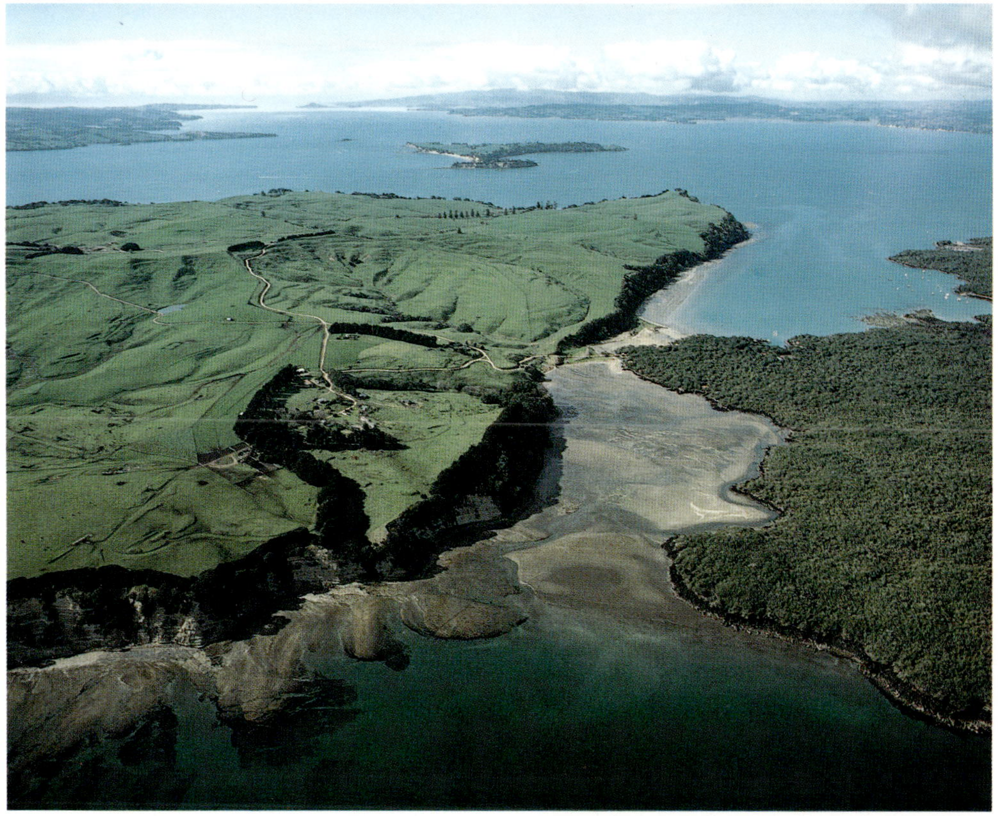

8

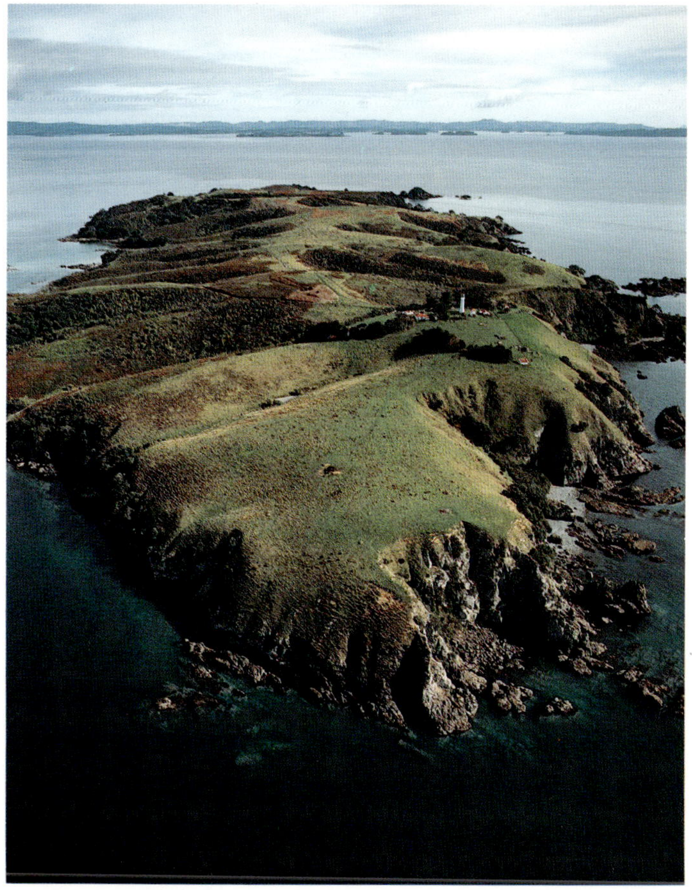

9

9 Tiritiri Matangi Island lies 20 km north of Rangitoto Island and 4 km off the Whangaparaoa Peninsula; this view, looking north-west towards the deeply-indented Rodney coastline, shows other distant islands of Hauraki Gulf Maritime Park – Motuora Island (centre) and Kawau Island (top right). The island consists of greywacke with a cap of Miocene sandstone, and shows a typical fretted greywacke coastline. It is one of the best examples within the park of a partly-eroded, uplifted marine terrace.

Tiritiri Matangi was grazed for over a century and has carried a lighthouse for 120 years. It is now the site of one of the most interesting experiments in the park – an attempt to revegetate it in indigenous forest, reintroduce rare native birds, and encourage the public to visit it as an open sanctuary where these species can be observed in the wild.

8 In all of Hauraki Gulf Maritime Park there is no clearer contrast between sedimentary and volcanic landforms than this contact zone between Motutapu Island (left) and Rangitoto Island (right). In this view looking south-east, Motuihe Island can be seen just beyond Motutapu with the Tamaki Strait separating Waiheke Island (top left) from the mainland. This western end of Motutapu Island consists of Waitemata Sandstone (Tertiary age) overlying greywacke of Mesozoic age. The cliffs and wavecut platforms in these sedimentary rocks predate the eruption of the basaltic lavas of Rangitoto.

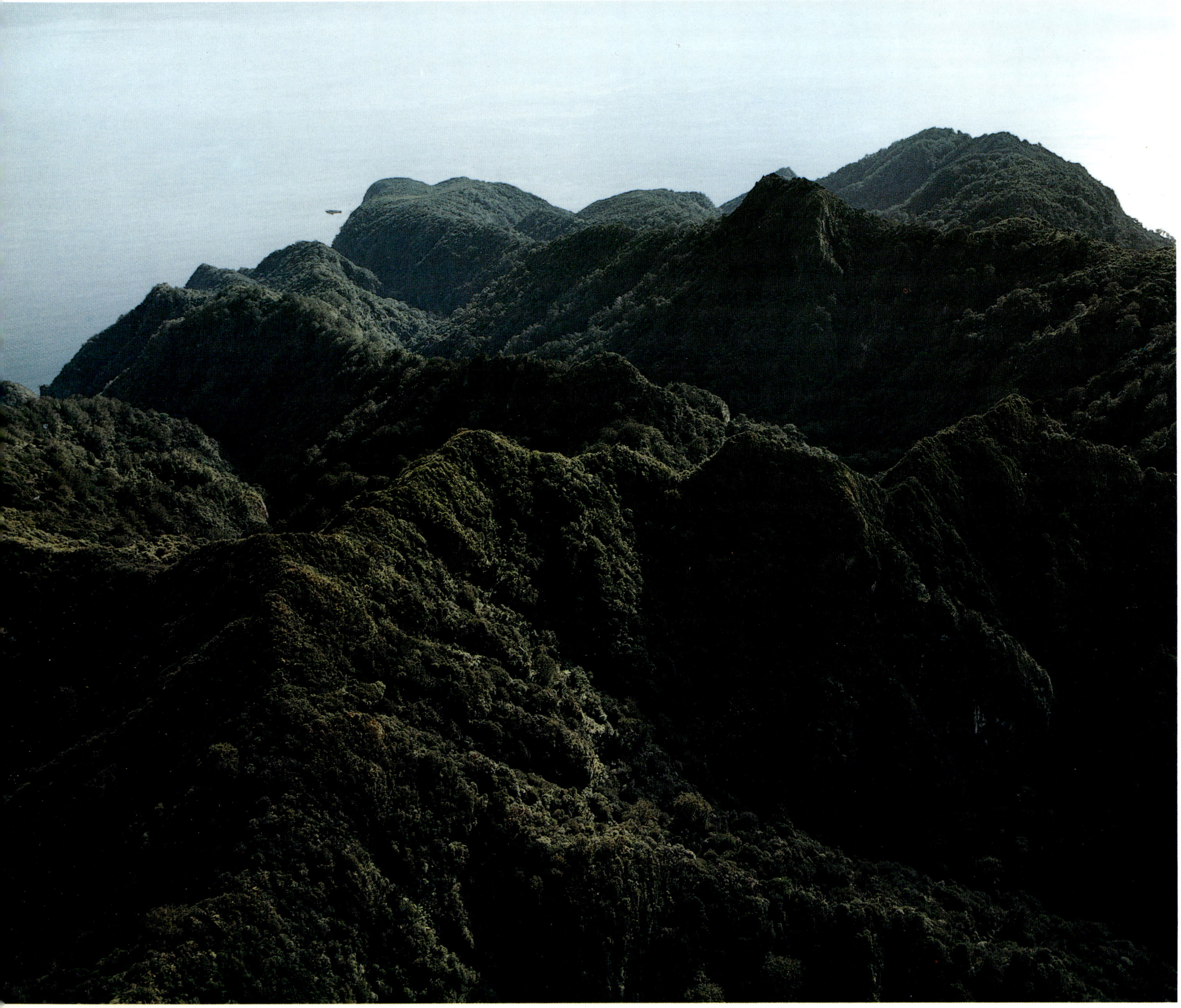

10

10 Little Barrier Island (Hauturu) is probably the most important wildlife sanctuary among the outer islands of Hauraki Gulf Maritime Park. It is a deeply eroded andesitic cone, roughly circular and covering 2817 ha. This view northwards across the summit (Mt Hauturu, 722 m) shows the rugged nature of the island's topography. There are only two small flat areas on the island – Te Titoki Point with its superb boulder bank of andesitic rocks, and Pohutukawa Flat behind Hingaia Point the site of an enormous rockfall from the cliffs 400 m above.

12 The Poor Knights Islands lie 25 km off the Northland coastline and 45 km north-east of Whangarei. They are the northernmost islands in Hauraki Gulf Maritime Park, their nearest neighbours being the Hen and Chickens Group just visible 50 km to the south (centre, distance). The Poor Knights lie at the outermost limit of the continental shelf and were not connected to the mainland during the last glaciation (in contrast to the other offshore islands of the gulf). Consequently, much of the flora and fauna is endemic to the islands.

The two main islands and the numerous rocky islets can be seen in this view looking south across Tawhiti Rahi to Aorangi. The islands consist of well-compacted, strongly jointed rhyolitic breccia and tuff of late Miocene age. The 150–200 m-high cliffs which ring the island are a striking feature of this rhyolitic landform. In places, the cliffs extend for 100 m below water, making landing very difficult.

A large Maori population lived on Aorangi Island in prehistoric times. The indigenous vegetation was almost completely cleared during this occupation but since then kanuka and pohutukawa regenerated all over the island. The waters around the Poor Knights have been designated as one of New Zealand's limited number of Marine Reserves because of the quality of their marine life.

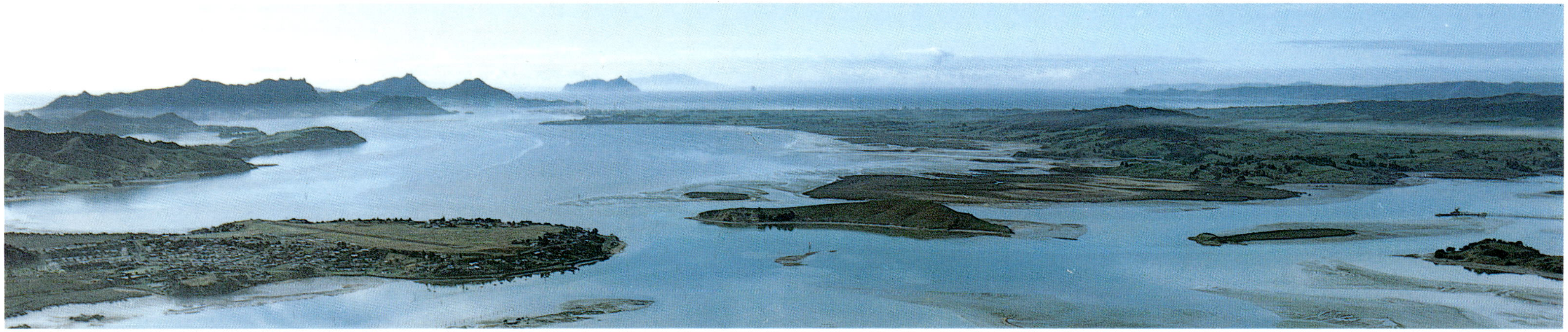

11

11 The view south-east across Whangarei Harbour contrasts the distant remnant volcanic cones (Mt Manaia, Bream Head, Taranga Island and Little Barrier Island) with the tombolos and sand dunes in the non-volcanic landscape of the harbour.

13 Taranga Island (the 'hen' of the Hen and Chickens Group) is the rugged 426 m high remnant of an andesitic volcano of Miocene age. Interestingly, the other five islands of the group (the Marotere, or Chicken Islands) are non-volcanic.

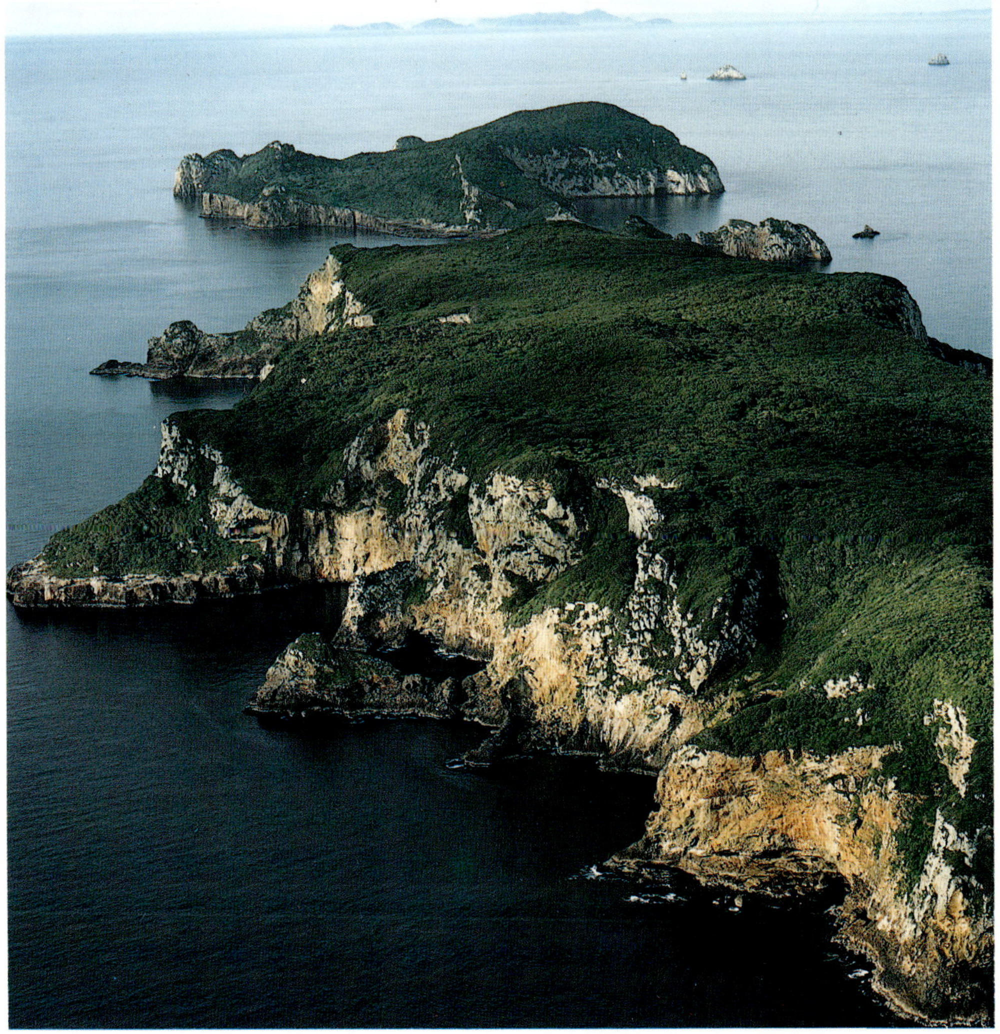

12

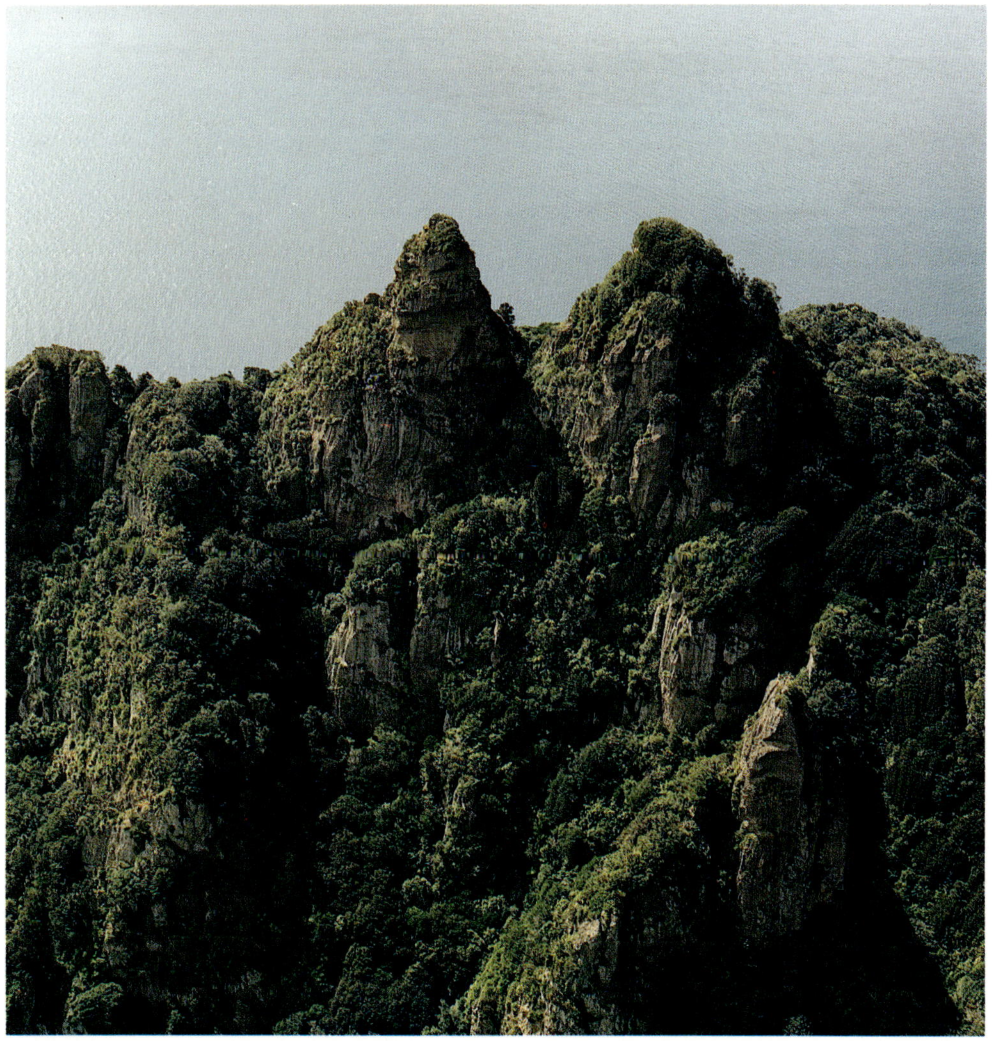

13

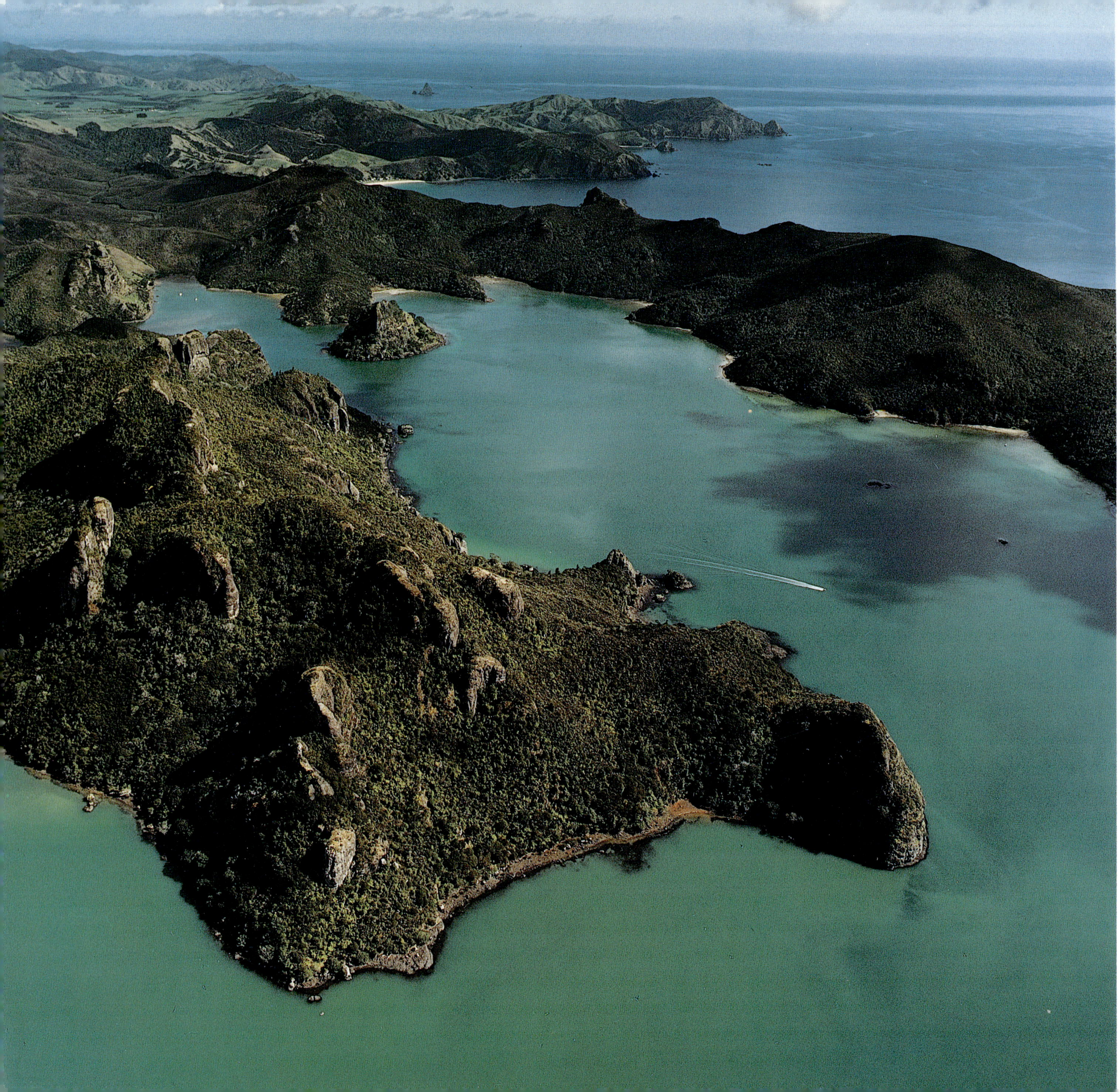

14 This landscape, around Pekapeka Bay on the northern side of the entrance to Whangaroa Harbour, consists of old volcanic rocks similar to the Miocene-aged rocks of Taranga Island in the Hen and Chickens Group (Fig. 13). The rounded exposed bluffs are the remnants of a sequence of andesitic breccia lahars that once formed a ringplain centred on tiny Wekarua Island (centre, distance). The bays were formed as the sea flooded back into the valleys at the end of the last glaciation. Most of the forested land in the photograph lies within Ranfurly Bay Scenic Reserve, the northernmost part of the Bay of Islands Maritime and Historic Park.

15 The central feature of the sprawling Bay of Islands Maritime and Historic Park is the Bay of Islands itself, here seen looking north-west across Manawaora Bay and Orokawa Peninsula. The island in the centre is Moturua Island and most of the larger islands within the photograph lie within the park. The Purerua Peninsula, the northern headland bounding the bay, can be seen in the top left.

The landforms of this part of the Bay of Islands have developed in the oldest known rocks in the North Island, greywackes of late Paleozoic to early Mesozoic age. The surface of the greywacke has been typically weathered to a considerable depth of yellow-brown clay; in places (such as Red Head on Okahu Island, top right) the greywacke underlying the clay has been weathered to a red colour. The gentle topography indicates the sustained weathering of the landscape and the flooding of the former river valleys as the sea level rose at the end of the last glaciation. Since the sea level stabilised at its present level 6000 years ago, sand tombolos have developed to link together some of the former islands.

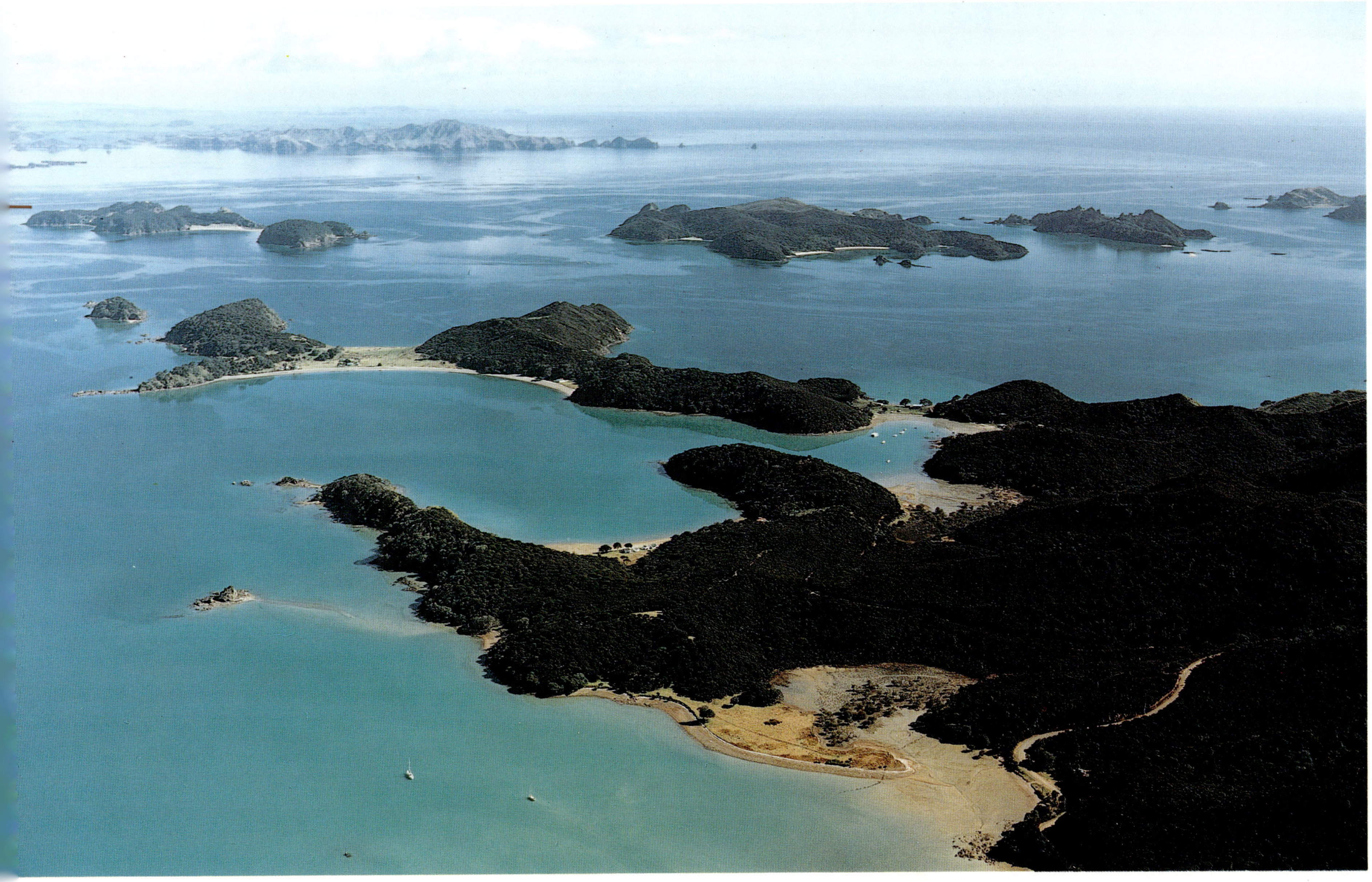

15

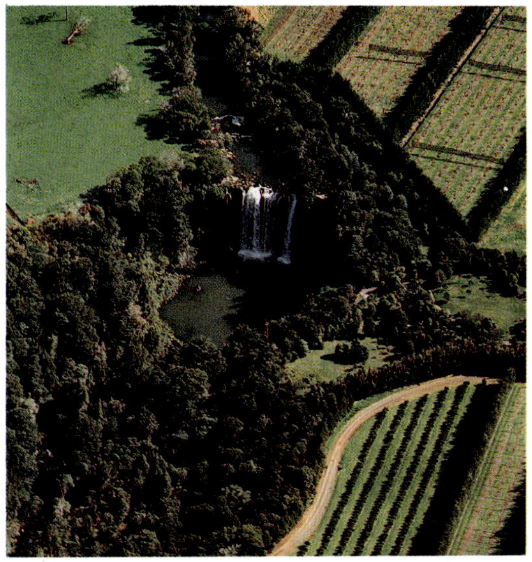

16

16 Rainbow Falls, 3 km up the Kerikeri River from Kerikeri township, is one of the most popular scenic features in the Bay of Islands park. Extensive lava flows poured down the river valleys around Kerikeri during the late Quaternary ice ages. The Kerikeri valley floor was filled with lava which gradually eroded back to create the present 27 m fall. Rock from this same lava flow was used to build the historic landmark of the Kerikeri stone store downstream.

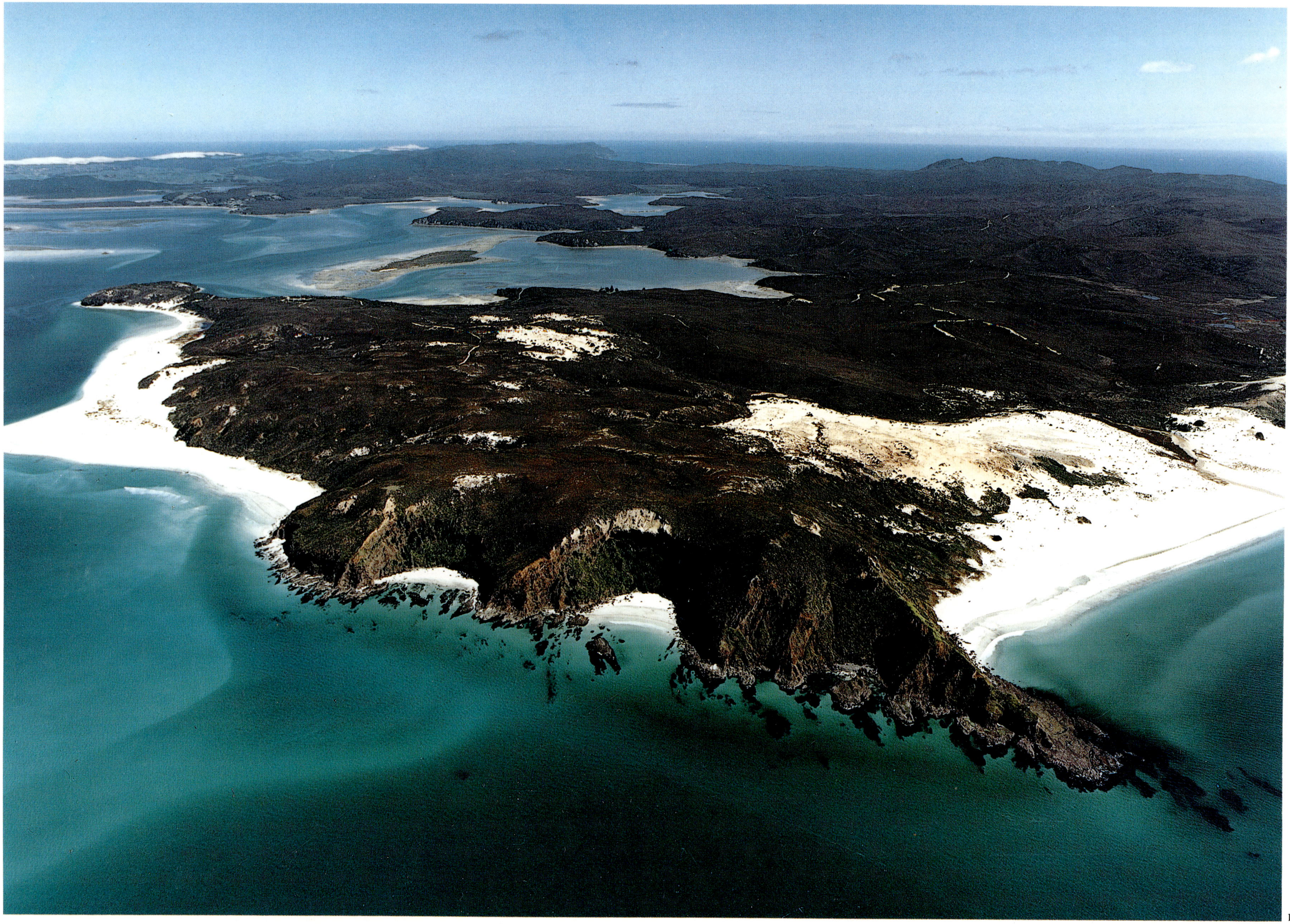

GLOSSARY

aa – basalt lava flow with rough jagged surface.
aggrading – landscapes (particularly river beds) which are built up by sediments eroded from the surrounding land.
amphibole – a group of dark-coloured silicate minerals, rich in iron and magnesium; example is hornblende.
andesite – a dark-coloured volcanic rock intermediate in composition between rhyolite and basalt.
arête – a narrow, often jagged, mountain crest created by the headward erosion of cirque glaciers on opposite sides of a ridge.
argillite – a rock formed by the hardening of mudstone or siltstone.
basalt – a type of volcanic rock which has a high iron and magnesium content but low silica. Molten basalt flows easily.
braided riverbed – the successive branching and rejoining of a stream channel, resembling the strands of a braid.
breccia – angular rock fragments in fine-grained material.
caldera – a large, basin-shaped volcanic depression.
Cambrian – the earliest geological period of the Paleozoic era, extending from 570 million to 525 million years ago.
cinder cone – a conical-shaped hill surrounding a volcanic vent.
cirque – a deep, steep-walled, amphitheatre-like ending to a valley; commonly caused by glaciation.
coal measures – any strata containing beds of coal.
conglomerate – a coarse sedimentary rock consisting of pebbles and boulders set in sand and silt.
continental shelf – relatively shallow belt of sea-bottom bordering a continental mass, usually to a water depth of 200 m.
couloir – narrow, steep gully leading up to a mountain ridge.
Cretaceous – the period of geological time extending from 135 to 65 million years ago.
cumulodome – dome-shaped accumulation of viscous lava which solidifies over a volcanic vent without a crater; also 'lava dome'.
delta – the low land, made up of alluvial deposits, at the mouth of a river, commonly forming a triangular or fan-shaped plain.
dendritic – drainage pattern which develops as a random network of tributary streams where the rock type is uniform and where faulting and jointing are insignificant.
Devonian – the fourth geological period of the Paleozoic era, from 395 to 345 million years ago.
diorite – a plutonic igneous rock of intermediate composition similar to andesite.
dip slope – a slope whose gradient and direction is the same as that of the underlying rock strata.
doline – circular depression in the surface of karst landforms; it is usually the point at which a stream disappears underground.
dolomite – a calcium magnesium carbonate mineral.
Eocene – an early period in the Tertiary era, from 53 to 38 million years ago.
exfoliation – the breaking-off of scale-like pieces from a large mass of rock.
feldspar – a very common group of rock-forming minerals, usually white or translucent. Example is orthoclase.
firn line – the uppermost line on a glacier above which the previous winter snowfall melts (ablates) during the summer.
fiord – long narrow arm of sea between steep slopes.
fluvioglacial – relating to meltwater streams flowing from glaciers.
frost-heaving – the lifting and disruption of soils (and rocks) caused by the subsurface freezing and thawing of water.
frost hollow – a depression susceptible to frosts through cold dense air draining downslope and accumulating in the hollow.
fumarole – a small volcanic vent from which steam and gases are ejected, often as jets and geysers.
gabbro – black, coarse-grained igneous rock.
glacier – an extensive body of land ice which flows downslope.
- cirque glacier – small glacier occupying a cirque basin.
- piedmont glacier – a broad glacier at the base of a mountain range, formed through a number of valley glaciers coalescing.
- valley glacier – a glacier which occupies a pre-glacial valley.

gleying – processes that occur mostly in wet soils, involve the reduction of iron and result in grey or bluish-grey colours.
gneiss – a hard metamorphic rock often similar in appearance and composition to granite; usually has some banding.
granite – a hard igneous rock that has crystallised deep below the earth's surface. It is rich in crystals of quartz, feldspars and shiny black and white micas.
granodiorite – a hard plutonic igneous rock, intermediate in composition between granite and diorite.
greywacke – dark grey sandstone, flecked with angular fragments of finer rock; formed by the hardening of deposits in ancient ocean basins; the major rock of central New Zealand.
hanging valley – a higher side branch of a mountainous river system now usually connected by a waterfall or series of rapids; origin of the valley is generally glacial (a smaller, feeder glacier).
hogsback – ridge with a sharp summit and similar steep slopes.
Holocene – the part of geological time extending from the end of the last glaciation (about 10 000 years ago) to the present day. Part of the Quaternary period.
igneous rocks – rocks that were once molten. If they crystallise deep below the earth's surface they are plutonic (e.g., granite); if they are erupted they are volcanic (e.g., rhyolite).
ignimbrite – thick sheets of rock formed by the welding together of extremely hot particles of rhyolitic ash.
interfluve – raised area between two adjacent streams.
interglacial – the period between two periods of glaciation.
kame terrace – a terrace lying between a valley glacier and the slopes of the valley; formed from fluvioglacial material deposited by meltwaters flowing along the sides of the glacier.
karren – blocks of limestone covered with narrow grooves caused by the dissolving action of water on the rock surface.
karst – a type of landscape characterised by sinkholes, caves and underground drainage; often formed in limestone.
kettlehole – a steep-sided depression in glacial deposits, often containing a lake or swamp; considered to form by the melting of large detached blocks of stagnant ice.
lahar – a flow of volcanic material, both ash and coarser products, mixed with water; often caused by the spilling over of a crater lake. Also used to describe mounds formed on the ringplain.
last glaciation – the last of the Pleistocene glacial advances which began about 80 000 years ago, reached a peak 20 000 years ago, and receded 14 000–10 000 years ago. Often termed the Otiran Glaciation after Otira.
leaching – removal of dissolved materials from soil by water.
limestone – rock composed dominantly of calcium carbonate.
loess – a blanket deposit of silt-sized material; usually carried by wind from dry river beds or outwash plains.
longshore drift – movement of beach sands and gravels along a shoreline through waves breaking obliquely on the beach.
magma – molten rock generated within the earth; on cooling, forms plutonic igneous rocks.
mafic – an igneous rock consisting of one or more dark-coloured ferromagnesian (iron and magnesium containing) minerals.
mammillated – rolling topography of bare rock which has been smoothed off by the passage of glacial ice.
marble – a hard metamorphic rock consisting predominantly of the calcium carbonate mineral calcite.
marine terrace – a platform, formed by coastal sea waves, which has been exposed by uplift, or by lowering of the sea level.
massif – a mountainous mass with fairly uniform rock type and geological structure.
Mesozoic – an era of geologic time extending from about 225 million years ago to about 65 million years ago.
metamorphic rocks – rocks that have been altered by heat and pressure deep below the earth's surface.
mica – group of minerals which often appear as shiny flakes in igneous and metamorphic rocks; includes muscovite (white mica).
Miocene – the period of geological time 25 million years ago to 7 million years ago.
moraine – mound or ridge of debris deposited by a glacier. Lateral moraine deposited at the sides of a glacier; medial between two tongues of ice, and terminal at the front end.
mudstone – soft sedimentary rocks formed from material which contains a large proportion of clay.
névé – area of freshly deposited snow in the accumulation zone (upper part) of a glacier.
Oligocene – an early part of the Tertiary era, from about 38 to 25 million years ago.
olivine – a greenish or brownish rock-forming silicate mineral; a magnesium iron silicate. Common in ultramafic rocks.
Ordovician – the second geological period of the Paleozoic era, from 525 to 440 million years ago.
orogeny – period of mountain building; in New Zealand there were three main periods – Tuhua, Rangitata, and Kaikoura, the last occurring 5–2 million years ago.
outwash – mainly sand and gravel washed out from a glacier by meltwater streams, and usually deposited near the moraine.
ox-bow – an almost cut-off loop of a stream. When the loop is cut off, an ox-bow lake is formed.
pakihi – a particular type of wetland found on the West Coast, South Island. Pakihi land is generally flat or gently sloping, carries a sedge/fern/restiad/rush/moss (and sometimes manuka) vegetation, occurs under a mean annual rainfall of more than 2200 mm, and is underlain by wet infertile soils.
Paleozoic – an era of geologic time extending from about 570 million years ago to about 225 million years ago.
peneplain – undulating plain from a long period of erosion.
peridotite – a hard coarse-grained ultramafic rock composed chiefly of olivine together with other ferromagnesian minerals.
periglacial – processes, areas or climate adjacent to ice sheets.
Permian – the period of geological time extending from about 280 to about 225 million years ago.
piedmont – lying or formed at the base of mountains.
pillow lava – rounded pillow-like masses of lava with a smooth skin; extruded under water.
plate tectonics – the theory that the Earth's crust consists of a number of rigid plates; the movement, interaction and destruction of these plates accounts for a wide range of phenomena including earthquakes, volcanism and mountain-building.
Pleistocene – part of Quaternary period extending from 2 to 3 million years ago to about 10 000 years ago.
Pliocene – Last part of the Tertiary period, extending from 7 million years ago to about 2 to 3 million years ago.
podzol – a soil often formed in a wet temperate climate under forest; characterised by very strong leaching.
polje – enclosed basin in a karst landscape, usually filled with alluvium; it may be drained by underground cave systems which become filled during times of high rainfall.
pumice – soft, light-coloured, frothy, glassy rock with the appearance of a sponge; usually formed by the trapping of bubbles of volcanic gases in molten rhyolite.
pyroclastic – general term for different fragments of rock ejected by volcano (e.g. lava, scoria, ash). Also tephra.
pyroxene – a group of dark silicate minerals similar in composition to the amphiboles. Example is augite.
quartz – crystalline silicon dioxide. A common, hard, rock-forming mineral, which weathers relatively slowly.
Quaternary – the period of geological time extending from 2–3 million years ago to the present.
rhyolite – a type of volcanic rock which is rich in silica, but poor in iron and magnesium. Molten rhyolite is very stiff and it usually gives rise to explosive volcanic eruptions with the emission of large quantities of ash.
ridge rents – slope failure about a fault trace on the upper part of a steep-sided ridge, generally induced by earthquakes; the scarp usually faces up-slope and lies parallel to the ridge.
ringplain – the lower and flatter part of the cone of a typical basaltic or andesitic volcano.
roche moutonnée – a protruding knob of resistant rock which has been sculptured by the moving ice of a glacier.
rock flour – fine-grained rock material produced by the grinding action of rocks held at the base of a glacier.
sandstone – sedimentary rock consisting of compressed or cemented sand-sized particles.
schist – a metamorphic rock that has developed distinct layering; can be split into slabs or flakes. Mica flecks common.
scoria – light-weight volcanic rock, usually formed by the trapping of bubbles of volcanic gases in andesitic or basaltic lava.
sedimentary rocks – rocks resulting from the consolidation of loose material that has accumulated in layers, usually on the bed of the sea, in lakes, or in rivers.
serac – a pinnacle of ice formed where crevasses intersect.
serpentine scrub – stunted scrub capable of existing on soils developed on ultramafic rocks; high levels of magnesium possibly make these soils toxic to many normal plants.
serpentinite – an ultramafic rock consisting of 'serpentine' minerals formed by the metamorphic alteration of olivine and similar minerals; usually greenish with greasy feel.
sill – igneous rock intruded as a near horizontal sheet.
siltstone – sedimentary rock formed mainly from silt.
sink-hole – funnel-shaped depression in the surface of a limestone landscape; marks the disappearance of a surface stream.
soil sequence – a group of soils usually chosen to have variation in only one soil-forming factor, e.g., a *chronosequence* (variation in time) or a *climosequence* (variation in climate).
soil texture – the relative proportion of the various sizes of particles (sand, silt, clay) that make up a soil.
stack – isolated rock pillar rising steeply from the sea.
striations – small grooves or scratches on the surface of rocks which have been scoured by rock embedded in glacial ice.
syncline – a large fold in rocks in which the strata dip downwards from both sides; often gives rise to a large depression.
talus – rock fragments lying at the base of a very steep slope.
tephra – a general term for all solid (rather than molten) materials ejected from a volcano during an eruption.
terminal (moraine) – ridge of glacial debris marking the maximum limit of an ice-sheet or glacial advance.
Tertiary – a term for geological time ranging from about 65 to 2–3 million years ago.
tholoid – dome of lava within the crater of a volcano.
tombolo – sandy or shingly spit linking an island to the mainland. May be produced by longshore drift of beach materials.
tor – an isolated pinnacle of bedrock exposed by erosion of overlying unconsolidated material.
truncated spur – valley-side spur which has been sharply cut off at its lower end by the action of a valley glacier.
tuff – a general term for consolidated volcanic tephras.
tundra – a term for the treeless plains of the high latitudes of the northern hemisphere; it should not be used to describe treeless areas at high altitudes in temperate latitudes.
ultramafic – relates to igneous rocks with very high contents of dark coloured minerals containing iron and magnesium.

17 The long fingers of the Parengarenga Harbour probe deeply into the Miocene sandstones and volcanic breccias, and Holocene sands of the northern end of the Aupouri Peninsula in the far north. The headland of Ohao Point in the foreground consists of volcanic breccia mantled with quartz sands. Note the high dunes (left, distance) at the northern end of Ninety Mile Beach near Te Paki to the west, and the Ponaki wetlands (centre, right), an important wildlife habitat. The soils in this locality are extremely infertile; some of them formerly supported mixed kauri forest, but they have since been further degraded by burning and gum-digging. The impoverished soils around Ohao Point now support an interesting community of dense stunted manuka/kanuka.

Ohao Point is 3 km south of Mokaikai Pa, one of many archaeological sites in this landscape of great significance to the Te Aupouri people of Te Hapua.

18 Cape Maria van Dieman at the north-western tip of the North Island is an old volcanic outcrop connected to the rest of the Aupouri Peninsula by a tombolo of golden sand high in feldspar minerals. The cape and the other volcanic stumps in this north-westerly view (Motuopao Island, centre distance; Taupiri Island, left; and Te Kohatu Point, right) are all remnants of a sheet of Cretaceous-aged seafloor pillow lava flows.

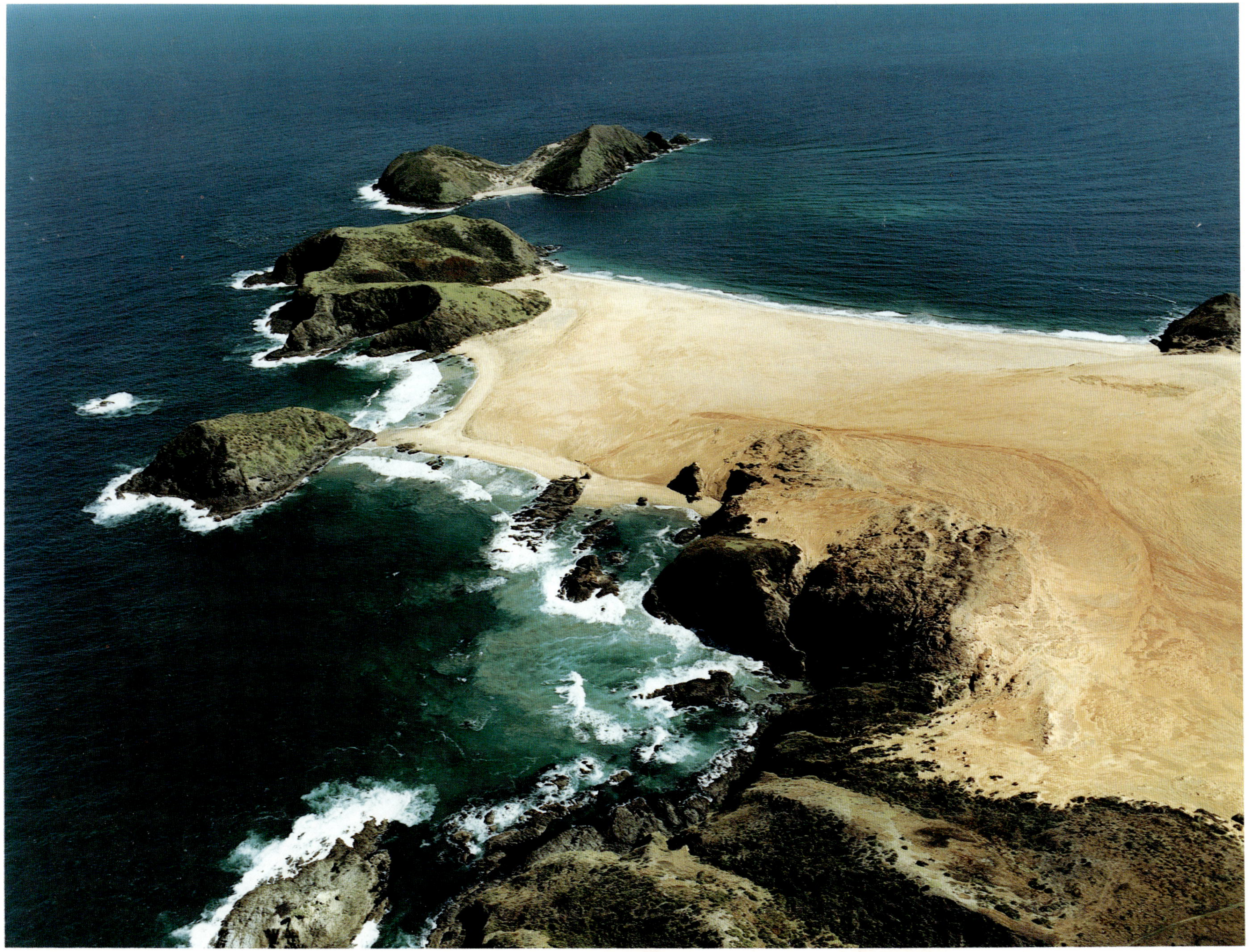
18